Praise for *God Was Right*

"Sublime and entirely original."

—Abigail Shrier, *New York Times* bestselling author of *Bad Therapy* and *Irreversible Damage*

"*God Was Right* shows how considering Torah wisdom through modern data produces fascinating reading and highly practical truths. This is a must-read for any leader—from a parent to a president—who wants to get the best out of his people and the most out of life."

—Joe Lonsdale, managing partner of 8VC, cofounder of Palantir, Addepar, OpenGov, the Cicero Institute, and the University of Austin

"*God Was Right* is a brilliant tour de force whose combination of ancient scripture and contemporary social sciences culminates in a fascinating book that delights, surprises, stimulates, and lights the path to living wiser, smarter, happier, and better."

—Marty Makary, MD, Johns Hopkins University professor and *New York Times* bestselling author of *Blind Spots*

"*God Was Right* is where the profound meets the practical. This simply brilliant book draws from a vast array of different disciplines to provide deep wisdom and incredibly useful guidance that will engross and enlighten every reader."

—Marc Siegel, MD, professor of medicine at New York University Langone Medical Center, medical director of Doctor Radio on Sirius MD, and Fox News senior medical analyst

"*God Was Right* reveals the Bible's essence: the ultimate guidebook for people of all faiths, ready to provide the path to the good, fulfilling, and happy life. A masterpiece that will enrich the lives of all believers and seekers."

—Robert Stearns, founder and executive director of Eagles' Wings

"Mark Gerson's new book, *God Was Right*, is a must-read for anyone seeking to understand the timeless relevance and transformative power of the Torah. Modern social science is now proving that the Torah will enable you to live your best life right now."

—Gordon Robertson, CEO of the Christian Broadcasting Network

GOD WAS RIGHT

Also by Mark Gerson

The Telling: How Judaism's Essential Book Reveals the Meaning of Life

GOD WAS RIGHT

How Modern Social Science Proves the Torah Is True

MARK GERSON

BenBella Books, Inc.
Dallas, TX

BenBella Books, Inc.
8080 N. Central Expressway Suite 1700
Dallas, TX 75206
benbellabooks.com
Send feedback to feedback@benbellabooks.com

BenBella is a federally registered trademark.

Printed in the United States of America
10 9 8 7 6 5 4 3 2 1

Library of Congress Control Number: 2024054641
ISBN 9781637746172 (hardcover)
ISBN 9781637746189 (electronic)

Editing by Joe Rhatigan
Copyediting by Michael Fedison
Proofreading by Cheryl Beacham and Marissa Wold Uhrina
Text design and composition by PerfecType, Nashville, TN
Cover design by Brigid Pearson
Printed by Sheridan MI

CONTENTS

PART TWO

Self-Improvement: How We Ought to Act

PART THREE
Self-Improvement: How We Ought to Think and Feel

PART FOUR

Together: How We Should Live with Others Communally

INTRODUCTION

The Torah, also known as the Five Books of Moses, is the most important book of all time. We Jews read from it three times a week, welcome our children into adulthood by their chanting from it, and consecrate homes, births, weddings, and funerals with its verses. We rise in its presence when it is taken out of the ark that houses it. We kiss it when it is paraded past us during Shabbat services. We dance with it annually. We bury it ceremonially when it becomes no longer fit for daily use. We have performed daring rescue operations of Torahs from political violence in Germany, Iraq, Siberia, Yemen, and Egypt and natural disasters in New Orleans, New York, Cape Town, and Antakya. We have studied its every theme and each detail—down to the word and even the letter—with care, consistency, curiosity, and reverence.

We have done all of these practices for several thousand years, enabling each Jew today (whenever today is) to be in active dialogue and relationship with Jews across geographies and through time. The Torah surely is, in the words of the German poet Heinrich Heine, the "portable homeland of the Jew."[1]

And it is not only *our* homeland. In Matthew 5:18 (The Sermon on the Mount), Jesus says that he came to "fulfill" the Torah, which should be followed to every "jot and tittle." The Quran considers Abraham to be the "father of prophets," Moses to be the prophet who "talked directly with God," and the Torah to be the source of "guidance and light" whose "fulfillment" is the path to "success."[2] And countless secular thinkers and leaders have issued testimony in effective agreement with that of President

John Adams: "The Bible contains the most profound Philosophy, the most perfect Morality, and the most refined Policy, that ever was conceived upon earth . . . [It offers] the only System that ever did or ever will preserve a Republick [sic] in the World."[3]

Yet the most audacious and ambitious commentary about the Torah comes from its most authoritative source. This is Moses, the Torah's central protagonist who the narrator of the Torah says in Deuteronomy 34:10 will be the greatest prophet ever to live.

In Deuteronomy 32:47, Moses tells us that the Torah is either "empty" or "your life." Consequently, we learn that Moses is telling us that the Torah is not just a good book, an interesting book, a helpful book, or an influential book. It is, Moses asserts, all or nothing—and should be accepted or rejected in full.

This is an astonishing claim, far from what anyone would broadly expect to be said about a book. If anyone—Homer or Shakespeare, Chaucer or Tolstoy, Rowling or King, truly *anyone*—insisted that his or her books encompassed "everything," we would consider the author to be a lunatic. But this is Moses, whose Torah has been the spiritual lifeblood of countless people for thousands of years. His claim deserves a serious assessment. This process can begin by moving outside of the realm of books and asking: What kind of things are all or nothing and must be accepted or rejected in full?

We can easily tell through other statements that must be accepted or rejected in full. For instance, the Denver Nuggets won the NBA title in 2023. If you throw a ball in the air, it will soon fall toward Earth. George Washington was the fifth president. Frank Sinatra learned his craft from Elvis Presley, who lived at Monticello. There is nothing partial about these statements. They are either true or false.

So, Moses is asserting that the Torah is *true*. This is an astonishing claim, with massive implications. If the Torah is true, then it deserves everyone's attention, devotion, and fidelity. If the Torah is interesting, instructive, wise, but not *true*—then it could be considered like other enduring but not essential works.

How can we determine whether Moses is right, and that the Torah is true? The first step, as with any book or even artistic expression, is to assess its genre. If one saw a Broadway rendition of *Death of a Salesman* and remarked that it wasn't very good because there was no dancing or jokes, a reasonable response would be, "Of course not. It is neither a musical nor a comedy. It is a *drama*, and so you shouldn't be looking for laughs!"

How might one get the genre of the Torah similarly right and wrong?

The Torah, as if anticipating its question of genre, answers it early on in its first book—Genesis. Genesis 1 is the story of God's creation of the world. On Day Three, God creates vegetation, plants, and fruit. On Day Four, God creates the sun. Of course, vegetation cannot exist without the sun. Does that disqualify the Torah before it really begins? Of course not.

The Torah is well aware of the biological difficulty of this sequence. But he is not trying to teach us about photosynthesis. Rather, he is teaching us what the Torah *is not*. It is not a science book that explains how plants flourish. Nor is it a history book that explains what comes before what.

Consequently, the Torah is not claiming that vegetation preceded the sun, the world was created in six days, that a snake talked Eve into eating fruit from the forbidden tree, that one man (Noah) built an enormous ark that survived a historic flood, that a donkey talked to a man—or any other historical or scientific claim.

If the Torah is not a history or science book, then what kind of book is it? The Torah reveals the answer in its name. The word "Torah," drawing from the Hebrew root *hora'ah*, means teaching, instruction, or guidance. So, the Torah is a *guidebook*. In Deuteronomy 10:13, Moses tells us just what kind of guidebook it is. It is intended, he says, "for your benefit." As we can only benefit from guidance that we can easily understand and act upon, the Torah must be comprehensible and practical. In Psalm 119:89, King David tells us how long we will be able to derive this benefit. His answer: "Forever." The Torah, by its lights, is a true *and* practical guidebook of eternal relevance—for everyone.

What is its guidance about? The answer is revealed in what the Torah addresses. The Torah provides instructions on how we should choose our spouse, teach our children, select our clothing, govern our nations, think about our past and our future, set the norms for our culture, structure our days and our week, spend our money, make decisions, relate to those near and far, and many other such topics. The Torah provides guidance about *everything*.

So, Moses is making quite an assertion about the Torah. He is saying that the Torah is the highly practical, comprehensive, and true *guidebook* for all people in all times. Given the importance of Moses and the centrality of the Torah in the lives, imaginations, and dreams of so many people and nations, an insistent question emerges: *Is Moses right?*

People throughout the world have been essentially asking that question for more than three thousand years. For almost all of that time, the answer could only be given on the basis of observation, experience, and faith—which are not the stuff of truth. Slowly, and then suddenly, everything changed.

The change started in the late nineteenth century when Professor Wilhelm Wundt of the University of Leipzig sought to determine how long it would take research participants to make a judgment. This marked the birth of social science, which uses the scientific method to ask questions concerning who we are, what we can be, and why we think and act as we do. The twentieth century saw departments of social science develop at thousands of colleges and universities around the world. Each of these departments had professors and researchers who, like Professor Wundt, conducted experiments and made assessments using the scientific method.

And then, about one hundred years later, came the internet. The advent of the accessible and advanced internet, with its related data collection capabilities, computing power, and analytical tools, made the twenty-first century the Golden Era of social science. The subject of these studies includes relationships, decision-making, clothing, time structuring, routine, reminders, how we think about the past and the future, and many others.

The usual place for scientific studies is in academic journals, and there are plenty of social science studies to be found there. But many of these studies have yielded findings sometimes labeled as "discoveries," that are so interesting, compelling, and relevant that they have escaped the standard confines of scientific discussion. Many have populated the front pages of major newspapers, graced the covers of mass-market magazines, and become the subjects of best-selling books and documentaries. Some have won their researchers Nobel Prizes.

The explosive popularity of social science in the era of big data cannot be attributed to it being fun to read, easy to share, or effectively marketed. There are plenty of subjects that would fit those criteria—but they have not captivated the fascination of such a diverse array of people. Social scientific studies have been so popular because they have consistently revealed important, interesting, and actionable *truths* about the human condition. These studies rarely (if ever) mention the Torah, but they are asking the *same* questions and addressing the *same* subjects as our portable homeland.

Consequently, we can now compare the claims of the Torah with the findings of modern social science, and finally—after three thousand years—answer the question with scientific confidence: Is the Torah true?

That is what this book will reveal.

One note, before we get started. This book is designed to be read in one of two ways. The reader can, of course, read it straight through from beginning to end. But the reader can also select a chapter on a subject that interests him in the moment and engage just with it. The Torah lends itself to this kind of experience, as each Torah story, law, and even verse contains a multitude of lessons. For instance, the reader will meet Jacob and the wrestling angel in the chapters on self-transformation and future orientation, Joseph and his brothers in the chapters on grudges and reframing and Moses and the Midianite women in the chapters on bystanding and noticing.

PART ONE

Reality: How Things Are

1

Why Moses Commands Incapability and Willpower Fails

The Torah and Science of Character

It is often said that Judaism is a religion of action. That is true, and is derived from the Torah itself. Leviticus 22:31 instructs us, "And you shall keep my commandments, and do them: I am the Lord." *Keep* and *do*: The verbs emphasize the importance the Torah places on action.

This insistence on action raises many questions. Does it matter *why* we do what we do? Does it matter *how* we do what we do? What is the most reliable way to ensure that we act as we should? Is the Torah *only*, or even *primarily*, a guide for action?

At the core of these questions is a larger discussion about how we should think about character—as independent of, even if expressed in, action. This notion is so important to the Torah that it is addressed in each of its five books. And it is so important to modern life that it is one of the most frequently addressed subjects in social scientific literature.

Genesis: Ethics vs. Etiquette in Noah's Family

It is in Genesis 6:13 that God, having noted that "the earth had become corrupt . . . [and] filled with robbery," decrees a flood that will destroy everything and everyone in the world. God exempts only Noah, Noah's family, and select animals. The method of survival will be a giant ark. God provides Noah with very detailed instructions about how to build the ark, and the text tells us twice that Noah "did according to everything God commanded." In Genesis 7, the text tells us that "Noah, with his sons, his wife and his sons' wives with him" entered the ark. The husbands and the wives, we see, come separately. It is not appropriate, God is teaching us, to make love during a catastrophe.

A year later, the flood is over and the waters have receded. God tells Noah to "go forth from the ark; you and your wife, your sons and your sons' wives with you." The husbands and the wives are instructed to leave *together*—it is time for them to re-create mankind. This time, Noah does not comply with God's instruction. The text tells us: "Noah went forth, and his sons, his wife, and his sons' wives with him."

Noah apparently has no intention of re-creating the world. Indeed, we soon find out what Noah instead intends to do. He plants a vineyard and gets drunk—so drunk that he falls asleep, naked, inside his tent. One of his sons, Ham, comes into the tent and sees his father naked. Ham does nothing to cover his father or otherwise preserve some modesty. He does the opposite. He leaves the tent to gossip about what he saw to his brothers, Shem and Japheth.

Shem and Japheth respond with thoughtful concern that behooves dutiful sons. The text tells us, "Shem and Japheth took a garment and laid it across their shoulders; then they walked in backward and covered their father's naked body." The Hebrew language offers an intriguing subtlety. The word for "took" (*va'yikah*) is in the singular. But Shem and Japheth both took the garment! We would thus expect the verse to say that *they* took (*va'yikhu*) it. Generally, actions undertaken by two people start with one suggesting it and the other agreeing—by one moving and the other following. Which brother—Shem or Japheth—is the subject of "he took"? Which one was the leader?

Shlomo Yizchaki (better known as Rashi) was an eleventh-century French rabbi who is widely acknowledged to be one of the greatest Torah commentators of all time. Rashi notes that Shem is mentioned before Japheth, and therefore indicates that Shem led, and Japheth followed. Shem, Rashi concludes, was the more devoted son. Rashi's position is supported by what happens next. When Noah awakens, he praises the Lord as the "God of Shem," and says that Japheth is to be blessed by dwelling "in the tents of Shem."[1]

Given that Shem and Japheth ultimately performed the same righteous act, why do Noah and the great Rabbinic interpreters care who went first? The twentieth-century sage Rav Joseph Soloveitchik suggests an answer. Shem acted out of "ethics," a desire to do the right thing. And Japheth, following him, acted out of "etiquette," the impulse to appear polite and kind. Both are deserving of blessing for *acting* righteously. But Shem's pre-eminence, in the eyes of Noah and our Rabbinic interpreters, reveals the Torah's conviction that the same action performed from a place of ethics (or character) is far superior to that action being undertaken of etiquette (or convention).[2]

Genesis: Abraham's First Test

It takes ten generations from Noah for the next major figure in the Torah to arrive. Abraham has a long, fascinating, and difficult life. Indeed, his life is so challenging that the ancient sages stated he endured ten tests.[3]

Moses ben Maimon (known as Maimonides or the Rambam) was a twelfth-century sage who is universally considered to be one of the greatest rabbis, Torah interpreters, and Jewish philosophers of all time. According to Maimonides, God delivers the first test in Genesis 12:1. It is, "Go from your country, your people and your father's household to the land I will show you."[4] God continues, telling Abraham that he will be the father of a great nation and will be blessed. Abraham follows God's instruction and leaves with his family and his wealth.

A question immediately emerges. Genesis 12 does not seem like a test. It should not be hard for anyone to follow God's explicit instruction, especially if it comes with a promise of a great nation, divine blessings, and the participation of friends and family. The nineteenth-century sage Yehudah Aryeh Leib Alter (known as the Sfat Emet) explains. The test is not whether Abraham will do as instructed. It is whether he will do as instructed out of a desire to please God or out of a desire to become wealthy and powerful. Abraham's *intention* is so important that it constitutes the test.[5]

Exodus: The Ultimate Commandment

One of the most familiar parts of the Torah is the Ten Commandments, which were given on two tablets in Exodus 20. From the moment the first readers noted that the Ten Commandments were given on two tablets, commentators have sought to understand the meaning behind their order and structure. Maimonides divided the commandments into two: the first tablet being obligations between man and God and the second between man and man. His contemporary Abraham bar Hiyya divided them in three: man/God, man/family, man/others. Rashi emphasized connections across tablets (the first/sixth, the second/seventh, etc.).[6]

As with every Torah verse, each of multiple interpretations can yield an intriguing and important truth. Here, there is at least a fourth explanation as to the ordering of the commandments. The first nine—including the prohibitions of murder, robbery, adultery, and idolatry and a commandment to honor one's parents—are about actions. But the *ultimate* commandment—the Tenth Commandment, the one to which they all build up to—is not an action at all. It is a prohibition on coveting. As the thirteenth-century sage Bachya ben Asher said, "It is known that coveting is a matter of the heart."[7]

Why would coveting, the one commandment that concerns a "matter of the heart" rather than an action, be the *ultimate* commandment? Does the placement of coveting suggest that it is the most important commandment and that the prohibition on coveting is more important than even the prohibition on murder?

Seemingly, yes—and for good reason. Coveting is at the root of most cases of stealing and adultery and many cases of murder, idolatry, and all the other commandments.

With this order, the Torah teaches us about coveting *and* character. Murder, robbery, and adultery seem like very different bad actions, but we see through the Ten Commandments how they derive from a single character trait: coveting. Get rid of one character trait, and lots of terrible actions are diminished or eliminated.

Exodus: Why the Golden Calf Angers God

Ten chapters after God gives us the Ten Commandments, Moses takes leave of the people for forty days to go up a mountain and commune with God. He is gone longer than the people anticipate. They respond to his absence by building a Golden Calf, which they simultaneously worship and turn into a centerpiece for an orgy.[8]

God sees what his people are doing and is furious. He exclaims to Moses, "I see that this is a stiff-necked people. Now, let Me be, that My anger may blaze forth against them and that I may destroy them, and make from you a great nation" (Exodus 32:9–10).

Why is God so angry? At first glance, it seems obvious: God is furious because the Jews have committed the sin of idolatry with the kind of behavior that often accompanies it.

As the twentieth-century sage Nosson Tzvi Finkel (known as the Alter of Slabodka) noted, the text suggests something very different. God's anger, as expressed in the divine criticism, is not directed at the worship of an idol, which is an *action*. Instead, God wishes to destroy the people for being "stiff-necked"—which is a character trait. Fortunately, Moses is able to convince God to spare the people.[9]

Jews revisit this concept of stiff-neckedness during our many prayer days devoted to self-improvement, most importantly Yom Kippur. In our liturgy during these days, we declare, "We are not so brazen and stiff necked so as to say before you 'we are righteous and have done no sin' rather, we and our fathers have sinned." The necessary prelude to self-improvement, we learn, is the refusal to see ourselves as better than we are.

Leviticus: "You Shall Be Holy"

In Leviticus 19:2, God tells Moses to address "the entire assembly of the Children of Israel." This may sound perfunctory, but it is actually extraordinary. God often tells Moses to address "the Children of Israel," but this is one of the few times when God tells his prophet to address *the entire assembly* of the Children of Israel.

What message, the reader is primed to wonder, is so important that God wants everyone to hear it directly and simultaneously from Moses in one moment? God does not leave us to wonder. He says, "You shall be holy, for holy am I, Hashem, your God."

This is a remarkable instruction for two reasons. First, other ancient cultures asked only the priestly class to be holy. But God, in the Torah, radically democratizes the holiness expectation in saying that it should be a universal goal. Second, "holiness" is not an action. It is a state of character. God, in Leviticus 19:2, is not asking anyone to *do* anything. He is telling everyone to *be* something—and that is holy.

The reader of the Torah, his awareness heightened by the call for the "entire assembly" to be "holy," is drawn to think: *What, God, do you mean by "holy?"*

God seems to have anticipated that. In Leviticus 19:3, God immediately launches from the command to be holy into the *actions* that constitute holiness. These include honoring parents and keeping the Sabbath, refusing idols and leaving a corner of the field for the poor, giving generously, speaking truthfully, paying one's workers immediately, taking responsibility for others, voicing one's grievances, rejecting superstition, not mourning excessively, being kind to the convert, being honest in weights and measures, and many more.

Leviticus 19:2–3 presents a strange juxtaposition. It would be easily understandable if the Torah told us to just "be holy." The Torah would be saying that he trusts us to know what is holy. It would also be easily understandable if the Torah just required compliance with a list of actions that constitute holiness as it would mean that the matter is too important to leave to our discretion. But why include *both*?

The many rules in Leviticus 19:3 must not be meant to be a comprehensive accounting of what constitutes holiness. They are meant to be *examples* of them. Add all the other rules in the Bible to them, and we still don't have a comprehensive accounting of what constitutes holiness.

This rolls up to a conclusion: The Torah has *too few* teachings. Life is too varied and complicated for any list of prohibited and permitted actions to be complete—even one drawn from the Torah. For instance: Let's imagine a man who does not compliment or express love to his children, does not address the doorman at his building by name, neglects to tell his daughter to invite everyone in the class to the party so no one feels left out, and starts every day with a breakfast of fries, cake, and beer.

The man will not have explicitly violated a Torah law. But the thirteenth-century sage Moses ben Nachman (known as Nachmanides or the Ramban), in his analysis of Leviticus 19:2, has a name for such a character. He is a "scoundrel with Torah license." One can, in other words, follow the rules of the Torah and still do all kinds of unholy and even barbaric things.

A second perspective is the Torah has *too many* teachings. The moral decisions that we have to make in our daily lives are so frequent and sudden that it is impossible for everyone (or perhaps anyone) to immediately, reliably, and flawlessly recall which teaching applies to which situation.

In comes Leviticus 19, which says essentially, "It's okay." Study and honor the rules, stories, and laws the Torah does provide—observe good people, and place yourself in a virtuous community, so that you become holy and act correctly even in the absence of specific direction and instruction.

So, in Leviticus 19:2–3, we learn that holiness, which is the epitome of good character, is both separate from actions *and* manifested in them. But that's not all. Character, the Torah insists, is manifested in our actions *and* in the way we do them. The intention and attitude in the performance of the commandments are core to the Torah, which develops a philosophy of each.

Numbers: The Broken Vow

In Numbers 30, the Torah provides the instructions that govern oaths. The text, reflecting the Torah's teaching that words are of the utmost importance, says that oaths are irrevocable. However, the Torah offers an exception. A father or a husband can effectively nullify the oath of his daughter or wife.

The Torah presents an interesting situation. What happens if a father cancels the vow, but the young woman—unaware that the father has done so—breaks the vow? If actions were all that mattered, nothing should happen to her—as the young woman's oath had been nullified prior to her transgression. This is not what the Torah says. The text specifies, "The Lord shall forgive her" (Numbers 30:6).

Why would the young woman need forgiveness if she has not violated anything? The Talmud explains that her father's successful plea does not negate the fact that she *thought* she was transgressing. The sin for which she needs to ask forgiveness is not in the act itself; it is in the intention. The intention to break the vow, distinct from the fact that the vow was invalid, manifests a character defect that requires repentance.[10]

The importance of intention, independent of action, would continue to intrigue thinkers in the Torah tradition. For instance, the twentieth-century American sage Rav Yitzchak Hutner addressed the question: What happens if one performs a good deed with the right intention, but later regrets it? One might think that nothing should happen as the good deed is done, and the reward would be deposited alongside it. Rav Hutner, drawing from the Talmud, wrote that such a person would lose all reward for the mitzvah. If the intention disappears into regret, so does the credit for the action.[11]

Deuteronomy: Joy, Fire, a Terrible Curse, and the Importance of Attitude

Arriving in the final book of the Torah, in Deuteronomy 28:48, Moses warns the Jewish people about something that might befall them: "Therefore, you will serve your enemies, whom the Lord will send against you, [when you are] in famine, thirst, destitution, and lacking everything, and he will place an iron yoke upon your neck, until he has destroyed you."

What will we have done to deserve such a punishment? The preceding line makes it very clear. "[You will be cursed] because you did not serve Hashem, your God, amid joy and gladness of heart."

> Why is it so important to God that we do what he wants with a joyful attitude? God explains his reasoning in Numbers 15:39, when he commands us to wear *tzitzit* (ritual fringes) to remind us to follow him. If we are not continually reminded to serve God, we risk exploring "after your heart and after your eyes." The heart, the seat of desire, comes first. We will ultimately do, God is saying, what we want to do—and then find the reasons to do it. Consequently, we are to find joy in doing what we should do. We are cursed for acting correctly without joy, because only joy will ensure that we do the right thing consistently and dependably.

Throughout the Torah, God deploys an easily relatable metaphor to describe how we should show joy—and other attitudes that are appropriate for specific situations. The metaphor is fire, the universal symbol for enthusiasm.

In Exodus 3:2, God appears to Moses *in* fire at the burning bush. In Exodus 13:21, God leads the people out of Egypt *by* fire. In Deuteronomy 9:3, Moses says that we will be prepared to enter the Land when we know "that it is the Lord your God who passes before you *as* a consuming fire." In 1 Kings 18, God "answers by fire." In Daniel 7, God's throne is described as "ablaze with flames." There are dozens of other associations of God with fire throughout the Bible.

Why does the Torah want us to associate God with fire? The twentieth-century sage Sholom Dovber Schneersohn (the fifth Rebbe of Chabad, known as the Rebbe Rashab) explains: Godliness is like fire. Torah study, prayer, and indeed all the commandments, he said, require a flaming heart. This idea is encapsulated by his famous statement that "between coldness and heresy stands an extremely thin wall." A belief held without enthusiastic expression is one susceptible to being abandoned, even for heresy.

The traditional enemy of the Jewish people is Amalek—introduced in Exodus 17 as the force that attacks when we are thirsty, quarreling, faithless, and mutinous. The Amalekites, in sum, attack us when we are at our weakest, and not engaging with—let alone bothering or challenging—anyone.

The early twentieth-century sage Moshe Soloveitchik explained that Amalek is not a particular people, but a force that presents in two forms. One is the external enemy: the Romans, the Inquisitors, the Nazis, the Soviets, Hamas, the Iranian regime.[12] The other is the internal enemy who attacks our character and leads us away from what we know is right and good.

How does the Amalek succeed in attacking us? The twenty-first-century American sage Rabbi Menachem Mendel Schneerson (the seventh Rebbe of Chabad) looked to what Moses, in his great summary and interpretation of the Torah that is Deuteronomy, commands regarding Amalek. Moses instructs, "Remember what the Amalekites did to you along the way when you came out of Egypt. How they happened upon you along the way, and struck from the rear, all the stragglers from behind you—when you were faint and weary; and they did not fear God."

The Rebbe notes that the word for "happened upon you" (*karcha*) can also mean "made you cold." Thus, the Rebbe said, Amalek as the internal enemy is the voice that says, "Do the commandments, but do so without fire."[13]

We see the centrality of attitude in the most important event on the Jewish calendar, the Pesach Seder. The Seder is the Jewish New Year celebration where we relive and retell our freedom story through a short book called the *Haggadah* (The Telling)—and contemplate who we want to be in the coming year. The entire freedom story occurs in the Book of Exodus. Yet, the Haggadah does not even reference the Book of Exodus in its description of our freedom story. It has us relive and retell this story through Deuteronomy, the book of the Torah where nothing new happens. Why?

Let's enter the text of Deuteronomy 26, which constitutes the body of the Haggadah. It is of an imaginary man in the future—a farmer coming to the Temple to offer his "first fruits" after a successful harvest and to tell the Exodus story. Moses says, "You and the Levites and the foreigners residing among you shall *rejoice* in all the good things the Lord your God has given to you and your household." The joy that the farmer must feel in doing this good deed is so important that it is the rare emotion that Moses commands. And we, in the Haggadah, tell the story through him—and like him.

We now see why the authors of the Haggadah chose Deuteronomy 26, rather than anything from Exodus, as the source text for our freedom story. The authors of the Haggadah are teaching us what they regard as a crucial lesson to define the year ahead. The *attitude* that we bring to something is as important as the thing itself. And when it comes to doing God's will, that attitude should be joy—expressed with enthusiasm.

What Is Life For?

The Torah concludes with the letter *lamed* (from the word Israel) and begins with the letter *bet* (from the word Bereshit). Together, they form the word *lev*—which means "heart." The essence of the Torah, we learn, is to win the hearts of its adherents.

This conviction is asserted in the earliest Jewish Torah commentary—the Bible itself. In 1 Samuel 16:7, we learn that God "looks upon the heart." Proverbs 23:26 tells us, "My son, give me thine heart." First Chronicles 28:9 instructs, "God searches all hearts and understands the inclination of all thoughts." And the Talmud encapsulates it all, saying: "God requires the heart."

Two thousand years after the Bible was concluded, Maimonides instructed, "And all these matters [the mitzvot] are to [help us to] overcome our negative inclinations and to correct our traits; and most laws of the Torah are instruction from afar from the Great Adviser [to help us] to correct our character traits and straighten our ways."[14]

The anonymous fifteenth-century German sage known primarily by the name of his work, the *Orchot Tzaddikim*, was even more insistent. "If you do not possess refined character traits, then neither do you possess

Torah and mitzvot, for the entire Torah depends on the refinement of character traits."[15]

In the eighteenth century, the sage Elijah ben Solomon Zalman, known as the Vilna Gaon, encapsulated the Torah's teaching on character: "The prime purpose of man's life is to constantly strive to break his bad traits. Otherwise, what is life for?"[16]

If Moses were writing a commentary on the Vilna Gaon (rather than the other way around), he would have certainly agreed—with an addition. In Deuteronomy 10:17, Moses tells us that God "accepts no bribes." By this point in the Torah, every reader knows that! Indeed, the Torah repeatedly forbids *everyone* from taking bribes. But Moses is so insistent that he provides an example thirteen verses later—when he says that one must not bring a "harlot's hire" or an "exchange for a dog" as an offering. Why, then, would Moses be telling us in his final speech that God takes no bribes—and offering examples?

Nachmanides said that harlots and men who raise brazen dogs that harm the public might excuse their behavior if they are allowed to contribute some of the proceeds to God. The sixteenth-century sage Obadiah Sforno expounded on this idea—saying that people will be tempted to bribe God by saying, *I will do this good thing so that I can do that bad thing.* The prohibition on bribing God, Sforno wrote, reveals a core Torah truth: "A mitzvah [good deed] cannot extinguish a sin."[17]

Why would someone who wants to sin bother trying to bribe God? After all, someone who intentionally sins is well aware that he is doing something wrong.

Why would he not just do the act—and save himself the moral gymnastics involved with bribing God? It can only be that people want to see themselves as fundamentally good—and are prone to convincing themselves that they can sustain their moral self-image while doing the prohibited act. And it must be a sufficiently common phenomenon to warrant Moses addressing it in his departing speech to the Jewish people.

As the Torah is about to end, Moses shows what can happen when we think and act from anything but character. In Deuteronomy 29, he says that our desires will draw us to things that we acknowledge to be "disgusting." This seems unnatural, and even bizarre. It would seem as if we should easily and even automatically be repelled by disgusting things!

Not so, Moses says. These disgusting things will become like "a root flourishing with gall and wormwood." In other words, we will convince ourselves that these "disgusting" things are *so good* that we will grow entire philosophies from them—and work to persuade others of them. We will make ideologies out of our sins.

Are we then doomed to rationalize our bad actions (by bribing God, or other means)—and to consider bad things to be so good that we want to socialize them with others? The Torah offers an insistent no. It does so in two ways. It offers a solution that will not work, and then offers one that will.

The Non-Solution: Willpower

In Genesis 39, Joseph is a late teenager far away from home and serving as the head slave in the home of Potiphar, a top official in the Pharaoh's regime. He is, the text tells us, "handsome of form and handsome of appearance."

Potiphar's wife "cast her eyes upon" Joseph and tells him, "Lie with me." He refuses, saying that he cannot do such a thing to Potiphar and sin against God. The traditional chant for the Torah places a cantillation mark (known as a *shalshelet*) over the word "refuse." The *shalshelet*, which is used four times in the Torah, indicates hesitation—in the context of one struggling to make the correct decision. Joseph's refusal is not easy for him.

Potiphar's wife does not give up. She solicits him every day, but downgrades her demand to increase her chances. She initially asks him to "lie beside her"—indicating that she is willing to settle for something less than sex. He refuses. She then asks him to "be with her"—indicating that she is willing to just be with him privately. He refuses again. At no point does Joseph make certain to avoid seclusion with Potiphar's wife—which he could have done by ensuring that a young slave or two were always by his side. He knows that having sex with Potiphar's wife would be wrong and is relying on his willpower to align his actions with his character.

The text then tells us Joseph enters the house one day to do his work and that "no man of the men" was there. "No man of the men" is as strange in Hebrew as it is in English. Some commentators believe this meant that there were no adult males in the household. But if it were only that Joseph was alone, the phrase "of the men" would have been superfluous.

What, then, could the Torah be telling us? We get a powerful clue in its next book. In Exodus 2:12, Moses sees a Jew fighting an Egyptian. He looks "this way and that way and saw no man." But there were other men present, as is demonstrated by the fact that his subsequent act (taking a side and killing the Egyptian) was widely known the next day. So what does the Torah mean by "no man"? It seems to be saying: Someone who refuses to act justly is not a man.

According to the fourth-century sage Rav Shmuel Bar Nachman, the phrase "no man" in Genesis 39 must refer to Joseph himself. His willpower having been depleted, Joseph enters the house with at least ambiguous intentions.[18]

Potiphar's wife sees Joseph and, rather than opening with words, grabs his garment before demanding: "Lie with me!" She grabs the garment so forcefully that it is partially torn off him. Seemingly taken aback by her aggressiveness, he flees outside with the garment in her hand.

As if anticipating Shakespeare's Lady Macbeth—"Hell hath no fury like a woman scorned"—Potiphar's wife tells the "men of the household" (more evidence that there were men in their vicinity) that Joseph attempted to rape her. Joseph, having relied on his willpower until it had significantly weakened, ends up in prison for twelve years. Through Joseph's ordeal, we learn that willpower can start strong, will inevitably weaken, and cannot be depended upon to protect us from doing tempting and wrong things.

As the Torah nears its conclusion, it returns to willpower—in a very different context. In Deuteronomy 23:9, Moses warns the people: "When you go out against your enemies, you shall guard yourself from every evil thing." The concept of "enemy" may be understood to include all forces that might damage us physically, mentally, and spiritually. We must, Moses instructs, "guard" ourselves from them—and never let them get into a position to harm us. Perhaps if Joseph had had access to Deuteronomy, he would have known to ensure that he was never alone with Potiphar's wife.

If willpower is a frail, progressively weakening, and ultimately unreliable way to ensure that one acts according to character, what can? The Torah gives us a clear answer.

Incapability: The Ultimate Character Goal

In Deuteronomy 12, Moses addresses tithing—the requirement that we give part of our harvest to the needy. Moses could have just told us that it is *forbidden* to consume the tithes—as we owe them to the poor. Instead,

Moses decrees, "You are *not capable* of eating within your cities the tithe of your grain." We see that Moses does not simply decree that we tithe out of obligation. Tithing is about developing our character to such a point where we are *incapable* of consuming that which we are obligated to give.

In Deuteronomy 22, Moses reminds us of the imperative of returning lost items to their owners. He does not only require that we perform the action of returning lost objects. He says that each person must get to the point where he is "*incapable* of hiding yourself [and not returning the object]."

The thirteenth-century Spanish sage Rabbeinu Yonah of Gerondi explored the significance of the clause "incapable of hiding yourself." Rabbeinu Yonah says that we are to return the lost object because we simply "*cannot* ignore it." We are to have internalized the righteousness of returning lost objects so deeply that it is just a part of who we are and what we do. It is not even a matter of choosing to return the lost object; it is a matter of not being *able* to ignore it.[19]

Moses thus tells us *how* we can refine our character. We need to develop an attitude of being *incapable* of sin. He wants us to be *incapable* of ignoring a lost object and *incapable* of misappropriating the tithe. He wants righteous conduct to be embedded so deeply in our character that we are *incapable* of acting otherwise. The true test of character, by the conclusion of Deuteronomy, is whether we are incapable of doing bad things and incapable of neglecting good things.

The Science

Death by Decision

Science is conclusive: Living *good* is a challenge. In 2015, Professor Wilhelm Hofmann of the University of Cologne wrote that we experience desires during half of our waking moments. Of those desires, 33 percent of them conflict with what we believe to be the correct actions. And we give into our illegitimate desires 13 percent of the time.[20]

This battle between our desires and moral action is waged all the time, with varying stakes. It is waged when we consider whether to sleep late or wake up and study, whether to spend discretionary income to help others or indulge ourselves, whether to spend an afternoon volunteering or watching television. And this battle can be a matter of life and death. A variety of studies using data from 2000 to 2010 found that more than 40 percent of all deaths and 55 percent of deaths of people under eighty are due to behavioral decisions that conflict with our vision of who we want to be. These include drugs, alcohol, tobacco, obesity, and careless accidents.[21]

The Self-Enhancement Effect

In the Spring 1950 issue of *Public Opinion Quarterly*, Hugh J. Parry and Helen Crossley of the United States Information Agency published a report titled "Validity of Response to Survey Questions."

That might be the most boring title ever written. Its subject and findings, however, are anything but. The study was a report on three questions that Mr. Parry and Ms. Crossley asked residents of Denver, Colorado. Do you have a library card? Did you vote in the last mayoral election? Did you give to the recent charity drive?

The researchers found that 20 percent of residents said that they owned a library card, 63 percent said that they voted in the last mayoral election, and 67 percent said that they gave to a recent charity drive. Mr. Parry and Ms. Crossley then went to the actual data. It showed that 13 percent of residents owned a library card, 36 percent voted in the election, and 33 percent gave to the charity drive. In each instance, people lied in ways that promoted themselves. The extent of the lying was in proportion to the moral weight of each question, with most people lying about the activity that speaks most profoundly to character (charitable giving).[22]

This was no mid-century phenomenon. In the 2010s, 50 percent more graduates of the University of Maryland reported having given a donation to the school than actually did, and American men and women reported using two to three times the number of condoms that are actually sold in a given year.[23]

Lying may usually be wrong and even stupid in that it predictably compounds the trouble that would come from telling the truth. But it often makes sense in the moment. Why, for instance, would a child lie to his parents about taking a cookie from the cookie jar? Obviously, to avoid the consequences of having violated a rule.

But why would an *anonymous* respondent lie in a survey where no one will ever know who he is or how he responded? It must be to the only person who will ever know about the response—himself.

Contemporary psychologists have identified a phenomenon that explains why a person may do this. It is called the "self-enhancement effect." This is a phenomenon whereby people rate themselves more highly than they deserve on positive measures. It is found everywhere—the 93 percent of Americans who say that they are above average drivers, the 94 percent of college professors who believe that they are above average teachers, and the 25 percent of high school seniors who rate themselves in the top 1 percent of students in "getting along with others."[24]

Those are not the only applications of the self-enhancement effect. In 2017, Professor Cindi May of the College of Charleston reported in *Scientific American* on the place where the self-enhancement effect is "most profound." This concerns what she called "moral characteristics." Indeed, a 1998 study by Jonathon Brown at the University of Washington found that 89 percent of people regard themselves more positively than others on qualities including friendliness, modesty, persistence, and responsibility.[25]

How ingrained is this self-enhancement effect? A 2012 study led by Professor Hofmann is illustrative. He and his colleagues had participants record how they felt each time during the day when they acted out of accordance with their long-term goals. He found that the pleasure that people experience from acting in accordance with an illicit temptation is significantly diminished by the knowledge that they are doing the wrong thing. For instance, a married man who spends the night with a woman he met on a business trip will find that his pleasure is significantly diminished by the "stressful inner conflict" that afflicts him as he cheats on his wife. The term "guilty pleasure" is precisely right—with the guilt extracting a lot of pleasure.[26]

The fact that the self-enhancement effect is so profound when applied to moral qualities yields an important revelation. Most people yearn not only to *do* the right things, but to *be* good. How, then, do people so consistently do what are obviously—even by their own estimation—the wrong things?

Rationalization

In a 2015 paper, Professor Shaul Shalvi and his colleagues at Ben-Gurion University asked an intriguing question: "[How can we explain] the prevalent, mundane, unethical behaviors committed by 'ordinary' people who value their morality highly but cut corners when faced with an opportunity to gain from unethical behavior?"[27]

They discovered that there is not one simple explanation. Instead, they found that we have constructed an elaborate system to align our actions with our character. Professor Shalvi and his colleagues cataloged "pre-violation" and "post-violation" justifications that we commonly use, with the "violation" being of our self-conception as good people.

The first pre-violation justification identified is *ambiguity*. Professor Shalvi and his colleagues offer the example of a man on a business trip who takes his father to an expensive dinner. The man considers expensing the dinner to his company. Should he do so? Of course not. Yet the businessman, for whom the question is not theoretical but a matter of real money, might say that the rules in such situations are not clear. After all, his father always has good business advice. By framing his father's role ambiguously (is he a dad or a business advisor?), the businessman has cleared the way to make the shareholders of his company pay his personal expenses.

The second pre-violation justification is *self-serving altruism*. This is particularly easy when the beneficiaries are apparent and the victims are diffuse. For instance, insider trading, which occurs when a market participant uses privileged information to gain an illicit advantage. The victims are his anonymous counterparties, who will, as a result of his trading, buy slightly higher or sell slightly lower than they otherwise would have. It is usually impossible to identify the specific victims. Thus, it would be easy for one with privileged knowledge to say: "I will make the trade, it won't really hurt anyone, and I will give most of my profits to the soup kitchen. Think of how many hungry people will eat because of my insider trading!"

The third pre-violation justification is *moral licensing*. This is exactly what Sforno said of Moses's declaration that God does not take bribes. Moral licensing occurs when one says: "The fact that I am generally good or just did a good deed gives me the license to do the bad thing that I really want to do."

Professor May provides an example: "An individual who volunteers to deliver food for Meals on Wheels, for example, may later find it acceptable to take home office supplies from work." She cites a variety of studies demonstrating moral licensing in consumer behavior, the workplace, and charitable donations.[28]

Our system of rationalization, Professor Shalvi writes, does not end with the sin (or violation). It adapts and activates again after the violation. One of the key ways it does so is through what Professor Shalvi and his colleagues call *comparison*. One might acknowledge that he has sinned, but convince himself that he is still a good person—by comparing himself to others. For instance, a husband might say: "Yes, I flirted with a woman at work, and there's no way around it—it was wrong. But compared to Bill Clinton, Eliot Spitzer, John Edwards, Donald Trump, King David, and God knows how many others, I didn't do anything!" The psychology behind this seemingly strange reasoning is clear. We strive to maintain the self-image of having a good character, regardless of what we do.

The Love for Disgust

Moses, as discussed, said that our proclivity to follow our desires is so powerful that it can lead us to do even things we regard as disgusting. Fast-forward to the twenty-first century. The three most popular websites, according to Statista, are Google, YouTube, and Facebook. A close fourth is Pornhub, and right behind it is Xvideos. The genre keeps coming in strong, with Xnxx and Spankbang also among the top fifteen.[29]

What can one expect to find on these sites? Writing in the *Free Press*, Isabel Hogben writes that her youthful discovery of Pornhub (the most mainstream of porn sites) included "simulated incest, bestiality, extreme bondage, sex with unconscious women, gangbangs, sadomasochism, and unthinkable physical violence."[30]

The data bears out her observation. A 2022 analysis of popular internet pornography videos found that 88 percent of them contained physical violence, 49 percent contained verbal aggression, 15 percent contained nonconsensual aggression, and 95 percent of actresses in violent pornography expressed pleasure or neutrality.

Surely, many of the consumers of this pornography know that what they are watching is disgusting—not to mention wrong, despicable, and immoral. Yet they do so anyway, in stunning quantities.

Why? Some morally license by saying that they have earned the moral credit to watch pornography by having done good things elsewhere. Others practice self-serving altruism by saying that their consumption of pornography supports feminist liberation, artistic expression, or the libertarian ideal of buyers and sellers willingly exchanging value.

But many do not even attempt those forms of rationalization. They know that pornography is disgusting but they watch it anyway. This leads to the question: Why don't people just summon their willpower and reject this pornography—among other disgusting and repulsive things? Why does the Torah (in the Joseph / Potiphar's wife story) assert the diminishing strength of willpower—to the point where it is effectively useless?

Willpower

The Torah, as we saw, is devoted to the cultivation of good character and the performance of righteous actions. Why, though, does the Torah not even mention or suggest one of the most common modern techniques—the exercise of willpower?

Contemporary science has produced a reason, and it is encapsulated in the title of a paper by Professor Michael Inzlicht of the University of Toronto: "Willpower Is Overrated." The science writer Brian Resnick, who reviewed the modern studies on willpower in an analysis that he published in *Vox*, is even more conclusive. He writes, "Studies have found that trying to teach people to resist temptation either only has short-term gains or can be an outright failure."[31]

And it gets worse. Willpower, a variety of studies have demonstrated, fails even when it supposedly succeeds. A 1998 study by Professor Roy Baumeister and colleagues at Case Western Reserve showed that people who resisted the temptation to eat a delicious cookie gave up sooner on solving an impossible puzzle than those who were not put in that position. This finding has been replicated in different contexts, with the same results.[32]

Why would resisting the temptation to eat a forbidden cookie compromise one's resolve to solve a puzzle? An analysis in *The Economist* explains, "Cognitive control, the umbrella term encompassing mental exertion, self-control and willpower, also fades with effort."[33] The exercise of willpower consumes our mental energy, leaving us with less energy to devote to the next activity.

In her 2013 book, *The Willpower Instinct*, Professor Kelly McGonigal of Stanford University shows just how depleting willpower can be. Her research found that students who use willpower to study eat less well, are prone to emotional outbursts and bike accidents, and even stop flossing. And it is not just students. She writes:

> Smokers who go without a cigarette for twenty-four hours are more likely to binge on ice cream. Drinkers who resist their favorite cocktail become physically weaker on a test of endurance. Perhaps most disturbingly, people who are on a diet are more likely to cheat on their spouse. It's as if there's only so much willpower to go around. Once exhausted, you are left defenseless against temptation—or at least disadvantaged.[34]

The biblical Joseph, reflecting in prison, would have understood.

Becoming Incapable

All of this might seem disconcerting. We want to align our behavior with our character but end up lying to ourselves and/or engaging in all kinds of rationalizations. We can exercise willpower, but it depletes our other sources of strength even when it works—which it rarely does.

Is, then, living a consistently good life simply impossible for most people? Professor Inzlicht does not think so. He writes, "Research makes clear that the best way to reach one's goal is not to resist temptations but to avoid temptations before they arrive; it further suggests that willpower is fragile and not to be relied on; and that *the best self-regulators engage in willpower remarkably seldom* [emphasis added]."[35]

In other words, willpower is weak. But it shouldn't matter, as we should seldom have to call upon it. How can that be when temptations abound? One answer will be familiar to those who recall Moses's instruction for us to become "incapable" of doing the wrong thing or neglecting the right thing.

First, we can decide to make forbidden things inaccessible. A dieter would be much better off keeping hot fudge brownies out of the home than depending on his willpower to resist them. If there are no hot fudge brownies around, the dieter will be incapable of eating them.

But this won't work with everything, as many temptations are either too subtle or too ubiquitous to reliably isolate and remove. For those, we have a 2012 study published in the *Journal of Consumer Research.*

The Power of "I Don't"

In 2012, Professors Vanessa Patrick of the University of Houston and Henrik Hagtvedt of Boston College had thirty working women sign up for a health and wellness seminar. All of the women were told to think of a long-term health and wellness goal that was important to them. The researchers had the women commit to doing a daily workout, and split them into three groups of ten.

The first group was told to "just say no" when they were tempted to lapse. The second group was told to say "I *can't* miss my workout" when they were tempted. The third group was told to say "I *don't* miss workouts" when similarly tempted.

These linguistic distinctions are significant. One who says "I can't" (about anything) is open to being convinced that, "Yes, you can." One who says "I don't" is saying, "I never have, and never would, do that kind of thing." It is essentially the same as the Torah's insistence of being "incapable" of neglecting the commandments.

The researchers tracked the participants for ten days. One out of ten in the "can't" group persisted in the daily workout commitment. Three of ten participants in the "just say no" group persisted. And eight out of ten in the "don't" group persisted.[36]

The unique power of "I don't" over everything else (even "I can't") is seen in that study—and in phenomena that range from eating to heroism.

The laws of Kashrut, by which Orthodox Jews abide, forbid the consumption of lobster, bacon, cheeseburgers, and other foods that many people find highly desirable. Yet, I have never heard of an Orthodox Jew struggling with the prohibition on non-kosher foods. Why? Eating bacon cheeseburgers is just something that Orthodox Jews *do not do*. They are essentially incapable of doing so. Consequently, Orthodox Jews do not have to call upon their willpower when they pass by a McDonald's. They do not have to think at all. Refusing cheeseburgers, for an Orthodox Jew, is an easy *non-decision*.

Orthodox Jews are also aware of the commandment in Deuteronomy 4:9 that states, "You shall guard yourselves very much." Most commentators understand this obligation to "guard yourself" as a mandate to take care of your body.[37]

This command does not come with a law prohibiting the consumption of specific foods. It does not ask for an "I don't" commitment. Orthodox Jews are permitted to eat potato pancakes, French fries, and cheesecake. Thus, Orthodox Jews can comply with Deuteronomy 4:9 by enjoying those foods (among others) in moderation.

Does the discipline that they exercise with non-kosher foods extend to these unhealthy kosher foods? Not at all. According to a 2012 study from Israel, male ultra-Orthodox Jews are *more* likely to have weight problems than their secular counterparts.[38]

This phenomenon is not limited to Orthodox Jews. According to a 2022 study by Professor Elisa Becker of the University of Exeter, people who decide to become vegetarians generally develop a "disgust" for meat within their first month of forsaking it. As with Orthodox Jews, this discipline often does not extend to eating generally. A 2005 study from Tufts University concluded that 29 percent of vegetarians are obese.[39]

Why do Orthodox Jews and secular vegetarians eschew hot fudge brownies with difficulty but bacon cheeseburgers with ease? In the former case, an Orthodox Jew or vegetarian who says, "I really *can't* eat that brownie," is vulnerable to the voice that says, "Yes, you can" because it is a small piece, it is a holiday, you did not have dessert yesterday, you are happy and deserve to celebrate or sad and need a culinary uplift. In the latter case, the Orthodox Jews and vegetarians simply say, "I *don't* eat bacon cheeseburgers." It is that voice—the voice of incapability—that works.

The power of incapability (or "I don't") extends beyond helping us avoid the bad. It can ignite remarkable courage and activate us for the greatest good.

On June 8, 2023, a Syrian refugee in France entered a playground and stabbed four children and two elderly people. His rampage was cut short by a slightly built man, Henri d'Anselme, who confronted the attacker with his backpack. Why did Mr. d'Anselme put his life on the line? He explained, "All I know is that I was not there by chance. It was unthinkable to do nothing."

Mr. d'Anselme explained why he was, essentially, incapable of not responding. He is a devout Catholic who felt "guided by providence and the Virgin Mary." And the implications of their guidance was so deeply embedded in his being that he did not need to think before risking his life. He explained: "The entire Christian civilization on which our country is built is a knightly message to defend widows and orphans." He was *incapable* of not acting in accordance with his expectations of Christian civilization.[40]

Cultivating Enthusiasm

The Torah, as we saw, maintains that a good character is fueled by an enthusiasm about doing what we should do. What does contemporary science reveal?

In recent decades, psychologists have discovered and developed the notion of "self-concordance." This concept, in the words of Professor Marina Milyavskaya and colleagues at McGill University, reflects "the extent to which individuals' goals reflect their personal values and interests."[41]

Individuals with high self-concordance, as Professor Milyavskaya wrote, "want to" do what they should—and are much more successful at acting in accordance with their character aspirations than are those with "have to" goals. Her 2016 study of college students who set three goals for a semester determined that students with self-concordant goals made more than 20 percent more progress toward them than students who did not. This finding coheres with a 2008 study by Professor Richard Koestner of McGill, who found that adults with self-concordance made 25 percent more progress toward their goals than those without it. This finding accords precisely with Moses's instruction that we enjoy our good deeds.[42]

How can we best develop a robust self-concordance? It turns out that there is an indispensable quality, familiar to those who have considered the references to "fire" in the Torah.

In 2009, the *Sporting News* named the greatest coach of all time. There was little or no dispute that they had chosen the right person: John Wooden, whose UCLA basketball teams won ten national championships, including seven in a row (1967 to 1973). What accounts for his astonishing success? There are many things, but it all starts with something that he began developing as a twenty-four-year-old coach in 1934. This was his Pyramid of Success. Most elements of the Pyramid changed over the years, but one thing didn't. This is *enthusiasm*. He wrote, "[Enthusiasm] brushes off upon those with whom you come into contact. You must truly enjoy what you are doing."[43]

Coach Wooden's experience is validated by the data on successful teachers generally—as is discussed in the chapter of this book on education.

Dr. David Sirota has long been one of the leaders in corporate behavioral research. In 2005, he and several colleagues reported on a study the firm conducted using a unique dataset: that of employee enthusiasm, which they had measured at 237 companies over the previous eleven years.

They determined that 14 percent of these companies had enthusiastic employees. They found that companies with enthusiastic employees outperformed the average prices of companies in the same industry by 250 percent. The stock prices of companies with unenthusiastic employees underperformed their peers by an even greater amount. Enthusiasm, Dr. Sirota found, is the key factor that leads employees to work harder and better—to the benefit of themselves and their organizations.[44]

Why is enthusiasm so powerful? If we are enthusiastic about something, we will want to do it frequently and better. As Coach Wooden said, we are apt to share what we are enthusiastic about. Therefore, there is an enormous difference between just doing the right thing and doing the right thing enthusiastically. No wonder that Moses said that we will be cursed if we serve God—but without "joy and gladness of heart."

Reflection

The Torah is clear that our actions are the most important, and indeed determinative, aspect of each person. Hence, the Torah is full of stories and laws that teach us what actions we should take (from giving to the poor to setting up a judicial system) and those we should not (from gossip to murder).

Our actions are so important that the Torah considers, in all five of its books, how we can most reliably do what we should and avoid what we shouldn't. It concludes, and emphasizes, that even the most determined attempts to robotically comply with a set of moral rules are unsustainable and will ultimately fail. We can attempt willpower, but it inevitably weakens until it dissipates. We can steel ourselves to overcome our desires and do what we should—but we will inevitably convince ourselves (even if no one else) that what we want to do is what we should do.

The way to ensure a durable commitment to moral and spiritual action, the Torah argues, is to develop our character—so that we want to do what we should, and are ultimately "incapable" of doing what we shouldn't.

Modern social science, from its studies on willpower to its development of concepts like moral licensing, has validated the Torah's claims.

The claims of the Torah and social science about the importance of character lead to two related inquiries. One is: Why do we act as we do? The second is: How can I improve my character?

The first question will be addressed in the next chapter, and the second will be addressed in the following section of this book, which addresses self-improvement.

2

Why God Loses Two Arguments and End-of-the-World Cults Thrive Past Destruction Date

The Torah and Science of Why We Believe and Act as We Do

God Loses Two Arguments

By Exodus 7, the Jews have endured more than two centuries of Egyptian slavery. God decides that it is time to free them and to begin the Exodus. But that is not the only, or even the main, goal of the Exodus. God, through Moses, announces in Exodus 7:5 that it is primarily to convince Egypt "that I am Hashem [God]." If Egypt knows God—if the most powerful empire in the world accepts the truth of ethical monotheism—then the rest of the world will likely follow, and God will have won the world.

God knows that he will have to win the argument through the only language that the Pharaoh speaks: power. God begins peacefully by having Moses and Aaron beat the Pharaoh and his sorcerers in a competition involving staffs and snakes. God, through Moses and Aaron, easily defeats the most talented sorcerers in Egypt. But the victory has no effect. God announces, "The Pharaoh's *heart* is unyielding."

After the peaceful competition fails to move the Pharaoh, God adopts a different tactic. He delivers nine punishing plagues, with each one seemingly directed against an aspect of the Pharaoh's religious system *and*

Egyptian society. The first plague (the Nile turning to blood) strikes at Hapi, the Egyptian god who is supposed to oversee and protect the river—the life source for the nation. The second plague (an infestation of frogs) strikes at Heket, the Egyptian god of fertility (whose head was a frog). This process continues until the ninth plague (three days of darkness), which strikes at Ra (the sun god) and causes every Egyptian to sink into what seems to be a clinical depression.

God defeats the Pharaoh overwhelmingly in every instance, simultaneously demonstrating the impotence of the Egyptian "gods" and raining pain upon the enslaving society. The Pharaoh is given an opportunity after each plague to free the Jews. Yet, he never does so. Why?

The text refers many times to the Pharaoh's "heart" being "weighted" or "hardened"—sometimes by God, sometimes by the Pharaoh. Yet, the text never even references his mind. It is very clear that God believes that he will succeed or fail in changing the Pharaoh by going for his heart. God apparently considers the mind irrelevant in the Pharaoh's decision-making process.

In Exodus 11, God decides to go all out. He announces the coming of the tenth plague: the slaying of the firstborn. He delivers, and every household of Egypt suffers a crushing fatality.

This plague succeeds in changing the Pharaoh's mind—for one day. A day after relenting, the Pharaoh sends his charioteers to chase the Jews and bring them back into slavery. Although he sends many chariots, the term the Torah uses for "chariot" is in the singular. This is the Torah's way of teaching us that the charioteers thought and acted with one mind. Despite each losing a firstborn—in addition to having suffered each of the previous plagues at the hand of a God no one doubted—the charioteers all persisted in agreeing with the Pharaoh and disagreeing with God.

The charioteers fail to bring the Jews back to slavery. By Exodus 12, God has freed the Jews. But he completely fails to convince the Pharaoh and the Egyptians that he "is Hashem" and deserving of being followed. God, and us readers, learn that not even divine authority expressed through ten plagues can change a mind that is made up.

The reader is left wondering: Is this inability or unwillingness to change one's mind a characteristic of ancient Egypt or of mankind generally? We will find out in Numbers 22, when the Moabite King Balak dispatches

Balaam to curse the Jews. Balaam is a world-famous gentile prophet who is acknowledged in ancient Jewish teaching for being as talented as Moses.[1]

Balaam, who is excited by the assignment because of the wealth it promises, is continually stymied by God in his effort to curse the Jews. He acknowledges that he does not have the power to do something that God explicitly forbids. He explains, "Even if Balak would give me his house full of silver and gold, I cannot go beyond the word of the Lord my God" (Numbers 24:13).

Even accepting God's authority and knowing God's will, Balaam does not change his mind about cursing the Jews. Balaam instead uses his creativity and determination to try different ways to destroy the Jews. God thwarts all of Balaam's schemes until he is eventually slain for having "turned against the Lord and his people" (Numbers 31:16).

Fast-forward to the Book of Joshua. Joshua declares, "Cursed be the man before the Lord, that rises up to build this city Jericho: He shall lay its foundation with his firstborn, and with his youngest son shall he set up the gates of it." Much later, in 1 Kings 16:34, a man named Chiel has the temerity to build Jericho. When Chiel lays the first brick, his firstborn son dies. He keeps building until all of his children are dead. He never changed his mind.

Why did the Pharaoh, Balaam, and Chiel persist in maintaining their beliefs, despite direct evidence from God that they were wrong? Why did their minds not change at all, even when it is clear (even to them) that their persistence would result in death and destruction?

God, it turns out, had already provided the answer.

From Feeling to Thinking to Acting

In Exodus 1, the Pharaoh announces his decision to commit genocide against the Jews by killing every Jewish baby at birth. These plans are set in motion in Exodus 2:1—where we learn that a man from the House of Levi marries a daughter from the House of Levi. The woman gives birth to a son.

They are able to hide the baby for three months, but after that, can no longer protect their infant from the Egyptian murderers. The boy's mother puts the baby in a wicker basket and sends him down the river. Would the baby, somehow, be saved?

At that time, the Pharaoh's daughter goes to bathe by the river when she sees the basket coming down the current. She opens the basket, sees the baby, and hears him crying. She does not stop there.

The Pharaoh's daughter, we read in Exodus 2:5, "took pity on him and said, 'This is one of the Hebrew boys.'" She then concocts a plan to save the baby, which involves her adopting him. The baby is Moses.

The order of events here is crucial. *She first feels* (she takes "pity" on him). *She then thinks* (she notes that the baby is a Jew). *She finally acts* (she adopts him). Her decision-making process is clear: It goes from feeling to thinking to acting.

Fast-forward to Numbers 15:39: God commands the Jews to wear *tzitzit* (ritual fringes) on the corners of our garments. God explains, "[You are to wear *tzitzit*] so that you do not explore after your heart and after your eyes after which you stray."

The order in the language is, as with the Pharaoh's daughter in Exodus 2:5, instructive. God stipulates that the emotion ("your heart") will *precede* the thinking (what the "eyes" observe), which will *precede* the action ("after which you stray"). This law applies to all Jewish men. God is essentially telling us that we are all like the Pharaoh's daughter—and the Pharaoh and Balaam. Again: we feel, *then* recruit reasons that comply with our emotions, and *finally* act accordingly.

By Deuteronomy 6:5, Moses has deeply absorbed this lesson from God. Moses commands us to "love the Lord thy God with all your heart, all your soul and all your might." First, we will feel (our heart). Then we will think (our soul). Then we will act (our might). Moses based this existential instruction on the premise that we all operate, in this sense, as the Pharaoh's daughter did in early Exodus.

In Deuteronomy 29:3, Moses shows us just how this process works. He says, "Yet until this day, the Lord has not given you a heart to know, eyes to see, and ears to hear." We might associate hearts with feeling and minds with knowing. But not Moses. He insists that the heart *knows. Then*, our our eyes and ears—the agents of the mind—get involved in service of the heart.

In none of these instances—the Pharaoh's daughter, the Pharaoh, Balaam, and the Jews described in Numbers and Deuteronomy—does the protagonist take in the data and make a reasoned conclusion based on it. In each case, the protagonist starts with an emotionally derived conclusion, adjusts reasoning, and executes actions accordingly.

From one perspective, the Torah's teaching that we think with our hearts and use our minds to recruit reasons to support our emotions is dispiriting. A reader might even ask: How can we criticize the Pharaoh if he was just driven by his emotions? What is the role of free will, which the Torah supposedly insists upon and celebrates, if we are slaves to our passions?

The Torah has the answer.

Foolish Wood and Wise Hearts

In Exodus 25, God gives the Jews an assignment. We are to build a Tabernacle, a portable temple that will accompany us on our journey through the desert. The holiest item in this sacred space would be the ark. It will contain several holy things, including the tablets of the Ten Commandments, Aaron's staff, and a jar of manna.[2]

God is very specific about how the Tabernacle and everything in it is to be built—down to the number of loops at the end of the second set of curtains. Therefore, it is not surprising that God specifies precisely what material the ark is to be made of. The core of the ark is to be made of acacia wood. Why? The Rebbe Rashab finds the answer in the fact that acacia wood, *shittim*, is etymologically related to the word "*shetut*," which means folly or foolishness.

Why would the ark be made of "foolish" material? The Rebbe Rashab explains that everyone is a fool for something. Everyone, in other words, is emotionally connected to something or someone beyond all reason. Thus, the Torah is instructing us to be a "fool" for the right things.[3]

Can an individual decide to become a "fool" for something good? The Torah answers this question ten verses later, in the description of the actual building of the Tabernacle. Moses commands, several times, that crucial tasks be performed by people with a "wise heart"—those who are emotionally invested in using their skills for a holy task.

Moses clearly believes that we can and should educate the passions of the heart to become wise. The ways we can do so are discussed at length in the chapters of this book on routine and changing oneself.

A Great Dissenter—and His Footnotes

None of this would have made any sense to Plato, the Greek philosopher who lived after Moses and before the Talmud. He identified three components of human behavior: the *logos* (reason), the *thymos* (spiritedness/emotion), and the *eros* (desire). Plato believed that a cultivated person would use his logos to instruct his thymos and his eros. He wrote, "That part of the soul, then, which partakes of courage and spirit . . . might hearken to the reason, and, in conjunction therewith, might forcibly subdue the tribe of the desires whensoever they should utterly refuse to yield willing obedience to the word of command from the citadel of reason."[4]

Plato's presumption that people ought to be driven by their reason led to his valorization of the intellectual elite. As the Cambridge philosopher Stephen Cave writes:

> Plato emerged from a world steeped in myth and mysticism to claim something new: that the truth about reality could be established through reason, or what we might consider today to be the application of intelligence. In *The Republic*, Plato concludes that the ideal ruler is the "philosopher king," as only a philosopher can work out the proper order of things. And so he launched the idea that the cleverest should rule over the rest in an intellectual meritocracy.[5]

In other words, Plato believed that reason can and should drive decision-making—especially among intelligent people. The most refined (the gods and the philosophers) will be able to make decisions entirely from reason.[6] Hence, respect and authority should be accorded to the most intelligent, who will use their cognitive capabilities to make the best decisions for themselves and society.

How important is the Platonic conception to how we think today? The twentieth-century Harvard philosopher Alfred North Whitehead said, "The safest general characterization of the European philosophical tradition is that it consists of a series of footnotes to Plato."[7]

As Professor Whitehead wrote, the philosophical and political program of the Enlightenment was based upon Plato's conception. It is embodied in the rhetorical question of the British poet John Milton: "Let her [Truth] and Falsehood grapple; who ever knew Truth put to the worse, in a free and open encounter?" Milton's presumption was that people with different convictions would meet in "a free and open encounter." The result would be the triumph of the truth, with those who had previously argued for the falsehood having changed their minds.[8]

This concept, as the University of Wisconsin economist Jeffrey Smith has shown, was used continuously in the freedom struggles in colonial America. Professor Smith wrote, "The specific proposition advanced by thinkers like Milton and Jefferson—that truth would overcome falsehood in free and open encounter—was one rationale for the general expansion of intellectual and political freedom that occurred in the 17th and 18th centuries."[9]

Consequently, there is no doubt that the wide acceptance of Plato's conception inspired one of the best ideas to ever bless mankind. This conception of the marketplace of ideas is probably the single most important basis for the First Amendment of the United States Constitution, which guarantees freedom of conscience and its expression.

However, the greatness of the First Amendment does not mean that Plato's claim—that people reason and then decide—was right. Mistakes often produce great outcomes. The discovery of plastic, Vaseline, penicillin, Viagra, Corn Flakes, the microwave, and the color mauve were all the result of fortuitous mistakes.[10]

Indeed, the Platonic conception was directly challenged by some Enlightenment thinkers who nevertheless appreciated the political outcomes that derived from it. Francis Bacon wrote in his 1620 book *Novum Oregnum*:

> The human understanding when it has adopted an opinion (either as being the received opinion or being agreeable to itself) draws all things else to support and agree with it. And though there be a greater number and weight of instances to be found on the other side, yet these it either neglects and despises or else by some distinction sets aside and rejects.[11]

The debate between the biblical and the Platonic views raged even in the United States. Thomas Jefferson favored frequent constitutional conventions. James Madison objected, saying, "The passions, therefore, not the reason, of the public would sit in judgment." Thomas Jefferson's views, he explained, were appropriate for "a nation of philosophers . . . but a nation of philosophers is as little to be expected as the philosophical race of kings wished for by Plato."[12]

Mr. Madison's contemporary, the great British theoretician of freedom David Hume, agreed with his philosophy. He wrote in his 1740 book *A Treatise of Human Nature*, "Reason is, and ought only to be the slave of the passions, and can never pretend to any other office than to serve and obey them." Moses would have nodded in vigorous agreement.[13]

The debate stage is set. Plato and his footnotes claim that reason, not passion, governs what at least highly intelligent people believe and do. The Torah, Francis Bacon, James Madison, and David Hume claim that passions, not reason, govern what everyone thinks and does.

Who is right? The stakes are no less than the fundamental understanding of human condition—what we believe, why we believe, and how we can change.

The Science

It's the End of the World

Professor Leon Festinger was one of the pioneers of American social psychology in the twentieth century. He was teaching at Stanford University in 1956 when he and several colleagues published what became a seminal work of social psychology: "When Prophecy Fails."

Their subject was end-of-the-world cults, which were prevalent in the 1950s. They asked: What changes in a believer's commitment to the cult when the world *doesn't* end?

Professor Festinger identified a cult that determined, based on messages from aliens, that the world would end on December 21, 1954. The cult members, though, would be okay because the aliens would pick them up in flying saucers and take them into outer space. The cult members acted on their convictions. Some gave up their jobs and possessions, which they would not need in outer space. They removed all metal from their clothing (such as zippers and brassiere wires) so as not to interfere with the workings of the spaceship.[14]

The world did not end. How did the cult members respond? A couple of members left, but a significant majority did not. And they had their reasons. Some concluded that the world did not end as a result of their having come together. Others found a calculation error and reset the end-of-the-world date. Others said that the event had been postponed to enable them to prepare to "meet their maker." These adherents did not question the premise of the cult, or the credibility of its leader. They became more convinced, and worked even harder to bring others into the cult.[15]

Someone learning about this response might wonder: Was it a function of the era or a unique characteristic of this particular cult? Or is it representative of a generalized phenomenon? Three decades later, we found out. In 1988, the former NASA engineer Edgar Whisenant published a book about his end-time prediction: *88 Reasons Why the Rapture Will Be in 1988*. He sold 4.5 million books and gave away another three hundred thousand to Christian pastors.[16]

The Rapture would occur, he guaranteed, on September 13, at the conclusion of Rosh Hashanah. When the world did not end, he explained that his prediction was thrown off by a fluke in the Gregorian calendar that year. He revised the date to September 15, and then October 3. When the world kept going on after October 3, he adjusted his calculations and came out with a similar book the next year. This process lasted until 1993.[17]

One might look at these two cases and say that belief in highly specific and near-term end-of-the-world scenarios is unconventional. Such believers might not be using much reason to arrive at their conclusions to begin with. Therefore, it is at least possible that the inability or unwillingness of their devotees to change their minds about the prophet after the prophecy fails relates to the particular psychology of those who might believe in end-of-the-world cults in the first place.

Fortunately, we have data from conventional college students on a quintessentially mainstream political topic: capital punishment. In 1979, Professor Charles Lord of Texas Christian University and his colleagues took two groups of college students. One group supported capital punishment. The other opposed it. The researchers presented each group with data on capital punishment. Those who supported capital punishment rated the pro–capital punishment data as "highly credible" and the anti-capital punishment data as "unconvincing."[18]

By itself, this is not interesting. It is to be expected that people find data that supports their side of an argument more convincing than data that opposes it. But there was a twist to the data. *It was all fake.* How did the students respond upon learning this?

They became more convinced of their initial positions. Those who had started out pro–capital punishment were now even *more* persuaded of its efficacy after learning that the reinforcing data was fake. Those who had opposed capital punishment rejected it with even greater fervor. Professor Lord explained:

> People who hold strong opinions on complex social issues are likely to examine relevant empirical evidence in a biased manner. They are apt to accept "confirming" evidence at face value while subjecting "disconfirming" evidence to critical evaluation, and as a result to draw undue support for their initial position from mixed or random empirical findings.[19]

The fake data study has been replicated many times, with many stories, fact patterns, and groups of participants. The only thing that is consistent is the result: Exposure to *any* data, even if it is revealed to be fake, strengthens the original belief of the adherent.

This phenomenon now has a name in psychology: "my side bias" or "confirmation bias." The role of new information in the thought process is to confirm preexisting beliefs and to amplify one's conviction in one's side. Professor Festinger explained:

> A man with a conviction is a hard man to change. Tell him you disagree and he turns away. Show him facts and figures and he questions your sources. Appeal to logic and he fails to see your point . . . Suppose an individual believes something with his whole heart; suppose further that he has a commitment to this belief and he has taken irrevocable actions because of it; finally, suppose that he is presented with evidence that his belief is wrong; what will happen? The individual will frequently emerge, not only unshaken, but even more convinced of the truth of his beliefs than ever before. Indeed, he may even show a new fervor for convincing and converting people to his view.[20]

So, the Pharaoh does not change his mind about freeing the Jews and accepting God even after ten plagues. Devotees of the end-of-the-world cults kept evangelizing after the predicted doomsday came and went. Balaam, who knew that the all-powerful God is protecting the Jews, persisted in attempting to destroy them until his efforts killed him. And college students became stronger in their convictions about capital punishment after learning that the data they were provided with in support of their position was fake. Professor Festinger was certainly correct: "A man with a conviction is a hard man to change."

Are We Scientists or Lawyers?

Professor Festinger's statement, along with his and the other examples, all pertain to how people think with their hearts even (and seemingly especially) in the presence of data and logic. But Moses's pronouncement that we will have "hearts to know, eyes to see and ears to hear" (in that order) applies to another kind of question as well. These are purely moral questions, which cannot be confirmed or rebutted with data. These questions do not ask whether something is good or bad, true or false; they ask whether something is right or wrong. How do our hearts and minds interact to yield moral decisions?

Enter Professor Jonathan Haidt of NYU, one of the great social psychologists of the twenty-first century. In and around 2010, he presented a (thankfully) hypothetical scenario to his students:

> Julie and Mark are siblings who take a trip together to France. One night they are staying alone in a cabin near the beach. They decide that it would be interesting and fun if they had sex with each other. At the very least, they reasoned, it would be a new experience for each of them. Julie is already taking birth control pills and Mark uses a condom. They both enjoy the sex, but decide not to do it again. They keep that night a special secret between them, which makes them feel even closer to each other.

Professor Haidt then asked participants in the study what they thought of Julie and Mark's decision to have sex. Only 20 percent of people approved. The other 80 percent offered reasons for their objections—for instance, that Julie could get pregnant and give birth to a deformed child.

However, all of the reasons the students offered against this incest were easily rebutted. There was no risk of pregnancy. The sex was consensual, and it deepened their sibling relationship.

The participants did not argue with these obvious rebuttals. They did not try to say that Julie could become pregnant or that the sex was nonconsensual. They did not come up with any other reason why Mark and Julie did something wrong. But their inability to find such a reason did not lead them to change their minds. Professor Haidt reported that they "seemed to be flailing around, throwing out reason after reason, and rarely changing their minds when Scott [his research assistant] proved that their latest reason was not relevant."[21]

How, then, do we handle objections to beliefs that actually cannot be sustained with *any* reasoned argument? Professor Haidt offers a few more hypotheticals.

Would it be okay to eat a family dog that had been hit by a car? Would it be okay to eat a human cadaver before it was incinerated? Would you sell your soul for $2—even when the "contract" specified, "This form is part of a psychology experiment. It is not a legal or binding contract in any way"?

Professor Haidt saw the same result as he did with the Mark and Julie hypothetical. The participants could not identify a sustainable reason why it was wrong to eat a dead dog or human or to "sell their soul." Similarly, they did not change their minds even when it was very clear that they could not come up with a reason to support their view.[22]

What was going on in the minds of these respondents? Their reason could not provide any coherent explanations but their emotions did. With their emotions having already made the decisions for them, their minds attempted to recruit reasons to support their conclusions—and kept trying, even after each argument was definitively rebutted.

Professor Haidt concluded, "When it comes to moral judgments, we think we are scientists discovering the truth, but actually we are lawyers arguing for positions we arrived at by other means."[23]

Or, as Moses said, we have "hearts to know, eyes to see, and ears to hear"—in that order.

Making and Losing Money

Is there any arena where we reliably think with our minds first? If there were, a good candidate would be the one where everyone, regardless of their religious, political, or philosophical orientation, wants the same thing:

money. There are a lot of ways to make money, and a few universal rules for how to do so.

One of those rules comes from the greatest investor in American history, Warren Buffett, who wrote in his 1988 shareholder letter: "Our favorite holding period is forever." In other words, an investor should buy and hold.[24]

Mr. Buffett's philosophy of buy and hold is widely supported and equally well known. The reverence that all investors have for Mr. Buffett is reflected in his nickname, "the Oracle of Omaha." Do investors follow his buy-and-hold philosophy?

The financial research firm Dalbar has the data. Investors trade so often that they lose an average of 3 percent a year due to what a *Financial Times* analysis calls "emotionally driven investment decisions"—with that number doubling during times of significant market volatility.

There are many triggers to emotionally driven investment decisions. Investors get excited about a company or a product. They become discouraged by a disappointing earnings report. They panic in bear markets and get exuberant in bull markets. Whatever the cause, professional investors—those paid to think rationally and act accordingly—suffer the same challenges. Consequently, around 80 percent of actively managed funds underperform the broad-based index in their sector.[25]

There is nothing technically difficult about buying or selling a stock. So, are stock market participants, who can act with a click or a call, uniquely vulnerable to emotionally driven decision-making? In 2012, American Express published a warning titled "Don't Fall in Love with Your Business." Many entrepreneurs, the analysis shows, indeed fall in love with their business ideas. This "love" overwhelms the entrepreneur and takes their focus away from the rational activities that often separate success and failure. For instance, "recruiting, operations, cash flow management and risk mitigation strategies."

And those are not the only problems that come with falling in love with one's business. This love, the American Express analysis shows, can hinder another discipline that every entrepreneur recognizes is crucial: adapting to market changes. Yet, large numbers of businesses fail because their owners are too emotionally connected with their idea to make these necessary changes. The analysis concludes, "If you are in love with your idea, it's time to grow up."[26]

The only problem with the conclusion is that there is nothing childish about making decisions based upon emotions. It is, at least according to the Torah, what adults do.

The Role of Intelligence

Plato would have conceded that most people allow their emotions to drive their decision-making. That is why he advocated the reign of philosopher-kings—highly intelligent people whose decision-making would be directed by their reason.

The Torah has a different position on this. There are plenty of people in the Torah who are portrayed as dullards—Esau, Lot, and Reuben, among others. But these are not the people whom the Torah highlights as maintaining a conviction against all evidence. The Torah's exemplars of this phenomenon are the Pharaoh and Balaam, who are distinguished for their intelligence. Why might the Torah use these intelligent men as examples of how people strengthen their beliefs in the presence of contrary evidence? To show us that such actions are not the result of intellectual deficiency.

An investigation can begin with an understanding of what intelligence is. In 2010, a team of neuroscientists from Spain, the United States, and Canada defined "intelligence." They enumerated several criteria—the *first* of which was "the mental ability for reasoning."[27] This explains why Plato, who believed that highly intelligent people would rationally analyze available information en route to reasoned judgments, supported rule by philosophers.

Are, as Plato believed, intelligent people more likely to use their reasoning ability to come to conclusions and make decisions? In 1991, Harvard professor David Perkins and colleagues did an experiment to find out. Professor Perkins presented students (in high school, college, and graduate school) of different levels of intelligence with a social issue they would likely have a strong opinion about—like capital punishment. He then asked them to write down all of the reasons supporting their side and the other side.

The participants at all education and intelligence levels came up with more arguments for their own side than the other. One would think, though, that a high-IQ person would be able to come up with more reasons than less-intelligent people. That proved to be *partially* true. The high-IQ participants came up with more arguments for their own side than did the lower-IQ participants. But they did not come up with more arguments for the other side. Professor Perkins and his colleagues concluded, "People invest their IQ in buttressing their own case rather than exploring the entire issue more fully and evenhandedly."[28]

The science historian Michael Shermer has the data to show it. He discovered that plenty of college graduates are likely to believe in things like telepathy, magnetic therapy, alien abduction, ghosts, astrology, and miracle cures. Reflecting on his research, Mr. Shermer concluded:

> Smart people believe weird things because they are skilled at defending beliefs they arrived at for non-smart reasons . . . Rarely do any of us sit down before a table of facts, weigh them pro and con, and choose the most logical and rational explanation, regardless of what we previously believed. Most of us, most of the time, come to our beliefs for a variety of reasons having little to do with empirical evidence and logical reasoning. Rather, such variables as genetic predisposition, parental predilection, sibling influence, peer pressure, educational experience, and life impressions all shape the personality preferences that, in conjunction with numerous social and cultural influences, lead us to our beliefs. We then sort through the body of data and select those that most confirm what we already believe, and ignore or rationalize away those that do not.[29]

Why Elliott Came to Ruin

Modern social science has enabled us to understand that, as the Torah teaches, we have a "heart that knows"—and a mind that provides it with reasons and justifications. It is joined by contemporary neuroscience, which describes *how* it is the heart—and not the mind—that determines what we believe.

Dr. Antonio Damasio is a Portuguese neuroscientist who has won seemingly every prize and award broadly available in his profession. He is an expert on damage to the ventromedial prefrontal cortex, which regulates emotion—a specific kind of brain damage that is caused by accidents and tumors. He found that these patients, following their injury, still maintained their IQ scores, and performed well on tests of moral reasoning, memory, and language.

This is not surprising—as these are rational functions, and only the emotional part of their brains was affected by their loss of function in the ventromedial prefrontal cortex. Equally not surprisingly, these patients had lost nearly all of their emotionality. They were not moved by even the most gruesome or joyous photographs. Unencumbered by emotions, these patients were paragons of reason. How would they perform when it came to making real-world decisions?

According to Plato, these people should have performed magnificently. After all, they no longer had emotion to cloud or compete with their reason. Without a working ventromedial prefrontal cortex, they were perfectly equipped to weigh all of the evidence before them and make sound decisions based only on the data.

How did they actually perform in making decisions? The story of Dr. Damasio's patient Elliott is illustrative. Elliott, as a result of a brain tumor, had lost the ability to emotionally process. A *Harvard Business Review* analysis provides details about Elliott:

> Faced with an organizational task, he'd deliberate for an entire afternoon about how to approach the problem. Should he organize the papers he was working on by date? The size of the document? Relevance to the case? In effect, he was doing the organizational task too well, considering every possible option—but at the expense of achieving the larger goal. He could no longer effectively reach decisions, particularly personal and social ones, and despite being repeatedly shown this flaw, he could not correct it.[30]

Of course, Elliott had to make decisions, even if it took him an inordinate amount of time to do so. He decided to get married, and then got divorced. He then married a woman everyone warned him about, and divorced again. His intelligence got him employed, but he rapidly lost those jobs. And he got involved commercially with a lowlife that ended with his bankruptcy.[31]

Consequently, Dr. Damasio concluded, "What is missing in a person who can pass an intelligence test with flying colors but can't even organize his own life? As our tests prove, the result is a lack of normal emotional reactions. I continue to be fascinated by the fact that feelings are not just the shady side of reason but that they help us to reach decisions as well."[32]

The Pleasure of a Confirmed Conviction

In 2004, Emory professor Drew Westen put supporters of George W. Bush and John Kerry under a functional magnetic resonance imaging (fMRI) machine to see how their brains reacted when their candidates contradicted themselves. Professor Westen found that the dorsolateral prefrontal cortex (which is affiliated with reasoning) was not aroused. This showed that partisans did not even process, let alone get disturbed by, their candidate's contradictions.

Other parts of the brain became quite active. These included the orbitofrontal cortex (which processes emotions), the anterior cingulate cortex (which monitors conflicts), and the posterior cingulate cortex (which is associated with addiction). And perhaps most tellingly, the ventral striatum of the participants was aroused. This is the part of the brain that is associated with pleasure—eating chocolate, receiving compliments, and achieving sexual climax.

Professor Westen concluded, "Essentially, it appears as if partisans twirl the cognitive kaleidoscope until they get the conclusions they want, and then they get massively reinforced for it, with the elimination of negative emotional states and activation of positive ones."[33]

The Hand of Compassion vs. the Calculus of Reason

As discussed, the Torah tradition posits that we think with our hearts (rather than our minds)—but does not despair over it. We can train ourselves, and educate our children, to become passionate for right things and to reject wrong things.

The question of whether or not this is true is best answered by a phenomenon from our recent history: the righteous gentiles—those who risked, and sometimes sacrificed, their lives in order to save Jews during the Holocaust. An analysis can begin with the findings of University of Connecticut professor Nechama Tec.

Nechama Tec became interested in the psychology of righteous gentiles because she was saved by one. Professor Tec, a Jewish girl born in Poland in 1931, survived the Holocaust by assuming the identity of a niece living with her Catholic family. Her experience led her to devote her academic career to studying a phenomenon that has intrigued many in the years since the Holocaust: why some gentiles in Nazi-occupied lands, who could have achieved relative safety by staying away from Jews, chose to risk everything to save Jews.

What accounted for the heroism of the righteous gentiles? Professor Tec's research found that there were no demographic dividing lines. She found that the rescuers could be illiterate or learned, religious or irreligious. The rescuers, regardless of their backgrounds or status, shared a decision-making process. "Whenever they extended the help, it never followed a long, prolonged deliberation."[34]

This finding was confirmed by the YIVO Institute for Jewish Research. The YIVO researchers discovered: "Indeed, most rescuers do not appear to have thought carefully about their actions or analyzed them; instead, they viewed their assistance to Jews as a natural reaction to human suffering."[35]

Perhaps the most succinct description of the rescuers' motivation came from Otto Springer—the son of a high-ranking German soldier who risked his life during the Holocaust to help Jews escape. Why did Mr. Springer, and other righteous gentiles, act with the quickness and courage of the Pharaoh's daughter in Exodus 2? He explained, "The hand of compassion was faster than the calculus of reason."[36]

These discoveries lead to a question. Was there a role for reason in this heroism? The answer is yes—and it was discovered by Professor Samuel Oliner of Humboldt State University.

Professor Oliner was born in Bielanka, Poland, a few months before Nechama Tec. He survived the Holocaust due to the heroism of Balwina Piecuch, a gentile acquaintance of his parents. In 1950, Oliner made his way to the United States, where he became a decorated soldier in the Korean War. He earned a PhD from the University of California at Berkeley, and devoted his life to studying why a relatively small number of people acted like Balwina Piecuch and most did not.

He (like Professor Tec) was able to rule out some obvious candidates: social class, wealth level, intelligence, religious commitment, closeness to Jews. Righteous gentiles, bystanders, and perpetrators were all composed of diverse groups. But there were some salient distinguishing characteristics of the righteous gentiles.

He wrote:

> Rescuers described their early family relationships in general and their relationships with their mothers in particular as closer significantly more often than did non-rescuers. Rescuers also felt significantly closer to their fathers than did bystanders. From such family relationships, more rescuers learned the satisfactions accruing from personal bonds with others.[37]

Professor Oliner also described what these bonds were made of: "the capacity for love and compassion . . . as well as a sense of self-esteem and efficacy (a sense of self that tells them that they can succeed at some task, even dangerous ones)."[38]

The rescuers, as Professor Tec showed, acted from the heart. They felt an emotional connection and commitment to vulnerable people they could have easily ignored. Professor Oliner found that this emotional imperative did not generate randomly. Instead, it came from a deep appreciation for their parents. And he found that the parents of rescuers had something in common. They taught their children, consistently throughout their childhood, to derive emotional satisfaction from forming interpersonal bonds based on love and compassion. This parental direction provided a deep-seated confidence that they could, when necessary, act to successfully create positive change regardless of the challenges. When the opportunity presented itself to help Jews escaping the Nazis, these men and women were emotionally ready.

These parents—again, from all backgrounds and statuses—shared one tactic of moral education. It was in the way they disciplined their children. Professor Oliner said of the rescuers, "As children, they were likely to have been disciplined by reasoning and taught to consider the consequences of their misbehavior." The emotional commitment of rescuers was constructed by a persistent and thoughtful education in the reasons why they, as emerging adults, should desire to do right and reject wrong. The rescuers, in the terms used by Moses in Exodus 35–36, had "wise hearts"—that were educated by the everyday reasons their parents taught them for why they should act as they should . . . and did, when it mattered most.

Reflection

So, the Torah proposes, and modern science validates, that we make decisions using our hearts rather than our minds. Yet, God has given us minds so complex and so impressive that even (and perhaps especially) the most accomplished neuroscientists are consistently amazed by its range, capabilities, and power. When it comes to making decisions, is this literally awesome three-pound thing residing in our heads good for anything except justifying the determinations that we have already made with our hearts? Is reason, as David Hume said, a slave to our passions?

The answer seems to be: not necessarily. If we are not mindful of the relationship between emotions and reason—between the heart and the head—we are likely to sentence our minds to a career of servitude to our passions. But if we are mindful of the Torah's teachings, which are validated by modern science, we can turn our reason from a slave into a partner.

Here are a few ways to do so.

Use Reason to Make the Right Emotional Commitments

The first role of reason derives from the Rebbe Rashab's interpretation of why the holy ark is made with acacia (foolish) wood. We are all going to be emotionally committed to something that will capture our hearts, draw our focus, and command our time, money, and commitment. We will, in Torah terms, be "foolish" for something, and then recruit reasons to support and refine our convictions.

This is not grounds for despair; quite the contrary. The parent (or expecting parent) can realize that their child will be passionate about—perhaps "foolish for"—something. And they have the power to significantly influence what this will be.

A parent who showers praise on her son for his athletic performance will likely create a child who is passionate about sports. A parent who emphasizes the importance of grades will likely create a child who is passionate about achievement. A parent who regularly and enthusiastically brings her child to volunteer opportunities and charitable fundraisers, explaining that they are fortunate to be able to serve the Lord who loves them, will likely create a child who is passionate about helping others.

What is an adult whose parents did not educate him toward the right passions to do? He should not blame his parents. Everyone can decide what to be passionate about—and then position himself to develop those emotional commitments. He can do so in one of two ways.

Let's say that a person decides that he would like to become passionate about serving others, and knows that he is good at building or just lifting things. He can join a community of people who spend Sundays working together to build homes for the poor. The satisfaction of creating something for someone else, amplified by the camaraderie and friendships that are created when people work together to accomplish something all agree is important, will produce that emotional commitment.

Let's say that another person has a passion, but knows that it is not being put to productive use. For instance, a person has a passion for football. His wife asks him if spending all Sunday in front of the television (and betting on the games) is really what he wants to model for their children. He could agree with her and decide instead to channel his passion for football by coaching children in the sport.

Use Reason to Amplify Emotional Commitment

In 2015, the leaders of the British charity Freedom from Hunger (FFH) wanted to determine how best to market the organization. Their one fundamental question was, "What is a better way to cultivate donors: a rational appeal or an emotional appeal?" An analysis from the British charitable support group Third Sector explains the parameters of the study that was done regarding it:

> It divided its donor list into two random groups. Those in one group received a conventional solicitation with an emotional appeal and a personal story of a beneficiary, with a final paragraph suggesting that FFH had helped that beneficiary. Those in the other group received a letter identical in all results—except that the final paragraph stated (truthfully) that "rigorous scientific methodologies" had shown the positive impact of FFH's work.[39]

The result: The non-donors and the low-engaged donors did not contribute more pursuant to the "rigorous scientific" findings. However, those who frequently gave significant amounts increased their gifts with the rational plea. Reason, the study found, will not generate a commitment. But it can help to confirm and to strengthen one's preexisting emotional commitment.

The insight from this study can be used by anyone with a passion for something worthwhile. An executive can use data on the company's growth to show committed employees why working even harder will build their careers and their wealth. A coach can present evidence to his team that they can win the championship if they play cohesively and spend more time in the weight room. A clergyman can cite scripture to his congregants to convince them to give more charity and better honor their biblical obligation to love the stranger. As long as the passion is there first, reason can help to amplify it.

Use Reason to Structure and Check Emotions

Every fan of American popular music will recognize a common subject across genres: the foolishness of love. The song might be "My Foolish Heart" (Bing Crosby / Rod Stewart), "Fools Rush In" (Elvis Presley), "Won't Get Fooled Again" (The Who), "Maybe I'm a Fool" (Aretha Franklin), "The Fool on the Hill" (The Beatles), or "Why Do Fools Fall in Love?" (Frankie Lymon and the Teenagers). In all cases, the theme is clear: Love is a very fertile producer of fools and foolishness.

Why would this theme resonate so universally? Everyone recognizes that romantic love—perhaps the quintessential emotion—can easily bypass or overwhelm reason and lead one to make very foolish decisions.

Someone, perhaps while listening to Frank Sinatra's haunting rendition of "I'm a Fool to Want You," might think: *Is there anything I can do to govern this emotion?*

The answer is yes—and it's very easy. For instance, let's say that a young Jewish man wants to have a Jewish home and to continue the faith into the generations. He knows that he can do so if he marries another Jew. He also knows that he could easily be attracted to and enthralled by beautiful women of all faiths. What should he do?

It's simple: If he only dates Jewish women, he will only become romantically attached to—and eventually marry—a Jewish woman. He might be a "fool" for a woman, but in the sense articulated by the Rebbe Rashab and not Frankie Lymon. He should be a fool for someone appropriate for his foolishness—in this case, a Jewish woman.

This same discipline can be applied to business, where emotional commitments also drive mistakes. In 2021, I cofounded a membership business called the Interesting Investment Institute (3i Members). The members are exited founders, family office executives, fund managers, and professional athletes who invest significantly, eclectically, and frequently in the private markets. We share private market deals in a structured process, perform group diligence on them, educate each other about business topics and opportunities, and identify partners, solutions, and co-investors. Everyone in the group is an experienced and successful businessperson who has learned the hard way, at some point, that the American Express analysis is right: Falling in love with a business or an investment is easy to do, and often leads to costly mistakes.

Consequently, we have built a forum where members—before committing to an investment—enter a (virtual) room with others considering the investment. Members, using data and speaking from experience, engage in vigorous discussions in which they explain why they are or are not favorable to the investment—or what more they have to learn to develop conviction. Sometimes, members who enter these discussions passionate about an investment emerge with greater conviction. Other times, they emerge with their passions doused and decide not to make the investment. In all cases, the members enthusiastically subject their passions to the test of reason—and report that the challenges they receive and observe in these forums have made and saved them a lot of money.

3

Why Aaron and High Achievers Stand Back

The Torah and Science of Impostor Syndrome

A Strange First Blessing

In Deuteronomy 28, Moses lists the blessings that the Jews will experience if we follow God's ways. The blessings are simply wonderful. We will be blessed in the city and in the field. We will be blessed with children, with fruit, meat, victories over our enemies—and many other things.

Before we get to the concrete blessings, Moses provides a strange context. In Deuteronomy 28:2, he says, "All these blessings will come upon you and overtake you, if you hearken to the voice of the Lord." What would it mean that the blessings will "come upon and overtake" us? Wouldn't we seek them out?

The nineteenth-century sage Haim Aryeh Leib of Jebwabne explained: Without divine help, we are likely to run away from our blessings. The blessing of Deuteronomy 28:2 is that they will overtake us despite our efforts to eschew them.[1]

This raises some interesting questions. Why would anyone run *from* a blessing? And why would running from blessings be so common that Moses would introduce Deuteronomy 28:2 with a statement that we will be blessed whether we want to be or not?

It turns out that Moses knew just what he was talking about, from long and varied experience.

Moses Rejects the Best Job Offer Ever

In Exodus 3, God has decided that it is time to free the Jews from Egyptian slavery. In order to do so, he needs a human partner. He identifies Moses, telling him, "And now, go, and I shall dispatch you to Pharaoh and you shall take my people the Children of Israel out of Egypt."

This is the best job offer anyone ever received. Yet, Moses rejects it no less than three times! He first says that he is inadequate. Then he says that he will be unable to convince the Jews to follow him. Finally, he says that he is not "a man of words." Commentators have, for millennia, discussed and debated what Moses meant when he said that he was not "a man of words." But one thing is for sure—he was not articulate, charismatic, or comfortable giving rousing speeches to big crowds. Therefore, he concluded, he was disqualified from leadership.

This is not all that Moses thought would disqualify him from leadership. Moses grew up in the Egyptian palace as the adopted grandson of the Pharaoh. His Egyptian identity is so pronounced that the group of women he saved from harassing men by a well in Exodus 2 refer to him as "an Egyptian man." He likely reflected on having lived a life of comfort and privilege in the palace and concluded, rightly, that his life experience could not have been more different from those of the Jewish slaves. How, Moses seemingly wondered, could he be the right person to lead the slaves in a revolt against the Pharaoh?

This all makes sense until the reader reminds himself of one thing. It is *God* who asks Moses to accept the leadership role! Still, Moses effectively tells God that he is wrong—and that he (Moses) is unqualified for the divine appointment. Why would Moses do that?

Moses likely felt like an *impostor*. And this feeling, we learn, is so powerful that even direct appeals from God could not overcome it. Moses eventually accepts the role, but only after God effectively forces him to do so.

The story teaches us about the constitution and power of what we now call *impostor syndrome*—which is the phenomenon where a person judges himself so unqualified for the position he is being considered for or holds that he actually feels like a fraud. As Moses shows, not even God's insistence that one is qualified for the job is enough to overcome his insistence that he is not.

God, as only he can, eventually compels Moses to accept the divine assignment. The way he does so is highly instructive. In Exodus 4:17, he commands Moses to take the staff that is "in your hand." Why would God need to instruct Moses to do so? There is nothing magical about Moses's staff; it was seemingly the one he always had. He had always used that staff to lead sheep, and would soon use it to lead people.

God's instruction to take what is "in your hand" speaks to much more than the physical tool. God is telling Moses, essentially: Stop focusing on your deficiencies and why you think they disqualify you. Start focusing on what is in your hand—your capabilities and strengths, which might help you understand why I chose you. If Moses had done so, he would have realized at least two qualities (discussed in other chapters of this book): his intolerance of injustice and his exquisite noticing.

The Torah shows a supreme irony that is often at the root of impostor syndrome: The quality that one believes *disqualifies* him (and makes him an impostor) is often the quality that others have rightly determined *qualifies* him.

The fourteenth-century Spanish sage Nissim ben Reuven (known as the Ran) pondered the deficiency that Moses said disqualified him from the role—not being "a man of words." God, the Ran taught, needs a leader whose message would last in perpetuity. If we accepted the Torah because of Moses's eloquence or charisma, the divine project on Earth would be superficial, fragile, and seriously imperiled. God, in choosing Moses, knew exactly what he was doing. God *needed* someone who was "not a man of words." It was Moses's difficulty with words that actually *qualified* him for the role.[2]

The same is true with Moses's upbringing. As the Torah makes clear from Exodus to Numbers, the Jews disqualify themselves from entering the Promised Land because of the slave mentality that persists after they achieve legal freedom through the Exodus. God knows what we would learn by Numbers: Only someone *without* a slave mentality could guide the way to freedom. As with his difficulty with words, this quality that Moses likely thought disqualified him from leadership was precisely that which qualified him for the role.

A Family Trait: Aaron "Comes Near"

A month after the Exodus, the Jews are still traveling in the desert. We are blessed by God with food, safety, and everything else we need as we prepare for freedom in the Promised Land.

God calls Moses to the top of the mountain to receive the Ten Commandments. Moses assures the people that he will be back in forty days. On what seems like the fortieth day, he is still gone—and the people panic. They decide to take their gold and to build a calf. It is unclear whether the calf is a substitute for God or for Moses. In either case, the act is unambiguously forbidden.[3]

Moses's older brother and partner, Aaron, the *religious* leader of the Jews, is on the ground. Aaron tells the people to come back the next day with their family jewels to celebrate a "festival for the Lord." Aaron presumably thinks that the people will sleep on it and ultimately decide not to sacrifice all of their jewelry to build a golden calf. He could win the argument without having it.

It is a clever plan—but it fails. The men deliver the jewelry enthusiastically. Aaron, ever avoidant of conflict, never makes the case for God and Moses and against idolatry. He never tells the people they are making a mistake. The people use their jewelry to make the golden calf and have an idolatrous orgy around it.

Moses descends from the mountain in "burning anger." He directs some of that anger at Aaron. God shares Moses's disappointment in Aaron. God, the Torah tells us, sends a plague "because of the calf that *Aaron* made." Three thousand people are killed. Aaron has catastrophically failed in his first test of spiritual leadership in the eyes of Moses, the people, and God.

God, because of Moses's insistence, does not give up on the people. Instead, God seemingly reflects on the sin and emerges with a recognition that human faith needs to be concretized. The people need a physical structure of religious significance. He concludes that the choice is not between a golden calf and nothing, but between a golden calf and something more edifying.

God has quite a "something" in mind. He instructs the people to build a portable temple—the Tabernacle. The people work very well together in this great act of construction. By Leviticus 9, it is time to inaugurate the structure where Aaron will serve as the spiritual leader of the Jewish people.

Moses says to Aaron, "Come near to the altar and offer your sin offering and your burnt offering and make atonement for yourself and the people; sacrifice the offering that is for the people and make atonement for them, as the Lord has commanded" (Leviticus 9:7).

One word in that statement has intrigued millennia of Torah students: "near." "Come near" implies that Aaron is far. Why would he be far?

Rabbi Jonathan Sacks, drawing from Rashi (who in turn drew from the Rabbis of the Talmud), has an explanation. Aaron, Rabbi Sacks wrote, is standing far away because he is "ashamed and fearful."[4]

What is he ashamed of? What is he fearful about?

Aaron is ashamed of how he performed when his religious leadership was tested at the Golden Calf. He is fearful of how he will perform as a religious leader on the highest stage. As Rabbi Sacks concluded, Aaron considers himself to be an impostor. Thus, the sages of the Talmud imagined Moses telling Aaron, "Come near—it is for this that you were chosen."[5]

The instruction to "come near," therefore, is Moses's way of encouraging his brother to reframe his experience at the Golden Calf—from that of having failed to that of getting prepared. Rabbi Sacks explained, by way of imagining how Moses might have explained the "come near" to Aaron:

> You know what sin is like. You know what it is to feel guilt. You more than anyone else understand the need for repentance and atonement. You have felt the cry of your soul to be cleansed, purified and wiped free of the stain of transgression. What you think of as your greatest weakness will become, in this role you are about to assume, your greatest strength.[6]

Overcoming Impostor Syndrome

Rabbi Abraham J. Twerski was a Rabbi and psychiatrist whose therapeutic insights were informed by his deep Torah understanding. In his 1987 book, *Let Us Make Man: Self-Esteem Through Jewishness*, he recognized a paradox in the human personality. "Of everything in the world," he wrote, "the human being is closest to oneself, and yet is often most distant from oneself. This remoteness results in distortion of the self-perception."[7]

The impostor syndrome is one of these distortions. The Torah, through the examples of Moses and Aaron, shows two ways in which it can be overcome. Moses does so because God forces him to accept the assignment. This is not a replicable model.

Aaron overcomes his impostor syndrome very differently, and in a way that reflects Rabbi Twerski's insight. Aaron does so when another person—in this case, his brother Moses—tells him, "Come near." This is replicable, for a reason articulated in the Talmud. The Talmud instructs, "A prisoner cannot generally free himself from prison, but depends on others to release him from his shackles."[8]

The Torah's diagnosis and solution for impostor syndrome is, thus, very clear. As each of us is distant from ourselves, we are prone to consider ourselves unqualified for tasks that others—even God—deem us right for. Consequently, a person who experiences impostor syndrome should seek the counsel of what the Talmud refers to as a "beloved friend"—one who offers informed, concerned, and caring guidance.

The Science

A Concept Is (Re)Born

In 1978, Pauline Rose Clance and Suzanne Ament Imes were practicing psychologists who taught at Georgia State University. They noticed a commonality in many of the highly successful women they counseled and worked with. "Despite their earned degrees, scholastic honors, high achievement on standardized tests, praise, and professional recognition from colleagues and respected authorities, these women do not enjoy an internal sense of success."[9]

Why? They discovered that these women had an "internal experience of intellectual phoniness." This experience manifested in a variety of ways. Some women thought that they were accepted into graduate school due to a mistake by the admissions committee, some believed that their abilities had been overestimated, and others maintained that their success was due to luck. They all had a self-conception that was misaligned with the conception that others had of them.

Drs. Clance and Imes came up with a term to describe what they observed: "impostor phenomenon."

Drs. Clance and Imes noticed that this impostor phenomenon (or impostor syndrome, as it has since come to be known) existed in the presence of abundant evidence to the contrary. For instance, one woman with two master's degrees, a PhD, and numerous publications to her credit considered herself unqualified to teach remedial college classes in her field. These "impostors" suffered from a clear cognitive distortion—their self-perception was untrue—and they could not talk themselves out of it.

However, Drs. Clance and Imes had significant success with these women in therapy. They described how:

> A group setting is also valuable because one woman can see the dynamics in another woman and recognize the lack of reality involved. Mary cannot believe that Jane thinks she is stupid. After all, Jane has a Ph.D. from an outstanding university, is a respected professor, and is obviously bright. In a group setting, the ways in which an individual negates positive feedback and maintains her belief system emerge in clear relief and can be brought to the attention of the client.[10]

As with Moses and Aaron, these patients struggled to have the confidence to acknowledge that they were qualified for their positions. But they also discovered the Torah's secret to overcoming it: surrounding oneself with the counsel of caring peers who deeply understood the full reality of the situation.

What Moses and Tom Hanks Have in Common

It is not surprising that Moses and Aaron were the biblical figures to suffer from impostor syndrome. Nor is it surprising that the identification of impostor syndrome in 1978 concerned those whom Professors Clance and Imes identified as "high achieving" women. Impostor syndrome is an affliction of high achievers, as it depends on one being in a position worthy of thinking that he or she does not deserve to be there.

And it is prevalent—with more than 70 percent of successful people having experienced it. Among the public figures who have recalled suffering from impostor syndrome are Sonia Sotomayor, Michelle Obama, Arianna Huffington, Lady Gaga, Albert Einstein, Tom Hanks, David Bowie, Serena

Williams, Robert Pattinson, Tina Fey, Howard Schultz, Matt Higgins, Helen Mirren, Sigourney Weaver, Sheryl Sandberg, and Maya Angelou.[11]

The impostor syndromes of these diverse high achievers likely share some characteristics, which were enumerated in a 2020 analysis in *Medical News Today*. Impostor syndrome causes people to suffer diminished work performance, assume fewer responsibilities, and avoid seeking promotions, which leads to anxiety, depression, and shame.[12]

How might one conquer his impostor syndrome? The *Harvard Business Review* guide for managers helping employees through impostor syndrome has an answer. It is: "Assign mentors wisely."[13]

How can these mentors (or other trusted counselors) help? Professors Brad Johnson of the United States Naval Academy and David Smith of the Johns Hopkins Carey Business School lay out the techniques that mentors of people with impostor syndrome should employ. These methods include normalizing impostor feelings (showing how common they are), directly challenging negative self-talk by emphasizing (especially by comparison) how qualified the protégé is for the task, and sharing one's own impostor stories.[14]

The widespread recognition of the effectiveness of the "assign mentors wisely" strategy to deal with impostor syndrome is reflected in a new profession—that of "Certified Impostor Syndrome Mentor."

Moses may not have been certified—but he was the first impostor syndrome mentor.

Reflection

Two stunning things about impostor syndrome are how easily it can affect anyone and how prevalent it is.

The Torah teaches this by using as its exemplars Moses and Aaron. They are the top two people in the desert, each with a position that God gave them, and yet they still feel like impostors. Modern social science has validated the Torah in its finding that more than 70 percent of successful people have experienced impostor syndrome. And both the Torah and modern social science demonstrated how serious it can be.

Moses's impostor syndrome would have caused him to refuse God's assignment to free the Jews and lead us to freedom had God not forced it upon him. And it causes people today to experience a range of problems from depression and anxiety to the rejection of career-enhancing opportunities.

What are some of the thoughts that a person with impostor syndrome might experience? He might ask: "Doesn't the coach, who just called the play for me, know that I missed my last two three-pointers?" "What if my congregant, who is coming to me for marital advice, knew what my wife thinks about me right now?" "Don't my bosses, who just gave me a promotion, know the product launch failure last year was under my leadership?" "How can I be a responsible parent when I feel as though I can barely take care of myself?"

There are two approaches (or strategies) for dealing with these thoughts. One derives from the words of the Midrash (ancient Rabbinic commentary): "It is for this that you were chosen," that the sages imagined Moses telling Aaron after needing to be told, "Come near." One who has marital problems might realize that he has become sensitive to and knowledgeable about the subtle things that generate marital tension—and is thus especially qualified to help someone in a similar situation. One whose last product launch catastrophically failed can realize that his bosses appreciate how much he had learned from his mistakes—and, quite reasonably, consider him the best person to lead the next launch. These just might be the strengths—the "staff that is in your hand," to quote God to Moses in Exodus 4—that are qualifying.

The other answer comes from André Malraux's 1967 book, *Anti-Memoirs*. André Malraux discusses running into a man with whom he had served in World War II who had subsequently become a parish priest. Mr. Malraux asked the priest what he, after years of hearing confessions, had learned about mankind. The priest told him that he learned two things. The first was, "Everyone is much less happy than he seems." (The second was, "There is no such thing as a grown-up person!")[15]

In the era of social media, everyone knows just how right the priest was. We all know people who post photos of their loving and happy family—camouflaging a reality that is far from what is being portrayed. Familial happiness is not the only thing that people exaggerate or even invent in their crafted image.

A retired congressman recently told me that people often come to the House of Representatives with a conviction that they are in the highest position they should occupy. That quickly changes when they get to know the people who hold positions they thought were beyond their capabilities.

The implications—from family to politics—are clear. If one thinks that she would be an impostor by assuming an important role, it is only because she does not really know the people who would otherwise have the position. And—as we learned from Moses and then from Aaron—the experiences or qualities that she thinks might disqualify her might be those that make her ideal for the role and its responsibilities.

4

How Joseph's Embrace of His Brothers Became the Current Gold Standard in Psychotherapy

The Torah and Science of Reframing

Joseph's Invention

Genesis 37:2 begins with an odd statement: "These are the generations of Jacob: when Joseph was seventeen years old." The problem is that Jacob had thirteen children. But the passage identifies Jacob's "generations" only with his youngest son, Joseph.

It does not take us long to learn the reason. Jacob, we are told in Genesis 37:3, "loved Joseph more than all his children, because he was the son of his old age, and he made him a coat of many colors." Jacob has a favorite child who he believes embodies the hope of the generations.

Joseph carries this status as an entitled teenager would. He brings bad reports of his brothers to his father, thereby increasing his advantage. He has dreams of his parents and siblings bowing down to him, and shares them with his family.

The brothers, we learn in Genesis 37:4, "saw that their father loved him more than all his brothers, so they hated him, and they could not speak with him peacefully." Jacob, like all parents, surely wanted his children to love and support each other. He sends Joseph to check on his brothers, who are shepherding in a field—perhaps hoping to generate a feeling of fraternal care and affection. It turns out to be a catastrophic miscalculation.

Joseph's brothers seize him. After initially resolving to kill Joseph, the brothers are persuaded first by Reuben and later by Judah that they cannot profit from killing Joseph. They decide to sell him instead. Joseph becomes a slave in the house of the Egyptian officer Potiphar and later, a prisoner in the royal jail. Through a most improbable and extraordinary series of events, Joseph's skills as a dream interpreter earn him the audience of the Pharaoh—who is tortured by a concerning dream. Joseph tells him the meaning of the dream. There will be seven years of plenty followed by seven years of famine. Egypt, Joseph recommends, should use the surplus of those first seven years in order to survive the seven lean years that will follow.

The Pharaoh is convinced. He gives Joseph the power and responsibility of administering the country through famine. Joseph, in an instant, goes from being a slave and prisoner to the number-two man in Egypt.

Thirteen years later—following another extraordinary sequence of events in Joseph's life—his brothers come to Egypt to procure food for their starving family in Canaan. Joseph recognizes them, but they do not recognize him.

Joseph, in perhaps the most stirring moment in literature, reveals himself to his brothers after a process that seems to take several months. They are stunned, and immediately think that he is about to make them suffer as payback for them attempting to sell him into slavery.

Joseph anticipates this concern, but then he does something extraordinary. He tells them that they should not worry. Joseph explains in Genesis 45:8:

> And now, be not distressed, nor reproach yourselves for having sold me here, for it was to be a provider that God sent me ahead of you . . . It was not you who sent me here, but God; he made me father to Pharaoh, master of his entire household and ruler throughout the entire land of Egypt.

Joseph's brothers respond with stunned silence. Why can't any of them say *anything*?

It is because Joseph had just brought something entirely new into the world: the idea of *reframing*. Joseph had just told them that he had taken his experience out of the frame of enslavement and put it in the frame of rescuing. While fully recognizing the truth of his experiences, Joseph explains that he does not interpret them negatively. He interprets it as being orchestrated by God in order to save the world from a global famine. This act of reframing enables him to transform a terrible situation into a redemptive one. It enables him to turn a curse into a blessing. And his brothers, like everyone else in the world at that time, had never seen anything like it.

Joseph's invention of reframing might have saved his brothers from starvation, but it also helps them and their families enjoy a prosperous life in Goshen, the suburb in Egypt where Joseph settled them. When their father dies, the brothers say, "Joseph will . . . surely repay us all the evil that we did to him" (Genesis 50:15).

They fling themselves at him and offer to be his slaves. Joseph responds by telling them, essentially, that his reframing is entirely sincere—indeed, divinely inspired. He says, "Fear not, for am I instead of God? Although you intended me harm, God intended it for good; in order to accomplish—it is as clear as this day—that a vast people be kept alive. So now, fear not—I will sustain you and your loved ones" (Genesis 50:19–21).

Despite the facts of their lives as reunited brothers, Joseph's invention of reframing is so radical that the brothers never quite believe it.

God Learns from Joseph

God has a vision for the world, articulated from Exodus to the Prophets. The Jews should, per Exodus 19:6, become a "kingdom of priests and a holy nation." In this role, we will inspire others to accept the truth of ethical monotheism, whose central tenet is that all people are created in the image of God.

But God has a problem. His vision requires people from all over the world—strangers—to learn from each other, work together, and ultimately worship the same God in unity. But strangers, naturally, have one of two reactions to each other.

The first is indifference. In 1759, Adam Smith published his classic, *The Theory of Moral Sentiments*, which offers a parable of a hypothetical "man of humanity in Europe" who hears that the "great empire of China . . . was suddenly swallowed up by an earthquake."

> He would, I imagine, first of all, express very strongly his sorrow for the misfortune of that unhappy people [and] he would make

> melancholy reflections upon the precariousness of human life . . . And when all this fine philosophy was over, when all these human sentiments had been once fairly expressed, he would pursue his business or his pleasure, take his repose or his diversion, with the same ease and tranquility, as if no such accident had happened . . . If he was to lose his little finger tomorrow, he would not sleep tonight; but provided he never saw them, he will snore with the most profound security over the ruin of a hundred million of his brethren, and the destruction of that immense multitude seems plain an object less interesting to him than this paltry misfortune of his own.[1]

The second natural response to the stranger is even worse than indifference. It is the process of "othering" and is exemplified in an English word: barbarian. The term "barbarian" debuted in Greece at around the same time as the Exodus took place. It referred to "people from out of town"—those with unfamiliar languages and customs. All people from out of town—all strangers—were regarded as "barbarians."

How, coming into a world where people ignore or despise strangers, would God achieve his vision of the Jews? We find out in Leviticus 19:34. God says, "But the stranger that dwells with you shall be to you as one born among you, and *you shall love him as yourself*, for you were strangers in the land of Egypt."

The commandment to love the stranger is, from Exodus to Deuteronomy, reiterated an astonishing thirty-six times.

The use of "stranger" in the second part of the verse ("as you were strangers in the Land of Egypt") is remarkable. The text of early Exodus describes us as being beaten and tortured, which is consistent with the description of Egyptian slavery in the historical record.[2]

For people in contemporary society, a stranger is the person walking toward us on a city street, the new kid in school, the guy sitting next to us on the bus. These do not describe our experience in Egypt. We were slaves. So why would God insist on us reframing our experience from being slaves to being strangers? There are two reasons.

First, God's reframing from being slaves to strangers teaches us to never consider ourselves as victims. This, as discussed in the chapter of this book on culture, is one of the most damaging things that one can do to oneself. Among other things, victims do not act based upon what they believe that they should do. The victim acts only in accordance with the demands of the perpetrator. Victims have no agency. By having us reframe our experience in Egypt as strangers rather than slaves, God liberates us from the despairing immobilization of the victim. He frees us to be independent agents capable of mighty dreams, audacious goals, and the ability to achieve them.

Second, God realizes that this act of reframing will enable us to do the impossible, which is *love* the stranger. If we reframe *our* foundational national experience from being "slaves" to being "strangers," we will regard *ourselves* as strangers. We will thus be able to conquer the natural inclination to ignore, fear, and despise the stranger. Instead, we will identify and empathize with him and ultimately, love him.

How to Love the Stranger

The Torah is not a collection of sayings to fit on bumper stickers or social media postings. It is a guide for life. As such, the Torah addresses the highly practical question of *how* we can actually love a stranger. It does so through a consideration of how the unnatural love (of the stranger) can relate to and be integrated with our other loves—most of which are natural and even instinctive.

In Deuteronomy 15:11, Moses says, "Therefore, I command you, saying, you shall surely open your hand to your brother, to your poor one [in your city] and to your needy one in the Land." The order, as always in the Torah, is instructive. We first love our family, then those in our city, and finally those in the entire land. Each love builds on the previous one and trains us for the next.

Our affections and commitments might *begin* at home—but, as we are instructed in Deuteronomy, they should not *end* there. The potential of love, the Torah teaches, is abundant. Like light and learning, love does not deplete when it is shared. It grows. As we love those closest to us most intensely, we develop the love that we are divinely obligated to devote to the stranger. The opportunity to follow this formula and do the otherwise impossible—to love the stranger—is made possible by the invention of Joseph and the application by God: of reframing.

Reframing and Truth

In considering reframing, it is important to recognize what it does—as well as what it does not do. The biblical invention of reframing enables us to derive meaning and purpose from bad situations and to achieve great things that would have otherwise been impossible. But reframing never asks us to forget, deny, or diminish the badness of an experience.

Joseph always knew exactly how he got to Egypt. The most important Jewish holiday, Pesach, is a celebration and exploration of our journey from slavery to freedom—not "strangerhood" to freedom. Observant Jews quite consistently recall being "slaves" in the daily prayers. The biblical vision of reframing, based entirely on truth, enables us to remember the bitter reality of an experience while turning it into an opportunity for growth, meaning, purpose, and service.

The Science

Logotherapy: Reframing in the Darkest Places

Viktor Frankl was born in Vienna in 1905. When World War II started, he was emerging as a leading psychotherapist. He was given the opportunity to leave Europe, but stayed to be with his parents. Dr. Frankl spent the war years in four different concentration camps, including Auschwitz. Yet, he emerged from the Holocaust to write *Man's Search for Meaning*, one of the most important books of all time.

In this book, Dr. Frankl encapsulates the philosophy of human possibility that he derived from his experience in hell on Earth. He wrote, "Everything can be taken from a man but one thing: the last of the human freedoms—to choose one's attitude in any given set of circumstances, to choose one's own way." We cannot, Dr. Frankl taught, always choose our situations. But we can always decide how to interpret and to frame them.[3]

Dr. Frankl cites an example of how this discipline can work. Following the war, he came to the United States where he established a counseling practice. He tells the story of an elderly patient who was severely depressed following the death of his wife. Dr. Frankl writes:

> I refrained from telling him anything, but instead confronted him with a question, "What would have happened, Doctor, if you

> had died first, and your wife would have had to survive without you?" "Oh," he said, "for her this would have been terrible; how she would have suffered!" Whereupon I replied, "You see, Doctor, such a suffering has been spared her, and it is you who have spared her this suffering; but now, you have to pay for it by surviving and mourning her." He said no word but shook my hand and calmly left the office.[4]

Dr. Frankl's patient was able to cope with the death of his wife once he reframed it as the only way that she would avoid the misery of living without him. As a result of the reframing, the patient was able to derive meaning and purpose from his suffering.

Dr. Frankl named his philosophy of therapy by reframing "logotherapy," which means "healing through meaning." Therapists who practice logotherapy encourage their patients to reframe their experiences, however painful they are, to find meaning in them. Studies from the United States to Iran have found it to be effective in a wide variety of circumstances—from parents whose children have cancer to those struggling with substance abuse.[5]

"The Current Gold Standard in Psychotherapy"

Logotherapy is one of the most important psychological developments of the past hundred years. But it is not the only one to be based on reframing, and it might not even be the most widely adopted. That designation probably belongs to an aligned school: Cognitive Behavioral Therapy (CBT), which was conceived and developed by Dr. Aaron Beck.

Aaron Beck was a psychiatrist whose hundred-year life began in Providence, Rhode Island, in 1921. A graduate of Brown University and Yale Medical School, a young Dr. Beck entered his residency intending to be a neurologist. He soon realized that the tools and remedies available for neurologists to help patients were limited, and that there was a need for more psychiatrists.

Dr. Beck became a psychiatrist, but a dissatisfied one. He concluded that psychiatrists could help people—but not with the theories and methods available at the time.

The dominant type of psychological treatment then was based on the teachings of Sigmund Freud. These treatments encouraged patients to identify the repressed sources of their pain and anxiety. Dr. Beck surmised that this technique was not helping patients. He invented a new form of treatment, one that he would subject to rigorous analytical and quantitative testing over the many years to follow—CBT.

The core tenet of CBT is what Dr. Beck termed "cognitive reframing" or "cognitive restructuring." Its insight is that all experiences can be accurately interpreted in multiple ways. Echoing Dr. Frankl, he insisted that we have the freedom to choose how we interpret these experiences. The choice of how to frame an experience will determine how we feel about it, what we learn from it, and how we live in accordance with that learning.

The opportunity presented by reframing is described through a case study interview with Dr. Beck published by the Beck Institute. A patient, a talented writer, came to see Dr. Beck. The patient, who considered himself a total failure, was depressed and even suicidal. Dr. Beck asked him for the evidence upon which this self-assessment had been based.

The patient explained that his wife had been "cross" with him, showing that she didn't love him. His teenage kids were misbehaving, showing that he was a failed father. The patient continued and explained that the sales of his book had suffered a sharp decline, showing that he was a failed writer. Moreover, the roof was leaking, showing that he could not even maintain his home.

Dr. Beck suggested that they separate these issues in a search for alternative explanations. With the guidance of Dr. Beck, the patient reframed each of the experiences. He concluded that his children might be misbehaving because they were normal teenagers, that his wife was cross with him out of frustration with their children, that the leaking roof was a common occurrence that could be fixed by calling a roofer, and that the book sales had declined because the paperback edition had just come out.[6]

At the conclusion of the sessions, the man's situation had not necessarily changed at all. His kids were still misbehaving, his wife was still sometimes cross toward him, and his hardcover book sales remained low. But he no longer used these facts to frame himself as a failure. By reframing his experiences, the writer was able to escape his despair—and cultivate the self-confidence and strength he needed to persevere and grow.

The psychological literature of reframing shows the extent of the problems that reframing has addressed. It is now used successfully to treat conditions including schizophrenia, depression, irritable bowel syndrome, chronic pain, anxiety disorders, eating disorders, alcohol dependency, psychosis, chronic fatigue syndrome, obsessive compulsive disorder, and tic disorders. This psychological technique, which Joseph and God effectively designed in Genesis, has become, in the words of Dr. Daniel David of the Center for Behavioral Oncology at Mt. Sinai Hospital in New York, "the current gold standard in psychotherapy."[7]

Reframing Wins an Olympic Gold Medal

In the 2020 Summer Olympics in Tokyo (held in 2021 due to Covid-19), the women kayakers were stationed behind Tokyo's Kasai Canoe Slalom Centre getting ready for a race. The Australian kayaker Jess Fox had been preparing for this moment for nine years. But there was a problem. She had eaten something that seriously disagreed with her. She ran behind the tent and vomited.

Ms. Fox told her coach (her mother, herself a former Olympian) what happened. They were not concerned. How could such a physical weakening not concern an Olympian who was about to compete in the highest-stakes event of her life? Because Ms. Fox and her mother were trained in kayaking *and* understood psychology.

Jess Fox recalled telling herself, "Whatever I had between the runs didn't sit well, and then I just thought, 'Okay, my body's ready, that's just my body telling me to get ready for something big.' So it's always about reframing those things and putting it into a positive."[8]

Jess Fox, by reframing a weakening illness as a signal from her body that it was *ready*, turned physical weakness into mental power—and won the gold medal.

Reframing Feeds the Poor

In 1969, Shirley Chisholm of New York City became the first black woman elected to Congress. When she arrived, she was assigned to the Agriculture Committee, which she considered completely irrelevant to her constituents in Brooklyn.

The disappointed congresswoman received a call from a constituent—the Lubavitcher Rebbe Menachem Schneerson. He asked her to visit. She did, and told him that she was upset at not being put in a position to help her constituents. The Rebbe responded, "What a blessing God has given you! This country has so much surplus food, and there are so many hungry people. You can use this gift that God gave you to feed the hungry."

Shortly after returning to Washington, Congresswoman Chisholm met Senator Bob Dole, a Republican from Kansas. She worked with Senator Dole to create the WIC (Women, Infants, Children) program, which uses surplus food to feed the poor. When she retired from Congress fourteen years later, Congresswoman Chisholm reflected, "A Rabbi who is an optimist taught me that what you may think is a challenge is a gift from God. And if poor babies have milk, and poor children have food, it's because this Rabbi in Crown Heights had vision." Indeed—the vision of reframing.[9]

Loving the Stranger

As previously discussed, God's great act of reframing is directed at enabling us to do the otherwise impossible and love the stranger. This would be God's most important project on Earth.

The substance of reframing—loving the stranger—is so revolutionary that it deserves a scientific consideration itself. Is God right that loving the stranger is a quintessentially unnatural act, and thus in need of reframing?

This question became one of international criminal justice in 2018. This is when the American missionary John Allen Chau went to proselytize among the people of North Sentinel Island in the Bay of Bengal, a protected area of India. The inhabitants of the island are, to this day, among the only people on Earth to remain completely isolated from modern technology, social practices, and ideas.

Mr. Chau, against Indian law, reached the island and was killed by its inhabitants. The islanders were not punished because the authorities recognized, essentially, that they are a premodern people whose natural instincts were untouched by any subsequent ideas about how to treat strangers. We might think that killing a stranger is barbaric, but the North Sentinel Islanders regard strangers as threatening and dangerous.

Was the presumption of the Indian authorities correct? To investigate this question, let us consider the cliché that "opposites attract." This cliché would suggest that loving the stranger is not hard—and is, to the contrary, natural. According to a report by Dr. Michael Johnson of the Marriage and

Family Studies Laboratory at Binghamton University, 86 percent of people looking for love believe that opposites attract.[10]

Is it true? Fortunately, more than 240 studies dating all the way back to the 1950s have addressed this question and yielded a definitive answer. As Dr. Johnson reports, there is "an irrefutable association between being similar to and being interested in the other person." Hence, the title of his review, "The Idea That Opposites Attract Is BS."[11]

Indeed, the extent of our homogamy (love of the same) in and out of the romantic context is so profound that it becomes simply weird. A 2016 study led by Professor John Jones of the United States Military Academy showed that people are attracted to others with similar names. The researchers conclude, "A wedding for Jesse Jefferson and Jennifer Jeffries may be just around the corner."[12]

A 2002 study led by Professor Brett Pelham of SUNY Buffalo (now called the University of Buffalo) shows that people are disproportionately likely to choose careers based on their names. For instance, the name Dennis is as common as the names Walter and Jerry. However, people named Dennis are significantly more likely to become dentists than are those named Walter or Jerry.[13]

And it gets even stranger. A 2013 study led by Professor Bruno Laeng of the University of Oslo showed that individuals think that their romantic partner is more attractive when a part of their own face is morphed onto it. This is not because the morphed face is, somehow, objectively more attractive than the natural one. Only the subjects reliably thought that their faces were more attractive.[14]

So, the evidence is clear. Opposites do not attract. People are attracted to the similar—so profoundly that it becomes weird. Love of the stranger is indeed novel, and the North Sentinel Islanders were reacting in the most naturally human way.

How to Love the Stranger

As discussed, Moses provides a counterintuitive and practical way to love the stranger. He explains we do not need to sacrifice love for those near in order to love the stranger. To the contrary, Moses teaches that we build our love for others on the foundation of love for our families. Those who first open their hand to their "brother" will then do so to the "poor one [in one's city]" and finally to the "needy one in the Land."

What does the data say?

Being a spouse and a parent are, of course, time-consuming commitments. One might think, therefore, that single and childless people who have more free time are more likely to volunteer than those with family commitments. In 2015, the Bureau of Labor Statistics compiled the data. It showed that married people are 50 percent more likely to volunteer than single people and that parents with children under 18 are 38 percent more likely to volunteer than those without children.[15]

People with families generally have more financial obligations than those who are single. Yet, the Indiana University Women's Philanthropy Institute found that "being married increases both the likelihood of giving and the amount of giving, regardless of gender."[16]

A 2015 analysis from the Philanthropy Roundtable reported that citizens of the top ten states for charitable giving give twice as much to charity as those in the bottom states (as a percentage of adjusted gross income). The top states: Utah, Mississippi, Alabama, Tennessee, Georgia, South Carolina, Idaho, Oklahoma, Arkansas, and North Carolina. The bottom states: Hawaii, North Dakota, Connecticut, Massachusetts, Rhode Island, New Jersey, Vermont, Maine, and New Hampshire.[17]

The difference? The states for the most and least charitable giving map almost precisely with the Pew Research Center data on the most and the least religious states. Indeed, research curated by the Philanthropy Roundtable shows that Americans with a religious affiliation give more than twice as much as those without a religious affiliation—and regular churchgoers give four times as much as those who do not attend church.[18]

This giving extends to what Karl Zinsmeister of the Philanthropy Roundtable has determined to be the fastest growing sector of charitable giving: international charities serving "the poorest of the poor." The reason for this growth is "soaring interest by Evangelical Christians." And religious giving extends to *secular* charities, as multiple studies have found that religious people give more to secular charities than do secular people.[19]

How about those who give profoundly with their time? The Philanthropy Roundtable found that religious Americans adopt children at 2.5 times the national rate and are particularly likely to foster and adopt troubled and hard-to-place kids. Religious institutions are also the most likely to run programs to mentor prisoners and care for their families; provide emergency shelter beds; and administer programs for substance abusers, the unemployed, and those suffering from HIV/AIDS—all with volunteers from the religious institution.[20]

So, the data demonstrates that Moses was right in saying that allegiances do not trade off but build—culminating in genuine acts of loving the stranger. The last word can belong to the *New York Times* journalist Nicholas Kristof, who has devoted much of his career to covering international humanitarian crises and those who work to alleviate them. He wrote in 2011:

> Evangelicals are disproportionately likely to donate 10 percent of their incomes to charities, mostly church-related. More important, go to the front lines, at home or abroad, in the battles against hunger, malaria, prison rape, obstetric fistula, human trafficking or genocide, and some of the bravest people you meet are evangelical Christians (or conservative Catholics, similar in many ways) who truly live their faith. I'm not particularly religious myself, but I stand in awe of those I've seen risking their lives in this way—and it sickens me to see that faith mocked at New York cocktail parties.[21]

Reflection

It is fitting that God's master class in reframing involved challenging one of our most natural instincts: being ignorant of or suspicious toward the stranger. That's because reframing is unnatural. If we are fired by a boss, dumped by a girlfriend, defeated by an opponent, or insulted by a friend, we will *naturally* respond negatively, in accordance with how we feel after defeat. It is only by reframing that we can transform realities like Victor Frankl's patient and Jess Fox did.

Reframing, though proposed in the Torah and validated by modern science, has a challenger. It is the claim that we should trust our instincts and follow our gut. When we "trust our instincts," we commit ourselves, *in principle*, to the first frame we place around an experience.

This commitment makes, essentially, three claims. First, the immediate interpretation of the person who is the most personally affected or emotionally wounded is right. Second, there is no role for purposeful reflection, long-term thinking, and strategic evaluation. Third, there is no value in advice from others who might be thoughtful, wise, and dispassionate—and might encourage us to challenge our first interpretation.

Which paradigm serves us best: that of trusting our instincts or reframing? First, it should be stipulated that both those who believe in trusting instincts and reframing can accept the full truth of what happened. Joseph never forgot that his brothers sold him to slavery. God knew that the Jews were slaves, and Jess Fox was aware that she had just vomited.

If each had trusted their instincts, what would have happened? Joseph would have probably taken revenge on his brothers. The Jews would have been trapped in a victim mentality. And Jess Fox would not have won her race.

Instead, they each reframed—while maintaining fidelity to the truth of their circumstance. Joseph was right that his brothers' treatment of him led to his becoming the viceroy of Egypt, enabling him to save them and the people of Egypt. God and Moses were right that the enslavement gave us the opportunity to "love the stranger"—and to show the world how this otherwise impossible idea is achievable, good, and right. Jess Fox was correct that "something big" was about to happen.

Consequently, reframing brings us to a remarkable and liberating realization: We *can* change the past. Of course, this does not mean that we can change *what happened* in the past. But that's rarely the most enduring or important aspect of the past Rather it is what we will do next with our understanding of the past.[22]

The ability of reframing to change the past exemplifies its remarkable power and potential. God, recognizing the potency of reframing, puts it to another use as well. By having us put our experience in Egypt into the frame of strangerhood, he enables us to approach the otherwise impossible state that is needed for the divine vision to be fulfilled. This is for us to love the stranger.

How, then, can one love the stranger? There are extraordinary examples. One can, like Dr. Tom Catena (inspired by his Christian faith), leave all of the comforts and necessities of American life behind to become the only physician in the Nuba Mountains of Sudan—serving over a million people in an environment without consistent power and running water. One can, like Dr. Rick Hodes (inspired by his Jewish faith), go to Ethiopia as a young doctor for a short mission—and stay for a lifetime, as the only spine doctor in a country with an enormous amount of spinal deformities. One can, like Mohamed Bzeek (inspired by his Muslim faith), become a foster parent to dozens of terminally ill children who have no place to go.

Most of us cannot love the stranger with the *completeness* of these heroes, but they cannot actualize their love alone. Dr. Catena has told me that without donors, he would be working with Band-Aids. This opens an opportunity. We can all discharge our biblical obligation to love the stranger by becoming the genuine and indispensable partner of those who do so with a completeness that we can just admire. We can all go to the websites of organizations such as African Mission Healthcare, Samaritan's Purse, and Watsi and join these heroes in loving the stranger—and make a *routine* of doing so. When we do so, we can express our gratitude to the Torah—as its concept of reframing is what ultimately taught us to do the otherwise impossible and love the stranger.

5

How Abraham Was Cool

The Torah and Science of Culture

What is culture? It is a word so common we often fail to consider what it actually is. The United Nations provides a fine definition: "The set of distinctive spiritual, material, intellectual and emotional features of a society or social group that encompasses not only art and literature but lifestyles, ways of living together, value systems, traditions and beliefs."[1]

Culture: Salvation or Destruction

"Noah was a righteous man," we learn in Genesis 6:9, "perfect *in his generation*." The text shortly thereafter tells us something about that generation. "Now the earth has become corrupt before God; and the earth had become filled with robbery [or violence]." God decides to destroy the world in a flood, saving only Noah and his family.

Seemingly every Torah commentator has developed an opinion as to what the tantalizing qualifier "perfect in his generation" says about Noah. Is the Torah pro-Noah in saying that his righteousness should be considered remarkable given that it existed in a generation otherwise devoid of it? Or is the Torah anti-Noah saying that he was righteous *only* by comparison with the others in his generation?

Commentators in both camps agree on at least one thing. The most important character in the Noah sequence might not be him. It is the *culture* of violence that was so pervasive and important that God determined that the world must be destroyed on its account.

The flood ends, and God changes much about his view of the world in its re-creation. The importance of culture, we learn through the very next major figure in the Torah, is not one of them. Another corrupt society and culture arise on earth. The cities of Sodom and Gomorrah are filled with corruption and violence, just like the whole world had been in the days of Noah.

"Because the outcry of Sodom and Gomorrah has become great," God tells Abraham in Genesis 18:20–21, "and because their sin has been very grave, I will go down to see whether they have acted altogether according to the outcry that has reached me; if not, I will take note."

Abraham offers quite a response. He asks God if he would destroy the city if there were fifty righteous people. God says he would not. Abraham, seeing that God is willing to negotiate, keeps going. He asks God if he will destroy the city if there are forty-five righteous people. God says no. Abraham keeps bargaining with God until God agrees not to destroy the city if there are but ten righteous people.

Then God departs. The negotiation is over. Even Abraham, who had so courageously and successfully argued with God, does not push the argument any further.

Why does Abraham stop? Why doesn't he try to bargain God down to seven people, five people, or even one righteous person? The Torah does not tell us because we already know from the story of Noah: People live within broader cultures. A good individual can, *heroically*, preserve his decency even within a culture filled with robbery or violence. But without at least a small virtuous subculture, the society will continually go from bad to worse. A thoroughly and pervasively bad culture, we learn from the stories of Noah and Sodom, is fit for God's reluctant destruction.

What It Means to Be a Firstborn

The Torah's consideration of culture continues into its next book. In Exodus 7:5, God announces the purpose of the plagues. It is not only to free the Jews from Egypt, which God could have done in a much more efficient way. He could have provided a magic carpet to bring the enslaved Jews from

Egypt to the Promised Land or put the Egyptian army to sleep while the Jews escaped.

The purpose of the plagues, we learn in Exodus, is so that "Egypt shall know that I am Hashem."

God subsequently delivers nine punishing plagues, and the Pharaoh does not free the Jews. But God does not give up on his re-creation project. He has the ultimate tactic ready, with the tenth and final plague.

God declares in Exodus 11:4, "Toward midnight I will go forth among the Egyptians, and every firstborn in the land of Egypt will die, from the firstborn of Pharaoh who sits on his throne to the firstborn of the slave girl who is behind the millstones and all the firstborn of the cattle."

At this point, the reader is drawn to stop and consider. Who is the firstborn? At first glance, the answer seems obvious: The firstborn is the child born before the others. But this cannot be. In Exodus 4:22, the prelude to the plagues, God tells Moses to tell the Pharaoh that the Jews are God's "firstborn." But we are not the oldest people in the Torah, or even close. Abraham, the first Jew, fights in a war involving *nine* other peoples. And those don't include some of the other peoples who also precede the Jews: the Amorites, Hittites, Perrizites, Jebusites, and others.

What, then, could God have meant by his desire for the Jews to be his "firstborn," and to destroy the Egyptian firstborn?

Anyone in a multi-child family can understand. If the firstborn in a family guides her siblings to follow the rules and live by the values of their parents, the family is likely to be calm and happy. If the firstborn guides her siblings to break the rules and contravene the values of their parents, the family will disintegrate into a constant state of dissension and conflict.[2]

The firstborn, in other words, is the culture carrier. God wants us to be his "firstborn" because he wants us to create a culture that others will want to emulate. Correspondingly, the firstborn in the Egyptian household is also the culture carrier—the one who embodies and evangelizes the culture that rejects God and enslaves and murders a people.

God's vision for the Exodus, we see, is centered around the destruction of one culture and the creation of another. His re-creation plan is all about culture.

The Divine Order

Fast-forward to Deuteronomy 20. Moses, who is preparing the people to continue after his passing, is focused on Zionist unity. He decrees universal military service, which ensures that everyone will contribute to the establishment and defense of the Jewish state. But he recognizes that universal military service is an ideal, and that there will be special circumstances that necessitate exemptions.

He enumerates four. One of those is for those who are "fearful and soft of heart." The significance of this exception is discussed in the chapter of this book on fear. The others are, in order: Those who have built a new house but have not lived in it, those who have planted a vineyard but not begun to enjoy it, and those who have become engaged to a woman but not yet married her.

The order of things listed in the Bible is always a teaching moment, with commentators having extracted lessons and guidance from it since the beginning of biblical interpretation. This is especially so with Deuteronomy 22:9. In his section of laws regarding "Human Dispositions," Maimonides called the order in which the exemptions are listed "the way of sensible men." One who does these things out of order is a fool who is likely to end up subsisting on charity.[3]

What else may be considered a "way of sensible men"? In Exodus, Moses decreed universal education. Therefore, it can be presumed that everyone in the biblical military (exempt or not) would have been educated. After being educated, the man gets a job that will enable him to secure the "new house." He then plants a vineyard—which shows some savings and/or personal financial diversification.

Given how small the vineyards could be in ancient times, he need not have advanced far in that step. He just needs to have the basic foundations of financial independence. After the man is educated, has received a job that enables him to provide housing and start saving, he is able to get married. The Torah and Maimonides do not mention having children, as they assume that having children will come after being married.

So, the order Moses decrees for the people is: Be educated, get a job, set the foundation for financial independence, get married, and have children.

And it was an order of such universal and eternal importance that Maimonides would consider it, simply, "the way of sensible men."

The Three Cultures

The Torah's persistent insistence on the importance of culture begs for a nuance. Our great guidebook could not say, broadly, to just seek good cultures and reject bad cultures. Culture comes in too many varieties for that to be worthy of the practical support that the Torah promises.

Sure enough, the Torah portrays three cultures that were dominant in biblical times and have remained so ever since. These are the same three cultures that Professors Bradley Campbell of California State University and Jason Manning of West Virginia University, in a remarkable 2014 paper in the journal *Comparative Sociology*, identified as characterizing the modern world. These are the honor culture, the victim culture, and the dignity culture.[4]

A consideration of these three cultures in the Torah can begin with one of its central ideas—that we should imitate or emulate God. In Exodus 34, God helps us understand who he is and provides assistance with the task of emulating him. In response to a plea from Moses, God reveals his thirteen attributes. The first two are compassion and graciousness. The third is "slowness to anger." And a consideration of biblical cultures shows why it would be a divine quality worthy of universal adoption.

How does "slowness to anger"—as a quality of God and man—prepare us to understand the Torah's view of culture? A hypothetical is illustrative. Let's say that Phil insults or otherwise offends Jack. How is Jack expected to respond? If he is expected to get angry and fight, he is in an honor culture. If he is expected to get angry and complain to a third party, he is in a victim culture. If he is expected to consider engaging with Phil's insult to be a distraction from what he really wants to be and do, he is in a dignity culture. A defining feature of each culture is how quick it is to anger.

God's slowness to anger reveals what he thinks of each of the cultures. But culture is too nuanced, pervasive, and determinative to leave it at that. The Torah offers, from the stories of Genesis to the summing up of Deuteronomy, a robust description of the choices offered by each kind of culture and the consequences of taking them.

The Honor Culture

The ancient world had a dominant culture. It was an honor culture. The ancient cultures of Rome, Greece, Egypt, China, India, and Japan were very different in some respects, but scholars of each have determined them to be honor cultures.

No one ever considered adding the ancient Jewish culture to this list. The reason is encapsulated in a Baraita. The Baraita are ancient Jewish teachings, drawn from the Torah, that were passed down orally until they were recorded almost two thousand years ago. Some are referenced in the Talmud—including this one:

> The Sages taught: Those who are insulted but do not insult others, who hear their shame but do not respond . . . the verse states regarding them: "And they that love him are as the sun going forth in its might" (Judges 5:31).[5]

The unpacking of this Baraita reveals the fundamental Torah perspective on the honor culture. One who is insulted or shamed and does not respond or reciprocate embodies the divine trait of "being slow to anger." Where does he derive the strength to ignore these insults? It is out of a "love for God" who has a mission for each of us, which requires our devotion and our focus.

The Torah models this "love for God"—manifested in a rejection of the honor culture—in three of its heroes. They are Abraham, Rachel, and Moses.

Abraham and Lot

In Genesis 12, God instructs Abraham to "go forth from your land, your relatives and from your father's house to a land that I will show you." Abraham has a divine mission and purpose—even if he does not yet know what either are.

He goes forth with a group of relatives and followers. One of the people he takes with him is his nephew, Lot. In Genesis 13:15, we learn about their relationship: "And Lot *also*, who went with Abraham, had flocks, and herds, and tents." Lot has become wealthy "also" as a result of going "with" Abraham. Abraham is the source of Lot's good fortune.

Lot does not respond with the gratitude of a protégé. "The land," the Torah tells us, "could not support them dwelling together for their possessions were abundant and they were unable to dwell together. And there was quarreling between the herdsmen of Abram's livestock and the herdsmen of Lot's livestock" (Genesis 13:6–7).

Lot, despite owing his prosperity to Abraham, allows tension and strife to foment between him and his uncle. It spreads to their employees. What would the logical, reasonable, and even predictable response of Abraham have been? Anyone who has seen *The Godfather* might suggest that Abraham would punish or even kill his nephew.

But this is not what Abraham does. Abraham does not even take offense. Instead, he says, "Let's not have any quarreling between you and me, or between your herders and mine, for we are close relatives. Is not the whole land before you? Let's part company. If you go to the left, I'll go to the right; if you go to the right, I'll go to the left" (Genesis 13:8–9).

Lot chooses the part of the land that is rich in material wealth but poor in moral resources. He soon finds himself embroiled in a regional war between multiple kings. Abraham marshals a small military force and executes a daring nighttime raid, which defeats multiple kingdoms. He saves his nephew.

The text gives no indication that Abraham ever gave a thought to the fact that Lot's trouble is caused by his decision about where to settle. Likewise, the text gives no indication that Lot ever apologizes to Abraham or shows any gratitude to Abraham for rescuing him. And the text gives no indication that Abraham ever expects such a response or is disappointed by its absence.

Abraham's sense of self, we see, is not validated or invalidated by what anyone else says or does. He takes nothing *personally* because nothing is about him. He is a man on a mission, and consequently refuses to allow any considerations of what he might personally deserve distract him from achieving it.

Why Jacob Loves Rachel

Years later, Abraham's grandson Jacob goes into exile to escape the murderous wrath of his twin brother, Esau. He soon thereafter meets the beautiful and lovely Rachel, and asks her father, Laban, for her hand in marriage. Laban agrees, provided that Jacob works for him for seven years.

After the seven years are over, Jacob says: "Give me my wife, for my time is fulfilled, that I may cohabit with her." Laban responds by tricking Jacob into marrying his older and less desirable daughter, Leah. Jacob, for reasons the text leaves us to wonder, does not realize who he has spent the night with until the next morning.

When Jacob realizes that he has married Leah instead of Rachel, he sternly expresses his feelings at having been "deceived" to Laban. Laban allows Jacob to marry Rachel as well, provided that Jacob works another seven years for him. Jacob agrees, and soon has both sisters as his wives.

Why does Jacob love Rachel so much? Yes, he notes in Genesis 29:17 that she is "of beautiful features and beautiful to look at." But this describes initial attraction, not enduring love. We can locate the source of his love thirteen verses later, where the text tells us that Jacob "also loved Rachel (*mee*) Leah." Many translations render *mee* as "than"—and thus read the verse as describing Jacob's preferential love for Rachel over Leah.

However, the eighteenth-century sage Abraham Chaim of Zlotchov notes that the Hebrew prefix "*mee*" primarily means "from." This translation makes more sense because we already know, by Genesis 29:17, that Jacob is completely in love with Rachel. If the Torah were telling us that Jacob loved Rachel "more than" Leah, it would not be teaching us anything new—which every passage does.

Rabbi Chaim's reading, on other hand, suggests that Jacob loves Rachel because of how she responds to Leah's having married Jacob. Rachel had every right to be angry with her sister for stealing her husband. But Rachel sublimates her disappointment at being cheated out of her husband to her sensitivity and concern for her less beautiful and seemingly unwanted older sister.[6]

Rabbi Chaim's insight is validated by what we learn in Genesis 30. Leah and Jacob's son Reuben goes into the field to get mandrake plants (a kind of ancient aphrodisiac) for his mother. Rachel, who has not yet conceived, asks her sister for some of the mandrakes. Leah sharply responds, "Wasn't it enough that you took away my husband? Will you take my son's mandrakes too?"

Rachel could have lashed out at her sister, pointing out that it was Leah who stole Jacob from Rachel—and not the other way around. But Rachel does not get angry or otherwise distracted by arguing with Leah. There is no indication that she takes her sister's insult personally at all. Doing so would have just distracted her from her mission—which is to, despite fertility problems, have a child who will continue the Jewish people. Her lack of anger, in Jacob's eye, validates Rachel as the perfect wife for him and the ideal matriarch of the Jewish people. Rachel, as Abraham before her, demonstrates a slowness to anger—and, in so doing, rejects the prevalent honor culture of the ancient world.

How Moses Responds to Insult

By Numbers 12, Moses has established himself as a great leader. He personally fought for justice for Jews and gentiles, demanded that the Pharaoh release his slaves, led the Jews in a daring escape from Egypt and into the desert, established education as the priority of the Jewish people, set up a judicial system, led the Jewish people in war, and demanded to God that he forgive the Jewish people after the sin of the Golden Calf.

But there is one thing we don't know about Moses. How will he respond if personally insulted? In Numbers 12, Moses's siblings, Miriam and Aaron, gossip about his love life. God is furious and summons them, harshly chastises them, and severely punishes Miriam with disease.

In an honor culture, Moses would have also been furious. Miriam had offended him in the most sensitive way for a man in such a culture—by insulting his woman. Moses, though, says only one thing. He beseeches God, "Please, heal her now."

This is not the only time in Numbers when Moses is confronted. In Numbers 9, nameless men demand to Moses that they be able to celebrate Pesach because they were unclean at the time of the holiday. In Numbers 27, five sisters tell Moses that the laws of inheritance are unjust. Both are direct challenges to God's law and Moses's authority. In neither case does Moses get offended, pull rank, or show any concern that such challenges will weaken his authority. To the contrary, he *welcomes* their challenges and brings them to God—who changes the law in accordance with the winning arguments of these ordinary citizens.

Moses, the Torah shows, consistently rejects the fundamental tenet of the honor culture—and refuses to even consider violence as a response to being publicly insulted. A man on a mission, he never allows himself to be fazed or otherwise distracted by personal affronts. Instead, he considers criticism a mechanism to help him achieve his mission.

Victim Culture

The honor culture is not the only culture of significant concern to the Author of the Torah. There is another one. It is the victim culture. Like the honor culture, the victim culture is marked by a quickness to anger. Instead of responding to anger by fighting, the participant in a victim culture responds by appealing to a third party. The quickness to anger that is cultivated and manifested in victim cultures accounts for many of its characteristics—particularly those it shares with participants in the honor culture. These include the development of a large and sensitive ego, which leads victim culture participants to focus on how others perceive them at the expense of how they can serve others and fulfill the divine mission that the Torah believes each of us has.

These and other consequences of the victim culture, the Torah posits, are pervasive, deep, and defining—for the culture and the individuals who comprise it. And the Torah has a rich description and an unambiguous and definitive take on it.

When God Doesn't Hear a Cry

In Genesis 16, Sarah, an old woman, has concluded that she cannot conceive a child. She encourages her husband, Abraham, to have a child with her maidservant, Hagar. The result of the union of Abraham and Hagar is the birth of a son, Ishmael.

In Genesis 21, Sarah miraculously becomes pregnant, and Isaac is born. Ishmael and Isaac grow up together, but all is not okay in this blended family. In Genesis 21:9, we learn that Ishmael is behaving inappropriately with his brother. We don't know exactly what Ishmael is doing, but it is enough for Sarah to tell her husband to banish Hagar and Ishmael. Abraham, after God intervenes, accedes to Sarah's demand that Ishmael must be exiled.

Hagar and Ishmael depart with water and other provisions that Abraham provides. They end up in Beersheba. Beersheba means either "Place of Seven Wells" or "Well of Oaths." In either translation, it is a town known for its abundant water.

A short while into their journey, the water that Abraham had provided is depleted. This is not a surprise. But nor should it have been a problem. Hagar and Ishmael were, after all, in a place famous for its water. But the implications of being in this "Place of Seven Wells" is lost on Hagar. She moves away from her son and says, "Let *me* not see the death of my child." Preparing to die of thirst, she sits "at a distance" from Ishmael and cries.

This is a good moment for the reader to pause. Hagar does not act to procure water for herself and Ishmael. Hagar does not cry because Ishmael is suffering. Instead, she cries about her own feelings and resigns herself to death.

The story continues. God, the text says, "heard the cry of the youth." We did not previously know that Ishmael had been crying, but it is reasonable that he had been. His mother, wallowing in her sorrow, has effectively abandoned him to die of thirst. Still, what about Hagar, who we know had been crying? God does not mention it; he only refers to "the cry of the youth." The reader is drawn to ask, *did God hear Hagar's cry too?* Apparently not. God, seemingly, does not hear the cry of one who makes herself into a victim.

God may be disappointed in Hagar, but he does not forsake her. Instead, God says to her, "What troubles you?"—as if nothing should. He shows why. He "opens her eyes," and she sees that there is a well with plenty of water for Ishmael. Despite the fact that God has just provided her with abundant water, Hagar does not praise or thank him. She does not say anything. The story ends.

In the Bible's first exploration of the victim mentality, we learn several of its characteristics. First, the victim renders herself completely incompetent. This incompetence is so profound that Hagar is unable to even notice a solution for her problem that is in front of her eyes. Second, the victim becomes a narcissist. This narcissism is so profound that Hagar focuses on her own feelings even when her son is suffering greatly. Third, the victim becomes ungrateful. This ingratitude runs so deep that Hagar does not even thank God when he rescues her and her son from the consequences of her narcissism and incompetence. Fourth, the victim becomes incapable of learning and growth. Hagar never shows any signs of positive development. And she does not teach anything either. Hagar never speaks with Ishmael about what he did to get them banished, or help him develop and improve.

Who Receives Deference?

Let's say that a student was given the assignment of defending Hagar. He would have a case. It would be that Hagar was poor, weak, and ostracized—and therefore is deserving of sympathy that would exempt her from the standards that could be fairly applied to others. It sounds plausible, unless the student also considered Exodus 23.

Exodus 23 is part of the sequence of laws that follows the giving of the Torah at Mount Sinai. In Exodus 23:3, God instructs: "You shall not show deference to a poor person in a dispute." It is followed, in Exodus 23:6, by another rule: "You shall not subvert the rights of your needy in a dispute."

These instructions are combined in God's instruction toward the beginning of the Holiness Code in Leviticus 19:15: "You shall not render an unfair decision: do not favor the poor or show deference to the rich; judge your kin fairly." These instructions, which obviously apply to professional judges, are not intended just for them. They are provided in a list of laws governing prosocial behavior, and therefore apply to the judging of people that everyone does all the time.

The guidance from the post-Sinai instructions and the Holiness Code is clear. One might be inclined to favor the rich and pocket an IOU from someone who can help later. One might be inclined to favor the poor and feel virtuous. The Torah is clear: Do neither. When it comes to whom we should respect or favor, one's status as being rich or poor—one's privilege or victimhood—is morally and legally irrelevant. We are to consider everyone and everything according to merit. This point is so important that it is not only articulated in Exodus and Leviticus—but is reiterated again by Moses, in his closing speech that constitutes Deuteronomy.

This rule is not only a core component of how the Torah wants us to conduct ourselves politically, judicially, and socially. It also has psychological ramifications. If a society privileges victims, it will encourage people to identify as victims. And this, the Torah tells us, is devastating in many ways.

Redemption: The Victim Mindset Politically

In Exodus 6:6–7, God is preparing to liberate us from Egyptian slavery. He instructs Moses, "Therefore, say to the children of Israel, 'I am the Lord, and I will take you out from under the burdens of the Egyptians, and I will save you from their labor, and I will redeem you with an outstretched arm and with great judgments. I will take you as my own people, and I will be your God.'"

These words constitute the four expressions of freedom (take you out, save you, redeem you, and take you as my people), which are immortalized through the four cups of wine we drink at the Pesach Seder.

The first two expressions (take you / save you) are physical, as they are about God's taking us out of Egypt. The fourth (take you as my people) is spiritual and about our relationship with God. The twentieth-century American Rabbi Chanoch Leibowitz notes that these three blessings, which cover the physical and the spiritual, seem comprehensive. What, then, could be the need for or the meaning of the third expression of freedom—that of redemption?[7]

We learn the answer in a variety of stories, laws, and teachings from Exodus to Numbers: It is the liberation from the slave mentality, which is a core component of the victim culture. And the importance of ridding ourselves of the slave mentality comes through precisely in Numbers 13.

In Numbers 13, the Jews are more than a year removed from slavery. Moses sends scouts to the land to prepare for the inevitable conflict to follow. The mission is a disaster. Ten of the twelve scouts return from the expedition saying that the divinely ordained mission to take the land is impossible. They explain, "We were like grasshoppers in our eyes, and so we were in their eyes." God concludes that this entire generation (but for Joshua and Caleb, who wish to enter) will die in the desert.

Moses, who is always ready and willing to argue with God on behalf of the people, does not object. Why? Because he recognizes that the Jews were not yet *redeemed* from slavery. Even with Moses's instruction and God's protection, we thought of ourselves as weak and fearful grasshoppers. We had left Egypt, but Egypt had not left us. We were partners with God under the leadership of Moses, but we still thought of ourselves as victims. And this mentality had become so pervasive that almost everyone accepted it. We had become a *victim culture*. A victim culture—a nation of Hagars—could never successfully confront the challenges of being a free people in the Promised Land. Consequently, God decrees that this generation would live out its days in the desert.

The story ends on a hopeful note. The people may not enter the Promised Land, but their children will. The victim mentality, and the culture it creates, need not endure in perpetuity. It can change.

The Victim Culture, Personally

As discussed in the chapter of this book on reframing, it is very clear in the Exodus story that we were slaves in Egypt. Yet in Exodus, Leviticus, and Deuteronomy, the Torah characterizes our experience in Egypt as that of a "stranger." Why would the Author of the Torah, who knew the difference between a slave and a stranger, have made this switch?

One is, as discussed, to provide us with the framework to do the unheard of—and love the stranger. The other is to help us shed the victim mentality that would come with perpetually seeing ourselves as slaves. In order to confront the challenges in the Land, en route to becoming (per Exodus 19:6) a "kingdom of priests and a holy nation," we will need to be confident people who act—and not victims who are acted upon.

The Victim Culture, Militarily

It is Numbers 20. Moses is leading the people through the wilderness and needs to pass through the kingdom of Edom. He says, "So said your brother Israel: You know all the hardship that has befallen us." He continues by describing the hardship—specifically that the people had just emerged from slavery in Egypt. Moses concludes by saying that the people just want to "pass through"—and will not "veer right or left." He promises that they will not touch a field, a vineyard, or even drink any water.

The king responds, "You shall not pass through me—lest I come against you with the sword!"

The "Children of Israel" respond, reiterating what Moses concluded with—that they will not touch anything. The king of Edom refuses again, this time "with a massive throng and a strong hand." Moses leads his people on a circuitous route, avoiding Edom.

This sequence is instructive for Moses. He learns that appeals from weakness, or those based on victim status, do not work. They breed contempt in the king of Edom, and he hardens his position.

In Numbers 21, a similar situation arises. The people need to pass through the Amorite kingdom. This time, Moses sends emissaries to its king, Sihon. The emissaries do not lead with a victim narrative, or otherwise speak from weakness. Instead, they just guarantee that they will not touch a field, a vineyard, or drink any water. Sihon, like the king of Edom, refuses. He goes to war against the Jews. Having shed their victim narrative, Moses and his people operate from strength. They win an astonishing victory, capturing the entire kingdom.

Biblical Success

The victim mentality, as we see explicitly with the scouts in Numbers and the litigants in Deuteronomy, leads to loss and failure. What, then, might lead to success? The Torah makes this an easy question—as it has only one person who is declared "a successful man." This is Joseph—who earns this designation twice. How did he achieve this prestigious designation?

Abandoned by his family and sold into slavery in a strange land, Joseph has the most legitimate claim to victim status of anyone in the Torah. Yet he does not complain. Instead, he marshals his innate talents and becomes the slave in charge of a prominent household. When the wife of the master of the household frames him for rape and he lands in prison, he again does not complain. In prison, he again marshals his talents and earns the respect of everyone around—to the point where even the warden believed that "God is with Joseph."

He eventually gets out of prison, as a result of interpreting the Pharaoh's dreams. He becomes the viceroy of Egypt—the number-two man in the kingdom, behind only the Pharaoh. He names his first son Manasseh ("God has made me forget all my hardship and all my father's household"), indicating that he will never maintain, let alone act upon, grievances from the past. And he continually expresses his gratitude to God, often by crediting God with his accomplishments.

Even as Joseph rises, falls, rises, falls, and rises again when he becomes the viceroy of Egypt, he always maintains great confidence in his own ability to effectuate positive change for himself and others. He is an emotional man who cries eight times in just a few verses—but never as a result of anything that happened to him. Despite being persecuted by his brothers and then by his master's wife, he clearly maintains his close relationship with God, continually grateful and focused on his unfolding mission. Joseph, in word and deed, continually and systematically rejects each tenet of the victim mentality and culture. In establishing Joseph as its quintessential anti-victim, the Torah sets him up to be the *only* person in the Torah to be designated a "success."

The Victim and Honor Cultures Converge

The honor culture and the victim culture seem quite distinct because their outward manifestations are so different. The fighting that characterizes honor cultures is entirely different from the complaining that characterizes victim cultures. But the Torah's presentation of these cultures enables us to see beyond their manifestations and into their fundamental similarities. And these begin with the rejection of the "slowness to anger" that God defines himself by.

Participants in both cultures take personally, and react viscerally, to the words, glances, and even silences of others. This quickness to anger betrays that they do not have an internally generated sense of self, but are instead driven by an ego that moves with the whims of outside influence.

Consequently, participants in both cultures are very sensitive to what outsiders—even people they do not know—think of them. They do not measure themselves by their character, actions, or accomplishments. They measure themselves by how they are perceived, with the only difference being the desired perception. Honor culture participants want to be perceived as strong and receive respect. Victim culture participants want to be perceived as aggrieved and receive sympathy. In neither case does the participant gratefully focus on what he owes. Instead, he focuses with resentment on the respect or sympathy he is owed. Fixated on how others perceive him and whether they are giving the respect or sympathy that he feels is owed, he cannot devote himself to a mission or live for a purpose that is greater than himself.

No wonder God decided that neither culture could be that which would be hospitable for a free people in their own land, en route to being a kingdom of priests and a holy nation.

Fortunately, the Torah presents an alternative.

The Dignity Culture

In Exodus 19:6, God articulates his vision for the Jewish society. We are to become a "kingdom of priests and a holy nation." This is a radical notion. The priesthood, and holiness, are not for a spiritual elite. They are an opportunity, and an expectation, for everyone.

Fewer than ten verses later, the Torah makes it clear what the preeminent virtue of the priest is. In Exodus 28:2, God tells Moses to give the high priest clothing appropriate for his "dignity and honor." As always, the ordering of the language is instructive. Dignity is the preeminent quality.

One of the best ways to know the importance of something in a society is to assess how it is treated when it conflicts with other things a society considers good. Enter Deuteronomy 24:10–13, where Moses declares: "When you shall claim a debt of any amount from your fellow, you shall not enter his home to take security for it. You shall stand outside, and the man from whom you claim shall bring the security to you outside. If that man is poor, you shall not sleep with his security."

This instruction seemingly conflicts with a crucial priority of the Torah society—which is the rule of law, as applied to commercial transactions. There is no question that the creditor can collect on his debt. After all, he can accept collateral to ensure that the debt will be paid. Why, then, is the creditor prohibited from entering the home to take the collateral? Why must he surrender his legal right to the immediate receipt of the collateral if the borrower is poor?

It is because of the culture in which these transactions must occur. To enter a man's home to take the collateral—to be searching for it or demanding it in front of his wife and children—would violate his dignity. Similarly, to make a poor man spend the night without something he *needs* (presumably a blanket or clothing) would violate the poor man's dignity as well. And dignity, we learn in Deuteronomy, trumps even the basic tenets of commercial law—which the Torah otherwise enumerates and embraces.

Other characteristics of what constitutes the Torah's ideal of dignity are explored in various chapters of this book. For instance, a dignified person embraces responsibility, gives generously, lives an ordered life marked by routine, is future oriented, interprets others generally, and dresses appropriately and strategically.

Those do not, however, provide a comprehensive accounting of the Torah ideology of dignity. It is probably impossible to provide a full enumeration of all of the Torah's characteristics of dignity because the concept is embedded in every component of its vision for a good person and a good society. But there are several crucial and defining components of dignity that the Torah emphasizes which are worthy of exploration. These include who we serve, what we admire, how we consider our agency, when we should act violently, when we should speak, and how we tell our story.

Be a Slave to God

In Leviticus 25:55, God says: "For the Children of Israel are slaves to me, they are my slaves." This is a startling statement. God identifies himself, from Exodus to Judges, not as the Creator of the Heavens and the Earth—but as the *liberator* of the slaves. The foundational act of the Jewish people is that of a slave revolt. If there is one thing in the Torah that is abundantly clear, it is that God hates slavery. Why, then, would God say that the Jews are to be "slaves"?

A slave is totally devoted and committed to his master, and acts only in accordance with his will. Consequently, a slave to God will need to ascertain what God wants from him—what, in other words, God put him in this world to do. A slave to God, solely concerned with what God wants from him, will not give heed to the slights, insults, and offenses that drive people in victim and honor cultures. He will not care where he is invited, where he is seated, or other measures of earthly status that are not related to his divine mission. And he certainly will not become jealous, envious, or covetous—as he will be focused on the mission that his divine master has provided, without regard to what the master has charged others with doing.

Perhaps most of all, the slave to God will be able to resist any temptation, distraction, or diversion from the will of God. The slave to God can live with the peace, confidence, and security of someone who cannot deviate from the word, mission, and expectations of her sole master and only real boss. Free from ungodly distractions, purposeless diversions, and useless comparisons, he will reliably and consistently live a life of dignity.

Embrace One's Agency and Determine the Future

In Genesis 49, Jacob, on his deathbed, is about to give his children their final blessing. He says, "Assemble yourselves and I will tell you what will befall you in the End of Days."

He concludes the blessings almost three dozen verses later without explicitly saying what will happen in the "End of Days." Why not? According to the Midrash, Jacob, apparently tempted to give an end of days prophecy, either stops himself or is stopped by God. The reason why either would do so is effectively revealed in Deuteronomy 18, when Moses forbids sorcery and divination. A dignified person does not seek prophecies, signs, or anything else to find out what the future holds. He knows that the future is open and waiting for his co-creation of it.

In chapter four of Pirkei Avot ("Ethics of our Fathers," an ancient text of Jewish wisdom), the first-century sage Ben Zoma asks four questions that, as South Africa's Chief Rabbi Warren Goldstein says, refer to qualities that everyone wants. The four questions (and their answers):

- Who is wise? He who learns from every man.
- Who is strong? He who subdues his evil inclination.
- Who is rich? He who rejoices in his lot.
- Who is honored? He who honors others.

These answers, as Rabbi Goldstein points out, are counterintuitive—as we normally answer them through comparison to others. Ben Zoma's answers share a crucial commonality: They are all within an individual's control, and are not expressed or validated in comparison to anyone else. Unlike participants in the honor and victim culture, those who answer as Ben Zoma suggests maintain an internal locus of control—and in so doing, exemplify Torah-based dignity.[8]

Self-Esteem

Everyone who has been involved in a communal building project or other charitable fundraising campaign knows what the economic logic of the endeavor dictates. The responsible party generally gets as much money as he can from the wealthiest people who might be interested. He then, sometimes using their commitment as an endorsement, supplements these contributions with much smaller gifts from a broad base of supporters. It is always good, for a variety of reasons, to involve as many people as possible—but it is often economically unnecessary.

This logic describes most such collective endeavors—but not the very first one. This is the building of the Tabernacle, the home for God that the Jews constructed in the desert in late Exodus. In the construction of the Tabernacle, every adult has to contribute a half-shekel. No one is allowed to contribute more or less.

What is the reason behind this strange fundraising technique? The Pardes Institute scholar Yiscah Smith says that the purpose is to provide everyone with the self-esteem that comes from having contributed to an important cause. The result of this mass cultivation of self-esteem: the creation of "a *dignified* home for the Divine."[9]

Why is the cultivation of self-esteem so important that God would supersede the laws of economics to establish it in the construction of the holy Tabernacle? A person with self-esteem will not crave the sympathy that drives a participant in the victim culture. He will not seek the outward expressions of respect that participants in honor cultures demand. He will, instead, have the confidence and competence necessary to focus on his mission from God and to execute as well as he can.

The Use of Violence

In Genesis 20, Abraham is a powerless Jew in a hostile land. The King of Gerar takes his wife. A generation later, his son Isaac is in a similar predicament. His wife narrowly escapes the clutches of a gentile king. These acts—surrendering one's wife to a king—are the epitome of *indignity*. The powerless Jew risks, or perhaps guarantees, indignity. There is an alternative.

In Exodus 2:11, Moses sees an Egyptian attacking a Jew. He saves the Jew by killing the Egyptian with his bare hands, and escapes to Midian to avoid the inevitable response of the Egyptian state. As soon as he arrives in Midian, he sees men harassing seven sisters by a well. Moses single-handedly drives away the men and rescues the women.

What does God think of Moses using violence to save the life of the Jewish man and to protect the dignity of the Midianite women? God soon chooses Moses to be his partner in his defining act—the liberation of slaves.

In Exodus 22:1, we see that the question of violence—and its relationship to dignity—is not just for great leaders like Moses. It is for everyone. In Exodus 22:1, a man is at home when a thief breaks in. What is he to do? The Torah is very clear: "If a thief is seized while tunneling and beaten to death, there is no blood guilt in that case." A homeowner need not retreat, cower in a safe room, or appeal to a third party. He can stand his ground, and defend himself, his family, and his property.

In 1974, Rav Joseph B. Soloveitchik reflected on this passage. He wrote:

> He [the thief] didn't come to kill him. For instance, I am in my bedroom upstairs, [on] the second floor, I heard someone opening the door and coming in; he came as a burglar. If I should not interfere with his burglary, he wouldn't kill me. But if I should interfere, he'll kill me, he'll commit murder. So what is the law? That I have a right to kill him . . . The covenantal community is not a community of meek ones. Not at all. It is not a community which offers the other cheek if I get slapped once. It isn't; it's not true.[10]

At around the same time when Rav Soloveitchik offered that interpretation of Exodus 22:1, the Israeli prime minister Menachem Begin met with a delegation of young Jewish leaders. They asked him about the lessons from the Holocaust.

Prime Minister Begin was the right person to ask. In the 1930s and early 1940s, Menachem Begin had seen the kinds of things that would soon horrify good people the world over. Jews forced to wear signs proclaiming, "I am a defiler of the race," and "I am a Polish pig." Jewish men watching their women and children beg for their lives from Nazi soldiers. Jews forced to cut each other's payot (sidecurls) in public. Jews stripping before being led to dig a mass grave into which they would fall after being shot . . . and countless other examples of otherwise inconceivable indignity.

Menachem Begin had a six-part answer ready. His third lesson was: "A Jew must learn to defend himself. He must forever be prepared for whatever threat looms."

Prime Minister Begin developed this point in his fourth lesson. He explained:

> Jewish dignity and honor must be protected in all circumstances. The seeds of Jewish destruction lie in passively enabling the enemy to humiliate us. Only when the enemy succeeds in turning the spirit of the Jew into dust and ashes in life, can he turn the Jew into dust and ashes in death. During the Holocaust, it was only after the enemy had humiliated the Jews, trampled them underfoot, divided them, deceived them, afflicted them, and drove brother against brother, that they then could lead them, almost without resistance, to the gates of Auschwitz. Therefore, at all times and whatever the cost, safeguard the dignity and honor of the Jewish people.[11]

A person of dignity, we see, imitates God in Exodus 34. It is not that he never angers, but that he is "slow to anger." He has the capacity for violence, but never uses it to settle personal scores. Instead, he uses it judiciously, strategically, powerfully, and infrequently.

Speech

In Leviticus 19:16, God prohibits gossiping. In Numbers 30:3, the Torah instructs, "If a man makes a vow to the Lord or makes an oath to prohibit himself, he shall not violate his word; according to whatever comes out of his mouth, he shall do."

A dignified person, accordingly, chooses his words carefully and does what he says. Just as a person who is careful about his purchases will buy less than one who is careless about them, a dignified person will follow the counsel of Proverbs 17:27 and "use few words." As King Solomon wrote in Ecclesiastes, "He that has knowledge spares his words: and a man of understanding is slow to anger."

A dignified person will also be careful about what he talks about. Yom Kippur, the day of atonement, is the holiest day of the Jewish year. One of the sins that we repent for on Yom Kippur is that of *veidat zenut*—"[participating in] discussions of lewdness." Lewd discussion—which manifests in crude talk about sexual matters, bodily functions, and plenty of other things—is considered by our Yom Kippur liturgy to be a violation of dignity, and a sin we need to repent for.

What We Praise

In Genesis 25:34, Esau sells his birthright (the crown of spiritual leadership) to his younger twin brother, Jacob, in exchange for a bowl of red stew. It would be understandable if Esau, with his hunger satisfied, regretted the sale. It would be mature if Esau, with self-awareness, said that he was satisfied with the transaction because he did not have the right disposition for spiritual leadership, which should belong to his more pious and studious brother. He does neither. Instead, the Torah tells us, Esau "disparaged the birthright."

This story reveals a crucial Torah teaching about dignity. A dignified person will admire and celebrate worthy things—and disrespect and disregard unworthy things. King Solomon encapsulates this teaching in Proverbs 27:21: "A man is tried according to his praise." The things we choose to value and praise say a lot about who we are as people.

Telling Our Story Truthfully

An important decision that every person—knowingly or not—makes is how they will tell their story. There are always so many things that happen in one's history and so many possible interpretations of what to include, exclude, and emphasize. The result often reveals the character of a culture.

The Jewish story, as told in the Torah, is one of patriarchs with moral failings, murderous sibling rivalry, attempted fratricide, prostitution, liberation followed by nonstop rebellion, mass hysteria that turns into idol worship, and mass seduction that turns into sex on the steps of God's Tabernacle.

One of the greatest heroes of the Bible is King David, who is descended in part from a sexual union between Lot and his daughter. King David is famous for having one of his soldiers killed so he can sleep with his wife. The scandalousness of our origin story is so striking that, as one commentator concluded, it must have been written either by an antisemite or by God.[12]

We can dismiss the idea that the Torah was written by Jew haters. That leaves a question: Why would the Jews tell our story with such brutal honesty?

Because, perhaps, this is simply what a dignified people does. A hallmark of a dignified culture, the Torah shows, is a people telling its story *honestly*. This means including and even emphasizing the moments of pride and shame, the rising and falling, the progress and the setbacks. A dignified people has no need to omit, exaggerate, or explain away. A dignified person or people honestly assesses past actions and learns and grows from them.

The Jewish Symbol

Many cultures have a symbol that embodies, and can serve as shorthand for, its moral ambitions, essential meanings, and cultural yearnings. Christians have Jesus dying on the cross, the Chinese have the yin and the yang, and Nordic culture has the World Tree.

In 1949, the municipality of Jerusalem had a contest to determine what the symbol of the city would be. The winner was a rampant lion standing with its paws facing outward. This lion stands in front of the Western Wall and is on the flag of Jerusalem today.

The choice of the lion is a demonstration of how Israel, even for those whose vision of the state is secular, is the *Jewish* state. On his deathbed, our patriarch, Jacob, gives his son Judah (after whom Jews are named) the blessing of rulership and bestows upon him what has become understood as the "messianic prophecy." The prophecy begins, "You are a lion's cub, Judah; you return from the prey, my son. Like a lion he crouches and lies down, like a lioness—who dares rouse him?" (Genesis 49:9). The Lion of Judah has become synonymous with the image of Jewish kingship.

In the Book of Kings, we read about King Solomon's throne. It was so extraordinary that "no such throne was ever made for any other kingdom." What does such a throne look like? The text explains: "Six steps led up to the throne, and the throne had a back with a rounded top, and arms on either side of the seat. Two lions stood beside the arms, and twelve lions stood on the six steps, six on either side" (1 Kings 10:19–21).

Even today, there is one symbol in synagogue art that endures despite the general hesitancy toward iconography. These are the two lions that surround the Ten Commandments. These lions often adorn the entrance of synagogue arks.[13]

Why, of all animals, does Judaism make the lion such a pervasive and insistent symbol of our cultural aspirations?

The Shulchan Arukh (the code of Jewish law codified in the sixteenth century) opens by instructing every individual to "arise like a lion to serve your Creator." Many readers might think that this is a command to arise quickly, but this is not so. The lion does not rise quickly and rush off. He wakes up slowly and surveys the environment as he seemingly ponders where he should go and what he should do.

When the lion decides that it is time to engage the world, he is ready. The lion has, due to a reflective layer of cells behind the retina, night vision that is able to make use of the faintest moonlight. The lion's nighttime vision is eight times better than that of humans. And the lion's spectacular vision is complemented by outstanding hearing. Lions can hear prey a mile away. The lion, in other words, has an outstanding command of the reality of his environment.[14]

And the lion confronts that reality with a characteristic that is described in the instruction of Judah ben Tema in Pirkei Avot: "Be strong as a leopard, and swift as an eagle, and fleet as a gazelle, and brave as a lion, to do the will of your Father who is in heaven."[15] The lion, in the Jewish understanding, is distinguished by its courage. This courage is embedded into the behavior of the species, and evident to all observers. Lions sleep with their eyes closed, a very rare trait among animals with eyelids.[16]

Moreover, the lion has no natural predators. That does not give him invincibility, as lions engage in plenty of battles and lose some. Lions battle fiercely to protect their young, even when doing so means engaging in a battle where the odds are against them.

When a lion decides to fight, he does so in the same manner that he awakens—carefully and thoughtfully. He joins other lions. Together, they stalk their prey for up to an hour, often hiding in the grass before they decide to pounce. The lion is, as God said of himself, slow to anger. But when the lion angers, she roars to battle—at close to 45 mph.[17]

The lion—the animal who awakens carefully, sleeps with his eyes closed, grasps reality, defends his young, and chooses his battles judiciously, fears no one, is courageous—is the model of *dignity*. As such, the lion is the symbol of Jewish culture—proudly adorning the Jerusalem flag.

The Science

From when God destroys the world in the time of Noah, and Sodom in the time of Abraham, the Torah makes clear that the character and constitution of a society's culture is the single most important determinant of its fortunes generally and those of its constituents specifically.

Culture is not the only preeminent determinant of the fortunes of an individual or his society. There are others. The rule of law is certainly one, and it constitutes the chapter of this book regarding corruption. Two others are intelligence and power dynamics. Which of these three forces (intelligence, power dynamics, and culture) determines the health and wealth (broadly defined) of individuals and their society?

Intelligence

The opening ceremony at the 2008 Summer Olympics in Beijing featured a celebration of what China calls the "Four Great Inventions." These inventions—of printing, papermaking, the compass, and gunpowder—are just some of the remarkable innovations that came out of the Chinese empire through the first millennia and a half of the common era. Other early Chinese inventions include fireworks, the folding screen, gas lamps, the adjustable centerboard keel, the restaurant menu, uses of paper in currency, playing cards, toilet paper, the belt drive, pest control, the blast furnace, drilling, mining, the candle clock, the wheelbarrow, and the zoetrope (a kind of movie).

Around 1500, this spectacular development stopped. Well before the twentieth century, China's achievements in technological development had been vastly surpassed by those of many, much smaller, European countries. What happened? The Chinese did not get dumber in the sixteenth century.

In 1500, the Ming Dynasty decreed the death penalty for building a ship with two masts. In 1551, China extended the death penalty for traveling in such a ship. These effective prohibitions on distant travel are manifestations of a cultural choice—what the scholar Mark Leonard calls the "Great Wall mentality." The consequence of China turning inward accounts for the spectacular reversal of fortune at the dawn of modernity.[18]

A very similar dynamic—of the development of a society being significantly slowed because of its imposition of a "Great Wall mentality"—has occurred in our time.

The early development of the US technology industry was equally concentrated in two areas: Route 128 in Massachusetts and Silicon Valley in California. The success of these regions accounts for the economic growth experienced by their respective states in the 1970s and 1980s. Indeed, Michael Dukakis, who served as governor of Massachusetts for much of this period, based his 1988 presidential campaign on what had become known as the "Massachusetts Miracle." However, by the time of his campaign, the "Massachusetts Miracle" was diminishing and Silicon Valley was ascending. What happened?

It was not anything that Michael Dukakis did or didn't do. People in Massachusetts did not become dumber. Professor Anna Lee Saxenian of the University of California at Berkeley figured out what was happening a decade before Mark Zuckerberg left Massachusetts for Silicon Valley to start Facebook. Route 128, she wrote, had developed a system of "independent companies that keep largely to themselves," where the prevailing ethos was one of "secrecy."

Silicon Valley developed a fundamentally different culture. Silicon Valley companies, Professor Saxenian wrote,

> . . . compete intensely while learning from one another about changing markets and technologies through informal communication and collaboration . . . the organizational boundaries within companies are porous, as are the boundaries between companies themselves and between companies and local institutions such as trade associations and universities.[19]

Consequently, Silicon Valley has produced companies such as Facebook, Salesforce, Google, and Tesla. And Route 128, which started at the same place, hasn't.

Intelligence, we see, is not the determinant between the success and failure of a society. Is power dynamics?

Power Dynamics

Another candidate for the distinction between successful and failed societies is power dynamics. Those who believe in this theory say that groups with power—and/or privilege—use the resulting prerogatives to grow their wealth and power at the expense of others.

Of course, this theory can be true. A dominant group with state power and totalitarian ambitions can quash, steal, and kill their way into achieving power and money at the expense of others. Short of that, how much do power dynamics explain about individual and group success?

One place to look is the Jewish people. In 1920, Jews were a small minority of the population of Europe. According to the theory that success and failure in a society is determined by power dynamics, we should have been a marginal group. In 1920, Jews constituted 6 percent of the Hungarian population—and 46 percent of the medical doctors, 40 percent of the factory owners, and around 20 percent of the painters, sculptors, musicians, and actors.[20]

And this dynamic is by no means limited to Jews. In the 1960s, the dominant ethnic group in Malaysia was the Malay. Yet the Chinese minority (comprising around a third of the country) had more than one hundred times the number of engineering degrees as the Malay majority.[21]

How about in the United States? In 1899, there were four academic high schools in Washington, DC. These high schools were segregated by race; three of the high schools were white and one was black. The students at the black high school outperformed the students at two of the white high schools, despite widespread discrimination against blacks.[22]

In the twentieth century, Asian Americans were not politically powerful. Chinese Americans were victims of explicitly discriminatory laws and violence that included assaults, expulsions, and massacres. Japanese Americans were interned in camps in the United States during the World War II years. Even as direct discrimination ended, these groups did not focus on politics—and never had much of an organized political presence in Washington or the state capitals.

Yet, they thrived to such an extent that they were so well represented in "elite" universities in the twenty-first century, that these institutions crafted policies and procedures to limit their enrollment—a practice that was declared illegal by the United States Supreme Court in 2023.

Despite abundant evidence showing that groups without power—and even groups who are being discriminated against—can and do significantly outperform the powerful, this explanation for success in society still persists. In the 2020s, this has been especially prevalent as it is the fundamental idea behind the claim of "white privilege." Under this theory, white people use their power and privilege to capture the wealth and other assets of society. What does the data say?

White Americans earn, on average, approximately half as much as Indian Americans. White Americans also earn less than Nigerian, Taiwanese, Lebanese, Syrian, Israeli, Australian, Filipino, Guyanese, and Tanzanian Americans. Why would such a diverse array of groups earn more income than "white Americans"—many of whose ancestors have been in the United States for a long time? It cannot be that Filipino, Syrian, and Tanzanian Americans use their "power" to the detriment of "white" people. What, then, could be an alternative explanation for the success of these and other groups around the world?[23]

Culture

In 2018, Professors Amy Hsin of Queens College and Yu Xie of the University of Michigan published a study that sought to ascertain why Asian Americans do better academically than whites. They found that Asian Americans are not different in general intelligence from their white peers. They also found that children from Asian American groups with poverty rates higher than whites still outperformed their native-born white peers.

What, then, could it be? They found that Asian American success can be attributed to a combination of motivation, self-control, attentiveness, work ethic, and persistence. Or, in a word—culture.[24]

In 1980, there were only 25,000 Nigerian Americans. Forty years later, there were 450,000 Nigerian Americans—meaning that this group comprises barely more than 0.1 percent of the American population. Eighty-five percent of Nigerian Americans were born in Nigeria. How have they done? Nigerian Americans are one of the most well-educated groups in the United

States. They are much more likely than the average American to work in a managerial or professional role, and enjoy significantly higher incomes than average. They are, according to a 2018 Oxy analysis, "the most successful ethnic group in America."[25]

Their success, which is growing, can be explained by many factors, but certainly not "Nigerian privilege" or any other expression of power dynamics. What might account for it?

One factor, which is accounted for in the data, was expressed by the renowned Nigerian American architect Chinwe Ohajuruka. Growing up in the 1970s in Nigeria, she recalls, "Nothing was more important than education." This cultural imperative, she says, is *increasing*. Education for Nigerians is, she says, "a tsunami with a slow and building movement that has not yet unleashed its full might."[26]

Another cultural fact that explains Nigerian success is the family. Just 4 percent of Nigerian children live in single-parent households. By contrast, the United States has the highest rate in the world at 23 percent, with massive variation among the different cultures that compose the United States.

The consequences of this most fundamental of cultural aspects—who raises the children—show up in all the relevant data. The poverty rate of single-parent households is *more than six times* that of married households. The 23 percent of children who come from single-parent households account for 63 percent of youth suicides, 90 percent of homeless and runaway children, 60 percent of rapists, 71 percent of high school dropouts, and 85 percent of youths in prison.[27]

The data is clear and unambiguous. The best anti-poverty mechanism is a cultural phenomenon: the two-parent household. But it is not the only mechanism. Isabel Sawhill and Ron Haskins of the Brookings Institution have determined that there is a sequence that, if followed, will reduce one's chances of poverty very significantly.

They called it the success sequence, and it is: graduate high school, get a full-time job, turn twenty-one, get married, and have children—in that order. It is, *precisely*, a modernized version of the sequence Moses articulated around military exemptions in Deuteronomy 20—whose rejection, Maimonides wrote, would lead to subsisting on "charity." The result: Only 3 to 4 percent of millennials in their late twenties and early thirties who have followed the success sequence are below the poverty line.[28]

No one has challenged the poverty data around the success sequence. Critics have said, instead, that it "focuses too narrowly on individual behavior."[29] However, its most prominent promoters are clear that it is not primarily about an individual's decision. The success sequence is about *cultural* norms. Wendy Wang and Brad Wilcox of the Institute for Family Studies write:

> We do not take the view that the success sequence is simply a "pull yourselves up by your own bootstraps" strategy that individuals adopt on their own. Rather, for many, the "success sequence" does not exist in a cultural vacuum; it's inculcated by an interlocking cultural array of ideals, norms, expectations and knowledge.[30]

So, the data certainly suggests that the Torah is right—and that culture is the most important determinant of one's individual and communal fortunes. The Torah also describes, and opines on, the three kinds of dominant cultural types: the honor culture and the victim culture (which it counsels against) and the dignity culture (which it supports). What does the science say?

The Art of the Duel: The Honor Culture in the United States

As discussed, the honor culture dominated the ancient world. Unlike many things that were prevalent thousands of years ago, it is very much with us—with many cultures and subcultures that can be clearly labeled as honor cultures. The difference is that now, we have twenty-first-century tools to understand and evaluate the honor culture—and to assess the Torah's radical condemnation of it.

The United States, of course, has a historically very important division: between South and North. There were, throughout much of American history, many things that sharply distinguished the South from the North. The most important, of course, was slavery—and then the segregationist policies that developed following the Civil War. Another is the very different perspectives on the honor culture.

In the early to mid-nineteenth century, a twenty-six-year-old Frenchman named Alexis de Tocqueville toured the young United States and recorded his impressions. The result was *Democracy in America*—a book that is, according to the Pulitzer Prize–winning critic Michael Dirda, "acknowledged by both liberals and conservatives as the best book ever written about our system of government and our national character."[31]

In *Democracy in America*, Mr. de Tocqueville wrote about what he learned on a trip to Alabama: "At the slightest quarrel, a knife or pistol comes to hand. These things happen continually; it's a semi-barbarous state of society." Indeed, the murder rate in rural South Carolina from 1800 to 1860 was four times that of urbanized Massachusetts.[32]

What accounts for Mr. de Tocqueville's observation and the supporting data? Professor Bertram Wyatt-Brown of the University of Florida attributed the high murder rate in the rural pre–Civil War South to an ethic of "primal honor." He defined primal honor as: "You identified yourself on the basis of what others think of you."[33]

Some of the killings were, as Mr. de Tocqueville described, the result of responding in the moment to a passing insult, offense, or affront with deadly force. But this quickness to anger became institutionalized, to the point where one of the South's most important practices was created because of it: the duel. If a self-respecting southern man was insulted, particularly concerning a woman, money, or politics, he would not ignore it or even sue for slander. Such suits, a 1937 analysis of North Carolina pre–Civil War culture declares, "were likely to be employed only by women, cowards and those religiously opposed to engaging in the more speedy process."[34]

The "more speedy process" was fighting—and, in its institutional and ritualized form, dueling. The mores and rules of dueling were set in quasi-law, like the 1838 dueling code drafted by South Carolina governor John Lyde Wilson. One man would offend another. Sometimes, this offense was concocted by a woman who wanted to test a potential beau. The offended man would take out an advertisement in the newspaper and challenge the offender to a duel. The challenged man, unless he deemed the offender unworthy of a response, would accept. The combatants would meet in an open field to duel with rules as clear as those that govern any sport. The Grateful American Foundation explains:

> In America, duels were most prevalent in the South, particularly among upper-class gentlemen. Men who were challenged to a duel were expected to accept; those who refused faced public embarrassment. One South Carolina general, recalling a duel in his youth,

> remarked, "Well I never did clearly understand what it was about, but you know it was a time when all gentlemen fought."[35]

These "gentlemen" included the society's leaders and culture carriers. Prominent Americans who killed or were killed in duels included President Andrew Jackson, Senator Thomas Hart Benton, Commodore Stephen Decatur, Secretary of State Henry Clay, Congressman John Randolph, Congressman Jonathan Cilley (who was killed in a duel by Congressman William Jordan Graves), and Treasury Secretary Alexander Hamilton (who was killed in a duel by Vice President Aaron Burr).

Manhood in Pre–Civil War North

Duels were much less prevalent in the northern states. The reason was articulated by one of the most well-respected men in the North, Benjamin Franklin. In 1784, Mr. Franklin wrote to Thomas Percival, the British doctor and author:

> It is astonishing that the murderous practice of dueling, which you so justly condemn, should continue so long in vogue . . . A Gentleman in a coffee house desired another to sit farther from him—why so?—Because, Sir, you stink.—That is an affront and you must fight me . . . How can such miserable sinners as we are, entertain so much pride as to conceit that every offense against our imagined honor merits death![36]

Benjamin Franklin and the northern culture that he represented, hated dueling because it was a manifestation of "offense against our imagined honor." Mr. Franklin would not even dignify what constituted the basis of southern culture with the term "honor." He called it "imagined honor."

And his example captures the essence of the honor culture. One man wants to move away from another in a coffeehouse because the latter fellow smells bad. The second person, instead of ignoring the situation and focusing on more important things, has "so much pride" that even this minor insult constitutes a matter worth fighting to the death.

Such are the consequences of a culture that presumes a quickness to anger, valorizes an externally determined sense of self, and expects that a real man will regard any insult as a matter worth fighting to the death for. And Benjamin Franklin—and those who followed and thought like him—hated it.

Benjamin Franklin's views on imagined honor and dueling were standard in the pre–Civil War North. And it was not as though the North lacked a concept of honor. The North had a robust concept of honor that was also an important aspect of the culture. It was just completely different from that in the South.

Brett and Kate McKay, thought leaders on the subject of manliness, explain:

> [In the North], the need to physically retaliate against anyone who impugned your honor began to seem silly; *un*-manly, in fact. Who cared what other people thought of you? A man could simply point to the fruits of his labors to rebut a critic. Gentlemen began to assert a self-worth that was less dependent on the opinions of others and more focused on the contents of his conscience.

By contrast to the honor culture of the American South, Mr. and Mrs. McKay write, "the watchword of Northern manliness was 'self-restraint.'"

When a northern man behaving in accordance with the highest ideals of his culture was insulted, his blood did not boil. To the contrary, he was "cool." This "coolness," the McKays explain, became "the defining quality of Northern honor." They go on:

> A Northern gentleman was to be cool in personal and physical confrontations; he didn't give in to extreme emotions, could laugh off the insults of others, and never caused a scene. A Northern man who suffered a lapse in his self-restraint and failed to be cool would often say he had "forgotten his manhood," or had been "unmanned" by the incident.[37]

"You Can't Jail a Man for Standing Up for His Rights"

In 1891, the state of Kentucky began a practice that continues to this day. All state officeholders are required to swear to a particular oath. The oath is: "I, being a citizen of this State, have not fought a duel with deadly weapons within this State nor out of it, nor have I sent or accepted a challenge to fight a duel with deadly weapons, nor have I acted as second in carrying a challenge, nor aided or assisted any person thus offending, so help me God."

Even in our partisan era, swearing to this statement is one thing that Democrat and Republican officeholders in Kentucky seem to agree on. The fact that this oath is uncontroversial demonstrates that the more *formal* manifestations of the honor code have diminished or disappeared.

But does this suggest that the cultural impulses that culminated in dueling have become as quaint as this oath? To answer that, we can turn to one of the great journalists of the twentieth century—Hodding Carter Jr. A son of Louisiana and a liberal, Mr. Carter devoted his career to understanding, chronicling, and changing the practices of the South. His 1950 memoir, *Southern Legacy*, is a masterpiece of the genre.

In this book, Mr. Carter recounts an incident from Louisiana in the 1930s. An "irascible, middle-aged Louisianian" lived near a gas station. The workers at the gas station persistently teased him, and the man told them to stop. They ignored his requests. One morning, the man had enough. He got his gun and shot them. He killed one, maimed another, and killed an innocent customer.

Mr. Carter wrote that no one except the relatives of the deceased were "particularly aroused by the slaying" because "passion killings were an old story." This killing was notable only because it was one of the few that resulted in a jury trial.

Hodding Carter knew about this case because he, at the age of twenty-six, was chosen for the jury. He was one of the three townspeople on the jury; the other nine were farmers. The trial lasted only three days because the prosecution and the defense agreed on the facts.

Mr. Carter, chosen as the foreman of the jury for reasons that he didn't fully understand, was the first person to speak in the jury room. He said the defendant was guilty. He expected it to be a quick deliberation, leading to a conviction.

The responses, he says, "were loud, immediate and confused." One juror explained, "Good God Almighty, bub. He ain't guilty. He wouldn't have been much of a man if he hadn't shot them fellows."

At the end of the short deliberation, Mr. Carter could only convince two other jurors—the other townspeople—to vote to convict. One of the farmers explained to Mr. Carter, "Son, you're a good boy but you got a lot to learn. You can't jail a man for standing up for his rights."

Mr. Carter, as foreman, announced the result in the courtroom: acquittal. The judge was appalled, and demanded that the jury be polled. When polled, the other two townspeople had decided to join the farmer. Mr. Carter's was the sole voice for conviction. The defendant, who according to Louisiana law at the time needed only eight votes to walk free, shook hands with the eleven jurors who were on his side and left the courtroom a free man.

Hodding Carter realized that he should not have been surprised. His father was liberal by the standards of his day and was no devotee of the unwritten honor code that governed southern culture. Still, the senior Hodding Carter instructed his son at a young age in a variety of rules about violence. If a fellow kid curses or provokes you—especially if he calls you "a son of a bitch"—young Hodding was to "fight fairly and immediately."

If the aggressor was older and Hodding was with others, the group was to fight the aggressor. If Hodding was caught alone with the larger aggressor, he was to find a weapon and fight. If an adult similarly bothered Hodding, he was to tell his father, and his father would fight. That happened several times, with the senior Hodding Carter always armed for the encounter.

As a young father, Hodding Carter Jr. was a soldier stationed in Maryland with his wife and sons. An adult neighbor accused one of his boys of stealing a helmet and threatened to slap him. Mr. Carter wanted to settle the matter peacefully, especially as he knew that there would be trouble following a fight between a soldier and a civilian. But he was a son of the South, and an adult had insulted his son. Mr. Carter took his son to the man's apartment and told the man that he had two choices: apologize or fight. He reflected that his father would not have approved, as "there was nothing in his set of rules that made an apology an easy way out."

The other man, "a surprised civil servant, apologized profusely and asked me in for the drink we both needed."[38]

The honor culture, we learn, dies hard or not at all—even for a liberal journalist who opposed its presumptions, who would have gotten in trouble for following its logic, and who devoted his life to changing the assumptions and practices of his native South.

The Power of an Insult

What happened to the southern honor culture in the years since Hodding Carter published his memoir? Everything is aligned against it. There are no feminist intellectuals arguing that the brothers of an aggrieved woman have the moral obligation to find the perpetrator and beat him up. There are no child-rearing experts who counsel parents to instruct their sons that they should respond to insults by fighting "fairly and immediately." There is no one in Kentucky calling for the state constitution to be amended to enable legislators to challenge their political opponents to duels. There are, simply, no intellectual or institutional defenses of the honor culture in the United States. Moreover, American culture has become less regional and more national—as is evidenced by the gradual disappearance of regional accents. The honor culture should finally be gone—or survive with only a few flickering embers.[39]

Enter Professors Dov Cohen and Richard Nisbett at the University of Michigan. In 1996, Professors Cohen and Nisbett enrolled eighty-three white male undergraduates from the North and the South from similar socioeconomic backgrounds. The students gave their saliva to be measured for levels of testosterone and cortisol—which are elevated when one is angry. The result: The baseline testosterone and cortisol levels were the same among the northern and southern students.

The students were then told to fill out a demographic survey, walk down a hallway, and deposit it into a file cabinet. As they put away the survey, a large man bumped each student, slammed the cabinet shut, and called him an asshole.

Observers, not knowing which students came from the North and the South, were milling about the participants. The observers were charged with judging the participants to be either angry or amused. The observers judged 35 percent of the northern students and 85 percent of the southern students to be angry.

Another researcher then administered a second saliva test to measure the cortisol and testosterone levels in the students again. The results: The levels of the northern students rose modestly above the baseline from the first test. These levels skyrocketed in the southern students.[40]

The quickness to anger that God had modeled against in Exodus 34, and that fuels the honor culture, remains measurably strong even as previous manifestations—such as fighting and dueling—have diminished or disappeared.

Hypermasculinity, the Aggressive Assertion, and Defense of Respect

Is the persistence of honor culture tendencies in the United States unique to white southerners? In 2015, Harvard professor Orlando Patterson published an op-ed in the *New York Times* called "The Real Problem with America's Inner Cities." He makes the point that American inner-city culture is deeply multicultural. He writes of American inner-city culture: "[It is] socially and culturally heterogeneous, and a great majority of residents are law-abiding, God-fearing and often socially conservative."[41] However, there is an important subculture that Professor Patterson noted from the data he analyzed. Professor Patterson writes:

> In all inner-city neighborhoods, however, there is a problem minority that varies between about 12.1 percent (in San Diego, for example) and 28 percent (in Phoenix) that comes largely from the disconnected youth between ages 16 and 24 . . . Their street or thug culture is real, with a configuration of norms, values and habits that are, disturbingly, rooted in a ghetto brand of core American mainstream values: hypermasculinity, the aggressive assertion and defense of respect.

A "culture" based on hypermasculinity, aggressive assertion, and defense of respect—that is a precise description of an honor culture. I brought this up with the Manhattan Institute criminologist Rafael Mangual. He said that it was right—from his research and his life experience growing up in the inner-city of New York. Mr. Mangual described a courtship practice where a young woman, after one date, would call the young man to say that someone was bothering her at the mall. This was a test. Would the young man come to the mall and fight for her honor? Similar tests occurred with items as meaningless as a coat—but the outerwear was not the real cause of the fight. Honor was. This anecdote shows in the data. The *Encyclopedia of*

School Crime and Violence reports that violence is 60 percent more common in urban schools than in suburban schools.[42]

Honor Culture: Live from the 94th Academy Awards!

At the 2022 Academy Awards, host Chris Rock made a joke at the expense of the actress Jada Pinkett Smith. Her husband, Will Smith, responded with a classic honor culture move. He rushed to the stage and hit Mr. Rock. The Academy responded by banning him for ten years.

The quickness of the banning showed how American elites, as embodied in the Academy, regard the honor culture. If the decision to ban Mr. Smith from the Oscars were put to a popular vote, it would have been more complicated. A 2022 survey conducted by the Democratic pollster Blue Rock Research showed that more than half of Americans believed that Mr. Rock was "more wrong" than Mr. Smith—with those who are less educated, less wealthy, and female most likely to side with Mr. Smith.[43]

The Wages of an Honor Culture

This is the twenty-first century—and so we have an abundance of data, both observational and quantitative, to assess the honor culture. We can, therefore, assess across three arenas whether the Torah is correct to consider it significantly adverse to human flourishing.

The first arena is crime. In 1958, the homicide rate in the South was three times greater than that in the North. How about two generations later—when so much about southern attitudes and practices had changed? In 2012, approximately 25 percent of Americans lived in the South. These Americans accounted for more than 40 percent of the violent crime in the country.

In 2022, Professors Michele Gelfand and Ying Lin of Stanford University published an analysis that incorporated two generations of studies of honor culture and violence in the United States. They determined that the honor culture is "a major driver" of school shootings, domestic violence, and gang violence. Their findings are a subset of the conclusion they cite from the renowned British anthropologist Julian Pitt-Rivers: "Honor has caused more deaths than the plague."[44]

The second arena is anger. Professors Cohen and Nisbet demonstrated through the second testosterone and cortisol tests just how angry a small slight makes people in an honor culture. We now know just what happens to our bodies when we are angry. The simple act of recollecting an angry moment diminishes one's immunoglobulin A, which is the body's first line of defense against infection, for six hours. In the hours following the actual experience of anger, one's chance of a heart attack doubles, one's chance of having a stroke triples, and one's chance of having a brain aneurysm increases by 600 percent. Longer-term effects of anger include lung problems (probably due to inflammation in the airways from the persistent release of stress hormones), high blood pressure, deepened depression, and exacerbated anxiety. The honor culture, which feeds on anger, is medically dangerous for all of its participants.[45]

A third finding about the honor culture is quite different from the first two. In 2022, *Condé Nast Traveler* published an article on the ten "Friendliest Cities in the United States." With the exception of San Juan, Puerto Rico, all of these cities are in states that a research team from the University of Oklahoma determined to be "honor states."[46]

Why are the most polite, charming, and friendly places in "honor states"? Why would an honor culture, which is defined by a quickness to anger expressed in violence, be so polite? The logic of an honor culture leads right to it. Most language and much behavior is subject to ambiguity and misinterpretation. This is tolerable when seeming displays of disrespect can be presumed to be ignored or subject to easy clarification. But neither describes an honor culture—where even perceived disrespect can easily lead to deadly violence. Thus, southern politeness is a linguistic adaptation to the honor culture. It is a highly effective way of signaling that one means no disrespect and therefore, doesn't want to fight.[47]

Twenty-First-Century Victims

The honor culture in the United States has diminished, but has not disappeared, since its heyday in the pre–Civil War South. How about the other culture repudiated by the Torah—the victim culture?

The first question to ask about victim culture is: What precisely is it? In 2020, Professor Rahav Gabay of Tel Aviv University and several colleagues published what became a major paper in the *Journal of Personality and Individual Differences*: "The Tendency for Interpersonal Victimhood: The Personality Construct and Its Consequences."

In the paper, they introduced a psychological concept called the Tendency for Interpersonal Victimhood (TIV), which measures the extent of one's victim mentality. TIV consists of twenty-nine characteristics that measure the victim mentality. The psychologist Scott Barry Kaufman, writing in *Scientific American*, condensed them into four. The stronger one identifies with one of the characteristics, or the characteristics as a whole, the greater one's victim mentality. These four statements of TIV, which follow, provide a helpful framework with which to evaluate the victim mentality—and the victim mentality writ large.

"It is important to me that people who hurt me acknowledge that an injustice has been done to me."

One with a victim mentality believes that he is constantly suffering from injustices perpetrated by those who would do him harm. Consequently, the currency of the victim—what he wants most from society—is *sympathy*.

The key part of this desire might not be the sympathy but rather the notion of being *owed*. One who focuses on what he is owed does not attend to, or perhaps even acknowledge, what he owes—which is the foundation of gratitude. We saw this in Genesis with Hagar, who does not thank God even after God "opens her eyes" to enable her to see the abundant water in front of her. And we see it today at Princeton University.

Princeton University houses the Carl A. Fields Center for Equality and Cultural Understanding. The Fields Center engages "professional facilitators" to train fellows to "educate and advocate for the Princeton community in relation to diversity, inclusion, and social justice through peer-facilitated workshops, training, consultation, one-to-one support, dialogues, as well as serving as informal support for students who experience discrimination and bias." It is a classic example of a common phenomenon: the cultivation and development of the victim mentality at an elite university.[48]

How is the Fields Center doing at educating members of the Princeton community on how to be victims? In November 2022, the Fields Center featured a poster with a photo and a quotation from Estela Diaz—who graduated from Princeton in 2014 and now teaches at Columbia University. Ms. Diaz said, "If you're only giving, there is time to be selfish. I want to teach other folks of color how to center themselves and their needs . . . If anyone ever tells you to be grateful, you can just smile and walk away."[49]

"It is very hard for me to stop thinking about the injustice others have done to me."

This statement of victimhood is a classic example of rumination—which is the psychological process of persistently revisiting and even reliving negative events. Mental health authorities have identified rumination as either causing or exacerbating depression, anxiety, insomnia, hypochondria, substance abuse, eating disorders, phobias, and PTSD. The American Psychiatric Association notes that rumination triggers a vicious cycle. They write: "The more a person ruminates, the worse they feel, which then contributes to more rumination." One with a high TIV ruminates constantly.[50]

Sometimes rumination, deriving from the victim mentality, has an even more profound and irrevocable effect. Patrick Prince is the associate vice provost for Threat Assessment and Management at the University of Southern California. His research shows that mass shooters do not surprise those who know them. They usually display, long in advance, characteristics that give away their likelihood to commit mass murder. One of the most salient characteristics, Provost Prince says, is "rumination over perceived injustices" and application of "a name and face to a grievance."[51]

"I think I am much more conscientious and moral in my relations with other people compared to their treatment of me."

One with a victim mindset is not concerned with identifying genuine suffering or alleviating it. Those with a victim mindset focus on establishing *themselves* as the victims. Sometimes, they do so by using specific language—with words such as "pain," "hurt," and "broken" being invoked to describe their normal, everyday situations. Other times, they do so by way of analogy—with a variant of "Nothing has really changed" when comparing their situation to a historical example of genuine oppression. However they describe it, those with the victim mentality *identify* as victims. This moral elitism manifests in two different ways.

The first manifestation is that discussed in our chapter on the importance of character. It is the concept of moral licensing. The variant of moral licensing that is relevant to the victim mentality was revealed in a 2010 experiment conducted by a Stanford University research team led by Dr. Emily Zitek. Dr. Zitek and her colleagues asked two groups of students to write for five minutes about a negative experience. One group was told to write about a time that they were bored. Another was told to write about a time they were wronged.

At the end of the experiment, all of the participants were asked to help the researchers with a project. Eighty-one percent of those who wrote about a time that they were bored chose to help. Only 60 percent of those who wrote about a time that they were wronged helped. In other words, writing about a time when one was wronged *for just five minutes* made the participants 33 percent less likely to help with a simple task. If this extremely light touch of victimization—writing about a memory of being wronged for a few minutes—triggered such a diminution in helpfulness, one can only imagine what more extensive victimization does.[52]

Why would those who think even briefly in a psychological experiment about being victims behave differently than those who do not? The victim says a variant of: “The world treats me badly. I am not going to be a sucker by being nice, caring, or generous when others are trying to persecute me.” The victim, therefore, provides himself with the moral license to be less nice, helpful, and sociable than if he did not have the victim mentality.

The second manifestation of moral elitism in those with a victim mindset is what the Bowling Green University philosopher Brandon Warmke calls “moral grandstanding.” Professor Warmke characterizes this as “people using talk of morality or politics to try to impress others with their moral qualities and gain social status.” He says that those who “want to be seen as the most affected by some injustice” (i.e., with the victim mentality) are likely to be susceptible to this.

Moral grandstanders are, as Professor Warmke explains, likely to do two things. They are apt to “pile on”—to join in the criticism when someone has “misspoken or engaged in a small infraction.” And they are apt to “ramp up”—to demonstrate their moral status by calling for increasing censure and punishment of supposed violators. This creates a logic of ever more extreme positions.[53]

“When people who are close to me feel hurt by my actions, it is very important for me to clarify that justice is on my side.”

One with a victim mentality, by definition, focuses on the wrongs done to him. He is, therefore, unlikely to acknowledge anything he has done to contribute to the unfortunate situation. Accordingly, he will not be able to repair the relationships that were damaged by his hurtful actions—or learn and grow as a result of his mistakes.

South Park Speaks

So, contemporary social science is aligned with what the Torah teaches about the victim mentality. A victim mentality makes people incompetent, ungrateful, self-centered, entitled, unhelpful, and sad.

Therefore, one might think we would reject the victim mentality and, by extension, the victim culture that celebrates, cultivates, rewards, spreads, and institutionalizes the mentality. An assessment of whether this is the case can begin with an assignment that the *New York Times* editors gave to some of its columnists.

The editors asked their columnists to select "the cultural artifact that best explains America."[54] The culture columnist Farhad Manjoo selected the television show *South Park*. Given the show's consistent popularity and importance since 1997—demonstrated in viewer hours and awards won—there is no doubt that Mr. Manjoo made a good selection.

In early 2023, the 321st episode of *South Park* aired—"The World Wide Privacy Tour." The main characters were a thinly veiled Prince Harry and Meghan Markle. But they weren't the only characters. There is also Kyle, who wants a reputation rebrand. He goes to a branding agency that specializes in reputation management. The agency runs Kyle's profile through a computer and comes back with a new brand: "Rugged. Vegan. Compassionate. Victim."

Kyle demurs, saying, "I . . . I don't think that's really me." The branding executive returns with another idea: "Sensitive. Outdoorsy. Frugal. Victim." Kyle demurs again, saying that he is not into the outdoors.

The branding executive reminds Kyle that the purpose of the brand exercise is not to describe who Kyle really is, but how he wants to be seen by others. The executive returns with a third suggestion: "Wealthy. Handsome. Multi-talented Grammy Award-Winning. Victim."

But there is a problem with this one, and it is not Kyle's choosiness. The executive retracts his suggestion, explaining, "Oh, that . . . that one's taken already."[55]

How did we get to the point where the parody show "that best explains America" would portray victimhood as the most valuable characteristic?

Enter Elijah Megginson.

The Victim Culture Starts: Diversity, Equity, and Inclusion (DEI) and Its Antecedents

In 2021, Elijah Megginson, a high school senior from inner-city New York, wrote an op-ed for the *New York Times* about his experience applying to colleges. Mr. Megginson describes being continually guided since the eighth grade, "You're smart and you're from the hood, you're from the projects, colleges will love you."

Mr. Megginson was uncomfortable with college admissions advisors constantly telling him to (in his words) "sell your pain." Mr. Megginson sought out a teacher and mentor, Nathaniel Sinckler, who graduated from Morehouse College in 2013. Mr. Sinckler identified with his student because he remembered (from a decade earlier) also feeling "pressured to write about something I could oversell."

That something was one's status as a victim. Mr. Megginson wrote that he, in the process of writing his personal statement in the way that everyone advised him to, realized, "I didn't want to be a victim anymore. I didn't want to promote that narrative. I wanted college to be a new beginning for me."[56]

Unfortunately for those who think like Elijah Megginson, it is highly unlikely that college would be that kind of "new beginning." Instead, he will likely find himself among a student body that regards—as observed by CUNY professor Ilya Bratman—life as a "victimhood competition."[57]

> This "victimhood competition" is not like many competitions, where people can choose whether to participate. This one, at least at the universities that Mr. Megginson likely considered, is not optional. It has been institutionalized through the teaching of the DEI philosophy that everyone is expected to subscribe to, and through a bureaucracy that is charged with its indoctrination, implementation, and enforcement. This is DEI: Diversity, Equity, and Inclusion—the world's greatest ever systematic attempt to inculcate individuals and institutions into the victim mentality.

The premise of DEI is that there are two kinds of people: perpetrators and victims (or oppressors and oppressed). Who, in an often idyllic campus environment, are the victims? They are members of large groups that, based on race, gender, ethnicity, or sexuality, are considered by DEI to be "marginalized," "oppressed," or "underrepresented."

How important a part of the university culture is DEI? In 2021, Claudine Gay became the Dean of the Harvard College Faculty of Arts and Sciences. Her top priority was "making more progress on diversity." In 2023, President Peter Salovey of Yale identified what the *Yale Daily News* called "the administration's five-year mission to improve diversity, equity and inclusion at Yale" as his *top* priority.[58]

As will be discussed in the chapter of this book on diversity, these universities execute on this top priority by hiring and empowering large and pervasive DEI bureaucracies. The main functions of these bureaucracies include cataloging students and faculty by race/ethnicity/gender/sexuality (so that spots and jobs can go to those who can claim victimhood), educating students into how they can identify as victims (particularly through trainings in subjects like microaggressions and implicit bias) and administering a biased instruction, reporting, and prosecution apparatus.

The existence of such an extensive DEI bureaucracy leads to some fundamental questions. Aren't most college students fundamentally nice young men and women looking to learn, grow, and have fun? If not, why are the admissions offices letting in so many haters? If so—if freshmen classes are *not* full of perpetrators looking for victims—then why would there be such a need for DEI staff?

The DEI philosophy and profession seems to have anticipated this question. The profession has answered with a fundamental redefinition of victim and perpetrator. Until very recently, everyone agreed that perpetrators intend to harm their victims, and victims know that they are being oppressed. Both were also well aware of why and how. A Jew who was sent to Auschwitz knew that he was a victim of the Nazis, who wanted to exterminate the Jews. A black man who was denied the ability to marry a white woman in the Jim Crow South knew that he was a victim of a racist system that wanted to preserve the "purity" of the races. A gay man subject to execution in Gaza knows that he is a victim of his society, which hates homosexuals. A woman being robbed knows that she is a victim of the mugger, who wants her valuables.

Victims and perpetrators do not need to be educated about who they are. It is all too obvious.

Then came DEI. The DEI redefinition of victimhood maintains that the oppressor does not need to intend any harm, and the oppressed does not need to know that he is being harmed. This concept is embodied in two terms that are core in the lexicon of DEI: unconscious bias and systemic bias—both of which serve to encourage more people to see themselves as victims.

Unconscious Bias

The concept of unconscious (or implicit) bias holds that people harbor all kinds of prejudice toward one another, often without either side knowing it. Most DEI bureaucracies use the Harvard Implicit Association Test (IAT) to assess the existence and extent of unconscious bias. According to this test, between 70 to 75 percent of white people hold racist biases. When other forms of prejudice are accounted for, the test reveals that 90 to 95 percent of people have illegitimate biases.[59]

For instance, Maureen Fitzgerald is one of America's most well-known authorities on implicit bias. In her TED talk on the subject, she provided an example of what concerns her. A father and a son are in a car accident and are rushed to the hospital. The surgeon says: "I cannot operate on him because he is my child." If the listener pictures a man as the surgeon, the listener harbors an implicit bias against women.[60]

If the vast majority of people hold illegitimate biases, then it stands to reason that those same people have acted against people in "marginalized" groups. These results certainly suggest that everyone in a "marginalized" group has been victimized by many people—and therefore can accurately and properly consider themselves to be victims. But that's not all. Given how easily, according to the IAT, we develop and deploy implicit biases, most people in "oppressor" groups have many biases. This means that someone who is in multiple "marginalized" groups—say, a black, gay woman—is victimized across multiple identities everyday, and therefore lives the life of a pervasively assaulted victim.

And being a victim of "implicit bias" is apparently very serious. According to Professor Anthony Greenwald of the University of Washington, "Implicit bias is widely understood to be a cause of unintended discrimination that leads to racial, ethnic, socioeconomic and other inequalities."[61] The lesson for Elijah Megginson and those like him is clear: Your non-black classmate who you think is your good friend or pleasant acquaintance likely harbors a significant bias against you. If he seems nice, it is because he does not know that he is biased against you or is hiding it. And the consequences for you are very significant.

Systemic Bias

The second expansion of the victim narrative is that of "systemic" bias. It shares with "unconscious bias" the idea that oppression can happen in the absence of intention of the perpetrator and knowledge by the victim. The difference is in who harbors the bias. With unconscious bias, the perpetrators are individuals. With systemic bias, the perpetrators are institutions.

For instance, in 2020, Princeton University president Christopher Eisgruber wrote that Princeton historically "intentionally and systematically excluded people of color, women, Jews and other minorities." He does not acknowledge any changes, aside from that "Princetonians . . . now take pride in the diversity of our community."

He writes: "Racism and the damage it does to people of color nevertheless persist at Princeton . . . Racist assumptions . . . remain embedded in structures of the University itself." He only identifies one specific manifestation of these "racist assumptions"—which is that Princeton has more programs about European languages and cultures than African languages and cultures.

Nonetheless, President Eisgruber proposed a massive expansion of DEI efforts—including hiring and contracting to favor "underrepresented groups." He also established a "trustee-level committee" focused on "renaming and other campus iconography" and "offerings regarding . . . bias response."[62]

The "Bias Response"

President Eisgruber's "bias response" offerings included education for students about whether they are victims. The DEI staff, as well as the instruction and training modules around "unconscious" and "systemic" bias, shed some light on how victimhood is cultivated. So do the guidelines published by numerous universities.

There are seemingly standardized guidelines for what students should look for to identify if they are victims. They include microaggressions, symbols, degrading language, posting or commenting on social media related to someone's identity in a biased manner, imagery objectifying women, or anything that can be considered "mocking." Sometimes, even those categories are too limiting. According to Princeton University and American University, bias is "a broad category of behaviors that demean or intimidate individuals or groups because of personal characteristics, beliefs, or expressions."[63]

The DEI personnel understand that such broad direction might not be sufficiently clarifying. For instance, what would constitute "demeaning a belief"? It is not apparent.

The DEI offices have a solution—and it is exactly what would be expected from a victim culture. The University of Minnesota counsels students who think that they might have been a victim of bias, but are not sure, to trust "their gut feeling or instinct." The students are encouraged to contact the Bias Response Referral Network, where a professional can "share related examples of bias." Brown University specifies that anyone who is unsure whether an incident constitutes bias should report it anyway.[64]

Princeton University's DEI office offers a FAQ. One of the questions is, "I experienced harassment, but the individual claims it was a joke. What are my options?"

The answer: "You are encouraged to discuss your experience with a confidential resource or to submit a formal report. Behavior will be judged by its impact directly on the person affected or a third party who witnessed the behavior, regardless of intent."

This is a classic victim culture move. The listener is discouraged from ignoring the matter, interpreting the speaker generously and concluding that the comment was a joke, talking it through informally with others in the community to gain perspective, or asking the speaker to clarify. He is, instead, to go right to a third party with the power to punish. And the power will be ready. The joker/perpetrator, the Princeton resource continues, will then be "investigated" by authorities in the Office of Institutional Equity and Diversity.

The Princeton FAQ continues: "How does Princeton support my well-being if I report my concern?" The support includes:

> Access to counseling services, rescheduling of exams and assignments, change in class schedule including the ability to transfer course sections or withdraw from a course, change in work schedule or job assignment, change in campus housing, imposition of an on-campus "no contact order," or "Persona Non Grata" order, administrative remedies designed to curtail contact and communications between or among individuals.

The next FAQ is, "What if I prefer to handle my experience independently without filing a report?" This is not prohibited, but it is discouraged. If the hurt party chooses to handle his "experience" directly, he is instructed to "document the conversation in writing"—presumably to buttress a claim against the perpetrator at a later point. In a victim culture, the ultimate currency—a victim claim—should at least be preserved, if not cashed in.[65]

Minority Student Satisfaction

The University of Michigan has been a national leader in DEI programs. According to a 2024 profile in the *New York Times*, the university has spent approximately $250 million on DEI programs since 2016. According to the *New York Times* report, "Michigan's DEI efforts have created a powerful conceptual framework for student and faculty grievances—and formidable bureaucratic mechanisms to pursue them. Everyday campus complaints and academic disagreements, professors and students told me, were now cast as crises of inclusion and harm, each demanding some further administrative intervention or expansion."

The result: "Students and faculty members reported a less positive campus climate than at the program's start and less a sense of belonging. Students were less likely to interact with people of a different race or religion or with different politics—the exact kind of engagement DEI programs, in theory, are meant to foster."[66] The data suggests that the University of Michigan data is not an outlier, but a feature of what can be expected from a culture of victimization. Texas A&M began an abundantly funded and comprehensively deployed DEI program in the early 2010s. In 2015, as these efforts were starting, the university reported the percentage of students who agreed that they "belonged." Ninety-two percent of white students, 88 percent of Hispanic students, and 82 percent of black students agreed. Texas A&M spent more than $10 million per year on DEI efforts in the subsequent years. In 2020, 82 percent of white students agreed that they "belonged"—as did 76 percent of Hispanic students and just 55 percent of black students.[67]

The purpose of DEI on campus is to make minority students feel welcome and empowered. Why would a *greater* investment in DEI lead to *less* minority satisfaction? We learned the answer in Numbers 13, when the scouts returned from their mission to the land. The scouts, still carrying the slave mentality they developed in Egypt, believed that they were "grasshoppers"—fearful and vulnerable to everything in the environment—in their own eyes, and thus in the eyes of others as well. With DEI telling minority students that they are victims, many of these students will inevitably feel like grasshoppers—under constant threat from those who would harm them intentionally or inadvertently.

Some student "victims" will, logically and understandably, not be able to focus on learning, relationships, or anything else that might otherwise be associated with college life. They will want to do something about their perpetrators. In 2016, Thedemands.org showed how. This site listed the "demands" from activists at dozens of colleges and universities related to "end[ing] . . . systemic and structural racism on campus."[68]

The Yale demands were prefaced with, "Next Yale, an alliance of Yale students of color and our allies, have come together to demand that Peter Salovey and the Yale administration implement immediate and lasting policies that will reduce the intolerable racism that students of color experience on campus every day . . . The harms are quantifiable."

Yale president Peter Salovey responded. He did not question the assumption that students at his institution suffered "intolerable racism . . . every day." He did not show any concern that his students, privileged to spend their days learning and socializing in an idyllic environment, were overwhelmed by grievance. He did not suggest that the students initiate a deliberative discussion where multiple views could be presented and assessed.

Instead, he responded with pride and appreciation for Yale's victim culture and its fruits. He stated: "In my thirty-five years on this campus, I have never been as simultaneously moved, challenged, and encouraged by our community—and all the promise it embodies—as in the past two weeks."

President Salovey was not just "moved." He committed tens of millions of dollars to diversity spending, and gave an award at graduation to two of the student demanders/protestors for having "provided exemplary leadership in enhancing race and/or ethnic relations at Yale College."[69]

How did this presidential endorsement of victim culture work? A 2021 essay by Caleb Dunson, the co-opinion editor of the *Yale Daily News*, is illustrative:

> [Yale] started off excluding women and people of color from its student body and now parades them around for diversity photos and social justice brownie points. Changes might be made at the University's margins, but Yale's fundamental nature will, in all likelihood, remain the same. Since we can't change Yale, we have to tear it down . . . To fix it, we must get rid of the University. Completely.[70]

Beyond the University: The Victim Culture in Intimacy, Business, and Politics

In his classic book *The General Theory of Employment, Interest and Money*, the great twentieth-century economist John Maynard Keynes wrote, "Practical men who believe themselves to be quite exempt from any intellectual influence, are usually the slaves of some defunct economist. Madmen in authority, who hear voices in the air, are distilling their frenzy from some academic scribbler of a few years back."[71]

How influential, among today's "practical men who believe themselves to be quite exempt from any intellectual influence," has the victim culture of universities become? An investigation of three different sectors of society are illustrative. These are intimacy, business, and politics.

Why Most Bisexual Women Under Thirty Only Have Sex with Men

One of the defining features of any culture concerns how it regards intimacy. In an honor culture, men are expected to fight over women. In a traditional religious culture, men and women are expected to have sex only after marriage. In a dignity culture, men and women speak about and treat each other with respect—and keep intimate activities private. How about in a victim culture?

Since 2008, the General Social Survey has surveyed people under thirty about their sexuality along five political dimensions: Liberal, Slightly Liberal, Moderate, Slightly Conservative, and Conservative. In the years between 2008 and 2016, there was not a strong correlation between one's politics and one's sexuality.

Then everything changed for one group: those who identified as liberal. In 2016, 88 percent of the liberal group identified as heterosexual, which was in line with the other four political categories. By 2021, the other four categories had remained greater than 85 percent heterosexual. However, only 66 percent of the liberal group identified as heterosexual.[72]

What accounts for the dramatic rise of young liberals who, by 2021, identified as something other than heterosexual? An additional data set from the General Social Survey and a study from the University of Oklahoma are illustrative. From 2008 to 2010, 13.3 percent of bisexual women under thirty had *only* male partners in the previous five years. From 2018 to 2021, 54.8 percent of bisexual women under thirty had sex with *only* male partners in the previous five years. The data speaks: A lot of young and straight people now claim to be bisexual.[73]

Why would they do so? The answer may come from a well-known graduate of the Brown University Class of 2020: Michaela Kennedy-Cuomo, the daughter of former New York governor Andrew Cuomo and Mary Kerry Kennedy.

Ms. Cuomo is a Divine Life Alignment coach who runs a store on Etsy where she sells her work, which includes Pride Month earrings, affirmation phone backgrounds, and wall art that enables her to "reclaim and redefine my power portal."[74]

In 2021, Ms. Cuomo did an Instagram livestream in which she said that she identified as a lesbian in elementary school, a bisexual in middle school, a pansexual in high school, and is now a demisexual. She explained that she is genuinely a demisexual, and was not just proclaiming it for social reasons.

These assertions lead to two questions. Why might she claim demisexuality (or any kind of sexuality) for *social* reasons? And why would heterosexuality not have been a stop on her tour of sexual self-discovery?

She explained, "It is hip or cool to not be hetero in my liberal bubble."[75]

Ms. Cuomo's observation, backed by the aforementioned data, leads to another question. An earlier version of liberalism said that one's sexuality is a private matter and should not lend itself to coolness or its opposite. What happened?

Michaela Cuomo explained in an Instagram post and Instagram Live video she published in 2021. Ms. Cuomo offered her love to those who have not "claimed their sexuality" due to "fear of physical, psychological or financial safety"—and criticized the management of Instagram: "If #bi weren't censored, maybe I could have accessed the information and tools that as a bisexual person I would need to protect myself from increased rates of sexual victimization, homelessness, hunger, unemployment, hate crimes, and mental health challenges."[76]

Stepping back: Are discussions or proclamations of non-heterosexuality censored on social media? No. Is it conceivable that Ms. Cuomo, a highly educated scion of two of the most successful political families in the United States, would be homeless and hungry because of her sexuality? Again, no. So what is Ms. Cuomo's logic?

As she said, it is "cool to not be hetero" in her culture. What else is "cool" in her culture? Asserting a "fear of physical, psychological or financial safety" is apparently one. Professing to be "bi" is another, and asserting that "#bi is censored" is another. There is one concept that encompasses all of these examples: being a victim—the defining characteristic of Michaela Cuomo's culture or, as she puts it, "bubble."

How to Interpret a Christmas Wreath

In 2022, LinkedIn published the results of its study of the fastest growing professions in the United States. The first was "vaccine specialist." The second was "diversity and inclusion manager."[77]

One of these diversity and inclusion managers is Mita Mallick from Carta, a major investor services company. In December 2022, the *Harvard Business Review* published her essay "How to Support Your Jewish Colleagues Right Now." She wrote of Jill Katz, the Chief People Officer for a consulting firm. Ms. Katz described arriving at the office in December to find that every office door had been decorated with a Christmas wreath and stocking. Her office did not, like the others, have a red stocking. It had a blue stocking (the color of the Star of David on the Israeli flag).

Ms. Katz could have concluded that while Jews don't decorate with wreaths, it was a nice and even touching gesture from her colleagues to include her in the holiday celebration. As DEI instructions show, people in victim cultures are trained to interpret ambiguities ungenerously. Sure enough, Ms. Katz felt "shocked and devastated."

Why would Ms. Katz be "devastated" by what could easily be interpreted as an inclusive sign of fellowship? Why would the *Harvard Business Review*—the quintessential mainstream business publication—use this as an example of how corporate leaders need to better "support Jewish colleagues"? Why did the article not cite anyone questioning that the blue stocking was a sign of oppression? Why, in other words, does everyone in this story (Jill Katz, Mita Mallick of Carta, the *Harvard Business Review*) endorse playing the victim? It must reflect the extent that American business has adopted the victim culture.[78]

The 2016 and 2020 Presidential Elections

In late October 2016, the journalist Norman Bell wrote a column for the Lowy Institute, saying, "America is poised to elect Hillary Clinton as President."

He was wrong about that. But he was right in saying:

> Clinton correctly called Trump on his habit of seeing himself as a victim. He's previously claimed rigged Republican primaries, rigged judicial processes in the matter of Trump University, rigged media, rigged polling, even a rigged process for deciding not to hand an Emmy award to his TV show. The good news for Trump (and the bad news for America) is that The Donald is not the only one who feels victimized.[79]

One of those who soon also felt victimized was Hillary Clinton. After she lost the election, Secretary Clinton claimed that she was the victim of Russian interference, "voter suppression laws," "sexism and misogyny," and others.[80] She also claimed to be the victim of electoral theft. She told a crowd in Los Angeles in May 2019, "You can run the best campaign, you can even become the nominee, and you can have the election stolen from you." She told CBS in September 2019 that Donald Trump was an "illegitimate president" who stole the election through "many funny things." She reiterated this claim to *The Atlantic* a year later, saying, "No, there was a widespread understanding that this election [in 2016] was not on the level."[81]

In 2020, President Trump lost his bid for reelection. He had learned, perhaps from Hillary Clinton, how to process a defeat in contemporary culture. He claimed that he was the victim of electoral theft. In his case, there were many perpetrators—including the Republican secretary of state and governor of Georgia.

President Trump stated that he was not the only victim in the 2020 election. He told his supporters at a rally on December 5, "They're trying to take it from *us* through rigging, fraud, deception and deceit. That's what we saw in the election . . . We will do something about it. We're going to do something about it quickly."

How should his supporters feel about the election being taken from *them*? Donald Trump, the master political marketer, knew exactly what idea to deploy. "We are all victims. Everybody here. All these thousands of people tonight. They're all victims. Every one of you."

President Trump was not going to let his army of "all victims" be victimized forever. He explained, "We'll be watching on January 5."[82]

A year later, President Trump announced his bid for the presidency. He defined himself in language that he knew would resonate with large swaths of the public: "And I'm a victim. I will tell you I'm a victim."[83]

Toward a Dignity Culture

Professors Bradley Campbell and Jason Manning, the authors of the previously mentioned paper in *Comparative Sociology*, offer a succinct definition of the dignity culture. It is manifest when its members have "an inherent [self]-worth that cannot be alienated by others."[84]

The "self-worth" of dignity cultures, Professors Campbell and Manning explain, manifests in a "thick skin." This thick skin enables people to exercise an "ethic of restraint and toleration." With a thick skin enabling "an inherent self-worth that cannot be alienated by others," one will not be easily angered. He will not focus on himself but, instead, on his mission and purpose. He will pay heed to what he contributes, and not to how he is perceived. He will be able to welcome criticism, accept rebuke, focus on his mission and purpose, search outside for advice and inside for affirmation. He will tell his story truthfully, as he does not care how others may interpret anything about him. He will tell, and even emphasize, the unfortunate and negative aspects of his history—as he considers them an indispensable source of learning and growth.

This idea that dignity derives from a deserved self-worth has its roots in the Enlightenment. Immanuel Kant declared that dignity is a concept of "unconditional and incomparable worth" that "admits no equivalent" and commands us to make choices that elevate us above animals and things.[85]

At around the same time when dignity was being discussed by the leading thinkers in the West, it was being put into action by leading political actors. One of the relatively rare invocations of the term "dignity" around the American founding was from James Monroe. In 1776, Monroe described his colleague George Washington as having "a deportment so firm, so dignified, but yet so modest and composed, I have never seen in any other person."[86]

President George Washington was a son of the South who hated the duels that were at the crux of its honor culture. Instead, he loved the Bible—and had one verse to which he consistently returned.[87] It was Micah 4:4: "Everyone will sit under their own vine and under their own fig tree and no one will make them afraid for the Lord Almighty has spoken."

This vision of dignity—of an independent soul, sitting under *his* vine and fig tree without fear—defined President Washington's personality and his politics. In 1790, he sent a letter to the Hebrew Congregation of Newport, Rhode Island, welcoming the Jews to America:

> May the Children of the Stock of Abraham, who dwell in this land, continue to merit and enjoy the good will of the other Inhabitants; while everyone shall sit in safety under his own vine and fig tree, and there shall be none to make him afraid. May the father of all mercies scatter light and not darkness in our paths, and make us all in our several vocations useful here, and in his own due time and way everlastingly happy.[88]

The word "dignity" does not appear in the Declaration of Independence—but the concept does. It is embodied in the famous preamble, "We hold these truths to be self-evident, that all men are created equal, that they are endowed by their Creator with certain unalienable Rights, that among these are Life, Liberty and the pursuit of Happiness."

The word "dignity" does not appear in the United States Constitution, either. However, the idea of dignity does. It enabled the negative rights (the "freedoms from") in the Bill of Rights. Americans can, pursuant to the Bill of Rights, speak their minds, assemble, publish, and worship as they desire without regard to what the majority thinks or tries to demand. A dignified political culture, the American founders believed, must protect these quintessential manifestations of self-worth and individual expression. As Professor Doron Shultziner of Hadassah Academic College demonstrates, many of the national constitutions established in the twentieth century have essentially adopted the American Bill of Rights—and frame them explicitly as an expression of dignity.[89]

If George Washington epitomized dignity in the first half of American history, Martin Luther King Jr. did in the second. Dr. King spoke specifically of dignity in his speech accepting the Nobel Prize and in his speech at the March on Washington—in reference to work, protest, and justice. His embrace of dignity—the word and the concept—derived from his deep identification with Moses. In his last speech, Dr. King channeled the commandment of Leviticus 25:55 to be a "slave to God" when he summarized his life goal: "I just want to do God's will." He continued:

> And He's allowed me to go up to the mountain. And I've looked over. And I've seen the Promised Land. I may not get there with you. But I want you to know tonight we as a people will get to the Promised Land. And I'm happy tonight, I'm not worried about anything. I'm not fearing any man. Mine eyes have seen the glory of the coming of the Lord![90]

Reflection

Culture, the Torah insists, is of paramount importance in determining the outcomes that an individual or society can expect and reach. Modern social science and experience have validated this finding. The Torah presents the same three cultures that the social scientists Bradley Campbell and Jason Manning identify in modern society. They are the honor culture, the victim culture, and the dignity culture.

The honor culture, which once defined the American South, no longer has institutional support or intellectual defense. Still, its manifestations abound with remarkable breadth. From support for Will Smith hitting Chris Rock, to surveys of the politest cities, to the cortisol levels of southern and northern men who were passingly insulted—the honor culture lives. Its persistent strength is a testament to why the Author of the Torah is so concerned about culture. Culture is so powerful that its mores, values, and practices can thrive generations after a specific form has been retired.

The victim culture, on the other hand, is in full blossom. Why do so many of the most privileged people—nobility, presidents, and scions, among others—persistently claim to be victims? The answer can only be that they must be making these claims within a culture where the victim mindset is taught, modeled, validated, and *rewarded*.

The Author of the Torah, as discussed above, despises both cultures. And modern science, having produced an abundance of evidence from helpfulness to heart attacks, from murder rates to rumination, from gratitude to brain aneurysms, shows why.

But even one who accepts the Torah and modern science on the honor and victim cultures has a question to answer. When is it acceptable and advisable—and even good and right—for someone to take offense, and act against a perpetrator or other kind of adversary?

The answer is in Exodus 34, where God describes himself as being "*slow* to anger." One who is slow to anger may feel the same urge to respond as one who is quick to anger. But the slowness provides just what he needs to strategically determine whether a contemplated response is both morally justified and practically good for him. More specifically: He has the time to decide whether the costs of exercising anger are worth the benefits.

For the honor culture, let's imagine a young man driving with his girlfriend on a highway. A man in another car cuts them off and makes a lewd gesture to his girlfriend. The young man's instinct is to run the guy off the road or otherwise punish him. Will he do so? If he is a participant in the honor culture, he will be quick to anger—and is likely to respond that way.

If he is slow to anger, he will give himself the time to do a cost-benefit analysis. The benefit: the psychic pleasure of punishing a jerk who insulted him and his girlfriend. The costs: the significant potential for an accident where he, his girlfriend, and bystanders could get hurt or killed, a fight that ends in pain or worse for him and his girlfriend, and trouble with the law.

If the young man is slow to anger, he will have decided that he—rather than a jerk on the highway—is in control of his emotions and the decisions they provoke. He will avoid the biochemical problems that are generated by anger. He will be able to continue to focus on his goals without what could be a major distraction. He will have, in so doing, chosen to act like a man of dignity.

For the victim culture, we don't have to imagine. We can go right back to my childhood in Short Hills, New Jersey. It was the summer of 1980, and I was seven years old. I had just spent a wonderful day with my friend and his parents at their country club. I came home and asked my parents if they could join the club. They said no. I asked why, is it too expensive? No, they said. It is because we are Jewish and the club does not admit Jews as members.

I remember being stunned. But it was the regular practice for several country clubs in and around the town. The question, at that moment in 1980 and in the subsequent years, was, What should we do about it?

My parents' position was very clear. We should do nothing. The policy of the country clubs was, they explained, inexplicable and wrong. But it was of no practical importance. I, like every Jewish kid in town, had plenty of gentile friends, classmates, and teammates—none of whom showed any antisemitism. Moreover, my parents emphasized, I was fortunate to grow up in a wonderful town in this truly awesome country—full of options and opportunity, where there were no limits on what I could be or do. There would be no getting distracted with the *narishkeit* (foolishness) of a country club's policy. Plus, if we cared—we could join Mountain Ridge, the nearby club founded in 1912 by Jews in response to not being able to join the gentile clubs.

This view was not unique to my parents. It was the prevailing belief in the Jewish culture of 1980s Short Hills. In 1984, the *Christian Science Monitor* (a national publication) ran an article on Jews in Short Hills. The article makes it clear that the Jews of Short Hills simply refused to pay much heed to the policies, or otherwise see ourselves as victims. Instead, the reporter said that the Jews he interviewed said that these policies "keep alive a Jewish identity in a society that tends to blur the traditional meaning of that identity."[91]

I agree with—and am grateful for—my parents' position, and the ideology it derived from. It taught me that my future in this great land of opportunity was my responsibility and would be determined by my choices. It taught me that I should focus on improving myself and helping others, and not on getting worked up over policies that would have no impact on my or anyone else's life opportunities. It taught me, most importantly, that I should never see myself as a victim.

This was not the only such example from my childhood. My parents' home in Short Hills, like all others constructed in town in the 1950s, has a restrictive covenant in it. It says that the house cannot be sold to a Jew. This once meant something. In the 1950s, my grandmother would drive my mother through Short Hills to look at the beautiful Christmas lights. All the houses had these lights because Jews couldn't live there.

By the time my parents bought the house in 1977, the restrictive covenant was a joke. Restrictive covenants were unenforceable, which was irrelevant because no one was trying to enforce them. Probably a quarter of the town was Jewish—with more Jews moving in. We still laugh at the restrictive covenant, and remark that the fact that it went from being a source of restriction to one of humor demonstrates what a great country we live in.

But others take it seriously. Every so often, the *New York Times* runs an article about how a nonprofit group or a lobbying body has formed to purge homes of restrictive covenants. For instance, the *Times* ran an article in 2021 about one such effort. The article quoted California State Assemblyman Kevin McCarty as saying of restrictive covenants: "They're harmful. To me it's akin to leaving a sign above a water fountain that says, 'White Only.'"[92]

Our family disagrees. The "Whites Only" signs in the Jim Crow South were an integral part of an evil state structure that systematically denied black people their constitutional and God-given rights and opportunities. The restrictive covenant in my parents' deed is *harmless*. Blacks in the Jim Crow South were victims of a terrible state system. Residents whose homes have meaningless legacy restrictive covenants in them are not victims of anything. The contention that the restrictive covenant (which no one supports or tries to act upon) is "akin" to a manifestation of Jim Crow is a hideous insult to those who suffered under it and to those who worked successfully to change it.

How can one distinguish between a restrictive covenant in the deed of a house in Short Hills in 2024 and a "Whites Only" sign in the Jim Crow

South? God provides the counsel in Exodus 34 in his instruction to be "slow to anger." One who finds out that his house has a restrictive covenant is likely be disturbed and taken aback. Assemblyman McCarty showed what one might do if he is also quick to anger. He will feel *harmed*—indeed, "akin" to a black person being denied fundamental civil rights in the Jim Crow South. Assuming the role of a victim, he will lash out against his perpetrators. If the perpetrators are long dead (like with restrictive covenants), he will spend lots of time and energy boxing against shadows. That may seem harmless, but we all only have so much time to live. One who spends time on meaningless things is depriving himself of spending time on meaningful things.

What if someone, finding a restrictive covenant in his deed, is slow to anger? He will likely do what my parents did and turn to appreciation and gratitude for the great county and lovely town in which change happened so quickly and completely.

Or he might do what Rabbi Moshe Scheiner of the Palm Beach Synagogue did. One of the main original developers of South Florida was Henry Flagler—who, in accordance with the practices of the time and place, was determined to keep Jews out (hence, the 1930s Miami hotel advertisements: "Always a view, never a Jew," and "Air-conditioned rooms available. Oceanfront luxury at low cost. Gentile clientele."[93] Flagler, who put now unenforceable restrictive covenants against Jews in his property deeds, has a museum (an official national historic landmark) devoted to him in Palm Beach.

Rabbi Scheiner, who leads a large and growing congregation in Palm Beach, did not wage a campaign to get the museum to change its name or its landmark status removed, purge deeds of unenforceable restrictive covenants, or lead an effort to get rid of the many statues to Flagler in South Florida. Instead, he held the thirtieth major anniversary celebration for his synagogue at the museum—where his congregants danced to Jewish music, raised money for Jewish charities, ate kosher food, and rejoiced in all they had done together and were committed to keep doing.

In every case, one who adopts the divine quality of being "slow to anger" will enable himself to be smart, disciplined, and strategic. He will realize that there are some things worth getting angry about and fighting for—but not everything. By being slow to anger, he can set the threshold for his emotional engagement and decide what crosses it and what does not.

And that's not all. One who is slow to anger will find his restraint rewarded with self-mastery, happiness, and health. One who explodes into road rage after being cut off or calls the campus bias line in response to a joke will find himself consumed by his anger and its ramifications. He will, therefore, deprive himself of the time, energy, mindspace, and relational capital to focus on things that he might have considered more worthy if he had given himself the chance to decide.

A slowness to anger, which facilitates emotional discipline and strategic deciding, just might be the beginning of dignity.

6

Why the Israelites Want to Return to Egypt and Patty Hearst Joined Her Kidnappers

The Torah and Science of Stockholm Syndrome

The Rape of Dinah

It is Genesis 34, and Dinah, the daughter of Leah and Jacob, left the family home to "see the daughters of the land." She is taken and raped by Shechem, the city's prince. Shechem, the text tells us, "became deeply attached to Dinah . . . he loved the maiden and appealed to the maiden's emotions." In an effort to legitimize his relationship with Dinah, Shechem appeals to Jacob and his sons. He asks them for Dinah's hand in marriage, and suggests that their peoples merge.

Dinah's brothers Simeon and Levi respond with cunning, and tell Shechem that he can have Dinah and that their nations can merge. The brothers have just one condition: that all of the men of Shechem get circumcised. Three days after the mass circumcision, when the men are weakened, Dinah's brothers enter the city and kill every inhabitant—saving Shechem and his father for last.

Dinah is now free to go home with them. No one is left to pose a threat to her or her family. And she does—but the text makes it clear that her escape is not so simple. After killing her rapist and his father, the text says, "Then they took Dinah from Shechem's home and left."

This is intriguing. Why do Simeon and Levi have to "take" Dinah? Why wouldn't Dinah have run into their arms and escaped as quickly as she could? The fourth-century sage Rabbi Yudan explained: "They dragged Dinah out of Shechem's house—against her will." She apparently had become so fond of Shechem—she had so thoroughly identified with him and his people—that she wanted to stay in his house after he was dead.[1]

How could Dinah have identified, to such an extent, with her oppressors? In the next book of the Bible, we see just how common this phenomenon is, as a similar dynamic afflicts the entire Jewish people.

The Jews in the Desert: On Empathy and Stockholm Syndrome

Jewish slavery under Egypt was brutal. Exodus 1:13–14 tells us that "the Egyptians made the Children of Israel serve with crushing hardness. They embittered their lives with hard work, with mortar and with bricks, and with every labor of the field."

The Jews are seemingly destined to be afflicted until they die—individually and nationally. But God, with his partner Moses, orchestrates the first slave rebellion in human history. In Exodus 12, the Jews are soon liberated from slavery and on our way to being a free people in the Promised Land.

Seven weeks later, God declares his everlasting partnership with the Jews, consecrated by his giving us the Ten Commandments at Mount Sinai. The Jews are under God's protection in the desert, preparing for sovereignty while having all our needs (including physical safety, delicious food, and adequate housing) provided for by God.

This is an awesome manifestation of divinely bestowed fortune. How did we respond? We said: "We remember the fish that we ate in Egypt free of charge; the cucumbers, melons, leeks, onions, and garlic." And we knew what we wanted to do with that "memory." "Let us appoint a leader and go back to Egypt" (Numbers 11:5).

Only a year removed from the Exodus, we yearned to return to our captors and slave masters.

How prevalent is this mentality? Enough to make it a subject of Moses's parting advice and commands to his people. In Deuteronomy 7:21, Moses provides us with instructions regarding the Canaanite nations, who were the enemy of the Jews. He says: "Do not *admire* them, for the Lord your God, who is among you, is a great and awesome God."[2]

Why might we *admire* the Canaanite nations? The Canaanite nations made their sacred symbols out of phallic representations, engaged in child sacrifice, and practiced bestiality and incest—among other things. We might admire them for the same reason that Dinah's brothers had to take her from Canaan—which is the same reason why we identified with our Egyptian slave masters and their "free" food. It is because of the psychological dynamic where people identify with, and even admire, their oppressors.

The Torah offers a solution to the problem it identifies. In Numbers 11:16, we learn God's response to our wanting to return to Egyptian slavery. He says: "Gather to Me seventy men from the elders of Israel, whom you know to be the elders of the people and its officers and bring them to the Tent of Meeting, that they may stand there with you."

God's general solution—have ex-slaves counsel other ex-slaves—fits into the general rubric of Jewish thought. As discussed in the chapter of this book on impostor syndrome, the Talmud teaches: "A prisoner cannot free himself from prison, but depends on others to release him from his shackles."[3] Redemption from suffering is likely to require the loving support of another person.

Why would God command the appointment of seventy *elders*? Younger people can be just as smart, reasonable, logical, and sensible as their elders. Any number of younger people could have easily made the case against returning to Egyptian slavery. But God only seeks the involvement of *elderly* people. And that's not all. God does not tell Moses to use the first seventy old people he finds. He tells Moses to select them, presumably for their wisdom. This coheres with the idea that the word the Torah uses for elders—*zaken*—bears the connotation of wisdom. The distinguishing quality that the elders had as a group was that they had been enslaved for a long time. They had endured the horrors and terrors of slavery—and would, with the *authority* that only experience can provide, have the best chance at convincing the rebels that their perspective was skewed.

The Science

"I'm Tania!"

William Randolph Hearst was the most influential media owner in the world in the early decades of the twentieth century. His empire consisted of newspapers, magazines, newsreels, and movies. He was also a major political figure, having served as a congressman and mayor of New York. The model for Charles Foster Kane in Orson Welles's *Citizen Kane*, Mr. Hearst's net worth was $30 billion in today's dollars. He died in 1951, and left a great fortune to his descendants. That made his granddaughter Patty a good kidnapping target.

In 1974, Patty Hearst was a nineteen-year-old college student living with her fiancé, Steven Weed. On February 4, they were at the home they shared. There was a knock on the door, and they answered. A group of armed men and women burst in, beat up Mr. Weed, grabbed Ms. Hearst, threw her into the trunk of their car, and drove off.

These were terrorists with the Symbionese Liberation Army, intent on igniting a war against the "capitalist state." They confined, tortured, and raped Patty Hearst. In the months that followed, Hearst had at least two opportunities to safely free herself and return to her previous life. She refused. Instead, she trained with the SLA in weaponry and crime.

On April 15, 1974, she entered the Hibernia Bank in San Francisco with a gun. She announced, "I'm Tania. Up, up, up against the wall, motherfuckers!" That was her first of several such crimes. She was arrested in September of 1974—and eventually pleaded guilty, explaining that she had been brainwashed. She was convicted and imprisoned anyway. Her sentence was commuted by President Carter, and she was ultimately pardoned by President Clinton.[4]

Patty Hearst's transformation from a privileged young lady to a kidnapping victim to a criminal who was psychologically captured by her kidnappers is an astonishing story. But by 1974, the public was not entirely surprised. There was a precedent to describe the Patty Hearst phenomenon, and a term had been invented to describe it: Stockholm syndrome.

Stockholm Syndrome

Jan-Erik Olsson, born in Sweden in 1941, was arrested for the first time in 1957. He spent much of the following sixteen years in prison for various violent crimes. On August 23, 1973, this thirty-two-year-old career criminal was on a furlough from prison.

He put on a mask, hid a submachine gun under his jacket, and entered the Sveriges Kreditbanken—a bank. He took four employees hostage and placed them in the bank vault. His condition for their release: three million Swedish krona ($710,000) and a getaway car.

Olsson did not want to work alone. He demanded the freedom of a criminal he met in prison and greatly admired (Clark Olofsson). The authorities freed Olofsson, and allowed him to join Olsson at the bank.

One hostage, Elisabeth Oldgren, complained that she was claustrophobic in the vault. Olsson put a rope around her, and allowed her to walk outside of the vault. She responded by thinking that he was "very kind to allow me to leave the vault."

Olsson, frustrated that he was not receiving what he wanted from the authorities, threatened to shoot the hostage Sven Safstrom in the leg. Mr. Safstrom responded by thinking that it was "kind of him [Olsson]" to threaten to shoot only his leg and to allow him to get drunk before getting shot. Even more, he thought of Olsson as "a kind of emergency God."

Another hostage, Kristin Enmark, got on the phone with the Swedish prime minister Olof Palme. She pleaded that she and the hostages should be able to leave in a getaway car—with the robbers. She explained: "I am not desperate. They haven't done a thing to us. On the contrary, they have been very nice."

A few days into the siege, the authorities had drilled holes in the vault—to send in tear gas. Olofsson and Olsson put nooses around the hostages, and threatened to hang them if the gas came in. On August 28, the gas came in. Olofsson and Olsson, thinking that the gas would give them brain damage in fifteen minutes, immediately surrendered. The authorities instructed the hostages to leave first. They refused. Ms. Enmark explained: "No, Jan and Clark go first—you'll gun them down if we do!"

When they were all out of the bank, the hostages hugged and kissed their captors. The hostages refused to testify against Olofsson and Olsson. Instead, they raised money for their defense.[5]

What were these hostages thinking? It seems to have been something very similar to what the ex-slaves in the Torah were thinking when they demanded to return to Egypt.

The early-twentieth-century psychologists Sándor Ferenczi and Anna Freud would have known. Writing independently in the 1930s, Drs. Ferenczi and Freud each discussed the phenomenon of "identification with the aggressor."[6]

The Swedish psychiatrist Nils Bejerot applied this insight to the events at the bank, and gave the phenomenon a name: Stockholm syndrome. According to psychotherapist Dr. Paul Hokemeyer, "Stockholm syndrome describes a powerful and loving connection [that] people who are oppressed develop for their oppressors."[7]

It has captured the public imagination in a way that perhaps no other psychological disorder has. IMDB lists the "Top Twenty-Five Movies About Stockholm Syndrome"—as there are many more to choose from.[8]

The kinds of cases that made Stockholm syndrome famous—those involving guns and kidnapping—are rare. But Stockholm syndrome is not limited to kidnapping—and is anything but rare.

The Cleveland Clinic has identified Stockholm syndrome in child abuse, coach–athlete abuse, relationship abuse, and sex trafficking. The National Domestic Violence Hotline reports, "We hear from many people who are in abusive relationships . . . that they love their abusive partner."[9]

Why does Moses, in his parting speech, warn the Jews to not "admire" our enemies? Why did the Jews in the desert, Patty Hearst, the hostages in the Swedish bank, and so many victims of domestic violence identify with their oppressors? The Cleveland Clinic calls Stockholm syndrome a "coping mechanism"—an example of the mind of an oppressed person tricking itself to enable the individual to endure an otherwise unbearable situation.

The Treatment for Stockholm Syndrome

How does one treat Stockholm syndrome? Dr. Hokemeyer says, "The key to getting away from an abusive partner is marshaling the courage and intellect that resides within you to connect with a positive force to transition you through a terrifying process."[10] *A positive force.* This is the individual the sages in the Talmud were thinking of when they wrote, "A prisoner cannot generally free himself from prison, but depends on others to release him from his shackles." But why would Moses have chosen his "positive force" to be of "wise elders"?

In 2018, a team of researchers led by Dr. Sarah Hargreaves of the University of Sheffield noted the proliferation of online forums to help people with all types of conditions and challenges. They found that the quality that enables maximal helpfulness is empathy. And they identified two different groups who will show the greatest empathy in service of assuaging the pain of others.

Teenagers, they write, send "emotional messages in a personal style," whereas older people employ a "more formal style." However, "older adults"—the kind recruited by God and Moses—expressed higher levels of concern for others than their teenage counterparts.[11]

So, age is a proxy for empathy. But that is not all. They identified another characteristic that maximizes empathy. They write:

> Empathy is stronger or more evident when users share similarities, such as going through the same experience. Similarity provides a basis for greater identification between users, increases the likelihood of an accurate understanding of the situation (empathetic accuracy), and fosters greater intimacy.[12]

The ideal group for a support forum, therefore, is an elderly person who has had the same experience as the people struggling from it. Moses's elders—who had endured slavery for the longest—were, by the lights of modern social science, the ideal choice to counsel the confused ex-slaves. But as noted, these must have been *wise* elders, capable of sharing Moses's difficult judicial and leadership duties. Why wise elders rather than just old people?

Pastor John Maxwell has been one of America's top leadership thinkers and coaches since the 1980s. In 2011, he reflected:

> We've all heard, 'Experience is the best teacher,' but it's simply not true. Experience is not the best teacher; it never has been and never will be. Maturity doesn't always come with time; sometimes age brings nothing more than wrinkles and gray hair. Experience is not

> the best teacher; evaluated experience is the best teacher. Reflective thinking is needed to turn experience into insight.[13]

No wonder why God wanted "wise elders" to perform the existential task of counseling the desert Jews out of their extreme slave mentality.

Reflection

We may think that the Stockholm syndrome portrayed in popular culture is a distant phenomenon. After all, being kidnapped is rare—and so identifying with one's captors must be rarer still.

But it is only the Stockholm syndrome of the biblical Dinah, Kristin Enmark, and Patty Hearst that is rare. We are all likely, at some point, to know someone who is in a relationship that is objectively unhealthy and perhaps downright dangerous. That person might believe, and insist, that her boyfriend/girlfriend/spouse/another really means well, is just emotional, is going through a lot, acted terribly just this once, or is improving. The Torah, amplified by social science, guides us to consider another possibility altogether. The person we care about might be entirely wrong—and is, at great peril, identifying and drawing closer to her abuser.

This prevalence and power of Stockholm syndrome should educate us to rush to help someone who is suffering from it. An initial intervention is an important start, and it can be followed by ushering the person suffering from it into a community of people who have suffered similarly. The more elderly and wise people in the community, the better.

The Torah, everyone agrees, does not chronicle everything—or even most things—that happened in the lives of its characters. The Torah, in its silences, offers much for our imagination. How were the wise elderly people that Moses called to help those struggling with Stockholm syndrome in the desert affected by their counseling role?

Modern evidence provides a clue. Gabe Cohen spent much of the twenty-first century in and out of prison and addiction centers. He founded the very successful Discovery Café, a program in Colorado that treats addicts. A journalist who studied Discovery Café attributed its success to the "true street credibility" of Gabe Cohen. Mr. Cohen describes his work in helping addicts: "The work I do today gives meaning to the wreckage of the past." The seventy elders of Numbers 11 probably felt the same way.

7

Why Noah's Ark Was Fish-Free and Teenagers Drive Recklessly

The Torah and Science of Peer Pressure

Why Are There No Fish on Noah's Ark?

In Genesis 6, we learn that God's heart was "deeply troubled." The problem: "Every inclination of the thought of man was evil all the time."

He has a tragic solution. "I will wipe from the face of the earth the human race I have created—and with them the animals, the birds and the creatures that move along the ground—for I regret that I have made them."

God exempts, among humans, only Noah and his family. God, after reiterating that he will "destroy . . . every creature that has the breath of life in it," issues another exemption. God instructs Noah: "You are to bring into the ark two of all living creatures, male and female, to keep them alive with you. Two of every kind of bird, of every kind of animal and of every kind of creature that moves along the ground will come to you to be kept alive" (Genesis 6:19–20).

Three things are clear. First, all the people (except for Noah and his family) must die. Second, all the animals (except for one male and one female) must die. Third, the fish—who do not "move along the ground" and do not "breathe"—will live.

This leads to two questions. Why were animals, who do not make moral choices, destroyed? Why were the fish exempt from the destruction?

The nineteenth-century sage Yosef Dov Soloveitchik had the answer. He said that the animals shared an environment with the people—and, consequently, were corrupted by the evil of mankind. The fish, however, were underwater and therefore did not share an environment with people and animals. Uncorrupted by the behavior in the environment aboveground, the fish were exempt from the divine decrees against the people and the animals.[1]

Most readers of the Noah story probably ask a variant of the same question. How could the animals—who, again, do not make moral decisions—have been corrupted by the environment, or anything else? The answer: Genesis 6 is not intended to teach us about what happened to animals in an ancient flood. It is intended, like all biblical narratives, to guide us to living and *being* better. Consequently, we are led to conclude that if even the animals can be corrupted by the doings of the people in their environment—how much more so each of us.

Tabernacle Seating and Melting Hearts

So, one of the first lessons of Genesis is that people are *very* sensitive to the influences of those in our environment. Two questions arise. How might this insight be manifest in human choices? What might be its consequences? The Torah addresses these in Numbers and Deuteronomy.

The Book of Numbers is, in large part, a chronicle of the Jewish people struggling with self-inflicted wounds and internally generated conflicts in the desert. One of these calamitous moments is that of Korach's Rebellion in Numbers 16. In this story, a man identified as "Korach, the son of Izhar son of Kohath son of Levi" incites an insurrection against Moses.

The text identifies Korach's conspirators as Reubenites. The rebels have no positive agenda. They do not have a single policy they would like to implement or abolish. Theirs is a populist revolution only about power. Still, it poses an existential threat to Moses's leadership. The story ends with Korach and his followers being burned and buried alive.

The first question from this story is: Why do the Reubenites, alone among the tribes, join Korach—a Levite? Rashi finds the answer in Numbers 2, which describes the seating arrangement around the Tabernacle. The Reubenites are seated right next to the Levites—specifically the family of Kehat to which Korach belonged. The Reubenites joined the rebellion because of peer pressure. They were corrupted by their neighbors at the Tabernacle.[2]

The peer influence that developed around the Tabernacle did not only affect the Reubenites. And it was not only negative. Importantly, it was pervasive—affecting lots of tribes, for good and for ill.

The Bible is clear that three of the tribes turned out very well. They are Judah, of whom the psalmist says, "Judah is my lawgiver." There is Issachar, of whom Chronicles says, "had understanding of the times." And there is Zebulun, of whom Judges says, "came from those who wield the scribe's quill." What accounts for the good outcomes for these three tribes? As Rashi points out, they were seated next to Moses and Aaron at the Tabernacle. They were the beneficiaries of *positive* peer influence.[3]

Moses will incorporate these lessons on peer influence in his parting speech to the Jewish people. In Numbers 1:45, Moses decrees mandatory military service for all Jewish men. This is intuitive, as one of the ways to unite a nation is through shared sacrifice in support of its common goals and existential needs.

But by Deuteronomy 20, he seems to have learned something that leads him to refine the rule. Moses says, "Who is the man who is fearful and fainthearted? Let him go and return to his house, and let him not melt the hearts of his fellows, like his heart." One coward in a unit, Moses suggests, can "melt the hearts" of an entire community of otherwise brave warriors.

This teaching from Numbers and Deuteronomy, that we will become like those whom we associate with, would become a major theme in subsequent Jewish thought and teaching.

In Pirkei Avot, Nittai of Arbela listed three ways to avoid moral trouble. The first two: "Keep a distance from an evil neighbor" and "Do not cleave to the wicked." He says that people absorb the behaviors of those near them as inevitably as a customer in a spice shop absorbs the aromas of the store. Therefore, he famously warned, "Woe to the wicked and woe to his neighbor."[4]

In the following three hundred years, a lot would change—but not this idea. Rabbi Yohanan asks his colleagues to comment on the "right way to which a man should cleave." Rabbi Joshua said, "A good companion." Rabbi Yose said, "A good neighbor."[5] Almost a thousand years later, Maimonides would reflect:

> It is natural for a man's character to be influenced by his friends and associates and for him to follow the local norms of behavior. Therefore, he should associate with the righteous and be constantly in the company of the wise, so as to learn from their deeds. Conversely, he should keep away from the wicked who walk in darkness, so as not to learn from their deeds.[6]

What should an individual do when he finds himself in a bad environment? Maimonides had a simple solution. The person must "migrate to a state where conduct is good." If it is not possible to migrate to such a place, he said that the individual must seek solitude—even in a cave, a cliff, or a desert. This is an extraordinary statement from any Jewish authority given the Jewish emphasis on relationships and community. But as untenable as it is to be alone, Maimonides considers being around bad influences even worse.[7]

Peer Influence and Communal Responsibility

So, the Torah and subsequent Jewish tradition insist that we are profoundly influenced by those with whom we associate. However, this presents a challenge. The Talmud, drawing from clear instruction in Genesis, teaches, "Every Jew is responsible for every other Jew." This has been widely interpreted to mean that every Jew has a responsibility for both the material and spiritual well-being of other Jews.[8]

This has a significant implication for a people who are continually educated in the Torah to be sensitive to peer influence. As with all peoples, there will always be Jews who are spiritually deficient—and show it through their actions and inactions. If every Jew is responsible for the spiritual obligations of every other Jew and there will always be spiritually deficient Jews, then every Jew will have to engage deeply with people who are corrupting influences. Given the Torah's doctrine of how we are so profoundly influenced by peer pressure, that should be a recipe for corruption and degradation.

What, then, are we supposed to do? Are we to always surround ourselves with positive influences? Or are we to stay enmeshed in a society with negative influences and fulfill our responsibility to elevate them?

The answer is so important that it surfaces in very different places throughout the Torah.

Incense, Heifers, and the Gladiator Games

In Exodus 30:34, God instructs Moses in the "incense" that are to be in the holy Tabernacle. One of them, galbanum, smells foul. This is strange. Why does God command the presence of a foul-smelling fragrance in the holiest of places?

The third-century sages Rav Hana bar Bizna and Rabbi Shimon Hasida explain that the presence of the foul-smelling fragrance is an education for how we should treat foul people—sinners or those off the path—in our synagogues and communities.[9] These people should be especially welcome in the synagogue, as it is an ideal place for them to be influenced positively.

This idea is embedded in the Hebrew language. The seventeenth-century Rabbi Nathan Nata Shapira of Krakow (known by the name of his work, *Megaleh Amukot*) observed that the word *tzibur* (community) is an acronym of the three Hebrew words *tzaddik*, *beinoni,* and *rasha* ("righteous," "intermediate," and "wicked"). Righteous people, the *Megaleh Amukot* deduced, must welcome the wicked into the community so that they can positively influence them.[10]

Numbers 19:2 is the verse that millennia of commentators (including King Solomon) have regarded as the Torah's most inscrutable passage. A review of the passage makes clear why. An individual becomes defiled. He goes to the priest, who takes an unblemished and unspotted red heifer and sacrifices it by throwing it into a fire with many other things. The priest uses the concoction to purify the contaminated man. The individual emerges purified, but the priest is now contaminated!

What is the meaning of this passage? The twentieth-century sage Rav Joseph Soloveitchik explains that while the process may be inscrutable, the lesson is not. It describes the obligation of the Jewish leader to sacrifice his purity in order to help purify others.[11]

This position is amplified in Deuteronomy 13, where Moses says that a "wayward city"—one in which the inhabitants have turned to idolatry—must be destroyed. The requirements for destroying the city are so high that the Talmud specifies that it never happened. What, then, is the purpose of the instruction in Deuteronomy? Maimonides explained that positive influences must be brought to a city before it can be condemned as "wayward."

Consequently, there must have been "wayward cities" that were *slated* for destruction—but which were subsequently saved.[12]

The Talmud offers a real-world example of how Jews should subject themselves to impurity in order to purify others. When the Romans conquered Israel, the main form of entertainment were gladiators—where men and beasts would attack each other to the delight of screaming fans. If a man was not killed naturally, a Roman authority would often ask the crowd whether the losing party should be killed—and act in accordance with the crowd's desire.

The Jewish authorities hated everything about this activity. Consequently, they banned Jews from attending the games—and even from selling animals to those who would subject them to these games.

However, Rabbi Nathan offered an exception. Jews could attend this quintessentially depraved activity in order to cheer for the life of the losing fighter and potentially influence the crowd and the Roman authority to save him. Jews could also attend to testify that a fighter had died so that the fighter's widow would be free to remarry.[13]

So, Jewish teaching is very clear. Peer influence is so important that we are to leave a community that is negative—even if that means living on a cliff. However, our responsibility to each other is so deep that we must welcome those who will be bad influences in order to provide them with a good influence. This sounds like a contradiction. Is it? The Torah provides the answer in two places.

Immunizing Ourselves from Peer Influences

In Numbers 14, God and Moses decide that it is time for the Jews to conquer the land. Twelve men go from the desert to "scout out the land." The mission fails catastrophically. The peer influence is so profound that the scouts are able to convince each other, and then everyone else, to defy the will of Moses and God. Yet two of the scouts, Caleb and Joshua, resist the peer pressure that led their colleagues into a collective spiral of fear and cowardice. How did they do it?

As the twentieth-century Israeli sage Rav Yosef Shalom Elyashiv noted, the answer lies in the text. God says, "And my servant Caleb . . . was of a different spirit" (Numbers 14:24). Peer influence naturally and powerfully aligns an individual's attitudes and behavior with the norms of the group. But Caleb shows that a different spirit can exist and resist even in environments where others are actively exerting a significant amount of peer pressure.[14]

This leads to a tactical question. How does one develop a "different spirit" strong enough to withstand even the most intense peer pressure? The Torah provides guidance. Caleb, importantly, does not resist peer pressure alone. He does so with Joshua.

Caleb is not the first to show how peer pressure can be resisted. He had an august predecessor, who had a different model. In Genesis 12, Abraham leaves his birthplace to evangelize on behalf of ethical monotheism. As the Torah records, he engages deeply with pagans as a part of this mission.

Yet, he does not engage with pagans alone. He begins his journey with his wife and others in a small community of united, tight-knit, like-minded people. He continually grows that community as he persuades people to embrace ethical monotheism. By engaging pagans from a base of what is always a good and growing (even if small) community, Abraham draws the strength to immunize himself from negative influences.

The Power to Resist

What should one do if he finds himself in a bad community without a positive subcommunity and cannot, per Maimonides, move to a better community? The Torah answers with three examples.

In Genesis 24, Abraham's servant Eliezer goes on a search for a wife for Isaac. It is an extraordinary assignment, as Isaac had been chosen by God to lead the Jewish people. The woman Eliezer finds, if he is successful, would be the next matriarch of the Jewish people.

Eliezer, as the chapter of this book on romantic love discusses, immediately meets Rebecca. Rebecca, the text tells us, is "exceedingly beautiful to look upon" and insists on personally fetching water for him and for all of his quite thirsty camels. After she demonstrates her extraordinary generosity and does not ask for any compensation, Eliezer gives her a lot of jewelry.

Rebecca brings this stranger home and introduces him to her family. Bethuel, who was identified in Genesis 22 as Rebecca's father, focuses intently on the jewelry. He is, we see, a man driven by materialism rather than generosity or any other divine characteristic. Her brother, Laban, is even worse. He is so bad that the Haggadah—the great guidebook of the Passover Seder—will describe him as "worse than Pharaoh."

Eliezer eventually takes Rebecca with him to marry Isaac. The Torah describes their union with intriguing language in Genesis 25:20. "Isaac . . . married Rebecca, the daughter of Bethuel the Aramean from Paddan-Aram and the sister of Laban the Aramean."

Why would the text, which has no redundancies, tell us *again* that Rebecca is the daughter of Bethuel and the sister of Laban? It would not do so to educate us about their relationship, which we already know. It must be telling us that one's influences are not determinative. A person raised in a terrible environment *can* transcend it and become a woman with the spiritual gifts to lead God's project on Earth.

Rebecca is, in the words of the scholar Leon Kass, the Bible's "woman of all seasons."[15] She is a hero, and heroes are rare. But the Torah is clear that her excellence, though remarkable, is replicable.

In Exodus 1, the Pharaoh decrees that all Jewish baby boys be killed at birth. The Pharaoh's daughter, nevertheless, saves, adopts, and rears the Jewish boy who will become Moses.

And then there is Korach's Rebellion—which was enabled by the peer influence that led the Reubenites to join in. There is no doubt that this peer influence was powerful. But was it determinative?

In Numbers 26:11, we learn: "Korach's sons did not die." They did not just survive, but are credited with writing ten psalms that Jews and Christians recite regularly. How did Korach's sons survive and thrive—writing eternal prayers about God? There is only one way. They must have resisted the influence of their father and all those around him to such an extent that they constructed an alternative philosophy.

The Science

When Smart People Fail Very Easy Tests

In 1951, the psychologist Solomon Asch had fifty students from Swarthmore College take a vision test to see which of three lines was the same length as another control line. It was as easy as it sounds. Only it was not a vision test. It was a psychological experiment.

In the first several trials, the only participants were students who were part of the experiment. They all answered correctly. In the next group of trials, the students were joined by people they thought were other students but were really actors. The actors, as instructed by Professor Asch, gave the wrong answer and selected a line that was clearly a different length.

The result was that more than a third of the students in the second group of trials gave the wrong answer. In the course of several trials with different tests, more than three-quarters of the students in this group gave a wrong answer to very easy questions. In the debriefing, almost all of the students who gave the wrong answer reported doing so because of the influence of the others.[16]

In 2005, the neuroeconomist Gregory Berns executed what was essentially a modernized version of this study. He assembled cohorts of five participants and asked them whether computerized 3-D shapes would match or clash when rotated. The question was easy, and the answer apparent. The twist was that four of the people in each cohort were actors, leaving only one real participant. The four actors all gave the wrong answer to this easy question. Consequently, only 30 percent of the real respondents gave the correct answers.

Why did these participants give the wrong answer in response to the peer influence? Professor Berns did what Professor Asch, in 1951, could not. He ran brain scans of the participants.

The brain scans revealed that the participants who answered correctly had their amygdala aroused. This is the part of the brain that is associated with fear, anxiety, apprehension, and other negative emotions.

By contrast, the brains of those who conformed to peer pressure and gave the wrong answer lit up differently. Their parietal lobe, which is the part of the brain that is responsible for perceptions, lit up. With concern for how they were *perceived* aroused, these participants gave the wrong answer. They were able to avoid the amygdala and the attendant discomfort. The lesson from Professor Berns's experiment is clear: It is more comfortable to join a group in being wrong than to be alone and right—and most people go with the comfortable choice.[17]

Why Teenagers Drive Recklessly, Use Condoms, Become Transgender—and Pretty Much Everything Else

A question that adults have long asked is: Why do teenagers make bad decisions? The traditional answer is that teenagers do not have fully developed frontal lobes, which is where the brain makes decisions.[18]

In 2013, Professors Laurence Steinberg and Jason Chein of Temple University and Dustin Albert of Duke University tested this theory. They conducted a variety of experiments to determine why adolescents make bad decisions such as driving recklessly (as determined by driving behavior in a simulator).

They found that adolescents, acting in isolation, "likely appear as risk averse as adults." However, adolescents in a driving simulation game took 50 to 200 percent more risks when they thought that they were being observed by their peers. The legendary teenage recklessness, Professors Steinberg and Chein concluded, is the largely the result of peer influence.[19]

Numerous studies have shown the dynamics and consequences of this phenomenon. Peer influence starts to become important for most children at around age ten, builds to age fourteen, and then escalates dramatically before it stabilizes. Peer influence has been shown to guide adolescents in everyday decisions, such as what music to listen to and what clothes to wear. Social scientists have discovered that it is the most significant determinant for all kinds of more important decisions that adolescents make. These include: whether to use condoms, identify as transgender, get pregnant, drink, use drugs, smoke cigarettes, graduate from high school, serve in the military, ruminate on the past, and commit suicide.[20]

Why Adults Reuse Hotel Towels, Get Divorced, Donate Organs, Feel Lonely—and Pretty Much Everything Else

Peer influence does not stop or even diminish when one becomes an adult. It continues to influence whatever life decisions adults make, from the mundane to the existential. Contemporary social science has demonstrated just how sensitive we are to peer influence and how broad the term "peer" can be for influence to be asserted.

In 2008, Professor Noah Goldstein of the University of Chicago published a study regarding why hotel guests reuse towels. Professor Goldstein found that 33 percent of hotel guests reused towels after being given a message about the benefits of saving water. Yet, 50 percent more guests reused towels after being told that most of the guests who stayed in the same room did so. Just being told that people who stayed in the same hotel room—about as loose a definition of "peer" as there is—was sufficient to change behavior.[21]

Peer influence among adults extends from the mundane (reusing hotel towels) to the profound. In 2013, Professors Rose McDermott of Brown University, James Fowler of the University of California, and Nicholas Christakis of Harvard published their analysis of thirty years of data on marriage, divorce, and remarriage. They found that people are 75 percent more likely to become divorced if a friend is divorced, and 33 percent more likely to get divorced if a friend of a friend is divorced.[22,23]

Between reusing towels and getting divorced, seemingly every adult decision is significantly mediated by peer influence. These include online purchasing, musical preferences, binge drinking, work habits, tax compliance, punctuality at doctor's appointments, eating to obesity, meat eating, vegetarianism, the assumption of responsibility for actions, organ donation, exercise frequency, and the exhibition of facial preferences.

Consequently, Professors Fowler and Christakis generally use a different term to describe peer influence. They use "social contagion." In fact, it is not only behaviors that travel through human networks. It is also how we feel. One might think that a person with robust social connections is unlikely to feel lonely. That is true, but a 2009 study led by Professor John Cacioppo of the University of Chicago revealed an important caveat. Even people with robust social connections are likely to feel lonely if their friends do.[24]

The Last Resort Is Always a Resort

So, modern social science has demonstrated that the Torah's teachings on peer influence are precisely right. It makes perfect sense, by the lights of modern science, that the seating at the Tabernacle influenced how the tribes behaved and what they became. Moses was equally validated in his decision to exempt fearful young men from military service on the grounds that their participation would "melt the hearts" of the other soldiers. And Nittai of Arbela was offering the right warning when he said: "Woe to the wicked and woe to his neighbor."

But the Torah, and the Jewish tradition, does not end its discussion there. It also emphasizes that we have an obligation to help those whose character and behavior have the potential to corrupt—and counsels that we can safely do so when supported by a small and virtuous subcommunity. And it concludes by saying that an individual can, despite the power of peer influence, resist it.

What does the modern data suggest?

One of the most vibrant movements in Judaism is Chabad-Lubavitch. Chabad rabbis, who are all fully Orthodox and live traditional lifestyles, are the opposite of insular. They are devoted to being "lamplighters"—to bringing a robust Jewish life to those who would otherwise be without. This commitment to reaching out is embodied in that their rabbis are called "emissaries." These emissaries *seek* cultures that are very different from (and often opposed to) theirs, in order to positively influence them. Yet, they always go with a small community—even if it is just their (usually large) family.

The result? I recently had a conversation with a Chabad rabbi who had just returned from a conference of rabbis from a variety of denominations. He discussed with colleagues from the Reform and Conservative movements their greatest concern for their children. His colleagues said that their greatest concern was that their children would intermarry. This concern is supported by the data. Seventy-two percent of the non-Orthodox Jews who married between 2010 and 2021 married gentiles.[25]

The Chabad rabbi was taken aback. He, like many other Chabad rabbis, had raised his children in a community full of intermarriage. Yet he, like other Chabad rabbis, was not at all concerned that his children would intermarry. The data validates his lack of concern. Only 2 percent of Orthodox Jews are married to gentiles, and the rate is lower within Chabad families (who are considered part of the ultra-Orthodox community, which have even lower rates). The conclusion is as clear as the data: It is possible to maintain countercultural values even so long as one is deeply enmeshed in a small subcommunity where those values are taught, discussed, honored, practiced, and modeled.

Still, a question remains. What if—like Rebecca, the Pharaoh's daughter, and Korach's sons—one finds himself morally alone and cannot do as Maimonides suggests and move? The example of Mosab Hassan Yousef is illustrative. Mr. Yousef, like the Pharaoh's daughter, is the child of an evil man—in his case, the Hamas founder Sheikh Hassan Yousef. Mosab Yousef grew up deeply enmeshed in the culture of Hamas, which is devoted to the destruction of Israel, the murder of Jews, the subjugation of Christians, the suppression of women, and the persecution of homosexuals. The young Mosab Hassan Yousef, as a result of participating in Hamas's violence against Israelis, spent two years as a young man in Israeli prisons.

In prison, he began to think independently about what he was taught and what he observed. He could have, like many Hamas leaders, left prison and become a very rich man with political power and popular support. Instead, he offered to work with Israel against Hamas. Given the code name of Green Prince, he used his position as the heir apparent to Hamas leadership to provide Israel with intelligence that saved countless people. When his situation became too precarious, Israel staged an arrest to take him away from those who would kill him.

He eventually became a Christian and an American citizen who devotes his life to educating the world about the genocidal intentions and capabilities of Hamas. Mosab Hassan Yousef, like the Pharaoh's daughter and Korach's sons, shows that the power of free will can be even greater than that of peer influence.

Reflection

The Torah and social science of peer influence irrefutably demonstrate that much of what we think, feel, and do is determined by others in our environment—very broadly defined, to include people we don't even know.

This discovery and rediscovery has profound implications. One of the most important ideas in the West is John Stuart Mill's "harm principle," which stipulates that people should be free to do whatever they want so long as it does not impact others. Our sensitivity and responsiveness to peer influence, as claimed by the Torah and validated by modern social science, calls into question the assumption behind this principle. There is very little, if anything, that we do that does not impact others. One who gains weight, stops smoking, gossips, gets divorced, feels happy, or even reuses hotel towels *significantly* influences others—even those one does not know—to behave or decide similarly. Accordingly, there is little (if anything) that others do that does not influence us.

This acknowledgment that peer influence is significant, pervasive, sensitive, and affects everything, can lead us in two directions.

First, it means that everything we say and do is likely more important than we realize. The impact of what we say and do is not limited to the identifiable consequences of our words and our actions. It also includes how others speak and act—and even how those whom they interact with speak and act. The Torah and the science of peer influence make it clear that the question "Is this a good thing for me to say or do?" is just part of any decision-making process. The question "Is this a good decision for me and lots of others to say or do?" is simply more accurate.

Second, it raises the stakes on the question of whom we associate with. Our chance at becoming who we want to be will depend, to a significant extent, on whom we spend time with. The Torah and social science are clear that even people who consider themselves strong and independent will determine what is normal, acceptable, good, expected, and special in accordance with what others in their environment say and do. Consequently, the question of who we want to be needs to be contemplated in combination with the question of who we want to be around.

At first glance, it might seem that the Torah and science of peer pressure guide us to completely avoid communities that are full of unfortunate influences. The logic of this is that spiritually deficient communities would, without the positive influences that saved the wayward cities of Deuteronomy, get worse and worse. However, the Torah and social science say that this is unnecessary. Fundamentally good people can, and perhaps must, engage with the spiritually deficient with enough depth and regularity to positively influence them. These good people can substantially inoculate themselves from being negatively insulated by engaging from within a tight-knit, unified, strong, and morally aligned community.

And what if one finds himself in a suboptimal community—and without a subcommunity like Abraham had when he left on his journey in Genesis 12? He can, per Maimonides, leave the community. If he cannot do that, he has the model of Pharaoh's daughter and Korach's sons—and can, with resolve, thrive counterculturally.

PART TWO

Self-Improvement: How We Ought to Act

8

The Blessings of Jacob, Pinchas, and Hank Williams Jr.'s Rowdy Friends

The Torah and Science of Changing Oneself

Jacob's Blessing

As the chapter of this book on character demonstrates, the Torah and modern science are aligned in believing that character is indispensable for living a good life. This assertion, however, does not settle a question or end a debate. Instead, it introduces what is perhaps the existential question and challenge. The question: Can we change our essential characters? And if so, how?

The word "behemoth" has been the subject and even the title of scholarly papers, popular movies, and books in genres that include science fiction, economics, and politics. "Behemoth" is an English word that describes a "giant monster." But its origin is in biblical Hebrew. Behemoth derives from the Hebrew word for "animal": *beheima*. Beheima is, according to the sixteenth-century sage Judah Loew ben Bezalel (the Maharal of Prague), a contraction of *bah mah*—which means "it contains what it is."[1] An animal, the Hebrew language explains, is what it is. It cannot change in any kind of moral sense.

If the Torah defines an animal by containing all it is, what is a man? God tells us with the name of the first man, Adam. The name Adam, as Rabbi Doniel Baron of Aish Ha'Torah writes, describes a man who is born *from* the ground and can rise. Men are distinguished from animals in that we are not meant or destined to stay who we are. We can change.[2]

In early Genesis, it is not apparent that man's capacity for change will be anything other than a latent potential buried deep in Adam's name. In Genesis 7, God, who is disgusted with mankind, destroys the world with a flood. In Genesis 8:21, God vows never to do so again—but not because he was wrong about mankind, and not because he sees any evidence that people can change. He says, "Never again will I doom the earth because of humans, for every inclination of the human heart is evil from youth." God refrains from destroying the world not because people are good or can change but because he is understanding.

Fast-forward to Genesis 27, where Jacob is fleeing the murderous wrath of his twin brother, Esau—whom he had tricked out of receiving his father's blessing. Twenty years later, Jacob concludes his exile. As he starts the next stage of his life, he must make amends with his estranged brother. He plans a reunion with Esau. The reunion is not looking promising, as Jacob receives word that Esau is approaching with an army of four hundred men.

Jacob spends what seems like could be his last night on Earth alone. He is confronted by a man or an angel who engages him in an all-night wrestling match. At dawn, Jacob is about to win the match. He says to his opponent, "I will not let you go without a blessing." This is the root of the Jewish idea that we will emerge from every struggle with a blessing.

The fight ends, and the angel/man says, "Your name will no longer be Jacob, but Israel, because you have struggled with God and man and have overcome" (Genesis 32:28).

There is, as Rabbi David Wolpe identifies, a problem with this story. Jacob tells the man/angel that he will only release him after getting a blessing. But Jacob, seemingly, lets him go without receiving one. There must have been a blessing that we missed! And, indeed, there was. It is given in the very act of the angel's changing of Jacob's name to Israel. It is the blessing of self-transformation.[3]

So which is it? Is man evil from his youth, or can he change? According to the Torah: both. Our hearts and actions tend towards evil, but need not go that way. The acknowledgment in Genesis that we can transform ourselves prepares us for a remarkable pronouncement in Leviticus. In Leviticus 19:1, God tells us: "You shall be holy, for I am holy." We can transcend our evil nature to such an extent that we can actually be "holy," *like God.*

This conviction would become a fundamental Jewish conviction. In *Laws of Repentance*, Maimonides says, "A person should not entertain the thesis held by the fools among the Gentiles and the majority of the undeveloped among Israel that, at the time of a man's creation, The Holy One, blessed be He, decrees whether he will be righteous or wicked. This is untrue. Each person is fit to be righteous like Moses, our teacher, or wicked, like Jeroboam."[4]

Everyone can change so profoundly that he can be as righteous as Moses! This audacious assertion leads us to ask: How can I do so?

The basic construct is simple. One can change by removing negative traits or by developing positive traits. The Torah offers clear and simple guidance for both.

Removing Negative Traits: The Art of Channeling

How can we remove negative traits? God provides the answer clearly in Exodus 32–34. In Exodus 32, Moses is on Mount Sinai communing with God and receiving the Ten Commandments. Moses does not return exactly when the people expect him to. They respond by building, worshipping, and having an orgy around a Golden Calf. God is furious. He tells Moses that the people are "stiff-necked" (meaning stubborn) and worthy of destruction. Moses, who is disappointed and irate with his people, nevertheless convinces God to spare them. But he doesn't reveal his reason for another two chapters.

In Exodus 34, the situation has calmed down. Moses and God are engaged in an intimate conversation, reflecting on the Golden Calf and their plans for a future together. Moses says to God: "If I have found favor in Your eyes, my Lord, may my Lord go among us, *because* it is a stiff-necked [stubborn] people."

This is seemingly strange. God had wanted to destroy the people because we were stiff-necked! That makes sense: stiff-neckedness (or stubbornness) is generally assumed to be negative. Yet, Moses asks God to save us not *in spite* of us being stiff-necked—but *because* we are stiff-necked. What is going on?

Enter Rav Yitzchak Nissenbaum. Born in Belorussia in 1868, Rav Nissenbaum was a Jewish leader serving in Warsaw in the late 1930s. He was given the opportunity to flee the Nazis, but insisted on remaining with his people. He was killed by the Nazis in 1942—but not before he imagined what Moses was thinking when he pleaded with God to save us *because* we are "stiff-necked" in Exodus 34. Rav Nissenbaum explained:

> Nations will call on them to assimilate, but they will refuse. Mightier religions will urge them to convert, but they will resist. They will suffer humiliation, persecution, even torture and death because of the name they bear and the faith they profess, but they will stay true to the covenant their ancestors made with You.[5]

The Jews being stiff-necked, Moses explains, is what would lead Jews to remain—proudly and strongly—as God's people in the difficult times. Yes, being "stiff-necked" caused us to behave as we did at the Golden Calf. But this same quality, *channeled differently*, can lead to an otherwise inconceivable loyalty and fidelity to God.

So, the Torah establishes that the trait of stubbornness that leads God to nearly destroy us can, *channeled differently*, qualifies us for eternal divine favor.

The Jewish tradition makes it very clear that there is nothing unique about stiff-neckedness, as it pertains to channeling. The Talmud offers another trait that is assumed to be negative. This is a propensity to draw blood—described by the fourth-century sage Rav Ashi as regarding people born under "the nature of Mars." Such a person, Rav Ashi said, might channel his nature into becoming a highway robber. Or he could channel the same trait toward becoming a butcher, a surgeon, or a mohel (one who performs circumcisions).[6]

The quintessential example of this transformation was another rabbi of the Talmud—Reish Lakish. As a young man, Reish Lakish was enormously strong. He used this physical capability to become a gladiator who killed others for the entertainment of cheering masses. Under the influence of Rabbi Yochanan, Reish Lakish transformed himself and used his past to become one of the great Jewish commentators on repentance.

But he never surrendered or degraded the physical qualities he once used to kill people for entertainment. When a great rabbi of the age, Rav Imi, was captured by bandits, Rabbi Yochanan said that nothing could be done to save him. Reish Lakish disagreed. He said, "Even if I am killed or I kill someone, I will go and I will save him with strength."[7]

The Torah and Talmud show that a moral assessment of stubbornness and a propensity to draw blood, which are generally presumed to be negative, depends upon how one chooses to channel it.

How about a trait that is presumed to be positive? The Talmud addresses the trait of kindness. The second-century sage Rabbi Elazar said, "He who is merciful to the cruel will be cruel to the merciful."[8] In other words, kindness, when applied to the cruel, is a vice and even a sin. Case in point: In 1989, the Hamas terrorist Yahya Sinwar was arrested by Israel for planning to abduct two Israeli soldiers and for torturing and murdering four Palestinians he suspected of "collaboration." His practice of killing Palestinians he suspected of being sympathetic toward Israel was so legendary that he earned the nickname "the Butcher of Khan Yunis." The medical providers who treated him in the Israel prison remarked on how spectacularly cruel and evil he was.

In 2010, Sinwar developed a brain tumor while serving time in an Israeli prison. Israel could have let him die naturally without killing him. Instead, the Israeli doctors performed complex and successful brain surgery on Sinwar. He repaid this kindness by masterminding the October 7th massacres.

The lesson from the Torah tradition is clear. There are no good and bad traits. There is just positive or negative channeling of neutral traits. If someone has a negative aspect of his character that he wants to change, he can identify the underlying trait that is causing the negativity. He should not try to eliminate it, but instead to channel it toward positive ends.

Developing New Traits: Pinchas Receives the Biblical Peace Prize

The channeling of qualities, in the Torah worldview, is a necessary aspect of positive transformation. But it is not sufficient. God insisted that we can all be holy, and Maimonides said that everyone has the ability to be as great as Moses. In order to do so, people will also need to develop *new* qualities. For instance, every good person has a significant measure of kindness, toughness, resoluteness, compassion, generosity, gratitude, and more. How, then, can a person who is *lacking* in a good quality develop it?

The Torah provides the answer in Exodus 24:7, when God gives the Jews the Torah. The Jews accept it with a single statement that is both simple, profound, and enduringly instructive: "We will do and we will hear." The "hear" can alternatively be translated as "understand" or "think."

The order of the verse, as always, is deeply important. First, the Jews tell God, we will *do*. Then, the Jews tell God that we will *understand/think*. Moses and God like the answer so much that they consecrate it with a blood covenant. The rabbis of the Talmud liked the answer so much that they imagined that an angel came to each Jew and laid two crowns on his or her head, one for "we will do" and one for "we will hear."[9]

Why does this simple response evoke such an enthusiastic response from God, Moses, and the rabbis of the Talmud? After all, it should not be that big a deal that the people would accept a gift that is clearly presented from God.

The insight is that we don't act in accordance with our thoughts. Instead, we think in accordance with our actions. The lesson is clear, profound, and important: If one wants a quality or character trait, he should not do much thinking or pondering about it. He should simply act in accordance with that quality or character trait, and soon it will be a part of him. In other words, one should fake it until he makes it—which, with enough actions, he will.

We see this point exemplified in the Book of Numbers. The idolatrous prophet Balaam, after trying unsuccessfully to curse the Jews, attempts to corrupt us by sending Midianite women to lure us into sexual immorality and idolatry. It works. In a brazen display of moral bankruptcy, Zimri, a leader of the tribe of Shimon, fornicates with the Midianite woman Cozbi in front of the Tabernacle. Out of nowhere, a man named Pinchas steps forward and thrusts a spear through the couple—killing them publicly.

God responds to Pinchas's vigilante act by giving him the "Covenant of Peace" (Numbers 25:12). Why does God give Pinchas, whom we know mainly through this killing, the Biblical Peace Prize?

The nineteenth-century sage Naftali Zvi Yehuda Berlin, known as the Netziv, said that this is a guarantee that "[Pinchas] would not become an agitated and angry person, for the nature of the act he did—killing a person with his hands—leaves a strong impression."[10]

In other words, the impact of our actions on our own character is so strong that God fears that Pinchas's act of violence would make him a violent person. God intervenes to arrest this process by providing the Covenant of Peace.

The insight that we add new qualities as a result of what we do would constitute a core part of Jewish ethical teaching. Two of the great works of Jewish law and practical advice are *The Sefer Hachinuch* (by an unknown thirteenth-century author) and *The Path of the Just* by the eighteenth-century Rabbi Moses Luzzatto, known as the Ramchal. These works were separated by five hundred years, but they similarly developed the Torah's teaching as to how people can add new qualities.

The *Sefer Hachinuch* is a book of Torah-based rulings and teachings—perhaps given by a father to his son. The *Sefer Hachinuch* says, "You must know that a man is acted upon according to his actions; and his heart and all his thoughts always follow after the actions that he does—whether good or bad."[11]

Five hundred years later, Rabbi Moses Luzzatto explained how this insight makes change far easier than it seems. He wrote, "The external movement rouses the inner one and certainly the external movement is more in his power than the inner ones. Thus, if he exercises what is in his power to do, this will lead him to also attain what is not in his power."[12] Developing a quality through contemplation or even abstract commitment is difficult—even beyond our "power." But everyone can act in accordance with what he decides to do. Therefore, we should just resolve to do things that reflect the quality we want to develop—and pretty soon we'll have it.

Two other canonical Jewish thinkers, separated by more than half a millennium, explained how this can work practically.

Maimonides, writing in the twelfth century, addressed the question of whether it is better to give one's annual allocation to *tzedakah* (charity) in one large gift or many smaller gifts. He ruled that it is preferable to give many small gifts of charity over one large gift because "the repeated act of generosity" will make the person a giver.[13]

The nineteenth-century sage Rabbi Yisrael Meir Kagan (known as the Chofetz Chaim) was once asked by a young devotee whether it would be better to take a job in the bank giving withdrawals or taking deposits.

The Chofetz Chaim told the young man to work in withdrawals, because the constant act of giving would make him a giver.[14]

The practical implications are clear. If, per Maimonides, one wants to be more charitable, he should simply start making small contributions every day and keep doing so. If, per the Chofetz Chaim, one wants to become a giver, he should just give frequently. A person who wants to change himself should, in other words, identify the behaviors that manifest the desired character traits, and make a *habit* out of doing them.

The Torah tradition is so insistent on the practicality of this method of character change that it even, through the third-century sage Rabbi Yochanan, is explicit about how long it takes for a habit to become embedded into one's character. The answer: thirty days.[15]

The Science

Hank Williams Jr.'s Rowdy Friends

In 1981, Hank Williams Jr., at age thirty-two, released one of the great country songs: "All My Rowdy Friends (Have Settled Down)." Surely, no listener responded, "That's amazing! How did all of his friends settle down?"

Instead, the song hit number one on the country charts in part because it triggered a recognition that people who are rowdy in their twenties can be expected to settle down by their early thirties. We can all look back on our younger selves and acknowledge how much we changed. The only question is whether those changes are thoughtful, intentional, and good.

We may intuitively recognize that rowdy friends can be expected to settle down, and acknowledge the reality of human change that Hank Williams's song suggests. But social science has revealed that this intuitive recognition is at odds with what we believe about human change.

In the early 2010s, Harvard professors Jordi Quoidbach and Daniel Gilbert and University of Virginia professor Timothy Wilson set out to determine how much people thought they changed in the previous decade, and expected to change in the subsequent ten years. They surveyed 19,000 people between the ages of eighteen and sixty-eight and found:

> Young people, middle-aged people, and older people all believed they had changed a lot in the past but would change relatively little

> in the future. People, it seems, regard the present as a watershed moment at which they have finally become the person they will be for the rest of their lives.[16]

They called their finding "the end of history illusion." And it is not just ordinary survey respondents who harbor the illusion that they will not change from now on—whenever now is. Until recently, social scientists thought the same thing. In 2008, Professors Brent Roberts of the University of Illinois and Daniel Mroczek of Purdue published a review of the scientific literature on adult personality change. They wrote that prior to the mid-1990s, many in the scientific community thought that personality traits stopped changing in adulthood.[17]

Since then, the earlier theories that personality traits become solidified in adulthood have been disproven. Professors Roberts and Mroczek write, "Research now shows that personality traits continue to change in adulthood and often into old age, and that these changes may be quite substantial and consequential."[18]

Maimonides, who said that the "undeveloped" and "foolish" believe that people cannot change—while the truth is that everyone can be as righteous as Moses or as wicked as Jeroboam—would have agreed.

The real question is not whether people change. We will. It is whether we will change mindfully or mindlessly. And, if we change mindfully—if we decide to become better—a question emerges. *How* can we do so?

Modern science suggests two ways. The first would have sounded very familiar to Moses, when he argued with God to save the Jews because we are "stiff-necked." The second would have sounded very familiar to those who contemplated why God gives Pinchas the Covenant of Peace.

The Science of Channeling

In 2019, a team of scientists at the Max Planck Institute for Human Cognitive and Brain Sciences in Leipzig found that 30 percent of people are born with an A1 mutation, which likely accounts for the trait of stubbornness. Most of us would instinctively conceive of stubborn people as closed-minded individuals who refuse to try new things or allow new evidence to influence their experiences, conclusions, and worldview.[19]

However, the team at BetterHelp, a large online psychological services company, offers counsel to stubborn people. They do not recommend that stubborn people conquer their stubbornness. Instead, they suggest that "being stubborn is not an inherently negative thing. In reality, stubbornness can be a very positive aspect of your personality, and this trait can help you make progress toward your goals."[20]

Stubbornness, the team at BetterHelp asserts, can be channeled to enable people to become determined and decisive, to be effective leaders, and to persevere in the face of adversity. For instance, a parent with the A1 mutation can be stubborn about where the family goes for dinner, or he can decide to *channel* his stubbornness into ensuring that his child receives a good education in spite of his learning challenges.

Does it work? In 1997, Clint Pulver was a ten-year-old student at an elementary school in Heber City, Utah. He had a problem. He could not stop tapping on his desk.

Clint's insistent tapping inhibited his academic performance and annoyed his classmates and teachers. He spent a lot of time at the principal's office. The principal had a solution: Clint should sit on his hands whenever he got the urge to tap. Clint tried this tactic, but it did not work.

During one of his tapping sessions in class, Clint was told by Mr. Jensen, his teacher, to stay after class. Clint thought that he was in trouble again. Instead, Mr. Jensen reached into his desk and handed him a pair of drumsticks. He asked Clint if he ever thought of drumming. Clint hadn't—but he took the drumsticks, and never put them down.

Clint Pulver put himself through college by drumming. He has directed the drumline for the Utah Jazz. He has since played with artists including Carrie Underwood, Tim McGraw, and the Blue Man Group. And he was able to do so because of Mr. Jensen, who, like Rav Ashi in the Talmud, recognized that there are no good and bad qualities—just good and bad applications of neutral qualities. By leading Clint to productively channel his need to tap, Mr. Jensen enabled his student to discover his calling.[21]

The Science of Developing New Qualities

In 2012, the Secretary of State of the Home Department in Great Britain issued a bold charge to the National Health Service (NHS). The NHS was to "take every opportunity to prevent poor health and promote healthy living by making the most of healthcare professionals' contact with individual patients."[22]

This seems like a typical bureaucratic pronouncement—bold and vacuous—that was more likely to generate urgent nods than meaningful change. This did not work for Professors Benjamin Gardner, Phillippa Lally, and Jane Wardle of University College London. They were determined to help the NHS genuinely determine how people could change their health habits. So they delved deep into the relevant research.

They determined that primary care doctors found "traditional behavior change strategies" related to health to be time-consuming to discuss, difficult to implement, and unsustainable. But there was an alternative, and it is epitomized in the title of the article "Making Habits Habitual," which Professors Gardner, Lally, and Wardle coauthored for the *British Journal of General Practice* in 2012.

Their contribution covers a study that incorporated two groups of people who wanted to lose weight. One group was given ten simple diet and activity behaviors, with the encouragement to perform them with regularity. The control group was wait-listed and not given any intervention.

After 8 weeks, those who were told to make small and consistent changes lost 2 kilograms (5 pounds) compared with 0.4 kilograms in the control group. At 32 weeks, completers in the intervention group had lost an average of 3.8 kilograms.. Those in the habit intervention group reported that the behaviors had become "second nature," that the practices had "wormed their way into their brain," and that they "felt quite strange" if they did not stick with the habits.[23]

This finding, they wrote, was emblematic of what had become the social scientific consensus. They wrote: "Decades of psychological research consistently show that mere repetition of a simple action in a consistent context leads, through associative learning, to the action being activated upon subsequent exposure to those contextual cues (that is, habitually)."[24]

This could be read as a modern restatement of what the *Sefer Hachinuch* wrote nine hundred years ago—and a perfect justification for why Maimonides told his followers to give small amounts every day and the Chofetz Chaim told a young man to work in withdrawals rather than deposits. Habits really do make the man.

We now know not just that they were right—but *how*.

The Power of Habit

As every mother knows very well, there is not much room for the child to maneuver out of the birth canal and into the world. Consequently, the adult brain is only 5.5 inches long, 3.5 inches wide, 4 inches tall, and weighs just 3 pounds. This is *small*—at least as compared to other animals, some of whose brains are up to seven times larger than ours.[25]

How, then, can we small-brained animals do so much? God had a solution. It is described by Charles Duhigg in his best-selling book *The Power of Habit*. The brain, he says, "is constantly looking to save effort." And it does so through awesome properties, which were described by Isaac Asimov, who called it "the most complex and orderly organization of matter in the universe." Seemingly every scientist who has studied the brain agrees.[26]

One of the enablers of the brain's efficiency is described by David Orenstein of MIT. The human brain, he writes, is "famously flexible or 'plastic.'" When one brain connection (called a synapse) forms, others weaken, *and the brain changes*. The result can be a personality change.

But how? The MIT neuroscientist Ann M. Graybiel explains that we can easily affect a change *by simply forming a habit*. She goes on to say that the brain is so plastic it becomes noticeably different after a week of a new habit being adapted.[27]

This is not a matter of merely theoretical interest. In 2015, Nigel Mathers of the University of Sheffield gave the Davis Lecture at Harvard University. His subject: "The Science of Kindness." His analysis of kindness could apply to any quality:

> Individual acts of kindness release both endorphins and oxytocin, and create new neural connections. The implications for such plasticity of the brain are that altruism and kindness become self-authenticating.
>
> In other words, kindness can become a self-reinforcing habit requiring less and less effort to exercise. Indeed, data from functional magnetic resonance (FMR) scans show that even the act of *imagining* compassion and kindness activates the soothing and affiliation component of the emotional regulation system of the brain.[28]

In the previous ten years, the Torah's claim that we become what we do has leaped out of academic journals and popular science publications and into mainstream intellectual culture. James Clear's book *Atomic Habits* has been deservedly parked on the best-seller lists for years, which is also populated by other books by Mr. Duhigg, Gretchen Rubin, and several others. Many of these books have the word "habit" in their titles, and subtitles referring to some variant of "small changes." And they explain just how we can stimulate the process so that we change in accordance with our actions.

The first step toward creating a new habit is to develop a simple, measurable, and specific goal. An insufficiently specific goal, Mr. Clear writes, is just a dream that will fall victim to the "little exceptions" that collectively and successfully conspire against the characteristic being developed.

The second step is a cue or stimulus. The brain, Mr. Duhigg writes, "spends a lot of effort at the beginning of a habit looking for something—a cue—that offers a hint as to which pattern to use." Mr. Clear states that if there is no cue, "your habit will never start." The cue need not be complicated. It could be something as simple as the time of day.

The third step in the process is the action. One who wants to improve his prayer life could commit to praying every time the clock hits 7 AM. One who wants to exercise could leave for the gym every day at 5 PM. One who wants to become more charitable could make an online donation every day when the sun sets.

Modern science has shown how this process, which is exactly the one brought from the Torah by Maimonides and the Chofetz Chaim, works. "The brain," Professor Graybiel writes, "has an absolutely fabulous system for getting reward signals."

The reward system is powered by dopamine, the chemical transmitter that is released when we expect a reward. Dopamine is, as Harvard Health reports, "most notably involved in helping us feel pleasure as part of the brain's reward system."[29] Dopamine, sometimes called "the anticipation molecule," is released during activities such as sexual activity prior to climax and smelling cookies baking in an oven. All of the many activities that activate dopamine *immediately* precede the reward; we release the dopamine when we smell the pizza, not when we imagine eating it next week.

If we set up the reward to follow a behavior, the brain will release the dopamine in anticipation of the reward. Consequently, dopamine is the ideal and indispensable ally in the formation of habits. If we want to establish a habit, we just need to create a reward that we will enjoy immediately after its performance. If one wants to volunteer every week and loves iced coffee, she should promise herself iced coffee after each volunteer session. When the habit is formed, she will no longer need the reward—as she (in the words of Professor Lally) will feel "quite strange" not acting accordingly. The character trait—in this case, service to others—will have become a part of who she is.[30]

This leaves a question, which was also asked by the sages of the Talmud: How long does it take before a habit becomes part of who we are? Rav Yochanan, as mentioned, said thirty days. Professor Lally and her colleagues determined that it is a range between 18 and 254 days, with the average being 66 days.[31]

Reflection

The teachings of the Torah and the rediscoveries of modern science agree: We can decide that we want to change and, fairly easily, accomplish the goal. The first way one might want to change is to get rid of negative traits. The Torah and modern science unite and say that we should keep the quality but channel it toward positive ends. For instance, let's imagine someone who simply loves making money, and is very good at it. Even more, he enjoys showing off his wealth—in part so he can talk with people about money. He can channel his love for money and recognition by making as much as he can—and giving it to charity intelligently, thoughtfully, and publicly—thereby inspiring others to give well and generously.

Let's imagine a young man who just loves danger and is a devotee of base jumping and wing suiting. He is not constituted to be an office worker who enjoys evenings at home—and shouldn't try. Instead, he should consider becoming a rescue diver, a firefighter, or a combat soldier.

In addition to turning the negative into the positive through channeling, we can just as easily achieve more positivity by adding new qualities. The way to do so was articulated by God in Numbers, Rabbi Yochanan in the Talmud, and Maimonides in his commentary on the Mishnah—and validated by scientists like Professors Lally and Mathers and popularized by authors such as James Clear and Charles Duhigg.

We can decide what qualities we want to be part of our character and act consistently in accordance with those qualities. These actions will become habits, which will define what we do and who we are.

How might one change through habits? It is both practical and easy.

a. Identify the characteristic you want to change. For instance, I want to be more generous.
b. Identify the action that you will take that embodies that characteristic. For instance, I will give more to charity.
c. Select a modest goal that can be done continuously and habitually. For instance, I will give $3 a day.
d. Choose a cue, such as, "I will make the charitable gift every night after dinner."
e. Do the act. Every day after dinner, make an online donation of $3 to a meaningful charity.
f. Gradually increase the extent: Every two weeks, give fifty cents more.

This will work with almost anything from giving to charity, remembering names, being nicer, being a more attentive friend, being a more loving spouse, getting in shape, keeping a diary, studying a subject, and praying/meditating.

And it will work fast. Whether it will take (per Rabbi Yochanan) thirty days or (per Professor Lally) sixty-six days probably depends on the individual and the habit. But the logic is indisputable. If we focus on one characteristic at a time, that means that we will be able to develop at least five new characteristics a year. The math of self-transformation works.

9

The Theology of Linen and Why the Pittsburgh Penguins Got So Many Penalties in 1980

The Torah and Science of Clothing

What might we expect the Torah—or any religious text—to say about clothing? Most of us would instinctively say: not much. Clothing, we might think, is superficial. Perhaps there is a role for clothing around the concepts of ritual and modesty, but it is not something that the Bible should have much to say about. The Bible should counsel us to focus on who we are and not what we wear.

However, we do not have to read far into the Torah to learn that this is not the case. In Genesis 3:21–24, God decides that Adam and Eve must permanently leave the Garden of Eden and begin a journey in the wider world.

The story of a parent sending a child on a journey is a common one. We would expect the grandest of all such stories to begin with the parent offering thoughts of deep yearning, articulating carefully considered words of wisdom, and perhaps providing a memento to serve as a reminder of home. God does not do any of that. Instead, he prepares for Adam and Eve "garments of skin." And God doesn't stop there. The text tells us, "He clothed them."

Why would God want *clothing* to be the focus of Adam and Eve's journey into the entirely new world? Why would God want his last role in the Garden to be that of a clothier? The Torah will answer this question.

Esau's Best Clothes

Fast-forward to Genesis 28. The great matriarch Rebecca has a problem. Her aging and blind husband, Isaac, has sent Esau (the "older" of their twin sons) to catch game and prepare a meal for him. After this, Isaac intends to bless Esau. This is not a difficult assignment for Esau. He is, the text tells us, "a man of the field." In other words, he is a tough guy who thrives by struggling with the challenges of the outdoors.

Rebecca knows what is really happening, and it has nothing to do with dinner. Isaac, by having his son make him dinner, is enjoining Esau to do a mitzvah (good deed) to honor his father. Having performed the mitzvah, Esau will be ready for the paternal blessing—which is the eternal leadership of the Jewish people.

But there is a problem. Esau, who has the advantage of being loved by his father, is completely unqualified to receive the blessing and carry on the family name. Esau had already sold his birthright to Jacob for a bowl of raw soup. Moreover, the text is clear that it is not the visceral act of a hungry man. After Esau eats the soup, the text tells us that he "disparaged the birthright." Esau demonstrates his disregard for Jewish continuity shortly thereafter when he marries two Canaanite women. These intermarriages are, we learn in Genesis 26:35, "a source of grief to Isaac and Rebecca."

So, Jacob, the younger son, must receive the blessing from Isaac in Esau's stead. But Rebecca has another problem. Jacob, her favorite son, is not qualified either. He is, the Bible tells us, a "simple" man who "dwells in tents." He has had no involvement with practical realities and tough choices, and is lacking in worldly sophistication. Could such a person lead the Jewish people in a corrupt and dangerous world, full of peoples who would seek to destroy us and crush our mission? Not a chance.

Rebecca has to do something. In fact, she has to do two things. She has to ensure that her husband blesses Jacob instead of Esau. And she has to toughen Jacob up, qualifying him to receive the birthright in a difficult world. Further, she has to do both before Esau returns from the field with the meal.

Rebecca thinks fast and commands Jacob to trick Isaac into thinking that he is Esau so that Isaac will bestow the birthright upon Jacob.

She acts. Rebecca prepares the meal that Isaac requested from Esau, and gives it to Jacob to provide to his father. She covers Jacob's soft hands and the smooth part of his neck with goatskins so that Isaac will sense that the one with him is his hairy son Esau. And she dresses Jacob, the text tells us, in the "best clothes of Esau, her older son."

Why would Rebecca do this? Isaac, who is blind, cannot see what his son is wearing. One reason is that she wants her husband to smell Esau's clothing, as will indeed happen in Genesis 27:27. But this can't be all, as it would not explain why she tells Jacob to put on his brother's "best clothes." Any of Esau's clothes would have conveyed the smell.

Another explanation is offered by *Daat Zekenim*, a thirteenth-century French commentary. The *Daat Zekenim* suggests that the success of Jacob's mission depends on him *feeling* like Esau. And Jacob, Rebecca surmises, will be able to feel like Esau, to act like Esau, and to *be* Esau if he wears his brother's most personal clothing.[1]

Rebecca's strategy works. Jacob, dressed as Esau, successfully acts against his timid nature and, with cunning, tricks his father into giving him the blessing.

Becoming a Priest

The Torah, as a great work of literature, rarely explicitly provides the meaning of its stories or laws. It ignites our imagination, and allows us to ascertain the guidance it offers. One exception, however, appears in Exodus, and another in Numbers. And both concern clothing.

In Exodus 28, the Jews, freed from Egyptian slavery, are ready to actualize their freedom by building God's Tabernacle. God, the owner of the Tabernacle (and the world), gives instructions to Moses, who is fulfilling the role of general contractor.

God begins the instruction by saying, "Make sacred garments for your brother Aaron (the high priest) for dignity and honor." He continues, issuing very specific instructions about what is to constitute these garments: a breastplate; an apron; a robe; a woven tunic; a turban; and a sash made of gold, blue, purple, and scarlet yarn and fine linen.

Why does God care so much about what the high priest must wear? The answer is in the beginning of the instruction: "for dignity and honor." For "dignity and honor." But of what—the priest or the Tabernacle? The absence of a specification implies both. The priest will bring dignity and honor onto himself—creating the capacity to think, say, and do things befitting of the Tabernacle—if he dresses in accordance with the instructions provided in Exodus. The clothing will enable the priest to feel like the priest and, thus, to *become* the priest.

The Lessons of Linen

In Leviticus 6, the priests get their first major assignment in the Tabernacle—to administer the sacrifices. But before it is given, God has an instruction for them: "The Kohen (priest) shall don his fitted linen tunic, and he shall don linen breeches on his flesh." The clothing, as the early rabbinic interpreters made clear, had to be directly on his body. There were to be no undershirts. This arouses two questions. First, what is with all the linen—both in the description of the clothing of the high priest in Exodus 28, and of all the priests in Leviticus 6? Second, why is the clothing so important that the Torah specifies it must be directly on his body?

First: the linen. The twenty-first-century American sage Rebbe Menachem Mendel Schneerson explains that linen comes from flax and that the flax plant yields one stalk per seed. This alludes to the intrinsic oneness of God. Thus, the priests are being instructed by the Torah to *wear* their faith in the oneness of God. The clothing, therefore, is the way in which the high priests—the religious leaders of the community—can always *be* men of pure faith.[2]

By Leviticus 6, the career of linen in the Torah is just starting. In Leviticus 19:19, God instructs: "Do not wear clothing woven of two kinds of material." In Deuteronomy 22, Moses makes clear that the prohibited mixture is wool and linen. The seriousness of this commandment is reflected in the Talmudic ruling: "One who discovers diverse kinds [*kilayim*, i.e., a prohibited mixture of wool and linen], in his garment, must remove them even in the public marketplace (he may not wait until he reaches home)."[3]

Taking off one's clothing in the marketplace is a rather surprising Talmudic instruction! Why did the rabbis of the Talmud believe that public embarrassment is an acceptable price for avoiding the prohibition of wearing a wool and linen mixture? Why, for that matter, does the Bible prohibit mixing wool and linen at all?

The answer becomes apparent when considering prohibitions in Leviticus that immediately precede that text. These are prohibitions against mixing two kinds of animals and planting two kinds of seed in the same field. All of these prohibitions are about mixing things that do not belong together. It is through this instruction where we learn that separation—the opposite of mixing—is so important that it takes precedence over even the most basic tenets of modesty.

Why would separation be important? The Hebrew word for "holiness" is *kedusha*. Its root means to separate, set apart, or distinguish. In order to make something holy, we have to separate it from everything else. We do this each Friday night, when we separate Shabbat from the other days of the week. We do this under the marital canopy (the *chuppah*) when the groom, at the moment of matrimony, declares his bride to be separate from all other women. By separating wool and linen in our clothing, we are able to *embody* this indispensable component of sanctity.

Tzitzit: The Significance of the Blue and the White

In Numbers 15:39, God decrees that Jews should wear ritual fringes called *tzitzit*. The fringes are primarily white, with a blue fringe set amongst them. Why does the Torah command Jews to wear this strange article of clothing? The Torah tells us explicitly that "it shall be to you as a fringe, that you may look upon it, and remember all the commandments of the Lord, and do them; and that you seek not after your own heart and your own eyes, after which you go astray."

The function of the *tzitzit* is clear enough—it is to enable us to always be reminded of the commandments. Why do they have to be blue and white? White, as the contemporary sage Rabbi Meir Soloveichik says, is the color of clarity. And blue? The Talmudic sage Rabbi Meir explains: "Because blue resembles the sea, and the sea resembles the sky, and the sky resembles God's Throne of Glory." White signifies clarity and blue signifies the heavens.[4]

What, then, is the significance of *combining* the blue and the white? Rabbi Meir Soloveichik explains that the combination of white and blue teaches us how we are to approach the Torah. We are to do so with a sense of awe and mystery—as we react when we contemplate the heavens. This is the blue. And we are to do so with the clarity that is produced by the successful exercise of our human reason. This is the white. Lest anyone think that our great guidebook for life is all mystery or all rationality—or that mystery and rationality are contradictory—the accessory that the Torah has Jewish men wear teaches a lesson: God wants us to combine and synthesize them.[5]

Observant Jewish men, by wearing *tzitzit*, are not only reminding themselves of the existence of the commandments. They are teaching themselves that the commandments are manifested through a synthesis of mystery and rationality.

The Science

The Penguins Switch Uniforms

The year 1979 was a great one for Pittsburgh sports. The Steelers won the Super Bowl, and the Pirates won the World Series. The Penguins started the hockey season with an expectant fan base. The Penguins, however, did not deliver. They won only nineteen of their first forty-nine games. They needed a change—and made the one that was entirely within their control. On January 30, 1980, they announced that they would change their uniforms. They would no longer wear white and blue. Instead, they would wear black and gold.[6]

The change did not work. They won only 35 percent of their remaining games. However, hockey analysts noted a different statistical change. Before the uniform switch, the team averaged eight penalty minutes a game. Following the change, they averaged twelve penalty minutes a game—a remarkable 50 percent increase.

This intrigued Cornell University professors Thomas Gilovich and Mark Frank. They asked whether or not there is a correlation between the uniform change and playing aggressively.

They examined the data from the National Hockey League (where all penalty minutes are the result of aggressive behavior) and the National Football League (where most penalty yards are awarded because of aggressive behavior). The period they examined was 1970 to 1986. Of the twenty-eight teams in the NFL, five wore black uniforms. These teams had the first, third, seventh, eighth, and twelfth most penalties. Of the twenty-three teams in the NHL, five wore black uniforms. These teams had the first, second, third, sixth, and tenth most penalties.[7]

So, can the color one wears determine—or at least massively influence—performance? Professors Gilovich and Frank devised an experiment. They told subjects that they were participating in a study about the psychology of competition. Half of the students were given white jerseys and the other half were given black jerseys. The teams then had to select from a list of twelve which game to play.

Some of the choices were aggressive activities (such as dart gun duels). Others were nonaggressive (such as shooting baskets). They found, in the words of a *Sports Illustrated* analysis, that "there was a huge difference" in what the teams chose. The teams that wore the black jerseys were far more likely to choose the aggressive games. Professors Gilovich and Frank concluded, "If the wearing of a black uniform can have such an effect in the laboratory, there is every reason to believe that it would have even stronger effects on the playing field (or rink)."[8]

These findings—from professional and amateur athletes—open the question: Is there anything unique about sports that makes athlete behavior susceptible to clothing choice? Or are the increased penalties that accrued to the Penguins and similarly attired teams emblematic of a much broader phenomenon?

"The Invasion of Body and Brain"

In 2012, Professors Hajo Adam and Adam Galinsky, then of Northwestern University, conducted an experiment. They conceived of "attention-related tasks" and divided undergraduates into three groups to perform them. They asked one set of students to wear a white coat described as a doctor's coat. They asked another set of students to wear the same coat but described it as a painter's coat. A third set did not wear the coat at all but instead had it placed in front of them on a table.

Given that the students were drawn at random from the same pool, there is every reason to expect that they would have performed very similarly. And that was true of two groups: the group whose participants thought that they were wearing a painter's coat and the group whose participants were not wearing the coat. The group wearing the "doctor's coat" performed significantly better. How did this happen? Professors Adam and Galinsky conclude, "Clothes invade the body and brain, putting the wearer into a different psychological state . . . You have to wear the coat, see it on your body, and feel it on your skin for it to influence your psychological processes."[9]

Clothes "invade the brain and body." This theory would explain why the ancient rabbis commanded us to strip in the marketplace rather than wear a combination of wool and linen. And additional social science research sheds further modern insight on this bold claim.

In 1998, Professor Barbara Fredrickson of the University of North Carolina at Chapel Hill and several colleagues put male and female college students in individual dressing rooms. They had half the students put on sweaters and the other half put on swimsuits. They then gave each of the students, individually, a math test. The result was that the women in the swimsuits felt "disgusted," "ashamed," or "disgraced"—or, as described by Professor Fredrickson, "objectified." The men just felt "foolish." The consequence: The women wearing the sweaters did significantly better than those wearing the swimsuits. There was no difference among the men.[10]

In 2014, Professor Michael Kraus and several colleagues had male Yale students engage in a mock negotiation over the buying and selling of a hypothetical factory. Those who dressed in the clothes they came with made an average profit of $1.58 million. Those who changed into sweatpants and sandals made an average profit of $680,000. Those who changed into suits made an average profit of $2.1 million. The difference can be attributed to the more formally dressed students being more confident in the value of the factory.[11]

These results were confirmed a decade later, in a study led by Professor Michael Slepian of Columbia Business School. Professor Slepian and his colleagues found that students in an experiment were better able to think creatively and have a broader conception of opportunities and challenges when dressed formally.[12]

The fact that clothing changes can profoundly influence activities as different as hockey playing, test performance, and mock negotiating validates the conclusion of Professors Adam and Galinsky that clothing "invades the brain." But this raises another question. *How and why* is clothing so psychologically impactful? The mechanism was discovered in 2006 by Professor Bettina Hannover of the Free University of Berlin. Professor Hannover divided student participants in an experiment into two groups. One was told to come ready to participate in an experiment while dressed in formal clothes. The other was told to come dressed casually.

The catch: The students, and the clothing they wore, were the experiment. When the subjects arrived, the researchers asked them to describe themselves by responding quickly to trait adjectives. The result was that those who dressed formally used words like "cultivated," "accurate," and "strategic" to describe themselves. Those who dressed casually used words such as "easygoing," "clumsy," and "tolerant." It seems, then, that our most fundamental self-conception is profoundly influenced by what we are wearing at the moment. And our self-conception is significantly responsible for how we perform or behave in almost all circumstances.[13]

Enclothed Cognition

In the 2010s, a new discipline began taking hold in universities: fashion psychology. There are now fashion psychology programs at Purdue, Pepperdine, Arizona State, the London School of Fashion, and other universities. One of the major focuses of study within fashion psychology is "enclothed cognition"—the study of how our clothing interacts with our thinking.

One of the leaders in the field of enclothed cognition is Professor Karen Pine of the University of Hertfordshire. One of the questions that Professor Pine and other enclothed cognition scholars have asked is: Why do we dress as we do? This question became important because of studies that show how the "aesthetic evaluation of garments" (how clothing looks) accounts for only 10 percent of our clothing decisions.[14]

A more significant determinant is revealed by a study from the University of Hertfordshire discussed by Professor Pine. In that study, forty-five young adults came to a venue wearing whatever they wanted. The students were photographed and completed a "Positive and Negative Affect Scale" to articulate their mood that day. The scale contained words that describe moods such as "ashamed," "excited," and "jittery." The subjects rated how their feelings corresponded with each word on a 1 to 5 scale.

The photographs, with the faces pixeled out, were presented to observers. This meant, Professor Pine explained, "That the observers were judging little more than a faceless, static, clothed body." Observers, she reports, were able to recognize when a subject was experiencing negative emotions and were even better at identifying people in a positive mood.

This discovery, along with that of Professor Hannover, leads to a conclusion about how we select our clothing in the morning. We open our closet with a set of feelings that match our self-conception. Then, we (probably unwittingly) select clothing that corresponds to our mood and self-conception. The result is manifest in how we feel, act, and perform throughout the day.

These discoveries lead to intriguing questions: Can we reverse the usual process? Can we first decide how we would like to feel, act, and perform, and then select clothing that will influence what we do and who we become?

NFL Hall of Fame cornerback Deion Sanders thinks so. He said, "If you look good, you feel good. If you feel good, you play good. If you play good, they pay good."[15]

Kesha Linder, a fashion merchandising expert who has worked at Gap, Victoria's Secret, and ThredUp, thinks so. She says, "If I'm feeling down, I usually dress up to feel more put together. Tuning in to how you feel each morning can help you dress for success."[16]

Are Mr. Sanders and Ms. Linder correct? Professor Pine concludes from her research that "when we put on a piece of clothing we cannot help but adopt some of the characteristics associated with it, even if we [are] unaware of it."[17]

The implications are very practical and just as profound. Professor Pine, writing about women, posits it is plausible to contemplate "a wardrobe of 'happy clothes,' as protection against ever feeling miserable again."

What would be in such a wardrobe of happy clothes that can be an antidote against "ever feeling miserable again"? Professor Pine suggests the following:

- A well-cut dress in a beautiful fabric
- Jewelry that will stand out and make one feel special
- Natural fibers (linen, cotton, silk, and wool) and colors such as sky blue, leaf green, and sunshine yellow that link us to nature
- Playful patterns that resurrect the carefree feelings of childhood
- Mismatched items (such as a leather jacket over a dress) to trigger the brain's desire for novelty

- Flat shoes that are associated with adventurous travel
- Flowered prints that "glow with health"

If changing one's clothes can easily make one happier, then is shopping a solution to depression? It need not be. The solution to the problem is likely in one's closet now. Professor Pine writes that women who are unhappy and stressed neglect over 90 percent of their wardrobe.[18]

Professor Pine's analysis pertains to how clothing can be a force against misery and for fostering happiness. How about the kind of commercial success that Professors Kraus and Slepian studied? A 2022 University of Texas analysis, drawing from multiple studies, concludes, "It's clear that the way a person dresses can affect how successful they are." The analysis recommends four practices:

- **Choose quality over quantity.** Start with the basics, like black dress pants, a tailored blazer, and a well-fitted pair of jeans. Avoid fast fashion, since they're usually poor quality and go out of style after one season.
- **Maintain a clean, tailored appearance.** Choose clothes that fit you perfectly, or get them tailored. Make sure your clothes are always clean and pressed. Take care of your clothes, always washing and storing them properly. Choose colors and patterns that complement each other. A clean, well-arranged outfit contributes to an elegant appearance.
- **Don't wear logos.** Choose clothes that are classic, versatile, and elegant but don't have any prominent logos.
- **Dress up.** If you always dress up just a bit more than necessary, you'll stand out and look like you're someone important. Nobody regrets being the best dressed in the room. That doesn't mean you have to wear formal attire all the time. But put effort into all of your outfits, and add accessories that show some personality and style.[19]

"Dressing Like Players? Really?"

Fashion psychology might be a new discipline, but its central insight has permeated popular culture for some time. Cosplay is a combination of the words "costume" and "play" and refers to the practice of dressing up as one's favorite fictional character such as Spider-Man or Harley Quinn. Cosplaying became a phenomenon in the 1980s among attendees at science fiction conventions. There are now an estimated five million Americans who participate in cosplay. This industry of clothing, makeup, and accessories exceeded $5 billion in 2021 and is expected to grow to almost $25 billion by 2030. And cosplaying is even more popular in China, South Korea, and Japan.[20]

Why do people spend so much time and money on cosplaying? Professor Robert Muller of York University wrote, "The psychological transformation of dressing like a beloved character is a compelling motivation and is cited by cosplayers as one reason it is fulfilling—the exploration of the identity of a fictional character."[21]

Even though the cosplaying community is quite large, it can still be considered a subculture. Yet, its foundational impulse—to become someone else through attire—has dominated the most mainstream of American activities.

In the 1970s, Jim Liebe was running his family business, the R. J. Liebe Athletic Lettering Company. His parents had founded the company, which designed team uniforms (particularly by sewing names and letters on the back of jerseys), in 1933.

Jim Liebe discovered that there was an alternative to sewing on the back of jerseys. This product, known as Vinflex, is a heat-transferring process that enabled names and numbers to stick to jerseys. Vinflex made the sewing obsolete and enabled the mass production of jerseys with names and numbers. Little did he know that his innovation would unlock or create a latent desire, and create a huge industry.[22]

A glance at photos of major sports events in the 1950s shows fans dressed in suits and ties. Today, fans at World Series games do not dress that way. One reason for the change is the general shift away from formal clothing, as men rarely wear suits and ties even to work. But the dominant attire at many professional sports games has not been replaced with nothing. It has been replaced by player jerseys, enabled by the process pioneered by Jim Liebe. The industry of licensed sports apparel is now over $30 billion a year.[23]

In 2016, Tim Layden analyzed fan attire for *Sports Illustrated*. He wrote, "Over the last four decades, American sports fans have transformed themselves from a populace that dresses almost exclusively in civilian clothing and pays to watch athletes perform in uniform, to one that dresses—in significant numbers—exactly like those athletes."

He continues: "Jersey-wearing by fans is such normative behavior in the modern sports culture that its absurdity—dressing like players? Really?—has long been snowed under by its ubiquity."[24]

Why do fans dress in the uniforms of their favorite players and teams? Mr. Layden answers in the title of his *Sports Illustrated* article: "We Are What We Wear."

Secrets of the Great Performers

Question: What do Peter Criscuola, Tiger Woods, Michael Jordan, and Tom Wolfe have in common? One answer: their excellence in their very different crafts. The deeper answer: the way they achieved that excellence.

Peter Criscuola was born in late 1945, in Brooklyn. He grew up wanting to play the drums like Gene Krupa—the great big band performer who played with Benny Goodman and Tommy Dorsey. Like Marion Robert Morrison (John Wayne), Lucille Fay LeSueur (Joan Crawford), Margarita Carmen Cansino (Rita Hayworth), Dino Crocetti (Dean Martin), and Anthony Benedetto (Tony Bennett), Mr. Criscuola took an Americanized name when he began performing. He assumed the name Peter Criss and became a star, but not through urbane songs like Goodman/Krupa's "Sing, Sing, Sing." He became the drummer for the metal band Kiss.

How did Peter Criss transform from a nice boy from Brooklyn into one of the wildest drummers of all time? Two words: "cat makeup." In his memoir, *Makeup to Breakup*, Mr. Criss explained:

> When I put on that cat makeup, I truly was transformed. Forget about Peter Criscuola, the kid from Brooklyn. He didn't exist. I believed I was a superhero, the most iconic cat of all cats, sitting up there overlooking my prey . . . It was insane power tripping. My arms felt stronger. I was really transformed into this powerhouse of

> energy. I couldn't hit my drums hard enough. It was almost scary to feel that much power.[25]

Golf fans have noted that Tiger Woods always competes wearing a red polo shirt on Sunday tournaments. He explains that his mother told him that it is his power color.[26]

Tiger Woods's sometimes golfing buddy Michael Jordan wore a new pair of sneakers before every basketball game. It was not because a once-worn sneaker would make him more effective. Mr. Jordan explained, "The reason I chose to do that is because . . . [when] you put those shoes on for the first time, it's like you feel energetic, you feel like you have something you can actually showcase. Well, I wanted that feeling every game."[27]

The new sneakers were not Mr. Jordan's only strategic clothing choice. He also wore his University of North Carolina practice shorts under his NBA shorts during every game. In doing so, he was able to channel his college coach Dean Smith, about whom he said, "He was more than a coach—he was my mentor, my teacher, my second father. Coach was always there for me whenever I needed him and I loved him for it. In teaching me the game of basketball, he taught me about life."[28]

Tom Wolfe, one of the greatest ever American writers, was famous for his white suits. Mr. Wolfe always wore white suits when out, but how about when he wrote his books in the privacy of his study?

I asked his daughter, Alexandra Wolfe Schiff, about her father's clothing convention. She replied:

> My father didn't wear a white suit to work but he did wear a navy, gray, or brown suit, or checkered. Later in his life he wore slacks with a beautiful silk paisley smoking jacket over his high collared Oxford shirt. And then his "casual" office attire was navy slacks with a white Cuban guayabera he had custom made. But he never wore jeans or sweatpants or anything casual for work. He'd even change to go to the gym and come back, shower and put the suit back on for dinner with my mother and then more work after dinner.[29]

Reflection

The Torah, as we have discussed, is not a history book or a science book. Nor is it a fashion catalog—but a guidebook that seeks to enable us to live happier, better, and more meaningful lives. For thousands of years, we might have wondered why a guidebook would focus so much on clothing. Why would God send Adam and Eve from the Garden with "garments"? Why would Rebecca dress Jacob in Esau's *best* clothes? And why was the prohibition on mixing wool and linen so important that we are to strip in the marketplace to comply with it?

In the twenty-first century, social science, exemplified by the practices of Michael Jordan, Peter Criss, the Pittsburgh Penguins, and sports fans everywhere, has demonstrated just what the Author of the Torah taught. We become what we wear.

The implications of this now proven Torah truth are profound. One of the great questions of human development is, *What can I do to make myself better?* This can, of course, refer to being happier, mentally healthier, more productive, more confident, or any number of other things. Many people have tried solutions from yoga to therapy, from meditation to medication, from gratitude journals to exercise.

There is a place for all of these techniques, and many others. Yet, the Bible and modern science are telling us that one of the easiest places to look for self-improvement is our closet. If a woman wants to feel happier, she can follow the instructions of Professor Pine and put a leather jacket over a floaty dress. If she wants to write with discipline, she can put on a blazer over a tailored skirt. If she is working from home, she should dress as if she is at the office. If she is playing in a big game, she can Be Like Mike and wear the pair of shorts given to her by the early coach who first told her that she is a winner. We can all choose to dress in accordance with our aspirations and reap the benefits of enclothed cognition.

10

The Core of the Commandments and the Dashboard Jesus

The Torah and Science of Reminders

In Numbers 6:5, God instructs Moses to tell the Jewish people, "A man or woman who wrongs another in any way, and so commits treachery toward Hashem, must confess . . ." At first, this seems like a passage that one would expect from any religious text. It is an instruction that people should not wrong each other, and if they do, they should confess.

Its other message, which is right there in the text, is completely stunning. It is embedded in the phrase "toward Hashem." By characterizing all acts of wronging another as a "treachery toward Hashem," the Torah is making the bold claim that one who wrongs another is not just committing an interpersonal foul. He is assaulting God.

Consequently, everything we say and do has moral consequences that rise to the level of divine interest. That certainly imputes a gravity to our decisions. But what does it imply about the *difficulty* of moral decisions? Perhaps everything. If the hundreds of moral decisions that we make every day were hard, we would drive ourselves crazy. Consequently, the vast majority of moral decisions must be easy.

Indeed, they are. We know that we should be honest in our dealings, patient with our children, faithful to our spouse, generous with our resources, truthful with our words, honorable to our parents, loving to strangers, and that we should eat responsibly, look both ways before crossing the street, never text and drive, and pick up the laundry from the bedroom floor.

The fundamental moral challenge, therefore, is not knowing what is right and wrong. It is getting ourselves to do what we know is right. And the Torah has a solution, which it introduces in early Genesis, and emphasizes and illustrates throughout.

The Rainbow

In Genesis 9, God announces a major decision. The flood, which had just destroyed the world except for Noah, his family, and the animals they were instructed to save, would be a onetime event. "Never again," God says, "will life be destroyed by the waters of a flood."

This is not to say that God will be satisfied with mankind. On the contrary, it seems as if God realizes that he will be inclined to destroy the world again. So, in Genesis 9:14–15, he announces a solution to the problem of being tempted to destroy the world after committing not to. "And it shall come to pass, when I bring a cloud over the earth, that the bow shall be seen in the cloud: *and I will remember My covenant*, which is between Me and you and every living creature of all flesh; and the waters shall no more become a flood to destroy all flesh." The purpose of the rainbow is to serve as a reminder to God.

Why, the reader is led to wonder, would *God* need a reminder? Surely he remembers even without the rainbow! The Torah is not a guidebook for God. It is a guidebook for us. And the purpose of the rainbow is to teach us that if even God needs a reminder to do what he knows he should and should not do, then so do we.

We learn in the Book of Numbers what our equivalent of a rainbow might be.

Quite a "Following Incident"!

As noted in in the chapter of this book on clothing, God commands Jewish men to wear ritual fringes (*tzitzit*). But why? God explains, "It shall be to you as a fringe, that you may look upon it, and *remember* all the commandments of the Lord, and do them; and that you seek not after your own heart and your own eyes, after which you go astray" (Numbers 15:39).

How might this work?

Rabbi Natan in the Talmud anticipates this question. He says, "Go and learn from the following incident concerning the mitzvah of ritual fringes."

The incident: A man once traveled overseas to visit a renowned prostitute. He sent the payment in advance—four hundred gold coins. After arriving at the prostitute's abode, he saw that she was the most beautiful woman he had ever seen. She was lying on the top of a bunk bed with several ladders to climb in between. The man began climbing with great anticipation and excitement. He was ready, she was ready, and then, as he ascended, his ritual fringes (*tzitzit*) slapped him in the face.

The young man, being reminded of the commandments, stopped in his place—painfully aware of the sin he was about to commit. He explained to the prostitute why he could not continue. The prostitute was so impressed that she ended up converting to Judaism and marrying the young man.[1]

The boy got the girl, and we received a lesson in the power of reminders. Even a single reminder, like the *tzitzit*, can enable a young man to conquer the most powerfully tempting sin.

The Core of All the Commandments

The ritual fringes are just one of the prominent reminders in Jewish practice. Other reminders include the festivals of Pesach and Sukkot, hearing the shofar, making kiddush on Friday night, reciting the Shema twice daily, and affixing a mezuzah to the doorpost. The importance of reminders in the biblical imagination is captured by the twelfth-century sage Abraham ben Meir Ibn Ezra. He said, "The core of all the commandments is the improvement of character—and the majority of them are essentially reminders."[2]

That, according to one of the most well-respected authorities in Jewish history, is the biblical vision for each of us: Improve your character, primarily through reminders.

Could reminders actually be that important a factor in our behavior and our character? Cue the twenty-first-century science.

The Science

Priming

In 1982, John Bargh of Yale University and Paula Pietromonaco of the University of Massachusetts published a study in the *Journal of Personal and Social Psychology* entitled, "The Influence of Trait Information Presented Outside of Conscious Awareness on Impression Formation."[3]

The title of the study probably never commanded the attention of any reader. But it is frequently cited, referenced, and discussed two generations later. Its importance can be attributed to it being one of the first inquiries into what became a major theme of psychological research and discovery: priming. Priming asserts that exposure to a stimulus (which might be just a word) *reminds* us of a set of related ideas—which, in turn, determines how we think or act.

Its applications are very broad.

A 1996 study by Professor Bargh showed that people who are primed with terms related to the elderly (gray, Florida, lonely, knits, forgetful, bald, and wrinkled) walked slower down the hallway than did those who were not primed.[4]

A 2006 study by Professor Dan Ariely of Duke University had students write down the last two digits of their Social Security number, and then participate in an auction. The students with higher Social Security numbers bid more than those with lower numbers.[5]

A 2010 study by Professors Spike W. S. Lee and Norbert Schwarz of the University of Michigan found that those who were told to lie to a hypothetical interlocutor in an email were more likely to buy soap than mouthwash, and people who were told to lie to a hypothetical interlocutor in a voicemail were more likely to buy mouthwash than soap.[6]

A study reported by Professor Daniel Kahneman of Princeton University in 2011 found that people who were primed to think about food were more likely to fill in so_p with a "u" than with an "a." People who were recently thinking about washing are likely to do the opposite.[7]

A 2012 study by Professors Promotesh Chatterjee of the University of Kansas and Randall Rose of the University of South Carolina primed one group of students to think about credit cards and the other to think about cash. Those primed with credit cards focused more on the benefits rather than the cost of the product and selected the more expensive items from among the available choices. Those primed with cash did the opposite.[8]

A consideration of the aforementioned studies of priming might, in the context of thinking about Torah guidance, lead one to say: "So what?" After all, it is of no great moral magnitude that students who are primed to think of their Social Security numbers bid more or less in an auction as a result.

Perhaps. But the larger message of priming is that we think and act in accordance with what we are reminded of. How might this discovery be morally consequential? Enter Harvard Business School professor Deepak Malhotra.

The Sunday Effect

In 2010, Professor Malhotra worked with an online charity auction company to assess when and why people raise their bids. He sent out a questionnaire, which included asking respondents if they attended religious services, and, if so, when. The result was that 73 percent of the respondents who attended a house of worship did so on Sunday.

Professor Malhotra then had the auction company send out messages to encourage respondents to rebid often. One message was oriented to their competitive spirit: "The competition is heating up! If you hope to win, you will have to bid again. Are you up for the challenge?" The rates of rebidding were the same among secular and religious respondents, on every day of the week.

The other message that he tested was oriented to their charitable spirit: "We hope you will continue to support this charity by keeping the bidding alive. Every extra dollar you bid in the auction helps us accomplish our very important mission."

The response rates to the charitable message were the same among secular and religious recipients on six days of the week. On Sunday, however, religious respondents were *four times more likely* to rebid pursuant to the charitable message than their secular counterparts. Professor Malhotra's conclusion was that religious people were "nicer" when "religion is on their minds."[9] Professor Malhotra termed his discovery "the Sunday effect."

In 2015, MIT professor Erik Duhaime studied how Moroccan merchants allocated money that he gave them. The merchants varied in their allocations except under one condition. When the Muslim call to prayer was audible—when Muslims were *reminded* of the expectations of their faith—*everyone* surveyed gave *all* of the money to charity.[10]

When Pornography Is Consumed

Since the dawn of the internet, every observer of online behavior has agreed on at least one thing: Pornography is popular. In 2023, the three most popular websites, according to Statista, were Google, YouTube, and Facebook. A close fourth was Pornhub, and right behind it was Xvideos. The genre keeps coming in strong, with Spankbang in eleventh and Xnxx in fourteenth.[11]

No wonder Pornhub reported that the amount of pornography uploaded to only its site would fill the memory of every iPhone in the world.[12]

In 2019, Harvard Business School professor Ben Edelman asked: Who is consuming all of this pornography? He determined that online pornography is popular in states with both high and low church attendance. After establishing that online pornography is popular everywhere, Professor Edelman then asked: *When* is it popular? One might think that usage would spike on the weekends when people have more time for such things.

Professor Edelman found that the purchase of pornography subscriptions declines on Sundays for one class of people—those who live in zip codes with high church attendance. This finding was confirmed in 2015 by data from the online pornography company adultempire.com, which disclosed that only 6.58 percent of its weekly visits occurred on Sunday (compared with roughly 20 percent on Saturday and Wednesday).[13]

So, when churchgoers are *reminded* of what they believe about pornography, their usage significantly declines. But the Sunday effect does not last even through Monday, which is Pornhub's busiest day of the week. Professor Edelman writes, "This analysis suggests that, on the whole, those who attend religious services shift their consumption of adult entertainment to other days of the week, despite on average consuming the same amount of adult entertainment as others."[14]

Reminders, the data suggests, can be very effective, but only if, like the *tzitzit* that the Torah commands Jews to always wear, they are deployed constantly.

Reflection

When we consider reminders, we often think tactically. We might put a reminder in our phone to ensure that we pick up milk before coming home. We might download an app that sounds an alarm when we leave a car to ensure that we do not leave a child there. We might ask the dentist's office to text us in six months to set up the next appointment.

These are all good, and important. But there are indications in our practices and culture that suggest that there is something more to reminders. For instance, every knowledgeable Jew is aware that gossip (*lashon hara*) is a grave sin. Strong prohibitions against gossip exist throughout the New Testament as well. So, is gossip still a common problem, even among observant Jews and Christians? We all know the answer.

Consequently, many observant Jews affix an anti-gossip sticker in a particularly vulnerable spot—the telephone. Others place their cellular phones in a case with the words "Lashon Hara Proof 100%" on it.

Another common problem is that of automobile safety. In 1955, automobiles had become a major part of American life. So did the consequences of breaking the rules of the road. By the mid-1950s, more than 35,000 Americans were dying in road accidents every year.

In 1955, Father Gregory Bezy lost a nephew and niece in a car accident. He responded by creating the Sacred Heart Auto League. The League was devoted to making driver safety a quasi-religious obligation. It deployed a variety of tactics and programs, including a pledge and a prayer. But it was something else that became wildly popular and enduring. This is the small statue of Jesus, meant to be affixed to the car dashboard.[15]

There have been many variations of the dashboard Jesus since its debut in 1955. One of those is being sold now by the online retailer Archie McPhee. Its marketing copy describes its essential function very well:

> Each 5-1/4" Jesus figure has a metal spring with an adhesive base and is ready to be a reminder to love thy neighbor, even if that neighbor does not use a turn signal when entering your lane. Jesus will not judge you for the car you drive, but he may remind you to be a good Samaritan if you see someone with a flat tire on the side of the road. This bobbler won't just inspire you to be a better driver, but also a better person.[16]

Reminders sure seem to be, per Ibn Ezra, "the core of the commandments"—whatever the commandments to which one has committed himself.

All this leads to the question: How might we deploy reminders to become the kind of person we wish to be?

1. Consider a characteristic or behavior one would like to do more or less of. It could be driving carefully, giving to charity, refraining from gossip, generally "being holy," or any number of other things.
2. Consider what might be a clear and sharp reminder of the activity. For driving carefully, it might be a statue of Jesus or a photo of your children. For giving to charity, it might be using "Charity18" as an online banking password. For refraining from gossip, it might be affixing an anti-gossip sticker to our phone. For generally "being holy," a Jew might put *tzitzit* under his shirt and a Christian might put a cross around his neck or a biblical verse tattoo on his arm.
3. Implement the reminder.

If this sounds simple, it's because it is. The Torah, in which reminders are "the core of the commandments," is a book of highly practical guidance intended to enable us to become "a kingdom of priests and a holy nation." It stands to reason that the Torah should emphasize reminders, the social science should validate them, and that they should be easy to implement.

11

Why Judah Gets the Kingship and Jim Calhoun Does Not Land a Prize Recruit

The Torah and Science of 100% Responsibility

After creating mankind, God has one simple instruction for Adam and Eve: "Of every tree of the garden you may freely eat; but of the tree of knowledge of good and evil you must not eat thereof; for on the day you eat of it, you shall surely die."

A serpent, who the Torah tells us is the most cunning animal in the Garden, convinces Eve to taste the forbidden fruit. Eve then shares the fruit with her husband. God takes notice and asks Adam, "Have you eaten of the tree, of which I commanded thee that you shall not eat?"

If there was ever an opportunity for someone to admit a mistake and take responsibility, this is it. But this is not what Adam does. Instead, he blames Eve *and* God: "The woman whom *You* gave to be with me—she gave me of the tree, and I ate."

God immediately turns to Eve and asks, "What is this thing that you have done?"

Eve responds, "The serpent deceived me, and I ate."

It is a cascade of evading responsibility, and God is furious. He visits eternal punishment on each evader of responsibility. The serpent loses its legs and gains the enmity of humanity. Eve and all women after her are sentenced to "hard labor" in childbirth. Adam and his male progeny will have to contend with "thorns and thistles" in order to eat. And they are all banished from God's oasis—the Garden of Eden.

This constitutes the Torah's first teaching of social morality: We are all responsible. It is a clear lesson from God, but it is not quickly learned.

Immediately after Adam and Eve are banished, we meet their children—Cain and Abel. They each bring an offering to God. Cain brings an ordinary offering, and Abel brings the "choicest of his flock." God turns to Abel's offering favorably, and Cain despairs.

God says to Cain, "Why are you angry and why are you crestfallen? If you do what is right, will you not be accepted? But if you do not do what is right, sin is crouching at your door; it desires to have you, but you must rule over it." God signals to Cain that he is ultimately responsible for his own lot, and that he has the ability to improve. Cain decides to neither take responsibility nor to seek to improve. Instead, he decides to kill Abel.

God responds by posing to Cain a rhetorical question: "Where is your brother Abel?"

Cain could have apologized, repented, or taken responsibility in another way. Instead, he begins with a lie: "I do not know." He follows God's rhetorical question with one of his own. It would become the world's defining statement of refusing responsibility. "Am I my brother's keeper?"

God is furious. He banishes Cain, just as he did to his parents when they evaded responsibility.

Why God Punishes Joseph

In Genesis 37, Joseph (the talented and favorite son of Jacob) has a set of dreams. They are thinly disguised tales of his whole family bowing down to him. Joseph, whose maturity does not match his talents, tells his family of the dreams. His brothers, the text tells us, hate him for it.

Right after the disclosure of the second dream, Joseph, as instructed by his father, goes into the field to meet his brothers. Alone with their younger, brilliant, arrogant, and immature brother, they do not counsel Joseph about the virtues of discretion, humility, or family unity. They do not teach him how to properly express and direct his abundant talents. Instead, they throw him into a pit and sell him into slavery in Egypt.

In Egypt, Joseph secures a prize position for a slave when he is assigned to manage the house of Potiphar, one of the most powerful men in the empire. Potiphar's wife, attracted to Joseph, who the text describes as "handsome of form and handsome of appearance," tells the young slave to "lie" with her. He refuses, but she entreats him daily.

One day, Joseph goes into the house "to do his work." It is tantalizingly unclear what he considers his "work" to be that day. Does he, as the biblical scholar Leon Kass suggests, consider the "work" to be having sex with Potiphar's wife?[1]

The text does not say. But we know that "no man of the household staff" is present. We also know that Joseph, as the lead slave, could have had other slaves accompany him into the house. It is highly unlikely that Potiphfar's wife would have sexually solicited him if he were surrounded by others.

Joseph enters the house alone, where he meets Potiphar's wife. She again instructs him, "Lie with me." Joseph, the text tells us, refused. But the Torah gives us a subtle insight into the psychological drama playing in Joseph's mind and body. The word "refused" is chanted with a cantillation mark called a *shalshelet*, a symbol of hesitation that appears four times in the Torah. So, Joseph refuses—hesitatingly.

Spurned and scorned, Potiphar's wife grabs Joseph's robe and rips it off. She uses it as evidence that he tried to rape her. The palace authorities believe her, and send Joseph to prison.

A while later, two prisoners (the Pharaoh's wine steward and baker) tell Joseph of strange dreams they have. Joseph, ever the master of dreams, tells the wine steward that he will soon be freed and back in the Pharaoh's employ. He asks the wine steward to plead with Pharaoh to free him as well. Joseph makes his case: "I have done nothing for them to have put me in the dungeon."

The wine steward is, exactly when Joseph predicted, freed from prison. But the wine steward fails to advocate for Joseph—leaving Joseph a prisoner for two more years. Joseph's continued imprisonment leads to a question. Why does God keep Joseph imprisoned for another two years? One theory is that Joseph was too reliant on the wine steward and the Pharaoh freeing him, rather than God.[2] But this theory is unsatisfying. The Torah is clear that God wants each person to be his partner, and will act only after we make the initial effort. If anything, God would have appreciated Joseph's making the case for his freedom.

So, if the additional two years in prison are not a punishment for insufficient faith, what are they a punishment for? The answer lies in Joseph's words to the wine steward: "I have done *nothing* for them to have put me in this dungeon." He accepts no responsibility for his imprisonment.

Is his rejection of responsibility correct? He is innocent of the allegation made against him (attempted rape) and should not have been sent to prison. And, of course, his brothers were wrong to throw him into a pit—the entire reason he was in Egypt to begin with.

But does all of this absolve him of responsibility for his imprisonment? Had Joseph not behaved with such immaturity and arrogance, his brothers would likely not have thrown him in the pit. Had he decided, upon entering the house, not to sleep with his master's wife, he would have entered the house with another member of the presumably abundant staff. She would not have solicited him, he would not have rejected her, and she would not have been scorned. It is, therefore, very unlikely that she would have hated him sufficiently to frame him for rape. If she did, she would not have had the material (his robe) with which to do so.

So, is Joseph correct that he did "nothing" to contribute to his imprisonment? In the Torah's understanding of responsibility, no. He is not *completely* responsible for his imprisonment, but so what? He is *partially* responsible for his situation. And yet, he says, "I have done *nothing* for them to put me in this dungeon"—absolving himself of *all* responsibility. Consequently, God keeps him in prison for another two years.[3]

Why We Are Called "Jews"

In Genesis 38, there is an excursus from the Joseph narrative. Joseph's brother Judah leaves the family to dwell with his friend Hirah. Judah marries a local woman, and they have three sons. Judah arranges for his eldest son, Er, to marry a woman named Tamar. Er, after sinning against God, promptly dies. Judah, consistent with the custom of the time (called levirate marriage), has his second son, Onan, marry Tamar. Onan, too, does evil in God's eyes and similarly dies.

Judah then promises Tamar his third son, Shelah, but intentionally stalls in providing him—as he is mindful of what happened to his previous two sons who married Tamar. Tamar is left widowed and childless, waiting for a man who she knows will never be given to her and unable to marry anyone else due to the laws of levirate marriage.

Sometime thereafter, Judah procures the services of a woman he thinks is a prostitute—and provides his signet, wrap, and staff as collateral. But the prostitute is actually Tamar, who has disguised herself in order to sleep with Judah and bear a child. She disappears with the collateral.

Several months later, Judah is told that Tamar has become a prostitute and is pregnant. He demands she be brought before him and executed. Just before she is burned, Tamar presents Judah with the collateral. At this moment, Judah could have denied any recognition of them. Tamar would have been executed, and he would have been spared all public embarrassment.

Instead, he says, "She is more righteous than me!" He has *taken responsibility*—even at the cost of his reputation and honor. This assumption of responsibility will come to characterize Judah as a person and a leader.

Years later, Judah and his siblings travel to Egypt to get food for their family. They get an audience with the viceroy of Egypt, but have no idea that it is their long-lost brother Joseph. Joseph tells them that he will provide food for them if they return with their brother Benjamin.

The brothers go home and tell Jacob what happened. Jacob, aware of what happened the last time he sent a child of Rachel with his brothers, refuses to allow Benjamin to leave the home. Judah, who had defined himself by taking responsibility with Tamar, knows just what to say: "I myself will guarantee his safety; you can hold me personally *responsible* for him. If I do not bring him back to you and set him here before you, I will bear the blame before you all my life."

Jacob relents and allows Benjamin to go to Egypt, where Judah's acceptance of responsibility is soon put to the test. After the brothers return to Egypt, Joseph engineers a situation in which Benjamin is framed as a thief. Joseph decrees that the others are to return home and leave Benjamin behind as a slave. The brothers have a choice. Will they abandon their half-brother Benjamin like they did Joseph years before, or will they take responsibility for him?

Judah answers on behalf of the brothers. "What can we say? How can we prove our innocence? God has uncovered your servants' guilt. We are now my lord's slaves—we ourselves and the one who was found to have the cup" (Genesis 44:16). None of the brothers disagree.

Judah, in this statement, does not merely make good on his promise to his father to be responsible for Benjamin. He also establishes himself as the leader of the family by accepting responsibility on behalf of *all* the brothers.

Moments later, Joseph dramatically reveals his identity and reconciles with them. The entire family then settles in Egypt under the care and protection of the Pharaoh.

Years later, Jacob, on his deathbed, gives a blessing to all of his sons. The question is: To which son will he bestow the "scepter"—the kingship, that of eternal leadership? The likely candidates are Reuben (the firstborn) or Joseph (the favorite and the most successful).

Jacob selects neither. He chooses Judah because, in the words of Rabbi Yehonasan Gefen, Judah demonstrated "greatness in the area of taking responsibility." The mark of a Jewish king—the example that God wants the Jewish leader to set for the Jews, and the Jews for the world—is that of taking complete responsibility. And we are reminded of this obligation and the divine importance of it, every time we recognize ourselves as Jews—named after Judah, who distinguished himself by taking responsibility. This will be exemplified by Judah's descendant King David who, upon being confronted with his moral failings, declares "I have sinned against the Lord."[4]

The "One Man" Who Sins

The greatest leader in the Torah is Moses. He is distinguished for many qualities—including humility, resilience, courage, audacity, faith, and commitment. But in very different circumstances in Exodus and Numbers, we see another quality in Moses. It is this quality that will qualify him, as with Judah, in leadership of the Jewish people.

In Exodus 6, Moses gives the people the good news that God has decided to free them from Egyptian slavery. The people do not respond as expected. The biblical narrator tells us, "They did not hearken to Moses because of their shortness of breath [or spirit] and because of their hard labor" (Exodus 6:9).

Three verses later, Moses recounts the story to God but offers a completely different explanation for why the Jews are recalcitrant. "The Israelites would not listen to me; how then should Pharaoh heed me, me—who has faltering lips?" (Exodus 6:12).

Exodus 6:9 is very clear that the Jews were recalcitrant because they were crushed and exhausted by the slave experience to the point where they could not conceive of a better future. Why, then, does Moses tell God that the Jews were recalcitrant because he is a bad spokesman? Because he has become a true heir to Judah's legacy, and takes responsibility for everything he conceivably can. In Numbers 16, we see just how embedded this quality is in Moses.[5]

Numbers 16 tells of a rebellion against Moses. This rebellion is led by Korach, a populist leader who has no positive agenda. He just wants power.

Korach is joined in leadership by On, Datan, Abiram, and 250 other men. By Numbers 16:22, God decides that he has had enough with these rebels. He tells Moses and Aaron to step aside so that he can kill them. Moses, as he had done several times before when under siege by rebellious people, prays on their behalf. He says to God, "O God, the God who gives breath to all living things, will you be angry with the entire assembly when only *one man* sins?"

This raises the question: Who is the "one man"? The easy assumption is Korach—the leader of the rebellion. But that conclusion is challenged by the fact that we were told, at the beginning of the story, that Korach is joined by many people. So, who could the one man be?

The nineteenth-century sage Rabbi Menachem Mendel Hager (known as the Immrei Chaim) suggests a resolution. The "one man" who Moses says is responsible for the rebellion must be Moses himself. He must have concluded that he led the people in such a way as to induce the rebellion, and thus takes responsibility for the terrible set of events.[6]

Punished for Unintentional Sins?

As the Torah progresses, its Author makes clear that this assumption of complete responsibility—of taking it even when it could reasonably be deflected—is the task not just of Jewish leaders, but of all Jews.

In Leviticus 4:2, God decrees the various penalties for sins committed "unintentionally." Why would a sin committed *unintentionally* result in any blame, let alone require restitution? Because sins, regardless of the intentionality behind them, generally do not just happen. They often occur because of thoughtlessness, carelessness, negligence, or lack of self-awareness. All of those things, as well as anything else that might have led to a sin, are grounds for the acceptance of responsibility.[7]

There is one type of person singled out in Leviticus 4:2 for unintentionally sinning. This is the Kohen, the priest-teacher. A Kohen may have a sacred role, but he is just a man who commits sins and makes mistakes like everyone else. Consequently, the Torah is instructing that even—and perhaps especially—a Kohen must atone for an unintentional sin with an offering.

The Kohen, the text continues, must make his offering in a particular way. Leviticus 4:12 states, "He shall carry to a clean place outside the camp, to the ash heap, and burn it up in a wood fire." But why must a Kohen's sacrifice be taken outside the camp?

The thirteenth-century sage Jacob ben Asher (known as the Ba'al Haturim) explained that everyone would see the sin offering outside the camp. In so doing, they would understand the importance for everyone—even the high priest—of taking responsibility for one's actions.[8]

An Affair to Remember

In Numbers 5:11–31, the Torah tells the story of a woman who secludes herself with a man who is not her husband and then does so again after her husband expresses his discontent. The marriage is headed for divorce and needs God's intervention to save it.

Who is to blame? The text is clear that the woman bears the responsibility of having secluded herself inappropriately and having possibly committed adultery.

But the language of Numbers 5:12 suggests that the allocation of responsibility is not so simple. The verse says: "A man, a man [sic] whose wife shall go astray" (Numbers 5:12). Why is the term "a man" used twice in a row? Rabbi Efrem Goldberg of the Boca Raton Synagogue offers a convincing answer. The double use of the term "man" indicates that he injected too much of himself into the relationship and became unbearable. Hence, the woman sought intimacy elsewhere.

Was the woman right to choose adultery (or even the appearance of adultery) as a response to the man's behavior? Of course not. But the man was similarly wrong to lead her to seek affection elsewhere. Both the husband and the wife, the text is guiding us to realize, should accept full responsibility for the situation.[9]

The Continuing Legacy of an Unclaimed Corpse

In Deuteronomy 21, a question is posed: What is a society to do when an unclaimed corpse is found in the field that is not in an incorporated city but in a no-man's-land? The Torah prescribes a ritual. The elders and the judges of the nearby cities shall go out and measure their distance from the corpse. When they determine which is the nearest city to the corpse, "all the elders"—every leader—of the closest city shall wash his hands and atone.

The existence of this question and the solution suggests several lessons. First, no-man's-land exists legally—but not morally. The lesson is clear: We must look beyond our clearly marked domains for problems in the community, and take responsibility for them. When the precise allocation of responsibility is difficult to ascertain, everyone takes it.

Moreover, the Torah does not say that the "city" or any other group has to atone. Why not? Because cities and tribes and nations cannot take responsibility. Only individuals can. Hence, all the elders must wash their hands and atone upon finding that the corpse was closest to their city.

The Culture of Responsibility

In Numbers 5:6, God instructs Moses to tell the Jewish people, "A man or woman who wrongs another in any way, and so commits treachery toward Hashem, must confess."

Maimonides analyzes the commandment to confess by way of reference to Proverbs 28:13: "One who covers his sins will not be successful." Thus, Maimonides rules that one who has sinned against another person must "repent and [express] regret" to the person he has wronged.[10]

But there is a practical problem with this requirement of confessing publicly. It is well expressed by the twentieth-century spirits entrepreneur Thomas Dewar. He said, "An honest confession may be good for the soul, but it is bad for the reputation."[11]

This is true for taking responsibility generally. The things that are difficult to take responsibility for are bad. Therefore, a person might reasonably conclude that he will be better off if he does not confess, leaving the allocation of blame to be ambiguous, unknown, or attributed to someone else.

How, then, can we encourage the taking of responsibility? The Torah tradition anticipated and answered this challenge. Perhaps not surprisingly, it involves the even greater taking of responsibility.

Maimonides, who said that one must express regret to a person he wronged, also ruled that this confession is just the beginning of a process. He wrote, "It is forbidden for a person to be cruel and refuse to be appeased. Rather, he should be easily pacified, but hard to anger. When the person who wronged him asks for forgiveness, he should forgive him with a complete heart and a willing spirit."[12]

Thus, one who wrongs another has an obligation to accept responsibility and confess. The recipient of the confession has an equal responsibility to graciously accept the confession. This responsibility is so profound that Maimonides ruled that the recipient of a confession must treat the affront, once apologized for, as if it never happened. He says:

> It is an utter sin to tell a repentant person, "Remember your previous deeds," or to recall them in his presence to embarrass him or to mention the surrounding circumstances or other similar matters so that he will recall what he did. This is all forbidden. We are warned against it within the general category of verbal abuse which Torah has warned us against as [Leviticus 25:17] states: "A man should not mistreat his colleague."[13]

Why do recipients of apologies have such a profound responsibility to graciously accept them? There are two reasons. First, we will be likely to take responsibility and apologize when we can expect that it will be met with gracious acceptance. Second, we will be even more likely to take responsibility and apologize when we believe that doing so will—to reverse Thomas Dewar's formulation—*enhance* our reputation.

The result of these twin dynamics is, simply, a *culture of responsibility*. And this culture of responsibility extends far beyond the important obligation to offer and accept apologies. This culture of responsibility is embedded in one of the Talmud's most familiar dicta: *Kol Yisrael arevim zeh bazeh*—every Jew is responsible for one another. This idea informs every aspect of Jewish life, practice, and hope.

The holiest day of the Jewish year is Yom Kippur. This is the day when, as Rabbi Shaul Rosenblatt describes succinctly, "We take responsibility."[14] We formally apologize for three kinds of sins: sins we are likely to have committed (e.g., "foolish talk"), sins that we might have committed (e.g., "eating and drinking [sinfully]"), and for sins that we very well might not have committed (e.g., "lewdness").

Why should a proper Jewish grandmother apologize for the sin of lewdness? The answer is revealed in how we all apologize for all of the sins. We do not atone in the singular and apologize "for the sins *I* committed against you through lewdness." Instead, we do so in the plural: "for the sins *we* committed against you through lewdness." The proper grandmother, when she makes this atonement, is not apologizing for personal lewdness. She is apologizing, on behalf of other Jews, and for her failure to sufficiently help other Jews to behave better. And this sense of mutual responsibility is so powerful that she is confessing as if she, herself, were lewd.

This culture of responsibility, as expressed through the teaching that every Jew is responsible for every other Jew, has ramifications that extend far beyond the confessing of sins. It accounts for why Jews in the West worked so hard and so effectively to liberate Jews in the Soviet Union; why the state of Israel takes extraordinary measures to bring home the few remaining Jews in places where they are unsafe; why Jews everywhere contribute funds to ensure that every Jew can enjoy a proper Pesach celebration; and why Jews around the world feel personally wounded when Jews anywhere are threatened or harmed.[15]

It is through this culture of responsibility, so clearly and fully articulated in the Torah and through the Jewish tradition, that there is such a thing as the Jewish people.

The Science

Someone Is Responsible . . . but It's Not Me

Rabbi Jonathan Sacks noted that a modern notion of responsibility has been largely determined by three men: Baruch Spinoza, Karl Marx, and Sigmund Freud. Although their philosophies were very different, each derived from the same premise: that man is not responsible for his actions. Spinoza believed that human action is determined by innate instincts and biological drives (now called genetic determinism). Marx believed that human action is driven by economic forces. And Freud believed that human action derives from childhood experience.[16]

Where might society be in this debate?

In October of 2021, the actor Alec Baldwin was filming a movie called *Rust.* While acting in a scene, he held a gun. This gun was, apparently unbeknownst to Baldwin, loaded. He aimed it straight at people in the crew and fired. A moment later, the cinematographer Halyna Hutchins was dead.

Mr. Baldwin soon thereafter gave a national interview to George Stephanopoulos about the event. He explained, "Someone is responsible for what happened . . . but I know it's not me."[17]

Alec Baldwin may not have been legally culpable for the crime of murder or manslaughter. But his abdication of *any* responsibility, despite the fact that he aimed and fired the gun, was not surprising to anyone who has lived in the broad culture from which that statement emanated.

Mr. Baldwin's claim is just a version of what Mark Memmott of NPR calls "the king of non-apologies"—the statement: "Mistakes were made." It has been uttered by Presidents Grant, Reagan, Bush, Clinton, and countless others in politics, not to mention other domains. And it is the opposite of the Torah's instruction that confessions must be made with reference to the specific sin.[18]

One who says, "Mistakes were made," receives a guarantee. His statement will not satisfy anyone and will lead to him being held in lower esteem. Yet the impulse to deny responsibility is so intense that people still say it all the time.

Why, then, would a presumably smart man like Alec Baldwin deny *all* responsibility for the death of a colleague he shot? Why would US presidents from both parties ranging across three centuries say, "Mistakes were made"? Why would respectable and intelligent people persist in denying responsibility when everyone knows that doing so will cost them the respect that they seek through their denials? There are at least four reasons.

1: Accepting Responsibility Is Bad for the Reputation

Per Thomas Dewar, apologizing is—outside of a culture of responsibility—bad for the reputation. An apology without a robust expectation of a full acceptance means that the bad act—which could have been denied, obfuscated, or ignored—remains attached to its doer and harms his reputation. One's reputation is a crucial determinant of whether he receives society's most prized tangible and intangible rewards—from a mate to a job. Consequently, people become so habituated to shirking responsibility that even intelligent and thoughtful people say transparently laughable things such as, "Mistakes were made."

2: Denying Responsibility Is in Our Evolutionary Nature

Stelian Nenkov is a regional research director of the investment firm WorldQuant. Mr. Nenkov points out that while people started evolving between 4 to 7 million years ago, the human brain is the same three-pound organ that our ancestors had 200,000 years ago. The problem: We only emerged from being hunters and gatherers 12,000 years ago.

Consequently, we have brains that are optimized for short-term thinking—the eating, mating, and avoiding of predators that governed the life of the hunter-gatherer man. But we live in a modern world that calls for long-term investments—financially, socially, and otherwise.[19]

What does this insight have to do with taking responsibility? A 2012 study led by Professor Tyler Okimoto of the University of Queensland in Australia and several colleagues is illustrative. They asked a fundamental question: Is it in one's short-term interest to apologize?

They split a research population into four groups and asked each to recall "a time when you did something that upset someone." Each group was then prompted to either recall a scenario where they either apologized, actively refused to apologize, or actively decided to do nothing. A baseline group was not prompted to think about their response. Participants then reported on a 1 to 7 scale how strongly they felt about themselves in regard to notions of power/control, value integrity, and self-esteem.

The results: Apologizing, they found, leads to a diminished sense of power/control, diminished feelings of value integrity (courageous, sincere, passive), and lower self-esteem. Indeed, they reported that "the harm-doers who recalled events where they had refused to apologize reported feeling more powerful." Consequently, they concluded that a rational, *short-term*, self-interest-maximizing actor would do well not to apologize and to deny responsibility.[20]

3: Denying Responsibility Helps Our Self-Conception

The second reason why people persist in denying responsibility was discovered by Dr. Carol Tavris. Dr. Tavris is a psychologist whose work over the past twenty years has centered around why, when, and how we do and do not accept responsibility for our mistakes. The title of her magnum opus (coauthored with Elliot Aronson): *Mistakes Were Made (But Not by Me).*

They found that an acceptance of responsibility concedes one of three things: that one did something stupid, bad, or wrong. The acceptance of any of these three often generates what psychologists call cognitive dissonance, with the dissonance being the distance between our self-conception (which is generally positive) and the reality of our having done or said something wrong. Dr. Tavris wrote, "To reduce dissonance, we have to modify the self-concept or accept the evidence. Guess which route people prefer?"[21]

4: Denying Responsibility Is Contagious

As discussed in the chapter of this book on peer pressure, the Torah posits, and social science demonstrates, that peer influence is a very pervasive and powerful determinant of what we say and do. In 2009, the University of Southern California professor Nathanael Fast and Stanford professor Larissa Tiedens published a study showing how peer influence works with taking responsibility.

One cohort of participants in their study heard California governor Arnold Schwarzenegger blaming someone else for a failure. Another cohort heard the governor accepting the blame. Those who heard the governor blame someone else were far more likely to blame others for a hypothetical failure of theirs. Indeed, Professors Fast and Tiedens found that the practice of shifting blame is as contagious as the 2009 H1N1 flu.[22]

Consequently, we learn that taking responsibility is not generally a preference or an isolated choice. It is a cultural facet. If a society deems abdicating responsibility to be acceptable or even tolerable, it will become the norm.

Hope?

Does this mean that there is no hope for taking responsibility? Are we, in other words, doomed to live in the world of "Mistakes were made"?

No, for at least two reasons that are entirely within our control.

Reason One: Lessons from Sports

Before entering the House of Representatives, Congressman Anthony Gonzalez was a wide receiver for the Indianapolis Colts. He, even as a Republican, was appalled at President Trump's rejection of responsibility for the 2020 presidential election result. Congressman Gonzalez processed President Trump's denials through something he learned from a Colts coach. A wide receiver or a tight end would, after missing a pass, come to the sidelines and complain that the safety had held him. The coach would simply say, "Why did you let him get close?" The offensive player, in other words, should take responsibility for not sufficiently outrunning his opponent and having to depend on a close call. With the power of incumbency and Joe Biden as an opponent, Congressman Gonzalez concluded, the election should not have been close.[23]

That Congressman Gonzalez's example comes from sports is not surprising. None of the many prominent people who have said "mistakes were made" are athletes or coaches. This is not a coincidence.

In 1993, the star freshman quarterback for the University of Florida, Danny Wuerffel, threw a crucial interception in a huge game that resulted in a loss for the Gators. The Hall of Fame Coach Steve Spurrier told him, "Danny, it's not your fault . . . It's my fault for putting you in the game."[24] Mr. Wuerffel, who would win the Heisman Trophy three years later, reflected on the moment in 2015 by saying, "Love you, Coach!"

In 2004, Providence University defeated the University of Connecticut in a basketball game where the Waterbury, CT, native, Ryan Gomes, scored 24 points and had 12 rebounds. A reporter asked the legendary University of Connecticut coach Jim Calhoun why he did not successfully recruit the hometown star. Coach Calhoun could have answered with any number of responses that referenced a complex and competitive recruiting process. Instead, he simply said, "I fucked up."[25]

These stories are typical for sports. Even in a culture of "mistakes were made," the best athletes and coaches rush to responsibility—well beyond where it is obviously warranted. Indeed, the reputations of the athletes and coaches are enhanced when they take responsibility and diminished when they do not. The world of competitive sports has what the broader society does not: a culture of responsibility. The question is thus ripe: How did sports become a culture where errors are much more likely to be explained with "I fucked up" than "Mistakes were made"?

Sports activities (games/matches) conclude after a short period of time with a winner and a loser. The goal of an athlete or a team is clear and inarguable: to win. Consequently, participants in sports seem to have determined without much discussion or debate that the chances of winning are optimized by everyone accepting 100% responsibility. And in so doing, they have created a subculture of responsibility within a general culture that often resists or rejects it.

Reason Two: The Imperative of Self-Improvement

The second reason why we are not doomed to live in the world of "mistakes were made" is also illustrated by sports. It is possible that *every* decent athlete has said, "I need to get better," and has taken significant actions to do so. And as Stanford professors Karina Schumann and Carol Dweck demonstrated, this might have everything to do with their willingness to take responsibility.

In 2014, Professors Schumann and Dweck surveyed forty-five participants to ascertain the effects of different theories of personality. The group was split in two. One cohort was given an article that posited, based on expert opinion, that personality can and always does change. The second group was given a different article that suggested, again based on expert opinion, that personality is largely fixed from early childhood. Participants in both groups were asked to summarize the point of each article and assess whether it was appropriate for high school students.[26]

Professors Schumann and Dweck then provided the study participants with a seemingly unrelated task. They gave them scenarios that asked them to see themselves in situations where they made mistakes. For instance, participants were asked to imagine that they had neglected to water their neighbor's plants (which they had agreed to do)—causing most of the plants to wilt and turn brown.

The participants were then assessed on several measures of responsibility. For instance: How bad did they feel about what happened? Were they likely to take responsibility? The researchers found that those who had been primed with the theory that people can change were more likely to accept responsibility than those who were primed with the theory that people cannot change.

So far, the fact that those who are likely to believe that people can change are more likely to take responsibility seems like an interesting correlation. But is there *causation*? In other words, why would people who believe in the possibility of change be more likely to take responsibility?

Professors Dweck and Schumann conducted another test to answer the question. Participants were asked to imagine having wronged somebody and were then asked whether or not they would assume responsibility for their action. They were then presented with part of a word that could be concluded in two very different ways, and asked to fill it in. For instance, "threa_."

They found that participants who did not take responsibility and thus did not believe in personal transformation were more likely to complete the word in a way that indicated stress. For instance, "threat" instead of "thread." It turns out that the acceptance of responsibility and the belief in the power of self-transformation are not only correlated—but build on each other and combine to produce a feeling of peace. Thomas Dewar was, it seems, very right. Taking responsibility may be (within some cultures) bad for the reputation—but it is good for the soul.

100% Responsibility—and Its Discontents

As discussed, the Torah tradition joins the commandment to take maximal responsibility with a requirement for the recipient of the apology to accept it with a forgiving spirit. This combination, continuously executed, culminates in a culture of responsibility—which requires both. Where does contemporary American culture line up with Maimonides's teaching that the refusal to forgive is cruel and forbidden?

In 2021, Alexi McCammond found out—as did the rest of us. Ms. McCammond was a rapidly rising young journalist who was named the editor in chief of *Teen Vogue*. After her appointment, some of her soon-to-be colleagues identified offensive tweets that she made ten years previously as a high school student. She renounced those tweets and apologized. Everyone agreed that she had changed and grown since she made those tweets, and that she no longer harbored the sentiments that she expressed as a youth. Still, she was forced to resign before she started.

The Atlantic journalist Elizabeth Bruenig took to Twitter to opine on the situation. She wrote, "As a society we have absolutely no coherent story—none whatsoever—about how a person who's done wrong can atone, make amends, and retain some continuity between their life/identity before and after the mistake. Complete clown show morally speaking, incoherent, arbitrary."[27]

Ms. Bruenig's comment is precisely right. Ms. McCammond's detractors did not articulate a theory of forgiveness that she did not satisfy. They advanced no theory of forgiveness at all. Instead, they essentially rejected the concept of forgiveness altogether.

The rejection of forgiveness has a casualty beyond a career death sentence issued at the moment of an offensive posting. It is described by the journalist Aja Romano, in an analysis of contemporary forgiveness in *Vox*: "[The lack of forgiveness] can also make the [apologizing party] even less likely to listen and learn the next time someone accuses them of doing something wrong because they've already been burned and they have less reason than ever to trust their accusers." In other words—just as the Torah tradition posits—people are only likely to take responsibility within a culture that expects, eases, and rewards it.[28]

How far are we from such a culture? Examples like that of Ms. McCammond suggest: very far. But there is a competing tendency. It is manifested, as discussed above, in sports—but its applications extend far beyond the fields and courts.

One of the most popular authors of all time is Jack Canfield—whose *Chicken Soup for the Soul* series has sold more than five hundred million copies. His books are not about the Bible, but he summarizes his philosophy on the site devoted to his enormously successful seminar and consulting business: "If you want to be successful, you have to take 100% responsibility for everything that you experience in your life."[29]

Mr. Canfield's exhortation to "100% responsibility" might have been interesting and inspiring to his readers and clients, but it was not new. "100% responsibility" is an expression and an idea that has been recently applied with astonishing broadness. It has been the topic of newsletters, corporate seminars, communications tactics, health advice, and inspirational speeches. It is the motto of Synovus Bank, which is consistently ranked by *Fortune* as one of the best companies in the United States to work for. It is the driving idea behind the outstanding best-seller by Jocko Willink and Leif Babin: *Extreme Ownership: How U.S. Navy SEALs Lead and Win*. 100% responsibility is an idea—a Torah-based idea—that has become a movement.

Reflection

In his 1881 novel *The Freebooters: A Story of the Texan War*, Gustave Aimard wrote, "In every human question, there is something more powerful than the brute force of bayonets. It is the idea whose time has come and hour struck."[30]

Beautiful, true, and relevant. Given how widely identified, deployed, popular, and intellectually uncontested the idea of 100% responsibility is, its hour might be now. We just might be ready for Moses's world—where a leader is one who takes full responsibility.

How can we build upon the foundation of 100% responsibility toward such a day? There are at least two solutions—which are simple, powerful, and tested.

The first derives from Matthew Crawford. He received a PhD in philosophy from the University of Chicago, and took a research position at a think tank. He could, he said, "write any nonsense whatever" without consequence. It was a job that spurned responsibility.[31]

This was not unique to his job. This lack of responsibility, he writes in what became a best-selling book, *Shop Class as Soulcraft*, is characteristic of knowledge work. Success in an office job, he writes, is often determined by contrived metrics detached from any objective standard. It is often conducted in the rubric of teamwork, which is a way of avoiding individual accountability. The whole culture of knowledge work has, Mr. Crawford writes, created a "poignant longing for responsibility."[32]

Mr. Crawford found a solution for his discontent, manifested in the literal sleepiness that he experienced doing knowledge work. He became a motorcycle mechanic, who, like everyone who makes or fixes things, has to take 100% responsibility. If the mechanic fails, the thing will not work or will soon break, with potentially catastrophic consequences for the customer and those nearby. So, the mechanic has to develop a rich sense of personal responsibility. His career, and often the lives of others, depend on it.[33]

One does not have to devote a career to making or fixing things to receive the spiritual satisfaction of 100% responsibility. Anyone who sets out to make or fix things (from motorcycles to computer code)—even as a serious hobby—will experience the discipline of 100% responsibility. And, consistent with the Torah and science that show that we become what we do, the acceptance of responsibility will make a formidable impact on one's character. With 100% responsibility becoming a part of his character, one will—like Anthony Gonzalez, the Indianapolis Colts receiver who went to Congress—be able to take 100% responsibility to places it has not yet permeated.

The second insight derives from a question asked by Rabbi YY Jacobson. What, he asks, should one do in a dispute with someone he cares about? The answer: apologize. What if one believes, even truthfully, that he is only minimally responsible for the rift? Forget about the allocation of blame, and apologize anyway.

This would be done without any compromise to the truth. Even if a person is 1 percent responsible for an interpersonal problem, he owes the other person an apology. If he withholds it, he is not paying what he owes. That he, too, is owed an apology has nothing to do with whether he has a responsibility to apologize. He can issue his apology as an expression of regret and responsibility.[34]

What will follow? People are unique and complex, so there can be no definitive answer. But it is at least highly plausible that the person to whom he is apologizing will respond in kind. And it is equally plausible that everyone involved with or around the apology will note, and be impressed with and thus influenced by, the invocation of 100% responsibility.

And that just might be the start to reversing what Thomas Dewar said. Taking 100% responsibility might be good for the soul *and* for the reputation. And that just might be the necessary ingredient for what we have been waiting for since Adam and Eve got kicked out of the Garden—the mass adoption of 100% responsibility.

12

Why the High Priest Wears Different Sets of the Same Clothes and How Industrial Accidents Can Be Avoided

The Torah and Science of Living in Routine

The GOAT Verse

Perhaps the sign that a human activity is appreciated is when it generates parlor games. Every sports fan has engaged in some kind of discussion about who the GOAT (greatest of all time) is, who constitutes the all-time starting five (or nine), and who delivered the best performance ever in a game. History buffs do something similar with ranking presidents.

The sages had a similar parlor game. The sixteenth-century work *Ein Yaakov*, compiled by the Spanish sages Jacob ibn Habib and Levi ibn Habib, records an ancient discussion between the sages where they asked, "What is the most important Torah verse?"

The first three entries are not surprising. The second-century sage Ben Zoma said that it was "Shema Yisrael—Hear O'Israel" (Deuteronomy 6:4). His contemporary Ben Nanas argued that it was "Love your fellow as yourself" (Leviticus 19:18). Then came Ben Pazi. His entry was from Exodus 29:39: "The one lamb you shall sacrifice in the morning and the second lamb you shall sacrifice in the evening."

The winner, according to Jewish tradition, is Ben Pazi![1]

This is stunning, for at least two reasons. First, we can only carry out the sacrificial service when the Temple exists. It does not exist now, and it did not even exist in Ben Pazi's day. It has not existed since the destruction of the second Temple in the year 70 CE. So, are our ancient sages concluding that the most important verse is one that can no longer be performed?

Second, Ben Pazi's contribution seemingly should not be the winner by the Bible's own logic. We are charged, per Exodus 16, with becoming "a kingdom of priests and a holy nation." This is to be measured, per Deuteronomy 6 and 28, by the "peoples of the world" beholding the Jews and concluding, "Surely this nation is a wise and understanding people," and seeing that we are "called by the name of the Lord."

Will the peoples of the world read "The one lamb you shall sacrifice in the morning and the second lamb you shall sacrifice in the evening" and be inspired to "call the name of the Lord"? It is doubtful. How, then, could Ben Pazi's chosen verse be universally regarded as the Torah's GOAT?

Rabbi Doron Perez, the leader of the Mizrachi World Movement, explains, "It is only through a continuous and consistent commitment, day in and day out, that change in ourselves and the world can truly be evoked . . . This is Ben Pazi's secret."[2]

There is a word for "continuous and consistent." It is "routine." The most important verse in the Bible, our sages determined, is the one that commands routine. And a routine sufficiently practiced becomes a habit.

Maimonides, as ever, articulated the importance of routine with authority, clarity, and succinctness. "Accustom yourself to habitual goodness, for character is dependent on habit, habit becoming as if it were second nature."[3]

Routine in Place

Genesis 19:27 tells us, "Abraham went early in the morning to the place where he had stood before the Lord," and Genesis 28:11 tells us, regarding Jacob's prayer, "He arrived at the place." These verses constitute, according to the Talmud, the beginning of prayer.[4]

Why would we be introduced to prayer with a conspicuous emphasis on the word "place"? As God is everywhere, can't we *pray* anywhere? Yes. But this does not mean that our prayer experiences will be equally reliable or robust everywhere. This explains why the Torah has Abraham and Jacob praying in "the place." And it explains why Jewish law stipulates that one should have a designated place to pray, even within one's home. The synagogue is, of course, another set place where Jews pray—but that's not all. Many Jews, encouraged by synagogue practice, have a regular place within the sanctuary where they sit.[5]

Why is the notion of a place so important? The answer is in a widely told and variously attributed Jewish tale of a child who goes to pray in the woods every day. An elder says to him, "Why do you go to the wood to pray? Don't you know that God is the same everywhere?"

The child replies, "God might be the same everywhere. But I'm not."

Jewish Practices and Routine

The Jewish year is structured around the *chagim*—the holidays. Whether we Jews are talking about Pesach, Rosh Hashanah, or Yom Kippur—we have all asked each other, "What are you doing for the holiday?"

It is a fine question—but it is imprecise. In Leviticus 23:4, the Torah speaks of the holidays together. And it does not call them holidays. The verse says: "These are the Lord's *appointed times*, which you shall designate in their appointed time."

As Rabbi Moshe Scheiner of the Palm Beach Synagogue points out, there is a major difference between "holidays" and "appointed times." A holiday means a vacation, describing an experience without rules. An appointed time describes something that is set in time—in fact, the same time every year. By calling holidays "appointed times," the Torah is guiding us to how we can get the most meaning and joy from a special day or a celebration. We need to make a plan and conduct it according to a schedule—with a structure that is always the same. Our appointed times—which can be very joyous—are routines.[6]

This ideology of appointed times defines Jewish life. Jewish men lay the same tefillin (ritual adornments that are worn on the arm and head) six days a week, and say the same prayers every morning, afternoon, and evening. Jewish women light candles every Friday night. And all Jews celebrate the same holidays, with a predictable regularity that enabled Randolph College professor Marc Ordower to determine that the secular calendar year of 3031 will not have a Hannukah. (But our great-something grandchildren need not be disappointed; 3032 will have two.)[7]

The observance of the holidays (or appointed times) is very important in Judaism, but there is something that is more important: study. There are many components to study—what one studies, how long one studies for, with whom one studies. However, the Jewish tradition does not consider any of these to be the most important aspect of study.

According to the fourth-century sage Rava, the question that we will be asked by the "Heavenly tribunal" is, "Did you set aside fixed times for Torah study?" Rava's heavenly tribunal will be primarily, or perhaps solely, concerned with whether one's study was a part of a *routine*.[8]

The Torah and Jewish practice involve many laws and rules. These offer guidance for how to uphold *mitzvot*, commonly translated as "good deeds." But the more accurate translation is "commandments." With so many mitzvot and a limited number of hours in the day, there will invariably be times when certain mitzvot co-occur with one another. How do we determine which *mitzvah* takes precedence, and therefore which to do first?

We might intuitively answer that whichever mitzvah occurs less frequently is more special, and therefore should take precedence. The Jewish answer, however, deriving from the ancient Mishnah, is clear: "The frequent one takes precedence." It is what we do most frequently that composes our routines, and our routines—the Mishnah teaches—are the most important things we do.[9]

The Problem with Routine

This insistence on routine, from the sacrifices to the prayers, from Torah study to ancient Bible verse contests, characterizes the entire Jewish experience. But there is a problem. It is presented in a passage in Deuteronomy 26, where Moses imagines a farmer. This farmer, sometime in the future, goes to Jerusalem to offer his "first fruits" in gratitude after a successful harvest. This story is so important that we use it (rather than anything in Exodus) to tell our freedom story in the Passover Haggadah.

After bringing his offering, the farmer says something apparently strange. He declares, "I have not transgressed your commandments, neither have I forgotten them." This seems redundant. If the farmer didn't transgress (and is aware that he did not transgress), obviously he didn't forget!

What is the Author of the Torah trying to teach us? The nineteenth-century sage Yehudah Aryeh Leib Alter (known as the Sfat Emet) explains that a person can do a good deed (or avoid a bad deed) just because it is part of his routine. That sounds good, and often is—but it comes with a potential problem. He can forget the entire reason that he was doing it, and therefore strip the religious practice of its spirit, meaning, and power to inspire others. This potential problem is sufficiently large for Moses to celebrate the farmer for not transgressing *and* not forgetting the commandments.[10]

What, then, might be the potential problem with performing routines in a *routinized* manner? The Torah identifies two and offers solutions to both.

God's Checklist

The Torah has a lot of people who excel at their jobs. Esau is described as a "skillful hunter," Joseph as a "successful man," Betzalel as a "master craftsman," and Moses is so talented a leader that the Torah tells us that there will "never be a prophet in Israel" like him. In none of these cases does the Torah tell us exactly how they did each aspect of their job. They knew how to do their jobs, and did them very well.

In Leviticus, we learn about a group of very successful people. These are the priests, the religious leaders of the community. They are charged with, among other things, bringing sacrifices to the Temple. This crucial task, which is performed daily, is one that requires a consistent and carefully executed routine.

The Torah, in its enumeration of the priestly activities, does something very different than it did with Esau, Joseph, Betzalel, and Moses. It lists the tasks that the priests must conduct in the performance of the sacrifice in painstaking and precise detail. The Yom Kippur sacrificial service is particularly detailed. *Some* of the tasks are: the priest procuring the animals for sacrifice, bathing in a ritual bath, donning his priestly garments, sacrificing a sin offering, bringing incense, drawing lots, sacrificing the communal offering, collecting the blood and sprinkling the blood eastward on the altar with his finger, and pushing the final offering off a cliff. The problem is that routines are conducted by human beings, who might be sick, tired, rushed, distracted, or even unduly confident on a particular day. Consequently, the priests (like anyone) might inadvertently skip one of the steps in the routine.

The solution: Give the priests a checklist. This checklist still allows the priests to capture the benefits of routine; they do not need to spend mental energy determining how to do the sacrifice. They just need to check that they have done each task, assuring that they conducted the routine while being mindful of each step.

Newness in Routine

The Torah presents the other problem of routine through the high priest. Leviticus 16 is devoted to the rituals of Yom Kippur, the most important Jewish holiday (or appointed time). God tells Moses to tell his brother Aaron, the high priest, to put on "the sacred linen tunic, with linen undergarments next to his body; he is to tie the linen sash around him and put on the linen turban . . . [and] bathe himself with water before he puts them on" (Leviticus 16:4).

Then comes a crucial twist. God instructs the priest to "remove his linen garments that he wore into the sanctuary, and he shall leave them there." The priest is never to wear those garments again. This is quite a statement, given that linen garments were expensive in the ancient world.[11]

Why was the high priest prohibited from wearing the same Yom Kippur outfit twice? Was God instructing the high priest to be a diva? Probably not.

Instead, the Author of the Torah was revealing how we should approach our everyday life. We need the consistency and constancy of a routine—hence, even the high priest needs to wear the same fashion every Yom Kippur. But there is, according to the twentieth-century sage Rabbi Norman Lamm, "a danger to routine." And that danger is boredom, which Rabbi Lamm said that the Torah considers "as poison to the spirit and the soul."[12]

The Torah's solution is that the priest must wear new clothes of the same fashion. In so doing, the priest is wearing—and teaching—a lesson for Jews to learn on this most holy of days. We are to bring, Rabbi Lamm said, "a new spirit, a new insight, a new intuition in [the routine things] we are doing."[13]

In other words, we are to make newness a part of our routine. Rabbi Lamm suggests several ways that Jews can make newness a part of our routine. The Jewish wife or mother lights Shabbat candles in the same way on Friday at sundown every week of her life. Yet, she should make "some novelty, some additional requests, some new insights and concern—perhaps for someone else's family" a part of the routine.

Observant Jews offer the same prayer over the bread at the conclusion of every meal. Yet, Rabbi Lamm advised, "we ought to vary the melody (if we do sing it) in order to challenge us to rethink our gratitude to the Almighty . . ."

Jews conduct a Passover Seder at the same time, with the same foods, and using the same book (the Haggadah) every year. Yet, we should have new discussions and thus "pour new meaning into old forms." Jews thank God for sight every day, but should seek out those with impaired or no sight to appreciate the purpose of the blessing—which is to "to be amazed and stunned, at the great miracle of being able to see!"

Perhaps the quintessential example of newness in routine is instructed in Leviticus 20:18. Here, we learn that a man must not have sex with his wife while she is menstruating. The second-century sage Rabbi Meir explains why:

> It is because if a woman were permitted to engage in intercourse with her husband all the time, her husband would be too accustomed to her, and would eventually be repulsed by her. Therefore, the Torah says that a menstruating woman shall be ritually impure for seven days, during which she is prohibited from engaging in intercourse with her husband, so that when she becomes pure again she will be dear to her husband as at the time when she entered the wedding canopy with him.[14]

The Torah's vision is for the same couple to make love on the same marital bed for, hopefully, a long time. But because of Leviticus 20, marital sex is set to always be new and exciting.

Does King David Dwell or Visit?

In Leviticus 26, God articulates the blessings that we will enjoy for following him. Many of these are easily understandable: God will grant peace in the land, remove wild beasts from our midst, give us many children, and dwell amongst us. Then there is, "You shall eat old grain long kept, and you shall clear out the old to make way for the new."

One might ask: Which is the blessing? Is it to take in the old or to replace it with the new? The voice from the Torah says that the blessing is to be able to do both simultaneously—to have the new incorporated into the old, and for newness to be a part of the routine.

When the Torah is returned to the ark in synagogue services, the congregation sings a verse from Lamentations 5:21 asking God to "renew our days as of old." This might seem like a contradiction. Which is it? Are we supposed to renew our days, or long for the old?

The answer is provided by King David, who prays to be able "to *dwell* in the house of the Lord all the days of my life and to *visit* His sanctuary" (Psalms 27:4).

King David yearned to *live* in the house *and* to experience it as if he were a *visitor*. When one dwells in a house, he is likely to establish the same routines every day. A visitor, by contrast, is excited by the newness in the place. King David yearned to dwell in the home with the spirit of a visitor—to experience familiar places, traditional ways, and ancient truths with the enthusiasm, excitement, and energy of newness.

Most clergymen today have not instructed their congregants about the doors through which they are to enter and exit the synagogue or church. That is because the prophet Ezekiel is not on the pulpit today. He said:

> When the people of the land come before the Lord on the times fixed for meeting, he who enters by way of the north gate to prostrate himself shall go out by way of the south gate, and he who enters by way of the south gate shall go out by way of the north gate; he shall not return by way of the gate whereby he came in, but he shall go out by that which is opposite it.[15]

Why would Ezekiel command that we enter and exit the temple at different gates after arriving at "fixed times"? It is because Ezekiel wanted us to follow a routine—and to inject newness into the routine to ensure that the routine does not become *routinized*.

The Temple was destroyed but has been replaced by two places: the synagogue and the home. The doorposts of synagogues and Jewish homes have *mezuzot*, in accordance with Moses's instruction in Deuteronomy 6:9: "And you shall inscribe them upon the doorposts of your house and on your gates." We think of the mezuzah as the item on our doorposts that contains a scroll. But that is imprecise. The word "mezuzah" *means* "doorpost."

The nineteenth-century sage Rabbi Yaakov Tzvi Mecklenburg notes that the word "mezuzah" comes from the root *zaz*—which means "to move." This, he says, is the message that the Torah wants us to understand when we enter and leave our home and gates. We are to move while fixed—to have a set routine and incorporate movement and variation within it.[16]

Rabbi Mecklenburg's insight is illustrated by a familiar activity that is conducted in both the home and the synagogue: prayer. The Talmud has much to say about prayer. But two of the most important stipulations about prayer seem contradictory. The Talmud says that there has to be a "fixed time" for prayer. The Talmud *also* says that it is forbidden to make our prayer "a fixed obligation."[17]

What could be the difference between a "fixed time" (required) and a "fixed obligation" (prohibited)? The sages Rabba and Rav Yosef in the Talmud explain. They understand a fixed obligation to be "one that lacks a 'new element.'"[18]

We must, in other words, make newness a part of the routine—by adding a "new element" to the same prayers we say every day, by exiting the same synagogue at the same times from a different door than the one entered, by ensuring that the same couple makes the same marital bed a place of excitement every month.

The Science

Addiction

In 1998, the United States government produced a guide for the treatment of cocaine addiction. The report, conducted by Dr. Delinda Mercer of the University of Pennsylvania and Dr. George Woody of the Veterans Affairs Medical Center, aggregated and synthesized findings from an enormous body of research conducted over the previous twenty years.

They identified some good news. "More than 20 years of research has shown that addiction is clearly treatable." Even better, Drs. Mercer and Woody identified the fundamental problem that addicts share, along with a solution. The problem is "a chaotic, disorganized lifestyle." The solution is to "help the patient to identify what he or she does each day and help to structure his or her days to encourage abstinence . . . The counselor must try to counteract this lifestyle, as well as restructure the content of the addict's daily activity, by trying to help organize the patient's daily routine."[19]

They then present routines for the addiction counselor to fill out together with their patient. The routines are very detailed, covering every hour of every day from when the patient wakes up at 7 AM until he retires at 11 PM.

Dr. Ellen Frank of the University of Pittsburgh is a physician with a very different specialty. She is a psychiatrist who specializes in the treatment of bipolar disorder. In 2006, Dr. Frank and several colleagues conducted a study where a cohort of patients were treated with the conventional combination of therapy and pharmaceuticals while another was also treated with social rhythm therapy, which emphasizes and regulates the routines of the patient.

Their conclusions state that "social rhythm therapy is associated with significantly reduced risk of recurrence of both depression and mania over a subsequent two-year period. Furthermore, we found that the protective effect of the treatment was directly related to the extent to which patients increased the regularity of their social rhythms."

The health benefits of these routines existed independently of what the routines were. The routines just had to be followed rigorously and consistently. Breaking them with even a weekend vacation risked triggering an episode.[20]

In 2010, Drs. Isabella Lanza and Deborah Drabick published a study of childhood behavior disorders in the *Journal of Abnormal Child Psychology.* Their subject was oppositional defiant disorder (ODD), which presents in children as hostile, uncooperative, and defiant behavior. The solution is to incorporate "high levels of family routine." And seemingly all of the literature on the treatment of attention deficit hyperactivity disorder (ADHD) involves the strict imposition of routines.[21]

Dreaming Soon

The imposition of routine does not merely lead people from destructive behavior toward normalcy. It leads from normalcy to excellence. The NBA Hall of Famer Dwayne Wade is an Olympic gold medalist, a three-time NBA champion, a thirteen-time All-Star, and an NBA Finals and All-Star Game MVP. He played on the 2008 Olympic team with other greats of his era. Yet one player stood out.

He recalls, "Everybody else just woke up. We're still stretching and yawning and looking at [Kobe Bryant] like, 'What the fuck?' We're all yawning, and he's already three hours and a full workout into his day."

It did not matter that Mr. Bryant was in Beijing with new teammates. He had the same routine he always carried out—whether he had just arrived in a foreign city or was having an ordinary family day in Los Angeles.[22]

A devotion to routine enabled Mr. Bryant's enormous success. It also describes how the great authors have been able to realize their creative gifts. Leo Tolstoy wrote every day because he concluded that his writing would be diminished if he allowed himself to "get out of [his] routine." Immanuel Kant's neighbors knew that it was 3:30 PM by seeing him leave his house with his gray coat and Spanish stick. Graham Greene wrote exactly five hundred words five days a week, before breakfast. W. H. Auden said, "Routine, in an intelligent man, is a sign of ambition"—and his friends described his routine as Mr. Wade did Mr. Bryant's. Maya Angelou wrote a semi-autobiographical book, *Daily Routines*.

And perhaps the most prolific and creative storyteller in American history, Stephen King, said that "the cumulative purpose of doing . . . things the same way every day seems to be a way of saying to the mind, you're going to be dreaming soon."[23]

The Author of the Torah, the Talmudic sages, Kobe Bryant, and Stephen King are in agreement that routine is essential for optimal human performance. But why?

Studies from the Cleveland Clinic in Ohio, the Salk Institute in California, Gazi University in Turkey, and other institutions have demonstrated that all mammals, including humans, have a circadian clock located in the hypothalamus area of the brain. This clock guides us through an approximately twenty-four-hour cycle, activating hormones and managing metabolism in line with the hour of the day. It is the body's natural way of setting routines, developed universally after infancy. Every international traveler has experienced the consequences of breaking it: This is jet lag. But there are much more serious consequences to breaking routine. These include obesity, diabetes, addiction, high blood pressure, and cancer.[24]

Why Accidents Happen

The DMV Written Test is a company that helps prepare would-be motorists for driving tests. One of the questions on the sample test is: "____% of crashes occur within 25 miles of home." The choices were 75 percent, 50 percent, 25 percent, and 15 percent. The correct answer is 75 percent.

So many people got it wrong that the DMV Written Test rated it "quite hard." But the question *is* easy. Everyone knows someone who has been in a car accident, and it is highly likely to have occurred near the person's home. The research bears this out. A study from the Progressive Insurance company determined that 77 percent of car accidents happen within fifteen miles from one's home, and a study from the University of Toronto found that the median distance of a car or motorcycle accident is 4.6 miles away from one's home. This is entirely predictable, as everyone could intuit what the United States Department of Energy determined: 90 percent of car trips are fewer than twenty miles.[25]

The fact that so many people got this wrong illustrates a fascinating misperception about routine. The respondents instinctively concluded that routines—the routes they normally travel near their home—are safe, and that danger presents in the new and unfamiliar. Indeed, the respondents probably thought that routinely driven routes are particularly safe because their challenges are known to the driver.

This disconnect leads to two questions. First, why do so many accidents occur on routes that people drive routinely? Second, what can be done to make routine driving safer?

"Nothing More Dangerous"

In 2013, Samuel Charlton and Nicola Starkey of the Transport Research Group at the University of Waikato in New Zealand published their research into driver safety. They had drivers placed in a simulator where they "drove" the same route seven times, with changes placed in the environment each time—such as changes to traffic signs. The participants judged the driving task to be easier as they became more familiar with the route. By the fifth and sixth sessions, the drivers reported that they were "driving without thinking about it," "zoning out," or "going on autopilot." By the seventh round, they were much less likely to notice changes in the familiar route like the removal of buildings or changes to traffic signs. Consequently, Professors Charlton and Starkey note, "Drivers [are] at greater risk on the roads they know best."[26]

This phenomenon is by no means limited to driving. *iMechanica* is a blog for mechanics and mechanicians. One of the topics covered on the site is "unsafe acts/conditions during routine tasks in platforms/offshore and how to avoid them."[27]

The heading for this topic is instructive. Why is there a robust discussion of "unsafe acts/conditions" during specifically "routine" tasks? Shouldn't a discussion about industrial accidents be about the dangers in *new* tasks or conditions?

A blog post by one respondent, Ike Precious C, says:

> I would like to add that there is nothing more dangerous than Routine activities, especially in the Oil and Gas industry. When one tends to do a particular task over and over again that he/she can tell a scenario without there [sic] is really dangerous. But I think it's high time that activities should be carefully analyzed to see if the element/factor of routine tasks [are] attached to it. The more routine the tasks are, the easier it is to break the safety rules surrounding this task/activity.

Bassey Kufre Peter replied, "I agree with you Ike, that most accidents in the industry are a function of routine activities . . . operators oftentimes overlook the safety requirements and guidelines of carrying out the most routine jobs."

Dike Nwabueze Chinedu followed with a comment noting that "routine tasks bring about laxity, lack of proper job assessment, misconduct, negligence and sometimes carelessness and the offspring of these is conspicuous unsafe practices in an offshore platform."

Foivos Theofilopoulos wrote, "At least from personal experience, I think that routine tasks are the ones where you have the most chances of something devastating going unnoticed."[28]

Interestingly, *no one disagreed*. The mechanics just contributed other examples, stories, reasons, and explanations for how serious hazards emanate from following routine.

These data, studies, and observations on the relationship between routines and driver safety / workplace accidents can be joined by another source. Modern neuroscience has revealed how our brains work with routines and new things.

We process a new skill through our prefrontal cortex, which resides in the very front of our brains. It allows us, as the behavioral therapist Benjamin Ruark writes, to

> focus our attention, plan, evaluate, judge, and store key information relating (as working memory) to whatever it is we're attending to at the moment. Our PFC does all the figuring out of what needs to be done when we learn a new skill, procedure, or behavior. It is aided by the hippocampi (HC)—a set of structures in the temporal lobes that form, organize, and store facts and events for possible future use.[29]

Once we perform the new skill several times, the prefrontal cortex hands off the task to the basal ganglia, which informs our "habit" memory and enables us to do things on "autopilot." This helps to make our brain the remarkably efficient system that it is. If we had to seriously consider and intently focus on everything we did, we would be limited in what we could do—and would not have the time or energy to learn many new things.

The problem is that the environments in which we perform routine tasks are not perfectly stable. A slight variation in the routine—say, a bicyclist crossing a street on which we have been accustomed to having only the occasional car—requires the prefrontal cortex. But it is effectively deactivated as we perform routines, as the basal ganglia is doing all the work.[30]

So, we now know just why—as the Torah teaches—routines are both necessary and dangerous. We need routines to be able to do the huge number of things that constitute the basics of human living. These routines allow us to focus less on familiar things, thus freeing us to devote our energy and attention to learning new things. This remarkably efficient system exists in a paradox. The same things that enable routines to set in, and life to function, can be dangerous—for two reasons.

First, a new thing (like a changed traffic sign) can pop up in the middle of a routine. The new thing is precisely what needs our attention, but our brains are set in "habit memory" mode.

Second, the brain in routine mode does not focus on what is distinctive about what it is considering. A person who is even slightly distracted, as we all are at various points, is susceptible to missing a part of the routine. Consequently, as the contributors to the *iMechanica* blog report, people doing routine tasks are vulnerable to carelessness, overlooking safety rules and misevaluating jobs.

And these results of living in routine—as we must—can be catastrophic. Thankfully, modern social science offers two solutions. And they will sound very familiar to those who know of the passages in Leviticus regarding the priest's checklist and Jewish couples refraining from sex while the wife is menstruating.

Checklists and "Changing Where We Sit"

In 1935, Boeing introduced new planes. The pilots had to learn their new features. The immediate result was a series of crashes. The risk mitigation expert Susan Koen reports on what the Boeing investigation determined. The crashes were not due to "the bells and whistles of the new plane"—but instead to the fact that the pilots, in focusing on the new features, had "straight-up forgotten important procedures, leading to a series of crashes." This is a classic example of the dangers of routine.[31]

The Boeing executives conceived of a solution. It was the implementation of checklists, which required the pilots to methodically review all of their tasks—especially the routine ones. Ms. Koen reports on how the checklists worked:

> It's not the step-by-step checklist alone that produces performance reliability in aviation. Rather, it's the recognition amongst pilots that they're fallible. It's the commitment to not operate from memory, because human memory is not reliable. And, most importantly, it's the system of having two people cooperate in working through and cross-checking each critical task.

Airline safety is just one of the crucial societal functions that has been improved by the modern debut of the checklists that God told the priests to use in Leviticus. In the 2020s, the three leading causes of death in the United States are heart attacks, cancer, and medical errors. Many of these medical errors are the result of a provider neglecting a part of their routine.[32] An important solution is revealed in the title of Johns Hopkins surgeon Atul Gawande's 2009 book: *The Checklist Manifesto: How to Get Things Right*.

Dr. Gawande tells the story of his colleague Dr. Peter Pronovost. In 2001, Dr. Pronovost decided to address mistakes associated with inserting central lines in the intensive care unit (ICU). Central lines are essential to caring for many patients in the ICU. They are placed in a large vein of the patient to deliver fluids, blood, and medications quickly. A mistake can lead to an infection—which can be debilitating or even deadly.

Dr. Pronovost isolated five routine tasks in the administration of central lines. Doctors should wash their hands with soap; clean the patient's skin with an antiseptic; put sterile drapes over the patient's entire body; wear a mask, hat, sterile gown, and gloves; and put a dressing over the insertion site once the line is in. These tasks, Dr. Gawande reflected, "are no-brainers; they have been known and taught for years"—just like the tasks that the priests performed when offering sacrifices in the Temple.

Dr. Pronovost empowered nurses to note how often one of these steps was skipped. The finding was that doctors skipped at least one step in a third of cases. So, Dr. Pronovost required doctors to check each step upon completion, and empowered nurses to assure compliance. A year later, the data was in. Dr. Gawande reports, "The results were so dramatic that they weren't sure whether to believe them: the ten-day line-infection rate went from 11 percent to zero . . . in this one hospital, the checklist had prevented forty-three infections and eight deaths and saved two million dollars in cost."[33]

Checklists work because they cause us to focus, even for a crucial moment, on routine tasks that might otherwise be missed. They cause us to be mindful of the things that constitute routines, while enabling us to focus primarily on the new things that will command our energy and intelligence.

If checklists are simple, the University of Hertfordshire Professors Ben Fletcher and Karen Pine suggest an even easier way to reset the brain to mitigate dangers posed by routine. They write, "Triggers for unwanted behavior often exist in our daily routines and the environments around us." The aforementioned data from machine accidents (including cars) show just how right they are. Their solution: "Literally changing where we sit can mean that we are not triggered to do what we would normally do in that place."[34]

In other words: Newness in Routine.

Reflection

The message from the Torah and social science is very clear. A stable and productive life requires routine. But routine, precisely because it enables us to perform a task without much thinking, can be dangerous. The Torah emphasizes the spiritual dangers and the science emphasizes the physical dangers of routine—but both come to the same solution. A combination of mindfulness about the components of the routine and an incorporation of newness within the routine preserve its benefits while eliminating its costs.

How might we live the wisdom of the Torah and its validation in social science?

First, we should attach a routine to every goal. If we decide that we want to get in better shape, we should resolve to work out for an hour every day or two days at a particular time. If we decide that we want to develop a greater sense of gratitude, we should keep a gratitude journal or write a book, and we should commit to doing so in the same place at the same time every day. If we decide that we want to get more involved in the church or synagogue, we should resolve to go to a service every weekend and an event every week.

Just the same, we should recognize the spiritual and physical dangers that accompany routines. We can solve this by maintaining mindfulness. Before we embark on a business trip that we make twice a month, we can use a checklist to ensure that we packed everything we need. When a loved one is getting ready for surgery, we can tell the surgeon how much we appreciate his experience—and verify that he is using a checklist.

And we should *always* make new things a part of the routine. If we drive from our home to our office every day, we should try a new route every Wednesday. If we sit down to write for two hours every morning at 7 AM in the same place, we can listen to different music in each session. If we say the same prayers every Friday night or Sunday morning, we can adorn the prayers with new yearnings, perspectives, and desires.

And then there is Dr. Ruth Westheimer's sage advice. Before Covid, Dr. Ruth came to our home for Shabbat dinner on most Friday nights. She often took the floor after the Shabbat prayer to remind the married couples in the room of the mitzvah to make love on Friday nights.

When issuing this reminder of a routine, Dr. Ruth always gave these married couples the same instruction: "Make love tonight—in a new position!"

Exactly.

13

Why the Israelites Hated the Perfect Food and IKEA Succeeds

The Torah and Science of Effort

Everyone who has been to a bris and has seen a baby circumcised is participating in a ritual that is introduced by God in the Book of Genesis. In Genesis 17:10–14, God tells Abraham, "This is the covenant which you shall keep between Me and you and your seed after you—every male child shall be circumcised." God tells Abraham that the circumcision shall occur on the eighth day of the boy's life.

The circumcision is the sign of the covenant—the everlasting relationship—between God and the Jewish people. Its importance cannot be overstated. How, then, would God and Abraham make it happen?

In Genesis 17:23, we find out. Abraham "took his son Ishmael and all those born in his household or bought with his money, every male in his household, and circumcised them, as God told him." Abraham circumcises his son, and every male in the household, by *himself*. This tradition persists until the present day. Jewish fathers are required to circumcise our infant boys by ourselves—unless doing so might harm the baby (in which case a *mohel* can perform the circumcision, pursuant to the specific and publicly audible instruction of the father).

This practice, and the text that inspires it, is intriguing. Why does Abraham circumcise the child himself? Abraham is a rich and powerful man who could have had lots of people do anything for him. Yet, he never considers delegating this essential task. Is this significant?

The Torah provides the answer unambiguously, starting with the next chapter. In Genesis 18, Abraham (by then an old man) is recovering from a painful circumcision. Sitting outside, he is greeted by three strangers. He quickly engages his wife (Sarah) and tells her to make them cakes. Abraham, we learn, does not assign the task to Sarah because he wants to relax. He rushes to the cattle, picks out a calf, and gives it to a servant to prepare. Abraham then *himself* collects all the components of the meal and serves the strangers—standing over them as they eat to see if he could provide them with anything else.

Abraham, though physically challenged by his circumcision, personally exerts effort that would have been impressive for a younger and healthier man. Four chapters later, Abraham is spiritually challenged. In Genesis 22, God appears to Abraham with what the Torah calls a "test." God tells Abraham to sacrifice his beloved son, Isaac, on the mountain.

Abraham awakes early in the morning to do so—and saddles his donkey. Then, he takes "his two young men with him and Isaac"—and Abraham (not any of the younger men) splits the wood for the offering.

Abraham, we see in early Genesis, is a wealthy man with lots of staff to do for him whatever he wants. But in good times (when he gets the blessing pursuant to Isaac's circumcision), tough times physically (after his circumcision), and difficult times spiritually (when God asks him to sacrifice his son), Abraham performs the same way. He exerts maximum effort *himself*.

The Torah is just getting started with one of its most important lessons.

When God Corrects Moses

Fast-forward to Exodus 14. Moses is leading the Jewish people out of Egyptian slavery, but the Pharaoh and his army have given chase and are right behind the escaping slaves. The people are confused and scared, as it seems like they are about to be recaptured into slavery.

Moses announces to his people, "Do not be afraid. Stand firm and you will see the deliverance the Lord will bring you today . . . The Lord will fight for you; you need only to be still" (Exodus 14:13–14).

God does not like this instruction. He says, "Why are you crying out to me? Tell the Israelites to move on." A divine command to *stop praying* is not something we would expect from a religious text. But God, at this moment when the Jews are transitioning from slavery to freedom, is providing crucial guidance about how to live as free people. We will not achieve freedom, or anything else, by relying on God alone. We need to act in all circumstances—even those where it seems like our efforts cannot possibly accomplish what needs to be done.

The Jews comply. By acting in partnership with God, we continue our journey across the Sea of Reeds. It is through God's miracles and our effort that we are redeemed.

A month later, God meets Moses on Mount Sinai. God hands Moses the Ten Commandments. Moses goes down the mountain and sees the people worshipping and seemingly having an orgy at a Golden Calf that they had constructed. Moses is furious and smashes the tablets God had given him.

Shortly thereafter, God summons Moses to come back to the top of the mountain. God gives Moses the Ten Commandments again, but there is a very important difference. God does not, as he did the first time, hand Moses the sacred tablets. He dictates them to Moses, who writes them with his own hand. These tablets would be the product of a partnership between God and Moses, and they would remain forever complete in the Ark of the Covenant. It is these tablets that are the product of human effort—not those that are handed to Moses from God—that achieve an enduring legacy.

The Effort of Architecture and Your Personal Torah

In Exodus 25, God provides precise instructions to the Jews regarding how to build the Tabernacle. In one of those instructions, God commands that there shall be no steps. Instead, there shall be a ramp.

Why does God care if there is a ramp rather than steps? The text provides one reason: so that the priests are not exposed as they ascend the steps. The Chief Rabbi of pre-Independence Israel in the twentieth century, Rabbi Abraham Isaac Kook, provides an additional explanation. In climbing steps, people can take a break. We can stand in one place. When climbing a ramp, one must always exert effort. Even if one stops when ascending a ramp, he must make an *effort* to balance himself and then to thrust himself forward. The approach to God always requires our effort.[1]

Fast-forward from Genesis and Leviticus to the end of the Torah. In Deuteronomy 31:19, Moses instructs the people to "write down this poem [a description of the Torah] and teach it to the children of Israel."

The Talmudic sage Rava issued an interpretation that is authoritative to this day: the passage obligates each Jew to write a Torah himself. As with circumcision, a Jew who believes that he is unqualified for this task can fulfill the obligation by helping a scribe to do so. Jewish tradition makes the instruction practical while maintaining the philosophy that one must do important things with his own hands.[2]

Why does Abraham have to perform the circumcision? Why do the tablets that Moses wrote endure, whereas the ones that God wrote do not? Why does the Tabernacle contain a ramp rather than stairs? Why does everyone have to write a Torah? All of these questions converge upon one answer—which God blasts through the text in Numbers 11.

What We Crave

After the Jews began their sojourn in the desert, God provides food in the form of manna. The manna was no ancient equivalent of the bland Meals Ready to Eat (MREs) that soldiers consume. In Exodus 16:31, we learn that the manna tasted like "wafers mixed with honey." In Numbers 11:8, we learn that it tasted like cream or oil cakes.

The manna was delicious either way, but which was it: wafers with honey or a cream-like dish? The ancient Midrash reconciles the passages, explaining that the manna tasted however the eater wanted it to. If one person wanted it to taste like wafers in honey, it did. If another wanted it to taste like cream, it did. If another wanted it to taste like roasted chicken seasoned with ginger and mustard seed, it presumably did too. The manna adapted to the consumer's taste.[3]

How did the Jews of the desert respond to being provided with the perfect food? In Numbers 11:4–6, we learn, "The people among them craved a craving, and the Israelites wept and said, 'Who will feed us meat? We remember the fish we ate in Egypt for free—also the cucumbers, melons, leeks, onions, and garlic. But now we have lost our appetite; we never see anything but this manna.'"

On the surface, this makes no sense. We are complaining about the perfect food and yearning for the rations that we were given to us as slaves in Egypt? Yes, and the reason for this can be found in the description that began the passage. We "craved a craving." This is not the way that we normally think of cravings. We do not think of cravings as things we crave—but as the opposite: things that we want to vanquish. One who craves ice cream might take a trip to the freezer or the parlor, and will be satisfied when his craving is gone a few scoops later.

What, then, could it possibly mean to "crave a craving"? The answer is provided in Numbers 11:8 when we learn what the Jews did with the manna. We "grinded, pounded and cooked it." In other words, *we worked it.*

Why would we have worked so hard on a food that was delivered every day, and tasted however we wanted? Our work could not have improved the food, which was, after all, perfect.

We were dissatisfied not by the food, but by the fact that we did not do anything to create it. We craved a craving—something, *anything*, that we could satisfy through our efforts. Without exerting effort for even our food, we yearned for the food and life of slavery in Egypt. Getting something for nothing made us go crazy.

According to the Effort . . .

The spiritual and existential importance of effort would become a major theme in post-biblical Jewish thought and practice. The Talmud records that Rav Kahana (a third-century sage) observed that a person prefers a *kav* (a measure of grain) of his own produce to nine *kav* of another person's. Why? A teaching from Ben Hai Hai from Pirkei Avot (Ethics of Our Fathers) explains, "According to the effort is the reward."[4]

Fast-forward to the twentieth-century sage Rav Eliyahu Dessler. In his magnum opus *Michtav M'Eliyahu* (Letter from Eliyahu), Rav Dessler writes: "Whether it is a child he has brought into the world, an animal he has reared, a plant he has tended or even a thing he has made or a house he has built—a person is bound in love to the work of his hands, for in it he finds himself."[5]

The teachings of Rav Kahana and Rav Dessler are embedded in a Talmudic teaching: *Mitzva Bo Yoter Mi-beshlucho* ("It is better to perform a *mitzvah* personally than through assigning an agent."). The Talmud illustrates this principle with an example that is still applicable today. It is permissible for someone to arrive at a set Shabbat table, without having been involved in the baking of the challah and the procurement of the wine. But it is better for one to have been personally involved.[6]

The Science

When Labor Leads to Love

The belief that we value things to the extent we work on them, so core to Jewish teachings, makes no logical sense. This is demonstrated by the true statement "Time is money." We all directly or intuitively decide how much our time is worth every time we consider paying someone to do something we *could* do ourselves—from getting groceries to clearing snow.

Basic economic logic dictates, therefore, that we should always be willing to pay more for items that require no work to procure than those that require work—and that we should especially appreciate free things. The difference in how we value an item that appears before us and one that requires our effort should be the value we put on our labor. For instance, let's imagine that a man values his time at $100/hour. He should, therefore, be willing to pay up to $200 more for a finished desk than one that requires him to spend two hours assembling.

We should attribute value to the labor we save, not the labor we contribute. This seems obvious and irrefutable. So, what does science say about the Torah's claim that the opposite is true—that we value things to the extent that we work on them?

In 2011, Professors Michael Norton of Harvard, Dan Mochon of Tulane, and Dan Ariely of Duke had one group of university students assemble furniture from IKEA, the store that sells furniture that requires customers to assemble it. Another group of students was shown a completed version of the furniture. The researchers then asked the participants to price the items. The results showed that the subjects who built the furniture were willing to pay 63 percent *more* than the ones who were given pre-built furniture.[7]

The professors termed their discovery the IKEA effect—which is well-described by the subtitle of their paper, which echoes the teaching of Rav Dessler: "When Labor Leads to Love."[8]

The IKEA effect and its proposition—that labor leads to love—has been tested with all kinds of things. Professors Norton, Mochon, and Ariely found it to be true with origami creations. A 2013 study by Professor Laura Hamilton of the University of California, Merced, showed that students get better grades in school to the extent that they (rather than their parents) pay for college.[9]

The IKEA effect explains why IKEA is a multibillion-dollar company. It also explains why people spend hours fixing cars they could take to the shop, build collections they could buy in full, and spend valuable time making hot sauce, tending gardens, and baking cookies. Contemporary businesspeople have made Ben Hai Hai's insight that "according to the effort is the reward" the core of their product marketing in Lego creations, fast-food sandwiches, stuffed animals, and coding.[10]

Anderson Cooper Answers Howard Stern

Ben Hai Hai's insight has also informed the thinking of many wealthy people about inheritance. A 2021 survey conducted by the Motley Fool showed that two-thirds of people who are in the position to leave large sums to their children are concerned that their children will be (in the words of *Shark Tank*'s Kevin O'Leary) "cursed" by receiving money they did not work for. These specific concerns include believing that the money will be used irresponsibly, that beneficiaries are ill-equipped to manage the money, and that the children will become lazy.[11]

This concern was clearly articulated in a conversation in 2014 that the television journalist Anderson Cooper had on *The Howard Stern Show*. Mr. Cooper is the son of Gloria Vanderbilt, the heiress to the Vanderbilt fortune.

Howard Stern told Mr. Cooper "it would seem to be loving" to leave a child a lot of money. Mr. Cooper, who grew up with a lot of rich kids on New York's Upper East Side, disagreed.

> I don't believe in inheriting money. It is an initiative sucker. It's a curse . . . Who has inherited money that has gone on to do things in their own life? If, growing up, I knew that there was some pot of gold waiting for me—I don't know if I would have been so motivated . . . There are a bunch of people who I grew up with who probably inherited a lot of money and I don't know what they are doing. I have not heard of them.[12]

Is Anderson Cooper's concern, embedded in the adage "shirtsleeves to shirtsleeves in three generations," warranted? According to a 2013 study by Boston University professor Jay Zagorsky, the answer is a resounding yes. Using data from the National Longitudinal Survey of Youth, Professor Zagorsky found that "the typical . . . respondent retains about half of his/her inheritance and either spent or suffered capital losses for the other half."[13]

Is this a unique problem of trust-fund kids who grew up with abundance they did not earn? We have another data source to assess: lottery winners. One might think that winning the lottery would cure financial problems and set people up for life. It does the opposite. Lottery winners are more likely than non-lottery winners to have significant financial problems after winning the lottery—with approximately a third of lottery winners actually declaring bankruptcy after their windfall.[14]

According to the effort is the reward, indeed.

Reflection

The great sociologist Max Weber, speaking of the increasing specialization in the world of 1920, said, "Does it mean that we, today, for instance, everyone sitting in this hall, have a greater knowledge of the conditions of life under which we exist than has an American Indian or a Hottentot? Hardly. Unless he is a physicist, one who rides on the streetcar has no idea how the car happened to get in motion."[15]

Professor Weber's insight is truer and more important than ever. Most of us still do not know how cars work, and the same goes for medicine, showers, elevators, airplanes, mobile messaging, artificial intelligence, and countless other things that define our lives.

On the one hand, this is a blessing. No one, regardless of how much he wanted to, could possibly understand how much of what powers our complicated world works. Our inability to understand much of what constitutes our world is the necessary accompaniment of the advances that can make our lives more connected, varied, wealthier, healthier, and longer.

But it comes with the risk described in the Torah and validated by modern science. If we get used to a world of things we can't understand and thus can't contribute to, we risk losing the appreciation and value that accompanies effort. And, as the complainers in Exodus showed, this is not psychologically sustainable. We will end up craving a craving, which might drive us crazy.

Hence, we have a conundrum. Human society, even in the ancient world of the Torah, requires specialization, which means that people will perform tasks for others. This necessarily increases with progress and complexity, which is good. No one should refuse a medication just because he doesn't understand its mechanism or can't create it himself.

Yet, the Torah posits and modern science confirms, that we value things to the extent that we put effort into them. How, then, should we each think about applying the IKEA effect in our lives?

The specific instances where God commands us to do tasks for ourselves provides guidance. God commands us to circumcise our boys and to write a Torah ourselves. These are all tasks related to our most important sources of connection, meaning, and sustenance.

How, then, could we determine which among the many things that constitute our lives require—by biblical principle—personal effort? We could identify the fundamental and existential sources of meaning and connection in our lives, and resolve to take personal action around them.

For instance, a parent might want to instill a love of his religious faith into his child. The parent, acknowledging that the church or synagogue could easily afford to pay a crew to construct a new deck, might suggest that he and his son build the deck themselves—along with other families who want to strengthen their commitment.

A parent who wants her child to connect with the biblical commandment to love the stranger could suggest that they volunteer together to make sandwiches in the food pantry, even when pure economic logic would dictate that they pay someone else to do the task instead. A Zionist family could go to the City of David (*Ir David*) in Jerusalem and engage in the sifting project, thus enabling children to themselves discover treasures from the First and Second Temples. A grandmother who wants to strengthen her connection with her grandson could suggest that they cook dinner for the family together every Sunday. A teacher who wants her students to be grateful can have her students keep a gratitude journal.

And one should always be very careful about leaving a child an inheritance—and not play the lottery!

14

The Magical 55

The Torah and Science of Work and Rest

In Exodus 12:2, Moses, at the instruction of God, has just warned the Pharaoh that the tenth plague—the slaying of the firstborn—is coming at midnight. This will be the final plague, after which the Jews will be freed from Egyptian slavery and begin our journey to the Promised Land to create a "kingdom of priests and a holy nation" that will serve as the model of the world.

What will the Jews do on this most consequential night? God has a carefully considered plan, which the Jews will reenact every year, forever, at our Passover Seder. Before he reveals his plan, he introduces it. He says, "This month is the beginning of months for you." This verse serves as the basis for the Jewish command to sanctify the new moon and to establish Rosh Chodesh—the head of the month—to maintain the Jewish yearly cycle.

The "beginning of months"—that is reasonable. It is appropriate to regard our first day of freedom as the ultimate beginning—and, thus, for it to become the first day of the year. Why, though, does God say that it is "the beginning of months *for you*"? How can a New Year be for—or not for—anyone? No one refers to January 1 as the New Year "for you."

The sixteenth-century Italian rabbi Obadiah Sforno explained that the qualification "for you" just might be the most important advice God can provide for any New Year. It is God's way of saying, "From now on, these months will be yours, to do with as you like. This is by way of contrast to the years when you were enslaved and had no control over your time or timetable at all."[1]

The essence of freedom, God is teaching, is to have control over one's time—to decide how to best allocate the hours, days, and years that constitute our lives. This divine teaching is consecrated through the holiday of Rosh Chodesh, the celebration of the new moon. The month would begin when, upon the testimony of two witnesses that a new moon had arrived, the head of the Beit Din (the Jewish court) would declare, "Sanctified!" Everyone in attendance would respond, "Sanctified! Sanctified!"[2]

So, we learn from Exodus 12 and from the declaration of Rosh Chodesh, a fundamental Jewish obligation to sanctify time. But the Torah wouldn't be a *great* guidebook if it merely instructed us to "sanctify" time. It would have to answer the question: *How* do we sanctify time and, in so doing, truly gain freedom? The Torah provides quite an answer to that question.

The Seven-Day Week

Most measures of time can be explained by nature. A day is the time the earth takes to rotate on its own axis. A month is the time it takes for the moon to orbit around the earth. A year is the time it takes for the earth to orbit the sun.

There is no such equivalent for the week. Consequently, ancient cultures defined the week very differently. The week was four days in West Africa, ten days in Egypt, and fifteen in China. The communists who ran the Soviet Union in the 1930s inaugurated a four- and then five-day week for the same reason that they banned church bells—"to facilitate the struggle to eliminate religion."[3]

Why do we have a seven-day week? From a secular perspective, it is not immediately obvious. A 2015 analysis of time by the popular science journal *Atlas Obscura* called the seven-day week a "totally random, basically meaningless division of time."[4]

This is *not* the perspective of the Torah. In early Genesis, God creates the world in six days and rests on the seventh. And it is not only that God works for six days. At the end of most days, he evaluates his work and deems it to have been "good" or "very good." God, we see, takes pride in his work and appreciates it having achieved its purpose.

Why does God go through such an elaborate process to create the world when he could have just willed it into existence without saying or doing anything? He provides us with an insight into his thinking in Genesis 1:27—when God announces that he has created man in his image. God structured his week as he did, to model for us how we should structure ours.

The seven-day week—structured with six days of work and a day of rest—is so important to God that he is not content to just model the behavior. In Exodus 20:9–10, God provides us with the Ten Commandments, which serve as the framework for all of his laws, teachings, and hopes for us. The first three commandments concern how we are to understand and relate to God.

The fourth commandment is the first to address how we are to live in the world: "Six days you shall work, and do all your work; but the seventh day is a Sabbath to the Lord your God, in which you shall not do any labor, you, nor your son, nor your daughter, your manservant, nor your maidservant, nor your cattle, nor your stranger that is within your gates." The Torah repeats a variant of this instruction several times—which is very rare for this text that has so much to impart in relatively few words. Why would God so insistently decree the seven-day week?

You Shall Work

God's revelation of the meaning of the seven-day week begins in how he phrases the first clause in the Ten Commandments. He says, "Six days *you* shall work." This is not the only, or even the obvious, way that the Author of the Torah could have commanded work. God could have said that work needs to get done, that tasks need to be completed, that things need to be created—and that we should ensure it happens.

Instead, God says: "*You* shall work." The object here is not the work. It is "you"—each of us. Why would work be so important for each of us that the Torah requires it for "*you* [us]"—indicating that its importance is independent of whatever the work accomplishes? The Torah, and the Jewish tradition that builds upon it, describes at least four benefits of work.

Dignity

The first is exemplified in the Talmudic story of Rabbi Yehuda. Each day, he would go to the Beit Midrash, the house of study. He did not bring a backpack or briefcase to the house of study, but a pitcher of water, which he carried on his shoulder. Why? It was not an idiosyncrasy but instead a manifestation of what seems to be an established practice. His contemporary Rabbi Shimon would go to the house of study carrying a basket on his shoulder. Rabbi Yehuda explained, "Great is work, as it gives dignity to the one who does it."[5]

Joy

The second benefit of work is articulated in the biblical book of Ecclesiastes (2:24): "There is nothing better for a person than to eat, drink, and enjoy his work. I saw that this too was from the hand of God." The imperative of enjoying one's work is not a theoretical goal.

The eighteenth-century Polish sage and founder of Hasidic Judaism, the Baal Shem Tov, said, "The ability to be joyous . . . is considered a biblical command." This was amplified by the twenty-first-century sage Rabbi Jonathan Sacks, who wrote, "Joy is the supreme religious emotion."[6]

Thus, the logic of enjoying our work is clear. In Genesis, Exodus, and Deuteronomy, God is clear that we must work six days a week. In Ecclesiastes, the enjoyment of work is given divine authority—and placed, as a human need, alongside food and drink. It is only possible to enjoy life if we enjoy what we do for six days a week.

Purpose

The third benefit of work is described by Moses in Deuteronomy 28:30, when he reveals the curses that will befall us if we do not heed the word of God. He says, "You shall plant a vineyard, but you shall not enjoy its fruit."

This curse is that our work will be meaningless. This is the opposite of the experience that God had in Genesis when he worked, evaluated, and determined that his creations were "good" or "very good." When work is the blessing that God intends it to be, it has a purpose and provides the worker with meaning and fulfillment.

Wisdom

The fourth benefit of work derives from the knowledge, understanding, and ultimately wisdom that it uniquely accords. Whether one's work emphasizes buying and selling, managing and mentoring, building and fixing, serving customers or treating patients, a job will provide an education into human challenges, yearnings, and potential. This is why even the most renowned ancient rabbis, who had the responsibility to transmit Torah and could have easily been supported by the communities who revered them, all had occupations. Rabbi Yochanan was a sandal maker, Rabbi Jose was a tanner, Rav Huna was a water carrier, Rabbi Joshua was a blacksmith, Rabbi Akiva was a shepherd, and Hillel the Elder was a woodcutter.

A thousand years later, the most renowned rabbis still had conventional jobs. Maimonides, Nachmanides, and Judah Halevi were physicians. Don Isaac Abravanel was a financier and statesman, and Rashi was a wine merchant. Many of their Torah commentaries and religious teachings are enriched by knowledge and insights that they derived from being so active in their professions. As Maimonides wrote of his profession, "The art of medicine is given a very large role with respect to the virtues, the knowledge of God, and attaining true happiness. To study it diligently is among the greatest acts of worship."[7]

The Torah is clear: Everyone should work for the dignity it dispenses, the enjoyment it brings, the meaning it provides, and the understanding that it enables. One might respond to such an ambitious goal and ask where one can find such satisfying work. The Torah provides an answer in two stories—one from Genesis and one from Leviticus.

Where Joseph Succeeds

A truth about work is that there is a huge variety in the kinds of activities that constitute it. One might then ask what jobs best yield the good life the Torah claims that work provides.

The Author of the Torah seems to have anticipated this question—as he answers it very clearly through the man who has its most varied career. This is Joseph. Joseph is a shepherd, a slave, and a prisoner—before establishing himself as the world's greatest dream interpreter and most important executive.

Joseph's achievements are such that he is the only person the Torah calls an *ish matzilach*—"a successful man." And the Torah calls him that *twice*—first in Genesis 39:2 and then again in Genesis 39:23.

If one were asked to guess when Joseph earned such a designation, there are some easy candidates. One might be when Joseph emerged from prison and correctly interpreted the dream of the Pharaoh that befuddled everyone else. Another might be when Joseph guided the entire world through a global famine.

But the Torah does not designate Joseph as successful either time! Instead, the Torah first calls Joseph "a successful man" when he is a slave in the home of Potiphar—and performs so well that he is appointed the head slave. Joseph is called "a successful man" again when he is a prisoner, and performs so well that the wardens put him "in charge of all that was done there."

The Torah, we see, identifies Joseph as a success when he performs well at the lowest of tasks and in the humblest of circumstances. Here, the Torah is providing its theory of success: Success should not be measured by the job one has, but by *how* one performs in his job.[8]

How is Joseph able to succeed in both places? He was, as was made clear almost as soon as we meet him, a talented person. But the Torah is full of talented people, and only Joseph is called "a successful man." There are two secrets to Joseph's success, and they are both presented very clearly in Genesis 39–40.

The first secret to Joseph's success is revealed in Genesis 39:5 (when Joseph is a slave in Potiphar's home) and Genesis 39:21 (when Joseph is a prisoner). In both cases, the text tells us that God has blessed Joseph. How has Joseph come to be blessed by God? Unlike his father, grandfather, and great-grandfather (Jacob, Isaac, and Abraham), Joseph never has a conversation with God. Instead, he constantly acknowledges and appreciates God, as one would a friend or a mentor who is always nearby. He always believed that his work, even as a slave and a prisoner, had meaning—so much that it was directed by God. This belief culminates in Genesis 45, when Joseph (then the viceroy of Egypt) reveals himself to his stunned brothers. He tells them not to be distraught at their role in his enslavement, as it is all part of God's plan.

Having always found meaning in his work, Joseph is prepared for the second attribute that will make him a success. The Torah reveals this attribute in Genesis 40:7, when Joseph approaches two of his fellow prisoners. He asks: "Why do you look so sad today?"

The presumption behind this question is astonishing. Joseph and the other inmates are living and working in prison. Yet, Joseph must have set such an example of being happy in his work that looking sad was *abnormal*. Indeed, they tell him the source of their sadness—which has nothing to do with their work in prison. Their sadness derives from having had perplexing dreams. They tell him their dreams, which Joseph interprets correctly. This establishes Joseph in Egypt as a master dream interpreter—which, two years later, led to the Pharaoh calling him from prison to interpret his disturbing dream. Joseph's convincing interpretation of the Pharaoh's dream results in him winning the ultimate promotion—the viceroy of Egypt, the number two in the entire land.

The story of Joseph, we see, reveals the biblical formula for worldly "success." Joseph finds joy, purpose, and excellence in what certainly seem like lowly, dead-end jobs: as a slave and as a prisoner. The fruits of his attitude toward his work do not present immediately. He spends around twenty years as a slave and a prisoner. No one would have predicted that a slave or a prisoner would ever become the viceroy of Egypt. But the career of a person who works hard, well, and joyously, will not—the Torah posits—be linear. Such a person, even in the lowliest job—can be a biblical "success"—and set himself up for a job that he could never have imagined himself in.

The Torah's Garbagemen

Joseph, as the only person in the Bible to be called "a successful man," is certainly special . . . but was he unique in being able to derive meaning, purpose, and joy in the humblest of jobs? In Leviticus 6:3, the Author of the Torah gives his answer.

The Jews are wandering in the desert en route to the Promised Land—and, at God's instruction, have built a holy Tabernacle that is led by the priest-teachers (called the Kohanim). God says, "The priest shall . . . take up the ashes to which the fire has reduced the burnt offering on the altar and place them beside the altar. He shall . . . carry the ashes outside the camp to a pure place." In other words, God commands the priests to take out the garbage.

How do the priests regard this assignment? The Talmud explains that the priests would race each other up the ramp of the altar to win the honor of removing more ashes. The priests were so excited to do this work that the Temple authorities had to set rules to prevent them from getting hurt as a result of rushing so enthusiastically.[9]

So, the Torah stipulates, "Six days *you* shall work"—declaring that we need to work, independent of what the work accomplishes. The Torah explains why. Work brings us dignity, purpose, wisdom, and joy. The Torah is clear that these benefits can be delivered by any job, and that a worker with this attitude sets himself up for upward mobility.

This seems like a good time to consider the seventh day of the week—Shabbat—which the Talmud declares to be "a taste of Heaven on earth."[10] The Torah, however, counsels us that the sanctification of time requires something in between. This is the attitude of anticipation.

Anticipation

In the Torah, in subsequent Jewish teaching, and in modern Hebrew, the six workdays have no name. There is no Monday, Tuesday, or Wednesday. Instead, there is Yom Rishon (first day), Yom Sheni (second day), and so on until the seventh day—which is the Sabbath, known as Shabbat. We are to enjoy, find meaning, and derive honor from our work while counting *toward* Shabbat, which is the day when work must cease.

Why do we have this strange day-naming convention? The answer is revealed by the fact that we are commanded several times in the Torah to be *shomer* Shabbat. This is often translated as an instruction to "guard" the Sabbath. That is a fine translation, so long as we understand what *shomer* (guard) really means.

One meaning is clear enough. We *protect* the Sabbath from all work-related tasks being performed on it. But that cannot be all. In Genesis 37:11, Joseph tells his family of his dreams of ruling over them. His father, Jacob, rebukes his son for relaying such a seemingly self-serving dream. But the text tells us that Jacob "*shamar et hadavar*." This is sometimes translated as "he guarded the matter."

However, one cannot "guard" a matter. So, what could the text mean? The answer can be found in the main function of a guard. It is to anticipate threats. Jacob was, as Rashi wrote, "anticipating" what would become of the dream.[11] Thus, to be *shomer* Shabbat is to both protect and anticipate the Sabbath.

This spirit of anticipation would become an integral part of the Shabbat experience. For instance, the singing of *Lecha Dodi*—which was composed by the sixteenth-century poet Shlomo Halevi Alkabetz. The song is sung in synagogues on Friday evening as the Sabbath approaches. "Let's go, my beloved, to meet the bride / Let us welcome the presence of Shabbat . . . / Come in peace, crown of her husband / Come O Bride! Come O Bride!"

This anthem is about *anticipating* the sacred day. The spirit of anticipation was resonant in a nostalgic reflection of the twentieth-century sage Rav Joseph B. Soloveitchik. He recalled the Jews of his youth in Europe who would go outside on Friday afternoons to greet the coming Sabbath "with beating hearts and pulsating souls."[12]

The Sabbath(s)—Plural!

On Friday at sundown, the weeklong anticipation is over as the Sabbath has finally arrived. We are ready to conclude our enjoyment of purposeful workdays by experiencing twenty-four hours of what our ancient sages called "a taste of Heaven on earth." How can we make this day as special, beloved, and holy as the Torah intends it to be?

The answer is revealed in the Shabbat commandment of Exodus 31:13: "You shall observe my Sabbaths." Why is the Sabbath referred to in the plural?

The answer is revealed in how the Shabbat is referred to throughout the Torah. We are instructed to "guard" *and* to "remember" the Sabbath. Remembering, in the biblical context, is never the opposite of forgetting. It is a call to action.

One Sabbath—that of "guard"—is the Sabbath of restriction. The Torah is clear, in several places, that we honor the Sabbath by refraining from creative work. However, that alone does not constitute the Sabbath experience. Rabbi Efrem Goldberg of the Boca Raton Synagogue says that one who experiences the holy day by just relaxing might be refraining from work—but is actually a *mechalel shabbat*: a Sabbath violator.[13]

What, then, does it mean to "remember" (or mark) the Sabbath that is entirely distinct from work? God teaches us in the creation story in Genesis 2:2. "On the seventh day God finished the work he had been doing; so on the seventh day he rested from all his work." So, was God creating ("finishing" his work) on the seventh day, or was he resting?

The reconciliation of these seemingly contradictory activities resides in what the Torah means by "rest." If it means simply not working, then God would not have had to create it. Absence cannot be created. It is what happens when the activity is not being performed. But God, by having "finished his work" on the seventh day, was obviously creating *something*.

What could that something be? Rabbi David Fohrman of Aleph Beta writes that God created a particular kind of rest called *purposeful* rest.[14]

The Jewish Shabbat practices, which have existed for thousands of years, show us what purposeful rest is. We usher in the Sabbath on Friday night by blessing God and our children, reciting an ode to the Jewish woman, making special blessings over wine and bread, and singing together. We then engage in a long and relaxed dinner with family and friends, discussing everything except business. Jewish married couples, acting in accordance with the strong encouragement of a variety of ancient teachings, will often conclude the evening by making love.[15]

On Saturday, we study Torah, pray, eat special meals, and play games or sports in fellowship and community. We also create and strengthen our relationships as we grow in mind and spirit. As the sun goes down on Saturday evening, we bid the Sabbath goodbye in a ceremony where we light special candles and pray for a good week ahead. Having rested purposefully on this *busy* day, we are refreshed, rejuvenated, recommitted, and ready to create in the subsequent six days.

How does purposefully resting on the Sabbath prepare us for the workweek ahead? The answer is revealed in a few hypotheticals. If an artist never stopped working on his painting to thoughtfully consider what to add next, how would the work turn out? If a business team never went off-site, would it perform better or worse? Would we want to go to a surgeon who operated all the time or one who operated frequently, had a fixed time to study her craft, and enjoyed fishing and playing ball with her children every Saturday?

The answer might be obvious to us—but that is only because we live in a world created by the Torah. In the fourth century BCE, the land of Israel came under the control of Alexander's Macedonian Empire. Several hundred years later, the Romans conquered Israel. The Greeks and Romans had their differences, but they agreed on at least one thing: The Jewish adherence to the Sabbath demonstrated that we were lazy. This view was articulated by the Roman poet Juvenal who, in his Satire XIV "Bad Parenting," ridiculed, "Those that . . . Revere the Sabbath . . . It's the father that's to blame, treating every seventh day / As a day of idleness, separate from the rest of daily life."[16]

It would be another 1,800 years before the practice of having time away from work was solidified in the idea of the weekend. And the early-twentieth-century Zionist poet Ahad Ha'am, reflecting on the miracle of continued Jewish existence, provided an explanation: "More than the Jews kept the Sabbath—the Sabbath kept the Jews."[17]

So, the Torah and the Jewish teaching and practice that are based on it tell us how to structure our time so that we can fulfill the ambition of Exodus 12:2 to sanctify time. We should find joy, purpose, and wisdom in and from our work—whatever our work is. As we do so, we should *anticipate* the Sabbath. From when Shabbat arrives on Friday night to when it departs on Saturday night, we should cease all work—and engage in *purposeful* rest.

What does science say about this remarkably distinctive conception of time?

The Science

In a recent discussion, Rabbi David Wolpe of Sinai Temple reflected on a lifetime of delivering eulogies. It is common, probably in all faiths, for the clergyman to meet with a family to discuss the life of a deceased loved one—in part to determine what to include in the eulogy. Rabbi Wolpe says that loved ones of the deceased often tell him that dad was a lawyer or an accountant—but *really*, he was a lover of English literature.[18]

Rabbi Wolpe reflects that he has found this sad. After all, the deceased spent tens of thousands of hours as a lawyer or accountant, which obviously constituted a large part of what he did and thus, of who he was. Yet, the implication of the eulogy wish is that all of the time spent working was just a funding mechanism to enable the deceased to be who he really was and to do what he truly enjoyed.

How prevalent might this attitude toward work be? One place to turn is American popular songs, whose lyrics often reveal what their broad audience thinks and feels about a subject of cultural importance.

From "Nine to Five" to "Overtime Hours for Bullshit Pay"

In 1980, Dolly Parton released "9 to 5," which was the theme of the 1980 movie by the same name. In the song, the employee and her colleagues work hard, but the boss is always taking and never giving. He denies the employee deserved promotions, and dashes her dreams. The employee feels as if she is a barely willing participant in a "rich man's game."

It immediately rose to number one on the charts and became, in the words of NPR, "an American anthem [that] unites workers across decades."[19] Indeed, in 2004, the American Film Institute named it one of the one hundred most important songs of the past hundred years. In 2017, it hit platinum status. Senator Elizabeth Warren used it as the theme for her 2020 presidential campaign, despite the devoutly apolitical Dolly Parton not having approved its usage.[20]

Dolly Parton's "9 to 5" was a huge hit, but not because it voiced anything original. It fit into the established genre of the American "hate work" song. In 1937, the Disney classic "Heigh Ho" from *Snow White and the Seven Dwarfs* incorporated what was basically the curse of Deuteronomy 28: "We dig up diamonds by the score / A thousand rubies, sometimes more / But we don't know what we dig 'em for."

In 1965, The Vogues soared to the top of the charts by singing about "trading my work for pay" in "Five O'Clock World." The protagonist tolerates his meaningless work because of the "long-haired girl" who "makes it all worthwhile."

In 1974, Bachman–Turner Overdrive released "Taking Care of Business," which spent twenty weeks on the *Billboard* Hot 100. It is about the worker who "gets up every morning" to "start your slaving job to get your pay."

In 2023, Oliver Anthony released his song "Rich Men North of Richmond," which debuted at #1 on the *Billboard* charts. He sang, "I've been sellin' my soul, workin' all day / Overtime hours for bullshit pay . . ."

The same themes are evident in The Beatles' "Hard Day's Night," Johnny Paycheck's "Take This Job and Shove It," Huey Lewis and the News's "Working for a Living," Kenny Chesney and George Strait's "Shiftwork," Cher's "Working Girl," and many other popular songs about work.

To put it mildly, no one in any of these songs describes deriving any dignity, joy, purpose, or wisdom from their work.

"A Profound Impact"

This is the twenty-first century, which means that we have more than music to assess what we think about work. We have data—and a lot of it. Each year, Gallup conducts a "State of the Workplace" study. In 2020, only 20 percent of respondents in this 142-country study reported being "actively engaged" in their work. This number might seem low, but it is a significant increase from previous years. The country that consistently ranks the highest in employee engagement is the United States. This seems promising for Americans, until one sees that we lead the world with a rate that is under 30 percent.[21]

The fact that most Americans (and others) are detached from their work—which is completely contrary to the biblical vision—arouses some important questions.

Is the biblical vision of purposeful work an unrealistic ideal? More fundamentally, if someone works an honest, unenjoyable, and meaningless job that provides him with time and money to spend with family, friends, community, and other interests, can he lead a happy and fulfilling life? Is it okay if a eulogy passes by the work of the deceased?

An investigation can begin with the research of Tom Smith of the National Opinion Research Center (NORC)—which is housed at the University of Chicago. In 2007, Dr. Smith published a report called "Job Satisfaction in the United States." After conducting detailed surveys of more than four thousand people, he concluded:

> Because of work's central role in many people's lives, satisfaction with one's job is an important component in overall well-being. For example, job satisfaction and general happiness are positively related with those saying they are very happy in general rising from 15.7% for those very dissatisfied with their job to 45.3% very happy among those very satisfied with their job.[22]

So: Those who are happy and satisfied at work are three times as likely to be "very happy" generally. And that's not all. In 2010, the psychologist Jessica Pryce-Jones published the results of her study of three thousand people from seventy-nine countries. She found that the happiest employees are 180 percent more energized, 108 percent more engaged, 50 percent more motivated, and 50 percent more productive than their less content colleagues. Of course, these qualities—being energized, engaged, motivated, and productive—are attributes that lead one to be successful at work (or any activity). Happier employees cultivate the attributes that lead to success at work.[23]

In 2011, Professor Teresa Amabile of Harvard Business School and the independent researcher Steven Kramer asked the same question about happiness at work with a different data set. Writing in the *New York Times* on "America's [work] disengagement crisis," they reported on a study they did of 12,000 diary entries of 238 workers at seven companies. With access to descriptive diary entries, they were able to understand why and how happy employees are better employees. They wrote:

> Our research shows that inner work life has a profound impact on workers' creativity, productivity, commitment, and collegiality. Employees are far more likely to have new ideas on days when they feel happier. Conventional wisdom suggests that pressure enhances performance; our real-time data, however, shows that workers perform better when they are happily engaged in what they do.[24]

What, in a dynamic economy, is likely to happen to workers who are more creative, productive, committed, collegial, engaged, motivated, and productive? Ms. Pryce-Jones explains, "Happiness at work is closely correlated with greater performance and productivity as well as greater energy, better reviews, faster promotion, higher income, better health, and increased happiness with life."[25]

The data is clear. The claim in "Five O'Clock World" that one can be dissatisfied with one's work but generally happy because a "long-haired girl" is waiting is largely mythical. The claim in the Torah, exemplified in Joseph—that the ability to find meaning and happiness at work is highly correlated with general happiness and upward mobility—is true.

No wonder Ecclesiastes says, "There is nothing better for a person than to eat, drink, and enjoy his work. I saw that this too was from the hand of God."

The Twenty-First-Century List of Essentials

These discoveries might lead one to ask: How can I be happy at work? One theory comes from Mary Crawford, a character in the 1814 Jane Austen novel *Mansfield Park*. She said, "A large income is the best recipe for happiness I have ever heard of."[26] The other is from the biblical Joseph, whose sense of mission and purpose is reflected in his continual conviction that his work is part of God's plan for him.

In 2010, Princeton professors Daniel Kahneman and Angus Deaton put this question to the test. They studied the results of the Gallup-Healthways

Well-Being Index from 2008 and 2009 and determined that happiness increases with income until $75,000 per year per household—after which more money does not lead to increased happiness. The $75,000 figure equates to approximately $108,000 in 2024 dollars. The data, they explained, applies to large cities with high costs of living. Consequently, the dollar figure could be adjusted downward for less expensive areas and upward for larger families. Subsequent studies have added a caveat—that naturally happy people are likely to become happier with greater incomes, but that naturally unhappy people plateau at the $75,000 mark.[27]

The fundamental insight of Professors Kahneman and Deaton is validated by Dr. Smith's NORC data. The job satisfaction survey found that the profession that produced the greatest satisfaction and the most happiness is that of the clergy. Firefighters ranked second in job satisfaction and third in happiness. Special education teachers ranked ninth in job satisfaction and fifth in happiness. The higher-paying jobs—engineers, salespeople, supervisors—were all below them in both categories.[28]

If compensation does not lead to job satisfaction, what does? The functions of the professions that lead in happiness and satisfaction give it away. Clergymen and firefighters are paid at around the American average. But they work in jobs that are laden with meaning and purpose.

This observation coheres with the discovery of Professor Shawn Achor of Harvard University that 90 percent of people would leave their job for one with less pay and more meaning. This matches the findings of Professor Amabile and Mr. Kramer, who write, "A clear pattern emerged when we analyzed the 64,000 specific workday events reported in the diaries: of all the events that engage people at work, the single most important—by far—is simply making progress in meaningful work."[29]

The biblical Joseph, who always found God in his work, became the Torah's "successful man." The relationship between meaning and success at work was the subject of analyses by the Brookings Institute in 2020 and McKinsey & Company in 2021. The Brookings study found that those who find meaning in their work are more likely to spend extra effort, seek additional training, and are less likely to call in sick. The McKinsey study reports that those who find their work "meaningful" are likely to seek close collaboration around difficult problems, be persistent and helpful, and associate the organization's success with their own. The qualities identified by the researchers at Brookings and McKinsey are, of course, those that set an individual up for promotions, raises, and other accoutrements of success. Indeed, the McKinsey study reports that those who find meaning in their work improve their performance by 33 percent.[30]

The social scientific findings on meaningful work led Professor Achor to conclude, "The 21st century list of essentials might be due for an update: food, clothing, shelter—and meaningful work."[31] Just as God said when he decreed: "Six days you shall work"—and Joseph exemplified this when he worked as a slave, a prisoner, and a viceroy.

The Lesson from Luke, a Hospital Custodian

So, the science suggests that there is a profound correlation between happiness, meaning, and success at work. Consequently, we are drawn to ask, What *kind* of work can be meaningful, enjoyable, and lead to upward mobility? The Torah—in describing the career of its only "successful man" (Joseph) and emphasizing how the priests rushed to take out the garbage—provides a definitive answer: any job.

What does the science say?

In the early 2000s, Professor Ann Wrzesniewski of the University of Pennsylvania studied how hospital custodians view their work. She found that some considered their work enjoyable and meaningful, while others viewed their work simply as a way to get paid. What accounted for the difference? It was not, she determined, the timing of the shifts or the background of the custodians. Professor Wrzesniewski finally figured it out and, she said in a Google Talk, "It stunned and inspired us."[32]

She found that the difference was in how the custodians characterized their tasks. One custodian, Luke, told Professor Wrzesniewski about an incident that occurred after he had cleaned the room of a young comatose patient. The patient's father, who had been keeping vigil at the bedside, took a break to go outside and smoke a cigarette. The father came back and, according to Luke, "just freaked out . . . telling me I didn't do it. I didn't clean the room and all this stuff. And at first, I got on the defensive, and I was going to argue with him. But I don't know. Something caught me and I said, 'I'm sorry. I'll go clean the room.'"

The interviewer said to Luke, "And you cleaned it again?"

Luke responded, "Yeah, I cleaned it so that he could see me clean it . . . I can understand how he could be. It was like six months that his son was here. He'd be a little frustrated, so I cleaned it again. But I wasn't angry with him. I guess I could understand."

Luke saw himself not as a custodian with a list of enumerated job requirements. His job, as he saw it, was not to just clean the room. It was "to make the patients and their families feel comfortable, to cheer them up when they were down, to encourage them and divert them from the pain and their fear, and to give them a willing ear if they felt like talking."

This attitude was not unique to Luke. Another custodian, Ben, said that he would stop mopping the hallway floor when a recovering patient needed to go for a walk. Ben's colleague Corey spoke of how he violated rules and refrained from vacuuming the visitor's lounge when family members of a patient were napping.

Another custodian violated her official duties and left her work area to walk the patients' families through the Byzantine maze of the hospital so that the sick person would not have to worry that his relatives would get lost. Another custodian consistently rearranged the decor in the room of a comatose patient, thinking that the patient might somehow respond to the newness in his environment. She did not say that these activities were part of the job. She said that they were "part of me."[33]

Job Crafting

Professor Wrzesniewski invented a term to describe this phenomenon: "job crafting."[34] Luke and Ben crafted—or reframed—their jobs to maximize its meaning. In deciding, truthfully, that they were not just trash collectors but the guarantors of the safe, sterile, and welcoming environment that the sick need to get better, they decided to become the "you" in the command of "Six days, *you* shall work." And they show us what Joseph in prison and the priests in the Tabernacle were doing: They were job crafting.

The potential of job crafting for happiness, satisfaction, meaning, personal prosperity, and organizational growth is so profound and promising that one wonders: In what jobs is job crafting available? Who can job craft, and where can it be done?

Professor Wrzeniewski shows how hospital custodians can job craft. In 1962, President John F. Kennedy toured NASA and was impressed by the diligence of a custodian. President Kennedy told the man that he was the best custodian he saw. "Sir, I'm not just a janitor," the man said. "I'm helping to put a man on the moon."[35] A 2019 analysis by the psychologist Catherine Moore references a customer service representative who escaped the boredom of entering orders by seeing herself as ensuring a positive customer experience. The analysis also describes a cook who framed his role as one of culinary artistry in a collaborative environment in service of providing a nourishing experience to others.[36]

It seems as if every job—from hospital cleaning to restaurant cooking—is open to crafting and its manifold benefits. All the worker has to do is to see himself, rightly, as a crucial part of an important process that creates something valuable and benefits others significantly.

Joseph, as the original job crafter, rises from being a slave and a prisoner to being the viceroy of Egypt. Is the Torah correct that job crafters set themselves up for career advancement? As Jessica Pryce-Jones demonstrated, happy workers are vastly more likely to be energized, engaged, motivated, and productive than others. These are the qualities that lead to career advancement. But we have more than this very good circumstantial evidence. In 2019, Professor Nina Fryer of the University of Leeds published a dissertation on the effects of job crafting (which she calls "task crafting") and promotions. She found that "logistic regression showed that task crafting at time 1 increased the likelihood of promotion at time 2."[37]

The "Old Adam" Becomes "Crazy Busy"

The "hate work" philosophy that has characterized so many popular songs is clearly at odds with the philosophy behind job crafting. Both tendencies exist in contemporary American life. There are hospital custodians who regard themselves as healers, and there is Oliver Anthony who laments "workin' all day for bullshit pay."

Which conception of work is ascendant? Are we set with a philosophy that regards work as what one must endure to receive a paycheck? Or are we moving toward a philosophy that embodies the Torah's "six days *you* shall work"—and its counsel to find meaning, enjoyment, joy, and dignity in that work?

Thorstein Veblen was one of the great American intellectuals of the late-nineteenth and early-twentieth centuries. An economist and a sociologist, he is perhaps the most valuable source for understanding how Americans perceived work in his era. In his 1899 classic, *The Theory of the Leisure Class*, he wrote, "Conspicuous abstention from labor . . . [has become] the conventional mark of superior . . . achievement."[38] Status, in Professor Veblen's era, was measured by not needing to work and not working—and demonstrating one's maximal engagement in leisure.

This vision of the good life was not just for the elite. In 1930, the great economist John Maynard Keynes of Cambridge University published a seminal essay, "Economic Possibilities for Our Grandchildren." Envisioning the economic culture of the twenty-first century, Professor Keynes said, "For many ages to come the old Adam will be so strong in us that everybody will need to do some work if he is to be contented [sic]."[39]

Professor Keynes, in his reference to "the old Adam," credits (or blames!) the Torah for the belief that people feel the need to work in order to be content. He believed that the Torah implanted, rather than identified, the idea that people have an existential need to work. Therefore, he reasoned, it could fade away. Indeed, Professor Keynes specified that the "old Adam" could be satisfied in fifteen hours a week of performing "small duties and tasks and routines."

A generation later, the legendary science fiction author Arthur C. Clarke went even further. He articulated his vision for the future in which machines would do all the work: "The goal of the future is full unemployment, so we can play."[40]

This vision, to put it mildly, is *not* the biblical philosophy embodied in "six days *you* shall work" or contemporary job crafting. Is this vision winning over the biblical conception of work?

One way to assess is through luxury marketing. Luxury marketers, with billions of dollars at stake, are charged with presenting the good (or aspirational) life to potential customers. Enter the advertising campaign of the 1980s and 1990s for Cadillac, named "Cadillac Style." This campaign was of rich people at leisure—playing polo, horse jumping, loading fancy dogs into a car, and diving off a yacht into the ocean.[41] Leisure, not meaningful work, is being portrayed as the aspirational life.

Another way to assess the prevalent ideology of work is through the rules set by elite private clubs. After I graduated from Yale Law School in 1998, I joined the Yale Club in New York City to have a place to meet people for the business I had cofounded (GLG). The Yale Club, I discovered, had a strictly enforced policy banning the use of documents, papers, or anything else that could constitute business activity in most public areas. Two people could talk quietly over a newspaper, but not over a business document. It was as if the existence of a business conversation in one corner of the room would pollute the Yale Club experience for members in another corner. This policy was the same at other similar clubs.

Messrs. Veblen, Keynes, and Clarke would have recognized the "Cadillac style" campaign and the Yale Club policy as an indication that the culture was heading in exactly the way they projected.

Sometime around the turn of the twenty-first century, everything changed. William Powers is the author of the 2010 best-seller *Hamlet's BlackBerry*. Mr. Powers, now of the MIT Media Laboratory, tells the story of his friend Marie. When he first met her in the mid-1990s, Marie was an immigrant learning English. When Mr. Powers asked her how she was doing, she would "flash a big happy smile and say, 'Busy, very busy!'"

Mr. Powers found it "strange, partly because she said it so consistently and partly because her expression and upbeat tone didn't match her words. She seemed pleased, indeed ecstatic, to be reporting that she was so busy." Her response soon became less strange to him. He writes:

> After a while, I figured out what was going on. Marie was copying what she'd heard Americans saying to one another over and over. Everyone talked so much about how busy they were, she thought it was a pleasantry, something that a person with good manners automatically said when a friend asked how they were doing. Instead of, "Fine, thank you," you were supposed to say you were busy.[42]

In a 2012 op-ed for the *New York Times*, the cartoonist Tim Kreider addressed the subject that Marie observed. He says, "If you live in America in the 21st century, you've probably had to listen to a lot of people tell you how busy they are. It's become the default response when you ask anyone how they're doing: 'Busy!' '*So* busy.' '*Crazy* busy.'"

Mr. Kreider noted that the people who say this are generally not those "pulling back-to-back shifts in the I.C.U. or commuting by bus to three minimum-wage jobs." The busyness of those who claim to be "crazy busy" is "self-imposed"—and their assertion, Mr. Kreider writes, is a "boast disguised as a complaint."[43]

A way to test Marie's intuition and Mr. Kreider's commentary is by returning to Cadillac commercials. By 2014, Cadillac ran a major campaign for its ELR Coupe featuring the actor Neal McDonough. In the advertisement, Mr. McDonough mocked rich people who accumulate "stuff" and ridiculed Europeans who use their wealth to take August off. He instead celebrated "crazy, driven, hard-working believers." The aspirational life presented by Cadillac in the 2010s was completely different from what it portrayed a generation before.

A 2016 study published by Harvard professors Silvia Bellezza, Neeru Paharia, and Anat Keinan showed why the most sophisticated marketing executives were portraying the aspirational lifestyle as one characterized by work by 2014. They found that wearing a hands-free Bluetooth headset connotes higher status than wearing a pair of headphones for music. They found that use of a time-saving delivery service connotes higher status than does shopping at a high-end grocery store. And they found that a man who "works long hours and always has his calendar full" is more highly regarded than a man who does not have to work and is often at leisure.[44]

The Yale Club and others like it have maintained their anti-work policies, with some making slight modifications (identifying limited spaces and hours where people can talk business). But they now have competitors. The twenty-first century has seen a boon in new private clubs in New York—including the Core Club, Zero Bond, Aman, the Soho House, and Coco's at Colette. These clubs do not prohibit documents, papers, or other accoutrements of work. Instead, they portray work as an indispensable part of any full or even aspirational life.

Zero Bond markets itself as "the piece you've been missing to perfectly complement city living, from workspace and business meetings to lively nightlife." Aman New York states that members are "encouraged to conduct calls, Skype, FaceTime, or video meetings in designated areas." Coco's at Colette co-locates a high-end co-working space with its dining and event facility. The Core Club speaks of enabling members to "endlessly cultivate themselves and enjoy an uncompromising quality of life" by "allow[ing] our members to seamlessly integrate work and play."[45]

55: The Magic Number

In the 2020s, the cultural tendency is clearly to value, celebrate, and even glorify work. While an appreciation of the value of work is now deeply incorporated in our culture, a dedicated time away from it is not. Those who celebrate being crazy busy often speak about how they work seven days. They do not, like Juvenal did two thousand years ago, ridicule Sabbath observers as lazy. Instead, they regard taking a day off from all work to be a lifestyle choice they reject on principle. They certainly do not, as the Torah does, regard the Sabbath as the ultimate win-win: a day of rest that enables people to work better in the subsequent six days.

Is the philosophy behind crazy busy right? Is the Sabbath an indulgence, a neutral lifestyle choice, or a boon for personal and professional vitality? Social science has provided the answers along three vectors: our physical health, our general capabilities, and our productivity at work.

In 2015, Professor Mika Kivimaki of the University College of London led a large team that reviewed dozens of studies related to working hours and health. She found that there are a certain number of hours that a person can work each week before a variety of unrelated maladies such as Type 2 diabetes, heart attacks, strokes, and sleep disturbance set in. It is fifty-five hours.[46]

These findings were confirmed in a 2021 study from the World Health Organization (WHO), which analyzed mortality and work hour data from around the world during the period of 2000 to 2016. The WHO determined that working more than fifty-five hours a week accounted for 745,000 deaths from heart attack and stroke in 2016—which represented increases of 42 percent (heart disease) and 19 percent (stroke) since 2000.[47]

And the effects of working more than fifty-five hours a week are not limited to health. A 2009 study led by Professor Marianna Virtanen of the Finnish Institute of Occupational Health, found that those who work more than fifty-five hours a week suffer a diminution in their vocabulary, their fluency, and their short-term memory.[48]

Could it be that risks to health and capabilities are prices we can consider paying for the increased output and societal wealth that come with working more than fifty-five hours? The first research into the area was conducted by the British Ministry of Munitions, which established a committee in 1915 to assess the work that resulted in equipping the soldiers in the Great War. They concluded that the British war effort required giving workers a Sabbath—*so that the workers would produce more.* The report states: "The evidence is conclusive that Sunday labour, by depriving the worker of his weekly rest, offers him no sufficient opportunity for recovering from fatigue, and is not productive of greater output except for quite short and isolated periods . . . seven days' labour only produces six days' output and . . . reductions in Sunday work have not in fact involved any appreciable loss of output."[49]

A century later, Professor John Pencavel of Stanford analyzed the data using modern tools. He determined that production correlated with work hours for the first forty-nine hours a week. The rate of production slowed significantly for hours fifty to fifty-five. However, there was no increase in output from hours fifty-six to seventy. *The Economist*, in reviewing Professor Pencavel's work, concluded, "That extra 14 hours was a waste of time."[50]

How universal is this finding? In 2018, *HR Magazine* stated, "Working longer than 55 hours a week is counterproductive and crushes productivity." Their source was Bruce Daisley, who derived his conclusion from his experience as a Twitter executive and the research that would inform his book, *The Joy of Work.* Mr. Daisley elaborated in a 2020 interview. He said, "It seems like anyone who's studied human cognition, human thinking, productivity, they struggle to see how productivity keeps going after we hit about 50 hours a week of work."[51]

Why does productivity diminish after fifty hours, and stop at fifty-five? A 2012 study by Professor David Strayer of the University of Utah is illustrative. He gave students a creativity test before and after a backwoods expedition. He found that they performed 50 percent better after the expedition. Taking time away from work on a regular basis, it is clear, dramatically improves the work—to say nothing for the spiritual development of the worker.[52]

So, it is seemingly undisputed that working more than fifty-five hours a week is bad for one's health and productivity. But why fifty-five hours? There is nothing about fifty-five hours that should make it the measure of seemingly all of these independently conducted and geographically distributed studies.

In a secular context, the fifty-five-hour limitation certainly seems arbitrary. But the biblical perspective, which starts with, "Six days you shall work, and on the seventh you shall rest," suggests otherwise.

A Sabbath observer can work a full day from Sunday to Thursday. The Talmud, drawing from Psalm 104, states that the workday lasts from sunrise (when the worker begins his commute) to sunset (when the worker begins his journey home). Given seasonal differences, and assuming a reasonable commuting time, the workday would be around ten hours. On Friday (when one must prepare for the Sabbath), a Sabbath observer can only work around half a day. Therefore, if a Sabbath observer works ten hours from Sunday to Thursday and five on Friday—he is working fifty-five hours a week.[53]

Why 55? The Neuroscience Speaks

So, the Torah and modern social science have converged on the propositions that meaningful and enjoyable work is necessary for a happy and fulfilling life, that such work is accessible for everyone, and that the most one should work is fifty-five hours a week—which is almost six workdays. What, then, does science suggest one should do on the seventh day?

In 2001, the University of Washington neuroscientist Marcus Raichle and his colleagues discovered an area of the brain they called the Default Mode Network (DMN), which is, as the mental health writer Debbie Hampton says, "the brain's resting state circuitry." It is "activated when you stop thinking about something specific [and] the best place to park a problem. In the DMN, your brain does some of its best, wisest, and most creative work."[54]

As the artificial intelligence researcher Max Frenzel notes, the DMN consolidates memories and searches for solutions to problems we identified in more active states. Dr. Frenzel writes, "As the DMN kicks in, our intuition takes center stage and our creativity and problem-solving skills become more nonlinear, making more distant associations. If you have ever had a powerful daydream or epiphany while on a walk or in the shower, you can thank your DMN for that."

The DMN may be "the brain's resting state circuitry" that generates creative breakthroughs, but it does not generate creative breakthroughs with just any rest. Dr. Frenzel writes that it gets clogged with distractions such as those generated by "zoning out in front of the TV, mindlessly swiping on Tinder, or clicking from cat video to cat video on YouTube."[55]

So, rest can provide the rejuvenation, freshness, and perspective that is needed for creativity and problem-solving—so long as it is not mindless. It must be, Dr. Frenzel says, "deliberate." The Author of the Torah, who created what Rabbi David Fohrman characterized as "purposeful" rest on the seventh day, would have understood.

Anticipation

The Torah effectively decrees that we are to work fifty-five hours a week, which is exactly the number that modern scientists have concluded is the number that maximizes productivity. The Torah decrees that we should have a day of purposeful rest following those fifty-five hours—which is what modern scientists have concluded is what the brain needs to maximize its creativity and problem-solving ability.

But the breakdown of the week into six days of work and a day of rest is not all the Torah decrees. It also tells us that we must *anticipate* the Sabbath. As noted, this idea is so embedded in the Jewish experience that we identify the weekdays not by names like Monday and Tuesday but by their distance from the Sabbath.

Why would the Torah, and its subsequent commentators, be so insistent that we must *anticipate* our sacred day? The answer might rest with the hormone dopamine. The Cleveland Clinic explains:

> Dopamine is known as the "feel-good" hormone. It gives you a sense of pleasure. It also gives you the motivation to do something when you're feeling pleasure. Dopamine is part of your reward system . . . As humans, our brains are hard-wired to seek out behaviors that release dopamine in our reward system. When you're doing something pleasurable, your brain releases a large amount of dopamine. You feel good and you seek more of that feeling.[56]

In 2014, the neuroscientist Robert Sapolsky conditioned monkeys to learn that they would receive a treat after they pushed a button in response to a light ten times. He measured the dopamine in their brains at each stage of the process. Professor Sapolsky found that the dopamine did not spike when the monkeys received the reward. It did so when they *anticipated* the reward. This correlation is so profound that dopamine has acquired a nickname in the scientific literature over the past several years: "the anticipation molecule."[57]

The implications of this finding are widespread. Research from university labs, medical facilities, and corporate marketing teams from around the world show that the dopamine-induced pleasure we derive from anticipation explains why drugs are addictive, why we enjoy the chorus in songs, and why shoppers prefer to wait for goods they buy online over receiving them immediately from an in-store purchase. We enjoy anticipation more than achievement, and the achievement significantly more so if we anticipated it.[58]

Another application can be easily intuited. If modern neuroscientists were asked, "What is the best way to get people to appreciate and enjoy a sacred day every week?" their answer would be simple: Make the day special and, just as importantly, construct a system where people *anticipate* it.

Reflection

One of the most common terms in discussions about the allocation of time is "work-life balance." This term betrays an ideology—which is that work and life are in opposition to one another and need to be "balanced." The Torah and modern science unite in their disagreement, stating that a fulfilled and happy life is not opposed to work, but requires it. The work just needs to be limited to fifty-five hours a week, followed by a day of purposeful or deliberate rest.

If we did not want to achieve work-life balance, but instead, to sanctify time in accordance with the consensus of Torah and science, what would one do? He would work a full week, and seek happiness, fulfillment, and purpose in that work. If one is in a job where such results seem elusive, he can follow the model of the biblical Joseph and the example of the hospital custodian Luke and job craft.

A corporate attorney can view his job as helping to ensure that commerce is conducted fairly, clearly, and justly within the rule of law—which is essential for an economy to prosper. A full-time parent can view his job as preparing the next generation to enjoy life, find their mission in the world, and impart sacred values to their children. A hospital security guard can view his job as a protector of the sick, injured, and their care providers. A school custodian can view his job as the guarantor of the clean and inviting environment that is necessary for students to learn and grow.

The worker can job craft, knowing that doing so will make him more fulfilled, happier, and best positioned for promotions and raises. Through the week, he would enjoy and derive meaning from his work *while* anticipating the seventh day. Why would he anticipate the Sabbath ideally with (as Rav Soloveitchik described of his youth) "a beating heart and a pulsating soul"? The activities of the seventh day, and the spirit they impart, should make it easily apparent.

When sundown on the sixth day arrives, the work activities would cease. He would welcome the new day—the Sabbath—with prayer and song, bless his children, glorify his wife, and thank God for the food and wine set before us. He, his family, and guests would then enjoy a long and leisurely meal, where they would discuss anything but work-related matters. After dinner, when the guests have left and the kids are asleep, he and his wife would retire to the bedroom and . . . not go to sleep immediately!

He would awake the next day and spend it learning, praying, and enjoying meals, games, sports, and discussions with family, friends, and neighbors. As sundown approached, he and his family would light a candle and sing a final song marking the transition from Sabbath to the workweek.

Refreshed and rejuvenated—and with the knowledge that we were now ready for optimal performance—he would enter the workweek, excited to perform the sacred acts of creation that characterize his work, and begin to anticipate the Shabbat that is six days away.

PART THREE

Self-Improvement: How We Ought to Think and Feel

15

Why Jacob Returns, the Butterfly Effect Exists, and the Patriots Dominated the NFL

The Torah and Science of "No Small Things"

Why Jacob Returns

It is Genesis 32, and Jacob is about to experience the most important encounter of his life. It is a reunion with his twin brother, Esau, from whose murderous wrath he fled two decades before. Jacob, his wives, and children cross the Jabbok River with "all of his possessions." Then, we learn, that Jacob is "left alone."

A question jumps from the text. How would Jacob have crossed the river with his family and all his possessions, and been "left alone"? Was he with his family and all their possessions or not?

Rabbi Elazar, in the Talmud, says that Jacob must have returned alone to the other side of the river to retrieve *pachim ktanim*—the "small jugs" that he left behind. Not valuable jugs, not heirloom jugs, not even beautiful jugs. Just "small jugs."[1]

How does this make sense? How could Jacob have left with all his possessions and returned for small things? Everyone who has left for a trip with "everything," only to realize that they left a small thing behind, understands Jacob's situation. The difference between us and Jacob is that we would rather buy the forgotten item in an airport store or train station, or just forget about it altogether, realizing that we do not *really* need it. The one thing we don't do is what Jacob, at least in the Talmudic imagination, did—which is return home for the small thing.

Why does Rabbi Elazar think that Jacob would have, on the most consequential night of his life, left his family to make this journey? The Torah will not answer the question in Genesis 32, but it will in Numbers 30—with an answer that is amplified throughout the teachings of the Torah tradition.

Numbers 30 is the section of the Torah governing vows. In Numbers 30:3, God commands, "If a man vows a vow to the Lord . . . he shall not violate his word, he shall do according to all that proceeds out of his mouth."

This seems clear enough: It is God's law that we should keep our promises. But Rashi notices something additional. He notes that the word for "violate"—*yachel*—comes from the root word *chol*- which means "mundane." A thousand years later, the Rebbe Menachem Mendel Schneerson explained the significance of Rashi's insight. The commandment "not to violate [*yachel*] his word" means two things. It means that one should not violate the terms of his vows and must fulfill his commitments. And it also means that one should not make his words and the actions that follow from them "mundane." The Rebbe said, "Even most mundane matters should be imbued with holy intentions and be consistent with the greater purpose for Creation."[2]

The Rebbe's insight enables us to understand why Jacob returned across the Jabbok River for "small things." If mundane matters are infused with holiness, what could be considered a mundane matter? If we need to ensure that our mundane activities are consistent with "the greater purpose for Creation," then do mundane matters and small things really exist?

The answer: No, there are no small things. Now we see why Jacob returns across the river for "small things"—because, for him, there is no such thing. Everything matters.

This seems strange. Of course, there are moments that are vastly more consequential than others. How is it, then, that the Author of the Torah is teaching us that there are no small things? The Torah offers at least four answers.

Reason One: One Man's Small Thing Is Another's Most Important Case

In Exodus 18, Moses's beloved and wise father-in-law, Jethro, comes to visit him in the desert. Jethro, witnessing his son-in-law's practices in the desert, is not impressed. He observes Moses judging all cases and says, "The thing you do is not good." Jethro advises Moses to judge the "great" matters himself and to delegate the "small" matters to others. Moses agrees to do so, and creates a system of intermediate judges.

Fast-forward to Deuteronomy 1:17, which occurs around forty years after Jethro's instruction to Moses. Moses recounts this incident in preparation for the Jewish people's entry into the Promised Land. Rather than speaking of "great and small matters," however, Moses instructs the judges that "if a matter is too *difficult* for you, bring it to me and I will hear it." The distinction that senior judges should make, he explains, is not between small and great, but between easy and difficult.

This narrative amendment is fascinating. In Exodus, Jethro tells Moses to appoint intermediate judges so that he could focus on the "great"—as distinct from the "small"—matters. Moses, in Deuteronomy, rejects the distinction between great and small altogether. The meaningful distinction, Moses suggests, is not between great and small, but between difficult and easy.

Why would Moses have changed the judging paradigm that he agreed with forty years previously? Moses must have learned something in four decades of judging that warranted the change. What could it be? There are two possibilities, both of which can be true.

The first derives from Exodus 22:9, where the Torah describes the laws for one who is safeguarding another person's "donkey, ox, sheep or any animal"—and the animal is injured, stolen, or dies. By stipulating that the laws of liability apply to "any animal," the Torah is emphasizing that even the "least valuable" animal is on par with the major farm animals used in commerce and agriculture.

The Torah's insight: No animal is "small" or without significant value to its owner. Correspondingly, every matter is important to those involved with it. To call a matter small risks (or guarantees) insulting, diminishing, or disrespecting a member of the society. And for Moses, whose fundamental charge is to construct a society of strong individuals who are united in mutual respect and shared vision, this is untenable.

A second reason why Moses may have altered the big-small paradigm, derives from Numbers 27, when five sisters come to Moses and say that they should be able to inherit in the land of Israel from their father even though they are female. One way to look at this is as a "small matter"—the estate law dispute of one family—hardly worthy of Moses's attention. But Moses hears the case and is joined by Elazar the Kohen (the high priest) and "the leaders of the entire assembly." The case is apparently both appropriate, and too difficult, for all of these men. Moses brings it to God, who rules that women should be able to inherit in the land. The result of this seemingly "small" estate law dispute is the biblical establishment and codification of egalitarianism. A small matter, we see, can have embedded within it principles whose adjudication can reshape a society.

Reason Two: Little by Little

The second reason for the Torah valuing seemingly small things is recorded in Deuteronomy 7, when Moses tells the people what will happen if we follow God's commandments. God will, Moses says, drive out our enemies. But *how* he says God will do so is deeply instructive. Moses says that God will drive them out "little by little."

Moses, of course, knew how the world can change with big events: Noah's flood, the destruction of Sodom, the splitting of the sea, and the giving of the Torah (among other things). Why, then, does he expect God to drive out our enemies "little by little" rather than all at once?

On July 30, 1978, the twentieth-century American sage Rav Joseph B. Soloveitchik gave a eulogy for Rebecca Twersky, known as the Rebbetzin of Talne. Rav Soloveitchik did not mention Deuteronomy 7, or even Moses at all. But in his discussion of what he learned from his mother, the Rav just might have explained why Moses said that God reveals himself "little by little."

Rav Soloveitchik said:

> I used to have long conversations with my mother. In fact, it was a monologue rather than a dialogue . . . I used to watch her arranging the house in honor of a holiday. I used to see her recite prayers; I used to watch her recite the sidra every Friday night and I still remember the nostalgic tune. I learned from her very much.
>
> Most of all I learned that Judaism expresses itself not only in formal compliance with the law but also in a living experience. She taught me that there is a flavor, a scent and warmth to *mitzvot*. I

> learned from her the most important thing in life—to feel the presence of the Almighty and the gentle pressure of His hand resting upon my frail shoulders. Without her teachings, which quite often were transmitted to me in silence, I would have grown up a soulless being, dry and insensitive.[3]

It is unlikely that Rav Soloveitchik's mother regarded her arranging of the house before a holiday or reciting a Shabbat prayer as a big thing. Indeed, Rav Soloveitchik did not cite one of them in particular. Instead, it was through years of observing his mother that he learned the lessons that helped make him into a great rabbi. Little by little, just as Moses instructed, Mrs. Soloveitchik taught her son what he needed to know to become Rav Joseph B. Soloveitchik.

That, it seems, is what Moses is revealing in Deuteronomy 7. Most of the changes in our lives happen "little by little," even, in each moment, imperceptibly. If something as big as the destruction of our enemies can happen "little by little," anything can—and probably will.

Reason Three: We Have No Idea What Is Small

A third reason for the Torah valuing small things can be found in the opening verse of Leviticus, which begins with intriguing language: "And He [God] called to Moses, and the Lord spoke to him." Any writing teacher would have edited this to something like: "The Lord called to Moses." Why does the Torah use such seemingly roundabout language instead?

The twenty-first-century Rabbi Yisrael Meir Druck explains. God, the Torah is teaching us, will speak with us—but not through fire and lights. God just might do so through a seemingly regular person, one designated with an ordinary "he." A *seemingly* small encounter might actually be one with the divine.[4]

Genesis 18 presents the quintessential example of this phenomenon. Abraham is sitting at the entrance of his tent following his circumcision in order to be prepared to help anyone who comes by. Three strangers pass by, which is an ordinary occurrence in the desert. Yet Abraham does not treat it as ordinary. He and his family, the text emphasizes, *rush* to give these strangers comfort, shelter, and a feast. It turns out that these strangers aren't just people, but angels. They have a message from God, which is that

Abraham and Sarah, who are both very old, will finally have their dream come true. They will become parents.

According to the Jewish tradition, there is nothing conceptually unique about this story. It describes how God interacts with people in the world. The Hebrew word for angel, *malach*, means messenger. Angels, accordingly, are ordinary people who God deputizes, even just for a moment, to carry his messages. These moments seem small to everyone involved and are easily and often ignored. But they are messages from God, meant to transform a life. Rabbi Marc Gellman explains:

> I want you to think about the angels who have come into your life. I want you to call to mind right now, among all the thousands of people you have met, those handful of people who clearly and absolutely changed your life for the better—not just parents and family, but often total strangers whose simple advice or gift or suggestion or admonition or question changed you forever. Perhaps it was the person who first gave you a book about science and sent you off on the road to become a scientist. Perhaps the person who told you that you would make a good lawyer or teacher or mother or friend or confidant at just the time when you had no intention of becoming anything like that. Perhaps it was the person who told you to watch out at just the time you needed to watch out. Perhaps it was the prayer in a hospital of a stranger who nobody saw on the floor but who came to your bedside and said everything is going to be all right and then it was all right even if the doctors did not understand why or how.[5]

Reason Four: We Live on Paths

In the Talmud, Rabbi Ben Azzai articulates a philosophy of small things that has become frequently cited. He says: "Run to perform [even] a minor mitzvah and flee from sin, for one mitzvah leads to another mitzvah, and one sin leads to another sin."[6]

Ben Azzai's claim derives from deep within the biblical tradition. After Adam and Eve are expelled from the Garden of Eden, God wants to be sure that no one goes near the tree of life. He assigns this task to angels.

God does not, as we might presume, have the angels guard the tree of life. Instead, he has them guard "the path" to the tree of life.

In Genesis 18, God declares his love for and trust in Abraham. He also tells us why. Abraham, God says, has instructed his children to follow the "*path* to do righteousness and justice." God could have admired Abraham for instructing them to do "righteousness and justice," but he doesn't. The path is crucial, and it will be emphasized throughout the Bible. From Deuteronomy to Isaiah to Jonah to the Proverbs—the Bible continues to speak of the "way of the Lord" or the "path of evil."

The message from the Bible is clear: We are either on a good or a bad path. If one is short with his children or rude to a parking lot attendant, it is not a small thing. It is a signal that he is on the wrong path. One who is on the wrong path for small things will be on that wrong path for *everything*, including unquestionably big things.

When "All" Means "All"

It is in the context of the philosophy of small things that we can understand the construction of some of Moses's parting words as he prepares for his death. In Deuteronomy 29:8, Moses instructs the Jews to "observe the words of this covenant and fulfill them, in order that you will be enlightened in all that you do." *All* that we do? Could this cover *every* expression and reaction, every word we choose to say and everything we decide to do and not do? Could Moses have really meant *all*?

King David thought so. In Psalm 56:9, he writes to God: "You keep track of *all* my sorrows. You have collected *all* my tears in your bottle. You have recorded *each one* in your book." He reiterates this sentiment in Psalm 106:3: "Blessed are those who act justly, who do right at *all times*."

All of his sorrows, *all* of his tears, *all* times?

David's son, King Solomon, also thought so. In Proverbs 3:6, King Solomon says, "Know God in *all* your ways."

What, one might ask, are the practical implications of "all"? The Talmud is very clear: "*Always*, a person should view himself as though he were exactly half-liable and half-meritorious." In other words, he should act as though the plates of his scale are balanced, so that if he performs one mitzvah, he is fortunate, as he tilts his balance of the scale to the side of merit.

If he transgresses one prohibition, woe to him, as he tilts his balance of the scale to the side of liability.[7]

In the twelfth century, Maimonides expounded on this idea, stating that everyone should consider the next thing that one says or does (whatever it is, without regard to whether it is supposedly big or small) to be the difference between "destruction . . . [or] salvation."[8]

The Science

Moses's Big/Small to Difficult/Easy Switch—in American Law

In 2012, David Mullins and Charlie Craig went into the Masterpiece Cakeshop in Lakewood, Colorado. They asked Jack Phillips, the cake artist who owned the shop, to make them a cake to celebrate their wedding. Mr. Phillips said that they were welcome to buy any cake in the store. However, he said that he could not deploy his artistic skills for a gay marriage, which he did not believe in. Mr. Mullins and Mr. Craig sued to force Mr. Phillips to make them the cake they wanted.

One way of looking at this is that this is a small dispute. The item at stake was a wedding cake. David Mullins and Charlie Craig could have, and probably did, just get the cake they wanted from another shop in Colorado. The Masterpiece Cakeshop is not exactly Walmart, whose policies affect millions. Mr. Phillips's shop is a tiny, independent local business.

Yet is this a small matter? It was not small to Mr. Phillips, who willingly lost 40 percent of his business rather than deploy his artistic skills for something that he did not believe in.[9] It was not small to Mr. Mullins and Mr. Craig, who believed that they were victims of discrimination. It was not small to the legal community, which generated countless law review articles, seminars, and discussions analyzing and assessing the case. It was not small to the United States Supreme Court, which in 2018, made the case one of the few it accepts every year. And it was not small to the American public, which consumed the abundant media commentary on the case over many years.

Because, as Moses seems to have intuited, big principles can live within small matters, thus collapsing the distinction between big and small. The principles in the Masterpiece Cakeshop case—which included artistic freedom, gay rights, anti-discrimination law, the free exercise of religion, coerced speech and public accommodation law—are anything but small.

The last word here belongs to Professor Scott Dodson, who directs the Center for Litigation and Courts at the University of California College of Law in San Francisco. In 2024, he and a colleague litigated a case before the United States Supreme Court. The case—*Stuart R. Harrow v. Department of Defense*—had $3,000 at stake. Professor Dodson said, "Despite it being kind of a nerdy, small-dollar-value, low-profile case, it is exactly the kind of case that the Supreme Court has taken every year for the last 20 years." Moses, whose frieze sits atop the United States Supreme Court, would have been proud.[10]

Little by Little: The Butterfly Effect

On a wintery day in the early 1960s, MIT meteorology professor Edward Lorenz was running some numbers related to predicting weather patterns. This was before the days of immediate computer calculations, so Professor Lorenz went out to get coffee before returning to see the results.

This experienced meteorologist knew roughly what results to expect. When he returned, he saw the result and was astonished by how inaccurate his prediction had been. What happened? He had rounded off one variable from .506127 to .506—and the predictions generated by his model were now way off.

What happened? By May 1963, Edward Lorenz explored the implications of this finding in a paper, "Deterministic Nonperiodic Flow," which he published in the *Journal of Atmospheric Research*. The title sounds comically boring, but it is one of the most important scientific papers of all time.

Professor Lorenz's ostensible subject was weather patterns, but he knew that his finding did not only concern them. It concerned how things happen in the world. He wrote, "Two states differing by imperceptible amounts may eventually evolve into two considerably different states . . . [meaning] an acceptable prediction of an instantaneous state in the distant future may well be impossible."[11]

In other words, the margin of error for the assumptions underlying any prediction is precisely zero. Why? Because any small difference in an assumption will yield a huge change in a future state. If small things yield huge changes, what have we learned about small things? That there *are* no small things.

Still, "Deterministic Nonperiodic Flow" seemed like an inconsequential paper after it was written. It received just three citations in publications outside of meteorology over the following ten years.[12] But a few colleagues recognized that this paper deserved more than the obscurity it was experiencing. In 1972, these colleagues asked him to discuss the old paper at the conference for the American Association for the Advancement of Science.

Professor Lorenz agreed to do so, and said that he would use the example of how the movement of a seagull can cause a storm. A colleague suggested that butterflies were more captivating. Professor Lorenz, recognizing that he was a meteorologist but not a marketer, agreed. He presented the paper "Predictability: Does the Flap of a Butterfly's Wings in Brazil Set Off a Tornado in Texas?" A seemingly small thing—the flapping of a butterfly's wings—can have a huge impact.[13]

After this presentation, Professor Lorenz's paper and its finding about small things was liberated from obscurity. Professor Gary Herman of Colorado State University wrote, "[Lorenz's finding] essentially makes long-range daily weather forecasting impossible to do accurately."[14] This is an unquestionably big finding. But the impact of Lorenz's insight went far beyond even weather forecasting. Professor Lorenz's conception of small things challenged the very understanding of science.

Jamie Vernon of the *American Scientist* explained in 2017:

> Lorenz's insight called into question laws introduced as early as 1687 by Sir Isaac Newton suggesting that nature is a probabilistic mechanical system, "a clockwork universe." Similarly, Lorenz challenged [the eighteenth-century mathematician] Pierre-Simon Laplace, who argued that unpredictability has no place in the universe, asserting that if we knew all the physical laws of nature, then "nothing would be uncertain and the future, as the past, would be present to [our] eyes."[15]

Professor Lorenz's paper did not only complicate long-term weather forecasting and challenge the fundamental premises of science. In 2022, a multidisciplinary team of scientists and mathematicians led by Professor Bo-Wen Shen published a paper: "Three Kinds of Butterfly Effects Within

Lorenz Models." They wrote, "Lorenz's studies laid a foundation for chaos theory, viewed as the third scientific achievement of the 20th century, after relativity and quantum mechanics."

So, Professor Lorenz's claim that the world works (in Moses's language) "little by little" is one of the top three scientific achievements of the twentieth century. And its implications have extended well beyond science. The Butterfly Effect has been used to guide acne treatment, assess Supreme Court litigation, and understand geopolitics. Moreover, the Butterfly Effect is the rare scientific presentation to have penetrated popular culture. It surfaces in popular and scholarly conversations of marriage, baseball, business, mental health, acts of kindness, and has inspired a major motion picture (*The Butterfly Effect* starring Ashton Kutcher) and a rap hit ("Butterfly Effect" by Travis Scott).

As important and popular as the Butterfly Effect is, contemporary manifestations of Moses's "little by little" prophecy go even beyond it. An age-old question is: What makes romantic relationships, including marriages, succeed and fail? Common answers following a breakup include: He/she had an affair, we fell out of love, we grew apart, the spark disappeared. These, and other expressions like them, speak of big things.

Dr. John Gottman is, according to a report from the University of California at Berkeley, "the nation's top marriage expert" and "the country's foremost couples researcher." Dr. Gottman's philosophy of relationships is encapsulated in the title of the podcast he does with his wife: *Small Things Often*. The tagline to the podcast is, "Successful long-term relationships are created through small words, small gestures, and small acts."

Or, as Moses (channeling God) said, "little by little."[16]

We Have No Idea What Is Small

According to a Columbia University analysis, approximately 9 percent of Americans suffer a "major depressive episode" each year.[17] One of the major causes of depression is rumination, which is the repetitive revisiting of negative thoughts.

How can one best stop ruminating? A team led by Gregory N. Bratman, now of the University of Washington, came up with an answer. It is not years of therapy, a drug regimen, or any other big thing. It is to take walks in nature. This practice "decreases [in] both self-reported rumination and neural activity in the subgenual prefrontal cortex [which processes rumination]." A nature walk might seem like a small thing, but not, as Professor Bratman discovered, for many people who suffer from crushing depression.[18]

If a walk in the park seems like a small thing, a smile might appear to be even smaller. Rebbetzin Esther Jungreis was born in Hungary in 1936. When she was eight years old, her family was deported by the Nazis to the Bergen-Belsen concentration camp. Upon entering the camp, her father (Rabbi Avraham Jungreis) gave her and other children an instruction: "Kinderlach, children, smile! When grown-ups see young children smiling, it will give them hope."[19] A smile from a child, Rabbi Jungreis knew, was no small thing. It could be the difference between life and death for those trying to survive in the worst place on earth.

Twenty-first-century science has demonstrated that Rebbetzin Jungreis's father was correct—and why. A variety of studies have demonstrated that smiling is as contagious as laughing—and more so than the flu. Someone who sees a smiling child is, therefore, likely to reciprocate the smile. The act of smiling releases neurotransmitters (dopamine, serotonin, and endorphins) that alleviate depression, lift moods, relax the body, and lower heart rate and blood pressure—no small things.[20]

Living on Paths: Why "Bigger Fish Come Along"

In 1982, the criminologists James Q. Wilson and George Kelling, building on earlier studies, authored an essay in *The Atlantic* entitled "Broken Windows: The Police and Neighborhood Safety." Citing data from cities throughout the United States, they suggested that police should not think in terms of big crimes and small crimes but order and disorder. When there is a culture of order all crimes will significantly diminish. Thus, a police force that attends to broken streetlights, littering, graffiti, public drinking, jaywalking, and fare-beating—"small" crimes that manifest disorder—will find that its jurisdiction has far fewer "big" crimes. In Torah terms, a city is either on a "path" of order or disorder.[21]

In the early 1980s, crime was destroying the New York City subway experience. Mayor David Dinkins hired Transit Police Commissioner William Bratton, who had become convinced by the Wilson-Kelling article.

Before Commissioner Bratton's arrival, turnstile jumpers were counted. Now, they were arrested. The findings of the NYPD, then and in subsequent years, was stunning. Almost half of those arrested for fare evasion had an open warrant for a prior crime—and around 10 percent of those who jumped turnstiles were found carrying a deadly weapon.

These findings stunned many observers. Fare-beaters, it turns out, are usually not law-abiding citizens who just want a free ride on the subway. They, like the rest of us, are on a path—an important concept that first surfaces in the Garden of Eden. In the case of fare-beaters, it is the path of lawbreaking. No wonder that, according to Professor Eugene O'Donnell of the John Jay College of Criminal Justice, routine fare-evasion enforcement enables the police to "ferret out more serious misconduct." Small and big crimes are on the same path—as are their alternatives.[22]

While the "broken windows" philosophy was developed to deal with crime, contemporary scholars are finding that it is not the only application. In 2023, the columnist Naomi Schaefer Riley declared, "It's time for a broken windows policy for schools."[23]

Why? In recent years, there has been an explosion of violence in schools. North Carolina schools experienced a 24 percent rise in violence from the 2018–19 school year to the 2021–22 year.[24] Denver experienced such a rise in violence that school superintendent Alex Marrero announced in 2023 that he was going to bring back armed guards, even though doing so would violate a policy set in 2020.[25] Akron experienced such an explosion in violence that teachers threatened to strike over it in late 2022.[26]

In 2022, Daniel Buck, a Wisconsin teacher who worked in charter, Catholic, and conventional public schools, published a book called *What Is Wrong with Our Schools?* He attributes the root of the problem to the way school administrators handle problems like inconsistent attendance and general disrespect. Administrators, he writes, are likely to respond to such things by saying that they have "bigger fish to fry." This, he says, is the problem. "If you don't deal with small things, bigger fish come along."[27]

"All Your Ways": What Makes a Champion

In 2009, the *Sporting News* named the greatest coach of all time. There is little or no dispute that they had chosen the right person: John Wooden, whose UCLA basketball teams won ten national championships including seven in a row (1967–73). Coach Wooden was able to achieve such consistent excellence by coaching in accordance with a famously thoughtful, considered, and well-articulated philosophy.

How did this quintessential philosopher coach start each season? By instructing his players how to tie their sneakers and put on their socks. Is it conceivable that Coach Wooden's players—high school and college champions who would become NBA Hall of Famers such as Lew Alcindor, Bill Walton, Jamaal Wilkes, and Gail Goodrich—did not know how to tie their sneakers and put on their socks? Did Coach Wooden know something special about avoiding blisters?

I put this question to Jamaal Wilkes, who played at UCLA before his Hall of Fame career with the Golden State Warriors and Los Angeles Lakers. Mr. Wilkes said, "No. Coach Wooden did not have special insights into blisters. He had special insights into people."

Coach Wooden's instruction, Mr. Wilkes explained, was not really about sneakers and socks. It was about small things. He instructed his players how to put on their socks and tie their sneakers to teach them that seemingly small things (like putting on socks and sneakers) constitute the difference between victory and defeat. And it was such an important lesson that Coach Wooden had his players, who generally played for all four years, do so at the beginning of each season.

This was no idiosyncrasy of Coach Wooden. According to ESPN, the greatest college football coach of all time was Bear Bryant, whose Alabama Crimson Tide won six national titles in his twenty-four years of coaching. His philosophy: "Little things make the difference. Everyone is prepared in the big things, but only the winners perfect the little things."[28]

In 2021, Athlon Sports published its list of the greatest NFL coaches of all time. Its top two were Vince Lombardi (Green Bay Packers, 1959–67) and Bill Belichick (New England Patriots, 2000–2024).[29] These men coached very different teams in different eras. But they shared a philosophy.

Coach Lombardi's philosophy is embodied in his "Game of Inches" speech. He said, "Life's a game of inches, and inches make the champion." One of his offensive linemen, Jerry Kramer, recalled of Coach Lombardi: "He ignores nothing. Technique, technique, technique, over and over and over until we feel like we're going crazy. But we win."[30]

Bill Belichick is renowned for winning six Super Bowls and for training a generation of outstanding coaches in the process. One of those coaches is Jim Schwartz, who received his initial training under Coach Belichick with the Cleveland Browns in the 1990s before he became the head coach of the Detroit Lions. Coach Schwartz told ESPN in 2016, "Probably the biggest thing I learned from Bill is that there isn't anything that is not important. Anything that touches the team is important. That philosophy of 'Don't sweat the small stuff'? Yeah, that was never his philosophy."[31]

One of the greatest rugby teams of all time is the All Blacks of New Zealand. In his book about the team, James Kerr identifies the secret to their success. Although writing about a different sport in a different culture half a world away, Mr. Kerr's description of their success sounds like it could have been written of Vince Lombardi's Packers or Bill Belichick's Patriots. "The players are taught never to get too big to do the small things that need to be done." For instance, every player participates in the cleaning of the locker room after each game.[32]

At the 1996 Olympic Games in Atlanta, the British cycling team was ranked seventeenth in the world and collected two bronze medals. In 2008, the British won fourteen medals; the next best team, France, won six. In 2012, the British won twelve medals, and the next best team, Germany, won six. What happened after 1996 to make the British so successful?

Simply: the hiring of Coach Dave Brailsford, and the implementation of his philosophy of "marginal gains." He explained to BBC in 2012, "The whole principle came from the idea that if you broke down everything you could think of that goes into riding a bike, and then improved it by 1%, you would get a significant increase when you put them all together."

Coach Brailsford continued, explaining what he sought to improve accordingly. These included "big" things like fitness and positioning, and also "small" things like sleeping in the right position, having the same pillow on the road, training in different places, and even being sure to tend to the inside of fingers when washing one's hands.[33]

The belief in "no small things," exemplified by the biblical Jacob when he returned across the Jabbok River, has defined the philosophies of the winningest coaches in basketball, football, rugby, and cycling. This belief also defined the philosophy of another winner: postwar Japan, in the field of global economics.

The Japanese economy was destroyed during World War II, and the country had to start anew. And it had to do so without abundant natural resources or arable land and with a moderately sized population. Yet, by 1968, it was the second largest economy in the world, with decades of significant growth still to come.

There are many factors that contributed to what became known as the "Japanese Economic Miracle." Yet, a major reason was provided by Masaaki Imai. Born in 1930, he spent much of his long life as Japan's leading management theoretician. In 1986, he published his major book *Kaizen: The Key to Japanese Competitive Success*. Kaizen, in the words of TechTarget's Diann Daniel, is "an approach to creating continuous improvement based on the idea that small, ongoing positive changes can reap significant improvements."[34]

The philosophy of kaizen, centered on appreciation of supposedly small changes that result in significant improvements, has been credited with the success of organizations such as Canon, Nestlé, Toyota, Mitsubishi Heavy Industries, Ford, the Mayo Clinic, Great Western Bank, the Gujarat Government, and Lockheed Martin.[35]

Reflection

The Torah, from Jacob to Moses, from Abraham to God, insists that there is no real category that could be called "small things." Modern science and experience, from broken windows to the Butterfly Effect, from the UCLA Bruins to the postwar Japanese economy, validates this biblical claim.

And it just may be the best parenting advice ever given. We can look back at our childhoods and ask: What were the moments that left a permanent impression, that taught an important lesson, that defined us in some important way?

Some of these moments may be the events we think about the most and prepare for the most: bar mitzvah ceremonies, confirmations, graduations, weddings, funerals, Christenings, brises, and baby namings. Others will be of major global events.

But do these constitute most of our vivid, important, pivotal, and *defining* memories from our youth? Probably not. Our most salient memories from childhood, and the enduring lessons we take from them, are often from conversations or experiences that no adult in the environment considered significant, lasting, or memorable. The moment may have been so small to the adult that he might not even remember it years, or even days, later. To the child, however, it might be everything.

The lesson is clear. A parent, or another adult who wants to guide a child, should regard every moment with a child to be the one that he or she will remember and be influenced by forever.

16

Why God Chooses Moses and Motorcycles Crash

The Torah and Science of Noticing

God Chooses Moses

In Genesis 1:26, God tells us how he plans to operate in the world. He says, "Let us make man." There has been plenty of discussion about who the "us" is. But perhaps the important fact is not who the "us" is, but why an omnipotent God would use "us" at all. The "us" is God announcing how he will operate in the world—He wants to work with a partner.

In early Exodus, God decides to do what he will consider his most important act ever—even more than the creation of the world. This is the liberation of the Jews from Egyptian slavery, known as the Exodus. A question emerges—who will be God's partner in this all-important act?

God seems to have his eye on Moses, who we meet in Exodus 1. Moses, who was born to a Jewish slave, was raised in the Pharaoh's palace. This is an important fact, as it means that Moses could feel the pain of the Jewish slave while leading with the confidence of an Egyptian prince.

In Exodus 2, the Torah reveals another qualifying trait. Moses sees an Egyptian beating a Jew, a Jew fighting another Jew, and gentile men harassing gentile women. He intervenes in each case—showing courage, conviction, and toughness. These are qualities that God will need in his partner in liberation. But still, he does not anoint Moses.

In Exodus 3:2, Moses is a shepherd in Midian. Walking in the desert, he comes across a bush that "was aflame, yet not being consumed."

Bushes frequently burn in the desert. Moses could have easily walked by, not noticing anything special. But he doesn't. He notices that the bush is on fire, but not being consumed. Moses stops, and says, "I will surely turn aside and see this great sight, why the bush is not aflame." This is astonishing for two reasons.

First: Moses could have simply said: "I will see this great sight." Why, then, does Moses preface his actions with, "I will surely turn aside"?

As Rabbi Efrem Goldberg of the Boca Raton Synagogue explains, this act reveals a crucial quality of Moses. He is a man who "turns aside." He is, in a word, a *noticer*.[1]

The second stunning aspect of Moses's statement in Exodus 3:2 is revealed in *what* he does with what he notices. The Torah tells us that the bush is aflame but is not being consumed. But bushes that are aflame *always* get consumed. Therefore, we would expect Moses to ask, "Why is this bush not being *consumed*?" Instead, he wonders, "Why is the bush not *aflame*?" But the bush, the Torah tells us explicitly, *was* aflame![2]

What is going on? Moses is essentially saying that all bushes that burn get consumed—but this bush, which is burning, is *not* being consumed. So, despite appearances, it must not be aflame! Moses has just provided a master class in noticing. A noticer, Moses teaches us, does not plug what he notices into his previous notion of reality. A noticer allows what he discovers to influence him, even to the point of transforming his previous notion of reality.

As the text reveals, Moses's noticing has impressed a rather important audience. In Exodus 3:4, we learn, "So when the Lord saw *that he turned aside* to look, God called to him from the midst of the bush and said, 'Moses, Moses!' And he [Moses] said, 'Here I am.'"

The way that God reveals himself is also deeply instructive. God, who is specifically impressed by Moses's noticing ("when the Lord saw that he turned aside to look"), emerges from Moses's place of noticing ("the midst of the bush"). God is found in what we notice.

God proceeds to tell Moses that he is going to be the leader who, in partnership with God, will free the Jews from slavery. God has determined that *noticing* is so important that it becomes *the* act and *the* quality that inspires God to pick the person who will be his partner in the Exodus. Why is noticing so important?

The Science

When Gorillas Play Basketball

In 2000, psychologists Daniel Simons and Christopher Chabris conceived of a game in which teenagers wearing white or black shirts toss basketballs to each other. An onlooker is told to count the number of passes conducted by those in the white shirts. Around halfway through the game, someone in a gorilla suit enters the scene and starts beating his chest. The gorilla, with all the subtlety one would expect from a gorilla beating his chest, stays for nine seconds.

Professors Simons and Chabris asked people how likely they would be, in such a circumstance, to notice the gorilla. Ninety percent said that they would notice the gorilla. However, the reality turned out to be very different. When they ran the experiment, only half of the participants noticed the gorilla. We are, they demonstrated, much worse at noticing than we think we are.[3]

Professor Simons was not satisfied arriving at a judgment about human noticing with just one experiment. Along with Professor Daniel Levin of Vanderbilt, Professor Simons ran a variant of the experiment with other scenarios. In one experiment, they had a researcher ask random people for directions. In the middle of the directions being provided, two colleagues of the researcher came between the researcher and the person offering directions. They were carrying a door, which made it impossible for the researcher and the person offering directions to see each other for the few seconds they were passing by.

During that time, the researcher slipped away behind the door, and a different person emerged to continue receiving the directions. This allowed the researchers to get the answer they wanted. How many respondents would keep on talking, indicating that they had not noticed that the person to whom they had just been offering directions had mysteriously been replaced by someone else?

The answer: Half of those offering directions continued after the door interruption as if nothing happened and they were talking with the same person.[4]

In another study, Professors Simons and Levin asked people if they would notice changes in a movie scene, from an actor alternating between wearing a scarf and not wearing a scarf to one actor replacing another. Eighty-three percent of people said that they would notice the change. But only 11 percent, when presented with real examples, did. The phenomenon, known as "change blindness," is, as an American Psychological Association analysis suggested, "shocking to most people."[5]

The fact that change blindness is so prevalent might explain why God, in Exodus 3, was so impressed by Moses's noticing at the burning bush. The fact that the Author of the Torah knew what Professors Simons and Levin "discovered" still leaves a fundamental question. Why should we care if we are worse at noticing than we think? Why does it matter if half of us do not notice a fake gorilla coming through a basketball drill? In other words, is God in the Torah correct that noticing is a surprisingly difficult *and* very important skill?

Road Safety

A 2013 study by the American Automobile Association showed that almost all Americans believe that speaking on a cell phone while driving is dangerous. However, that concern significantly dissipates when respondents are asked about speaking on a hands-free cell phone. Seventy percent of Americans believe that driving while having a telephone conversation on a hands-free device is at least a reasonably safe activity.[6]

It is safe to say that no driving safety researchers are included in the 70 percent. An abundance of research, from places as different as the United States and Iran, has concluded that both hands-free *and* handheld cell phone usage degrade the driver's acceleration, reaction time, stimulus detection, and lane deviation. Drivers on cell phones, on the road and in labs, are vastly less likely to notice road signs, red lights, and swerving cars, regardless of whether they are holding the phone.[7]

Why is hands-free telephone speaking when driving problematic? Because the problem with speaking on a cell phone while driving has little to do with the hands and much to do with the brain. This is known in the literature as "inattentional blindness." It is a close cousin of the change blindness that Professor Simons identified.

In both cases, we become "blind" to important things in our environment because we simply do not pay attention. We do not, in a word, notice. The consequences? According to Professor David Strayer of the

University of Utah in his analysis of driving while speaking on a phone, this failure to notice causes us to miss things and leads to outcomes that are "potentially lethal."[8]

Why Motorcyclists Are the Best Car Drivers

Motorcycles are sometimes known as "donorcycles," because the people who ride them are the group most likely to be in a near-term position to have all of their organs donated. This term is backed by the data. According to the Insurance Information Institute, motorcyclists are twenty-nine times more likely than passenger car occupants to die in a crash per vehicle mile.[9]

Why are motorcyclists 2,900 percent more likely to die in a crash than car riders? With a statistic that big, there are inevitably many factors. Some are due to the inherent characteristics of motorcycles. An analysis by the Idaho-based Rossman Law Group explains that motorcyclists have less protection, less control over their vehicle, and less braking capability than car drivers.[10]

But none of these reasons are what Professor Kristen Pammer of the University of Newcastle and several colleagues determined to be the leading cause of motorcycle accidents. Instead, they identify car drivers who "looked but failed to see," which is abbreviated in the psychological literature as LBFTS.[11]

Looking but failing to see sounds impossible. When we look at something, don't we see it? To the detriment of motorcycle riders, apparently not. In 2018, Professor Pammer had drivers look at a series of photographs of a route. In the final photograph, they inserted a motorcycle or a taxi, neither of which had been in the previous photographs. The result: 31 percent of the respondents failed to notice the taxi, and 65 percent failed to notice the motorcycle. This problem, according to Professors Simons, Chabris, and Levin (of the gorilla and door experiments), also afflicts bicyclists. In all cases, respondents generally noticed what they expected to see, to the detriment of what was actually there.[12]

So, there is no doubt that looking but failing to see—being really bad at noticing—is a common problem, with terrible ramifications. Is it, then, inevitable? Are drivers, accustomed to seeing other cars on the road, *necessarily* and *inevitably* going to fail to notice motorcyclists? No. There is one group of drivers that, according to the data, tends to notice cyclists, and drive better generally. David Newman, the CEO of the Irish insurance company Carole Nash, said, "We have proven beyond doubt that, based on the actual claims experience, motorcyclists are safer on the road [when driving cars]."

Mr. Newman explains:

> If you've got a steel cage, a car, around you, then it tends to be more forgiving if you make a mistake on the road. With a bike, it's not. If you come off, then very often you've hurt yourself: You do learn very quickly that you've got to be very road aware. So when someone gets off two wheels and goes behind the wheel of a car, they take that with them.[13]

In other words, motorcyclists have trained themselves to be excellent noticers—and thus, better drivers.

Finance

The world's largest ever investment fraud was the Ponzi scheme perpetuated by Bernie Madoff. He perpetuated this fraud over four decades, and claimed thousands of victims at a scale of more than $60 billion before he was caught in 2008. A fraud of this length and magnitude leads to questions: How did he do this? Was he an evil genius?

The financial journalists at *Barron's* did not think he was a genius. In 2001, *Barron's* ran an analysis entitled "Don't Ask, Don't Tell: Bernie Madoff Is So Secretive, He Even Asks His Investors to Keep Mum." In the same year, *MARHedge* published an article called "Madoff Tops Charts: Skeptics Ask How." Those articles alone were enough for investors and regulators to know that Madoff was a fraud. Indeed, many institutions and individuals (from Goldman Sachs to my friend Jeff Leventhal, who redeemed his investment when Madoff could not answer basic questions about the option strategy that supposedly produced the stated results) immediately identified the impossibility of Madoff's returns, and refused to engage with him.[14]

The accountant Harry Markopolos did not think that Madoff was a genius either. Indeed, Mr. Markopolos submitted his first memo of concern to the Security and Exchange Commission (SEC) in 2000 and continued to do so until the fraud was exposed in late 2008. In 2005, Mr. Markopolos submitted a memo to the SEC entitled "The World's Largest Hedge Fund Is a Fraud."

Mr. Markopolos enumerated twenty-nine "red flags," and that is conservatively counting, as several of his red flags included subpoints. Much of what he found was downright obvious. For instance, the Madoff business model was completely nonstandard, his borrowing rates were inexplicably high, he was hedging more options himself than were available in the market for everyone, he subsidized down months, he would not allow performance audits, his investment staff was composed entirely of family, his investors claimed to have special access, and his basic finance was fatally flawed.[15]

Some of Madoff's victims were unsophisticated investors who would not have known what to notice. We can put them aside. Others were highly sophisticated individual investors and financial institutions who employed professional investment teams. They either did not notice the obvious fraud or noticed and stayed in—expecting that the regulators would not notice. Sure enough, the regulators who examined Madoff's books, even after hearing from Mr. Markopolos, missed the fraud. It ended in the financial crisis when investors, for liquidity reasons unrelated to the fraud, wanted their money—which wasn't there.

How was Madoff able to develop such a broad and long-lasting fraud among sophisticated investors? There is just one answer. Some did not notice and others noticed but did not act. They did not learn from Moses, who noticed and allowed his noticing to transform his understanding of reality.

Relationships

The psychologists John and Julie Gottman are perhaps the leading experts on what makes marriages succeed and fail. As discussed in the previous chapter (on small things), their prescription for creating a good and lasting relationship is articulated in the name of their podcast: *Small Things Often*. In 2023, they wrote of what they learned after studying forty thousand couples. It illustrates, essentially, how to execute the small things philosophy. They write, "A thriving relationship requires an enthusiastic culture of appreciation, where we're as good at *noticing* [emphasis added] the things our partners are doing right as we are at noticing what they're doing wrong."

By noticing positive things, participants in relationships are able to identify what they should appreciate. The knowledge of what to appreciate enables people in relationships to deploy what the Gottmans call "the number 1 phrase in successful relationships": Thank you.[16]

Reflection

God taps Moses after he establishes himself as a noticer in full. Moses notices that the bush is burning but is not being consumed, *and* respects noticing so much that he allows it to change the way he views the world.

Modern social science has offered evidence from basketball-playing gorillas to road safety data to relationship advice to demonstrate just how rare *and* important good noticing is.

But it need not be rare. As we see in the case of motorcyclists who become safer car drivers, it is entirely possible to train oneself to be a good noticer. The life coach Sandra Possing offers practical advice that enables anyone to train himself to be a better noticer. Her suggestions include:

- Photograph your surroundings, as every thoughtful photograph is the product of the photographer noticing something interesting.
- Explore new places. We are generally inattentive in our customary environments. One way to improve is to go to new places where we have to notice things just in order to get around.
- Get rid of distractions. If we are always on our devices, we are training ourselves not to notice what is in our physical environment.
- Ask yourself questions. These include: "How is this person really feeling?" "What is the difference between what he is saying and what he is really feeling?" and "How many people in this room are in a good mood?" By doing so, we will train ourselves to notice discrepancies and subtleties.
- Use all of your senses to observe. This will certainly result in you hearing, seeing, smelling, and feeling things you otherwise would not have.
- Watch a foreign movie with subtitles. We have to notice a lot in order to construct a story of what is happening.
- Play observational games such as "Where's Waldo?"[17]

These techniques, and others like them, will condition the brain to notice until we become noticers. But that's a half Moses. Becoming a full Moses would also involve enabling what we notice to change how we see the world.

What might be the practical consequences of becoming full-Moses noticers? We will notice hazards in our environment, adjust our behavior accordingly, and have fewer accidents. We will notice potential medical problems and be able to address them before they become more serious. We will notice the signals that scammers inevitably leave in their treacherous wake. We will notice subtle changes in our loved ones and be able to address problems before they become catastrophic.

We will, in essence, be able to more quickly, honestly, and accurately assess the truth of situations and reap the benefits that knowledge of the truth inevitably brings.

17

Guarding to Observe the Sabbath and Why What Bleeds Leads

The Torah and Science of the Negativity Bias

Manasseh and Ephraim: The Lesson from Switched Hands

It is Genesis 37. Joseph is sold into slavery and begins an extraordinary career. He becomes a slave and then a prisoner before rising to become the viceroy of Egypt and the second most powerful man in the world.

When he becomes a viceroy, the Pharaoh gives Joseph a wife, Asenath, which means "she belongs to her father." Joseph and Asenath have two sons. Joseph, the text tells us, names his older son Manasseh, saying, "God has made me forget all of my hardship and my father's household." He names his second son Ephraim, for "God has made me fruitful in the land of my suffering." This is all the Torah tells us about these boys.

By telling us nothing else about these boys, the Torah calls our attention to what we do know—their names. The name Manasseh, Joseph's first child, serves to remind him of the negative experiences and bad people that Joseph has overcome. The name Ephraim, the second child, serves to remind Joseph of his accomplishments, opportunities, and creative potential. In short, the name of the first son (Manasseh) is about overcoming the negative. The name of the second son (Ephraim) is about achieving the positive.

Many years pass, and Joseph demonstrates that he has earned the Pharaoh's trust and authority. Joseph administers the Egyptian state so that there is plenty of food during a devastating global famine. After an incredible series of events, Joseph is eventually reunited with his brothers and then his father, Jacob.

As Jacob is about to die, he calls Joseph to his deathbed. Joseph, accompanied by his sons, arrives at his father's side. In Genesis 48:5 Jacob blesses Joseph, and says, "And now thy two sons, Ephraim and Manasseh, shall be mine, just as Reuben and Simeon are mine."

In blessing his grandchildren as he does his children, Jacob carries out a sort of adoption of Manasseh and Ephraim. It might have been a little late in life to adopt a child, but Jacob's adoption is not an act of paternity. It is an act of legacy.

Given that Joseph was always Jacob's favorite son, this is not surprising. The surprise was in how he articulates his adoption. He recognizes Ephraim before Manasseh! Is this an intentional act, or just a manner of speaking? If the former, is it the confusion of an old man or the acuity of a wise elder? We soon find out.

Joseph brings his two sons toward Jacob to receive their own blessings. Jacob places his right hand on Ephraim, and his left on Manasseh. This is significant, as the right hand signals primacy.

Joseph, thinking that his father cannot identify which son is which, attempts to rearrange Jacob's hands so that his father would place his right hand on Manasseh, his firstborn. But Jacob knew exactly what he was doing. He keeps his hands in place, explaining to Joseph that "the younger brother will be greater."

The significance of this moment is demonstrated by how it has become embedded in a widespread custom in Judaism. Every Friday night, at the beginning of the Shabbat meal, many Jews bless our children. We do not bless our sons to be like Abraham and Moses, Isaac and Jacob, Joseph and David, or any other Jewish hero. We bless our sons to be like "Ephraim and Manasseh"—in that order—just like Jacob did.

There are several reasons why we do this, which are discussed in the chapter of this book on future orientation. However, a different question is ripe now. Why does Jacob bless Ephraim first, and give him primacy over his older brother?

He does so to teach his family (and all of us) a crucial lesson. Confronting and overcoming the negative is important. Indeed, it is an activity worthy of a blessing. Even people as brilliant and good as Joseph will naturally put it first. But that is not, Jacob teaches, where negativity belongs. It belongs second, behind the positive, for reasons that God will demonstrate in Exodus.

Why We Guard and (Then) Observe the Sabbath

In Exodus 31:13, God says, "Speak to the children of Israel saying: you shall greatly guard My Sabbaths." The use of the plural to describe the Sabbath leads the reader to ask, "What does God mean by two Sabbaths?" There is, of course, only one Sabbath each week.

God explains in Exodus 31:16. "And the children of Israel should *guard* the Sabbath to *observe* the Sabbath for generations." This seems like a clunky expression. First, why is the term "Sabbath" used twice in the same half sentence? Second, wouldn't it be simpler for Exodus 31:16 to read: "And the children of Israel should *guard and observe* the Sabbath for generations," rather than "guard to observe"?

There is one period of the week that extends from sundown on Friday to nightfall on Saturday. But the passage in Exodus teaches us there are really *two* Sabbaths on the same day. One is the Sabbath of the negative: *guarding*, which refers to the activities that we cannot do on Saturday—ranging from talking on the telephone to using money and conducting business. The other is the Sabbath of *observing*. This is the Sabbath of the positive. Observing refers to activities we should do on the Sabbath: studying, praying, enjoying long meals, playing games, and otherwise engaging in activities that will refresh and rejuvenate us.

Which is more important? The text makes that very clear. We guard *to* observe. We refrain from the usual activities of the week in order to be able to focus on the special activities of the Sabbath.

This idea will animate the many prohibitions in the Torah. We are prohibited from mixing milk and meat to inculcate a respect for parenthood that would be violated if we risked boiling a kid in its mother's milk. We are prohibited from eating *chametz* (leavened products) on Pesach so that we will always remember the Exodus and contemplate and focus on the things that we want to be permanent in our lives. We are prohibited from eating on Yom Kippur so that nothing distracts us from this sacred opportunity to repent and connect with God. In all cases, we start with the negative to achieve the positive.[1]

Why Mention the Fins?

In Leviticus 15, God gives us a dietary law. We can only eat fish that have both "fins and scales." The rabbis of the ancient Mishnah noted something strange about this verse. All fish that have scales also have fins. Why, then, does the Torah not simply say that we can eat fish that have scales? The Talmud explains that the inclusion of fins enables us to "increase the Torah and beautify it."[2]

How does the seemingly redundant inclusion of fins increase and beautify the Torah?

The Rebbe Menachem Mendel Schneerson explained: Scales are protective; they keep away the negative. Fins move the fish forward; they enable the positive. As the purpose of kosher is to align what we eat with the character traits we seek (the earliest notion of "You are what you eat"), the Rebbe instructed that we should never eat, or be, only scales.[3]

The Rebbe's insight also explains why the Torah writes of "fins and scales"—and not "scales and fins." We need both, but the fins, the positivity, must come first.

The Blessings and the (Many More) Curses

The Author of the Torah devotes Leviticus 26 to encouraging us to follow his decrees. He has two tools: blessings and curses. As the twenty-first-century sage Rabbi Jonathan Sacks points out, the section on the curses is almost three times as long as the section on the blessings. And the curses are so visceral (for instance, that we will eat our children) that they are said in a low voice during that section's Torah reading. The blessings are not accompanied by singing, dancing, or anything like that.

Why is this? Rabbi Sacks explains, "The reason the curses are so dramatic is not because God seeks to punish, but the precise opposite . . . The curses were meant as a warning. They were intended to deter, scare, discourage." And that, the Author of the Torah apparently believed, is intended when the things we should not do are described abundantly and very negatively.[4]

Zionism

Many people say that the purpose of Israel is to be a safe haven for the Jews—protection against the damage that Jew haters will want to inflict upon us. David Ben-Gurion, a leading founding father of the state of Israel, was not one of those people.

In his book *The Will to Live On*, the American Jewish author Herman Wouk discussed a dinner that he had with Israeli prime minister David Ben-Gurion in 1955, following the Tel Aviv production of *The Caine Mutiny* (adapted from Mr. Wouk's book). Mr. Wouk had to take the trip from Tel Aviv to Ben-Gurion's desert home in Sde Boker in an army vehicle with military escorts. As the meal concluded, Prime Minister Ben-Gurion said, "You must return to live here, this is the only place for a Jew like you. Here you will be free."

Mr. Wouk replied: "Free? With enemy armies ringing you, with their leaders publicly threatening to wipe out the Zionist entity, with your roads impassable by sundown—free?"

"I did not say safe," Prime Minister Ben-Gurion replied. "I said free."[5]

Prime Minister Ben-Gurion was, in this dialogue, not dismissing the role of Israel as a "safe haven" for Jews. He spent much of his life identifying Jewish communities in danger, leading extraordinary operations to bring them to Israel, and building a powerful IDF to protect the Jews in Israel. His point to Herman Wouk was that Jews need a *safe* haven so that we can be *free*. The safe haven is not the end of the story. We need a safe haven primarily to fulfill our biblical charge to be a "kingdom of priests and a holy nation"—with all that it entails.

So, the Torah's view on negativity is simple and elegant. Negativity is so powerful that even a genius like Joseph will end up prioritizing it over the positive. We will gravitate to it, and emphasize it in our decisions. The Torah does not seek to diminish how seriously we take negativity. Jacob still blesses Manasseh; God instructs us to guard the Sabbath and that only fish with "fins *and* scales" are kosher—even though the categorization is redundant. The Torah guides us to acknowledge and appreciate the negative and to channel its power to enable us to do the positive.

What does the science say?

The Science

"One of the Most Understated Effects in All of Cognitive Science"

In 1982, Professors Barbara J. McNeil and Amos Tversky put forth two scenarios for someone with lung cancer. In scenario A, having the procedure would provide a 66 percent chance of living. In scenario B, having the procedure would provide a 34 percent chance of dying. Of course, the chances of survival in A and B are the same. Yet, respondents were approximately 2.5 times more likely to opt for the procedure when it was described in terms of living rather than dying.[6]

Thirty years later, Professor Alison Ledgerwood of the University of California at Davis asked a group of respondents how they would consider a new surgical procedure with a 70 percent success rate. She asked another group how they would consider a new surgical procedure with a 30 percent failure rate. Consistent with the findings of Professors McNeil and Tversky, those informed of the 70 percent success rate favored the procedure significantly more than those told it had a 30 percent failure rate. But Professor Ledgerwood added a twist.

She then told those in the 70 percent success rate group that they could also think of it as having a 30 percent failure rate. The procedure became much less popular. She also told those in the 30 percent failure rate group that they could think of it as having a 70 percent success rate. The procedure stayed just as unpopular.[7] Why would respondents, as in these experiments and many others, so value the negative more than its equivalent positive, even at the cost of logical thinking? Professors Paul Rozin and Edward Royzman of the University of Pennsylvania came up with the operative term in 2001: the "negativity bias," which, in the words of Michael Shermer of *Skeptic* magazine, is "one of the most understated effects in all of cognitive science."[8]

A 1998 study led by the University of Colorado neuroscientist Tiffany Ito identified significantly increased electrical activity in the brain when subjects were exposed to negative images compared to positive and neutral ones. This activity manifests in how we think. In 2005, the National Science Foundation determined that people have up to eighty thousand thoughts a day, and that 80 percent of them are negative.[9]

Why does such a profound negativity bias exist? The Decision Lab explains: "Negativity bias is assumed to have been a natural adaptive evolutionary function, developed by humans thousands of years ago. By continually being exposed to immediate environmental threats, our ancestors developed a negativity bias to survive."[10]

How sensitive and strong is this evolutionary function? A 1981 study led by Professor A. W. Logue of SUNY Stony Brook about food aversion is illustrative. Professor Logue surveyed 517 students from both Stony Brook and Harvard to learn about food aversion. She found that 65 percent of the students reported having at least one taste aversion.

Some of these aversions were with the students from birth. But most of the aversions were likely to have developed between the ages of thirteen and twenty, long after a genetic explanation would have predicted and after one's taste preferences naturally expand. Moreover, 74 percent of those aversions developed after a negative experience with the food. A generation later, Professor Arianna Maffei and her colleagues at SUNY Stony Brook found the reason why. They discovered that a single bad food experience can change the way the taste and threat processing centers of the brain interact, and make us hate a food we previously enjoyed. There is nothing similar with a positive food experience.[11]

Why is it common and adaptive for one bad food experience to change our brain chemistry forever, with no corollary for a positive food experience? Simply, one bad meal or wrong step can cause a serious illness, a devastating injury, or death. One good meal or right step cannot cure, repair, or save anyone. Evolution has done us well by giving us such a sensitive and potent negativity bias.

However, we also see the negativity bias at work in our lives in arenas well beyond food, and with far more complicated ramifications.

What Consumers, Believers, Lovers, Psychologists, and Voters Have in Common

People running small businesses routinely pay significant sums of money to deal with bad online reviews. They do this even when the overwhelming number of their reviews are positive. Why can't they take comfort in the majority of the reviews being positive, and ignore the negative ones as the grumblings of complainers and competitors?

The entrepreneur Andrew Thomas has calculated that it takes forty positive customer experiences to make up for one negative experience. The best-selling author and CEO of NP Digital, Neil Patel, explains how and why a negative review is so much more powerful than a positive one. A negative review triggers the customer to *imagine* worst-case scenarios. With the mind of the potential customer imagining all of the bad things that could happen because of the purchase, it is very hard to win his business.[12]

Online reviews are not the only domain with such stark negative-positive imbalance. Dr. John Gottman has determined that a healthy marriage requires what he calls "the magic ratio." Happily married couples have twenty positive interactions to balance out a single negative interaction. Even when in a conflict, a happy couple needs to have five positive interactions for every negative interaction to maintain stability.[13]

In 2013, Professor Azim Shariff of the University of Oregon published the results of a huge study encompassing more than 140,000 people in 67 countries. He determined that societies with a strong belief in hell have significantly lower crime rates. As for societies whose people believe in heaven but not hell? There is no such correlation.[14]

A study led by Professor Kennon Sheldon of the University of Missouri determined that a bad day carries into the next day's mood, while a good day does not similarly transfer. A study led by Dr. Dwight Riskey found that we evaluate bad actions far more than good actions when we assess one's character. An analysis of 17,000 psychological research papers by Professor Janusz Czapinski of the University of Warsaw found that 69 percent of them focused on negative issues. This might help explain why, as discussed in the chapter of this book on anti-fragility, there is so much more discussion of trauma than resilience, in both the popular and professional literature.[15]

Each election season in the United States offers numerous uncertainties, and two certainties. The first certainty is that pundits, with the support of much of the public, will decry the proliferation of negative campaigning. The second is that the campaigning will be negative.

For instance, many people remember the 2012 presidential election as an exercise in civility, especially before the fireworks of the 2016 election. The data suggests otherwise. Professor Mitchell Lovett of the Simon Business School at the University of Rochester found that 90 percent of the ads in 2012 were negative. Sixty-four percent were "purely negative," meaning that the advertisement did not say anything positive about the sponsoring candidate.[16]

Why would that campaign, like so many others, have been so relentlessly negative? A 2019 analysis by Robyn Schelenz of the University of California says, "Our brains respond to it." She explains:

> If you come to an issue negatively, but are later reminded of the policy's positive aspects, you will still think it's a bust. And if you start out thinking favorably about the policy, but are reminded of its downsides, your positive perception will be swept away and a negative one will take its place. Once we think the proverbial glass is half empty, it's hard to remember that it is also half full. In other words, our brains are hard-wired to seek out and remember negative information. That fact isn't lost on politics and political parties.[17]

Consequently: Negative advertising works. Professor Brett Gordon of Northwestern University determined that negative advertisements are 50 percent more likely than positive advertisements to win the support of an undecided voter. As the negativity bias would suggest, we are much more moved by a negative political message than by a positive one.[18]

Is this unique to politics, which is a zero-sum game (if someone wins, the other person loses)? In 1989, Eric Pooley of *New York* magazine laid down a marker. He wrote, "If it bleeds, it leads." Is he right?

In 2020, Professor David Rozado of the New Zealand Institute of Skills and Technology and several colleagues published an analysis of headlines from left-leaning, centrist, and right-leaning publications from 2000 to 2019. This is an instructive period, as this is the era when the technology revolution made it much easier for publishers to understand what their customers gravitate to.

Professor Rozado and his colleagues found that headlines were slightly net positive in 2000. In 2019, neutral headlines had become much less prevalent than they were in 2000, while headlines that conveyed disgust, anger, fear, and sadness were vastly more prevalent. This was especially so in the right- and left-leaning sources, and in the years following 2013.[19]

Social media companies, which thrive by using advanced analytics, also adapted in accordance with the discoveries regarding the negativity bias in media. From 2016 to 2019, Facebook had an angry emoji. Seeing how captivated angry users were, the company weighted anger emojis at 500 percent of likes in what it served to users. The consequences included what the *Washington Post* called "misinformation, toxicity, and low-quality news"—as well as a more engaged user base.[20]

Why would media companies emphasize the negative, even when it results in "misinformation, toxicity, and low-quality news"? In 2014, Professors Marc Tressler and Stuart Soroka of Vanderbilt University published the results of a study where they asked participants to state their preference for positive or negative news. They then presented the participants with positive and negative stories and observed which they selected.

They found that participants who said that they wanted positive and negative news had at least one thing in common: They overwhelmingly selected negative news. Professors Tressler and Soroka explained, "In short, news may be negative . . . because that is the kind of news that people are interested in. And results suggest that behavioral results do not conform to attitudinal ones. That is, regardless of what participants say, they exhibit a preference for negative news content."[21]

In 2019, Professor Soroka and several colleagues published the results of what was essentially a follow-up question: *Why* do people, regardless of what they say, prefer negative over positive news? They examined the psychophysiological reactions of over one thousand people from seventeen countries on six continents to real video news content. Respondents watched seven randomly ordered *BBC World News* stories on a laptop while wearing noise-canceling headphones and sensors on their fingers to capture skin conductance and blood volume pulse. Subtitles were used when necessary.

They found that the heart rate and the nervous systems of people from every country responded the least to the positive stories and the most to the negative stories, with the neutral stories in between.[22]

So, modern science has demonstrated that we engage more, respond more, and act more in response to negative commentary and media than with the positive. No wonder Moses, wanting to engage generations of his followers for eternity, included three times as many curses as blessings in his media platform—the Torah.

Triumph of the Negativity Bias: Why Americans Stopped Smoking

God, by stating in Exodus that we are to *guard* the Sabbath to *observe* it, showed how the negativity bias need not be eliminated, but can be effectively channeled to allow us to live our best lives. God, by emphasizing the curses over the blessings in Leviticus, made the case that the path to change is more effectively paved with the negative (emphasizing what we shouldn't do) than with the positive (emphasizing what we should).

What does the science say? We can start by taking a look at smoking.

It is a myth that we only recently appreciated the dangers of smoking. Pope Urban VII served as the leader of the Catholic Church for less than two weeks in 1590. That was enough time for him to enact a worldwide smoking ban. Fourteen years later, King James I published "A Counterblast to Tobacco," calling smoking "a custome loathsome to the eye, hatefull to the Nose, harmefull to the braine, [and] dangerous to the lungs." He imposed a 4,000 percent tax on tobacco products.[23]

Smoking bans in the seventeenth and eighteenth centuries were imposed in Russia, Sweden, Germany, Massachusetts, and other places. Those who supported and enacted the bans noted, along with King James I, that smoking causes severe health problems. By 1950, scientists from the United States, Germany, and England had clearly and irrefutably demonstrated the connection between smoking and lung cancer. In 1964, the United States surgeon general, Luther Terry, issued a report on the dangers of smoking. The report cited seven thousand studies. When Surgeon General Terry published his report, more than 42.4 percent of American adults smoked cigarettes regularly.[24]

In response to the 1964 surgeon general's report, Congress required cigarette manufacturers to put a message in small print on one side of the box. It read: "Cigarette smoking may be hazardous to your health."

The message was negative, but mildly so ("*may* be hazardous"). A federal law passed in 1970, in response to the 1964 surgeon general's report, forbade cigarette advertising on television. Still, cigarettes were a major part of aspirational culture. Cigarettes were presented as the epitome of feminist cool in the Virginia Slims campaign of the 1960s and '70s: "You've Come a Long Way, Baby." They were presented as the embodiment of manliness in the Marlboro Man campaign, which ran from 1954 to 1999.

Jimmy Carter, after winning the presidency in 1976, sent a framed photograph to the head of corporate relations of Philip Morris saying, "Your help on my campaign made this day possible." Four years later, Ronald

Reagan won the presidency. The White House, consistent with a practice that began with President Kennedy, gave cigarette boxes with the presidential seal as a regular gift.[25]

In 1980, 33.2 percent of American adults smoked cigarettes. This showed a decline from when the surgeon general's warning first appeared sixteen years prior, but it did not satisfy public health authorities. A 1981 *New York Times* article explained: "The staff of the Federal Trade Commission, after five years of study, has determined that the current warnings against smoking that appear on cigarette packages and in advertisements are not effective and that a new warning system may be necessary."[26]

In 1985, the mandates started changing. They got progressively more negative, warning of fetal injury, carbon monoxide poisoning, lung cancer, and emphysema. By then, the Reagan White House had replaced cigarettes with jelly beans as its favored gift.[27]

The Family Smoking Prevention and Tobacco Control Act of 2009 went further. Tobacco companies were to include "color graphics depicting the negative health consequences of smoking" to accompany nine different messages for health warning labels (HWLs) that would cover 50 percent of the front and back of cigarette packages.

The messages consist of the word "WARNING" paired with one of the following: "Cigarettes are addictive," "Tobacco smoke can harm your children," "Cigarettes cause fatal lung disease," "Cigarettes cause cancer," "Cigarettes cause strokes and heart disease," or "Smoking during pregnancy can harm your baby."[28]

In 2020, the FDA required that these warnings be replaced with more negative messages. Cigarette boxes throughout the United States, as required by the United States Food and Drug Administration in 2020, warned that smoking could lead to impotence, amputation, stunted fetal growth, bladder cancer (which, the box tells us, presents in "bloody urine"), and blindness, all accompanied with graphic photos. The warnings are just as dire, and the photographs are more graphic in Europe, Asia, Australia, Israel, and elsewhere.[29]

How effective was the barrage of negativity against cigarettes? Perhaps the hardest thing to change is an addiction, and cigarettes are highly addictive. And, as discussed, huge amounts of money and creativity were poured into portraying cigarettes as the epitome of cool—for men and women.

Yet, by 2003, only 11.5 percent of Americans were smoking cigarettes. And the data gets better. In 2021, only 1.9 percent of high schoolers smoked a cigarette in any given month. This more than qualifies as a "smoke-free generation"—whose threshold is 5 percent.[30]

This is an astonishing fact. It is unlikely that anyone until well into this century could have predicted that fewer than 2 percent of high school students would smoke cigarettes. It is also highly unlikely that this lifesaving fact would have been possible if the messaging from the surgeon general were positive, such as: "Quitting smoking is good for your health." The official messaging in the astonishingly successful anti-smoking campaign was entirely negative. The more negative the messages, the more they worked.

Yet, there is a crucial nuance. In 2013, WebMD reviewed anti-smoking techniques and identified the "#1 tip" that people who want to quit smoking should heed. It is *entirely positive*: "Find Your Reason." The posting suggests an array of potential reasons, from desiring to look younger to wanting to protect one's family from secondhand smoke. WebMD specifies that it does not matter which one a would-be quitter chooses so long as it is "strong enough to outweigh the urge to light up."[31]

This insight from WebMD completes the story of how the anti-smoking movement was so successful. The more negative the messaging, the more people quit smoking. Yet, the messaging was never directed at *smokers*. It was always directed against *smoking*. The ideology of the movement was clear: People should quit smoking because cigarettes are widely destructive and severely damaging (the negative), *and* smokers have so much to live for, contribute to, and be enthusiastic about (the positive). In other words, guard (refrain) in order to "observe"—just as God counseled regarding the Sabbath in Exodus 31.

Smoking's Rival

As bad as smoking is, it has a rival as a danger to health: obesity.

The CDC reports that those who are overweight or obese are at increased risk for medical problems that include high blood pressure, high LDL cholesterol, low HDL cholesterol, high triglycerides, type 2 diabetes, heart disease, stroke, gallbladder disease, osteoarthritis, sleep apnea and breathing problems, many types of cancer, mental illness, body pain and difficulty functioning physically, and all causes of death (mortality).[32]

The risks keep coming for people of all ages. In 2023, the *Washington Post* ran an analysis to determine why Americans are getting shorter. The UCSF pediatric endocrinologist Louise Greenspan found a culprit: childhood obesity. Fat, she explains, leads to an increase in estrogen, which results in an earlier fusion of growth plates. In 2024, a team from Lund University in Sweden researched the causes of more than three hundred thousand cases of cancer over four decades. They determined that thirty-two cancers had an obesity link and that there is a connection between excess weight and cancer in 40 percent of the cases.[33]

In 2019, Dariush Mozaffarian (dean of the Tufts University Friedman School of Nutrition Science and Policy) and Dan Glickman (President Clinton's secretary of agriculture) published an essay in the *New York Times*, "Our Food Is Killing Too Many of Us." They reported that obesity kills five hundred thousand Americans a year and consumes an astonishing 9.3 percent of the gross national product of the United States. And they are being conservative. A study from the Center for Science in the Public Interest concludes that their analysis undercounts the death toll of obesity by around 35 percent.[34]

According to the CDC, over 40 percent of Americans are obese. According to Harvard Health, 69 percent of Americans are either overweight or obese. Obesity is not only prevalent among older people with slower metabolisms, little time to exercise, and habits that are difficult to break. The CDC reports that 22.2 percent of adolescents—young people who generally have fast metabolisms, built in time to exercise, and have not lived long enough to form long-lasting habits—are obese.[35]

These obesity numbers represent an entirely new phenomenon, as obesity rates have tripled in the past sixty years. There is no mystery as to why this happened. The CDC reports that the size of a fast-food meal (burger, fries, and a soda) is four times as large now as it was in 1950.[36] These numbers are reflected in the calorie data. In 1960, the average American consumed 2,880 calories a day. This number was not meaningfully different a decade later. But change was soon afoot. By 2023, the average American was consuming almost 4,000 calories a day. And the types of calories we consume optimize for obesity. The consumption of oils, breads, and corn sweeteners has skyrocketed since 1970, while calorie intake from proteins has remained constant.[37]

Why would obesity, and the behaviors that lead to it, have risen so dramatically? Let's consider several possibilities.

One theory (prominently advanced in a 2023 segment of *60 Minutes* featuring Dr. Fatima Cody Stanford of Mass General Hospital) is that obesity is fundamentally a genetic disease, and that behavioral choices have little or nothing to do with it. It is true that one's genes powerfully influence one's *propensity* to become obese. Different genetic dispositions likely explain why a man who consumes 4,000 calories a day might be thin while another might be obese. However, this would have been the case a generation ago when obesity rates were dramatically lower. While genes can change over time (this is called genetic drift), there is no way it would have happened quickly or profoundly enough to account for the dramatic rise in obesity in one generation. Nicotine addiction is also highly heritable, yet no one attributes the dramatic decline in smoking to genetic changes in a generation.[38]

A second theory (popularized by Michelle Obama) is that many Americans are living in "food deserts," which are neighborhoods without nearby supermarkets and superstores that offer healthy foods. Under this theory, people would choose a healthy diet, but do not have access to one. Studies in 2012 from the Rand Corporation and the Public Policy Institute of California determined that it is false. The *New York Times* science journalist Gina Kolata encapsulated the findings of these studies: "Such neighborhoods not only have more fast-food restaurants and convenience stores than more affluent ones, but more grocery stores, supermarkets, and full-service restaurants, too. And there is no relationship between the type of food being sold in a neighborhood and obesity among its children and adolescents." The evidence is clear: Food consumption in the United States is driven by demand, not supply.[39]

A third theory is that people are insufficiently aware of what foods are likely to cause obesity, and would eat more healthily if they had better information. This theory informed the requirement, implemented in New York and California in 2008, that restaurant chains post calorie counts next to the menu offerings. These efforts failed. In 2015, Professor Aaron Carroll of Indiana University Medical School summarized the results of several studies: "At no time did the labels lead to a reduction in the calories of what diners ordered. Even if people noticed the calorie counts, they did not change their behavior." There are many reasons for this. Some people associated fewer calories with worse taste, and opted for the higher calorie meals. Others used their eating lower calorie meals from the restaurant as license to consume more calories later. Others did not notice the calorie labels, or care about them when they did notice.[40]

The obesity epidemic, therefore, cannot be explained by the lack of information about which foods (and how much of them) lead to it. Similarly, it cannot be attributed to a lack of knowledge about the dangers of obesity. A 2013 study from the Associated Press-NORC Center for Public Affairs Research found that 75 percent of Americans reported obesity to be a major health problem in the United States. This should come as no surprise as more than 10 percent of Americans suffer from type 2 diabetes, and presumably almost all of them (and those they are close with) know that it is often caused by obesity. And the awareness does not end there. A 2014 study from Gallup reports that 45 percent of Americans regard themselves as overweight or obese, representing two-thirds of those the data suggest qualify.

So, why would so many Americans be obese, even as they know that it is a major health problem? The data and lessons from America's cigarette experience are highly instructive. A Gallup poll from 1954 found that 70 percent of Americans recognized that smoking was harmful, effectively the same percentage of Americans who today know that obesity is harmful. At the same time, 45 percent of Americans smoked, effectively the same percentage of Americans who are obese today.[41]

We know that smoking and obesity have something else in common. It is very difficult for habitual smokers to quit and for obese people to lose weight. Yet, we know what enabled the astonishing reduction in cigarette smoking. It was the triggering of the negativity bias, through progressively more negative warnings and their reverberations in the culture.

Where does the negativity bias stand with regard to obesity? Two seemingly different stories—one involving a company (WeightWatchers) and one involving a politician (New York City mayor Eric Adams)—are instructive and illustrative.

When WeightWatchers Became "WW"

WeightWatchers, which started in 1963, pioneered the discipline of calorie counting. Calorie counting has its nuanced critics, but the fact remains that it is a highly effective way to structure a weight program. A man who consumes 2,500 calories a day is likely to be in a healthy range, while a man who consumes 4,000 calories a day is likely to be overweight, and a man who consumes 7,500 calories a day is likely to be obese. Consequently, WeightWatchers has long provided food products to enable people to count calories effectively and strategically.

In addition to its great brand and long history, WeightWatchers has other attributes any business owner would yearn for. Its longtime spokesperson (and major shareholder) is Oprah Winfrey, the country's most beloved television personality, and one who is widely known for having lost a lot of weight. The market size for WeightWatchers is the 69 percent of Americans who are either obese or overweight—*plus* those who are formerly in those categories and those who want external discipline to stay healthy. WeightWatchers has all the makings of what should be a large and growing business.[42]

In 2018, the company was doing great. Its stock had grown by twenty-five times in the previous three years. The board of WeightWatchers responded by . . . changing the name of the company to WW. WW offers a nod to the old name, but it would no longer mean "WeightWatchers." It would be shorthand for "Wellness That Works."[43]

Why did the board change the name and fundamental purpose of the company when it was doing so well? The decision was not financial. A 2018 article on the WW name change in *Vox* explains: "It's not surprising that WeightWatchers is distancing itself from dieting . . . Talking openly about dieting is becoming taboo, and the body positivity movement is on the rise."[44]

In the subsequent five years, the stock of WW crashed back to where it was before the escalation. How did the company respond? One might think that WW—perhaps like Coke after the "New Coke" fiasco of 1986—would change its name back to WeightWatchers. But the company did not do this.

Why? Let's turn to the story of Eric Adams.

In 2020, Eric Adams was the Brooklyn borough president and the quintessential New York City political centrist leader. He published a book, *Healthy at Last*. The title is a clear reference to Martin Luther King's "I Have a Dream" speech, where his famous refrain was "free at last." The book is about his journey of liberation from being unhealthy to healthy.

He describes in detail how he became unhealthy, starting with his days as a New York police officer. He explains, "I'd roll my patrol car through the McDonald's drive-through at midnight for a double cheeseburger, swing by KFC at 2 AM for coffee and fried chicken, and throw back a few slices at Pizza Hut before dawn . . . For years and years, it was the same routine: fast, cheap, and easy meals, or comfort food, as you might know it."[45]

This became problematic. He explains, "Ronald, Wendy, and the Colonel may have helped me through some tough times, but they were taking their toll on my body. First the weight piled on, and then came the aches and pains—small ones, then big ones. My back hurt getting out of bed. My feet hurt walking to the subway. I was constantly tired. All of this became normal."

In 2016, Mr. Adams woke up one morning with a bloodshot right eye and blindness in his left. His blindness was a symptom of what he learned was his diabetes and he "was likely suffering from the early stages of heart disease."

Determined to get better, he learned the science. He found: "Type 2 diabetes is a lifestyle disease; it doesn't happen unless we let it happen. When we gain weight from an unhealthy diet, fat builds up in our muscle cells, which blocks insulin from ferrying glucose to our cells."

He transformed his diet and lost thirty-five pounds. He became fit and healthy, his diabetes went away, and his sight was restored.

Yes, he conceded, there "are some lucky people out there who eat nothing but Big Macs and sundaes and live forever. But let me be clear: the scientific evidence overwhelmingly indicates that no matter your genetic predisposition, type 2 diabetes and heart disease can almost always be prevented, and in many cases reversed, by eating a healthy diet."[46]

He emerged determined to share his experience with his constituents and to inspire others to join his journey from obesity and its consequences. He had that opportunity in 2023. That is when New York City passed a law putting "weight" alongside race, gender, age, religion, and sexual orientation in anti-discrimination law, and Eric Adams was mayor. Mayor Adams supported this law, stating, "Science has shown that body type is not a connection to if you're healthy or unhealthy. I think that's a misnomer that we're really dispelling."[47]

What precipitated his changed belief in the correlation between obesity and health? There were no scientific discoveries in the early 2020s suggesting that one's weight has nothing to do with one's health. Instead, the explanation by the bill's sponsor, City Councilman Shaun Abreu, makes more sense. He credited a movement that began fifty years ago when "hundreds of body positivity activists gathered in Central Park."[48]

Body Positivity

What is body positivity? According to an analysis on Verywell Mind, "Body positivity refers to the assertion that all people deserve to have a positive body image, regardless of how society and popular culture view ideal shape, size, and appearance."[49] According to this logic, there is no legitimate grounds for saying that anyone should ever regard their body size as negative. Instead, everyone should regard his body as "positive"—and, therefore, not in need of change.

The body positivity movement does not stop with asserting that all bodies are the size and shape they should be. Instead, it links any claims that fat or obesity are negative to the most sinful beliefs in society. The Boston Medical Center defines "anti-fat" as the "implicit and explicit bias of overweight individuals that is rooted in a sense of blame and presumed moral failing . . . Anti-fatness is intrinsically linked to anti-blackness, racism, classism, misogyny, and many other systems of oppression." A 2020 *Forbes* "Editor's Pick" article ran the headline "The Unplugged Collective Explores How Diet Culture Is Rooted in Anti-Blackness." A 2021 analysis in *Science Friday* explores "How Racism Shapes Our Perception of Healthy Food." A 2021 analysis of body positivity in *Shape* magazine (a fitness magazine with an audience of fourteen million) concluded that "diet culture is heavily rooted in racism."[50]

In 2019, the UC Santa Barbara sociologist Sabrina Strings published the book *Fearing the Black Body: The Racial Origins of Fat Phobia*. The book received much acclaim. A review at the UCLA Barbra Streisand Center for the Study of Women praises it for telling "the story of how our world has come to be dominated by fatphobia, or a fear of fatness, and the deeply anti-Black roots that this fear entails."[51]

One of the people inspired by this book was Virginia Sole-Smith, an heiress to a pharmaceutical distribution fortune and a health journalist. In 2023, she published a book called *Fat Talk: Parenting in the Age of Diet Culture*. It became an instant best-seller, and Ms. Sole-Smith, the subject of a long profile in the *New York Times* a year later. Ms. Sole-Smith, the profile explains, does not use the term "obesity" (she instead says "ob*sity"), as she considers "obesity" to be an expression of "anti-fat bias." She claims that people do not have "much control over weight" . . . even as she tells her children's friend's parents that they can expect their child to eat "nine Oreos" at her house. This fits with her beliefs that there are no good and bad foods—she equates kale and donuts—and that limiting cookie consumption inhibits children from figuring out how to eat in accordance with their bodies' needs.[52]

Is there any room for negativity toward excess fat, combined, perhaps, with a deep respect for people who are struggling with their weight? Ms. Sole-Smith runs a very successful newsletter called *Burnt Toast*. No comments suggesting anything positive about weight loss are allowed.

The full mainstreaming of the ideology of *Burnt Toast* is evident on the covers of our most popular magazines. In 2021, *Cosmopolitan* ran a cover story featuring a clearly obese woman. The headline: "This Is Healthy."[53]

No wonder *Time* magazine declared in 2024, "No one knows how to talk about weight loss anymore."[54]

That being said, there are at least a few people who are neither intimidated nor confused by the idea that we have to be positive about a preventable and deadly condition. The *New York Times* profile of Ms. Sole-Smith cites doctors who are "infuriated" by the claim that obesity is acceptable and even healthy—as it is "approaching a myth" that an obese person can have a "healthy life" and a "normal lifespan." In 2019, the comedian and social critic Bill Maher saw what was developing. He commented:

> In August, fifty-three Americans died from mass shootings. Terrible, right? Do you know how many died from obesity? Forty thousand. Fat shaming doesn't need to end. It needs to make a comeback. Some amount of shame is good. We shamed people out of smoking and into wearing seat belts. We shamed them out of littering and most of them out of racism. Shame is the first step in reform . . . We've gone to this weird place where fat is good. It's pointing out that fat is unhealthy, that's what's bad. Fat shame? We fit shame. Really.

He went on to call those who oppose negativity with regard to obesity "the NRA of mayonnaise."[55]

In 2024, a team of reporters at the *Washington Post* and The Examination (a public health nonprofit organization) published an investigation of the body positivity movement. They told the story of Jaye Rochon, a Wisconsin-based video editor who struggled with her weight for many years. She lost a lot of weight, and then began seeing what the *Post* called "a juggernaut" of influencers advocating "health at any size." These influencers urged her to stop dieting and listen to her "mental hunger." Hearing that any negativity directed against fatness is illegitimate, she reengaged with cupcakes and was soon, again, three hundred pounds.

The *Post* team wondered: Who is funding these campaigns? It was not hard to locate the source: the food companies, such as Rich Foods (which makes whipped cream) and General Mills (which makes Pillsbury dough products, Lucky Charms, and Coco Puffs). General Mills, the investigation found, sponsors "dieticians" who post with hashtags such as #NoBadFoods, #FoodFreedom, and #DitchtheDiet. The investigation told of a General Mills executive who was asked at the leading industry trade show about the company's position on efforts to require the FDA to label foods as high in sugar and fat. The executive replied, "We're doing everything we can to prevent that from happening. Shaming is what I call it."[56]

This statement is a fine articulation of a claim of the body positivity movement, which is something that even the most enthusiastic smoking spokesmen did not say (or believe) in the heyday of cigarettes: The body positivity movement makes no distinction between obesity and obese people. To the contrary, it asserts that one's fat is, and should be, a part of one's identity, if one chooses. The suggestion that there is anything negative about fat is an act of prejudice against and even aggression toward fat people.

Consequently, United States policy does not discourage obesity or anything that could promote what all honest physicians agree is a healthy body size. To the contrary, the United States spends $4 billion a year subsidizing sugar production.[57] We also subsidize its consumption. Approximately forty million Americans receive SNAP benefits, otherwise known as food stamps. The government allows SNAP spending for any food except for hot or prepared meals. Thus, an eligible person can use food stamps to buy candy, cookies, and soda, but not a fresh and warm plate of grilled chicken, steamed vegetables, and brown rice.

The consequences: In 2023, Chip Edwards of the Cato Institute found that approximately 25 percent of SNAP benefits are spent on "junk food." His reference to "food" includes drinks. In 2018, NPR reported that 10 percent of food stamps are spent on sugary drinks. A 2022 analysis of Coca-Cola's finances by Calley Means shows that more than 40 percent of the company's US revenue comes from SNAP.[58]

This would explain the experience of Florida state senator Ronda Storms, who, in 2013, tried to have her state prohibit SNAP spending on soda. She said, "The biggest opponents I have right now are Coca-Cola, the soda companies, the chip companies, and the convenience store operators."[59]

Without the ability to trigger the negativity bias against obesity and toward health, Ronda Storms had no chance against those opponents.

A Lost Nuance

Bill Maher did not say anything negative about obese people. Neither did the aforementioned *Washington Post* reporters, Dariush Mozaffarian, Dan Glickman, or Eric Adams in *Healthy at Last*. They are not against fat people. They are against fatness. Their thinking is exactly in line with those who led the anti-smoking movement, which held that people should stop smoking in order to live longer and healthier as parents and grandparents, community members and citizens—that they should, in Torah terms, guard in order to observe.

However, the body positivity movement has conflated fatness with fat people, making fatness a part of one's identity (like race, gender, and sexual orientation). It has thus rendered the deployment of the negativity bias against obesity to be illegitimate. Consequently, obesity extracts a staggering cost on the United States and its citizens in terms of economic impact, health effects, and premature death.

Reflection

A concept that entered the popular lexicon in the 1990s is the "theory of change." According to the Center for the Theory of Change, it is "essentially a comprehensive description and illustration of how and why a desired change is expected to happen in a particular context."[60]

The ability to change—the potential of any individual or institution to get better—is our fundamental blessing, given by God in Genesis 35 when he tells Jacob that his name will now be Israel. This gift—what Rabbi David Wolpe calls the "blessing our self-transformation"—is discussed in the chapter of this book on character.

The Torah offers a three-part theory of change.

a. Change is both hard *and* necessary for us to flourish spiritually, morally, and materially.
b. Change requires us to say, mean, and do the following: This habit, practice, or trait (or policy, dynamic, or trend) is negative—or at least worse than I would like it to be. I want to adopt better (and thus different) habits and traits. Therefore, I am willing to invest the effort and endure the sacrifice to get from the negative to the positive.
c. The negativity bias, ungoverned, will lead us to focus on the negative at the expense of the positive. Properly governed, the negativity bias will enable us to be necessarily sensitive and attentive to the things that could inhibit us—so that we can change for the better and do positive things.

For instance, every parent should want his child to grow up to become a competent, confident, and secure adult. An ungoverned negativity bias will lead parents to emphasize the risks and potential dangers that exist at each stage of a child's emerging independence. Such people are vulnerable to becoming helicopter and snowplow parents who focus on the physical and emotional risks that exist all around them. These parents, having succumbed to the negativity bias, will unwittingly inhibit their child from pursuing the kinds of activities and relationships that will prepare him to become a competent, confident, and secure adult. The consequences of this succumbing to the negativity bias in this way are discussed in the chapter of this book on anti-fragility.

18

Judging Righteously and Predicting Divorce

The Torah and Science of Generous Interpretation

The Jewish Golden Rule

In Deuteronomy 16:18–20, Moses issues a very intriguing instruction. He says, "You shall place judges and law enforcement officials for yourself in all your cities that the Lord, your God, is giving you, for your tribes, and they shall judge the people [with] righteous judgment."

There are several intriguing aspects of this passage. First, why does the Torah instruct us to "place" judges in our cities? The Author of the Torah, for instance, wants priests in the Tabernacle, but he never instructs us to "place" them there.

Second, what is the meaning of "yourself"? Of course, the existence of judges and police officers benefits oneself—they benefit everyone. The passage could have read, "You shall have judges and law enforcement officials in all your cities," and been entirely comprehensible.

The eighteenth-century sage Rabbi Yaakov Yosef of Polonne reasoned that the passage is not *only* speaking about professional judges who serve in a legal context. As everyone judges people all the time, the passage applies to professional judges and each of us in our everyday judging.

Rabbi Yaakov Yosef explains that we can understand the significance of "place" and "yourself" by analyzing them together. He suggests that the verb "place" means "that which you put on others." The Torah is telling us, therefore, to judge others as we want them to judge us.[1]

How, we are drawn to ask, do we want to be judged?

The answer is provided through Hillel the Elder's statement in the Talmud, which has become the Jewish Golden Rule: "What is hateful to you, do not do to your fellow."[2] *Everyone* uses their words in context to convey something specific, and everyone hates having their words divorced from their intention. Everyone hates having their well-meaning words, actions, or inactions interpreted maliciously. Therefore, the reading of "place" as "that which you put on others," is a clear instruction that each of us should interpret the words and actions of others generously.[3]

Leviticus 19:15 records a different law of judging. The text says, "Judge your people fairly." That sounds obvious. Would God ever want us to judge *unfairly*? The Torah never wastes our time by instructing us in the self-evident. This passage, like all passages, must teach something important and nonintuitive.

Maimonides explains that the passage means that judges are commanded to treat litigants equally by allowing them all to speak for "a long time or a short time." Once again, this might seem like a rule for the courts, to ensure that everyone can air all of the arguments and evidence that could lead to the truth. And it is. But in Maimonides's reading, the passage goes further. He writes, "This mitzvah also includes the law that one is required to judge one's fellow favorably, and to explain his words and actions only in a good and kind way."[4]

Why Moses Refuses Joshua's Demand to "Stop Them"

In Numbers 11, God instructs Moses to select seventy elders who will help him judge the people and generally share the burden of leadership. These men are to be endowed with the spirit of Hashem. Sixty-eight of them report to Moses for duty. Two, Eldad and Medad, remain in the camp to prophesy.

Joshua, Moses's protégé and top aide, exclaims, "Moses, my Lord, stop them!" We are not told what aroused Joshua's concern, but there are not many possibilities. He must have interpreted their continuing to prophesy as a challenge to the religious authority of Moses and perhaps even God.

Moses, who has the same information about the incident as Joshua, has a very different interpretation. He says, "I wish that all the Lord's people were prophets and that the Lord would put His Spirit on them!"

This vignette is especially interesting because it does not advance the plot of the Torah. The Torah seems to emphasize this, as Eldad and Medad are never heard from again. So, what could the purpose of the story be? It must be to show us how similarly situated people with the same information could arrive at very different interpretations, one generous and one ungenerous. And that leads us to ask: Which is the better approach?

The Torah is clear about the answer. Joshua does not challenge Moses, indicating that he learned from his mentor that an ambiguous situation should be interpreted generously.

Why the Most Important Mission in the Torah Fails

In Numbers 13, it is time for the people to fulfill the divine mission of conquering the land and beginning the project of becoming "a kingdom of priests and a holy nation" in the Promised Land. The people decide that they would like to scout the land before conquering it. This is unnecessary, as the text is clear that God wants them to conquer the land and will personally guide them on the way. But God and Moses allow them to scout out the land, anyway.

The mission is a disaster. The scouts return, conceding that the land is spectacular. However, they say that they cannot conquer it because, among other reasons, "it is a land that devours its inhabitants."

Why would they have identified it as "a land that devours its inhabitants"? The ancient rabbis recorded that the men must have observed a lot of funerals—a reasonable conclusion given the number of inhabitants who were apparently devoured. The fourth-century sage Rava wrote that the scouts could, upon observing the funerals, have chosen to arrive at one of two conclusions. First: God arranged for many to die during the scouting mission so that the inhabitants would be preoccupied with burying their dead and wouldn't notice the Jews scouting the land. Second: The funerals were a result of the land having "devoured" its inhabitants. The people chose the ungenerous interpretation. This decision leads to a chain of circumstances that culminate in God forbidding that generation from ever entering the land.[5]

Why Dathan and Abiram Get Swallowed into the Earth

Three chapters later, we arrive at the greatest political threat to Moses's leadership in the Torah. Korach "separates" himself in order to start the most threatening rebellion against Moses in the desert. He is joined, the text tells us, by Dathan and Abiram.

Moses first tries to convince Korach that his rebellion is wrong and will be defeated. But he fails completely in that attempt. Moses then appeals to Dathan and Abiram, but in a very particular way. The Torah reports in Numbers 16:12, "Moses sent to call Dathan and Abiram." What does Moses mean by "call"? One of the standard tactics to understand the meaning of a word in the Torah is to consider its meaning in previous narrative contexts. As the nineteenth-century Rabbi Samson Raphael Hirsch noted, Moses heard the term for call (*kri'ah*) before. This was in Exodus 2:20 when Jethro, upon hearing that Moses saved his daughters from being assaulted, invites him to dinner with a "call." Jethro became Moses's father-in-law and beloved mentor. Accordingly, Moses's "call" to Dathan and Abiram is just like that of his father-in-law: positive, affectionate, and welcoming.[6]

Dathan and Abiram waste no time in responding. They say, "We shall not go up!" What are they thinking? Moses has called them in the same gentle and loving manner as Jethro had called him, and they are responding with a "We shall not!" Moreover, why do they add the word "up"? There is no indication that Moses is higher than them physically. And we know from Moses's legendary humility that he would not have considered himself "higher" than anyone else.

It is clear that Dathan and Abiram have *decided* to interpret Moses's words as a demand rather than an invitation—in a word—ungenerously. Having decided to interpret ungenerously, Dathan and Abiram become fueled by righteous indignation. They say, "Is it not enough that you have brought us up from a land flowing with milk and honey to cause us to die in the wilderness, yet you seek to dominate us, even to dominate further?"

This might be the most bizarre statement anyone utters in the Torah. Egypt is the land of milk and honey? Moses led the people from Egypt not so that they could get to the Promised Land, but so that they could die in the desert?

Dathan and Abiram are soon swallowed by the earth, their names forever living in infamy. The *choice* to interpret ungenerously, we learn, will warp one's sense of reality and ultimately lead to catastrophic consequences.

"The Best Way to Live"

In Pirkei Avot 1:6, the sages tell us, "Joshua ben Perahiah used to say: appoint for thyself a teacher, and acquire for thyself a friend and judge every man [with the scale] weighted in his favor."

The contemporary Israeli scholar Rabbi Joshua Kulp notes that the first two clauses (appoint a teacher and acquire a friend) don't obviously belong with the third. Why, then, did Rabbi Joshua ben Perahiah combine them? Rabbi Kulp explains, "One who is constantly skeptical of others' actions and motives will certainly not be able to have the friends or teachers mentioned in the previous two clauses of the Mishnah." This sequence represents, according to Rabbi Kulp, "some of the sagest advice the Mishnah can give in teaching a person to succeed in society."[7]

Another piece of sage advice regarding generous interpretation is found in a very different context. One question that every culture considers is, what constitutes beauty? The sixteenth- and seventeenth-century sage from Prague Ephraim ben Aaron Luntschitz (known as the Kli Yakar) notes that the Talmud refers to a "beautiful bride" as one who has "beautiful eyes." As there are all kinds of physical attributes that could signify beauty, why do the rabbis of the Talmud select the eyes? The eyes are, of course, what enable us to see. Therefore, the Kli Yakar concluded, the rabbis of the Talmud were equating beauty with having a generous perspective.[8]

This interpretation is supported by the second-century sage Rabbi Eliezer. When asked the existential question "What is the best way to live?" he had a simple answer at the ready. He said, "[With] a good eye."[9]

A thousand years later, Maimonides addressed the issue of interpretation in his *Guide for the Perplexed*. He wrote that correct biblical interpretation is based on the principle of interpreting generously in that we should consider "figuratively" passages that do not line up with scientific facts. Then, he immediately applied the principle to a seemingly different domain—that of interpersonal relationships. He wrote: "Whenever the words of a person can be interpreted in such a manner that they agree with fully established facts, it is the duty of every educated and honest man to do so. Only a fool or an ignoramus would refrain from doing it."[10]

One of the most successful Jewish movements of all time has been Chabad. Chabad, while fully Orthodox in its doctrine and practice, has established 3,500 centers in 100 countries, where hundreds of thousands of Jews (from the unaffiliated to the devout) learn, pray, and engage in community together. Moreover, Chabad runs one of the best Jewish learning sites (chabad.org), has 285 centers on university campuses, and serves the social services needs of Jewish prisoners, special needs children, sick children, widows, orphans, and the needy.

There are a lot of factors that account for Chabad's impact, as there is for any organization that has been so successful. An organizational psychologist would find Chabad's success to be mystifying, as it has not had a leader since the Rebbe Menachem Schneerson died in 1994. But we can isolate a fundamental principle of what made this organization so successful. It comes through in a story that Rabbi Moshe Scheiner, the Chabad Rabbi who founded the Palm Beach Synagogue, tells of an exchange that happened several decades ago.

The Rebbe once received a letter from a man who was disturbed by the fact that the Chabad House he attended tolerated the presence of a man who always wore flip-flops and read the newspaper through services.

The Rebbe wrote back saying that he was not disturbed and, indeed, had great respect for the man in flip-flops. The Rebbe explained that he assumed that the man was a secular Jew who did not relate to prayer, but came to the synagogue in case he was needed for a minyan (the ten-person quorum necessary for a prayer service). This spirit of generous interpretation applied even to seemingly obviously breaches of decorum, has come to define Chabad and all who come into its wide orbit.[11]

The Science

The Principle of Charity—and Its Progeny

In October 1958, the Canadian philosopher Neil Wilson delivered a paper at the UNC/Duke Philosophical Colloquium. The paper was published as an essay in the *Review of Metaphysics* the following year.

Such presentations are generally obscure exercises that are not noticed by anyone outside the room and, maybe, a tenure committee. But not this one. It was here where Professor Wilson developed a principle that would be quoted, cited, and studied decades later by academics across a range of disciplines. It is the "Principle of Charity"—defined by Itamar Shatz of the University of Cambridge in the twenty-first century as "the philosophical principle that denotes that, when interpreting someone's statement, you should assume that the best possible interpretation of that statement is the one that the speaker meant to convey."[12]

The Principle of Charity has spawned a number of similar ideas, which amplify its point and bring it to other domains. For instance, Hanlon's Razor, which was contributed by Robert Hanlon to *Murphy's Law, Book Two* (1980). Hanlon's Razor states, "Never attribute to malice that which can be adequately explained by stupidity."[13]

In his 1991 essay "Three Varieties of Knowledge," the philosopher Donald Davidson addressed the question, What are we to make of others, considering that our knowledge of them is limited? He proposed two ideas that accord with the Principle of Charity. There is the Principle of Coherence, which "prompts the interpreter to discover a degree of logical consistency in the thought of the speaker."

And there is the Principle of Correspondence, which "prompts the interpreter to take the speaker to be responding to the same features of the world that he (the interpreter) would be responding to under similar circumstances."[14]

The Principles of Charity, Coherence, and Correspondence command just what the Bible instructs. When interpreting a speaker's words, arguments, or perspective, we are to interpret generously. This principle has been amplified and developed in subsequent philosophy.

As the Bible shows, this theory is often put to the test. Has our culture reacted like Moses, or like Dathan and Abiram?

Microaggressions

In 2007, Professor Derald Wing Sue of Columbia University wrote of boarding a plane with an "African American colleague." He described the plane as a "small 'hopper' with a single row of seats on one side and double seats on the other" and as "sparsely populated."

The flight attendant, whom he identified as white, told Professor Sue and his colleague that they could sit anywhere. They chose two seats across from each other at the front. Shortly thereafter, "three white men in suits" came on the plane and were similarly directed by the flight attendant. They sat in three seats in front of Professor Sue and his colleague. The flight attendant asked Professor Sue and his colleague if they would move to the back of the plane. Professor Sue recounts his reaction:

> Although we complied by moving to the back of the plane, both of us felt resentment, irritation, and anger. In light of our everyday racial experiences, we both came to the same conclusion: The flight attendant had treated us like second-class citizens because of our race. But this incident did not end there. While I kept telling myself to drop the matter, I could feel my blood pressure rising, heart beating faster, and face flush with anger.

Professor Sue accused the flight attendant of racism. She was stunned and offended, and said that she was asking him to move only to balance the plane. He recounts, "For the rest of the flight, I stewed over the incident and it left a sour taste in my mouth."[15]

Why would Professor Sue have decided to interpret the flight attendant's request to be derived from racism rather than safety concerns? It is possible that the flight attendant was a racist. But it is well known and intuitive that a small plane needs to have its weight balanced. So why would Professor Sue interpret the flight attendant's request as racist? The answer is revealed in the idea he has devoted his career to, and is famous for. This is the idea of microaggressions. The concept was invented in the 1970s by Harvard professor Chester Pierce, and developed and popularized in the twenty-first century by Professor Sue.

Professor Sue defines microaggressions as "brief and commonplace daily verbal, behavioral, or environmental indignities, whether intentional or unintentional, that communicate hostile, derogatory, or negative racial slights and insults toward people of color." The "microaggression" can be, as Professor Sue wrote, unrelated to the intention of the speaker. A "microaggression" can also, according to an analysis by the American Psychological Association, be "so subtle" that neither the "victim nor the perpetrator" recognizes it as an aggression at all.[16]

These definitions and analyses create something of a riddle. What kind of act could be so "subtle" that it could be undetectable by the perpetrator *and* the victim, and yet still qualify as an aggression? The answer: one that could be interpreted either generously or negatively, and that the recipient (whom the APA calls "a victim") chooses to interpret negatively.

As Professor Sue demonstrated, the potential to interpret ungenerously, and experience microaggressions, occurs all the time. For instance, asking someone where he or she is from. One might consider this a pleasant bid for connection or an indication of interest in the other person. But not according to the American Psychological Association. The APA states that this conveys "the message that they are perpetual foreigners in their own land."[17]

Professor Lewis Schlosser is the chief psychologist for the New Jersey Association of Chiefs of Police. In 2008, he gave a presentation entitled "Microaggressions in Everyday Life: The American Jewish Experience." He said, "Ascriptions of Intelligence"—assuming that Jews are smart—is an antisemitic microaggression. Likewise, Professor Schlosser says that a gentile who says, "You need to get yourself a good Jewish lawyer," is a microaggressor.[18]

Is there another way to interpret a presumption that Jews are smart—or a comment from a gentile that he wants a Jewish lawyer? In 2015, Shaquille O'Neal gave an interview to the journalist Graham Bensinger. Mr. O'Neal discussed being a young man who, as a result of his basketball stardom, had become very wealthy. He lost $80,000 in a deal and decided that he needed a financial advisor. He interviewed several advisors. A couple of advisors pitched him on turning his $40 million into $200 million in a year or two. He quickly dismissed them.

Then an entirely different kind of financial advisor came to meet with him. This advisor was, Mr. O'Neal recalls, "one little small beautiful Jewish man." This advisor told Mr. O'Neal that he would put him in savings bonds and set up a subchapter S corporation so that the basketball player could deduct his business expenses.

Shaquille O'Neal decided right then who his financial advisor would be. "I said, 'Shalom, Baruch Hashem. I'm going with you, sir.'"[19]

Was Shaquille O'Neal, by referring to his financial advisor as "small, little, and Jewish," committing an antisemitic microaggression? Mr. O'Neal did not think so. Indeed, the interview continues with him describing in a quaking voice the relationship that he has had with this financial advisor, who, he says, "is like a father to me."

Aish.com, one of the most widely respected Jewish learning sites, doesn't think so either. Aish featured the interview with Mr. O'Neal, calling it a "Kiddush Hashem." Kiddush Hashem, which means "sanctification of God's name," is the highest praise that a Jew can offer.[20]

Interpreting Generously at Yale Law School

Where is society headed regarding interpreting generously? In the direction of Shaquille O'Neal and Aish or that of Professors Sue and Schlosser? Let's take a customary question: "Where are you from?" It might seem like a nice conversation starter, particularly in a society that values diversity. Yet CNN, the American Psychological Association, *Business Insider*, the *Harvard Business Review*, and Pfizer have all deemed it a "microaggression." And commentary from the same and similar institutions is clear that there is really nothing "micro" about "microaggressions." NPR has proclaimed microaggressions to be "a big deal." The US Education Department, Justice Department, National Cancer Institute, and the Cleveland Clinic (which consider microaggressions to be a significant *medical* issue) all agree.[21]

If there is any institution that should be devoted to interpreting generously, it is a law school. A good lawyer must understand the best arguments from the other side so that he will be able to anticipate and refute them with the rigor necessary to convince a neutral third party. And a good judge must also appreciate both sides of a case so that he can satisfy all parties with a fair ruling. Indeed, Harvard Law professor Joseph Singer recalls being a young law clerk, and being told by his judge that the "most important audience for any opinion is the losing side. He wanted us to write an opinion that showed we listened to the losing side's arguments. The idea was to give an argument that they could accept."[22]

Enter the institution that US News has consistently deemed "the No. 1 Best Law School"—Yale Law School. In 2021, the students, faculty, and administration at Yale Law School were given an opportunity to live (or not) the principle of interpreting generously. In the fall, Trent Colbert, a Yale Law School student who heads the institution's Native American Law Students Association (NALSA), sent an email to his classmates inviting them to a "Constitution Day Bash" sponsored by NALSA and the Federalist Society.

The Federalist Society is a national organization of conservative law students and scholars with chapters at most law schools. The activities for the party, the invitation said, included consumption of "Popeye's chicken, basic-bitch-American-themed snacks (like apple pie, etc.), a cocktail station, assorted hard and soft beverages, and (most importantly), the opportunity to attend the NALSA Trap House's inaugural mixer!"

Within minutes, the president of the Black Law Students Association condemned the invitation, in a Yale forum, as racist. Within hours, nine other students filed discrimination and harassment complaints about the message. Within twelve hours, deans Yaseen Eldik and Ellen Cosgrove summoned Mr. Colbert to the law school's Office of Student Affairs.

The deans did not know that the young man was recording the conversation. In that meeting, the "Diversity Director," Yaseen Eldik, told the student that the term "trap house" connotes crack, hip-hop, and blackface. Those "triggering associations," the dean continued, "[were] compounded by the fried chicken reference," which "is often used to undermine arguments that structural and systemic racism has contributed to racial health disparities in the US."

The deans demanded that Mr. Colbert sign a confession, apologizing for any "harm, trauma or upset" caused by his email and committing to "actively educate myself so I can do better." He refused. Deans Cosgrove and Eldik responded by emailing the student body accusing Mr. Colbert of using "racist language" and condemning his invitation "in the strongest possible terms."

The justification for the charge of racism, as discussed by Dean Eldik and others, was fourfold. It is a master class in *rejecting* the principle of generous interpretation.

First, the students claimed that the term "trap house" refers to a "crack house." That is one interpretation. Another interpretation, as shown in a liberal podcast, *Trap House*, is what the journalist Liz Wolfe identifies as "a place with a fun party."[23]

Second, it is unclear why one who regards a "trap house" as a "crack house" would interpret it as racist. But given that most crack users are white, it would seem racist to assume that a "crack house" refers to a place where blacks congregate.[24]

Third is the reference to "Popeye's chicken"—not, as the dean erroneously quoted Mr. Colbert as saying, "fried chicken." There is a Popeye's on campus from which the students apparently intended to order. It is unclear why anyone would interpret the inclusion of Popeye's chicken at a party to be racist.

Fourth, Dean Eldik said that the mention of the Federalist Society is "very triggering for students . . . that of course obviously includes the LGBTQIA community and black communities and immigrant communities." The school administrator is educating the students that they should interpret the involvement of the nation's conservative legal society—one that has chapters at two hundred law schools, professors from the right and left speaking at its conferences, and seventy thousand members including six Supreme Court justices—as akin to acceptance of homophobia, racism, and anti-immigrant sentiment.[25]

The results of Trent Colbert's email were clear and widely reported. Racial and social tensions were heightened, and accusations pitted students and faculty against one another for the remainder of the year. This was so sad and unnecessary. I graduated from Yale Law School in 1998, and friendships were created and sustained over a lifetime among people who disagreed on all kinds of issues (from the O. J. verdict to abortion to candidates running in elections). This was made possible by the culture of Yale Law School then, which was of interpreting generously. There is a happy ending to this story. I recently gave a talk to the conservative students at Yale Law School, and they reported that the "Trap House" era is over, and a renewed spirit of interpreting generously—with broad-ranging friendships—is back.[26]

Dean Spellman Is Forced to Resign

Claremont McKenna is a highly selective liberal arts college located in a beautiful area of Southern California. In 2015, Lisette Espinosa, a neuroscience and gender studies student at the school, wrote an article for the school newspaper.

She was unhappy. She wrote that she felt like an "imposter" as she wondered if she was admitted in order to fill a quota. She felt objectified by young men. She was so ashamed of Claremont McKenna's racist attitudes that she never invited her parents to visit. She said that the professors she admired felt "devalued" and even "harassed" on account of their "gender or sexual identity," and she accused the school culture of being "primarily grounded in western, white, cisheteronormative upper to upper-middle class values." She discussed visiting another college's "Communities of Resources and Empowerment Center" so often that people thought she had transferred.[27]

The Dean of Students, Mary Spellman, read the article. Concerned, she emailed Ms. Espinosa right away. Dean Spellman wrote:

> Lisette—Thank you for writing and sharing this article with me. We have a lot to do as a college and a community. Would you be willing to talk to me about these issues? They are important to me and the staff and we are working on how we can better serve students, especially those that don't fit our CMC mold.
>
> I would love to talk with you some more.
>
> Best,
>
> Dean Spellman

Lizzie Espinosa was infuriated. Why? Dean Spellman wrote about "fitting the CMC mold." Ms. Espinosa was joined in her interpretation of Dean Spellman's response by other students. One student, Taylor Lemmons, wrote, "'Fit the mold' only compounds the instances where she and her office have failed to respond to violence that marginalized students have experienced on this campus."[28]

These students came up with a response: a hunger strike. A classic "struggle session" followed the hunger strike. Dean Spellman and her colleagues were castigated by a large crowd of students. One student asked Dean Spellman, "How can we change your heart?" Another cried, "How can you learn to identify? We're hearing the same shit all over again." Another woman spoke, accusing Dean Spellman of falling asleep during the struggle session—when she was clearly covering her eyes to stop her tears.

Dean Spellman apologized multiple times. But it didn't matter. No one in a position of authority at this renowned liberal arts college seriously defended her—or suggested that her email to Ms. Espinosa should be interpreted differently. She was soon gone, having been effectively forced to resign.[29]

How a Word Goes into Forced Retirement

The word "master" derives from the Latin *magister*, meaning "teacher"—which in turn derives from the Latin *magis*, meaning "greater."[30] It has been used to describe a leader in an academic context since at least the thirteenth century, when Oxford, responding to a town-gown dispute that descended into a riot, put students into residential halls under the leadership of "masters."[31]

The term "master" later became a mark of academic distinction, as is expressed by the term "master's degree." Harvard University was established in 1638 with a frame house, a yard, and a "master." Subsequently founded universities, such as Yale and Princeton, also used the term "master" to describe their academic leaders.

In 2013, New York State launched a "Master Teacher Program." This program recognizes and rewards experienced and excellent STEM teachers. Participants receive professional development and are given opportunities to mentor younger teachers and to recruit people into the profession.[32]

One of the most successful education companies founded this century is MasterClass, which sources well-known authorities to lecture on a subject related to their expertise and experience. The "masters" include Bill Clinton, Hillary Clinton, Cornel West, Nikole Hannah-Jones, Pharrell Williams, and Judy Blume—offering instruction on leadership, philosophy, music, writing, and other subjects. There is also a series where masters present on "issues of social injustice and systemic racism, offering education and inspiration on ways to impact change."[33]

The term "master" seemingly did not bother anyone until the fall of 2015. That was when students at Yale, Harvard, and Princeton decided that the term "master" (which was used to describe the leaders of their residencies) was racist. They were quickly joined by professors. By the end of the year, the administration had to decide.

President Peter Salovey of Yale University wrote in a letter to the Yale community, "The term [master] derives from the Latin *magister*, meaning 'chief, head, director, teacher,' and it appears in the titles of university degrees (master of arts, master of science, and others) and in many aspects of the larger culture (master craftsman, master builder)."

Professor Salovey could have followed that statement by imploring his students to interpret generously, or at least to understand words in context. He chose otherwise. He abolished the title "master," as did his counterparts at Princeton and Harvard.[34]

This idea—as those that originate from universities generally do in one way or another—would have far-reaching impact. In June of 2020, the Houston Association of Realtors banned the use of the term "master bedroom" from its multiple listing service and elsewhere, on the grounds that it could be legitimately interpreted as racist and sexist.[35]

Housing professionals around the country quickly agreed with the new interpretation of "master." Cathy Taub, the founding chairperson of New York Residential Agent Continuum (NYRAC), said, "While there are certain benign connotations of the word master (e.g. in academia, a master's degree), the more typical association with the word 'master' is a person who controls or dominates another person, which is an incredibly negative connotation and one that should not be perpetuated in the nomenclature of real estate."[36]

Within a few weeks, the national real estate authorities were similarly convinced. Donnell Williams, the president of the National Association of Real Estate Brokers, said of the term "master": "It's a repetitive reminder of slavery and plantations. I don't feel that it's proper, and I'm glad that someone brought it up."[37]

The practice of interpreting so ungenerously that one would hear the word "master" in the context of bedrooms or colleges and think of slavery extends well beyond that one term. In 2024, JP Morgan officially discouraged or forbade the use of terms such as "grandfathered," "manpower," "good school/neighborhood," "conflict in Ukraine," and "cakewalk." All of these terms, in the context that they are *always* used, have no conceivable offensive or even negative connotations. Yet, the JP Morgan executives focused on the ungenerous interpretations that cast those terms as problematic. They said of "cakewalk": "Like 'white glove treatment,' this term is rooted in the history and mistreatment of enslaved African Americans in the United States. Instead use 'easy to do or achieve.'"[38]

The impulse to interpret ungenerously can be so profound that its adherents will misinterpret history in order to be able to do so. Cakewalks were sophisticated dances conceived by slaves *to mock* the culture of the slaveholders. They remained a popular and important part of black culture for generations following slavery, with competitions held at the Paris World

Fair in 1889 and Madison Square Garden a decade later. The cakewalk also inspired the great black musical genre of ragtime.[39]

The Demonstrable Effects of Interpreting Generously

Many people, contemplating the slow retirement of the term "master," might ask: Why does it matter? If some people take the term "master" out of context and are offended by it, why is it harmful to retire it? After all, there are other ways to describe instructors and the bedroom where the parents sleep.

That question would be a subset of a larger one, which is: Why is interpreting generously so important that the Torah would address it in narrative and law, with persistent amplification throughout generations of Jewish teaching?

First: *physical health.* In Dr. Sue's telling of the situation on the plane, his blood pressure rose and his heart started beating faster as his face became flush with anger. These are textbook signs of cardiovascular problems that lead to heart attacks and strokes.[40]

Of course, this single incident would not subject Dr. Sue to any lasting medical harm, and he may never again be on a small airplane where he is asked to move. But our reactions are products of our dispositions and even philosophies. A philosophy of ungenerous interpretation, which will lead to frequent experiences of anger, is sure to result in many instances where the blood pressure rises, the heart beats faster, and the face flushes. Over time, this can have serious medical consequences.

Second: *happiness.* In 2015, the *Washington Post* published an article that featured a photograph of a Harvard student who looked sad, exhausted, and defeated. Why would a Harvard student present this way? The young woman in the photograph was holding a sign that said, "'I <u>don't</u> see <u>COLOR</u>' . . . Does that mean you <u>don't</u> see <u>Me</u>?" The student was saying that those who believe that race should not be a factor in the allocation of society's privileges, such as college admissions, are really saying that they don't "see" her—and are racists.[41]

Of course, there is no reason to believe that one who is committed to the principle of color blindness is really saying that he does not "see" this young woman, or anyone else. The young woman in the photo made a choice to interpret the support of color blindness as meaning that she is unseen. This young woman would have certainly been happier if she did not assume that all of the (many) people who oppose racial preferences are really saying that they don't "see" her.[42]

Indeed, the correlation between interpreting generously and happiness would be demonstrated in a multinational study four years later. In 2019, a research team from universities in Poland, the United States, and Japan had 707 participants imagine scenarios such as being ignored by a colleague or stood up in a café. The participants were asked to evaluate the situation based on how much they thought the other person acted intentionally, how much blame they assigned to them, and how angry they were. They then filled out a questionnaire about how happy they considered themselves.

The study found that those who always interpreted generously were the happiest, those who sometimes interpreted generously were next, and those who never interpreted generously were the least happy. These results were the same in all three countries, which are very different from one another.[43]

Third: *community solidarity*. The development of any community depends on members building trust en route to achieving common aims. This requires that members have free, open, and vigorous conversations with one another. These relationships are very difficult to forge when members of the community legitimately fear that other members may dissociate words from context and intention and accuse them of terrible things. And these relationships become functionally impossible when community authorities indulge and even reward the practice of ungenerous interpretation.

Fourth: *relational health*. Interpreting generously is necessary for creating relationships, and also for maintaining them. Drs. John and Julie Gottman are two of the most important, influential, and insightful relationship psychologists in the modern era. The Gottmans distinguish couples into two categories: masters and disasters. The Gottmans can observe couples for fifteen minutes and predict, with 94 percent accuracy, whether the couple will be a master (and stay together) or a disaster (and get divorced).[44]

How can the Gottmans be so accurate with so little information? In 2014, the journalist Emily Esfahani Smith researched the work of the Gottmans and interviewed them to determine how. She writes:

> From the research of the Gottmans, we know that disasters see negativity in their relationship even when it is not there. An angry wife may assume, for example, that when her husband left the toilet seat up, he was deliberately trying to annoy her. But he may have just absent-mindedly forgotten to put the seat down.
>
> Or say a wife is running late to dinner (again), and the husband assumes that she doesn't value him enough to show up to their date on time after he took the trouble to make a reservation and leave work early so that they could spend a romantic evening together. But it turns out that the wife was running late because she stopped by a store to pick up a gift for him for their special night out. Imagine her joining him for dinner, excited to deliver the gift, only to realize that he's in a sour mood because he misinterpreted what was motivating her behavior. The ability to interpret your partner's actions and intentions charitably can soften the sharp edge of conflict.[45]

In other words, masters deploy the "good eye," which Rabbi Eliezer in Pirkei Avot taught is "the way to live."

Fifth: *personal development and self-actualization.* Professor Itamar Shatz has identified several ways that the practice of interpreting generously can help any individual grow intellectually and achieve her goals:

- Implementing the Principle of Charity enables us to better understand others, as we become able to figure out what people are trying to say—and, thus, who they are.
- Implementing the Principle of Charity makes our own thinking more rigorous, as we have to contend with the best of the opposing position.
- Implementing the Principle of Charity makes us more agreeable, as people will prefer to engage with someone who is genuinely trying to understand another person and his positions—rather than just trying to "beat" their arguments and "win" a discussion.[46]

Reflection

Maimonides, channeling the teachings of the Torah and the Talmud, said that only a "fool or ignoramus" would interpret ungenerously. This is, to say the least, not a widely accepted belief today. In his book *Making Loss Matter*, Rabbi David Wolpe writes that people in modern society often associate cynicism—a form of interpreting ungenerously—with intelligence.[47] Intelligent and sophisticated people, this belief goes, are able to see the hidden agenda, the bad intentions, and the insincerity of others. It is, *pace* Maimonides, the fools who look at the same set of facts and assume the best.

The choice of whether to have a "good eye" or not—to align with Maimonides or Derald Sue—is one of the most pervasive and important each person will make. As Rabbi Yaakov Yosef of Pollone said, we are all judges. We judge words, actions, situations, and people all the time. Indeed, judging might be the most serious act of thinking we do on a regular basis. Is an unreturned email an indication that the recipient missed the message or that they do not care to respond? Is someone's failure to say goodbye at a wedding a sign of his rudeness or his desire not to overwhelm the bride and groom with meaningless small talk on their special day?

There is no way of knowing. If one decides to view either situation with what Rabbi Eliezer calls a "good eye" and interpret generously, he may be correct. If one decides to adapt the philosophy of Derald Sue and interpret ungenerously, he may also be correct. What, then, should one do?

If one interprets generously, he will encourage more speech and enable deeper relationships—as people will not self-censor out of concern that their words will be taken out of context and interpreted negatively. If one interprets generously, he will be offended less—with benefits accruing to his cardiovascular health, personal growth, interpersonal relationships, and overall happiness.

19

Burning Them Both and Fueling Depression

The Torah and Science of Grudges

Having an Ax to Grind: The Obligation to Move On

The Torah instructs, in Leviticus 19:18, "You shall not take revenge nor bear a grudge against your countrymen, and you shall love your neighbor as thyself. I am God." The first thing to note about this verse is precisely who it is referring to. It is not referring to someone who committed a crime against you; there is a justice system for that. It is not referring to someone who has committed a tort against you; there is a civil court system for that. And it is not referring to war, for which there is an entirely separate set of rules. It is referring to "your countryman"—the neighbor, family member, friend, or colleague with whom a conflict has developed.

The second thing to note is that it refers to revenge *and* a grudge. The distinction between taking revenge and bearing a grudge seems difficult to decipher. Yet, the Torah is clearly asserting a difference between the two. The Talmud explains:

> What is revenge and what is bearing a grudge? If one said to his fellow: "Lend me your sickle," and he replied "No," and tomorrow the second comes [to the first] and says: "Lend me your ax," and he replies: "I will not lend it to you, just as you would not lend me your sickle" that is revenge. And what is bearing a grudge? If one said to his fellow: "Lend me your ax," and he replied "No," and

> tomorrow the second comes and says: "Lend me your garment," and he replies: "Here it is. I am not like you who would not lend to me." That is bearing a grudge.[1]

This distinction is expressed well by the English word "begrudgingly." The person in the Talmudic example of bearing a grudge *gives* his fellow the ax—but does so *begrudgingly.* A grudge, therefore, does not refer to an action but an attitude. The attitude consists of remembering a slight or offense, and letting that memory influence one's mindset at a later point.

The importance of attitude is underscored by a close examination of the Talmudic example. It is *permitted* to refuse to lend a countryman an item in the first place, so long as the countryman is not poor. But it is *prohibited* to lend him the item with a begrudging attitude. This seems odd. The borrower might very well prefer to receive the object from a begrudging lender than to not receive it all. Yet, lending begrudgingly is still prohibited. Why does the Torah consider grudges to be so bad that they are prohibited, even to the point of stopping a mutually agreed-upon transaction?

First, holding onto grudges prevents the formation of genuine community. This derives from the fact that the counterparty of the grudge is a "countryman." This term is one that speaks to citizenship—to fellow membership in a society. By forbidding grudges among "countrymen," the Torah is telling us that a good society cannot be constructed by individuals who keep a mental catalog of their grievances against each other.

Second, holding grudges is a sure way to guarantee unhappiness. The anonymous fifteenth-century German sage who is known by the title of his book *Orchot Tzaddikim* noted that there are no expiration dates on grudges. He explains where this leads. "The grudge-holder never overlooks a grievance and never forgives his companions who have wronged him, and this attitude drags after quarrels and hatred, and you already know how good and how pleasant is the quality of peace."[2]

In this analysis, the *Orchot Tzaddikim* reaches deep into the Jewish tradition and emerges with several explanations of how grudges lead to unhappiness. One who holds grudges, the *Orchot Tzaddikim* warns, will inevitably be consumed by them. The grudge holder will find them everywhere, assuring that he is perpetually generating new causes of conflict and resentment.

The grudge holder will also, in "never forgiving," be constantly looking back and finding negativity. This looking back for negativity—known today as rumination—is a major problem in the Torah tradition. In the Jewish evening service, we ask God to "remove the Satan from before us and from behind us." The Satan in front of us is an obvious danger; he is the one that tempts us to commit sins today, and in future days to come.

Who, then, is the Satan behind us? He is the one who tells us to attend to past insults, slights, mistakes, and regrets. One who holds a grudge issues an unconditional invitation to the Satan behind him. Satan will accept, and continually fill the person with reminders of the offenses that led to the grudge, filling his precious mind space with unproductive thoughts, and making him deeply unhappy.[3]

Third, grudges become morally distorting. The thirteenth-century French sage Hezekiah bar Manoah, known as the Chizkuni, builds on the intriguing fact that a potential lender could refuse to lend for almost any reason—but cannot lend if he does so with a grudging attitude. What kind of person, the Chizkuni asks, would generally lend? The answer: a person of generosity and goodwill. If a generally willing lender does so begrudgingly, he will have demonstrated what holding grudges can do: They can transform a person of generosity and goodwill into one of skeptical reluctance. Grudges, therefore, can turn one's character for the worse.[4]

The Torah is clear and explicit that we cannot hold grudges against our "countrymen." Grudges make the grudge holder an unhappy and diminished person—while corroding the basis of society. What, then, is the alternative? How are we supposed to act when wronged in a way that does not qualify for a tort, a crime, or an act of war?

The Alternatives to Grudges: Withdrawing, Forgiving, and Separating

The Torah offers three alternatives to grudges. They are framed in the verse that immediately precedes the prohibition on grudges. This is Leviticus 19:17, which prohibits "hating your brother in your heart." A hatred in the heart is, of course, the stuff of which grudges are made.

The text of Leviticus 19:17 is jarring and invites an immediate second read. Does the Torah really say that one can hate his brother, so long as he does not do so in his heart? It might seem strange for a religious text—but, apparently, yes. As long as one articulates his hatred, he is complying with the spirit and the letter of the Leviticus text. Why? Rabbi David Fohrman explains that one of several responses will follow. These responses also constitute the Torah's response to grudges.[5]

One might, in the process of expressing his hatred, realize just how petty he sounds. He will respond by withdrawing his hatred. In that case, the grudge is gone. Alternatively, the offending party, in hearing the expression of the hatred, may conclude that he harmed the speaker. He is then ready to participate in the process of forgiveness.

Brought into the world by Joseph in the Genesis, forgiveness is rigorously developed in the Jewish tradition. Forgiveness, in the Jewish imagination, is not just a matter of saying, "I'm sorry"—and everyone moving on. Maimonides wrote that a person seeking forgiveness must enter into a rigorous four-step process. He must stop sinning, feel genuine regret, confess out loud (to the aggrieved and to God), and resolve to never do it again.[6]

Having walked those four steps, the offender's responsibility is fulfilled. But the process is not completed. The person from whom forgiveness is being sought *must grant it*, which, of course, is incompatible with holding a grudge.[7]

This process is almost magical. Maimonides said that one who has repented and been forgiven should believe: "I am now another person, and not that person who perpetrated those misdeeds." This sentiment was reiterated by Rav Joseph B. Soloveitchik, who said that forgiveness is a re-creation of the self, and by Rabbi Abraham Isaac Kook who said that forgiveness is an act of vacating who one temporarily was and returning to one's true self. The grudge, pursuant to the Jewish process of forgiveness, is completely wiped away, as the person who committed the offense no longer exists and is instead "another person."[8]

There is a third possibility that happens when one articulates a hatred. Both parties might still maintain that they are right. It seems like the grudge is stuck! But it cannot be, as grudges are prohibited. What is one to do? Simply follow the model of Abraham.

In Genesis 13, the relationship between Abraham and his nephew Lot (and their respective parties) deteriorated to where they "quarreled" so much that they "could not live together." Abraham does not hold a grudge. Instead, he says, "Let us part company," and will never speak negatively about Lot. Therein lies the third solution for a grudge: Separate, and in so doing end (or pause) the relationship—without a sustaining grudge.

This is not the only time the Torah presents separation as an alternative to holding a grudge. Moses is clear, in Deuteronomy 24, that a married couple can get divorced. What they cannot do—whether they stay married or not—is hold a grudge.

Remembering and Forgetting

One of the most powerful statements in favor of forgiveness and against grudges in the Jewish tradition appears in the ancient Mishnah: "If one is a penitent, another may not say to him: Remember your earlier deeds." One who reminds a forgiven person of his previous deed is, the Mishnah rules, guilty of "verbal oppression."[9]

This statement, which is consistent with the idea that a forgiven individual is a new person, contains a tantalizing word: "*Remember*." Remembering is integral to grudges, as grudges depend on their holder recalling the offense. And here, the Mishnah is commanding us *not* to remember.

In the context of Judaism, forbidding remembering is stunning. Our daily prayers and our most important ritual (the Pesach Seder) are centered around *remembering* the Exodus. The great modern Jewish historian Yosef Hayim Yerushalmi encapsulated the centrality of remembering to the Jewish experience: "Only in Israel and nowhere else is the injunction to remember felt as a religious imperative to an entire people." He points out that the injunction to remember exists an astonishing 169 times throughout the Torah.[10]

If remembering is "a religious imperative" of Judaism, then why would grudges—a product of the memory—be forbidden? The answer is revealed in Deuteronomy 32:18, as Moses delivers his concluding words to the Jewish people. Moses predicts that the Jewish people will stray from God's word and explains what will motivate this sin. He says, in a translation rendered by the nineteenth-century sage Menachem Mendel of Kotzk (the Kotzker Rebbe), "The rock [God] who gave you the gift of forgetting, you forgot the God who formed you."[11]

Could forgetting, even for a people devoted to memory, be a "gift from God"? The eighteenth-century sage and founder of Hasidic Judaism, the Baal Shem Tov, certainly thought so. The holiest day of the Jewish year is

Yom Kippur and, as Jewish teaching instructs for all important events, it requires preparation. The Baal Shem Tov counseled that Jews should do three things in approaching the holy day. First, write down on one stack of paper everything that you did for everyone in the previous year. Second, write down the names of everyone who wronged you on the second stack of paper. Third, *burn them both.*

This discipline, which the Baal Shem Tov prescribed for remembering and forgetting generally, is especially applicable with grudges. As Rabbi David Wolpe, reflecting on this teaching, said, "If you remembered every pain, insult, and fatigue, you'd never get out of bed."[12]

The Science

The modern understanding of grudges can begin with its etymology. The wellness writer Sarah Vanbuskirk points out that the word "grudge" derives from the Old French word *grouchier*, which means "to grumble" and is related to the English word "grouch."[13]

The University of California at San Diego psychology professor Michael McCullough reports that grudges have been identified as a cultural phenomenon in almost every ethnographic study ever conducted. The universality of grudges suggests that they have developed because they are evolutionarily adaptive—their presence helps humans survive. Indeed, Professor McCullough says that grudges are effectively "etched into the wiring of our DNA"—and present in the brain as a "craving."[14]

Why are grudges so prevalent and deeply held? One theory is that they enable us to differentiate friends from enemies and distinguish between those who would help or harm us. An aligned theory is that they prepare us to retaliate, which is essential for both winning and avoiding conflict (through deterrence). Whatever the evolutionary mechanism, the science is clear that everyone will naturally form grudges, which will, unmanaged, become an important part of one's life.

The Torah—concerning holding a grudge against a "countryman"—takes an absolutist view. Is the Torah right?

The Health Effects of Grudges

What happens when we consider a grudge? Angela Buttimer of the Thomas F. Chapman Family Cancer Wellness Center at Piedmont Healthcare, explains: "Your brain doesn't know what is real and what is imagined. When you replay in your mind an experience you had six months ago, your body reacts as if you're having the same experience over and over again."[15]

A Johns Hopkins Medical School analysis comes to a similar conclusion, explaining that grudges are experiences in "chronic anger." We respond to this chronic anger by going into "a fight-or-flight" response—exactly as if we were experiencing a real-time danger.[16]

Our bodies can tolerate the fight-or-flight response for a short and rare period of time, as when we are responding to an immediate threat. But it is entirely different when the fight or flight is constant, as when we revisit our grudges. In 2001, Professor Charlotte V. O. Witvliet and colleagues at Hope College discovered what happens to the body when we just *contemplate* a grudge. They had one cohort rehearse a time when they nursed a grudge, and another cohort rehearse a time when they let go of a grudge. The thoughts of the grudge-holding group prompted emotions such as fear and anger, as well as significantly higher skin conductance, heart rate, and blood pressure changes from baseline. These effects lasted into a recovery period.[17]

These responses are indicators of medical trouble. Teams from Johns Hopkins and the Medical College of Georgia have determined that people who hold grudges are disproportionately likely to suffer from heart attacks, weight gain, high blood pressure, stomach ulcers, compromised immunity, back problems, headaches, and chronic pain.[18]

A 2018 report from the Americans' Changing Lives survey—a longitudinal study of American adults—showed that those who hold grudges are significantly more likely to experience cognitive decline than those who do not. An analysis by Professor Everett Worthington of Virginia Commonwealth University suggests why. Grudges cause the brain and body to be in constant stress. We respond to stress by producing the hormone cortisol. Persistently elevated levels of cortisol shrink parts of the brain—including the hippocampus, which turns experiences into memories.[19]

The Psychological Effect of Grudges

So, grudges impact us physically, but how about psychologically? A 2014 study done by a team of psychologists from the United States, Singapore, and the Netherlands found that participants who reminded themselves of grudges were more likely to perceive hills as steep. In addition, these participants could not jump as high as those who reminded themselves of when they let go of grudges. The reason: the maintenance of a grudge results in the changing of perception, which is the key to weighing data points properly, establishing control over one's life, and ultimately making good decisions.[20]

In 2018, the University of Washington psychologist Dr. Meghann Gerber wrote about the experience of holding a grudge. She explains, "Part of holding a grudge is replaying the story over and over in your head and thinking about all of those emotions associated with it." This is the concern of the *Orchot Tzaddikim*: A grudge holder gives precious mind space to a negative experience that, when consistently relived, will make it impossible to have peace of mind.[21]

There is a psychiatric term for Professor Gerber's "replaying" of a negative story "over and over." It is rumination; in Jewish liturgical terms, it is "the Satan behind." A variety of studies have identified rumination as a common instigator of major depressive disorder, PTSD, generalized anxiety disorder, obsessive-compulsive disorder, and a variety of other severe mental health conditions.[22]

There are at least two other ways in which grudges affect us psychologically. First: They lead to the mistreatment of others. In 2005, Professor Brad Bushman of Ohio State University found that people who ruminate on previous bouts of anger are prone to "displaced aggression"—expressing anger toward people not involved in whatever caused the grudge. In other words, people who hold grudges are likely to lash out at innocent bystanders. Holding a grudge, therefore, makes a person worse.[23]

Second: Grudges lead to self-destruction. In our Torah study group's discussion of grudges, Rhonda Kirschner, who lives part-time in Saltaire (Fire Island, NY), spoke of her experience as the volunteer magistrate for that four-hundred-person town. A young woman was pulled over for the crime of riding a bicycle at night, a sensible law given the state of the streets and the ease of a driver not seeing a rider there. The fine was $25.

Rather than pay or challenge the $25 fine, the defendant had another idea. When the officer asked the biker for her name, she said that she was someone else. The someone else was the new girlfriend of her ex-boyfriend. Thus, instead of facing a maximum fine of $25, the defendant's holding a grudge against the new girlfriend (not even her ex-boyfriend!) exposed her to a host of crimes including identity theft and lying to a police officer.

The Three Alternatives: Withdrawing, Forgiving, and Separating

As noted, the Torah suggests three alternatives to grudges, all of which derive from the commandment to articulate the hatred that is the source of grudges. The first alternative is the withdrawal of the grudge. This can happen after one articulates his hatred and experiences the clarity that comes with putting one's thoughts to words—helping him realize that his hatred is unjustified. This is always available, and should be the first point of call.

The second alternative is forgiveness, which is the process that follows the offender realizing that the hatred is justified. At the conclusion of this process, the parties reconcile with a stronger relationship based on the fact that the offender is now a changed person. As a changed person, the individual who committed the sin no longer exists. What does science say?

In 2021, Daniel Foster of the U.S. Combat Capabilities Development Command Army Research Laboratory and several colleagues from across the world published the results of a study they conducted of 971 workers through Amazon's Mechanical Turk. The study found that people would rather interact with those who insulted and then apologized than with those who did not insult them at all. In short, Professor Foster and his colleagues determined that an apology does not just repair a relationship, but actually creates a new and stronger one.[24]

A review of studies on forgiveness led by Professor Jichan J. Kim of Liberty University found that forgiveness decreases anger, depression, and anxiety—while increasing self-esteem and hopefulness for the future. Another review of the studies on forgiveness by Johns Hopkins Medicine shows that forgiveness "can . . . lower the risk of heart attack; improve cholesterol levels and sleep; and reduce pain, blood pressure and levels of anxiety, depression and stress [for the person who forgives]."[25]

The operative word in the Johns Hopkins analysis is "can"—and not "will." Forgiveness is not a magic potion. Professor Jim McNulty of Florida State University studied newlywed couples for two years. He found that forgiveness was beneficial when the negative behavior was infrequent, but backfired when the negative behavior persisted—when, in other words, the person had not genuinely changed. Professor McNulty wrote that successful forgiveness exists through a "process"—just as Maimonides counseled.[26]

There is now a term for forgiving quickly and immediately, and without anything like the process Maimonides recommended. The term, created by Professor Laura Luchies of Daemen College and several colleagues, is "the doormat effect." The "doormat"—one who unilaterally forgives—risks experiencing a diminished self-conception, being susceptible to manipulation and *increased* resentment.[27]

The third and final alternative to grudges happens when neither party considers himself to be wrong, and the hatred is mutually sustained. This alternative, modeled by Abraham, is separating from the source of one's hatred. When the parties are genuinely separate, they do not think about each other at all, thus removing the grounds for a grudge.

We now have a term to describe relationships between people who persist in their grudges and do not separate: toxic relationships. In 1985, a research team led by Dr. Roberto De Vogli of University College London began a longitudinal study to assess the impact of being in a toxic relationship on coronary heart disease. They isolated toxic relationships from other potential causes, from obesity to depression. The result: Those in toxic relationships had a 34 percent greater likelihood of a significant cardiac problem. Other studies have revealed that persisting in toxic relationships increases the frequency of common colds; diminishes self-esteem; exacerbates inflammation; causes breathing problems, tiredness, nausea, and headaches; and leads to engagement in "spite-based" competitive behavior.[28]

The consensus among therapists about how to deal with toxic relationships is expressed through an oft-quoted maxim: "The only way to win with a toxic person is not to play." Just as Abraham, as seen in his parting with Lot, models.[29]

Forgetting Can Make You Smarter

The Torah, as we discussed, is a text devoted to the cultivation of remembering. The celebration and appreciation of memory is shared by other philosophies. Memory has been compared to a palace by thinkers as diverse as the ancient Greek poet Simonides of Ceos, St. Augustine of Hippo, and the Scottish novelist Arthur Conan Doyle. And it is not just philosophers, but scientists as well.

But the Torah couples a veneration of remembering with a sacred notion of forgetting. The quintessential manifestation of this is grudges, where the Torah tradition says that one who has gone through the process of repentance and forgiveness should be considered as an entirely new person. And the quintessential expression of sacred forgetting is in Deuteronomy 32, where Moses praises "the gift of forgetting"—and considers its abandonment to be a "curse."

What does science say about balancing remembering and forgetting? In 2017, Science News published an analysis entitled "Forgetting Can Make You Smarter." Encapsulating the results of a study conducted by the Canadian Institute for Advanced Research, Science News reported: "the inability to remember was long believed to represent a failure of the brain's mechanisms for storing and retrieving information." However, this scientific consensus has been shaken in recent years.[30]

In 2019, the science writer Tom Siegfried analyzed the literature on forgetting for *Knowable Magazine*. He wrote: "Twenty-first century scientists who study memory have identified an important point to remember: Even the most luxurious palace of memory needs trash cans."

He cites the University of Glasgow neuroscientist Maria Wimber as saying, "There are memories that we don't want and we don't need. Forgetting is good and an adaptive thing."[31]

Why might that be? Paul Frankland of the Hospital for Sick Children in Toronto and Blake Richards of the University of Toronto have an idea. In a 2017 analysis in *Neuron*, they wrote, "Memory should not be viewed simply as a means for high-fidelity transmission of information through time. Rather . . . the goal of memory is to guide intelligent decision-making."[32]

Remembering too much, they and other scientists have concluded, can easily lead to *bad* decision-making. Professor Oliver Hardt of McGill University notes that we acquire huge amounts of information every day, from how our socks felt when we put them on to the color of the shirt of the guy next to us in the subway. The vast majority of this information is irrelevant to any decision we will have to make. Consequently, a healthy mind will forget a lot so that it can recall and process the inputs that lead to good decisions.[33]

The freeing of the mind from irrelevant and unhelpful facts is just one of the benefits of forgetting that scientists have recently discovered.

Professor Anne-Laure Le Cunff of Kings College in London lists ten ways in which memory can lead to bad decision-making. These include:

- Rosy retrospection bias—remembering the past better than it was
- Mood-congruent bias—recalling memories that are consistent with our current mood
- Egocentric bias—remembering our role in a positive event at the expense of the contributions of others
- Recency bias—remembering events that happened recently better than equally relevant events that happened further back in time
- Choice supportive bias—remembering chosen options better than rejected ones[34]

This enumeration of the benefits of forgetting is not exhaustive, especially as social scientists are discovering more all the time. Professor Ronald Davis of the Scripps Research Institute in Florida said in 2019, "We're at the very, very beginning of trying to understand the neurobiology of active forgetting . . . five years from now . . . hordes of neuroscientists will start invading this field." They could start with Deuteronomy 32.[35]

Reflection

Every instance of being ignored, offended, insulted, afflicted, or otherwise angered presents an opportunity to hold a grudge. Grudges can provide the guards we need against people who have wronged us once, and who may do so again—a useful function to be sure. Still, the Torah and social science unite in saying: Don't do it—and not because of some abstract moral problem. Grudges distract, damage, and ultimately diminish the person who holds them.

The Torah and social science unite again on the solution. We should either withdraw the grudge, forgive the offender (following a rigorous process), or separate from him. In each of these cases, we preserve the function of a grudge while liberating ourselves from its physically, socially, and psychologically destructive ramifications. And we also enhance our ability to enjoy "the quality of peace" that the *Orchot Tzaddikim* rightly said a thousand years ago, "you already know how good and pleasant [it] is."

20

Why God Tells Moses to Tell Aaron to Strike the Nile and How We Can Raise Our Baseline Happiness

The Torah and Science of Gratitude

Leah Names Her Son "Thanks"

Observant Jews begin the day by saying: *Modeh Ani*. This means, "Grateful am I." This is as strange a locution in Hebrew as it is in English. One would think that the way to express gratitude is by saying: *Ani Modeh*, "I am grateful."

But the placement of "grateful" before "I" is entirely intentional and deeply purposeful. In saying "grateful" before "I," we acknowledge the existence of gratitude before ourselves. In the words of Rabbi Shai Held, "Modeh Ani" is used "as if to suggest that there is no self without gratitude, that I do not become fully human unless and until I convey my gratitude to the One who created the gift that I am, and the even greater gift that I inhabit."[1]

It is appropriate that the first thing that observant Jews do in the morning is to acknowledge gratitude, and not only because it defines how we should experience the day ahead. The Torah makes it clear that gratitude literally describes and defines what it means to be a Jew.

In Genesis 29, Jacob meets Rachel and loves her immediately. He works for her father, Laban, for seven years in order to marry her. When the seven-year period concludes, Laban tricks Jacob into marrying Rachel's older sister, Leah.

Quite naturally, Leah feels unloved. She tries to win her husband's affection by deploying a doomed, tragic, and apparently ancient technique. She gets pregnant. She has three sons. She names her first son Reuben, stating, "Surely the Lord has looked upon my affliction; now therefore my husband will love me." She names her second son Simeon, "Because the Lord has heard that I was hated, He has therefore given me this son." Her third son, Levi, is named in the hope that "now this time will my husband be joined to me."

All these names reflect Leah's personal needs and the things she hopes to achieve from the birth of the new child. Yet none of these children give her the happy marriage she desires. She then has a fourth son and names him Judah, saying, "This time I will praise [or thank] the Lord," modeling for us, in the words of Rabbi Held, that we should be grateful even in the midst of our disappointment. It is from Judah that we receive the name "Jew."[2]

And that's not all. The absence of punctuation in the Torah creates a pathway for an additional understanding. The early-twentieth-century Belarusian sage Rav Yerucham Levovitz punctuated this verse as a rhetorical question: "[*Only*] this time, I will thank the Lord? Therefore, she named him Judah." Leah, in this reading, is saying that her fourth son's birth is so great that she cannot thank God just this time. By naming him Judah—or "Gratitude"—she will be reminded to thank God every time she sees him.[3]

How important is this idea in the Jewish mind? In Genesis 49:10, Jacob reveals his deathbed prophecy. He tells us that the Messiah will come from Leah's fourth son, the one that she named, essentially, "Thanks."

How the Jewish Freedom Story Is Inaugurated: Moses and the Nile

In Exodus 2, the Pharaoh decreed that all baby Jewish boys be drowned in the Nile. A Jewish mother puts her son in a basket and sends him down the river. The waters of the Nile delivered the baby safely to the waiting arms of a righteous gentile, the Pharaoh's daughter. The Pharaoh's daughter names the baby Moses.

By Exodus 7, that baby has grown up to be quite a man—indeed, the person God selects to guide the Jews from slavery to freedom. In Exodus 7:17, God decrees the first plague: the turning of the Nile River to blood. This is a fitting plague. The Pharaoh had previously ordered the drowning of all baby Jewish boys in the Nile. In so doing, the Pharaoh had turned the Nile, his country's life source, into a killing field. By turning it to blood, God will have shown the Egyptians just what the Pharaoh had made the Nile into.

What is surprising is *who* God tells to carry out the act. God tells Moses to tell Aaron to strike the river. Why doesn't God just have Moses do the striking himself? The answer is provided in Exodus Rabbah, an eleventh- to twelfth-century exegetical commentary on the Torah. Exodus Rabbah explains that Moses owed the Nile a debt of gratitude for delivering him safely to the Pharaoh's daughter, and therefore could not strike it.[4]

This explanation raises an obvious question. How can one owe gratitude to a river? Rivers cannot decide anything, let alone whether or not to comply with a leader's genocidal order. In this strange instruction to Moses, God is teaching us something profound. If Moses owes gratitude to a *river*, how much more must we owe gratitude to all of those people in our lives who *can* accept it? It is with this recognition of gratitude to a river that the freedom story of the Jews begins.

How the Jewish Freedom Story Is Celebrated: The Career of Gratitude

The most widely celebrated Jewish holiday is Passover. Passover is the authentic and biblically ordained Jewish New Year, whose central ritual is the Seder and whose guiding text is the Haggadah. We gather at the Seder to tell the story of the Exodus to our children and, with the guidance of the Haggadah, make commitments and assume responsibilities that will help us to become better Jews in the year to come.

If one were asked what would be the ideal passage to discuss the Exodus from Egypt, they would likely answer: the Book of Exodus! After all, the entire story of the Exodus is in the second book of the Bible. The book is literally named for this event! But the geniuses who wrote the Haggadah chose an altogether different source. And their choice reflects a desire to teach us how a Jew should experience the Exodus, and life itself.

They chose Deuteronomy 26, which appears near the conclusion of the Torah. The protagonist in Deuteronomy is not Moses, Miriam, Aaron, Joshua, or any other famous hero of the Jewish freedom story. In fact, the protagonist had not even been alive at the time of the Exodus. He is a farmer who lives far in the future and comes to the Temple, upon the completion of a successful harvest, to make an offering. The offering is of "the first of every fruit of the ground." The farmer makes the following declaration:

> My father . . . went down to Egypt with meager numbers and sojourned there; but there he became a great and very populous nation. The Egyptians dealt harshly with us and oppressed us; they imposed heavy labor upon us. We cried to Hashem, the God of our ancestors, and Hashem heard our plea and saw our plight, our misery, and our oppression. Hashem freed us from Egypt by a mighty hand, by an outstretched arm and awesome power, and by signs and portents, bringing us to this place and giving us this land, a land flowing with milk and honey. Wherefore I now bring the first fruits of the soil which You, Hashem, have given me (Deuteronomy 26: 5–10).

The farmer is awash in gratitude. And gratitude, we see, is not just an emotion or a response. It is an outwardly focused disposition that molds a character and even creates a personality.

After the farmer brings his first fruits, Moses instructs him, "You shall rejoice with all the goodness that Hashem, your God, has given you and your household, you and the Levite and the proselyte [convert] who is in your midst" (Deuteronomy 26:11).

Gratitude, we learn, leads to joy. But the effects of gratitude do not end there. Gratitude evolves into generosity. "When you have finished setting aside a tenth of all your produce in the third year, the year of the tithe, you shall give it to the Levite, the foreigner, the fatherless and the widow, so that they may eat in your towns and be satisfied" (Deuteronomy 26:12).

After giving to the poor and the Levite, the farmer asks something big of God: "Look down from heaven, your holy dwelling place, and bless your people Israel and the land you have given us as you promised to our ancestors, a land flowing with milk and honey" (Deuteronomy 26:15).

God, seemingly inspired by the gratitude, joy, and generosity it has inspired, complies. "He [God] has declared that he will set you in praise, fame, and honor high above all the nations he has made and that you will be a people holy to the Lord your God, as he promised" (Deuteronomy 26:19).

This is the divine pathway, articulated through the farmer in Deuteronomy and reinforced for Jews at our New Year's celebration. Gratitude leads to joy, which leads to generosity toward the poor and the needy, which leads to a special closeness to God, which leads to us becoming "a people holy to the Lord."

This course of gratitude has been reflected throughout Jewish thought. Rabbi Nachman of Breslov said, "Gratitude rejoices with her sister joy and is always ready to light a candle and have a party."[5]

There is nothing theoretical or abstract about this "party." It is expressed through the Jewish custom of *seudat hod'ah* (thanksgiving feast). From ancient times until the present, we have had this celebration of gratitude when one survives a danger, after a birth, and at other moments when we burst with gratitude and joy.[6]

Happiness and Satisfaction: A Crucial Distinction

From Genesis to Deuteronomy, the Torah guides us to gratitude and is very clear that it will culminate in joy and happiness. And joy, as the Baal Shem Tov said, is a "biblical command."[7]

Does being grateful and happy mean that one is satisfied? The Torah gives its answer through the biblical Jacob. The Torah tells us, several times in Genesis, that Jacob "settled" in one place or another. This is always a prelude to disaster and is no coincidence, but a core teaching. The twentieth-century sage Rabbi Adin Steinsaltz, surveying the widespread rabbinic criticism of Jacob for wanting to "settle," concluded, "God bestows many favors and gifts upon the righteous . . . but tranquility is not one of them."[8]

The enduring relevance of this philosophy was best articulated by Shimon Peres, who lived the greatest Jewish story of the past two thousand years (the rebirth and flourishing of the state of Israel) from his birth in 1923 until his death in 2016. He was a founding father of Israel who became the prime minister of Israel and eventually the president of the country. As an old man, he was asked, "What is the greatest Jewish contribution to humanity?" Shimon Peres had a lot to choose from. Yet he had a confident and singular answer: "Dissatisfaction."[9]

The space between gratitude, happiness, and satisfaction is explained in the seminal book of Jewish ethics, *Pirkei Avot*. Ben Zoma asks, "Who is rich?" The answer: "He who is satisfied with his lot." Yet, satisfaction should never breed complacency. The nineteenth-century sage Rabbi Yisrael Salanter explained: "A pious Jew is not one who worries about his fellow man's soul and his own stomach; a pious Jew worries about his own soul and his fellow man's stomach."[10]

This conception of satisfaction, which encourages contentment with one's material state and discontentment with that of others, flows directly from the Torah's logic of gratitude. Gratitude produces the joy that diminishes one's personal material ambition and amplifies social responsibility.

The Jewish Freedom Celebration Continues: The When and How of Gratitude

The Haggadah continues with a seemingly obscure and even weird debate between three rabbis—Rabbi Yosi the Galilean, Rabbi Eliezer, and Rabbi Akiva. It is about the number of plagues (or miracles) that enabled the Jews to escape from Egypt. The debate goes from 60 to 200 to 250, with Rabbi Akiva arguing for the highest number.

This strange passage, a miracle counting contest, leads us to ask: Why are they engaging in this debate in the first place? Why is a seemingly idiosyncratic activity (a miracle counting contest) in the Haggadah, which exists to help us live better, fuller, and more meaningful lives today?

The answer lies in who gets the final word—Rabbi Akiva. Thus, we learn that we should count as many miracles as we can. Everyone who tries to do so will realize the feeling that results from counting many miracles. It is gratitude. It is this sense that the authors of the Haggadah want to cultivate in us—at the Jewish New Year celebration, when we contemplate how to approach the year ahead.

Immediately following the miracle-counting contest in the Haggadah is Dayenu, a Seder favorite. The song is titled after the refrain, which translates to "It would have been enough for us." Just as the miracle-counting contest teaches us to express gratitude often, the song Dayenu instructs us how to do so.

First: a review of the lyrics. We sing that if God had split the sea but not led us through to dry land, it would have been enough for us. We sing that if he had led us through to dry land but had not drowned our oppressors, it would have been enough for us. We sing that if God had provided for our needs in the desert for forty years but did not feed us manna, it would have been enough for us.

This leads to a series of questions. If God had not led us to dry land, we would have drowned. If God had not drowned our Egyptian oppressors, they would have recaptured and enslaved us. If God did not feed us manna in the desert, we would have starved. So why would we express gratitude at each stage?

The Exodus, we are led to realize, is a system composed of many parts that eventually constitute the whole. A quick contemplation reveals that there is nothing distinctive about the Exodus here. Most important things occur as part of a process, which is a necessary component of a system. For instance, our bodily functions—which may seem very different from the Exodus. How appreciative should we be to have a beating heart, a functioning brain, or flowing blood? We need them *all* for the body to function. A dead brain and a healthy heart have the same result as a dead heart and a healthy brain. Given that our life depends on the functioning of each component of the system and we are grateful for life, the logic of gratitude in a system is clear: We owe maximal gratitude to each of its components.

And that's not all. If, instead of its fifteen verses, Dayenu just said, "God, thanks for everything," would the message of gratitude have been conveyed? Technically, yes, as "everything" would have incorporated all of the component parts that the song addressed. But would such a song have been satisfying and earned the enduring love that Dayenu has? No chance. This is because of what Dayenu teaches us about *how* gratitude should be expressed—specifically and frequently.[11]

Gratitude may be the theme of the Haggadah, which guides us through our New Year's celebration, but it is not only an annual exercise. It is a way of being. Observant Jews *formally* express gratitude one hundred times every day—from the kitchen to the bathroom—for everything from having water to drink to being able to relieve ourselves. Gratitude is the central theme of the dawn blessings, when we thank God for the human body and the physical world. And it forms the core of the *Amidah* (the central part of every prayer service) in which everyone must stand and declare, *Modim anachnu lach* ("We give gratitude to you [God]"). This theme continues through the Jewish prayer experience. It is acceptable to say "Amen" in response to the prayer of a leader in a synagogue service, with one exception. This is the prayer of Thanksgiving, which everyone must say himself.[12]

The Wages of Ingratitude

In Deuteronomy 26, Moses, as discussed, codifies a gratitude ritual that will lead to joy, generosity, and ultimately, a deeper relationship with God, the quintessential blessing. But that is not all that Deuteronomy tells us about gratitude. Indeed, it is only half of it. Elsewhere in Deuteronomy, Moses tells us what will happen if we are *ungrateful.*

In Deuteronomy 8, Moses tells us to always remember what God did for us. This includes rescuing us from Egypt, guiding us through the wilderness, providing us with manna, giving us the Torah and clothes that did not wear out. Despite decreeing that we are to live in a culture and with a spirit of gratitude, Moses is concerned that we will not do so. He is worried that we will forget God and attribute our fortune to our own power and the strength of our hands. If this happens—if we become ungrateful and narcissistic—Moses lays bare the consequences: "You will surely be destroyed."

The Torah is clear: If we are grateful, we will be blessed. If we are ungrateful, we will be cursed. Is there a third state, one in which a person is neither grateful nor ungrateful? There is nothing in the Torah that suggests that such a neutral space exists. There is no Hebrew word that suggests a neutrality between gratitude and ingratitude. In the Torah worldview, there is just gratitude and ingratitude.

The Science

Resetting Happiness

Everyone wants to be happier, but the way to increase happiness is often illusive. An instinctive assumption is that happiness is determined by external events. For instance, we assume that we will become happier if we achieve or become something—if we win a promotion, if we get married, or if we become wealthy. Similarly, we assume that we will become less happy if we get fired, get divorced, or lose money.

Numerous studies from around the world have shown that these events and accomplishments can profoundly affect our happiness . . . for a short time. People generally revert to their normal state of happiness within three months of the event. University of California, Riverside professor Sonja Lyubomirsky calls this "the happiness set point," which is significantly (though not entirely) genetically determined.[13]

If even winning the lottery does not produce sustained happiness, is there anything that can raise our happiness set point and transcend our genetics? Professor Lyubomirsky identifies fourteen "evidence-based happiness-increasing strategies whose practice is supported by scientific research." These include cultivating optimism, practicing acts of kindness, learning to forgive, and taking care of your body. Yet, none of these are the number one way, which is "expressing gratitude."[14]

A 2003 study by Professor Robert Emmons of the University of California, Davis showed just how sensitive our happiness is to expressions of gratitude. He determined that keeping a simple gratitude journal—just writing down five reasons for gratitude each week for ten weeks—is enough to raise one's baseline happiness by 25 percent. This study also found that people who kept the gratitude journal exercised more, slept better, and had fewer physical symptoms of bad health—all of which contribute to the sustained raising of the happiness set point.[15]

Dozens of subsequent studies have augmented Professor Emmons's findings. These studies have demonstrated that consistent expressions of gratitude help people to reduce pain, focus more, become more resilient after experiencing a potentially traumatic event and educational setbacks, perform healthy activities, and seek help for health concerns. Expressions of gratitude also enable athletes to develop self-esteem, help victims of bullying to be emotionally resilient, make people more energetic and productive and less envious and materialistic.[16]

Why would gratitude be uniquely capable of raising our happiness set point? The answer might lie with dopamine, which an analysis in Harvard Health describes as "the feel good transmitter." The UCLA neuroscientist Alex Korb explains that "feeling grateful activates the brain stem region that produces dopamine." Moreover, Professor Korb explains, the experience of gratitude increases the production of serotonin, which stimulates the reward center of the brain, leading to feelings of well-being and happiness.[17]

It is no wonder that the meditation expert Emily Fletcher calls gratitude our "natural anti-depressant" and the certified Gottman therapist Zach Brittle says that gratitude is "the secret that could put therapists out of a job."[18]

Why Gratitude Begets Giving

We read in Deuteronomy 26 that the farmer, having offered his first fruits, will be inspired to give to the widow, the orphan, and the proselyte. Gratitude, in other words, will not only make us *happier*, it will also make us *kinder*. Why might this be so?

In 2006, Monica Bartlett and Professor David DeSteno of Northeastern University had students perform a tedious task on a computer. Right when the task was about to be completed, the computer "crashed." The participants were predictably frustrated. In some of those cases, a disguised confederate of the researchers popped up nearby to help "fix" the computer, earning the gratitude of the unwitting participant.

The participants in both cohorts (those who were helped and those who were not) finished the experiment and left the room. The confederate who had offered help to one cohort asked each student for help collecting data. The result was a "dramatic difference" in the amount of time the students who received help were willing to offer, compared with the students who did not receive help.

But Professors DeSteno and Bartlett still had a question. Did the dramatic difference reflect only the gratitude that the student felt to the person who helped him? If that were the case, the prosocial behavior could simply be understood as repayment of a debt.

The professors ran the experiment again. This time, the person who "fixed" the computer was *different* from the person who was outside asking for help in collecting data. How, if at all, would the gratitude that the students felt toward one person transfer to another?

The result: "People who were feeling grateful as they left the building were not only more likely to agree to help the stranger but spent significantly more time doing so than did people who weren't feeling any emotion in particular." The effect in both cases was so powerful that the professors deemed it "dose dependent"—i.e., inject a dose of gratitude, and count on a prosocial result immediately following.[19]

Subsequent research has shown how the logic of gratitude-giving is embedded in our brains. In 2017, University of Oregon neuroscientist Christina Karns conducted a study in which participants had to fill out a questionnaire that determined how generally grateful they were. Professor Karns put the study participants in a brain scanner and had them watch as money was either deposited into their account or into that of a food bank. She found that those who had rated themselves as more grateful showed a stronger response in their brain when the money was given to the food bank than when it was deposited into their account. The more grateful the respondents were, the more they delighted in giving to others. Given that people will inevitably gravitate toward what brings them joy, the science is clear: Gratitude leads to giving, and continues with more giving, just as Deuteronomy predicted.[20]

Professor Karns then asked another question. Is this kind of gratitude innate, or can such gratitude be cultivated? She had a sample group begin a three-week exercise of keeping a gratitude journal, and had the control group write about other events in their lives.

She found that practicing gratitude shifted the value of giving in the ventromedial prefrontal cortex. It changed the exchange rate in the brain. Giving to charity became more valuable than receiving money yourself. After the brain calculates the exchange rate, you get paid in the neural currency of reward, the delivery of neurotransmitters that signal pleasure and goal attainment." These effects were significant but not sustained, demonstrating that at least the prosocial benefit of gratitude depends upon its continual expression.[21]

In other words, a short practice of gratitude makes a person more grateful. And this gratitude changes her, to where she becomes more concerned about and generous toward others—just as the Torah teaching on dissatisfaction suggests.

Where Is the United States Headed?

As in Hebrew, there is no word in English to describe a third state that is neither gratitude nor ingratitude. English is a rich language that has lots of synonyms to precisely describe many things, and the absence of such a term indicates that there is no concept of a state between gratitude and ingratitude.[22] Therefore, we can ask: Are Americans tending toward gratitude or ingratitude?

As the United States is a large and diverse country, it would be overbroad and thus inaccurate to say that Americans are either grateful or ungrateful. A 2012 study from the John Templeton Foundation found that 90 percent of Americans express, when asked, gratitude for our families. However, this is far from the Torah ideal of expressing gratitude ubiquitously and continuously. The study reports that 52 percent of women and 44 percent of men express gratitude on a regular basis.[23]

As the Templeton data shows, there are many Americans who express gratitude. But there are two tendencies that suggest that the culture is moving in the other direction. One is narcissism and the other is the victim mentality.

Where Ingratitude Leads: Narcissism

As discussed, Moses was deeply concerned that we, amidst our prosperity, would forget God. This ingratitude would present as narcissism, as we attributed our fortune to the power and strength of our hands. This attitude would ultimately lead to our destruction.

Moses was joined in this concern several thousand years later by another great liberator. On March 30, 1863, President Abraham Lincoln issued Proclamation 97, to take effect a month later. It was: "Appointing a Day of National Humiliation, Fasting and Prayer." He wrote:

> We have been the recipients of the choicest bounties of Heaven; we have been preserved these many years in peace and prosperity; we have grown in numbers, wealth, and power as no other nation has ever grown. But we have forgotten God. We have forgotten the gracious hand which preserved us in peace and multiplied and enriched and strengthened us, and we have vainly imagined, in the deceitfulness of our hearts, that all these blessings were produced by some superior wisdom and virtue of our own. Intoxicated with unbroken success, we have become too self-sufficient to feel the necessity of redeeming and preserving grace, too proud to pray to the God that made us.[24]

President Lincoln, echoing Deuteronomy, made a profound claim about ingratitude. One who thinks that his success or bounty comes from his own efforts alone, without regard to the "gracious hand" of God, will develop and exemplify a particular personality trait: narcissism.

But why? Professor Emmons explains that "people who are ungrateful tend to be characterized by an excessive sense of self-importance, arrogance, vanity, and an unquenchable need for admiration and approval. Narcissists reject the ties that bind people into relationships of reciprocity. They expect special favors and feel no need to pay back or pay forward."[25]

How does our culture regard this opponent of gratitude? Enter a 2011 analysis by Professor Nathan DeWall of the University of Kentucky: "Hit Songs Offer [a] Window into Society's Psyche." The title is right; music preferences reveal what people sing to themselves in private, dance to in public, dream about and think about generally—and are therefore culturally revealing.[26]

What insight into "society's psyche" did Professor DeWall identify in popular song? In 2008, he found himself listening to the Weezer song "The Greatest Man That Ever Lived (Variations on a Shaker Hymn)." The lyrics include, "I'm the baddest of the bad / I'm the best that you've ever had / I'm the tops, I'm the king / All the girls get up when I sing, yeah / I'm the meanest in the place."

Professor DeWall reflected, "Who would actually say that out loud?" The answer was—a singer who knows what his audience will appreciate. He thought, "They're marketing this toward an audience who has never loved themselves more."

As a social scientist, he designed a test for his hypothesis. He analyzed the *Billboard* 100 from 1980 to 2007. He found that the more recent songs were far more likely to reference "I" and "me" than "you" and "us" when compared to previous eras. On average, there was a 20 percent increase in the use of first-person singular pronouns and an 18 percent decrease in the use of first-person plural pronouns for each year of the twenty-seven-year period examined. Professor Jean Twenge and several colleagues, using a Google database, did a similar study on books from 1980–2008—and found similar results.[27]

That was far from Professor Twenge's first or last foray into the study of narcissism; she has devoted much of her career toward understanding it. The benchmark that she uses to measure narcissism is the Narcissism Personality Inventory (NPI), which was invented by Professors Robert Raskin and Calvin Hall of the University of California, Berkeley.

The NPI uses responses to several questions to determine narcissism. These include: "I can usually talk my way out of anything *or* I try to accept the consequences of my behavior"; "I like to be the center of attention *or* I prefer to blend in with the crowd"; "I can read people like a book *or* People are sometimes hard to understand"; and "I like to show off my body *or* I don't particularly like to show off my body."[28]

Professor Twenge's review of the literature surrounding the NPI has shown that there has been a "significant increase in college students' NPI scores" between 1982 and 2009.[29] In 2010, the same year when Professor DeWall published his study of popular music, Professor Twenge proclaimed that we are living amidst a "narcissism epidemic."

She explained a decade later: "Narcissism, an inflated view of the self, is everywhere. Public figures say it's what makes them stray from their wives. Parents teach it by dressing children in T-shirts that say 'Princess.' Teenagers and young adults hone it on Facebook, and celebrity newsmakers have elevated it to an art form. And it's what's making people depressed, lonely, and buried under piles of debt."[30]

Professors DeWall and Twenge began writing about their findings at the dawn of the social media era. Social media offers an unprecedented mechanism for people to portray an image of themselves to a large audience and receive immediate feedback. It is, as it sounds, ideally suited for narcissists. Studies from 2018 and 2020 have demonstrated that those with high NPI scores tend to have significant social media usage, and that those who use social media frequently develop increased narcissistic tendencies. Consequently, a variety of analyses of social media usage among millennials have declared that they constitute a "me, me, me generation" and ask questions like "Is Social Media Turning Everyone into a Narcissist?"[31]

And "everyone" means everyone—not just the younger generation who constitute much of the social media landscape. In 2019, the UK's Co-op Funeralcare compiled a survey of its thirty thousand funeral homes to ascertain the most frequently requested song to accompany people to their final resting place. The winner was not "Time to Say Goodbye," "Over the Rainbow," or "Four Seasons," although those were on the list. It was, in the words of Scott Maslow of *GQ*, "The obnoxious, ubiquitous ode to self-satisfaction, 'My Way.'"[32]

Mr. Maslow is in good company with his characterization of "My Way." The song was made famous by Frank Sinatra, the eternal Chairman of the Board. This epitome of mid-century grace and cool realized what the song was saying about and doing to the culture. And he hated it. Mr. Sinatra told a Carnegie Hall audience that it was written by an eighteen-year-old Frenchman named "Jacques Strappe" and introduced it in a 1979 concert in Atlantic City by saying, "I hate this song. I HATE THIS SONG! I got it up to here [with] this God damned song!"[33]

Why did Frank Sinatra hate it? The answer is revealed in how its lyrics compare to those in so many of his other songs, such as "Thanks for the Memories," "It Was a Very Good Year," "That Is What God Looks Like to Me," "For Once in My Life," and "My Kind of Town." In these and so many other songs, Mr. Sinatra expresses his gratitude to a love, to a city, to parents-in-law, to God, even to an ex-girlfriend. But there is not a word of gratitude in "My Way." Instead, there is "For what is a man, what has he got? If not himself then he has naught."

Where Ingratitude Leads: The Victim Mentality

One variant of ingratitude uttered by the narcissist is: *I owe nothing, because my good fortune is the result of having done things my way.* There is another variant that goes even further. It says: *I owe nothing; instead, the world owes me.* This is the view of a victim, whose mentality and worldview, as discussed in the Torah and social science, are considered at length in the chapter of this book on culture.[34]

The depth of the connection between ingratitude and victimhood can be seen in a classic elite university institution—Princeton University's Carl A. Fields Center for Equality and Cultural Understanding—as discussed in the chapter on culture. The Fields Center purports to "promote a sense of belonging that permeates throughout all aspects of the Princeton community by encouraging people, specifically those whose identities are marginalized and underrepresented, to embrace their autonomy and agency in spite of oppression." The Fields Center conducts this education through "professional facilitators" to train fellows to help Princeton students understand who is victimizing them and how.[35]

How are they doing toward this goal? In November of 2022, the Fields Center proudly displayed on its doors a poster with a large photograph and a quotation. It is of Estela Diaz, who graduated from Princeton in 2014 and now teaches at Columbia University. The quotation reads: "If you're only giving, there is time to be selfish. I want to teach other folks of color how to center themselves and their needs . . . If anyone ever tells you to be grateful, you can just smile and walk away."[36]

How Proud Are You to Be an American?

The dramatic rise in narcissism and victimhood arouses a question: How has it affected gratitude? One way to look at this is with regard to a poll that Gallup conducts every year. The subject is very simple: How proud are you to be an American?

This question is a fine proxy for gratitude for a simple reason: The United States is an incredible country, the envy of the world, and for an abundance of good reasons. Every American can (and should) find something, or lots of things, they want to improve in the country. That is part of being a good American, as the United States always welcomes new and constructive voices for change in the spirit of continual improvement and growth that characterizes this blessed nation. But that same quality is also a reason for expressing gratitude and pride, as America grants its citizens this voice that so many around the world lack. Therefore, a fine test of one's gratitude is: Are you proud to be an American?

In 2003, Gallup reported that 70 percent of Americans reported being "extremely proud" to be an American. There was a discrepancy along party lines, with 85 percent of Republicans and 62 percent of Democrats reporting being "extremely proud." In fewer than twenty years, the responses shifted drastically. In 2022, only 38 percent of respondents reported being "extremely proud" to be an American. The same party discrepancy existed—with 58 percent of Republicans and 26 percent of Democrats attesting to this level of pride.[37]

There is at least one consequence to this decline in gratitude that is suggested by the data. In June of 2020, a report from the General Social Survey determined that only 14 percent of Americans reported being "very happy"—the lowest percentage, by far, for that response in the fifty years of the study. And this decrease in happiness is not evenly distributed. In 2021, the journalist E. J. Dionne published an analysis of several studies, entitled "Conservatives Are Happier Than Liberals. Discuss."[38]

Some might say that June 2020—given Covid and the response to it—was not a representative time for assessing baseline happiness. But in March 2019, a University of California at Berkeley analysis of happiness suggested that American adults have been getting less happy since 2000—with adolescents experiencing more depression, suicidal ideation, and self-harm since 2010.[39]

In June 2022, Christopher Ingraham of the *Washington Post* considered the most recent data on happiness on the other side of Covid. He concluded, "New Data Shows Americans More Miserable Than We've Been in Half a Century."[40]

The UN World Happiness Reports of the twenty-first century show that this is *not* a global phenomenon. In 2019, the UN report cataloged the change in happiness from the period of 2005 to 2008 and from 2016 to 2018. Happiness *increased* in Israel, Burundi, Benin, Nicaragua, and 108 other countries. The United States was not one of them—not even close. Americans became so much less happy during that period that only 20 of the 132 countries surveyed registered a greater happiness decrease. These were South Africa, Italy, Afghanistan, Saudi Arabia, Malaysia, Jordan, Iran, Ukraine, Spain, Egypt, Rwanda, Malawi, Tanzania, Greece, Central African Republic, Yemen, India, Botswana, Syria, and Venezuela.[41]

Why would Americans be among the leaders in declining happiness? The answer just might lie in the Torah's connection of gratitude to happiness.

Reflection

In 2012, Oprah Winfrey wondered why, after having achieved such fame, fortune, and importance, she was no longer as happy as she once was. Specifically, she "no longer felt the joy of simple moments."

She opened her journal from October 12, 1996. She saw that she had recorded being grateful for running with a breeze that kept her cool, eating a cold melon on a bench in the sun, enjoying a "long and hilarious chat" with Gayle King about her blind date with Mr. Potato Head, eating "sorbet in a cone, so sweet that I literally licked my finger," and Maya Angelou calling to read her a poem.

As her life got busier, she had stopped her practice of acknowledging these causes of gratitude. She concluded that she could get that old happiness back if she resumed her practice—and wrote, "I'm back to journaling—electronically—and whenever there's a grateful moment, I note it. I know for sure that appreciating whatever shows up for you in life changes your personal vibration . . . In the next few weeks, we'll all be getting ready to cast a vote for the candidate of our choice. But I've learned from experience that if you pull the lever of gratitude every day, you'll be amazed at the results."[42]

The Torah and the social science of gratitude show that Ms. Winfrey's experience is predictable and replicable. The seemingly difficult and often elusive task of increasing one's happiness is actually very simple. We just have to follow the logic of Leah, who named her son "Thanks"; the miracle-counting contest in the Haggadah; the Jewish practice of blessings (which requires an expression of gratitude around every ten minutes); and the research of Professor Robert Emmons—acknowledging the numerous sources of gratitude that constitute our lives every day. It is so easy to do. Within two minutes of waking up, we should thank God—or otherwise express gratitude—for being alive, for being able to see, for having had a comfortable place to sleep, for being able to relieve ourselves, for being able to walk.

If we continue the day like that, we will certainly be happier. And, as the Torah and social science suggest, we will also become more outwardly focused, generous, and giving.

21

The Blessing of *Yisrael Saba* and the Marshmallow Test

The Torah and Science of Grandparents, Future Orientation, and Why They Are Related!

Our Relationship with Time

When we consider the relationships and associations we have in our lives, we often think of family, friends, colleagues, institutions, places, and even ideas. The Author of the Torah adds one kind of relationship that is key to living a thoughtful, meaningful, and good life. This is our relationship with time and, specifically, to the three units that constitute it: the past, the present, and the future.

Everyone, intentionally or unwittingly, will have a relationship with each of the three *and* a primary orientation toward one of them. The Torah, from Genesis to Deuteronomy, insists that the state of time we select for a primary relationship, the one we orient ourselves toward, is one of the most important decisions we will make. And the Torah offers decisive guidance as to the state of time that it is best for everyone to orient themselves to.

Past Orientation

In Genesis 19, God has determined that he must destroy the city of Sodom, but will save Lot and his family. He has one instruction for Lot and his family on their way out: "Don't look back."

Lot and his family begin their journey when Lot's wife violates the divine order and looks back. God immediately turns her into a pillar of salt. This might seem like a strange punishment, but it explains the prohibition on looking back. Salt was the ancient preservative; it's what we use when we want things to stay the same. This is valuable for food, but not for people. The Author of the Torah wants us to always be thinking and moving *forward*, as the only alternative is being stuck in the past. And Lot's wife, because she is oriented to the past—because she, when set on a journey forward, looks back—is transformed into a pillar of salt. Her wish is granted; she will stay the same forever.

This concern about living in the past, or even visiting the past too frequently, would become a fundamental tenet of Torah teaching. As previous chapters in this book demonstrate, the Torah forbids grudges and strongly leads us away from victimization—both of which are manifestations of being oriented toward the past.

The concern about being oriented to the past is also a major part of Jewish prayer. Every night, observant Jews recite the *hashkiveinu* ("cause us to lie down") blessing as part of the evening service. One line in the prayer is beseeching God to "remove the Satan from before and behind us." The "Satan from before us" is easy enough to understand—it is the negative influences and temptations that may lead us astray. Who, though, could the "Satan from behind" be? Whoever it is, it seems we are past it!

Rabbi Efrem Goldberg of the Boca Raton Synagogue explains that the "Satan from behind" are the regrets and the could-haves/should-haves that are technically in our past but plague us through the mental space that we grant them. This Satan, which is so ubiquitous and powerful that we pray to be free from it every night, is the "looking back" that God forbade for Lot and his family.[1]

Present Orientation

If Moses is the most well-regarded Jew in the Torah, Korach is the least. In Numbers 16, Korach leads a rebellion against Moses—but it is hardly the only resistance to Moses in the desert. So, why is Korach uniquely despised in the Jewish religious tradition?

Perhaps the answer lies in what Korach says in Numbers 16:3: "All the community are holy . . . Why then do you raise yourself above the Lord's congregation?"

Why does saying that "everyone is holy" qualify Korach for eternal disgrace? After all, God often issues a variant of the same instruction: "You shall be holy, for I, the Lord, am holy." Isn't Korach identifying with this great statement of Jewish aspiration?

While similar at face value, Korach's statement is actually an inversion of the Torah's instruction. God's statement that "You *shall be* holy" is an expression of future orientation. It reflects a constant striving to increase in holiness. Korach's articulation that "All the community *is* holy" is an expression of present orientation and suggests that everyone has already arrived at their destination.

In Isaiah 22:14, the prophet presents what has become the quintessential expression of present orientation. Isaiah introduces someone who says, "Eat and drink, for tomorrow we die." God's response is immediate and decisive. "This iniquity shall never be forgiven you."

This perspective on present orientation continues through the Talmud. The Talmudic term for a heretic is *Apikores*—an Epicurean. This term is a reference to the Greek philosopher Epicurus, whose philosophy is encapsulated in his statement "Pleasure is our first and kindred good . . . we [should] make the feeling the rule by which to judge every good thing." Such heretics, the Talmud states, will have "no share in the world to come."[2]

Future Orientation

Every Friday night, Jewish parents welcome the Sabbath by blessing our children with the same blessing that generations of Jews have done before us. The Jewish educator Lori Palatnik calls it a "magical, eternal moment for parents and children." Anyone who ushers in Shabbat with this ancient practice would likely agree that she is absolutely right.[3]

At the beginning of the blessing, we ask God to make our daughters like Sarah, Rebecca, Rachel, and Leah. We do not ask God to make our sons like Abraham, Isaac, and Jacob—their husbands and our patriarchs. Nor do we ask God to make our sons like Moses, Judah, Joseph, Aaron,

David, or any other well-known biblical hero. Instead, we bless our children to be like Ephraim and Manasseh. A reasonable response to this would be: *Who?* These are the sons of Joseph, but neither says a word in the Torah. Why, then, did the sages who designed this prayer, choose these obscure biblical characters as those we want our sons to be modeled after?

There are several reasons, each of which is true and instructive. One is that they maintained their Jewish identity in the diaspora. Another is that these are the first complete set of siblings in the Bible who appear to have had a harmonious relationship, despite a good reason not to, as their grandfather seemed to favor one over the other.

And there is, perhaps, the most important reason. The Torah's explanation for it begins long before we meet Ephraim and Manasseh. In Genesis 32, God changes Jacob's name to Israel. This has precedent: In Genesis 17, God had changed the names of Jacob's grandparents Abram and Sarai to Abraham and Sarah. But Jacob is the only one whom God calls by his original name after the change. Indeed, God himself uses both Jacob and Israel in a single verse in Genesis 46:2. Why would God change Jacob's name—and keep calling him by his old name?

In Genesis 47, Jacob's son Joseph has become, through an extraordinary series of events, the viceroy of Egypt. He has rescued his family from famine and brought them to Egypt. Joseph introduces his boss (the Pharaoh) to his father. Joseph does not offer his father's name, but the text does. The Pharaoh asks *Jacob*, "How old are you?" *Jacob* responds that he is 130 and that "my years have been few and difficult, and they do not equal the years of the pilgrimage of my fathers." This is the answer of a man who is focused on the past.

In the next chapter, Joseph is called by his ailing father to receive a deathbed blessing. *Jacob* (who, we are told, has failing eyes) notices two young men with Joseph. He asks Joseph who they are. Joseph tells his father that they are his sons—the Manasseh and Ephraim whom we recall every Friday night when we bless our children.

In the presence of his grandchildren, the text offers only one name for our patriarch: *Israel*. Israel blesses his grandchildren by saying that great nations will come from them. His blessing to them is seemingly complete, but he continues, instructing Jews for eternity how we are to bless our children. He says, "In your name will *Israel* pronounce this blessing: 'May God make you like Ephraim and Manasseh.'"

Why would our patriarch be required to bless his grandchildren as *Israel*? Why would our patriarch instruct each of us to imitate *Israel* in blessing our children to be like Ephraim and Manasseh? The answer is provided at the very beginning of the next book of the Bible. In Exodus 1:1, the Torah describes our trip to Egypt: "And these are the names of the sons of *Israel* who are coming to Egypt; with *Jacob*, each man and his household came."

This is, on its surface, a strangely worded phrase. The first and second clause of the line seem to convey the same information. It is a preface to the names of the descendants of Jacob/Israel who had come to Egypt. But every Torah commentator agrees that the Torah never wastes a word or has a redundancy, and that everything in the Torah exists to teach us something. What could this *seeming* redundancy teach us?

The first clause describes *Israel* as "coming." The second clause describes *Jacob* as having "come." The difference? One who is "coming" has not yet arrived; he still has more to do and, therefore, is oriented to the future. One who "came" is finished. His journeys are in the past. The experience associated with *Israel* is quintessentially one of *coming*, one of future orientation. The Torah's call for us to be future oriented is so important that we are called many times, throughout the subsequent books of the Torah, "the children of Israel"—not "the children of Jacob."

We now can understand the Shabbat blessing that Jewish parents offer to our sons. We are giving them the blessing of future orientation, and we are giving them the blessing of a grandparent. The latter is not incidental. Israel's status as a grandfather is glorified in the Jewish tradition through his ancient nickname: *Yisrael Saba*—"Israel the Grandfather."[4]

One question remains. What is the connection between grandparents and future orientation? It is not intuitive that we should convey the blessing of future orientation through a grandparent. To the contrary, it is downright curious. Grandparents usually have lived most of their years. What, then, could be the profound connection between grandparents and *future* orientation? The Torah, and the Jewish teaching that is based on it, explains.

The Torah Grandparent

In Deuteronomy 4:9, Moses describes the fundamental role of the grandparent. It is not to entertain or spoil the grandchildren. To the contrary, it is an existential *responsibility*. Moses says: "Do not forget the things your eyes have seen or let them fade from your heart as long as you live. Teach them to your children *and to their children after them*." The grandparent, in the Torah's imagination, is obligated to educate his or her grandchildren in service of transmission of Jewish teachings and traditions, with the goal of ensuring that Judaism thrives long after the grandparent passes.

The Talmud shows how seriously our sages understood this obligation. Rabbi Chiya bar Abba once saw Rabbi Yehoshua ben Levi rushing to bring his grandchild to synagogue. Rabbi Yehoshua explained his rushing by citing texts that lead to the conclusion that "teaching Torah to one's grandchild is tantamount to receiving the Torah at Sinai."[5]

This belief animates a debate in the Talmud. Is the greatest privilege *teaching* Torah to one's grandchild or *learning* Torah from one's grandchild? This debate presumes an agreement that learning Torah *with* one's grandchild constitutes the greatest privilege.[6]

The second connection between future orientation and grandparenthood is articulated by the twenty-first-century sage Rabbi Jonathan Sacks. Rabbi Sacks points out that the blessing of future orientation on the Sabbath not only starts with the blessing that we give to our children, it also concludes it. We bid adieu to Shabbat with a prayer: "May you live to see your children's children—peace be upon Israel."

This is a curious prayer. What is the connection between being a grandparent—and "peace"? Rabbi Sacks explains: "Those who think about grandchildren care about the future, and those who think about the future make peace. It is those who constantly think of the past, of slights and humiliation and revenge, who make war."[7]

How God Describes Himself

The Torah's insistence on future orientation is conveyed not only through the stories of its heroes. It also constitutes God's self-identification. In Exodus 3, Moses says to God, "Suppose I go to the Israelites and say to them,

'The God of your fathers has sent me to you,' and they ask me, 'What is his name?' Then what shall I tell them?"

As we saw with Jacob/Israel, a name in the Torah is not just a pleasant-sounding designation. It is the revelation of an essential quality. God responds, "I will be what I will be." God is essentially saying, "My name is Mr. Future Orientation." As we are created in God's image, the Torah is telling us that we should, as well, be future oriented.

This idea is subtly reiterated throughout the Torah. Events in the Torah are often introduced with either, "And it shall be" (*vehaya*), or "And it came to pass" (*vayehi*). These may seem similar, but an ancient Midrash (commentary) notes that verses introduced with "it shall be" introduce a "joyous event," whereas those that begin with "it came to pass" cue the reader that something bad is about to happen.[8]

What is the essential difference between these two phrases? The phrase "It came to pass" reflects an orientation to the *past*, while "It shall be" reflects an orientation to the *future*. The Torah, through these phrases and their contexts, lays it out very clearly and simply: Future orientation is positive and past orientation is negative.

Days of the Week: Counting in Future Time

The importance of experiencing time through future orientation comes through in the very ways in which Jews describe the days of the week. As discussed in the chapter on work and rest, there is no Monday, Tuesday, or Wednesday. Instead, there is Yom Rishon (first day), Yom Sheni (second day), and so on until the seventh day, the Sabbath. This naming custom guides us to always *anticipate* the Sabbath, and to be oriented to the future joy that the upcoming Friday night ushers in.

This spirit comes through in a central Shabbat song, *Lekha Dodi*, which was composed by the sixteenth-century poet Shlomo Halevi Alkabetz. This song is sung in synagogues on Friday evening as the Sabbath is approaching. It is more about anticipating the Sabbath (referred to as a bride) than celebrating the Sabbath itself—making it an ode to future orientation. Its lyrics: "Let's go, my beloved, to meet the bride / Let us welcome the presence of Shabbat . . . / Come in peace, crown of her husband / Come O Bride! Come O Bride!"

May You Keep Doing Good Things!

The Torah never directly mentions the afterlife, as commonly conceived. Scholars seeking to discern the Jewish view of the afterlife find secondary and tertiary meanings in various biblical passages.

Perhaps one reason why Judaism does not have much of a notion of the beyond is because it is not where the ultimate future happens. Genesis 18:1 begins a new parsha (Torah portion) called *Chaye Sarah*—The Lives of Sarah. It begins with her death. Genesis 47:28 begins another new parsha called *Vayechi*—And he lived. It is about the death of Jacob. The ideology: Our goal, in emulating Sarah and her grandson Jacob, should be to live forever—through those we have inspired and influenced. A good life, we learn, never ends—on earth.

Fast-forward to the story of another hero of the Torah: Moses. Moses's life goal was to guide the Jewish people into the Promised Land. Then came Numbers 20 where God tells Moses to speak to a rock and bring forth water from it. Moses instead strikes the rock. God responds by telling Moses that he is forbidden from ever leading the people into the Promised Land. Therein might be the lesson for each of us. A life well lived—one worthy of Moses, who the Torah stipulates will be the greatest prophet to ever live—will involve setting and working toward a goal that we will not achieve in our lifetime.

This anti-ending philosophy will become a key theme and teaching of Judaism's essential book: the Passover Haggadah. The Haggadah is the book that guides us through the Passover Seder, which is the most important event of the Jewish year. One piece of guidance that the Haggadah offers is through what it omits. The Haggadah, in relating the covenant that God makes with Abraham in Genesis 15, *omits* its final component: "Your descendants will return here to the Land."

The Haggadah famously features four questions, four sons, and four cups of wine, each relating to one of the four expressions of redemption in Exodus 6:6–7. But there are *five* expressions of redemption in the Exodus passage.

And the Haggadah, as discussed in the chapter of this book on gratitude, tells the story of our liberation through the farmer's declaration. The passage in the Haggadah starts in Deuteronomy 26:5 and goes through 26:8, and *stops* before 26:9, which describes our having arrived at the destination.

This philosophy and practice of resisting endings exists throughout the Jewish year. Five times a year, we complete a book of the Torah. When we finish each book of the Torah, we say the same thing: "Chazak, Chazak, V'nitchazek—Strength, Strength, May We Be Strengthened." In other words, we mark the conclusion of each book by looking to the next source of strength, and declare that this practice strengthens us. As Rabbi Mark Kaiserman of the Reform Temple of Forest Hills says in his analysis of this statement, "We celebrate the past at the same moment we look to the future."[9]

The ideology of "Chazak, Chazak, V'nitchazek" resonates in a common expression in modern Hebrew. In American English, we often congratulate someone by saying, "Well done." This implies that the action has been completed in the past. The commensurate Hebrew expression is very different. It is, "Yashar Koach," which means, "May your strength be continued." Thus, Jews communicate "Well done" by saying, "May you keep doing good things!"

Why does Judaism resist endings—the ultimate repudiation of the future—so insistently and ubiquitously? The answer, perhaps, relates to the nature of an ending. An ending is a declaration that the task is completed and the journey is done. It is a declaration that there is no future. And that is an idea that a people called the "Children of Israel"—the children of *Yisrael Saba*—just cannot abide.

As Rabbi Jonathan Sacks wrote:

> Human beings are the only life form capable of using the future tense. Only beings who can imagine the world other than it is, are capable of freedom. And if we are free, the future is open, dependent on us. We can know the beginning of our story but not the end. That is why, as He is about to take the Israelites from slavery to freedom, God tells Moses that His name is "I will be what I will be." Judaism, the religion of freedom, is faith in the future tense.[10]

The Divine Resolution

So, the Torah makes a definitive and insistent case against past orientation and in favor of future orientation. What does this suggest about how we should relate to the past and the present? The Torah provides the answer in Genesis and Deuteronomy.

In Genesis 28, Jacob, while fleeing his murderous twin brother, Esau, finds himself alone in the desert. He goes to sleep and has a dream of angels climbing a ladder, firmly planted on earth and ascending to heaven. One message of this existential passage is that we are to be firmly planted in the present, while being oriented to the future.

In Deuteronomy 32:7, Moses instructs, "Remember the days of yore, consider the *changes* in the generations"—effectively telling us that we are not to live in the past. But neither should we ignore the past. To the contrary, we should strategically consult the past with a sensitivity to the changes between generations, in order to guide how we live in the present and move toward the future.[11]

The Science

Past Orientation: Rumination

In Genesis, we learned of Lot's wife who turns back and is transformed into a pillar of salt. We now have a term that describes having one's mind stuck in a negative past—rumination, a concept that we have discussed in the sections of this book on grudges and culture. Rumination presents, according to the American Psychiatric Association, as being "hopeless about the future."[12]

We now know how common this condition is. According to a 2022 study led by Professor Amy Joubert of the University of New South Wales, 21 percent of people report "being unable to stop themselves from ruminating."[13]

This rejection of future orientation—this "being hopeless about the future"—is the cause of a stunning array of psychological problems. The scientific literature associates it with depression, anxiety, phobias, mood swings, appetite disturbances, eating disorders, excess fatigue, and suicidal ideation.[14]

Present Orientation: "The Battle Cry of a Generation"

In 2011, the rap artist Drake introduced what was, at the time, the most popular new term that rock star Adam Levine of Maroon 5 called "the battle cry of a generation." It is YOLO, an acronym for "You only live once."

There is nothing inherently problematic about YOLO. It could be understood as: "You only live once; therefore, do as many good deeds as you can each day so that your influence stretches far into the future." But it doesn't. The Drake song that popularized it is about clubbing, casual sex, admiring a girl's backside, and piling up tens of millions of dollars for no discernable reason. YOLO became the twenty-first-century iteration of the ideology so despised by the biblical Isaiah: "Eat and drink, for tomorrow we die."

The ideology of YOLO has a variety of manifestations in this century. In 2012, the rapper Ervin McKinness tweeted, "Drunk af [as fuck] going 120 drifting corners #FuckIt YOLO." Moments later, the car that McKinness was driving while drunk crashed into a wall, killing him and his four passengers.[15]

In 2021, Reddit participants in "WallStreetBets" used the term as they encouraged each other to take out debt to drive up the shares of GameStop and AMC. Štefan Lyócsa of the Slovak Academy of Sciences called the phenomenon "YOLO trading." The result of YOLO trading? Each stock rose dramatically before falling by more than 90 percent.[16]

The Marshmallow Test

In 1972, Stanford professor Walter Mischel and his colleagues conducted what became one of the most famous and important psychological experiments of all time: the Marshmallow Test. They put a favorite treat (marshmallows, pretzels, or cookies) in front of children whose mean age was 4½. They told the child that he would be left alone for fifteen minutes. If the child could deny himself the treat for fifteen minutes, he would receive twice the portion of the treat. Thus, any child who was oriented to the future—which was fifteen minutes away—would benefit massively (at least from the perspective of a toddler!).

The researchers recorded which children resisted the treat in the moment to receive a greater reward in the future and which did not. Years later, the Stanford team reconnected with the participants, and found that those who were future oriented as small children were more competent, had higher SAT scores, had a healthier body mass index (BMI), and were better able to cope with frustration and stress than those who could not wait for the treat.[17]

A variety of other studies have amplified these discoveries. In 2016, Professor Sarah Lindstrom Johnson of Johns Hopkins Medical School and several colleagues published a review of studies about adolescent future orientation. They found that adolescents who are future oriented have less drug use, less sexual irresponsibility, lower violence involvement, and improved educational and vocational outcomes.[18]

Heroin addicts in the United States, alcoholics in Finland, suicidal Hungarian college students, depressed Chinese college students, underperforming Iranian students, students who did not show resilience to Covid in Italy, and depressed Chinese workers in a food processing company seem like very different groups. But a variety of studies show that they have one thing in common: a lack of future orientation.[19]

Perceiving One's Future Self as a Totally Different Person

All, or at least some of this is intuitive. One who is future oriented—one who believes in hope—will forsake current pleasures to reap benefits later. It does not take much imagination to see how such people will become healthier, happier, wealthier, and more successful. Why, then, might the Torah insist on a future orientation that we could have intuitively arrived at on our own?

In 2022, Professors Eirini Kapogli and Jordi Quoidbach of the Universitat Ramon Llull in Spain found the answer. Using modern neuroscientific research about the parts of the brain that are aroused by different stimuli, they made an astonishing discovery: We regard our future selves more like strangers than we do as extensions of our present selves. They wrote:

> People who are not currently experiencing pain, cold, hunger or a powerful emotion will have a hard time imagining themselves feeling different in the future . . . [Moreover], *perceiving one's future self as a totally different person* [emphasis added] can lead to impatient decision-making such as foregoing larger monetary rewards for immediate smaller gains, less ethically sound decisions, and poor choices such as smoking and overspending.[20]

So, future orientation may seem obvious—but it is profoundly unnatural. It is no wonder that the Torah insistently makes future orientation so central, ubiquitous, and important.

The Epitome: Anticipation

No discussion of future orientation could be complete without a discussion of how we most often experience it—through anticipation. Much of what follows is also discussed in the section of this book on work and rest—which is fitting, as the Jewish calendar is oriented toward us anticipating the Shabbat ahead.

Future orientation is, as Professor Kapogli and Quoidbach determined, so unnatural that our brains actually register our future selves in the same way that they do strangers. But contemporary science has discovered an asset that can help us to overcome our natural disinclination to future orientation: dopamine. The Cleveland Clinic explains:

> Dopamine is known as the "feel-good" hormone. It gives you a sense of pleasure. It also gives you the motivation to do something when you're feeling pleasure. Dopamine is part of your reward system . . . As humans, our brains are hard-wired to seek out behaviors that release dopamine in our reward system. When you're doing something pleasurable, your brain releases a large amount of dopamine. You feel good and you seek more of that feeling.[21]

Dopamine is great. So, how do we get more of it? In 2014, the neuroscientist Robert Sapolsky found out. He conditioned monkeys to learn that they would receive a treat after they pushed a button in response to a light ten times. He measured the dopamine in their brains at each stage of the process. Professor Sapolsky found that the dopamine—the source of pleasure—did not spike when the monkeys *received* the reward. It spiked when they saw the signal, and *anticipated* the reward.[22]

In 2022, the Coleman Institute for Addiction Medicine reported, "Scientists are now naming dopamine 'the anticipation molecule.'" Pleasure, we have learned, exists in the anticipation for the reward more than in the reward itself. It comes from the blessing of Israel in Genesis—that of future orientation.[23]

The implications of this finding are widespread. In 2020, Professor Francisco Tigre Moura of the IU University for Applied Sciences wrote that the pleasure that we derive from anticipation explains why we gamble, why people get addicted to their smartphones, and why the chorus is so effective in music appreciation.[24]

The science of anticipation explains the finding of the marketing firm Razorfish. In their 2015 report *Digital Dopamine*, they found that approximately 75 percent of people in four global markets are more excited when goods arrive via online shopping than when they get the goods in a store. They explain:

> While it might seem logical to assume that an age of instant gratification means we want what we want immediately, that isn't always the case. Sometimes immediacy isn't enjoyable. While one might presume that waiting for purchases to arrive is a disadvantage for online shopping versus shopping in-store, it appears that people actually enjoy the anticipation involved in waiting for purchases to be delivered.[25]
>
> It is no wonder why the Torah tradition, which privileges joy to such an extent that the Baal Shem Tov called it a "Biblical command" incorporates anticipation in the way that we experience the days of the week.

The Grandmother Hypothesis

The Torah celebrates, emphasizes, and guides toward future orientation. And the Torah connects it with grandparenthood so tightly that the Shabbat blessing Jewish parents give our sons is one of future orientation from the quintessential grandparent, *Yisrael Saba*. Why would the Torah make this nonintuitive association?

The first remarkable thing about grandparents is that they exist at all. According to a 2023 analysis by Professor Pat Monaghan of the University of Glasgow in the *Journal of Zoology*, there are only six species that live past reproductive age: four species of whales, the Asian elephant, and humans. Considering that there are approximately 8.7 million species in the world, it is clearly rare for an animal to know his grandchildren. The general absence of grandparents is easily explained by evolution. As our primary evolutionary purpose is to reproduce to maintain our species, it makes sense that we would expire when that job is complete.[26]

The question, therefore, is not why grandparents are so rare; it is why they are so common among humans. In 1998, the University of Utah professor Kristen Hawkes and several colleagues published a paper in the *Proceedings of the National Academy of Sciences* seeking to answer this question. Their paper, "Grandmothering, Menopause and the Evolution of Human Life Histories," became one of the most influential and frequently cited articles in anthropology.

Professor Hawkes and her colleagues reviewed a variety of theories that sought to explain human longevity, and found them wanting. There was one that they settled on. It is known as the "Grandmother Hypothesis." The Grandmother Hypothesis starts with one of the fundamental (and traditional) responsibilities of the mother: to gather food for herself and her children. The problem is that mothers forage significantly less at around the time of the arrival of a newborn.

This problem is alleviated, or even solved, by what often happens. The grandmother does the foraging that her daughter cannot do when tending to an infant. With the grandmother doing the foraging, her daughter is liberated to have more children. Consequently, we have evolutionarily adapted to live long enough to serve as active grandparents and enable the comfortable raising of more children.

How has the Grandmother Hypothesis held up in the modern era, when young mothers generally don't forage? In 2014, professors Janice Compton of the University of Manitoba and Robert Pollak of Washington University in St. Louis found that the labor force participation of American married women with small children is 4 to 10 percentage points higher when there is a grandparent living within twenty-five miles.[27] A 2023 study by Miguel Ángel Talamas Marcos of the Inter-American Development Bank estimated that the death of a grandmother reduces her daughter's labor participation rate by 27 percent and lowers her earnings by more than 50 percent.[28]

Grandparents, evolutionary psychology makes clear, enable parents to do the quintessential future-oriented activity: have more children. And that's only the beginning of the scientific discoveries of the connection between grandparents and future orientation.

Grandparenthood: Good for Grandparents

So, it certainly seems true that one reason human beings live long lives is to be able to serve as grandparents who are active in the rearing of grandchildren. For some grandparents, this activity consists of caring for the children so that the mother can work. While that function is crucial for some families, it is inapplicable to many others. Is there a general rule, therefore, as to what makes for a good grandparent?

An analysis can start with a commentary on the elderly by Pastor Chanda in Zambia. He writes:

> The more I thought about this, the more I realised [sic] that we were all in danger of becoming cynics as we grew older because this world is very unkind. As we go through life, we encounter people who leave us with scars. These experiences turn us into skeptics . . . Perhaps it could have started in your courtship and early-married life when your spouse cheated on you. Since then, you cannot trust a man or woman . . . Yes, life leaves us with scars that make us pessimists. I remember meeting a man who upon seeing one of our former Presidents on television immediately said, "Bakabolala!" [i.e., "thieves"]. One bad politician in his life has made him think that all politicians are thieves.[29]

There is a cure for this cynicism, and it comes naturally. A past-oriented grandparent who persistently criticizes the current generation and its practices will quickly discover that their grandchildren aren't interested. Grandparenting works when grandparents find joy in the enthusiasm, the promise, the discoveries, the potential, and even the challenges of their grandchildren. This often presents in a common goal of grandparents: to live to participate in a *future* event such as a bar mitzvah, a confirmation, a graduation, or a wedding.

We know that grandparents allow parents to have more children and produce for their family. What is the impact of active and engaged involvement on the grandparents themselves?

A good place to begin is with the Berlin Aging Study, which, beginning in 1990, studied the development of 516 participants starting at age seventy for three decades. This study found that grandparents who cared for their grandchildren on a *noncustodial* basis had a 37 percent lower risk of dying over twenty years than did grandparents who were not deeply involved with their grandchildren. This finding has been widely confirmed. Studies from the Survey of Health, Ageing [sic] and Retirement in Europe and from the North American Menopause Society indicate that grandparents who spend significant (but not full) time caring for their grandchildren maintain their verbal fluency and cognitive abilities better and longer than those who do not.[30]

Those are just the easily measurable benefits of active grandparenting. According to the American Grandparents Association, 72 percent of grandparents say that being a grandparent is the "single most important and satisfying thing in their lives." This is a remarkable finding, given that all grandparents are also parents—which is rather important and satisfying! This is just what we would expect for people who are devoted to meaningfully making a significant impact on the future.[31]

Grandparenthood: Good for Grandchildren

Active grandparenthood is very good for parents *and* grandparents. But the blessing of the biblical Israel was to his grandchildren. What does contemporary social science say about grandchildren who have a close relationship with their grandparents? In 2020, Professors Tianyuan Li and Pok-Man Siu of the Education University of Hong Kong had adult participants assess their relationship with their closest grandparent. They found that those who had strong relationships with their grandparents had more positive views of aging. Those with more positive views of aging were able to live a healthier lifestyle and be less impulsive.[32]

That's not all. Professors Li and Siu also found that adults with a strong grandparent relationship had a more robust appreciation of "future consequences" for present action. In other words, the good grandparent transmits her future orientation to her grandchildren, and it stays with them well into adulthood.

The benefits of this transmission of future orientation are manifold. A plethora of studies from BYU, Boston College, Oxford, and other universities have demonstrated that children with strong relationships with their grandparents are more likely to be engaged in school, more social, better able to overcome the effects of maternal depression, more self-confident, more secure, more able to deal with trauma, less likely to become depressed and anxious, kinder, more compassionate, and more caring than their agemates without such a relationship.[33]

It is no wonder why the Torah instructs us to bless our children with the blessing of a grandfather, *Yisrael Saba*.

Reflection

Lot's wife manifests past orientation by rejecting God's instruction and "looking back." She is turned into a pillar of salt. Korach manifests present orientation by saying, "All the people are holy"—and gets, along with his confederates, swallowed into the earth. God shows the alternative, by naming himself "I will be what I will be." And *Yisrael Saba* guides us to instill this idea through how we bless our sons every Friday night.

Modern science has demonstrated that future-oriented grandparenthood is magical for grandparents and grandchildren, while enabling mothers to have more children and a more robust career. It has also demonstrated that our greatest pleasures do not come from receiving the reward, but from anticipating it. Modern science has also shown that a healthy future orientation keeps people away from drugs, prevents suicide, provides a bulwark against cynicism, increases school performance, and provides resilience against disease. The Torah and social science are in complete agreement that future orientation often makes the difference between success and failure, happiness and unhappiness, hope and despair.

It seems clear that the Torah and social science converge on the fact that we should live according to the principle of future orientation. What are some practical ways we can do so and thus fulfill the blessing of future orientation that we give our children every Friday night?

1. **Goal:** The Torah, the Haggadah, and Jewish practice hate the idea of endings. If important things do not end, we will always be relating to them through the lens of future orientation. This gift is available to each of us. We should, as God modeled by not allowing Moses to enter the Promised Land, set a goal for ourselves that we cannot accomplish in our lifetime. It might be providing excellent medical opportunities for everyone in Africa. It might be creating a drug-free environment for every American child. If our life goal

is one to which we will make continual progress but will die not having achieved, we will be gratified by progress and continually inspired to keep working toward an improved future. And we will remain future oriented until the moment of our death.

2. **Always Look Forward to Something:** Before Covid, Dr. Ruth Westheimer came to our home for dinner almost every Shabbat—when she was in her eighties and nineties. At one of those Shabbat meals, one of our other guests was Cantor Howard Stahl, a brilliant clergyman who enjoyed a remarkable career at three synagogues in New York and New Jersey. Dr. Ruth asked him what he does. Howard replied: "I just retired." Dr. Ruth gave him a look we will never forget—it was as if he had confessed to a terrible crime. She said: "You can rewire, but you must never retire!"

   She never did. Every time we saw Dr. Ruth, she was working on something—a documentary, a book, a class she was teaching at Yale, a speech she was giving. Erica and I visited Dr. Ruth in her apartment in May of 2024. It was clear that she would never, at least without great effort, be able to leave the apartment again. Yet she was excitedly telling us about her book on loneliness coming out in September. As we rode the elevator down, Erica and I remarked to each other that she was the most future-oriented person we know. Dr. Ruth passed away in July 2024, at age ninety-six.

   Around when Dr. Ruth passed away, I got a call from Pat Boone. Pat is one of the great singers of the twentieth century—with hits in numerous genres. He is also one of the foundational American Christian Zionists, and the song he is proudest of is the theme song for Exodus, which he calls "the second Jewish national anthem." Pat, who is ninety years old, called to tell me about a plan that he had for Israel and about a book he is writing and an album he is working on that draws inspiration from Bob Dylan. The reason why Pat is able to strategize, write, and sing new songs at ninety is because he is strategizing, writing, and singing new songs at age 90.

   The lesson from Dr. Ruth, Pat Boone, and other such role models: The key to being healthy and vibrant at ninety is to be creating something that will blossom in the future. It does not have to be the same thing one would have done ten, thirty, or fifty years ago, but it should be *something*. As Dr. Ruth said, "We can rewire—but not retire."

3. **Anticipation:** We can, as the naming of the days of the Hebrew calendar does, embed future orientation into our relationship with time. If we live our lives in constant anticipation of a special holiday or an anniversary, a birthday or a wedding, a graduation or a game, a presentation or a trip, and especially the Sabbath—we will find that we are always living with anticipation. Simply, there should always be something—and, ideally, multiple things—to which we are looking forward and working on.
4. **Stay close to grandparents:** We should give our children the blessing of *Yisrael Saba*—literally on Shabbat, and also by enabling the grandchild–grandparent relationship to be maximized. Grandparents—living the future orientation that is at the core of close relationships with their grandchildren—will live longer, healthier, and happier golden years. Grandchildren will grow up to become more resilient, better able to negotiate all kinds of challenges, kinder, and more confident. And parents will, consistent with the Grandmother Hypothesis, have increased professional and relational freedoms—and be able to experience the joy generated through the connection of the generations.
5. **Reinterpret YOLO:** YOLO does not need to be about casual sex, leveraged day trading, and drunk driving. It can, and should, be a philosophy of future orientation. With the recognition that we will only live once, we can devote ourselves to saving as many lives, ameliorating as much pain, or creating as many opportunities for the poor as we possibly can. In so doing, we can emulate the biblical Sarah and Jacob so that our lives can continue on earth long after we die.

PART FOUR

Together: How We Should Live with Others Communally

22

God Diagnoses and Cures the 2023 "Massive Deadly Epidemic Hidden in Plain Sight"

The Torah and Science of Relationships

Between Genesis 1:1 and 1:27, God has a busy five days. He creates light and darkness, the sun and the moon, the sea and land animals—among other things. He declares most of these creations to be "good." And he wasn't done.

In Genesis 1:27, God "created man in his image."

Although man is created in the image of God, the text has a striking omission. Man is not immediately said to be "good"—let alone "very good," as we might expect.

Why? God seems to reveal the answer in Genesis 2:18, in another invocation of "good." God, observing Adam, says, "It is *not good* for man to be alone."

So God creates (in Genesis 2:18) a "help against him"—a woman who becomes his wife. Man, no longer alone, has the ability to be good and to live well. The significance of God introducing the concept of spousehood by calling Eve "a help against him" will be addressed in the next chapter.

This is not the only time in the Torah when something is said to be "not good." There is just one other time—in Exodus 18:17. Here, Moses (in partnership with God) has just led millions of Jewish slaves to freedom. His beloved father-in-law, Jethro, comes to visit. Jethro notices that Moses is hearing cases "from morning until the evening"—because there are no other judges. Jethro is not pleased. He says, "The thing that you do is *not good*." Aloneness, it seems, is considered to be "not good" regardless of the context—from romantic relationships to judicial obligations.

The Torah's insistence that it is "not good" to be alone invites a question: How does God want aloneness to be cured? At first consideration, it seems obvious. Just surround yourself with others. But the text in Genesis encourages us to keep thinking. If aloneness just described the absence of another person, God had a number of options. He could have created a bunch of friends for Adam. Or God could have just created Eve as he did Adam—from the dust off the earth. Adam would have had someone to procreate, gather food, relieve loneliness, and stay safe with.

Instead, God puts Adam into a deep sleep and creates a woman out of Adam's *side* (not, as is often misinterpreted, his rib). This very particular way for God to alleviate Adam's aloneness raises yet another question. Why does God choose the first human relationship to be between two people who were initially connected physically? He does so in order to model the essence of a relationship. The model relationship is not of two people, fully formed, coming together. It is not just having someone around to alleviate loneliness. It is more than having someone to do tasks with—a "partner." The essential relationship, the Torah tells us, is about having someone to complete you.

God's Yearning

The English word "prayer" derives from the Latin root *precari*, which means "to beg or to ask." The Hebrew word most frequently translated as "prayer" is *tefila*. Tefila derives from the root *tafal*, which means to bind or connect. When we do *tefila*, we are connecting with God. And the Talmud, drawing from another verse in Deuteronomy, stipulates that Jews should connect with God through blessings a hundred times a day.[1]

Who would crave connection and want a hundred check-ins a day? Any parent can understand. A hundred check-ins would be desired by someone who craves or even *needs* a continuous, deep, and ongoing *relationship*.

We see this divine yearning throughout the Torah, even in unlikely places. Leviticus 22, for instance, is devoted to the creation of the Tabernacle. God declares, "I will be sanctified in the midst of the congregation of Israel." God reiterates this yearning in Leviticus 26:12, when he says, "My sanctuary [will be] *among* you." God, we learn, is not sanctified outside of the congregation—in heaven or somewhere else—but "in the midst of the congregation," where he can be in relationship with us and us with each other.

God, it seems, is completed by his relationship with us—as we are with him.

God's Relationships

To say that God wants a "relationship" with each of us is too general to be meaningful or guiding. That is even the same among people, as there are so many different kinds of relationships—and degrees within each one.

What, then, could God mean in his insistence that he wants a relationship with each of us? A clue comes from Maimonides, who invoked the Talmudic concept that God writes in the language of man. God makes it clear, throughout the Torah, that he desires such a deep and multifaceted relationship with us that no single analogue will suffice. He borrows imagery from all of our meaningful relationships to describe the kinds he wants with us.

God as Parent

In Exodus 4:22, God begins the process of revealing himself to Moses, Pharaoh, and subsequently, the whole world. He does so as a parent. "And you shall say to Pharaoh, thus says God, Israel is my son, my firstborn."

One of Judaism's quintessential prayers, which dates to Talmudic times and with which Jews conclude Yom Kippur in synagogues throughout the world to this day, is *Avinu Malkeinu*. It means, "Our Father, our King." Referring to God as a king is understandable, given the common biblical conception of God as the one with the ultimate power to reward and punish. It is interesting that the first—and primary—description of God in the prayer is not as a king, but as a parent. And, specifically, a father—with all of its connotations and expectations of love, discipline, teaching, protecting, providing, sacrificing, and advising.

God's role as a parent is not confined to fatherhood. In Deuteronomy 32:18, God is referred to as "The Rock who birthed you." God's maternal qualities are referenced in Psalm 131, Hosea 11, and Isaiah 66, where the prophet has God saying, "As a mother comforts her child, so will I [God] comfort you; and you will be comforted over Jerusalem."[2] God also wants to be our mother, with all of the connotations and expectations of a keeper of the home who exemplifies love, tenderness, generosity, resourcefulness, competence, guidance, kindness, and compassion.

God as Friend

One of the heroes of the Exodus narrative is Reuel, Moses's beloved mentor and father-in-law (also referred to as Yitro/Jethro in the Torah). Reuel means "*Friend* of God." Reuel was not the only friend of God in the Bible.

Another hero of the Bible is King David. David's closest relationship, celebrated in the Book of Samuel and subsequent commentary, is with Jonathan, his *friend*. When Jonathan dies in battle, David says some of the most poignant words in the Bible: "I am distressed for you, my brother Jonathan; you have been very pleasant to me; your love to me was wonderful, surpassing the love of women."

The notion of a soul friendship would return in the next generation, with God as the friend. The prophet Nathan, after learning that David's wife Batsheva was pregnant, told David that their son would be Yedidya ("Friend of God"). That son, whom David named Solomon ("Peaceful One"), would go to build the First Temple, write several books of the Bible, open Israel to international trade, and be renowned for his wisdom—making him, as Nathan prophesied, a true friend of God.

God as Spouse

The greatest moment in the Torah is, perhaps, in Exodus 19:17 when God gives us the Torah on Mount Sinai. God could have, of course, chosen any imagery to illustrate the moment. The imagery used comes through in an examination of the verse: "Moshe brought the people out of the camp to meet with God; and they stood under the mountain."

The problem, the rabbis of the Talmud pointed out, is that people cannot stand "under" a mountain. So, what did the Author of the Torah mean? According to the Talmud, God "raised the mountain above them as a vat." The Torah is describing a wedding scene. God lifts the mountain so that he could marry the Jewish people under a *chuppah*—a wedding canopy. The gift he gives us under the canopy—our "ring"—is the Torah. And the Jewish people—God's betrothed one—enthusiastically accepts and commits with the declaration "we will do, and we will hear."[3] The defining interaction between man and God is filled with the imagery of a spousal relationship.

Indeed, it is this relationship that will characterize the relationship between man and God in messianic times. In Hosea 2:18, the Bible declares of the messianic time, "And in that day—declares the Lord—You will call [me] husband, and no more will you call Me master." And we don't have to wait for messianic times to experience this relationship. God is, as Jewish men say every morning when donning tefillin states, our "betrothed."

God as Neighbor

By Exodus 25, God had, in a series of acts that awed the world, smote the Egyptians and freed the Jews. That established God as a mighty and powerful deity. But we see in Exodus 25:8 that God wants us to deepen our understanding of who he is. This is when God, in commanding the construction of the Tabernacle, says, "And let them make Me a sanctuary that I may dwell among them."

The twenty-first-century sage Rabbi Jonathan Sacks explains that the word for "dwell," *v'shachanti*, comes from the root *shachen*, which means "neighbor." God, who is capable of doing the most spectacular things, wants to dwell *among* us—just like a neighbor.[4]

What God Cares About in a Relationship

Following the Exodus, the Jewish people wander in the desert en route to the Promised Land. Our behavior in the desert leads God to determine that we were not yet ready to live as a free and independent people. We would stay in the desert for forty years, and would, of course, need to eat. God could have solved this by giving us some ancient equivalent of military MREs (Meals Ready to Eat)—food that would have kept us nourished, but be no more. Instead, he gives the people manna.

The manna, per Exodus 16:31, "tasted like honey wafers." Numbers 11:8, however, describes the taste as that of "oil cakes." Which is it? To solve this discrepancy, the rabbis cited a tradition that the manna tasted different for different people. It was, in a sense, engineered to taste as each person wanted. The manna was thus an attempt to satisfy individual diets and desires. No king or master would be concerned with satisfying such desires. God, in relationship with each of us, cares that we *enjoy* our lunch.[5]

In Deuteronomy 26, God declares that he heard "our affliction, our toil and our oppression." The toil refers to the work we did as slaves. As the Bible does not repeat itself, "affliction" and "oppression" cannot be the same thing. The ancient biblical commentary *Sifrei* explains the distinction. "Affliction" applies to our physical suffering, evident to all observers. "Oppression" applies to our internal suffering, evident perhaps only to ourselves. Everyone suffers different things, and God cares about it all.[6]

This divine comprehensiveness is reflected in Psalm 91, which Jewish tradition holds was written by Moses. The psalm declares, "He will call on me, and I will answer him; I will be with him in trouble; I will deliver him and honor him."[7]

The "trouble" is not specific. It is unbounded. It applies to public troubles and private struggles. God's relationship with us, whether as a parent, a king, a spouse, or a friend, is for all seasons, all places, and all reasons.

When God Needs

In the Book of Numbers, God shows what happens when we are *truly* in a relationship. In Numbers 27:16, Moses (acknowledging his advancing age) turns his focus to a successor. Moses says that the people without a strong leader will be like "sheep without a shepherd" and asks God to choose his successor. God selects Joshua and assures Moses that Joshua will have constant access to him through Elazar the priest.

Immediately thereafter, God tells Moses to ensure that the people make offerings to him twice a day and additionally on every Jewish holiday. Why would God insist on such frequent offerings at this juncture? Moses tells God that the Jews need God, and God immediately responds by telling Moses that God *needs* the Jews.

This is surprising. Need flows from lacking. How could God, who is all powerful and all knowing, *need*, and by implication, *lack* anyone or anything?[8]

Because, as the prophet Jeremiah quotes God as saying, "I have loved you with an everlasting love."[9] What does God's love have to do with God's needs? One might think that a loving relationship *satisfies* needs. It does. A loving relationship enables us to alleviate loneliness, to find meaning, and to create the bonds of trust necessary to build anything from a family to a business. But God is showing us something additional about a loving relationship. It also *creates* needs.

Every parent experiences this. Two people create a child. Though the baby did not exist previously, the parents' most painful thought immediately becomes contemplating life *without* her. It is not the pain caused by losing something the parent just likes, values, or even loves. It is the pain caused by losing what the parent existentially *needs*. And the love a parent has for a child only causes this need to deepen over time.

And the love/need connection is by no means unique to parents and children. It is a function of any loving relationship. One young man tells his girlfriend that he loves her but, though it may take some adjustment, would be fine without her. Another tells his girlfriend that he simply cannot imagine life without her—as she completes him. Which young man, all other things being equal, would the parents of the young lady want for their daughter?

The obvious answer is illustrated in a prayer that observant Jews recite after eating certain foods: "Blessed are you, Lord our God, King of the universe, Creator of numerous living beings *and their needs*." Why would we thank God for creating our *needs*? One might think that we would instead thank God for our independence—our *lack* of need. But we do the opposite. We express gratitude to God for creating our needs, as they exemplify what it means to be in a relationship.

L'Chaim

In 1926, the great Harvard philosopher Alfred Lord Whitehead gave the prestigious Lowell lecture. His subject: religion. He said, "Religion is what the individual does with his own solitariness."[10]

It is unknown if Professor Whitehead was thinking about Judaism when he said that. If he were, it might be the worst ever description of Judaism. Everyone who has uttered Judaism's most famous toast, "L'Chaim," is acknowledging the falsity of Professor Whitehead's words. Many think that "L'Chaim" means "to life"—but it doesn't. There is no way to say "to life" in Hebrew because there is no singular word for "life" in the language. L'Chaim means "to *lives*." There is no word for *a* life because, in the Jewish imagination, life cannot be lived or even conceived of in the singular. One can *exist* in the singular, but one can only *live* in a relationship.

And the Bible and the Jewish tradition that follows manifest this principle in some of our most important activities—where it is not at all obvious that togetherness is important.

What happens when someone tries to reason alone? Proverbs 18:1 is clear. "A man who isolates himself seeks his own desires; he rages against all wise judgment." The cultivation of wise judgment comes when people come together in respect to seek the truth, whereas one who insists on coming to conclusions in solitude remains ignorant.

What happens when someone tries to study alone? Proverbs 27:17 states, "As iron sharpens iron, so one person sharpens another." Rabbi Chanina Bar Chama in the Talmud took this to mean that just as one piece of iron sharpens the other, so also do two Torah scholars sharpen each other.[11]

This formed the core of the Jewish study practice—that of studying with a *chavruta* (a study partner). In the Talmud, Rabba bar bar Hana considers the words of Jeremiah: "Is not My word [the Torah] like fire?" Rabba bar bar Hana concluded that this means that "just as one stick cannot make a fire by itself, one person cannot learn Torah by himself." He concluded that "matters of Torah are not retained and understood properly by a lone scholar who studies by himself." His colleague Rabbi Yosei went even further, saying that those who "study by themselves grow foolish from their solitary Torah study."[12]

Just as one, unaided by the biblical tradition, might think it is possible and even advisable to reason or study alone, many people think that we can effectively pray alone. This is certainly possible. God seeks a deep and *constant* relationship with each of us. If one wants to pray before a meeting, a free throw, or going to sleep, he should do so. But the monumental prayers that constitute the legal category known as "Words of Holiness"—including the central Kaddish, Kedusha, and Barechu—can *only* be offered in a minyan (a group of ten or more). This practice reflects the conviction that we best express our relationship with God while in relationship with each other.[13]

This requirement of relationship as a core component of so many sacred activities is quite radical. Many other religions and faith communities celebrate solitude. The term "hermit" now describes people who are asocial. It derives from the profession of being a hermit—Christian clerics who live lives of devotion in solitude and silence. There are also equivalents of the hermetic life in Buddhism, Jainism, Hinduism, and Islam.

There is nothing like this in the Torah. To the contrary, the commandment in Leviticus, "You shall be holy," is given to "the *whole* congregation of Israel." We learn here that holiness is available to and incumbent upon everyone, and it can only be achieved within the entire congregation of Israel, full of people in relationship with each other.[14]

The Reality of Relationships

It is instructive that God's ultimate plea for a relationship comes in Leviticus (when God declares that he will dwell "in" us) and in Numbers (when God declares his need to be in relationship with us). Long before Leviticus, God knew about the fraught reality of relationships with and among people.

In Genesis 4, the first fraternal relationship ends in murder as Cain kills Abel. In Genesis 13, Abraham and his nephew Lot decide to separate when the relationship between them and their respective camps is destroyed by the wealth that Abraham created. In Genesis 21, Abraham banishes his son Ishmael. In Genesis 27, Jacob tricks his father, Isaac, into giving him the blessing intended for his twin brother, Esau. When Esau finds out, he is determined to kill Jacob. This does not happen only because Jacob flees into exile. In Genesis 37, Joseph's brothers—following a buildup of sibling jealousy that turns into "hatred"—throw him into a pit and debate only whether to kill him or sell him into slavery.

The story of Genesis shows that human relationships—including within families—can be expected to be fraught. As the story of family dysfunction that characterizes Genesis transitions to Exodus, we see that this has not changed. It is just shifted, with God now at the center of the relationship troubles.

In Exodus 15, the Jews had just been freed from Egyptian slavery by God and had sung songs of triumph and gratitude to him. Immediately after the song, they could not find water. The people, we learn, did not pray to God; instead, they "complained *against* God."

In Exodus 32, the people perceive that Moses is a day late in returning from Mount Sinai, where he is communing with God. They react by building a Golden Calf and then worshipping and seemingly having an orgy around it. God is so angry that he tells Moses he wants to destroy the Jewish people and start over again with Moses.

God knew that a relationship could easily bring discontent, disappointment, and even anger so intense that he would regret having entered into one at all. Yet God, with the conviction of one who reserves the designation "not good" for aloneness, unambiguously decides in favor of relationships—the deeper, the better.

The Fundamental Relationship

In Leviticus 21, the Torah lists the kinds of funerals that a Kohen (priest) may attend; these are exemptions from his normal prohibition against coming into contact with dead bodies. The Kohen, we learn, may attend the funeral of "the one closest to him," a parent, a sibling, and a child. The Talmud explains that "the one closest to him" refers to his wife. Why, then, would the Torah not just say "wife"? Probably to tell us that God wants us to regard our spouse as our closest relationship—to contemplate what that means, and to act accordingly.

This notion is reflected throughout Jewish teaching. Rabbi Elazar stated in the Talmud that "a man without a wife is not a complete person." Rabbi Elazar's point is amplified in another section of the Talmud where Rabbi Yosef says, "A man's wife is like his own body."[15] This kind of marriage—one of complete unity—was epitomized by the twentieth-century Israeli sage Rabbi Aryeh Levin, known as the "Tzaddik [righteous man] of Jerusalem." Rabbi Levin took his wife to the doctor for an infection of her foot and explained, "Our foot is hurting us."[16]

The Torah's philosophy about *what* to look for in a husband and a wife will be addressed in the next chapter (on courtship). But there are a few reasons why the Torah regards marriage as our most important relationship—and can be addressed now, in the context of what God wants in a relationship with each of us.

One is quite practical. The Talmud says of a man who "is twenty years old and has not married a woman . . . all his days are with sinful thoughts." By getting married and not having to think about sex all the time, a young man will be liberated to pursue professional and spiritual growth.[17]

A second reason hearkens back to Eve being created from Adam's side. The Talmud recounts the story of a Rabbi Yosi, who met Elijah the prophet. Rabbi Yosi asked Elijah, "In what manner does a woman help a man?" Elijah said that a man without a wife is just raw material. He needs a wife to turn him into a man, just as wheat needs someone to turn it into bread, and flax needs a person to turn it into clothing. Elijah continued, "Is his wife not found to be the one who lights up his eyes and stands him on his feet?"[18]

Why might a husband *need* a wife, and vice versa? The Torah provides a clue in the introduction of spousehood in Genesis 2 where Eve is described as "a help against" Adam. A spouse, the Torah teaches, should lovingly counsel, criticize, and guide his or her spouse. A spouse, in other words, should make one better at everything he or she does.

None of this is to say that marriage is magic and will simply solve problems and create opportunities while providing perpetual bliss. Every notable marriage in the Torah is full of significant challenges. Adam introduces us to the institution of marriage by talking *at* his wife and not *with* her. Eve, understandably, turns to the snake for companionship with catastrophic consequences for humankind forever. Noah is so disinterested in his wife that we never learn her name. He refuses God's instruction to re-create the world with her and instead gets drunk by himself. He ends up a dissolute old man, perhaps molested by his son.

Abraham and Sarah are the original Jewish couple and enjoy many decades of marriage. Yet, even they have communication problems at a pivotal moment in their lives—when God tells Abraham to sacrifice his son, Isaac. Abraham, without consulting Sarah, does as told until God calls off the operation. He subsequently lives apart from her until she dies.

Their son Isaac marries Rebecca and they enjoy the best marriage in the Torah. Still, Isaac and Rebecca seemingly fail to discuss even the most important questions with each other: how to raise their very different children, divide their inheritance, and assign the responsibilities of Jewish leadership and perpetuation. This communication failure culminates with their son Esau attempting to kill his brother Jacob, and with Jacob fleeing for his life into a decades-long exile.

Jacob's son Judah marries the "daughter of Shua." The fact that we don't know her name is, as with Noah, a bad sign. Sure enough, they name their children Er (childless), Onan (mourning), and Shelah (disappoint). The text makes a point to tell us that Judah is absent for the birth of their third son. Judah does not consult his wife when he makes a huge decision for the family and tells Onan to marry Tamar, the widow of Er. (This was the practice of levirate marriage—encouraged but not required.)

Judah's wife dies many years later. As a widower, he seeks the company of his friend Hirah. Judah sees a prostitute and makes a "detour" to solicit her services. He sleeps with her, not realizing that she is his daughter-in-law Tamar, who has impersonated a prostitute in order to deceive Judah into impregnating her. We can learn a lot from this remarkable story, including how even an imperfect marriage anchors a man. It is only after his wife dies that Judah goes astray in this most extreme manner.

Those marriages all come from Genesis—which stands to reason, as Genesis (unlike the other books) is fundamentally a family story. Moses is the great hero of the rest of the Torah. When his family joins him after the Exodus, he rushes to greet his father-in-law—not his wife, Zipporah. Moses remains distant and detached from Zipporah until they seemingly get divorced.

The Torah, as we learn in Deuteronomy, regards divorce as the necessary outcome for some marriages. In Deuteronomy 24, the Torah explicitly permits, and articulates a process for, divorce. The first-century sage Rabbi Akiva said that the altar in the Temple cries when a couple gets divorced—but, as with all of the other great commentators and authorities, he believed that divorce was sometimes the right outcome.

So, the Torah is anything but pollyannish about marriage. It simultaneously and enthusiastically states that marriage is the only solution to the existential problem of loneliness—and the indispensable structure through which individuals can improve and complete themselves.

The Science

The Beloved Volleyball

In the 2000 movie *Cast Away*, Chuck Noland (the character played by Tom Hanks) is stranded on an island. He is totally alone with only a few items from his plane, including a volleyball. Noland befriends the volleyball, whom he names Wilson, and almost ruins his own rescue in an attempt to save the volleyball.

Is it strange that a man, alone on an island, could develop a close relationship with a volleyball? Americans did not think so. The movie was a huge hit, and the Wilson company, which made the ball, sells 20,000 to 25,000 *Cast Away* balls a year. The original *Cast Away* ball, when put up for auction, sold for over $300,000 in 2021.[19]

Why did Americans gravitate to the story of a man who develops a deep relationship with a volleyball? Because they empathized with a man who, absent any human relationships, would create one of any kind—even with a ball. Moreover, Americans do something similar in normal circumstances. Between 2018 and 2022, mainstream publications such as the *New York Times* and *The Guardian* have covered the phenomenon of *adults* who go to sleep with, confide in, and get through their troubles with a stuffed animal. The title of *The Guardian* essay about the relationship of an adult and a stuffed animal was "I Love Him So Much I Could Cry."[20]

Why might people look to volleyballs and stuffed animals as beloved and needed companions? A 2014 study by the University of Virginia psychologist Timothy Wilson is illustrative. The study design was simple enough. They had their subjects sit alone in a room with nothing to do for six to fifteen minutes. Erin Westgate, then a graduate student working on the study, describes their hypothesis. "We thought it would be great. People are so busy that it would give them a chance to slow down, sit quietly, and daydream for a few minutes."

This vision of aloneness turned out not to be true. In one round of the experiment, participants were given a machine and told that they could choose to self-administer an electric shock if they so wished. Two-thirds of the men and a quarter of the women gave themselves an electric shock to alleviate the boredom. Later studies demonstrated that people are willing to alleviate their loneliness even through repulsive activities, like grinding bugs in a coffee grinder.[21]

Why would someone prefer to be electrically shocked than to be alone for up to fifteen minutes? Because, it seems from the study, loneliness is so painful and dangerous that people will do just about anything to alleviate it.

Loneliness

In 2020, Professor Siu Long Lee and colleagues at University College London published a study on the psychological effects of loneliness. They constructed a loneliness score composed of answers to these questions: How often do you feel you lack companionship? How often do you feel left out? How often do you feel isolated from others? The respondents answered with a 1 (hardly/never), 2 (some of the time), and 3 (often).

Professor Lee and colleagues found each one-point increase on the loneliness scale was linked with a 16 percent increase in average depressive symptom severity score. And this loneliness can be long-lasting. Loneliness can, the National Institute for Health Research determined, significantly raise one's risk of depression for up to twelve years.[22]

The negative impacts of loneliness are not only psychological. According to a study from the University of York, loneliness elevates the chance of a heart attack by 29 percent and a stroke by 32 percent.[23] The Centers for Disease Control in the United States cautions that loneliness raises the risk of dementia by 50 percent. A survey from Cigna Health showed that it has the same impact on mortality as smoking fifteen cigarettes a day. A variety of other studies show that loneliness leads to decreased physical activity, high blood pressure, gambling, binge eating, substance abuse, and diminished energy levels.[24]

The American public health authorities who have looked at loneliness have come to the same conclusion. Dr. Marty Makary, the Johns Hopkins surgeon and best-selling author of books on public health, declared, "Loneliness has become a public health crisis." Dr. Atul Gawande, the Boston surgeon who leads Global Health for USAID, says, "We have a massive deadly epidemic hidden in plain sight: loneliness."[25]

Dr. Vivek Murthy served as the surgeon general of the United States under President Obama and again under President Biden. In traveling the country and studying the data as America's doctor, he identified a systemic problem—what he, like Dr. Gawande, called the "epidemic of loneliness." Dr. Murthy concluded that this epidemic afflicts 40 percent of Americans. He describes meeting a wide variety of Americans, including factory workers, high school students, small business owners, and doctors. In 2017, he wrote:

> During my years caring for patients, the most common pathology I saw was not heart disease or diabetes; it was loneliness . . . I found that loneliness was often in the background of clinical illness,

contributing to disease and making it harder for patients to cope and heal.[26]

In the time since Dr. Murthy made his observation, research has made it clear that his observations reflected a deep scientific truth. Dr. Jeffrey Lam of the Brown University Medical School led a large research team that showed loneliness is associated with "altered structure and function in specific brain regions and networks." Loneliness, in other words, damages the brain—probably through a persistent stress and immune response. The effects of loneliness of the brain account for the cardiovascular problems that Dr. Murthy described as well as dementia and Parkinson's disease. And that's not all.

Dr. Ellen Lee of the University of California at San Diego says brain changes wrought by loneliness cause it to be "a persistent emotion that then shapes their behavior." The behaviors induced by loneliness include a lack of compassion, an inability to enjoy positive experiences, and what a 2024 *New York Times* analysis reports as "hypersensitivity to negative social words, like 'disliked' or 'rejected,' and to faces expressing negative emotions."[27]

Relationships, Relationships, Relationships

Perhaps the greatest psychological study of all time is the Grant Study at Harvard Medical School. The study, which has had four directors, started in 1938 with the intention of monitoring the lifetime happiness and wellness of 268 college sophomores from the classes of 1938 to 1944. Participants included *Washington Post* editor Ben Bradlee and President John F. Kennedy. In the 1970s, pursuant to a merger with another longitudinal study, 456 young men from inner-city Boston were added to the Grant Study.

The immediate past and current lead researchers of the study came to the same conclusion. A person's lifetime happiness and health is not primarily determined by one's cholesterol level at age fifty or any other metabolic factor. The primary determinant was identified by Harvard professor George Vaillant, who led the study from 1972 to 2004.

In 2017, Professor Vaillant stated, "When the study started, nobody cared about empathy or attachment." Relationships were not even considered as a factor in one's lifetime health or happiness. By the end, the researchers had determined the three ingredients for a long, happy, and healthy life. Professor Vaillant listed them: "Relationships, relationships, and relationships." And Professor Vaillant's successor as the study's leader, Robert Waldinger, noted that happiness-inducing relationships can be familial or communal, so long as they include a "commitment."[28]

A large and longitudinal dataset like the one generated by the Grant Study can answer many questions in addition to predictive factors for happiness. What, for instance, is most closely correlated with acquiring wealth? One candidate is body type. Professor Vaillant found that there was nothing financially predictive about whether a man was muscular, skinny, or plump. Another is economic background. Professor Vaillant found that there was no difference in the earnings of the Harvard men who came from rich families and those who came from working-class families. Another is intelligence. Professor Vaillant found that the Harvard men in the study with IQs between 110–115 earned as much money as those with IQs over 150.

What, then, might be a better predictor for wealth? He found that men who had good relationships with siblings earned an average of $51,000 *more* per year (in 2009 dollars) than those who had poor relationships with siblings or no siblings at all. He found that those who came from cohesive homes made $66,000 more than those from unstable homes. And men with warm mothers earned $87,000 more. The men with the warmest maternal relationships earned 2.43 times that of those with ordinary relationships.[29]

Why God Didn't Just Give Adam a Golfing Buddy

By modeling a variety of relationships, God demonstrates the high regard he has for a variety of relationships that people have as siblings, friends, parents, children, teachers, and pupils. Yet when it comes to alleviating loneliness, he gave Adam one particular type of relationship: *a wife*. Is the Torah correct that marriage is *indispensable* in alleviating loneliness?

For most of American history, the prevailing assumption has been that marriage is indispensable. The statistician Wendy Wang from the Institute for Family Studies analyzed census data and found that in 1970, 9 percent of Americans aged twenty-five to fifty had never been married. This data includes gay people who lived accordingly and could not get married—implying that almost all straight Americans between 25 and 50 in 1970 were married, divorced, or widowed. In 2018, 35 percent of Americans between those ages had never wed—and that is years after gay marriage was legalized in every state.[30]

The decline in marriage coheres with the emerging ideology of the day. A 2020 Pew report found that only 16 to 17 percent of Americans believe that being married is "essential" to living a "fulfilled" life.[31]

We now know, through social science, the consequences of being unmarried. For several decades, the statisticians Bernard Cohen and I-Sing Lee of the University of Pittsburgh have been valuing and analyzing thousands of risks. They have determined that "one of the greatest risks in our society is remaining unmarried." The risks they enumerate for unmarried men include suffering or dying from tuberculosis; stomach, intestinal, lung, and genital cancer; diabetes; stroke; heart disease; cirrhosis of the liver; motor vehicle accidents; other accidents; suicide; and homicide. This coheres with the data found by University of Chicago professors Linda Waite and Lee Lillard, which shows that 90 percent of married men at age forty-eight will live to sixty-five—compared with only 60 percent of single men at the same age. The data is similar for divorced and never married women—although widowed women fare better than widowed men.[32]

Why is marriage so important for mortality? In 2016, Professor Robert Shmerling of Harvard Health conducted a review of the medical literature around health and marriage. He showed that marriage brings longer life, fewer strokes and heart attacks, lower depression, earlier cancer detection, and better survival rates of major operations. A finding from Professor Waite can be added to this list: the abuse of alcohol and drugs drops significantly for men who marry. No wonder that Professor Waite reflected to the *New York Times*: "Marriage is good for everyone. But I'm battling a deeply entrenched, if dangerous and false, belief."[33]

The benefits of marriage do not just concern living, but living *well*. In 2023, Professor Sam Peltzman of the University of Chicago published his analyses of data from the General Social Survey from 1972 to 2022. He worked from a "happiness scale"—with people recording where they were between –100 (very sad) and 100 (very happy). Americans, he found, have been getting consistently less happy since 1970—with a significant decline starting in 2000. What accounts for the decline in happiness? He found a consistency in the data over each of the past fifty years—married people are always around 30 points happier than unmarried people. Professor Peltzman writes that "the recent decline in the married share of adults can explain (statistically) most of the recent decline in overall happiness." He goes so far as to say that the *only* people who are consistently happy over fifty years are married.[34]

"Married people," a 2023 analysis by Olga Khazan in *The Atlantic* concluded, "are happier. Period."[35]

Social scientists keep discovering reasons why married people are happier than their single counterparts. Single and divorced women are four to five times as likely to be victims of violence than are wives, and single men are four times as likely to be violent crime victims than are husbands. Married men earn 40 percent more money than their single counterparts, even after controlling for education and job history. Married men also have retirement accounts that are almost three times the size of their single counterparts. Moreover, married people of both genders have fewer mental health challenges, a lower suicide rate, and more and vastly better sex than do single people. They even, when elderly, feel less emotional and physical pain following an affliction.[36]

If the data on singlehood seems familiar to the data on loneliness, the Author of the Torah would not have been surprised. The Torah, from early Genesis, specified that marriage is the unique and indispensable bulwark against loneliness. But, as we have seen, behavior has not followed the data with marriage. As Americans are marrying less (and, as we'll see in the next chapter, later), a question emerges: What has taken the place of marriage?

Friendship

For the first two generations of American television, the ideological foundations of the most popular shows would have reflected some of the family values of even the most ancient societies. These portrayed people who were deeply committed in multigenerational relationships, laden with obligations and responsibilities. This was true of *I Love Lucy*, *Ozzie and Harriet*, *The Brady Bunch*, *Happy Days*, *All in the Family*, *The Cosby Show*, *The Fresh Prince of Bel-Air*, and many others. These families were sometimes idealistic, troubled, or even dysfunctional—much like those in the Torah—but they represented life as it had been lived in families for thousands of years.

But then the new millennia approached, and everything changed. There were three shows that, like important art often does, both reflected current culture practices and projected a vision of the good life. These shows, which also happen to be number 1, 2, and 3 on the *New York Post's* list of greatest NYC sitcoms, are *Seinfeld*, *Friends*, and *Sex and the City*.[37]

On September 21, 1995, the 111th episode of *Seinfeld* aired. It opens with George breaking up with his girlfriend because she beat him in chess. His recounting of the breakup leads to a deep discussion between George and Jerry:

> Jerry: What is this? What are we doing? What in God's name are we doing?
>
> George: What?
>
> Jerry: OUR LIVES!! What kind of lives are these? We're like children. We're not men.
>
> George: No, we're not. We're not men.
>
> Jerry: We come up with all these stupid reasons to break up with these women.
>
> George: I know. I know. That's what I do. That's what I do.
>
> Jerry: Are we going to be sitting here when we're sixty like two idiots?
>
> George: We should be having dinner with our sons when we're sixty.
>
> Jerry: We're pathetic . . . you know that?
>
> George: Yeah, like I don't know that I'm pathetic.
>
> Jerry: Why can't I be normal?
>
> George: Yes. Me too. I wanna be normal. Normal.
>
> Jerry: It would be nice to care about someone.

In the next scene, Jerry tells Kramer about his conversation with George. Kramer, intuiting that Jerry and George considered being married, has a ready answer:

> Kramer: They're prisons. Man-made prisons. You're doing time. You get up in the morning. She's there. You go to sleep at night. She's there. It's like you gotta ask permission to use the bathroom. Is it alright if I use the bathroom now?
>
> Jerry: Really?
>
> Kramer: Yeah, and you can forget about watching TV while you're eating.
>
> Jerry: I can?
>
> Kramer: Oh, yeah. You know why? Because it's dinner time. And you know what you do at dinner?
>
> Jerry: What?
>
> Kramer: You talk about your day. How was your day today? Did you have a good day today or a bad day today? Well, what kind of day was it? Well, I don't know. How about you? How was your day?
>
> Jerry: Boy.
>
> Kramer: It's sad, Jerry. It's a sad state of affairs.
>
> Jerry: I'm glad we had this talk.
>
> Kramer: Oh, you have no idea.[38]

Seinfeld was, as ever, capturing an emerging trend. As Maya Salam wrote of *Seinfeld* in the *New York Times* in 2023, a "refusenik sensibility is threaded through the entire series, and any attempt by the characters to sublimate themselves to social norms fizzled quickly and often in grand fashion."[39]

The "refusenik sensibility" was directed at marriage. Its paradigm—which was shared in *Friends* and *Sex and the City*—is that one can better achieve happiness and fulfillment with friendships instead of marriage and children. These shows were so popular and influential that they led to what a *Vox* analysis called "a legion of copycats" within a new genre of "conflict-less hangout comedy."[40]

The belief that thriving without attachment is possible, or even beneficial, did not come out of nowhere. A late-twentieth-century feminist slogan was, "A woman needs a man like a fish needs a bicycle." The libertarian alternative from Ayn Rand is "Freedom (n): To ask nothing. To expect nothing. To depend on nothing." The apolitical self-help literature agrees, as is evidenced with articles in popular magazines like: "11 Reasons Why You Need to Be More Independent" and "7 Signs You Don't Want a Life Partner, and Why That's OK."[41]

One might respond: Good for the new culture! The characters in *Friends*, *Seinfeld*, and *Sex and the City* might not have chosen the Torah's ultimate relationship and gotten married. Phoebe, Jerry, and Carrie did not have spouses, but they had independence and good friends. Can't friendship, which can be enjoyable and meaningful, provide the benefits of marriage while avoiding at least some of Kramer's concerns about attachment?

As ever, the data is instructive. In 1990, 3 percent of Americans reported to Gallup that they had no close friends. In 2021, that number had quadrupled. Another 37 percent of Americans in 2021 reported having one to three close friends. In 1990, a third of Americans reported having ten-plus close friends. In 2021, only 13 percent of respondents answered that way. The decline in marriage, we see, has not been accompanied by more close friendships—but by fewer. Americans are, according to the Survey Center on American Life, in a "friendship recession."[42]

This friendship recession and marriage decline has been accompanied by the diminution of another bulwark against loneliness: associational engagement. In 1995, the Harvard sociologist Robert Putnam published a seminal essay that he developed into a classic book in 2000—"Bowling Alone." He identified that bowling participation had increased while participation in bowling leagues had decreased. This was not an isolated phenomenon. He also found that engagement in religious institutions, veterans groups, civic associations, fraternal organizations, and volunteer activities had also decreased. This trend has continued and shows up in the data regarding friendship.

A 2021 American Community Survey report found that people with more friends are more likely to attend religious services, attend local events, invite guests to their home, and talk with someone they don't know well. The decline in the number of friendships and civic participation are highly correlated. We create friendships through associational participation, and participate in associational life with friends. The phenomenon of "bowling alone" that Professor Putnam identified in 1995 has become the "loneliness epidemic" that Surgeon General Murthy identified in 2017.[43]

While we are in a "friendship recession," many people *do* have close friendships. The value and delight in close friendships is celebrated in the Bible. As discussed, God wants to be a "friend" of man. David and Jonathan were described as having their souls "knitted" together. But what does social science tell us about these friendships—especially, as portrayed in the canonical shows, as a substitute for marriage?

The sociologist Gerald Mollenhorst of Utrecht University in the Netherlands analyzed survey data from a cohort of 1,007 people aged eighteen to sixty-five over a seven-year period. He found that individuals maintained the same number of friendships in each year. But only 30 percent of the friendships that existed in year one existed in year seven.[44]

Professor Mollenhorst's statistics will not be surprising to most people. A 2019 study by Evite showed that 82 percent of people reported that lasting friendships are hard to sustain. This is not because friends "break up." Instead, the diminution of friendships is typically gradual and undramatic. The American Survey Center found that most friendships are formed at work; these friendships are challenged when people change jobs, which they do frequently. Other friendships gradually diminish when the time previously spent with a friend is reallocated to one's children. For those reasons and others, the kind of friendship that builds relationship capital—which makes it easy and comfortable for people to share deeply with each other—is rare.[45]

Everyone can recognize the inherent instability and weakness in friendships in how we speak. If, say, one is asked, "How is your friend John? You and he were once inseparable"—a customary answer might be, "I really don't know. I haven't talked with him in a while." It is not a happy answer, but neither is it devastating—as we all acknowledge that friendships can fade and change, and are not made for durability.

If one asked: "How is your wife?" "How is your sister?" or "How is your daughter?" there are a lot of potential answers. Some are wonderful, some are tragic, and some are catastrophic. But perhaps the saddest is "I really don't know. I haven't talked with her in a while."

I Can Send Myself Flowers

As the leader of the Grant Study put it, the three words that illuminate the path toward human happiness are: "Relationships, relationships, and relationships." Given the slow decline of its most profound form (marriage) and the insufficiency of its main alternative (friendship), what are Americans doing? The teachings from American popular music are illustrative.

One of the great genres in modern popular music is the breakup song. The canonical breakup song is Neil Sedaka's "Breaking Up Is Hard to Do." The most beautiful breakup song is Frank Sinatra's rendition of "Softly as I Leave You." The most popular breakup song is now Miley Cyrus's "Flowers." It was released in early 2023 and debuted at the top of the *Billboard* Global 200 chart, reaching number one in dozens of countries and becoming the fastest song in Spotify history to reach one billion streams.

It is an entirely new kind of breakup song in that the replacement for Miley Cyrus's ex-boyfriend is . . . Miley. She realizes that she can buy herself flowers, talk to herself for hours, take herself dancing, and "love me better than you [the ex-boyfriend] can." In 1963, the Beatles famously sang, "I Want to Hold Your Hand." Miley Cyrus, two generations later, is delighted to have discovered that "I can hold my own hand."

If Miley Cyrus's dating herself goes well and she wants to take it to the next level, she has an option: sologamy (marriage to oneself). This relationship type made its popular debut in the 2003 episode of *Sex and the City* when Carrie decided to marry herself. She even registered at Manolo Blahnik. Other considerations of sologamy appeared in *Glee*, *The Exes*, *Cow and Chicken*, *Doctors*, and *Zoolander 2*.

Sologamy may have been new and avant-garde in the early 2000s, but it is mainstream now. In 2017, *Vogue* ran an article by Patricia Garcia, a near-forty-year-old woman. Ms. Garcia married herself, explaining, "I felt marrying myself is something fun, deep, and meaningful that I can do to recognize my arrival to adulthood." The Brazilian supermodel Adriana Lima also married herself in 2017, in a ceremony in Monaco. In 2020, *Essence* ran a feature of sologamy—calling it a "growing trend." In 2021, *Brides* magazine ran a guide to having a sologamous ceremony. In 2022, *Insider* ran a profile on sologamy featuring a woman who burst into tears upon receiving an engagement ring from herself. In 2023, CNN ran a major feature on women from their thirties to seventies who have married themselves.[46]

Sologamy is not the only way to be unconventionally attached. There is also "consensual non-monogamy." According to a 2021 study led by Professor Amy Moors of Chapman University, 4 to 5 percent of Americans in a romantic relationship do so as part of a "consensual non-monogamous relationship"—with 12 percent of Americans identifying consensual non-monogamy as the ideal type of relationship.[47]

Those who want to engage in a consensual non-monogamous relationship have a variety of options. There are throuples, in which three people are romantically committed to each other. There are quads, where four people are committed to each other. And there are polycules, which can incorporate dozens of people. A 2024 *New York Times* analysis of polycules reports, "It's not clear when the word was coined, but it seems to have started catching on around 15 years ago to suggest an intricate structure formed of people with overlapping deep attachments: romantic, sexual, sensual, platonic."[48]

The popularity—and even availability—of these alternative relationships is certainly an artifact of online living. In the pre-internet era, it is unlikely that most people would have ever heard of sologamy, throuples, quads, and polycules—even if they had existed. If someone had heard of, say, a throuple, it would have been difficult to easily find two other people who also wanted to enter one . . . and with you.

Now, the tools to identify, organize, and socialize an idea are readily available. Consequently, we can expect sologamy, throuples, quads, polycules—and other such previously inconceivable alternatives to marriage—to continue to grow. The one thing that is difficult to imagine is how adding a third, fourth, or twentieth person to a romantic relationship will make it easier, happier, or more durable. Perhaps the data will be in soon.

Reflection

A student of the Torah and social science reflecting on relationships might say, "Okay, relationships are important for human happiness and fulfillment." But isn't twenty-first-century technology driving us in that direction? The average Facebook user has 295 Facebook friends. The average Facebook friend has 359 Facebook friends. And the average Facebook user is interacting with his friends for twenty hours a month—with many doing so much more frequently. And that's just Facebook. So, one might conclude, we *are* investing in relationships![49]

The correct way to assess this is to ask a much more fundamental question: What is a relationship?—a *real* relationship that will alleviate the existential loneliness that led God, upon observing Adam, to say, "It is not good for man to be alone." The answer goes back to Numbers 27, where God and man declare their need for each other—a moment so important that it is reinforced in our daily prayers. A genuine relationship, the Torah is clear, is based on need.

The popular literature on relationships also incorporates a philosophy of need. It is expressed in the aforementioned statements from feminists and libertarians celebrating independence. Independence makes the claim: "I don't need anyone, and no one needs me." If independence suddenly sounds unappealing, so does its seeming opposite: dependence. The claim of dependence is: "I need others, but no one needs me." That, too, is unappealing. But there is an alternative to dependence and independence. It is *interdependence*—a state where we both need and are needed, in all kinds of ways by all kinds of people.

What kinds of relationships can be interdependent? An interdependent relationship cannot be about any variant of "conflict-free hanging out." One could enjoy his golf buddies, fantasy sports league participants, or Tinder dates, but any of those could be replaced or substituted without a problem. A relationship that enables its participants to escape the existential problem of aloneness, and need each other, is best formed when it is about something greater than the pleasure of just being together.

One who joins an EMS force will build relationships in the context of saving the lives of their neighbors. One who starts a company will build relationships around bringing something new, important, and valuable into the world. One who volunteers at a suicide hotline, an alcohol rehabilitation center, or a homeless shelter will build relationships in the context of helping the most vulnerable. One who becomes a fundraising leader or volunteer coordinator at her church or synagogue will build relationships in the context of supporting the sacred work of the institution. In each of these endeavors, the participants need each other in order to accomplish their missions.

The ultimate relationship—the one that creates, among other things, the strongest needs—is marriage. Yet, a prevailing modern view is that a couple can get married and the spouses can maintain their independence. We can see this view in the nomenclature of our largest state. California does not recognize a first lady/gentleman or even spouse, but instead a "First Partner."[50] The notion of a "partner" is one where both sides come together for some purposes but maintain their independence. It is the opposite of the Torah vision of a spouse as one who completes the other, exemplified in the Talmudic vision of a wife and husband as one body.

How did we arrive at the point where California has a "First Partner," people sing about buying themselves flowers, and some marry themselves?

One culprit: the Phil Dunphy Problem. Phil Dunphy, a character on Modern Family, famously told his television daughter: "Trust me, I had plenty of fun in my time. Then, I met your mom."[51] The sentiment that dating is fun and marriage is drudgery is a consistent theme in popular culture—and is often expressed in personal discussions and communications. The journalist Karol Markowicz reports, "Married friends don't sit around over margaritas praising their spouses. Few talk about how amazing and fulfilling it is to have children. Instead, people highlight the struggles of marriage and family so as not to make anyone else feel bad about how incredible it actually is. We hear about only the negative aspects of family and only the absolutely blissful part of singlehood."[52]

The Torah, by showing challenges in even the best marriages and among its greatest heroes, fully acknowledges that the quintessential human relationship can be very difficult. But why should the fact that marriage can be difficult lead us to avoid it? Every success, joy, triumph, and accomplishment comes with significant difficulties . . . and yet we, quite properly, seek them out. Moreover, every choice is accompanied by an assessment of its alternatives. And the data is clear that the alternatives to marriage guarantee many more risks and predict much less happiness than marriage, which uniquely provides the opportunity for each of us to be completed.

Still, one question remains. How can one select the right spouse to optimize the chance that marriage will be the completing experience the Torah suggests that it can be? The Torah and social science have a lot to say about that, which is the subject of the next chapter.

23

The Courtship of Isaac and Rebecca and Its Discontents

The Torah and Science of Love and Marriage

It is Genesis 23 and the matriarch Sarah has just died. Immediately after the mourning process concludes, Abraham assumes a paternal responsibility to find a wife for his son Isaac. He gives the assignment to his trusted servant Eliezer, who heads off to complete the task. He has one criterion for Isaac. The woman must be, Abraham instructs, "from the land of my birth." That land is Haran.

Why did Abraham specifically want a woman from Haran? We know only two things about it. The first is that Abraham's journey begins there in Genesis 12, with God commanding him to leave it. However, it had at least one redeeming quality. When Abraham and Sarah leave, they do so with "the souls they made in Haran." Haran, whatever its other faults were, must have had people who were open to God and to Abraham's divinely inspired leadership.

Eliezer stops by a well after a day's journey. A beautiful young woman gives water to him and his camels. Her generosity toward this stranger and his animals astonishes him. The young woman is Rebecca. All he knows is that she is "very fair to look upon," generous, and from Haran. Those three qualities are enough for him to decide that she is the right woman for Isaac. He conveys his intentions to Rebecca and her family.

Eliezer is ready to make his case for Isaac to Rebecca and her family. He tells them that Isaac is the dutiful son of a wealthy family that loves God.

Those two qualities—providership and piety—are enough for Rebecca and her family to agree that she should marry Isaac.

Eliezer brings Rebecca to meet the man she has agreed to marry. True to Eliezer's description, Rebecca's first sighting of her husband-to-be is while he is praying in a field. Isaac, we read in Genesis 24:67, "married Rebecca. So she became his wife, and he loved her; and Isaac was comforted after his mother's death."

That one short verse, along with the story of how they met, constitutes the Torah's guidance as to how to choose a spouse.

In the story of how they met, Rebecca and Isaac had established a fundamental compatibility. They had done so on the basis of identifying *just two or three* qualities about each other. These qualities are not idiosyncratic or random. They are directly related to those that will make for a suitable spouse.

The three qualities identified by the man (Isaac, through Eliezer) are being from a community open to God, being attractive, and acting generously. The two qualities identified by the woman (Rebecca) are providership and piety. With these criteria met for each, they are ready for the next steps, which are clearly articulated in Genesis 24:67. These steps are—crucially, *in order*: Get married. Become a spouse. Experience love.

The distinction between getting married and becoming a spouse is curious. One might assume that getting married and becoming husband and wife are the same thing, and thus happen simultaneously. But the Torah lists them separately, suggesting that they happen consecutively. Consequently, the biblical author apparently thinks that one can be married and not be a spouse.

What, we are led to ask, does it mean to be a spouse as distinct from just being married? It must be doing spouse-like things. But this just begs another question. What are spouse-like things? What, in other words, does it *mean* to be a spouse?

The Torah does not make it hard to figure out. One is modeled by Rebecca as soon as we meet her: a generous spirit that manifests in giving to others. Another is introduced by the way that God alleviates Adam's existential loneliness. God creates, out of Adam's "side," a wife—Eve. However, Eve is not described as a "wife" but as a "help against" Adam. In Numbers 16, the Torah illustrates just what it means for a wife to be "a help against" her husband. Numbers 16 begins with Korach planning what will be the greatest rebellion in the desert. Korach has no policies he wants to enact or other idealistic reasons to rebel; his is purely a populist revolt for power. He is joined by Datan, Abiram, and On.

Datan and Abiram stay with the rebellion and are prominent figures in its execution and eventual failure. On, however, disappears from the story immediately after his initial mention in Numbers 16:1. The rabbis of the Talmud provide a reason that fits within the Torah tradition: On's wife, realizing the danger and futility of her husband's involvement with Korach and his conspirators, takes action to prevent him from participating. According to the Talmud, On's wife gets him drunk so that he falls asleep in the tent. She then sits outside the tent with her hair uncovered, a sign of immodesty in that culture. Korach's followers, being respectful of female modesty, refuse to approach or enter the tent to look for On. As a result, On is spared from the consequences of the rebellion.[1]

In God's definition of a wife in Genesis and its illustration in Numbers, we learn a fundamental role of a spouse. It is to make the other spouse *better*—a responsibility that includes offering guidance, advice, criticism, and sometimes taking bold action.

As important—indeed, defining—as "being a help against" yourself is, it is not the only activity the Torah expects of a spouse. The other crucial component of being a spouse is revealed by what happens when a husband and wife are genuinely spouses. This is the notion of being in love.

This just raises another question—one magnificently captured by the great American songwriter Cole Porter: "What is this thing called love?"

We can arrive at the Torah's answer through the principle of biblical interpretation known as "the law of first mention." This holds that the first mention of anything in the Bible reveals its essence and meaning. The first mention of love is in Genesis 21, and it is not in the context of romantic love. It is of God telling Abraham to sacrifice his son Isaac. Consequently, the law of first mention posits that the essence of love is sacrifice.

The expectation of sacrifice is revealed in the Hebrew word for love—which is *ahava*. The root of *ahava* is *hav*—which means "give." The twentieth-century sage Rav Eliyahu Dessler explained the Jewish idea embodied in this word. He wrote that people often mistakenly believe that we give to those we love. The correct view, he said, is that we love those to whom we give.[2]

In this vein, Rabbi David Wolpe characterizes love not as a feeling or emotion—but an "enacted emotion" that derives from acts of giving and sacrifice. Rabbi Wolpe says, "When we ask whether someone is in love, we often ask, 'What do you feel?' We might better ask, 'What would you give?'"[3]

The Torah articulates a simple formula for courtship and marriage. Identify two or three genuinely important characteristics in a spouse. When you find someone who possesses these traits, get married. Then, become a spouse by generously giving and offering tender counsel that will help the other person grow continually. True love will emerge and deepen, leading to a relationship where the spouses become interdependent, each essential to the other, like one half of a body to the other. Is the Torah correct?

The Science

Falling in Love

A consideration of the contemporary American courtship philosophy and practice offers a fine way to assess the Torah's proposition, because it offers such a pure contrast. This consideration can begin with a common American expression in which the contrast is especially bright—that of "falling in love." The expression "fall in love" may be the most memorable idea in American popular song, and consequently, the American romantic imagination. In 1928, Cole Porter's song "Let's Do It, Let's Fall in Love," became the signature song of his first Broadway success, *Paris*. In 1931, Harold Arlen released a song, "Let's Fall in Love," which was so enduring that it became a hit for Frank Sinatra in 1961 and Art Garfunkel in 2007. In 1956, Nat King Cole released what became his signature song, "When I Fall in Love." The hit song from the 1961 Elvis Presley movie *Blue Hawaii* is "Can't Help Falling in Love with You."

This expression would have made no sense to the Author of the Torah. He would have said: People might fall to the ground, or for an April Fool's Day joke. But they don't "fall in love." They *cultivate* love through repeated acts of giving and sacrifice. What could you possibly mean, *fall* in love?

The difference in the two philosophies stems from a fundamental disagreement about the nature of love and marriage. The songwriters, who define, reflect, and amplify cultural perceptions, believe that love is fundamentally a feeling over which the parties have no control—hence the use of the word *falling*. The Author of the Torah believed that love is fundamentally an enacted emotion that is the result of iterative acts of giving and sacrifice. Even more fundamentally, the contemporary understanding is that love *precedes* commitment. The Torah's understanding is that love *follows* commitment.

There is an irony to this celebration of falling in love. Plenty of young people "fall in love," but do not plan on getting married anytime soon. Therefore, they must realize that this kind of "love" is too unstable to warrant a commitment. How, then, does one bridge the gap between this kind of love and the commitment of marriage?

The contemporary answer to that question reveals another fundamental difference in the courtship philosophies of the Torah and contemporary American society. And this difference is captured in a conversation between President Biden and a young woman he met in California.

President Biden's Advice

In October 2022, President Biden conducted an event on inflation and pharmaceutical costs at Irvine Valley College in California. He approached a young woman and offered unsolicited advice on a different topic. "Now a very important thing I told my daughters and granddaughters—no serious guys until you're 30."[4]

President Biden's advice expresses a philosophy of courtship. Young people should date a lot, and not think about marriage. Instead, young men and women should spend their twenties dating casually before turning thirty, and then get "serious." He did not say *what* it means to date casually, *why* young women should wait until thirty before getting "serious," or *how* spending ten to fifteen years dating casually will help one select or become a good spouse. President Biden's advice, offered spontaneously, reflects a commonly shared assumption in contemporary culture that is validated by the data. In 2018, fewer than 30 percent of Americans under thirty-five were married.[5]

Why might President Biden, clearly speaking from the mainstream of dating philosophy and practice, offer this advice? There are two prominent ideas in discussions of contemporary dating that explain it.

The first: You should not get serious, let alone commit, until you first know yourself. One can and should, according to this theory, spend her twenties getting to know herself, after which she will be prepared to get serious.

The second prominent idea is compatibility. When young people start to get serious, they look for *compatibility*, which consists of vastly more qualities than Rebecca and Isaac needed. The contemporary literature on the characteristics of compatibility that young people should seek before committing include: family, attraction, musical tastes, vacation preferences, sense of humor, cognitive and emotional intelligence, openness to experience, team playing, libido, extroversion, emotional intensity, career support, independence, confidence, response to feedback, adventurousness, charm, grooming, and shared interests.

How long does it take someone to determine whether their girlfriend or boyfriend is sufficiently compatible for marriage? A 2018 study from eHarmony found that the process of first date to engagement takes an average of 2.8 years—with a wedding following between twelve and eighteen months later. And that number is increasing. The millennial cohort in the eHarmony data date and are engaged for an average of 6.5 years before getting married.[6]

This data presents clear challenges from physical science—particularly for the young woman whom President Biden advised to date casually until age thirty. Data from the Stanford University School of Medicine demonstrates that women who have children in their thirties are at significantly higher risk for miscarriage, chromosomal problems, birth defects, high blood pressure, and gestational diabetes. These problems can be mitigated by egg freezing, but that procedure is physically burdensome and costs an average of $30,000 to $40,000 (inclusive of treatment and storage).[7]

Young men often think that they are exempt from the biological realities that women face as potential parents, but the evidence suggests otherwise. Normal male fertility never hits zero, but it declines significantly as men age. For instance, men under thirty-five are twice as likely to have a successful artificial insemination experience (after six cycles) than men over thirty-five, which is explained by an up to 23 percent decline in male fertility that starts at age thirty-nine.[8]

The risks and challenges of older fathers are not limited to fertility. A 2019 study from Rutgers Medical School professor Nancy Phillips concludes that children born to older fathers are at a higher risk of premature birth, late stillbirth, low Apgar scores (a health screen performed immediately after birth that measures heart rate, respiration, and muscle tone), low birth weight, higher incidence of newborn seizures, and birth defects such as congenital heart disease and cleft palate. The problems don't end at birth. Professor Phillips also found that children of older fathers have an increased likelihood of childhood cancers, psychiatric and cognitive disorders, and autism.[9]

Still, one might conclude that these challenges are a necessary price for enjoying a vibrant youth and securing a stable, happy adulthood with the right spouse. In this light, President Biden's recommended approach to dating may have several advantages: It can be enjoyable, offering the chance to connect with many different people; purposeful, as it aims to find a life partner; revealing, as it encourages self-discovery; instructive, helping one to understand others better; and prudent, allowing one to avoid poor decisions with lasting negative consequences.

Each of these aspects can be examined within the context of three alternatives to the Biblical model: casual dating, long-term serious relationships, and cohabitation.

Casual Dating: "The Purest Thing There Is"

The founding philosopher of the modern dating culture is Erica Jong. Her 1973 book, *Fear of Flying*, sold twenty million copies and served as an anthem to the exhilaration promised by the new possibilities of long and often casual dating. She was particularly enthusiastic about one prominent aspect of this process: casual sex. Ms. Jong celebrated what she called the "zipless fuck"—defined as "when you came together, zippers fell away like rose petals, underwear blew off in one breath like dandelion fluff. For the true ultimate zipless A-1 fuck, it was necessary that you never got to know the man very well."

She continued: "The zipless fuck is absolutely pure. It is free of ulterior motives. There is no power game. The man is not 'taking' and the woman is not 'giving' . . . No one is trying to prove anything or get anything out of anyone. The zipless fuck is the purest thing there is."[10]

Two generations into the Sexual Revolution, we can ask: Was she right?

Sex Without Commitment

In 2019, Kate Julian analyzed the state of sex among young and single people for *The Atlantic*. She wrote, "These should be the boom times for sex." Young people are dating for long periods of time without kids to slow them down. Outside of a few subcultures, there is no stigma associated with premarital sex. And the internet and dating apps have made it very easy to identify and connect with potential sexual partners. We live in an era optimized for the joy, anticipation, and excitement that Erica Jong dreamed of.

Yet, the late relationship anthropologist Helen Fisher, who directed the annual Singles in America survey for Match, said in 2018: "The whole Match company is rather staggered at how little sex Americans are having—including the Millennials."

Kate Julian, acknowledging Helen Fisher's observation along with the other data on the subject, concluded that we are in a "sexual recession." The number of young Americans who engaged in casual sex declined by 36 percent from 2007 to 2017, and the rate of young Americans who reported having no sex in the previous year doubled in roughly the same period. Moreover, the General Social Survey from 2010 to 2016 shows that married people in every age group have more sex than unmarried people in the same age group.[11]

Why would there have been such a decline in non-marital sex? One answer: Young men have found substitutes. One is video games. A British study from 2009 found that a third of men regularly prefer video games to sex, with 72 percent preferring a newly released video game to sex. This phenomenon was confirmed in a 2021 study by Professor Lei Lei of Rutgers that similarly found the rising popularity of video games is significantly responsible for the decline in casual sex.[12]

Video games are not the only popular substitute for sex. The University of Montreal researcher Simon Louis Lejeunesse found that the average single man watches two hours of pornography a week—in three forty-minute episodes. The presumed conclusion of these forty-minute episodes, of course, reduces a young man's desire for real-life sex. But the impact of pornography on sexual desire is not only physiological. There are at least two others.

One was identified by the psychologist Marty Klein. He explained in *Psychology Today*, "While previous generations of young people felt that much of sexuality was mysterious, today's young adults understandably but erroneously feel they've seen it all via porn, and so they're simply less curious and less motivated to investigate it."[13]

Another was articulated by the psychologist Dr. Robert Weiss. Dr. Weiss, having reviewed the studies on the subject, concludes: "Basically, research tells us that the more porn one uses, the more likely sexual dysfunction is." He explains that men who experience the variety and intensity of experiences offered by pornography develop a hormonal baseline that no actual person can match. He continues: "Even worse from a relationship standpoint, the constant fantasy/satisfaction cycle that occurs with heavy porn use leads to an emotional and psychological disconnection with even the most loving and valued of partners."[14]

Aside from video games and pornography, young men in the contemporary dating economy have another challenge. They report that women are "hard to please."[15]

Is it true that women are hard to please? When it comes to sex outside of a committed relationship, the data is in. A study by Zava—a company that sells sexual enhancement medication—determined that 81 percent of American and 84 percent of European women are dissatisfied with their one-night stands. It is not only women who find casual sex dissatisfying. The Zava survey also showed that almost two-thirds of men are similarly dissatisfied.[16]

This data, particularly concerning women, has been confirmed by seemingly every other quantitative and qualitative analysis. One of those who agreed is an older Erica Jong. In 2011, she told the *Huffington Post*:

> I mean we always wish it [the purity of the "zipless fuck"] would happen. We never completely give up the fantasy but I think it's rarer and rarer and when I look back on my life for the most part the best sex of my life has always been with people that I was with for many years and had a lot in common with . . . When I look back at the one night stands and zipless fucks, they were terrible.[17]

Consent

Another challenge that emerged, seemingly surprisingly, with contemporary dating practices can be encapsulated in one word: consent. Indeed, the aligned term "date rape" (which describes sex among acquaintances in the absence of consent) was first used in the mid-1970s, and became gradually more prevalent in the 1980s as casual dating practices developed. It did not become a widely discussed phenomenon until 1991, when William Kennedy Smith was indicted (and ultimately acquitted) of rape.

Soon thereafter, the issue of consent was widespread in the culture, especially including the question of what constituted it. Consent became such a widespread issue that there are now countless books, and even more articles, essays, and discussions, on the subject. There are even software products devoted to affirming and recording it. By the 1990s, most colleges implemented policies governing consent—including guidance that "grinding on the dance floor is not consent for further sexual activity."[18]

In 1993, *Saturday Night Live* ran a skit with Shannen Doherty, Phil Hartman, and Chris Farley parodying a college's consent rules—for instance, by having a young man ask the woman for permission to "praise you for your halter top." This is followed by a request for a kiss and then a request to "elevate the level of sexual intimacy by feeling your buttocks." The message was clear: Sexual relationships outside of a committed relationship are so fraught and complicated that they need rules and practices that are laughably bizarre.[19]

Within a decade, the complicated nature of uncommitted sexual relationships was no longer just the stuff of clumsy rules and late-night television parody. In 2003, the Supreme Court of California determined in the case *People v. John Z* that a woman can withdraw consent in the middle of sex. If her request is not immediately granted, the man is guilty of forcible rape. Many other states have followed.[20]

The decision drew substantial commentary, reflecting a wide variety of views. In 2014, *New York Post* humorist Frank Fleming wrote on X (formerly Twitter), "Conservatives should be happy about California; they're just one step away from requiring a marriage license to have sex."[21] Others have noted that it is ironic that feminists are taking positions that can be considered "neo-Victorian" or "neo-Puritan." Indeed, the psychologist Pamela Peresky reports that young men are eschewing sex because they are concerned about being falsely accused of sexual assault. Dr. Peresky's assessment is supported by data from the Kaiser Foundation, which reported that only 17 percent of college-aged men believe that the prevailing "Yes means yes" standard is "very realistic." The others are, as Dr. Peresky suggests, afraid of being later held to a standard they do not regard as very realistic.[22]

All the ambiguities aside, there is no doubt that consent is a very serious issue. The estimates of the prevalence of sexual assault on campus extend from 13 to 27 percent of women. This broad range is explained by the fact that almost half of sexual assault victims among college women do not report them, and that there can be ambiguity over what constitutes consent and counts as sexual assault. Wherever the number is in that range, there is one thing for sure: The sexual assault prevalence is hideously high—so much so that it makes one wonder why parents proudly spend a fortune to send their daughters to a place that promises a significant chance of her being assaulted.[23]

The question of consent, as currently discussed, is not referenced in the Torah or the Jewish teachings based on it. This is not because the Author of the Torah was unaware of the evils of sexual coercion; indeed, one of the foundational stories in the Torah concerns the rape of Dinah (the daughter of Jacob and Leah). It is because consent is generally not an issue in committed relationships—particularly marriage. But it has emerged as a very important source of anxiety and other negativity—including a rape epidemic—in the culture of casual dating and sex.

Long-Dating: Lessons from Cyberball

The aforementioned dynamics generally apply to non-serious dating—of which casual sex is a frequent component. How about long and serious dating? With the exception of the lucky few who have what George Gershwin called "beginner's luck" ("I've got beginner's luck / The first time that I'm in love / I'm in love with you"), people in the dating economy invest themselves in emotionally meaningful relationships, only to have their hearts broken. And this happens, in a typical modern dating career, many times.

How, then, should we think about the psychological costs imposed by this constant cycle of exhilaration, emotional connection, and rejection? Until recently, we didn't. Professor Mark Leary of Duke University said in a 2012 study of rejection: "It's like the whole field missed this centrally important part of human life."[24] That has changed, and the results are startling.

In August 2022, the *New York Times* published a feature called "'A Decade of Fruitless Searching': The Toll of Dating App Burnout—Ten Years After the Launch of Tinder, Some Long-Term Online Daters Say Endless Swiping Has Been Bad for Their Mental Health."

The article quotes the author and podcaster Shani Silver, who describes her experience of "endless swiping."

> When you are consistently disappointed by a space that was sold to you as a path to love over and over and over again—for many of us, for years at a time—you never really stop to ask yourself: "What is this doing to my mental health? What is this doing to my well-being?" . . . Imagine anticipating receiving something good for *years*. Existing in that state of "any day now" for an extremely extended period of time is incredibly unhealthy.[25]

Professor Kipling Williams of Purdue University would understand. In the early 2000s, Professor Williams invented the game of Cyberball. In the game, three people play Frisbee in a park. Then, two of the people start to exclude the third.

At the end of the experiment/game, Professor Williams performed a functional MRI on all three players. The excluded players routinely showed significantly higher levels of activity in the dorsal anterior cingulate and the anterior insula of the brain. These are the parts of the brain that are activated in response to physical pain.

A 2010 study led by Professor Ethan Kross of the University of Michigan found that these regions of the brain are similarly activated when people are shown photographs of a recent and significant ex-boyfriend or ex-girlfriend who had broken up with them. Another study reported by Dr. Sophie Mort showed that people whose dating profiles are rejected generate natural opioids, which are the body's *painkillers*. And that is just from having a profile passed over by a stranger—not being dumped by someone with whom one is emotionally invested and may even love. No wonder modern dating culture—where rejection is a feature and not a bug—generates so much depression, anxiety, and sadness.[26]

The Ultimatum

The literal pain of breakups may seem bad enough, but there is another common phenomenon within modern dating that is just as agonizing. This is staying together in a relationship that involves the ultimatum. The ultimatum, usually delivered by the woman, is: *We either get married or break up.*

Women in dating relationships are often forced to play a game that resembles high-stakes poker. The man, having dated the woman for months or even years, tells the woman that he needs more time to determine whether they are right for each other. The man, by the standards of modern dating culture, is not doing anything wrong. Indeed, he is supposedly being prudent in looking for dozens or hundreds of characteristics over a long period of time before committing.

The woman, mindful that her fertility (and thus, desirability in the dating economy) is diminishing as she gets older, has a choice. She can endure in silence. This might work for a short period of time, but silence in a relationship about a fundamental issue is unsustainable. If she chooses silence, she might blow up over something unrelated—leading the man to conclude that she is an irritable and irrational woman with no sense of proportion.

The alternative is giving him an ultimatum. An analysis of ultimatums by PsychCentral cites experts as saying that they are the equivalent of forcing someone to make a decision at "gunpoint," or else a manifestation of desperation.[27]

This quintessentially unromantic gesture will be met in one of three ways. He proposes, out of something resembling distress. He decides to keep his ultimate intentions ambiguous, and she reveals both that she is desperate and that her ultimatum was a bluff. Or he simply rejects the ultimatum, and they break up.

As any gambler, even an occasional one, knows, high-stakes betting is stressful. For poker players, this stress stems from the fear of losing money. Unsettling as it is, it rarely becomes life-altering. In contrast, women facing an ultimatum are forced to wager much higher stakes—their futures as potential mothers and wives. Unlike poker players, they did not choose to enter this game; they find themselves in it due to the culture that dismisses the biblical model of courtship. Regardless of the outcome, they must endure the significant and well-documented psychological and physical effects of negative stress.

One of the promises of modern dating culture was that it would provide a woman with freedom (even "liberation") to do whatever she wants romantically, sexually, and emotionally. One woman who decided to opt out of this culture and remain a virgin until marriage is Olympic hurdler and bobsledder Lolo Jones. She says that being a virgin in modern dating culture is "harder than training for the Olympics." Why?

Primarily, this beautiful, accomplished, and principled woman says, "I keep getting my heart broken."[28] This is the logic of modern dating culture.

With most women in the dating economy willing to have premarital sex, the young men will gravitate to them. The woman who wants to wait until marriage (or at least substantial commitment) will find that doing so excludes all or most of her potential suitors.

Cohabitation

Even after enduring serial rejection and finding a satisfying someone, marriage is far from inevitable. There is another highly popular option in today's society: cohabitation.

Until the sexual revolution began in the late 1960s, it was socially discouraged and hence rare for couples to live together and then marry. This is no longer the case. According to a 2019 Pew study, 69 percent of Americans say that cohabitation is acceptable *even* if a couple does not intend to marry. An additional 16 percent say that it is acceptable if the couple intends to get married.

Americans are acting accordingly. In the 1970s, only 0.2 percent of Americans lived in cohabiting relationships. This arrangement was forty times as popular in 2022—and especially among those between twenty-five and thirty-four (where 17 percent of individuals were cohabitating). There are now significantly more Americans under the age of forty-four who have cohabited than have married. Moreover, cohabitation is often more than a temporary arrangement for couples to save on rent in the months leading up to their wedding. Professor Arielle Kuperberg of the University of North Carolina at Greensboro found that 70 percent of first marriages in the 2011–2015 period started with a period of cohabitation that lasted an average of thirty-two months. As an analysis in *Psychology Today* points out, "What once was an extraordinarily rare living arrangement for a dating couple is now commonplace."[29]

Young couples cohabit for one of two reasons: as a substitute for marriage or a test for whether they should get married. The findings are clear for both situations.

First: cohabitation as a substitute. This idea began in the Sexual Revolution, with couples saying that they "don't need a piece of paper" to ratify their union. It was always an odd statement, as the same people who say this value other "pieces of paper"—from diplomas to awards. A 2019 study found that 85 percent of Californians with a college or graduate degree endorse "family diversity"—which is far higher than among those with a high school or some college education. Yet, 68 percent of these educated Californians said that it was also "personally important" to them that their children marry—and were the group most likely to have children after getting married.[30]

The data on children is important for a discussion on cohabitation as a substitute for marriage. One might respond that it is acceptable for a couple to cohabit—with widows and widowers in mind. Still, children have long been considered to be a primary purpose of marriage. This has changed. A 2019 Pew Report found that 59 percent of Americans believe that "couples who are living together but not married can raise children just as well as married couples." This is especially true among Democrats—where 73 percent agree with that statement.[31]

Is cohabitation an acceptable substitute for marriage? Do children raised in cohabitation settings fare as well as children with married parents? There is a lot of data to go by. Married individuals are 33 percent more likely than cohabiting individuals to report that they are "very satisfied" with their relationship—and 41 percent more likely to report that their mate is the person they "feel closest to." The reasons are clear. Married people are significantly more likely than cohabiting individuals to be satisfied with the division of household chores, work/life balance, and communication in the relationship—and to report that their mate is faithful, trustworthy, acts in their best interest, and is financially responsible. Married people are also significantly more likely than cohabiting people to approve of their mate's approach to parenting.[32]

The last finding is especially important, and cuts to the question of whether children are better off with married parents than with cohabiting parents. While just 6 percent of American children were born to cohabiting parents in the 1980s, more than 25 percent are today. The expected outcomes for these children are profound. A 2015 analysis from Princeton University and the Brookings Institute reported that children born to cohabiting couples experience three times as many family transitions as those born to married couples. And family stability, according to comprehensive reviews of the research from scholars at both the Brookings Institute and the University of California at San Francisco, is highly predictive of the physical, emotional, academic, and economic outcomes a child can expect. A child who lives with cohabiting biological parents is more than three times as likely to be abused and four times as likely to be neglected as one living with married biological parents.[33]

The second common reason why couples begin to cohabit is as a test for whether they should get married. A 2016 study by the Barna Group shows that 84 percent of those who support cohabitation say that it provides a test of "compatibility" before marriage. This fits with CDC data, which reports that a significant majority of men and women believe that cohabitation reduces the risk of divorce.[34]

Is this assumption borne out by the data? In 2010, a team of psychologists from the University of Denver and Penn State published a review on the literature on cohabitation. They concluded, "For first marriages, cohabiting with the spouse without first being engaged or married was associated with more negative interaction, higher self-reported divorce proneness, and a greater probability of divorce compared to cohabiting after engagement or marriage (with patterns in the same direction for marital positivity)."[35]

The risk of divorce for cohabiting couples is so profound that, according to an analysis in the *New York Times*, it has a name: "the cohabitation effect." This designation is supported by recent data. A 2023 study by Professors Galena Rhoades and Scott Stanley of the University of Denver found that couples who cohabit before engagement have a 50 percent greater risk of divorce than those who do not.[36]

Why does cohabitation—which seems like a good test for whether a marriage will work—lead to even worse marriage outcomes than conventional dating? The prevailing theory is "the inertia hypothesis," which is sometimes described as "sliding, not deciding." If, as the songwriter Neil Sedaka posited, breaking up is hard to do—it is even harder when it involves one person moving out of one home and into another. Consequently, cohabiting couples who might otherwise break up slide into marriage because the exit costs are so high.[37]

Divorce

After all of this dating, with or without cohabitation, many couples decide to get married. How, given the extent to which they have gone to seek compatibility, do they fare?

The best data point to start with is the divorce rate. As every divorce ends an unhappy marriage, the inverse of the divorce rate provides a ceiling on the number of happy marriages.

Approximately 41 percent of first marriages, 60 percent of second marriages, and 73 percent of third marriages end in divorce. These numbers might sound high, but they are down significantly from what they were in the 1980s. And that, according to Belinda Luscombe, the author of *Marriageology: The Art and Science of Staying Together*, "may not actually be good news."[38]

First, the number of people who have married has plummeted. A report from the Joint Economic Committee of the United States Congress showed that the marriage rate (the percentage of people who marry in a year) in 1972 was three times higher than it was in 2018. Marriage, as Professor Brian Hollar of Marymount College has shown, used to be a general practice. It is now increasingly favored by religious people, who are less likely to divorce.[39]

Second, the lower divorce rate does not account for a new, large, and fast-growing cohort: those who engage in "endless separation." These are couples who are permanently separated but have no plans of getting divorced anytime soon. A 2010 *New York Times* article on the subject titled "Why Divorce? Just Stay Separated," articulates many reasons for this phenomenon. These include keeping joint health insurance, the difficulty of disentangling finances, the desire to avoid a burdensome and expensive legal process, and the freedom it provides from the temptation to remarry.[40]

How prevalent is endless separation? Approximately 20 percent of couples who separate do not get divorced. Yet, they count as "married" in the divorce rate statistics, meaning that what could be called the "real" divorce rate is significantly higher than the formal rate.[41]

If we add the divorces, the endless separations, and the 7 percent who psychologist Ty Tashiro reports stay together but are "chronically unhappy," an approximate marriage happiness rate of around 30 percent emerges.[42]

Why do so many couples, despite extensive dating, end up unhappy? A survey by the Institute for Divorce Financial Analysts aimed to identify the primary causes of divorce. The results showed that parenting issues and substance abuse each accounted for 0.5 percent of divorces; emotional or physical abuse for 5.8 percent; financial problems for 22 percent; and infidelity for 28 percent. The leading cause, responsible for 43 percent of divorces, was "basic incompatibility"—the same reason that, according to a

Barna Group study, 84 percent of cohabiting couples choose to live together before marriage.[43]

How Much Information Is Necessary to Make the Right Decision?

The main reason why so many couples date for such a long time (sometimes cohabiting), is to ensure that they are sufficiently "compatible" for marriage. Yet, the divorce rate is largely due to "basic incompatibility." The explanation for this tragic irony lies beyond courtship and derives from a question of information theory: How much information is needed to make an optimal decision?

In 2020, a team of researchers from the Stevens Institute of Technology published a study in the journal *Cognitive Research* called "How Casual Information Affects Decisions." They began the study by presenting three groups of people with one fact pattern:

Jane just started college and is adjusting to her busy schedule of classes and extracurricular activities. She has heard about the "freshman 15," where new college students gain fifteen pounds during their first year of college. Jane wants to avoid this, while also having fun, making new friends, and leaving time for homework and studying.

What is the *one* thing you think Jane should do to achieve her goal?

- A. Go for a thirty-minute walk every weekend
- B. Maintain a healthy diet
- C. Avoid hanging out with friends
- D. Watch less TV

One group of people was given no additional information. The second was provided with textual guidance explaining that a healthy diet, consistent exercise, and social pressure can all contribute to weight gain or loss. The third group was presented with the same information in visual form.

The results were that 88.8 percent of participants with no additional information selected the right answer: maintain a healthy diet. The participants who received more information barely broke 80 percent, with no meaningful difference as to whether the information was presented textually or visually. This finding, the researchers reported, was "contrary to our expectations."

The researchers then conducted a series of other experiments to determine whether people with prior knowledge of a subject (type 2 diabetes and personal finance) performed differently. They found that those with no prior knowledge of a subject did better when given additional information, and those with prior knowledge did worse when given the additional information.[44]

Why did these study participants with knowledge make worse decisions when given more information? It probably manifests a concept that was identified by Hunter College professor Bertram Gross in his 1964 book, *The Managing of Organizations*: *Information Overload*. Information overload is described by Interactive Design Foundation as "the excess of information available to a person aiming to complete a task or make a decision. This impedes the decision-making process, resulting in a poor (or even no) decision being made."[45]

In essence, there is an ideal amount of information necessary for effective decision-making. Anything beyond this optimal level becomes "excess," which will lead to poorer decisions. The key to making good decisions, therefore, is to identify the essential inputs, stop seeking additional information, and then make a choice. This concept has been applied, seemingly without dispute, in fields such as commercial banking, telecommunications pricing, and industrial design. Perhaps the author of Genesis 24:67, by modeling the choice of a spouse based on just two or three criteria, was suggesting that we apply this principle when choosing a spouse as well.

How Love Becomes "Twice as Strong"

The biblical formula for love and marriage posits that young people should look for a few qualities in another person that are directly relevant to their potential as a spouse, get married, start doing spouse-like things—and then they will experience love. Potential spouses do not wait to be "complete" to marry; instead, they are completed by marriage. And love does not precede commitment; it derives from it.

The modern formula for love and marriage completely rejects every aspect of the biblical guidance. It is based on the premise that people should be completed before they wed, and should get married only after they "fall in love." The logic of this philosophy is clear: Young people should date a lot of people before getting "serious" about one, and then date the one they are "serious" about for a long time before determining if they are sufficiently compatible to wed.

The results of this process are now in: Broken hearts that lead the body to produce natural painkillers, sex so dissatisfying that even young men prefer video games to it, hideous numbers of acquaintance/date rape (among other problems of "consent"), the quintessentially unromantic conversation (the ultimatum), late marriage that results in fertility challenges and birth complications and a marital unhappiness rate of approximately 70 percent.

So, is there a modern version of biblical courtship whose results can be measured? There is. It is called "arranged marriage without coercion," and it is opposed to "love marriages." Its dynamics are *exactly* like that experienced by Rebecca and Isaac in the Torah.[46]

Many people will consider arranged marriages, with or without coercion, to be a relic of a faraway era. That is a mistake. A 2019 United Nations report showed that 55 percent of marriages in the world today are arranged, including 90 percent of marriages in India.[47]

Why would so many people in India (among other countries) still be practicing arranged marriages? Indians have enthusiastically embraced many aspects of Western culture, including medicine, finance, clothing, and education. But a 2013 survey conducted by IPSOS for the Taj Hotel Group found that around 75 percent of eighteen- to thirty-five-year-old residents of ten Indian cities favored arranged marriages over love marriages.[48]

A 2021 commentary from the *Times of India* explains:

> Very few people opt for love marriage in India due to a number of reasons like religious disputes, cultural differences, non-agreement of families and other critical matters. It has been reported that people give into arranged marriages even if they initially wanted to marry their loved one. This brings us to the speculation that arranged marriages are indeed superior and more powerful than love marriages in Indian society.[49]

The analysis continues to state that arranged marriages without coercion provide equal stature, financial stability, cultural identity, and "the same opinions among partners and families," so there is less chance of dispute.

How are these marriages doing? The estimates for divorce rates among arranged marriages globally range between 4 and 6 percent. The divorce rate in India is approximately 1 percent. Haredi Jews in Israel, who essentially follow the model of Isaac and Rebecca in their courtship practices, have a divorce rate of 6.6 percent.[50]

In 2022, *Brides* magazine—a distinctly Western publication—posed the question: Why is the data on arranged marriages significantly better than that of "love" marriages? The analysis explores a common explanation that may come to mind for anyone reflecting on this issue. The hypothesis suggests that participants in arranged marriages, particularly women, "have no other options and are essentially trapped." According to this logic, India's low divorce rate is due to the limited exit options available to women. If women had more freedom, they might end their marriages in India at rates comparable to those seen in the West.

How many arranged marriages would actually break up but for the woman being "trapped"? *Brides* magazine suggests some, but not many. The analysis continues: "There are plenty of positive explanations for the low divorce rates of arranged marriages. Couples feel more inclined to work through issues and are more dedicated to each other. Mutual admiration develops. They don't make rash decisions to marry someone because of passion or lust."[51]

This reasoning can also be applied to the Haredi (ultra-Orthodox) community in Israel, which, in accordance with the availability of divorce under Torah law, has established numerous organizations dedicated to supporting women seeking divorce. The divorce rate within the Haredi community is consistent with the global divorce rate for arranged marriages in India. Similarly, it applies to religious Muslims in the United Kingdom, where arranged marriages result in significantly higher rates of marital stability compared to their non-Muslim counterparts whose marriages are not arranged. Justice Paul Coleridge, Chairman of the Marriage Foundation in the United Kingdom, commented on arranged marriages among Muslims in a manner similar to *Brides* magazine. Judge Coleridge noted, "They enter marriage without artificial and unreal 'celebrity' expectations or a belief that they merely have to bump into a perfect partner . . ."[52] In 2010, Dr. Robert Epstein, a psychologist with the American Institute for Behavioral Research and Technology and the former editor in chief of *Psychology Today*, published an analysis in *Scientific American* on the science of enduring love. He highlighted India's remarkably low divorce rates and referenced a study by

Professors Usha Gupta and Pushpa Singh from the University of Rajasthan. Using the Rubin Liking and Loving Scale, Professors Gupta and Singh evaluated the depth of love in both arranged and love marriages in India. Dr. Epstein summarized their findings:

> Love in love marriages in India does exactly what it does in love marriages here: it starts high and declines fairly rapidly. But love in the arranged marriages they examined started out low and gradually *increased*, surpassing the love in the love marriage about five years out. Ten years into the marriage the love was nearly twice as strong.

Dr. Epstein writes that this finding was confirmed by a paper that the student Mansi Thakar of the University of Southern California presented at the November 2009 meeting of the National Council on Family Relations. Ms. Thakar, who studied arranged marriages from nine countries and five religions, found the depth of love within them more than doubled over approximately twenty years.[53]

The data is in and the implications are clear. The divorce rates among modern arranged marriages, which follow the biblical formula of Isaac and Rebecca, might be higher if divorce were more socially acceptable. The divorce rates among love marriages would also be higher if the endlessly separated and the chronically unhappy couples were counted as divorced as well. There is no basis to conclude that one rate is more depressed than the other. Consequently, we can conclude that the courtship practice of Isaac and Rebecca—identify two or three relevant characteristics quickly, get married, become a spouse, and experience love—is far superior to its contemporary competitor.

Reflection

The data on contemporary courtship and marriage reveals a clear, sad, and ironic truth. The Barna Group found that 84 percent of those who cohabit do so mainly to evaluate "compatibility." It's reasonable to assume that couples who date for extended periods without committing are also assessing compatibility. However, the Institute for Divorce Financial Analysts identified "basic incompatibility" as the leading cause of divorce. Tragically, young people are spending an enormous amount of time (often years per relationship) trying to identify features of compatibility that have nothing to do with what optimizes for a happy marriage.

Arranged marriage without coercion is a widely known, tested, and successful alternative to the long, iterative dating that characterizes modern life. The reality: modern Westerners are, for better or worse, simply not going to adopt the courtship practices of the Torah and contemporary India.

Are young people destined to continue enduring the frequent misery caused by modern courtship practices? Not necessarily. Young Americans can adapt Torah-based courtship practices—proven by social science to be more successful than contemporary methods—in a way that feels comfortable, inviting, and appealing to today's generation. What might this look like?

Americans should graduate from high school and resolve to date seriously, which means having an eye to marriage. They should identify the *few* characteristics that they want in a spouse. It is not hard to do; there are not many meaningful characteristics to choose from.

One of these will be a baseline of physical attraction. They can select two or three others. Generosity, competence, kindness, shared faith, providership, and love of children are good candidates. Taste in music and whether he or she prefers vacations in the sun or the snow are not.

When a couple, having dated for a short amount of time, concludes that that the boyfriend or girlfriend has this small number of carefully and strategically chosen characteristics, they should get married. They should then begin sacrificing for and giving to each other as they build a family together. They can expect love to emerge and to continually deepen into a state of need and interdependence.

Does this mean that young people will get married with lots of unknowns ahead of them? Sure. Does this encourage young people to make the quintessential commitment when they know little about themselves—and less about their boyfriend or girlfriend? Yes—and that is the way it should be. The lesson from the Torah and the Jewish tradition that is based on it is clear: Don't expect to be completed before marriage. Instead, become completed through marriage.

At first glance, getting married young after a brief dating period may seem risky. However, marital unhappiness data suggests that extended dating does not diminish the risk of marrying the wrong person. A few months of dating is sufficient for a young man or woman to determine whether the other person possesses the two or three key qualities he or she should seek in a spouse. It also provides enough time to understand the other person's values, character, aspirations, priorities, and commitments—all one needs before making the ultimate commitment.

Is there any point in dating for longer than these few months? Will this lead to a better marriage? Let's consider what generally happens in a marriage.

Parenting, financial stress, geographic moves, work/life balance questions, family issues, and health challenges—and the many decisions that are caused by them—are some of the most common and challenging aspects of a marriage. These issues, and others like them, rarely emerge during dating—whether it lasts for several months or years. And they never emerge in dating with the same intensity as they do in marriage, which has vastly higher exit costs and a sense of irrevocability.

The limited insight into how a potential spouse will respond to these challenges typically appears within the first few months of dating. It is uncommon for anything learned or experienced during a long dating period to accurately predict how a couple will function as husband and wife. The numerous details a young person may learn about their partner during dating—such as vacation preferences, whether friends are amusing, entertainment tastes, spontaneity, or enjoyment of long intellectual conversations—are largely irrelevant to what contributes to a successful marriage. In fact, thinking about (let alone focusing on) any of these things could easily lead to information overload and cause someone to end a relationship with a potential great spouse for an irrelevant reason.

Thankfully, there is an alternative—that offered by the Torah's Isaac and Rebecca, whose courtship practices have been shown by modern social science to optimize for a happy and fulfilling marriage.

24

Why Abraham's Army Won and the 2004 US Men's Olympic Basketball Team Lost

The Torah and Science of Synergy

In Genesis 13, God promises Abraham, "I will make your offspring like the dust of the earth, so that if anyone could count the dust, then your offspring could be counted." God reiterates this promise in Genesis 26, telling Abraham that his offspring will be as numerous as "the stars of the sky."

Fast-forward to Deuteronomy 7. Moses tells the Jews, "The Lord did not . . . choose you because you were more numerous than other peoples, for you were the fewest of all peoples."

A reader considering these verses might emerge very confused. Are the Jews going to be as numerous as the dust or the fewest of all peoples?

Rabbi Jonathan Sacks, reviewing the centuries of commentary on the juxtaposition of these two verses, offers a reconciliation. A nation's size does not have to be measured by its population. It could be measured by its contributions. And the Jews, by lots of measures, *are* a small people whose contributions can be compared to the stars of the sky or the dust of the earth. But this just leads to another question. How can a small people have outsized contributions—and in a way so dependably that God would bet his career on earth on it?[1]

The answer is provided in Leviticus 26:8 in the form of a blessing that God says will come to us if we act according to his aspirations. "Five of you shall give chase to a hundred, and a hundred of you shall give chasc to ten thousand."

The math is fascinating. In the first clause, we learn that five Jews can give chase to a hundred enemies. That would suggest that the ratio required for a successful chase is 1:20. However, the second clause tells us that it will take a hundred to successfully chase ten thousand. That would suggest that the ratio for a successful chase of a larger group is 1:100.

Why, in the biblical imagination, would a larger group be five times as powerful per person than a smaller group?

If Leviticus 26:8 was just a mathematical equation, it would not make sense. The blessing, as mathematician Alex Klein explains, is that the relationship between the number of people in a society and their strength will not be linear. Rather, the strength of the Jewish people will grow exponentially, far surpassing their numbers.[2]

The blessing of Leviticus 26:8 has an English name. It is *synergy*—the ability to combine so that the impact of one plus one is greater than two. This blessing of synergy is, perhaps, God's most fundamental blessing, as "the smallest of people" can only achieve God's awesome aspirations for us if we embody and live by it.

The Biblical Creation of Synergy

The concept of synergy raises the question: How can we create it? The Torah appears to have anticipated this, outlining the components of synergy clearly from the very beginning.

In Genesis 14, we encounter a scenario where four kings subjugate and wage war against five neighboring kings and their people. The four kings swiftly defeat the five. The king of Sodom, one of the five defeated leaders, flees, as all the wealth of his city is taken by the victors. The victors also capture Lot, Abraham's troubled nephew, who is living in Sodom at the time.

Abraham, despite his contentious relationship with his nephew, endeavors to save him. The Torah, in Genesis 14:14–16, tells us:

> And when Abram heard that [Lot] was taken captive, he armed his students, born in his own house, three hundred and eighteen, and pursued them unto Dan. During the night Abram divided

> his men to attack them and he routed them, pursuing them as far as Hobah, north of Damascus. He recovered all the goods and brought back his relative Lot and his possessions, together with the women and the other people.

The first remarkable detail about this stunning military victory is how few people Abraham had. His force consisted of just 319 men (including himself), the size of a single battalion. Yet, this small battalion managed to defeat several armies in a single night. Achieving such a victory with a small group against a much larger force requires synergy. This passage provides a blueprint for how to achieve that synergy.

Abraham's men, as we learn, were his "students." The term used in Genesis 14 is *chanichav*, meaning "those he educated." This indicates that their education was more moral than military. As individuals morally educated by Abraham, they shared the same background, worldview, and vision. In this sense, they were "armed" with his principles, which they collectively embraced.

Additionally, these students were described as "born in his own house." Does this mean they were all biologically related? Not necessarily. What matters is that they had grown up together and lived around each other; they were at least *like family*. Thus, they experienced *continuity*. This continuity presumably gave each person a deep tacit knowledge of each other—which enabled them to anticipate how their fellows would act, react, and communicate. And that's not all. There is a word that encapsulates individuals educated by a single teacher and essentially "born in his own house." Such people, who share a continuous relationship, are *unified*.

The Torah tells us that Abraham's men were "trained" and "armed"—in other words, they were *prepared*. Their preparation paid off, as seen in their tactical creativity when they divided into smaller units to launch a daring nighttime raid. They were *coordinated*, demonstrated by the ability of these small groups to—despite being separated and lacking modern communication—drive back much larger enemies all the way to Damascus. They were also highly *motivated*, as their mission was to rescue Lot—Abraham's nephew and, as one "born in the same house," a brother.

Abraham's small force was able to defeat much larger armies because they were unified, coordinated, prepared, motivated, and had continuity.

This creates the blessing of synergy described in Leviticus: that our strength will grow disproportionately to our numbers, just as Abraham's force did.

The Science

The Ringelmann Effect: What Happens When People Come Together Randomly

In 1913, the French agricultural engineer Max Ringelmann published one of the first social science studies. It was based upon data that he had collected in the 1880s. It became so important that his findings earned a designation used in social science to this day: The Ringelmann Effect.[3]

Professor Ringelmann conducted an experiment where participants pulled on a rope, and he measured the force they exerted using a pressure gauge. He discovered that individual effort consistently and significantly decreased as group size increased, from two participants up to eight. In groups of eight, individuals exerted only half the force they did when pulling alone. Professor Ringelmann attributed this phenomenon to two main factors: lack of coordination ("the lack of simultaneity in their efforts") and lack of connection ("[not] trusting his neighbor to complete the task as needed").

The Ringelmann Effect, as described by Spotify product design lead Tobias van Schneider, "describes the tendency for individual productivity to decrease as group size increases. And it doesn't just happen in tug-of-war games: It's present in companies like Google and Facebook more than a century after Ringelmann's discovery. And chances are, it's happening in your workplace, too." In other words, it is *normal* for organizations to be *less effective* than the sum of their individual contributions would suggest.[4]

Why is diminished effectiveness (known by psychologists as negative synergy) the norm for larger communities and organizations?

In 1974, psychologist Alan Ingham and his colleagues at the University of Massachusetts replicated Ringelmann's experiment with a variation to explore the impact of *perceived* group size on individual effort. In Professor Ingham's experiment, participants were placed in groups of six. Unbeknownst to some of them, only a portion of the group was actively pulling—with three of the six "pullers" merely *pretending* to pull the rope. Professor Ingham found that even the mere *belief* that one was participating in a larger group diminished personal contribution.

Professor Ingram's discovery was soon given a name: "social loafing." There have since been more than eighty studies of social loafing, on subjects ranging from brainstorming to poetry rating to Lego construction. They have largely confirmed Professor Ingham's findings.[5]

One such study was conducted by Professor Jennifer Mueller of The Wharton School at the University of Pennsylvania. In 2011, she published a paper in the journal *Organizational Behavior and Human Decision Processes* titled "Why Individuals in Larger Teams Perform Worse." Her dataset consisted of the diaries of members from twenty-six corporate design teams working on projects ranging from dental floss to airline purchasing to creating a cut-resistant fiber for factory workers.

Professor Mueller reported:

> On a smaller team, people knew what resources were available and felt they could ask questions when things went wrong . . . But in these larger teams, people were lost. They didn't know who to call for help . . . Even if they did reach out, they didn't feel the other members were as committed to helping or had the time to help. And they couldn't tell their team leader because [it would look like] they had failed.[6]

Negative synergy, therefore, derives from social loafing, lack of coordination, motivation, and solidarity—which can be grouped into what Professor Mueller called "relational losses." These losses, more common in larger teams, made it difficult for individuals to identify reliable sources of support, left people feeling isolated, and created stress that drained cognitive resources and impaired memory capacity.[7] If newspapers and contemporary historians existed in the time of Abraham, that just might have been a description of how his enemies performed against his much smaller force.

Abraham's Lesson: Taught by the 2004 US Men's Olympic Basketball Team

The 2004 US Men's Olympic Basketball Team was led by Allen Iverson and Tim Duncan—two all-time greats who, between them, had won the MVP award in the three previous seasons. The team had three other future Hall of Famers in LeBron James, Dwayne Wade, and Carmelo Anthony and was filled with All-Stars such as Stephon Marbury, Shawn Marion, Richard Jefferson, and Amar'e Stoudemire.

The other teams, combined, had only a few players who would ever contribute in the NBA—Manu Ginóbili (Argentina/Spurs), Luis Scola (Argentina/Rockets), Pau Gasol (Spain/Lakers), and José Calderón (Spain/Raptors). Only two of the international players, Pau Gasol and Manu Ginóbli, were as good as *anyone* on the American team. In addition to their sheer talent, the Americans had reason to be optimistic. The United States had won the gold medal in 1992, 1996, and 2000 without losing a game in any of the tournaments.

In 2004, the United States team lost to Puerto Rico by nineteen points, Lithuania by four points, and Argentina by eight points—en route to a bronze medal. Italy, which did not have a player who ever made an NBA team, won the silver. Argentina won gold. What happened?

In 2012 and 2019, *GQ* and ESPN surveyed a lot of the participants from the 2004 team to assess why they lost to teams whose best player was nowhere near as good as the worst player on the US team. The coach, Larry Brown, said that the team had "no time to prepare, no time to practice." Luis Scola said that the US team was "obviously extremely talented" but complained a lot about the slightly different international rules instead of adapting to them. Contrary to the principles of synergy taught by Abraham, the American team was *unprepared*.

Paul Bragna, a waiter on the ship that brought the team from the United States to Greece, noticed a lack of discipline: "They ate too many hamburgers. They were always in [the food] line. That's why they lose. They cannot jump anymore." They were, unlike Abraham's men, *unmotivated*.

The basketball analyst Bill Simmons recalled, "I looked at our team and I was like, 'Stephon Marbury is gonna be playing, who's the other guy? The backcourt is Marbury and [Allen] Iverson? We're screwed! Those guys are gonna be in fistfights for the ball.'" They were not *coordinated*.[8]

Abraham's Lesson: Taught by the Lakers, the Nets—and the Warriors

Going into the 2021–2022 NBA season, the favorite in Las Vegas sportsbooks to win the championship was the Brooklyn Nets followed by the Los Angeles Lakers. Everyone else was far behind.

It would have been a good time to place an out-of-the-money bet. The Nets lost in the first round of the playoffs, and the Lakers did not even make the playoffs.

How did they underperform so spectacularly? The answer just may be in the data compiled by Basketball Reference. One statistic they track was clearly ignored by gamblers—at least in 2021. It is that of "roster continuity," which is "calculated as the percentage of a team's regular season minutes that were filled by players from the previous season's roster."[9]

Most teams typically have a continuity rate between 60 percent and 80 percent. In 2022, the favorite—the Brooklyn Nets—had a continuity rate of just 50 percent, the fifth lowest in the league. The lowest continuity rate belonged to the Los Angeles Lakers, at 25 percent. Among teams with a lower continuity rate than the Nets, only the Chicago Bulls made the playoffs. The Bulls were eliminated in the first round.[10]

If he could have bet on the NBA, it is doubtful that Bob Myers would have placed his money on the Lakers or the Nets. As the general manager of the Golden State Warriors, Mr. Myers crafted the most successful basketball dynasty of the twenty-first century. He revealed his secret to Grantland in 2014: "If you've played basketball, you know there is a hard-to-quantify element of continuity. Playing together with the same group of people for a long time makes you better. It just does."[11]

Los Angeles Lakers star Kobe Bryant would have agreed. He won plenty, but his Lakers team was stymied five times between 1999 and 2014 by the San Antonio Spurs. In 2014, Mr. Bryant told ESPN what he envied about the Spurs. It was not the fact that the Spurs had a power forward and a point guard better than his team had. He said of the three Spurs stars and the coach, "I don't know if I can express to you how jealous I am of the fact that Tim, Tony, Manu, and Pop have all been together for all those years . . . I can't express to you how jealous I am of that. Not all this up-and-down stuff."[12]

Mr. Bryant's insight is not unique to basketball. Tom Brady, who won seven Super Bowls in the twenty-first century, said, "I've always said continuity is key in the NFL."

The football analyst Scott Smith explained why. "You can't prepare for every possible situation every week, so having had a lot of experience together helps you handle that." Groups that work together for a long period of time develop a tacit knowledge of each other that is, essentially, *preparation* for the unpredictable events that characterize everything from sports to business to the war that Abraham and his small force won over the five kings.[13]

The Jews

In 2015, the College of Charleston posed what it called the age-old question: Why have the Jews been so successful in the modern world? Data from almost every field—science, technology, medicine, statecraft, business, literature, entertainment—validates the premise of the question. The Jews are, per Deuteronomy, "the smallest of peoples" and yet have accomplishments and influence that reflect the blessing of being as numerous as "the stars in the sky." There is no doubt that this biblical prophecy has come true.

What is the answer to this age-old question, then? In 1828, the German poet Heinrich Heine called the Torah "the portable homeland of the Jew." He was exactly right. From the moment it was received, the Torah became the canonical source for living a good Jewish life, shared by Jews everywhere and in all times. As such, it became the ultimate resource for synergy and for the same reasons as articulated in Genesis 14.

The Torah kept us *motivated* by guiding us to yearn for the same land, pray for the coming of the same Messiah, and seek to create the same "kingdom of priests and a holy nation."

The Torah kept us *coordinated* by having Jews chant the same verses, study the same passages, and experience the same holidays at the same time every year. This practice has Jews ask the same questions and ponder the same challenges at the same time everywhere.

Moreover, the Torah has been our source of *unity* much like Abraham demonstrated in Genesis 14. Jews achieved our unity by being, in essence, "born in the same house." Across all places and generations, Jews share a deep and abiding relationship with the same matriarchs (Sarah, Rebecca, Rachel, and Leah), patriarchs (Abraham, Isaac, and Jacob), and homeland (Israel). This bond is reflected in how we speak of our ancestors, using affectionate terms typically reserved for family: Mama Rachel, Grandpa Jacob, Father Abraham, and Moses our Teacher.

The result of this motivation, coordination, focus, and unity—this synergy—has enabled the Jews to (just as prophesied in Genesis, Leviticus, and Deuteronomy) do far more than our numbers would suggest. And it is no mystery how this synergy has worked. It was discovered in the Cairo Geniza. The Geniza was the storeroom of the Ben Ezra Synagogue in Egypt. A huge number of documents, covering much of Jewish history, miraculously survived in the Geniza and was discovered by the Scottish sisters and scholars Agnes Lewis and Margaret Gibson in 1896.

One of the most remarkable finds was a check from probably two hundred years *before* the proliferation of paper money. The check, written by a Jew in Baghdad to a Jew in Cairo sometime around the tenth century CE, read, "Please give Joseph, the bearer of this check, a hundred coins." The only basis for this transaction, and countless others like it, was the trust and unity of a people who felt that they were "born of the same house," were prepared to support each other and motivated to do so. This deep sense of trust, possibly unmatched by any other group regardless of size, is the very quality that sociologist Francis Fukuyama identified as essential for "the creation of prosperity." It is, therefore, unsurprising—at least to those familiar with Leviticus 26—that Jews have achieved significant success, both financially and in other areas.

The synergy lived by the Jews also accounts for the greatest Jewish miracle of the past two thousand years: the creation of the modern state of Israel. On May 14, 1948, the armies of Egypt, Syria, Jordan, Lebanon, Saudi Arabia, and Iraq simultaneously attacked the nascent state of Israel. Israel was at a huge and seemingly unsurmountable disadvantage. A 2018 analysis of the war by Lt. Christian Heller of the United States Marine Corps Expeditionary Warfare School outlined Israel's "three strategic deficits." Young Israel did not have a "professional military capable of defending its sovereignty." Its "population was a fraction of the size of its combined Arab opponents." And it lacked "geographic space in which to maneuver its forces."[14]

The military leaders around the world, most notably US Secretary of State General George Marshall, were convinced that Israel would be promptly destroyed. The Arabs agreed. A 2009 analysis in Al Jazeera cites the Syrian political analyst and historian Sami Moubayed as saying, "The advisors to President Quwatli [of Syria] and King Farouk [of Egypt], for example, were telling them that this will be a piece of cake for the Syrians and Egyptians."[15]

The nascent, tiny, and sparsely populated state of Israel defeated the six Arab armies. How? Lt. Heller explains that the Jews "were united politically, motivated to fight and . . . relied on strong communal institutions for organization."

These Jews were able to reverse the logic of mathematics and achieve the synergy of Leviticus 26—just like their father Abraham did several thousand years ago.

Reflection

Almost every organizational leader has likely asked one or more of these questions: How can we achieve more with fewer resources? How can we outperform richer, more talented, or more numerous competitors? How can I maximize my team's potential so that the whole becomes greater than the sum of its parts? How can we scale effectively, making growth work to our advantage rather than against us?

The first principle for any leader to understand is the Torah's approach to group dynamics: "Five of you shall give chase to a hundred, and a hundred of you shall give chase to ten thousand." This teaching suggests that no one should feel intimidated by a larger, wealthier, or more talented opponent—nor should anyone feel secure simply because they possess those advantages. As demonstrated by the Ringelmann Effect, teams often become less effective as their size increases.

This does not mean that small teams have an *automatic* advantage over larger ones. But they have a potential one. They will, generally, have an easier time of achieving the magical math of Leviticus by following Abraham's example in unity, motivation, preparation, coordination, focus, and continuity. The outcome can be achievements that appear as vast and numerous as "the stars in the sky." These opportunities are, consistent with the Torah as the great guidebook for all mankind, open to everyone—from a basketball team to a corporate division to a global people.

25

The Biblical Serial Killer and Wernicke's Area

The Torah and Science of Words

God could have created the world in any way. He could have breathed, blinked, nodded, or thought the world into existence. Instead, God created the world using a strange tactic. He created the world through nine *utterances*.

Why would God have chosen to create the world with so many utterances? As the Torah is not a history book or a science book but instead, a guidebook, it must be to teach us something. If God can create the world with words, and we are created in his image, then we, too, can create our world with words. And the power of creation always brings with it the potential for destruction. If worlds can be created with words, worlds can be destroyed with words. This is far from intuitive. Because words are very easy to create and deploy, our instinct might be to consider them along with everything else that is abundant and reproducible—as without much value. The Hebrew language itself argues with that intuition. The Hebrew word for "word" and "thing" is the same (*davar*). Words and things, the language seems to suggest, are equally real and share practical and even material significance.

And, the Torah makes clear, words might be our most precious things. Enter Numbers 30:2–3. The Torah records that "Moses said to the heads of the tribes of Israel, 'This is what the Lord commands: When a man makes a vow to the Lord or takes an oath to obligate himself, he must not violate his word but must do everything he said.'"

There are at least three major teachings on words (or speech) that derive from that verse.

First: The nineteenth-century sage Rabbi Moses Sofer (known as the Chatam Sofer) notes a unique and telling aspect to the verse. Moses and God command things throughout the Bible. But they rarely preface it with, "This is what the Lord commands." Why, then, does Moses do so here? To show us, with divine authority, that if our word is meaningless, then everything else the Lord commands is meaningless.[1]

Second: We learn at least one reason why Hebrew has one word for "word" and "thing." All kinds of things—a painter's brush, a carpenter's hammer, a soldier's weapon—can transform other things. So can words. How so? One way is through a vow. For instance, one can transform potato chips that are, for better or worse, kosher. If a person makes a vow that he will not eat them for the next year, they become (pursuant to Numbers 30) as prohibited as bacon and shrimp. With a few words, a food item goes from being permitted to prohibited. This, Rabbi Zeidel Epstein writes, shows not only the power of words, but also the respect that God has for us. In Numbers 30, he gives us the opportunity to transform things through the words we decide to use.[2]

Third: Rashi writes that the translation "violate" (*yachel*) is insufficient. He understood the word *yachel* as deriving from *chol*, meaning "mundane."[3] Thus, the Torah is telling us not to treat our words as "mundane." Everything one says is important, as is *how* one says it.

A Due Date—Not a Deadline

A quintessential example of the importance in *how* we speak (in addition to what we say) is in Genesis 7:2. The Torah says, "Of all the clean animals you shall take for yourself seven pairs, a male and its mate, and of all the animals that are not clean, two, a male and its mate." The rabbis of the Talmud noted an oddity in the verse. It would have been more succinct and seemingly clearer to say "unclean" rather than "those who are not clean." Why, then, would the Torah use the more cumbersome phrase? Because it wished to use a gentler tone—referring to a positive quality the animals were lacking rather than characterizing them as simply negative.[4]

This lesson was especially important to the twentieth-century sage, Rebbe Menachem Mendel Schneerson. When asked to bless a hospital in

Israel, he agreed on the condition that its leaders would not use the standard Hebrew term *bet cholim*, meaning "house of the sick." Instead, he insisted it be called a *bet refuah*—a "house of healing." He believed that patients would have a better experience in a "house of healing" than in a "house of the sick."

Similarly, the Rebbe would never speak of a "deadline," but instead called it a "due date." A deadline and a due date make the same point—that a task needs to be done by a certain time. But a deadline references death whereas a due date references birth, thus creating a different reality and mentality for the project and its creators.[5]

Gossip

While the Torah establishes that all words are important, there is one type of speech that earns the greatest emphasis. It is gossip—and the Author of the Torah *hates* it.

Indeed, the Author of the Torah hates gossip so much that the Talmud actually has a nickname for it: "triple speech." The reason is also provided in the Talmud. "Gossip kills three: the one who says it, the one who listens, and the subject of the gossip." A gossiper, in Jewish terms, is a mass murderer.[6]

Eve, Moses, and "the Wrath of Hashem"

We are introduced to gossip in the story of the first people. In Genesis 2, God tells Adam that he may eat of any tree in the Garden except for the tree of the knowledge of good and evil. The next chapter opens with Eve relaying the conversation to the serpent—in a clear act of gossip. The serpent convinces Eve to violate God's word. The result: divine fury, resulting in the serpent being forced to live in dust, women to suffer pain in childbirth, and men to have to live by the sweat of their brows.

In Exodus 1, a similar theme emerges. Moses sees an Egyptian attacking a Jew. He intervenes to save the Jew, killing the Egyptian in the process. The next day, Moses sees two Jews fighting. He again intervenes. One man says, "Who made you ruler and judge over us? Are you thinking of killing me as you killed the Egyptian?"

In just one day, gossip about Moses killing the Egyptian had spread so quickly and widely that it was immediately on the mind of one of the two men he encountered. As a result, Moses becomes "afraid" and flees Egypt.

Later, in Leviticus 14:35, we learn about a mysterious condition called *tzaraat*. Although often translated as "leprosy," it cannot be leprosy because it affects not only people, but also houses and clothing. *Tzaraat* is a spiritual affliction with physical symptoms. The primary sin associated with *tzaraat* is gossip, as seen in Numbers 12 when Miriam suffers from *tzaraat* after speaking about Moses's love life behind his back. The Torah describes this as provoking "the wrath of Hashem."

In Leviticus 13–14, the process for cleansing someone afflicted with *tzaraat* is described as involving a week of exile. The gossiper doesn't simply leave and return quietly after the period ends. Instead, he must declare himself "Unclean! Unclean!" The Torah describes this as a purification process for two important reasons. First, it subjects the gossiper to the public humiliation of loudly leaving the community, mirroring the embarrassment he inflicted on the person he gossiped about. Second, the exile symbolizes the social rupture he caused, as he is separated from the community, reflecting the division his gossip created.[7]

This sequence in Leviticus highlights the seriousness of gossip and underscores the importance of how we speak about it—an approach that applies to all forms of communication. When someone identifies *tzaraat*, he is instructed to tell the priest, "It seems to me that there is a plague in the house."

This phrasing is curious. *Tzaraat* is marked by obvious white blemishes, making it easy to identify. Why, then, does the person speak so tentatively with, "It seems to me"? Rabbi Moshe Scheiner of the Palm Beach Synagogue, citing the Mishna, offers an explanation: it is an education for the individual who has misused words. By saying, "It seems to me," the speech offender learns humility and the importance of being cautious with his words.[8]

Cursing the Deaf

Leviticus 19:14 decrees, "You shall not curse the deaf." Cursing, in the Torah's view, is very serious. As Rabbi Geoffrey Dennis writes, "A curse is a verbal invocation pronounced to bring harm, evil, or detriment to another. More than a threat or a wish, a curse is assumed to have the power to make the desired harm a reality."[9]

Why would cursing be invoked here? There is no indication in the Torah or later sources suggesting that cursing actual deaf people was a widespread problem in ancient society that required a Torah prohibition. Additionally, the act of cursing a deaf person seems not only bizarrely cruel but also illogical, as the deaf person cannot hear the curse. So, what is the purpose and lesson behind this commandment?

The answer lies in a broader understanding of deafness. We are all "deaf" to what is said about us in our absence. Thus, Leviticus 19:14 serves as a Torah prohibition against speaking negatively about someone behind his back. While this behavior is already prohibited elsewhere in the Torah, the specific commandment against cursing the deaf offers a deeper lesson. It teaches us to view gossip not as harmless or even mildly harmful speech, excused by the fact that the subject may never hear it. Instead, it frames gossip as deeply cruel—equivalent to cursing a deaf person—and fully deserving of God's anger.

"You Shall Not Travel as a Talebearer"

Why is gossip so cruel? One overarching reason is found in Leviticus 19:16: "You shall not travel as a talebearer among your people, neither shall you stand by the blood of your neighbor." This commandment provides two insights into the nature of gossip.

The first insight is revealed through the use of the word "travel," an unusual choice to describe speech. This term is intentional, emphasizing that words move freely, quickly, inevitably, and uncontrollably. The Torah teaches that when we share information about someone, we must assume it will continue to spread far beyond our control.

This idea is illustrated in a well-known Jewish story about a repentant talebearer who asks his Rabbi how he can undo the harm he has caused. The Rabbi instructs him to cut open a pillow and scatter its feathers, then attempt to collect and put all the feathers back inside. The man tells the Rabbi that this is impossible. Right, the Rabbi says—when you gossip, it "flies on the wings of the wind, and you can never get it back." The victims of gossip are permanently wounded.[10]

The second lesson about gossip that is embedded in this verse is that the prohibition does not distinguish between positive and negative or true and false talebearing. It prohibits all gossip.

Why would the Torah prohibit gossip that is *true*? Because true information can be just as harmful as false rumors. Let's say that Jane tells

Amanda she is excited to have started dating Jim. Let's also stipulate that Amanda knows that Jim cheated on a test in the sixth grade, got drunk as a college freshman ten years ago, and does not close the blinds when he gets dressed in the morning. Is there a conceivably *constructive* reason for Amanda to share this *true* information? No.

Let's say that Amanda shares her knowledge anyway. Even if Jane dismisses the information, it might still color her perception of her promising beau as it is impossible to unhear something and difficult to resist the influence of what one knows. This is especially true with negative information, which, as discussed in the chapter on negativity bias, we are evolutionarily prone to accept. Even if Jane manages to resist the influence of what Amanda told her, she will likely think less of Amanda for sharing this gossip. In all cases, the outcome of the gossip is negative for one or more of the relationships at play. That example covers true but negative gossip. How about *positive* gossip? Enter Proverbs 27:14: "He that blesses his friend with a loud voice, rising early in the morning, it shall be counted as a curse to him."

Why should a blessing ever be counted as a curse? In his discussion of this proverb, Rashi focused on the "loud voice" aspect in the verse. He said that this speaks to a prohibition on "excessive praise."[11] Why would "excessive praise" be prohibited? Because it can lead to unforeseen negative consequences for the subject of the praise.

Imagine someone at a group dinner telling a friend that he wants to set him up with Yael, describing her as "the most brilliant and beautiful young woman you'll ever meet." It's not hard to picture someone else chiming in, saying that Yael isn't as smart as Priscilla or as beautiful as Gladys. Similarly, if a youth basketball coach calls a player "the next Ray Allen," it's easy to imagine someone responding that they've seen plenty of kids who are better shooters. Before long, the excessive praise has triggered a wave of criticism.

In his discussion of positive gossip, Maimonides does not disagree with Rashi. But he does not focus on "excessive praise" as the core issue in positive gossip. Instead, he explains that we must be mindful of the *context* in which we discuss others positively. One may not speak someone's praises in the presence of the subject's enemies, as an adversary is always looking for an opportunity to turn a positive into a negative. In the right context, however, positive speech about another is acceptable.

For instance, it is one thing for a churchgoer to tell the pastor's wife, "I saw Pastor John playing tennis, and he is really good!" It is another for a churchgoer to say the same thing at a larger social event. One person might wonder aloud how the pastor has so much time to work on his game, while another might say that men of God should focus on more important things, and a third might say that this explains why the pastor seems distracted during his sermons.[12]

The Exception

Let's return to the example of Jane, Amanda, and Jim. It is clear in the Torah's understanding that Amanda should not share with Jane that Jim cheated on a test in sixth grade. But what if she knows that Jim cheated on his last two girlfriends, is dishonest in business, or currently has a drinking problem?

The eighteenth-century sage Chaim ibn Attar, known as the Or Ha-Chaim, provides the universally accepted answer—which is based on Leviticus 19:16. He notes that the prohibition on talebearing is immediately followed by the prohibition against standing by the blood of one's neighbor. Why would the Torah present these seemingly unrelated directives in the same breath?

The Or Ha-Chaim states that the second verse articulates an *exception* to the first. We can (and, indeed, *must*) engage in gossip if the failure to do so would result in standing by the blood of our neighbor. Amanda's knowledge that Jim has recently cheated on his girlfriends, has a drinking problem, or is dishonest in business is pertinent to whether Jane should pursue a relationship with him. If Amanda were to refrain from sharing this relevant and important information, she would be standing by the "blood" of Jane and exposing her to potential harm.[13]

The Or Ha-Chaim's position on this is shared by all significant rabbinic decisors. There is also universal agreement that this exception should be narrowly construed and carefully invoked. The speaker of the *lashon hara* must investigate the situation to ensure that she is right (i.e., that Jim *is* a cheater or a drunk), have pure intentions (i.e., her goal is just helping Amanda), and must avoid a continued conversation about the matter.[14]

Gossip can obviously harm the reputation of the subject, but how can gossip also harm the speaker—qualifying it for "triple speech"? The nineteenth-century sage Rabbi Yisrael Meir Kagan (known as the Chofetz Chaim) pointed to Leviticus 24:20, which stipulates, "Anyone who injures their neighbor is to be injured in the same manner: fracture for fracture, eye for eye, tooth for tooth."

The Chofetz Chaim applied this instruction to the gossiper. The gossiper, according to his interpretation of the verse, will suffer the reputational damage akin to that which he caused through his words. The Torah, it seems, is suggesting a boomerang effect inherent in gossip.[15]

The Science

"A Single Word"

At the very beginning of Genesis, when God created the world with nine utterances, the Author of the Torah established the principle that, just as God creates the world with words, so too do we create our world with words.

In 2012, Andrew Newberg of Thomas Jefferson University and Mark Waldman of Loyola Marymount University published their book *Words Can Change Your Brain*. The word "Bible" does not appear in the book. But their central conclusion might have caused the Author of the Torah to nod in agreement. They write, "A single word has the power to influence the expression of genes that regulate physical and emotional stress."[16]

Contemporary science has shown just how profound and extensive this influence can be. Kory Floyd of Arizona State University has found that speaking positively to others (such as saying "I love you") leads to lower stress hormones, lower cholesterol, and a stronger immune system. The transformative power of words extends to those far less profound than "I love you." Professor David Tod of Aberystwyth University showed that positive self-talk enables young men to achieve greater angular velocity around the knee and jump higher.[17]

The power of words to transform reality works as much with the negative as it does with the positive. A negative word can interrupt the normal processing of language in the brain section known as Wernicke's area that enables us to understand the meaning of words in their context (like whether a "bank" refers to a river or a financial institution). A hostile word can disrupt the genetic expression in the brain that protects us from stress. An erotic word will trigger intimacy-related thoughts and (less intuitively!)

conflict resolution strategies. The name of a loved one stimulates the brain circuits associated with passion, whereas that of a friend does not. How important are these discoveries? Professors Newberg and Waldman write:

> Our own brain-scan research shows that concentrating and meditating on positive thoughts, feelings, and outcomes can be more powerful than any drug in the world, especially when it comes to changing old habits, behaviors, and beliefs. And to the best of our knowledge, the entire process is driven by the language-based processes of the brain. By changing the way you use language, you change your consciousness, and that, in turn, influences every thought, feeling, and behavior in your life.[18]

We Actually Love Gossip

There is one kind of speech that is more common than all of the others. A variety of studies of conversation has found that 65 to 80 percent of our conversations are gossip, which is characterized by University of California, Riverside professor Megan Robbins as "talking about people who aren't present."[19]

Today's popular media is as fixated on gossip as was the Torah, but the assessment has changed. Headlines from recent years show trending *support* for gossip: "Gossiping Is Good" (*The Atlantic*, 2018), "Why Gossip Can Be Good for You, Even If It's Mean" (*The Independent*, 2019), "Feeling Socially Rusty? Try a Little Light Gossiping" (*New York Times*, 2021), "Why Gossiping at Work Is Good for You" (BBC, 2021), and "Gossip Is Good for You" (Yahoo! Life, 2021).

Are the aforementioned headlines—and the analyses beneath them—correct? Is, perhaps, the biblical teaching on gossip antiquated or even plain wrong?

A consideration can start with an investigation of why gossip is, and apparently always has been, so prevalent. Oxytocin is called "the love hormone," as it is released after sex (earning its other nickname—the "cuddle chemical"). We also release oxytocin when we pet a dog, hug a teddy bear, sing together, and give birth. Its function is to engender trust, intimacy, and generosity. We are primed to engage in activities that generate oxytocin.[20]

What does this have to do with speech? In 2017, Professor Natascia Brondino and colleagues at the University of Pavia had a group of students engage in gossip and in a neutral conversation the following day. They measured, via saliva tests, the oxytocin levels of the students on both days. They found that those in the group who engaged in gossip had secreted significantly more oxytocin than those in the group who had not gossiped.[21]

So, we enjoy gossip because we are conditioned by evolution to do so. Gossip, the University of Oxford evolutionary psychologist Robin Dunbar says, "makes human society as we know it possible." Gossip enables us to live in societies that are larger than our immediate circles, when all reputational knowledge can be procured firsthand.[22]

This argument, which is at the core of the contemporary defenses of gossip, is entirely sensible. In a very small community, we might know that Jill is a cheater or that John is a thief. We would adjust our dealings with them accordingly. The development of a broad and complex society requires us to interact in groups too large for this knowledge to be procured firsthand. But the importance of the knowledge does not diminish with the growth of the group. Gossip fills the void and enables us to know who we are interacting with within a larger society.

What would the Author of the Torah have said? He would have likely agreed that gossip *feels* good; after all, that explains why people do it so often. He would have also agreed that gossip can serve the social function described by Professor Dunbar and others. That is why talebearing is required in cases where refusal to do so would constitute standing by the blood of one's neighbor.

The question, therefore, is not whether gossip *can* be good; it's whether gossip is generally good or bad. This question can be addressed by way of reference to the "triple speech" in the Talmud. What is the nature of the impact on each of the parties involved in gossip: the speaker, the subject, and the listener?

The Speaker

Why do individuals gossip? Professor Jack Schafer of Western Illinois University wrote in 2021:

> People . . . like to gossip because it gives them a sense that they possess secret information about another person, which gives them a sense of

> power. People want to be seen as being in the know when it comes to the latest gossip about others. If knowledge is power, gossip is turbocharged power. In order to display their power and reinforce their egos, people must share the information with other individuals.[23]

So, people gossip to be perceived as knowledgeable and important en route to being more well-liked and powerful. That sounds like gossip is good for the gossiper. Is that so?

In 2011, Professor Sally D. Farley of the University of Baltimore conducted a study of 128 people to assess the relationship between gossip, power, and likability. She determined that "high frequency gossipers" were actually 135 percent *less* liked than "low frequency gossipers," and that this difference existed regardless of whether the gossip was positive or negative.[24]

Professor Farley's demonstration that gossiping is bad for the reputation of the gossiper is reflected in our language. Gossip is usually a verb, as in: "He gossiped about her." But it is also the rare verb that becomes a noun, and in this switch, defines the person. A person who eats a lot is not called "an eat," and a person who travels frequently is not called "a travel." We recognize that even a person who *loves* eating or traveling cannot be reduced to the object of their desire. This is not so for gossiping. One who gossips is often called "a gossip"—reflecting that one who gossips is characterized and defined by their habit. And "gossips" are always among the least-respected people in a community.

Why would gossips be unpopular? Recipients of gossip, though they may enjoy the information in the moment, seem to intuit that *anyone* could be the next subject of gossip from the high frequency gossiper. Consequently, community members punish the gossip with distrust, dislike, and disrespect. And that is not the only cost of gossiping for the speaker.

In 2019, Professors Elena Martinescu of King's College London and Onne Janssen and Bernard A. Nijstad of the University of Groningen published a comprehensive review of the modern social scientific literature on gossip. They found that subjects of gossip develop an intent to retaliate against the gossiper, generating what one study called "spiraling aggression." The gossiper, therefore, is likely to find himself unpopular and untrusted, and as the target of the person he gossiped about.[25]

Those Gossiped About

Rehtaeh Parsons (seventeen years old, Nova Scotia), Amanda Todd (fifteen years old, British Columbia), Phoebe Prince (fifteen years old, Massachusetts), Jamey Rodemeyer (fourteen years old, New York), and Megan Meier (thirteen years old, Missouri) have one thing in common. They all committed suicide after being gossiped about.

Why would gossip drive teenagers to feelings of hopelessness, helplessness, and desperation that can, in extreme cases, make them suicidal? Professor Martinescu and her colleagues who studied the literature on the psychology of gossip found that those who hear negative gossip about themselves are highly likely to develop both self-directed negative emotions (guilt, shame, blameworthiness, anger at self) and other-directed negative emotions (hostility, irritability, and anger). In short, victims of gossip are made to feel worse about themselves and worse about others.[26]

The negative impact of gossip upon the subject is not only felt when the subject hears, or is even aware of the gossip. In 2009, Professor Maryanne Fisher of St. Mary's University had men rate the attractiveness of women on a scale of 1 to 7 without any input from others. They were again asked to do so, after learning what others said. This was an instructive test, because there is no reason why another person's commentary about a woman's looks should have anything to do with how attractive one considers her to be. However, the gossip did prove to be important. Professor Fisher determined that just one negative statement reduced a woman's score by 10 percent.[27]

Professor Fisher's finding provides an evolutionary explanation for why people hate being gossiped about. It is damaging to mate selection even if we don't know about it.

The Listener

Modern social science has confirmed the ancient Jewish teaching that gossip is devastating for the gossiper and the subject of the gossip. How about the third category of people who Rabbi Ishmael says is "killed" by gossip—those who are neither the purveyors nor the subjects of gossip, but those who just listen to it?

A 2012 study by Shimul Melwani (now a professor at the University of North Carolina) of students at the University of Pennsylvania examined the effect of gossip on students engaged in a group project. Dr. Melwani enrolled students in the study who, as part of their required management course, needed to complete a semester-long consulting project in teams of four or five.

At the end of the course, each team needed to give a presentation. Throughout the semester, Dr. Melwani surveyed the students in each group and collected measures of gossip (both about people within and outside the group) and team cohesiveness. She found that intra-team gossip "negatively influenced team outcomes such as psychological safety, cooperation, and viability and increased team-level perceptions of politics."[28]

And the consequences can be profound. In 2014, Professor Katerina Georganta and colleagues at the University of Thessaloniki Medical School in Greece surveyed 532 healthcare workers in six European countries to assess the relationship between gossip and job performance. They found that "negative gossip was positively correlated with emotional exhaustion and depersonalization." Consequently, "negative gossip also correlated positively with suboptimal care . . . and patient safety."[29]

In other words, people perform less well at their jobs if their work environment tolerates gossip. This of course harms the employee and also those the employee serves. The patients at the hospitals in the University of Thessaloniki study probably had no idea if the hospital workers gossiped, but the results affected their care. We see that just being around gossip—as a mere listener—has profoundly negative consequences.

Reflection

God, who could have created the world in any way or no way at all, did so with nine instances of "God said." A few words—"Good job," "I'm proud of you," "You disappoint me," "I love you"—can create, destroy, transform, inspire, discourage, and lots of other things. It is often unknowable when, with whom, or to what extent a word will have such an impact. The only thing we do know and that is within our control is that we each carry *enormous* power on our tongues.

The power of words, as the Torah intuits and modern science confirms, frequently applies to gossip. The contemporary popular literature on gossip often treats it as something unserious, or even positive. The Torah and modern social science completely disagree, and instead characterize gossip as a vicious triple threat: to the gossiper, to those who are gossiped about, and to those who listen to the gossiper.

This threat is vulnerable to a counterthreat, which is the one who resists gossip. Anyone can, and should, resist gossip. One who resists gossip would resolve to be thoughtful and mindful about his speech, to ensure that he is not gossiping. He would also refuse to listen to any gossip. And, with the conviction that words are important and gossip is virulent, he would explain *why* he is leaving a conversation that involves gossip.

One who resists gossip would also, in accordance with the prohibition on standing by the blood of one's neighbor in Leviticus 19:16, speak of others when there is a clear and necessary purpose. This might apply to warning a young woman that her potential beau is a cheater, an employer that a potential employee is a thief, or a coach that her talented player is using performance-enhancing drugs. These warnings should be targeted, purposeful, short, and accompanied by an explanation as to why they are more stilted and abrupt than most conversations.

Resisting gossip need not be a selfless act. It is a good strategy for everyone seeking to build his reputation and influence. His commitment to principle, his discipline, and the regard for others that he shows in his refusal to gossip will earn him the respect of those with whom he interacts. Moreover, when he does say something about someone else, in accordance with the biblical exceptions, he will be taken very seriously. Most importantly, his refusal to gossip will do what gossip does—it will travel. His commitment to treating words with the respect that is commensurate with their awesome power, especially as deployed with regard to other people, will inspire others and help create a culture where gossip is a source of shame.

26

Pinchas and Lenny Skutnik Become Heroes

The Torah and Science of Bystanding and Upstanding

Moses the Upstander

In Exodus 3, God chooses Moses for the most important mission in the history of mankind. Moses will lead the Jewish people out of Egyptian slavery (both physically and psychologically) and into freedom in the Promised Land. It is there that the Jews can fulfill God's dream for us to become "a kingdom of priests and a holy nation" and inspire the world to follow in the ways of ethical monotheism.

The greatness of this task warrants a great founding leader. Why, the reader is led to ask, does God choose Moses for this role? We know little about Moses going into God's decision, but the little we do know provides ample insight into the divine decision.

In Exodus 3, we read of how God selects Moses after the latter *notices* a bush that was burning but was not consumed. The characteristics and importance of this act are discussed in the chapter of this book on noticing.

But the burning bush was Moses's *final* test before God chooses him. By that point, Moses must have been a very good candidate for Jewish leadership. We can see why in Exodus 2 when Moses, a Jew adopted by the Pharaoh's daughter, wanders outside. He sees an Egyptian slave master beating a Jew. Moses stops. He has three choices. He can activate his Jewish allegiance and defend the Jew. He can activate his Egyptian allegiance and support the Egyptian. Or he can refuse to intervene, perhaps telling himself that he does not know the full story—that a dispute between two strangers should not concern him, that intervention is potentially dangerous, or that getting involved could compromise his status as an Egyptian prince.

Exodus 2:12 tells us, "He looked this way and that way and he saw that there was no man." One way to read this is that Moses was alone. But this explanation is challenged by the fact that there were at least two other men around (those in the fight) and seemingly, as we'll see, others who will tell the story. Another explanation is presented to us by way of the Hebrew language.

There are several words in Hebrew for "man." One is *zachar*, which means something like "male." There is *adam*, which can be approximated as "mankind." Another is *ish*, which is used by Hillel the Elder in Pirkei Avot 2:5 in the following way: "In a place where there are no men, strive to be a man." The connotation here is exactly as it is in American English, as when one tells another, "Be a man about it."

The word for "man" in Exodus 2 is not *adam*—but *ish*. Moses's observation, therefore, is that there were other adult males around but, because they weren't intervening, they were not *men*. Moses intervenes; he kills the Egyptian and saves the Jew.

The next day, Moses goes outside again. He sees two Jews fighting. Again, he intervenes and stops the fight. In the process, one of the men says, "Who made you ruler and judge over us? Are you thinking of killing me as you killed the Egyptian?" News of the events of the previous day had spread—presumably by other adult males who had witnessed it, or perhaps by the one who had himself been saved.

Moses has no time to contemplate the cynicism and ingratitude of his fellow Jew. He realizes that people know that he killed the Egyptian the day before, which means that he is in danger. He flees to Midian and sits down by the well.

His "sitting" turns out to be anything but contemplative and solitary. He sees a group of shepherds harassing Midianite women. It's several against one, but Moses does not seem to consider the odds. Again, he intervenes and saves the women. This is the last major event we learn about involving Moses until we meet him again at the burning bush. What could have impressed God to warrant him giving Moses the final test?

In these moments, Moses could have stood by in the face of injustice—with easy excuses and rationalizations for each of the three occasions. But he refuses to do so, and stands up each time. In doing so, he refuses to be a bystander and becomes *a man*. God deems him ready for the final test: to lead the Jewish people toward the Promised Land.

Bystanding: Molech and Baal Pe'or

The next book of the Bible is Leviticus, which is primarily concerned with ritual laws. In Leviticus 19:16, God instructs us, "Do not stand idly by the blood of your fellow." We have to wait only a few verses for the Torah to illustrate why this was a significant concern.

In Leviticus 20:1–3, God decrees the death penalty for anyone who sacrifices his child to Molech (an ancient deity associated with child sacrifice). But God is not done. He says, "If the members of the community close their eyes when that man sacrifices one of his children to Molech . . . I myself will set my face against him and his family and will cut them off from their people together with all who follow him in prostituting themselves to Molech."

Those who know about the sacrifice of a child and do nothing receive the most severe punishment in the Torah, aside from the death penalty. They are cut off from both God and the people.

That is not the only time in the Torah when God addresses bystanding in the context of the worship of foreign gods.

In Numbers 23–24, the king of Moab tries multiple times to destroy the Jews, only to be stymied each time by divine intervention. By Numbers 25, the Moabites have a different tactic. Their women seduce the Jewish men. The nation of Israel, we learn, "became attached to Baal Pe'or," the false deity of Moab.

This is an existential moment for the Jewish people. By this point in the Torah, the Jewish mission is very clear. We are to worship the one true God, honor him through righteous behavior, and in so doing, inspire others. In Numbers 25, the people are radically straying from that path by becoming attached to the false deity of Moab and violating the religious and moral integrity of the Jewish nation.

If the situation were not righted immediately, we likely would have assimilated into the idolatrous peoples around us. There would be no Jewish people, no nation of Israel, and no one to live by and model the truth of ethical monotheism. God's project on earth would be finished.

This would have been obvious to the Jewish desert community. But no one says, or does, anything. The nation, at this point, is one of bystanders.

God gets involved. He tells Moses to identify the people who are sinning and to hang their leaders. Moses delegates the task to the "judges of Israel," saying, "Let each man [judge] kill his men who were attached to Baal-pe'or."

Even with a direct order from Moses, nothing happens. The judges do not say or do anything.

A Jewish man named Zimri, identified as a prince of the tribe of Simeon, brings a Midianite woman named Cozbi to the steps of the Tent of Meeting, the religious sanctuary. In "the sight of Moses and in the sight of the entire assembly of the Children of Israel," Zimri and Cozbi begin to have sex on the Temple steps.

There is really no real modern analogy that can help us understand the severity of this act. Sex on the steps of a presidential inauguration would be an outrageous mockery, but it would have an amusing quality that would soften its scandalousness. Sex on the pulpit in a synagogue or church service would ruin that service (and the career of the institution's security director) but would not threaten the integrity of the faith. But sex on the steps of the Temple violated *everything*: the sanctity of the sanctuary, the integrity of the Jewish family, and the moral framework of the community. Everyone observing Zimri and Cozbi knew that, but no one does anything—until one man does.

Pinchas, the grandson of Aaron and the grandnephew of Moses, "followed the Israelite into the tent. He drove the spear into both of them, right through the Israelite man and the woman's stomach."

God responds, "Pinchas the son of Eleazar, the son of Aaron the priest, has turned back my wrath from among the Children of Israel, because he was zealous with my zeal among them, so that I did not consume the Children of Israel in my anger" (Numbers 25:11).

The twenty-first-century sage Rav Yisrael Druck notes two questions raised by the text. Why is God angry with *all* of the Children of Israel—so angry, indeed, that he is tempted to "consume them"? It is clear that not everyone was having sex with the Moabite women and worshipping their idols. It is because, Rav Druck notes, everyone (until Pinchas acted alone) was bystanding. The choice to be a bystander is so problematic for God that he was ready to kill everyone had Pinchas not stood up and effectively redeemed them.

Rav Druck's second question is triggered by God's saying, "Pinchas . . . has turned back from my wrath among the *Children* of Israel." Why does God not just say, "Pinchas . . . has turned back my wrath"? What is the significance of God adding "the Children of Israel"?

Because, Rav Druck explained, God is not only praising Pinchas for stopping the sex acts, the idolatry, and all they represent. He is also praising Pinchas for educating "the Children of Israel" to act when there is wrongdoing in one's midst, to be an *upstander* and not a *bystander*.[1]

God follows up his declaration with action. He rewards Pinchas with "the covenant of peace." This is the only time in the Torah that God gives anyone this divine award. Many people might have been qualified for it at various points—Abraham, Jacob, Rachel, Joseph, and even Esau were all candidates for this Biblical Peace Prize. But God reserves "the covenant of peace" for the upstander.

Pinchas will have a starring role at one of the most important Jewish rituals. Every Jewish boy, at eight days, is circumcised in a ceremony known as a *brit milah*. One blessing that the baby boy receives is the one that God gave to Pinchas. The blessing we give to all of our boys is that they should be upstanders.

Why the Temple Was Destroyed

The importance of not being a bystander continues long after the Bible. Perhaps the most tragic event in early Jewish history was the destruction of the Temple in Jerusalem. All subsequent persecutions of the Jewish people occurred because we were a stateless people, constantly at the mercy of the great world empires. Why was the Temple destroyed? The Talmud tells us that it was because of the sin of "baseless hatred."[2]

But the Talmud does not stop there. It describes the baseless hatred that led to the Temple's destruction by way of a narrative. A man, Bar Kamtza, was accidentally invited to the party of his enemy. Bar Kamtza shows up. The host, his enemy, demands he leave. Despite his pleas and protestations, he is forcibly removed from the party. He leaves so humiliated that he begins plotting his revenge. He tells the Roman emperor that the Jews are plotting a rebellion against him, and the Romans proceed to destroy the Temple in Jerusalem and exile the Jews.

What drives Bar Kamtza to existentially imperil his Jewish brethren? The Talmud tells us what Bar Kamtza said: "Since the Sages were sitting there and did not protest the actions of the host, although they saw how he humiliated me, learn from it that they were content with what he did."[3]

Bar Kamtza did not instigate the plot to destroy the Jewish nation because of how he was treated at the event. He did so when he saw the rabbis being bystanders to his humiliation. It was bystanding that constituted the "baseless hatred," and led to death, destruction, and exile.

The Thirteenth and Ultimate Commandment

Many modern concepts of justice and righteousness (from the separation of powers to anti-corruption laws) are based on biblical precedent. But the notion of bystanding as elucidated in the Torah, seems not to have penetrated modern society. Rabbi Efrem Goldberg of the Boca Raton Synagogue notes that an American can observe his fellow suffering, do nothing, and remain a good citizen. However, as the Torah's teachings on bystanding illustrate, one who observes the suffering of another and does nothing has committed a terrible act against his fellow, against the community, and against God.[4]

It is this understanding that enabled the twentieth-century sage Rabbi Joseph B. Soloveitchik to understand an otherwise inscrutable biblical verse. Psalm 37:25, which is assumed to have been written by King David, is commonly translated as, "I have been young and am now old, but I have never seen a righteous man abandoned, or his children seeking bread."

On its face, this makes no sense. The Bible never suggests that people who obey its tenets will be rewarded with happy lives free of any suffering. Such a notion would obliterate the concept of faith and transform service of God into a crude transaction. It would also be cruel to the many righteous people who *have* experienced the suffering of their children. So, what could King David have been talking about?

Rav Soloveitchik explained that the Hebrew phrase "I have not seen" should be translated as "I have not been able to stand by and watch." King David, reflecting on a long and full life, is asking to be remembered for never being able to see a righteous man abandoned, or his children seeking bread, without responding.[5]

The final Jewish word on bystanding belongs to Yehuda Bauer. In 1939, Yehuda was thirteen years old and the Nazis invaded his country, Czechoslovakia. His family fled to Poland and then Romania before traveling to Mandatory Palestine. Yehuda went to high school in Haifa, where he became inspired by a teacher to study history. He fought in the War of Independence in 1948, and then began a career as one of Israel's great historians.

In 1998, Yehuda Bauer was invited to address the German Parliament. He said, "I come from a people who gave the Ten Commandments to the world. Time has come to strengthen them by three additional ones, which we ought to adopt and commit ourselves to: Thou shalt not be a perpetrator; thou shalt not be a victim; and thou shalt never, but never, be a bystander."[6]

The Science

A Drowning in Florida

In 2017, a thirty-two-year-old Florida man, Jamel Dunn, fell into a lake in the town of Cocoa. He was clearly drowning. The potential saving grace for Mr. Dunn was the presence of five teenage boys at the side of the lake who had seen him fall. But the saving grace turned out to be irrelevant. None of the boys jumped in or did anything else to help. Instead, they filmed the event, and their recording explains why they acted as they did.

One teen can be heard in the recording saying, "Bruh's drowning, what the heck." Another teen is heard saying, "Ain't nobody gonna help you, you dumb fuck." A third teen says, "We're not going to help your ass." The conversation continued in this vein until one teen said, "He's dead"—followed by more laughing.[7]

Also in 2017, a fifteen-year-old girl from Chicago was gang-raped. The rape was witnessed by forty people who were watching on Facebook Live. None of the viewers reported anything or did anything to help the victim.[8]

On September 16, 2019, a sixteen-year-old boy named Khaseen Morris was approached by several other teenagers at a mall in Long Island, New York. The teenagers began to attack Mr. Morris. There were between fifty to seventy onlookers. No one intervened, but several took photographs and videos of what turned out to be a murder.[9]

In none of these cases were the bystanders arrested—and not because of prosecutorial irresponsibility. They had broken no law. They were well within their legal rights to watch someone raped or killed, and not even take out a phone to call for help.

These examples illustrate the "bystander effect," which describes when people, particularly in groups, choose to stand by rather than help when their involvement is acutely needed. It is by no means limited to matters of life and death as discussed above. For instance, the explosion of cyberbullying, which is often observed by lots of people who do not interrupt it, is a particularly modern, frequent, and often devastating manifestation of the bystanding that so disturbed the Author of the Torah.[10]

When People Bystand: A (Largely) Group Phenomenon

In 1968, the psychologists John Darley of Princeton University and Bibb Latané of Columbia University conducted an experiment to assess how people might respond in emergency situations. They asked Columbia University students to go into a soundproof room alone and discuss the personal problems of another student over an intercom. The intercom was used to maintain the anonymity of the student with the problems and the soundproofing prevented distractions, allowing the students to focus on the task.

Students were divided into two groups. One cohort of students was told that they were having a one-on-one discussion. Another cohort was led to believe that they were having a discussion with three or six people.

A confederate of the researchers then staged a medical emergency.

Among the participants who thought that they were in conversation with just one person, 85 percent called for help within two minutes and 100 percent called for help within six minutes. Among the participants who thought they were in conversation with multiple people, only 31 percent called for help within two minutes and 62 percent called within six minutes.

In another study, Professors Darley and Latané had participants fill out a questionnaire. After completing two pages of the questionnaire, the room began to fill with smoke that was piped in through a vent. Within a few minutes, smoke had filled the room. Participants who were alone reported the smoke 75 percent of the time. Participants in groups of three reported the smoke 38 percent of the time. Participants with two passive confederates reported the smoke 10 percent of the time.

In a third study, Professors Darley and Latané had a researcher administer a questionnaire. This time, the researcher left the room, and participants heard the sound of a crash and a person crying out. The results were similar. When alone, 70 percent of people helped. In groups of three, 40 percent helped. When there were two passive confederates, the duo helped 7 percent of the time.[11]

Fast-forward to the era of modern technology. In 2001, Professors Greg Barron, then of Technion Institute of Technology, and Eldad Yechiam of the University of Haifa, also set out to determine whether people are more likely to help others when in groups or alone. They used a technique that was unavailable to researchers in 1968. They set up a Yahoo email account for a fictitious person named Sarah Feldman. "Sarah" wrote an email:

> I am a graduate student of biology and am considering continuing my studies at the Technion. Do you know if there is a biology faculty at the Technion?
>
> Thanks in advance,
> Sarah Feldman

One batch of emails was sent to individual people at Technion, without anyone else included or cc'd. Another batch was sent to five people at Technion, each of whom could see that others were also addressed in the message. Every recipient of the email at Technion would have been able to easily answer the question correctly.

Professors Barron and Yechiam grouped the responses into four categories:

1. No response
2. A response without the requested information ("Find the web page and look yourself!")
3. A helpful response ("Yes, there is a biology faculty at the university")
4. A very helpful response ("Yes" followed by specific URLs, phone numbers, etc.)

The result: Individuals who were the only respondents were twice as likely to respond at all, and 50 percent more likely to offer a "very helpful response."[12]

These studies have confirmed what the Torah teaches—that people, especially in groups, are likely to become bystanders even when they know they should intervene. The question remains—*why* do people choose to be bystanders? Why did the other men witnessing the fight between the Jew and the Egyptian in Exodus 2 do nothing? Why did the vast majority of the Jewish nation stand by as a small group worshipped at the Golden Calf? Why did everyone but Pinchas stand by at Baal Pe'or? Why did dozens of people simply watch an attack at a Long Island mall? Why did so few people, when addressed alone, respond to Sarah Feldman's email?

Why do people resist saving others at the moment and in the circumstances when they are most capable of doing so—when they can work together as a group?

Why People in Groups Bystand

Social psychologists, guided by the pioneering work of Professors Darley and Latané, posit three reasons for why good people stand by while terrible acts occur. One was identified by Professors Barron and Yechiam in the aforementioned study—a phenomenon they termed the "diffusion of responsibility." When one is alone and something needs to be done, there is no easy way to deny or off-load responsibility. But when many people are around, it is easy to convince oneself that the problem can, should, and will be solved by someone else.

The second explanation for bystanding is "evaluation apprehension." This is manifested when one refuses to act, out of a concern that his words or actions will fail and that this failure will impose a social cost upon him such as public embarrassment.

The third cause of bystanding in groups was identified by Princeton professor Deborah Prentice and Stanford professor Dale Miller in a 1993 study. They found that most college students were uncomfortable with the amount of drinking on campus. These students also thought that most other students were comfortable with it. They termed their discovery "pluralistic ignorance"—which is the phenomenon where individuals in a group *incorrectly* think that their views are abnormal.[13]

Its relation to bystanding was described in a 2014 analysis in *Wharton Magazine*: "Contributing to the bystander effect is 'pluralistic ignorance,' which interferes with our ability to recognize that we are witnessing an emergency situation. We often look to others for cues to the acceptable social response, and if we see that others are not responding, it makes us less likely to take action."[14]

The Upstander

On January 13, 1982, what was then called Washington National Airport in DC was closed in the morning because of snow and ice conditions. It reopened at noon, when conditions eased. Air Florida 90, en route to Fort Lauderdale, was delayed as were many other flights behind it. It was further delayed by the taxi line of other aircraft.

By 3:59 PM, Air Florida 90 was ready to take off. However, the snow had resumed, and the conditions were punishing. If the flight got off, others could follow. If it did not, the airport would be shut down again.

The conversation on the runway was, as is customary with cockpit conversations, recorded.

15:59:32 Captain Wheaton: Okay, your throttles.

15:59:35 [SOUND OF ENGINE SPOOL UP]

15:59:49 First Officer Petit: Holler if you need the wipers.

15:59:51 Wheaton: It's spooled. Really cold here, real cold.

15:59:58 Petit: *God, look at that thing. That don't seem right, does it? Ah, that's not right.* [Emphasis added]

16:00:09 Wheaton: Yes, it is; there's eighty.

16:00:10 Petit: Naw, I don't think that's right. Ah, maybe it is.

16:00:21 Wheaton: Hundred and twenty.

16:00:23 Petit: I don't know.

16:00:31 Wheaton: V1 [measure of speed]. Easy, V2.

Air Florida 90 sped down the runway. It took off. As soon as it was in the air, one passenger—Joe Stiley, a private plane pilot—told his seatmate and colleague Nikki Felch to assume a crash position.

Thirty seconds later, the plane crashed over the 14th Street Bridge and plunged into the icy and frozen Potomac River. Most died upon impact or before. Five passengers, including Joe Stiley and Nikki Felch, were able to hang onto the tail section of the airplane. Within moments, there were many people, including some professional rescuers, at the shore. The rescuers sent a rope from a helicopter. One of the passengers desperately trying to hold onto the rope was Priscilla Tirado. Her husband, Jose, and baby, Jason, were already dead, and she was too weak to hold on. She was back in the frozen water, without anything to save her.

One of the onlookers was Lenny Skutnik, a twenty-nine-year-old functionary at the Congressional Budget Office. Seeing Ms. Tirado alone in the water, Mr. Skutnik threw off his coat, took off his boots, and jumped into the river. By that point, television crews were all over the scene and recorded Mr. Skutnik saving the lives of strangers.

The next week, he became the first ever presidentially invited guest at a State of the Union Address, where he sat next to Nancy Reagan. Subsequently, all presidential guests at the State of the Union Address are called "Lenny Skutniks."

Mr. Skutnik retired from the Congressional Budget Office in 2010. The CBO recognized his decades of service in, primarily, copying reports. His heroism on that terrible day in January of 1982 has led many to question why he, alone among hundreds of people (many of whom were more qualified for a rescue), conquered the bystander effect. He said, "I didn't have any profound thoughts. I just did it. When I got out of the water, I was satisfied. I did what I set out to do."[15]

Mr. Skutnik's explanation may be unsatisfying to people (indeed, most everyone) who appreciate a good story and value comprehensible explanations. We would have liked to hear of divine inspiration, of military training kicking in, of a grandparent's prayer echoing in his ear, of how the victim reminded him of his sister. But no. He said, "Nobody else was doing anything. It was the only way."

Lenny Skutnik might not have been able to teach us why people upstand, or provide anything approaching a methodology about cultivating upstanding in our children. But he taught us something even more important: that even a force as powerful as that drawing people to bystand can, and should, be overcome by anyone.

Reflection

Given the importance of upstanders to every society, a question naturally comes up: Can we require it, at least in the cases where one can safely and reasonably respond? After all, every American jurisdiction has a Good Samaritan Law that shields upstanders from liability. For instance, a physician who responds to a call on an airplane, "Is there a doctor onboard?" cannot be successfully sued if he attempts to help and the victim dies.

Could there be a Bad Samaritan Law requiring people to respond? Yes. Minnesota, Rhode Island, and Vermont impose a broad duty to rescue. Hawaii, Washington, and Wisconsin require citizens to report crimes to authorities. But these laws are rarely, if ever, enforced. Even supporters of these laws, such as Professor Ken Levy of Louisiana State University, are clear that their primary benefit is "symbolic."[16] Why are these laws so rare and seldomly enforced when they exist?

First, laws work best when they apply easily and clearly to everyone at all times. It is not clear how that principle might work here. Would a prosecutor have wanted to punish the boys who filmed the Jamel Dunn video? In theory, sure. But what if they were not confident swimmers? What if they feared—as would be reasonable in Florida—that the river had alligators? While we might consider someone who jumps into alligator-infested waters to rescue a stranger a hero, would we consider one who doesn't to be a criminal?

Less abstractly, there are easily foreseeable and unintended consequences to Bad Samaritan Laws. Professor Eugene Volokh of UCLA points out that Bad Samaritan Laws disincentivize witnesses from cooperating with the police, as observers will be less likely to report what they know if they could be prosecuted for lack of involvement.[17]

Another challenge with Bad Samaritan Laws concerns how they, unwittingly, diminish the obligation to be an upstander by limiting it to extraordinary events. The decision about whether to be an upstander or a bystander is not limited to dramatic moments such as those exemplified by Pinchas and Lenny Skutnik. A child who sees a friend being teased or bullied has the choice about whether to be a bystander or to intervene and become an upstander. One who hears friends gossiping has the choice about whether to be a bystander or to intervene and become an upstander. Someone who sees teenagers littering in the park has the choice to be a bystander or intervene by talking to the youths or picking up the garbage themselves and setting an example.

No one would want to arrest a child for not standing up for a classmate, her father for allowing gossip to occur unimpeded, or her mother for doing nothing about teenagers littering. Yet everyone who accepts the teachings of the Torah and social science on bystanding should want them to intervene enthusiastically. No one should think that the obligation to be an upstander is limited to those circumstances that could conceivably be covered by a law.

The obligation to be an upstander is a moral one that should be encouraged through our educational, cultural, and social institutions. How can we do this?

We can turn to Pinchas. All we know about Pinchas before Baal Pe'or is that he is the son of Eleazar and the grandson of Aaron. That doesn't tell us too much, as none of Aaron's other children or grandchildren intervene. Pinchas *never says anything* in the Torah, and no one says anything about him. We have no idea whether Pinchas was smart, learned, married, a father, generally calm, enthusiastic, rebellious, or pious—nothing.

Lenny Skutnik, before his upstanding at the 14th Street Bridge, was similarly anonymous. He did clerical and analytical work at the Congressional Budget Office, which is not a job that predicts heroism. Indeed, he had no idea why he was able to do what the judges at Baal Pe'or, the Columbia students in 1968, and the others at Washington National Airport on that freezing day in 1982 could not do. If Mr. Skutnik had said that it was because of his childhood clergyman's sermons or the mentorship of his high school football coach, we might think we were near the secret formula for being an upstander. But he offered no such answer.

With no easy answers, how can we orient society toward upstanding? How, more specifically, can we raise our children to be upstanders and to uphold Yehuda Bauer's haunting statement in the German Parliament: "Thou shalt never, but never, be a bystander"?

The fact that no quality—not piety, not intelligence, not anything else—can be identified as the key to upstanding yields a huge and inspiring realization. Anyone can fulfill Yehuda Bauer's commandment and become an upstander. It just takes an independent mind, an unwillingness to tolerate needless suffering and/or evil, and the courage to act accordingly. One thing is for sure: It has nothing to do with what is commonly characterized as intelligence. The judges at Baal Pe'or and the Columbia students in the Darley-Latané experiment had at least one thing in common: They were smart. They had likely participated in serious and erudite discussions of justice, fairness, responsibility, and social obligation. It begins with education. Parents and others who influence children should instruct them, consistently, that they will see and hear bad things. Others will likely ignore the situation, perhaps saying "Boys will be boys," "It's none of my business," I don't know the full story," or "I don't want to get involved." The inaction of others is not an excuse to stand by. It should trigger the realization that this is the moment to become an upstander. A parent who communicates the importance of upstanding when an elementary school classmate is being teased gives his child a moral education that will serve him when more dramatic moments present later.

In the 2010s, Nicholas Wu and his male friends at Princeton University made a pact. Specifically, they pledged to practice "bystander intervention"—to, among other things, rescue women from potential sexual assault. The journalist for the *Princeton Alumni Weekly* who reported this asked him if he was concerned about the risks of bystander intervention—"violence, social ostracism, awkwardness." Mr. Wu replied, "The consequence of not doing it is worse." The Author of the Torah would have agreed.[18]

27

Giving Leads to Wealth

The Torah and Science of Giving to Charity

Tzedakah

In Psalm 24, King David declares: "Unto God is the land and all that fills it."

This evokes two fundamental questions. What, actually, is King David asserting? And what are we to *do* pursuant to that assertion?

The answers to both questions are widely acknowledged within the Jewish tradition. The first cuts right to the heart of our relationship with property. We are to consider property to be God's. God has entrusted some of it to each of us, with the expectation that we use it in a way that would make him proud and glorified.

How are we supposed to do that? There are many ways—but the most important one is encapsulated in one word: *tzedakah*. This is sometimes mistranslated as "charity." While acts of *tzedakah* and charity both describe giving to the poor, they reflect fundamentally different frameworks. Charity, as it has been understood in the English-speaking world for at least eight hundred years, means "an act of kindness through philanthropy."[1]

The Torah does not command charity, which is given when one feels like acting kind. Instead, it insists on *tzedakah*, which more accurately means "righteousness." The distinction is essential. Giving to those in need is not just something nice to do; it is an *obligation*. It is an act incumbent upon all of those who seek righteousness. *Tzedakah* can and should incorporate kind acts and sentiments, but the biblical obligation exists *independently* of how anyone feels about the recipient.

This obligation is of such importance that the Talmud declares, "Greater is *tzedakah* than all of the sacrifices."[2] The rabbis of the Talmudic age had already come up with substitutes for sacrifices as the Temple had been destroyed by the time of its recording. These substitutes—prayer, study, and acts of kindness—took the place of the Temple offerings. So, the Talmud is declaring that *tzedakah* is actually greater than *all* of the most important biblical obligations and Torah practices.

The fact that *tzedakah* is such an important biblical obligation does not mean that the Torah tradition regards it as easy. Indeed, the expression "it's only money" does not have Torah resonance or roots. The most dramatic prayer of the year, the *Unetaneh Tokef* that is recited on Yom Kippur, refers to God as the one who will determine "who will live and who will die, who will become impoverished, and who will become wealthy." The most important prayer in the daily service, the Amidah, contains a plea for material prosperity. And the Hebrew word *damim* means both "blood" and "money," implying that parting with money can be as meaningful and as difficult as losing one's own blood.[3]

It is because giving *tzedakah* is so important and difficult that God goes to remarkable lengths to facilitate it. He even overturns the laws of faith and economics.

Deals with God: The Divine Exception

One of the core tenets of Judaism is spelled out in Deuteronomy 6:16: "You are not to test God." God is not an ATM where we can punch in the right code (in words or deed) and receive what we want. There are several reasons why such a view of "faith" accords with general Torah teachings, and is even a logical necessity.

First, God seeks a partnership with us—not a transaction. If we punch the right code into the ATM and cash does not come out, it is right to conclude that the machine is faulty and to seek another one. If we ask a vendor for a product that the vendor cannot deliver in a satisfactory time, manner, or condition, it is appropriate to seek another vendor. These responses are fine because they are transactions. But if we request something from a spouse or a colleague, and she says no or not yet, we will not just move on, because that is not how one behaves with a partner.

Second, we have no idea what to expect from God. Let's say that a young man wants to marry a particular woman or to get a certain job. He prays and does good deeds in order to convince God that he is worthy. However, it is possible that God has a plan for the young man that involves a woman he has not met or a career he has not conceived.

Third, what happens if God is asked for contradictory things? It is entirely possible that two young men could be inclined to promise God that they will do all kinds of good deeds if only he would inspire the same young woman to return their affections. What is God supposed to do in that circumstance?

So, making deals with God is fundamentally antithetical to the Jewish experience. But there *is* an exception, which is described in Deuteronomy 15:10. Moses, in describing how one should deal with a "destitute brother" instructs: "You shall surely give to him, and let your heart not feel bad when you give him, for in return for this matter, Hashem, your God, will bless you in all your deeds and in your every undertaking."

There is nothing abstract about any biblical blessing. They all have practical and material ramifications. When God blesses Isaac's crops, it grows a "hundredfold." When God blesses Joseph's household in Egypt, it becomes wealthy. When God blesses Hannah's womb, she has children. When God blesses Abraham, Abraham becomes the father of many nations.

So, Moses is clearly saying in Deuteronomy 15:10 that if we give to the destitute *enthusiastically*, we will be *materially* rewarded in "all your deeds and your every undertaking." This can be understood in basketball terms. If a player consistently assists and scores to achieve victory for the team, the coach will ensure that the ball is always in his hands. In the biblical worldview, God will provide to those who choose to support the poor with what they need to be his valued partners—and then some.

The spirit and seriousness of this guarantee is embedded in an exchange between Rabbi Yochanan and the young son of his study partner Resh Lakish, as recorded in the Talmud. Rabbi Yochanan asked the boy what he learned in school that day. The boy said, *Aser ta'aser* ("A tithe shall you tithe"). The boy asked Rabbi Yohanan as to the meaning of the double language.

Rabbi Yohanan, employing a wordplay, replied, "Take a tithe [*aser*] and you will become wealthy [*tit'asher*]."

The boy asked the great sage how he could be sure that this was true. Rabbi Yohanan told him to *test it* and see for himself: Take a tithe, see what happens.

The boy retorted, "Is it permitted to test the Holy One, Blessed be He? Is it not written, 'You shall not test the Lord your God'?" (Deuteronomy 6:16).

Rabbi Yocḥanan recited a companion verse to Deuteronomy 15:10—Malachi 3:10: "Bring the whole tithe into the storehouse, so that there may be food in my house. Test me in this and see if I will not throw open the floodgates of heaven and pour out so much blessing that there will not be room enough to store it."[4]

Subsequent Jewish teaching has built on this position. In his Mishneh Torah, Maimonides issues this bold claim: "No one ever became poor from giving *tzedakah* nor did anything bad or any harm come from it."[5]

In the twentieth century, the Rebbe Menachem Mendel Schneerson explained how this works. He said, "My father-in-law, the previous rebbe, said that when a Jew commits to giving an amount which seems totally unfeasible to him from a financial perspective, God opens a new conduit for him to help him fulfill his good resolution amid joy and gladness, which means that he is given several times more in order to be able to give that amount happily."[6]

Given that it is acceptable to make a deal with God when it comes to *tzedakah*, a question that pertains to all deals is raised. What return can we expect for giving *tzedakah*?

The answers are very practical. The third-century sage Rabbi Yitzchak stated that one receives six blessings for every coin and eleven for every word of comfort that he gives to another. The twelfth-century sage Yitzchak ben Asher Halevi (known as the *Riva*), looked to Genesis 26:12: "Isaac sowed in that land and reaped a hundredfold the same year. God blessed him and the man grew richer and richer until he was very wealthy." The Riva reasoned that Isaac's 100x yield was due to his planning to provide tithes to the poor. The Rebbe Menachem Schneerson said that the return is four to five times what one gives financially.

The only disagreement between these great sages separated by two millennia is whether a gift will pay out at 4x to 6x, 11x, or 100x.[7]

Giving as Taking: The Divine Exception

As the term *damin* (blood/money) reveals, the Author of the Torah knew that parting with money is difficult. Seemingly anticipating the tension between the difficulty of giving money and the commandment to give *tzedakah*, God steps in with another exception. This exception is to the most basic law of economics.

The law is that of zero-sum: If Jill gives Pete something, Jill will have less of it and Pete will have more. This seems obvious and immutable, but God creates an exception to it. It is introduced in Exodus and culminates in Moses's parting guidance to us in Deuteronomy.

In Exodus 25:2, God provides a very detailed description of how the Tabernacle is to be constructed and furnished. As with all major capital projects, this one is expensive. How would it be financed? God has a very specific plan. "Speak to the children of Israel; they are to *take* for me an offering."

God then specifies the kinds of offerings that the people are to *take*. They include gold, silver, bronze, yard of blue, purple, and scarlet; goat hair; red ram skins; olive oil; spices; and fragrance.

Why does God use the word "take" when he seemingly should be telling them to "give"? Is God really telling the Children of Israel to build the Tabernacle by *taking*? Apparently, yes—and in doing so, God is teaching us a fundamental lesson. When one gives *tzedakah*, it is *the giver* who actually receives.

This teaching is reflected in the Hebrew language. The Hebrew word *natan* means "give." In both Hebrew and the English transliteration, it reads the same backwards and forwards. The Christian author Linda Cox calls it "God's palindrome," suggesting that giving is inherently reciprocal—a mutually beneficial act, where it becomes unknowable, and ultimately irrelevant, who benefits more.[8]

Giving as Retaining: How a Person Is Measured

God amplifies his claim that giving and taking are indistinguishable acts of mutual benefit in Numbers 5:10. God instructs, "And each shall retain his sacred donations: each priest shall keep what is given to him."

This is a curious statement. How does one *retain* his donations? In the Talmud, the fourth-century sage Rav Nachman bar Yitzchak explained. A man only really has what he gives.[9]

A story attributed to the nineteenth-century financier and British patriot Sir Moses Montefiore shows how deeply this teaching is ingrained in the Jewish mind. Sir Moses was once asked what he was worth. He named a figure that the questioner responded to quizzically, as he knew that it was much less than his net worth. The financier replied, "You didn't ask me how much I own. You asked me how much I am worth. So I calculated how much I have given to *tzedakah* this year."[10]

This is an entirely logical claim. If one loses money, it's gone. But if one gives, the goodness enabled by his gifts is his forever. If one gives money to feed the poor or to heal the sick, the poor are fed and the sick are healed, regardless of whatever happens later.

A Community of Givers

In Exodus 30, God tells Moses how to conduct a census of the people. Everyone is to bring a half shekel to the Temple, where the funds are to be used in the construction of the sacred structure. By requiring that *everyone*—even recipients of *tzedakah*—contribute, God is teaching us two lessons.

The first is hinted at in the nature of the donation, which must be specifically a *half-shekel*. As Rabbi Moshe Scheiner of the Palm Beach Synagogue teaches, the message of a half denomination is that we become complete by giving in communion with others.[11]

The second lesson is raised by the question: Why does everyone—including recipients of *tzedakah*—give? It must be that *tzedakah* is not only about the wealthy supporting the poor and communal institutions. It is also about ensuring that society is not one of givers and takers, but a community of givers, where *everyone* experiences the dignity, goodness, and joy of giving.

As the Torah seeks to create a culture of giving, it prescribes that everyone must give with an entirely positive attitude. Moses is clear that *tzedakah* should be given "generously and without a grudging heart." The Talmud expands on this, stating that one must give with three components: a cheerful countenance, joy, and a full heart. Indeed, the Talmud stipulates that one who gives with a begrudging or otherwise negative attitude "loses all merit for the mitzvah of giving *tzedakah*."

The eighteenth-century sage Yedidiah Tiah Weil from Prague provided an example of how one is to give.

> One should empathize with the needy person in his misery and speak to him with consolation. This is what the prophet Isaiah wrote: "and you offer your compassion to the hungry and satisfy the famished creature." This means that one should first speak to the needy person and ask him about his troubles . . . He should placate the poor person and encourage him to come to his house. But once the meal begins, he should not speak about the other's poverty; rather he should treat him as if he were the host's best friend and happy to be with him. They should eat and drink happily together. When the poor guest prepares to leave, once again his host should console him with soft words and tell him that God will help him and that he will see better times just as we all wait for the final redemption.[12]

Where, How Much, and What to Give

The consecration of a *community* of enthusiastic and compassionate givers leads to three questions that speak to its implementation. These are: Where should I give? How much should I give? What should I give? The Torah offers clear guidance for all three.

Where Should I Give?

The Torah, which could not enumerate and prioritize every giving opportunity in each community in perpetuity, nevertheless offers a framework. In Deuteronomy 15:11, Moses says, "Therefore, I command you, saying, you shall surely open your hand to your brother, to your poor one and to your needy one in the Land."

As ever, the order of the things enumerated in the verse is instructive. We should, Moses guides us, first give to our "brother." The "brother" is not designated as destitute, and therefore, might be embodied in communal institutions such as schools and synagogues, where people come together regardless of their economic status.

"Your poor one" and "your needy one in the Land" sound similar, but their being distinguished from each other in the text indicates that the

Author of the Torah considers them differently. The Torah makes it simple to understand. The "poor one" must be in our immediate vicinity, as the "needy one"—as is indicated by his being "in the Land"—must refer to those we do not know. As there would have been no way to give to people outside the Land, this third category comes close to applying to international giving.

Importantly, the Torah commands all three types of giving—to our brother, to the poor in our vicinity, and to the needy in the more general "Land." The commandment to engage in all three types of giving explains the order in which they are listed. Giving is not a tradeoff; it builds and grows. We start by giving where it is easiest—to those with whom we are closest, including the communal institutions that nourish us. We grow as givers as we give to the poor in our wider communities. And we are completed as givers when we give to the poor with whom we have no personal or even communal connection. This final act enables us to fulfill our biblical obligation—reiterated dozens of times in various forms in the Torah—to "love the stranger." *Tzedakah*, the Torah is clear, *begins* at home, but it does not end there.

What Should One Give?

Everyone, the Torah is clear, must give money to support the poor both in and out of one's community. But God is clear that the gifts he desires are not limited to money. In Exodus 25, God enumerates what must be contributed to the Tabernacle. These items include gold, silver, spices, fragrances, and embroidered materials—all the works of craftsmen. We see that giving requires each person contributing money *and* from the special capabilities that they have.

Rabbi David Wolpe, citing the Rebbe of Ger, asks a fascinating and very Jewish question. He thought of the generation in the desert, which had manna and all other necessities provided directly and regularly by God. How, then, did people give *tzedakah*? Rabbi Wolpe suggested that they offered gifts of their imagination. As manna could taste however anyone wanted, Rabbi Wolpe imagined that the desert Jews shared ideas for how the food could taste and were thus able to give and take from each other in this unique time of universal plenty.[13]

During the darkest days in Jewish history, Rabbi Avraham Halevi Jungreis showed just how giving could be done in the opposite context: when no one has anything. In 1944, he, his family, and approximately five hundred thousand other Hungarian Jews were sent by the Nazis to concentration camps. When they arrived at Bergen-Belsen, he told his four children, "Kinderlach, children, smile. When grown-ups see young children smiling, it will give them hope." One of his daughters, Esther, was eight at the time and grew up to be one of the great Jewish scholars, teachers, and leaders in twentieth-century America. She reflected on her father's teaching that they, even as child slaves, had a unique gift to give, which would have lifesaving capabilities for the community.[14]

How Much Should One Give?

This question of how much to give is answered explicitly in the Shulchan Arukh, the sixteenth-century code of Jewish law. It is a misnomer that Jews should just tithe and give one-tenth of their income. To do so, the code declares, "is the average disposition." But no one should strive to be average. Therefore, the Shulchan Arukh rules, "If one can afford, let him give as much as needed. Under ordinary circumstances, a fifth of one's property is most laudable."[15]

A wealthy person, by definition, is not in an "ordinary circumstance." Therefore, he should give much more than 20 percent.

How much more than 10 or 20 percent should each person give? The Torah, as an eternal guidebook, does not offer a precise formula that everyone in every conceivable financial situation, anywhere, and at any time, should follow. But it does offer a principle that can guide us in our decisions.

Much of the Book of Leviticus is devoted to sacrifices. In Leviticus 2:1, we are instructed, "When anyone offers a grain offering to the Lord, their offering is to be of the finest flour." In other words, we are not to give to God what we no longer want, what is left over, or what we otherwise do not value. We are to give our "finest."

This commandment is reiterated in Leviticus 22:19 and Deuteronomy 15:21 where we are commanded to offer animals without blemish. The prophet Malachi, speaking around eight centuries after the Torah was given, emphasized the imperative of giving one's best: "'When you sacrifice lame or diseased animals, is that not wrong? Try offering them to your governor! Would he be pleased with you? Would he accept you?' says the Lord Almighty."

The aforementioned verses in Leviticus, Deuteronomy, and Malachi apply to sacrifices to God (often as atonement). In Leviticus 23, God makes it clear that this same ideology applies to our giving to the poor.

In Leviticus 23:19–21, God tells us about how and when to offer lambs as part of a sin offering. In Leviticus 23:23–25, God tells us about how and when to offer the fire offering of Rosh Hashanah. Leviticus 23:22, which serves as a break in the instructions for the lamb and fire offerings, tells us: "When you reap the harvest of your land, do not reap to the very edges of your field or gather the gleanings of your harvest. Leave them for the poor and for the foreigner residing among you. I am the Lord your God."

The interjection of this law of *tzedakah* in the middle of these two laws of sacrifice seems bizarre. Why would the Torah include what seems to be a glaring non sequitur? The ancient commentary *Torat Kohanim* explains. The Torah is teaching us that giving to the poor is not just a nice, good, or right thing to do. It is the equivalent of having built the Temple and offered sacrifices. One should regard giving to the poor just as one does giving to God.[16]

Knowing the instructions in Leviticus on giving, we can return to the question of how much we should give. In Leviticus 22, we learn that we should give from our best and that giving is done in the context of sacrifice. Therefore, we are giving enough when doing so constitutes a *sacrifice*—when our gifts lead us to do without something that we would otherwise enjoy.

Giving Intelligently

The Torah is clear that God wants us to give generously, joyfully, enthusiastically, and creatively. But that is not all. He also wants us to give intelligently.

In Exodus 23:5, God says: "If you see the donkey of your enemy fallen down under its load, do not leave it there; you shall surely help with him." The verse could have said, "You shall surely help him." But it doesn't. It says, "You shall surely help *with* him."

Why would the Torah include the "with"? The Talmud explains, "If the owner of the animal went and sat down . . . he [the one who would otherwise help] is exempt."[17] If the recipient will not appreciate the gift or participate in the act of giving, there is neither an obligation that one should give nor an expectation that he should anyway.

Twelve verses later, the Jews commit one of our greatest sins in the desert. Anxious about Moses's apparent delay in returning from Mount Sinai, the Jews use all of our gold and silver to construct a Golden Calf. We worship around the calf and seemingly have an orgy.

Most commentators have seen the behaviors at the Golden Calf as constituting sins of idolatry, impatience, and a lack of faith. They are correct. But in the Jerusalem Talmud, Rabbi Abba bar Acha identified another problem—one pertaining to a defect in what he called the "character of the people."[18]

He said: "They're solicited for the Golden Calf and they give. They're solicited for the Sanctuary and they give." The sin, according to Rabbi Abba bar Acha, is indiscriminate giving.

According to Rabbi Abba bar Acha, it didn't matter to the people whether the collection was for an idol or God. They gave indiscriminately. Through both the story of the Golden Calf and the law concerning helping your enemy, the Author of the Torah is imparting another fundamental lesson about giving. It also has to be done *intelligently*—with thoughtfulness, rigor, and regard to whether it will solve, do little about, or even exacerbate the problem the giver seeks to address.

The Science

The Phenomenon of Giving Leading to Wealth

In his 1871 book, *The Descent of Man*, Charles Darwin expressed a conundrum. His theory of evolution was based on the premise that species (including humans) adapt to optimize for survival. It explains why people like sex, snakes have no legs, mice have big ears, giraffes have long necks, and Tibetans have large lung capacity. But it doesn't seem to explain why people give without expecting anything in return—a phenomenon that Mr. Darwin noted extends even to one man giving his life for another to whom he is unrelated.[19]

Evolution is not the only theory confounded by charitable giving. There is also socialism. In 1981, the socialist mayor of Burlington, Vermont, Bernie Sanders, said, "I don't believe in charities." He explained that he disagreed with the "fundamental concept on which charities are based," which is that citizens, as distinct from the government, should care for the poor. The Republican governor of Vermont at the time, Richard Snelling, seemed confused. He responded, "Charity is not a dirty word. We have discovered that you can't buy caring."[20]

Most Americans agree with Governor Snelling that "charity is not a dirty word." Around 75 percent of Americans give money to charity—adding up to approximately half a trillion dollars in 2021.[21]

Just as charitable giving is prevalent, so is financial concern. In 2022, approximately half of Americans described their financial condition as "bad." This is not surprising, given that a third of Americans report that an unexpected expense of $400 would cause significant financial distress.[22]

Because personal financial distress is such a ubiquitous concern, there is abundant commentary pertaining to its causes and solutions. Investopedia lists ten reasons why people hit financial trouble: excess/frivolous spending, debt, buying a new car, spending too much on a house, borrowing too much against the house, living paycheck to paycheck, not investing, paying off debt with savings, and not having a plan.

Donating to charity is not one of them. But could it be subsumed under excess spending? The examples of excess spending given by Investopedia suggest not. These are dining out, buying cigarettes, and ordering specialty coffee.[23]

An analysis by GOBankingRates found twenty-three reasons why people end up in financial hardship. Many of the twenty-three are those listed by Investopedia—as well as others, such as paying too much for cellular phones and service. Even this more comprehensive list does not list giving to charity as a reason why people hit financial trouble.[24]

The host of *The Dough Roller Money Podcast*, Rob Berger, provided one hundred ways to improve one's financial situation. Many of his recommendations involve saving money—for instance, refinancing debt, "thinking twice" before lending to friends and family, conducting a home energy audit, and using cashback sites for online purchases. Mr. Berger includes a recommendation on charity. He says that one can improve his financial situation by *giving more*.[25]

Why would Rob Berger state so matter-of-factly that giving to charity is a way to *improve* one's finances? A 2007 analysis in *Entrepreneur* explains why. The researchers at *Entrepreneur* worked with the dataset of the Social Capital Community Benchmark Survey—a survey of about thirty thousand people in more than forty communities across the United States. They assumed that volunteer activity, regardless of income, is a proxy for charitable giving. This is a reasonable assumption. A 2009 study by the Fidelity Charitable Gift Fund found that volunteers give ten times as much to charity as do people who do not volunteer.[26]

The *Entrepreneur* team, equipped with the volunteering and income data, concluded: "Imagine two families that are identical in size, age, race, education, religion, and politics. The only difference is that this year the first family gives away $100 more than the second. Based on my analysis of the S.C.C.B.S. survey, the first family will, on average, earn $375 more as a result of its generosity."

The math of compound interest growth explains how significant the *net gain* of $275 that is enjoyed by givers can be over time. Let's say that a person decides to give just $1,000 more to charity than the average person in his community. He will, according to the aforementioned study, gain $2,750. If he continues doing this for forty years, and assuming an average stock market return, he will have approximately $1.3 million more than he would have if he donated the average.

The researchers at *Entrepreneur* were staggered by this finding. They explained it by asking: "Is it . . . a metaphysical phenomenon?"

Well—the Torah is clear that people who give enthusiastically will have made an outstanding financial investment. But that does not make the *Entrepreneur* finding metaphysical. God, as Maimonides said, works his miracles in the world—and within nature. Consequently, we should be able to figure out why giving makes people wealthier. And thanks to twenty-first-century social science, we can. In fact, we know five ways in which giving leads to wealth.

Giving Leads to Wealth #1: Through Increased Happiness

In 2006, Jorge Moll and colleagues at the Cognitive and Behavioral Neuroscience Unit of the D'Or Institute for Research and Education in Brazil put subjects under an MRI. They measured the activity of the mesolimbic reward system in the brain when people were given money for themselves—and then for the purpose of giving it to charity.

The researchers found that the reward systems were positively activated by pure monetary rewards—i.e., when they got to keep it themselves. This is not surprising. Everyone would be happy to receive a raise, discover a long-forgotten bank account, find a $100 bill at the bottom of a drawer, or learn that they are the beneficiary in the will of a long-lost relative.

What is interesting and surprising is another of their findings. They write, "Remarkably, more anterior sectors of the prefrontal cortex are distinctively recruited when altruistic choices prevail over selfish material interests."[27]

In other words, the part of our brain that generates pleasure—that provides rewards—is more active when we give than when we receive.

This finding was so counterintuitive and important that social scientists continued to test it. In 2007, Professor William Harbaugh and his colleagues at the University of Oregon gave $100 to participants under a brain-scanning machine. They found that the participants were happy when they received the money, happier when they were told that the money was going to a food bank, and happiest when they voluntarily contributed the money to the food bank.

An analysis of the brain chemistry of giving by the Cleveland Clinic, reports that the reward system of the brain produces dopamine (which provides pleasure) and oxytocin (known as "the love hormone") when we give. These are the same stimuli we generate when eating chocolate and having an orgasm.[28]

The studies of brain chemistry show how giving generates pleasure in the short term. How about longer-term pleasure?

One of the great datasets in social science is the Wisconsin Longitudinal Study, which measured the lives of ten thousand graduates of Wisconsin high schools from 1957 until 2011. This large dataset of the same cohort of people through most of a lifetime enables researchers to identify correlations with attitudes and behaviors in the past to outcomes in the present.

Professor Donald Moynihan of the University of Wisconsin–Madison and several colleagues found that the individuals who, in the early 1970s, had reported being more giving at work were the most likely to consider themselves happy in the 2000s. Professor Moynihan and his colleagues reflected, "Our findings make a simple but profound point about altruism: helping others makes us happier. Altruism is not a form of martyrdom, but operates for many as part of a healthy psychological reward system." The

Author of the Torah, who referred to giving to the Tabernacle as *taking*, would not have been surprised.[29]

An observer might look at these findings and discoveries and conclude: Okay, so giving makes us happy. But what does being happy have to do with being wealthy? There are at least two answers. One relates to how happy people perform at work. The other relates to how people feel about their wealth and how that feeling impacts wealth accumulation.

In 2022, Professors Paul B. Lester (Naval Postgraduate School), Ed Diener (University of Illinois), and Martin Seligman (University of Pennsylvania) analyzed what accounts for outstanding performance at work. They came up with a singular answer. "Top performers have a superpower: happiness."

A variety of studies have confirmed their finding, showing that happiness correlates with professional and financial success. This finding has been found to apply to people as diverse as soldiers, corporate employees, and investors. Happy people earn more because they are more likely to be optimistic, take fewer sick days, are more productive, are more likely to solve problems rather than complain about them, and invest in their professional growth.[30]

The formula is clear. Giving leads to happiness, and happiness leads to wealth. And that is far from the only reason that twenty-first-century social scientists have found for why giving leads to wealth, as God promised in Deuteronomy.

Giving Leads to Wealth #2: The Extra Milers

In 2015, Professor Ning Li and his colleagues at Johns Hopkins studied the performance of eighty-seven teams of laborers at a petroleum plant. Each team had approximately eight members. Through a review of performance and interviews with employees, these researchers identified the "extra milers" in the company—those employees who displayed the "highest frequency" of collaboration and the attitude of giving it reflects. They found that "even a single extra miler in a vital position plays a more important role in driving team processes and outcomes than do all the other members."[31]

In a *Harvard Business Review* analysis, Professor Rob Cross of Babson College and Professors Adam Grant and Rob Rebele of Wharton showed that the dynamic of the extra miler is common. And the impact of the extra milers is powerful. The 3 to 5 percent of an organization who are the extra milers account for between 20 and 35 percent of the collaborative work. These givers become known in the organization for their generosity, and are constantly sought by their colleagues.[32]

Why would extra milers and other prosocial individuals earn more money than their colleagues who do not share those characteristics? Professor Kimmo Eriksson of Mälardalen University in Sweden explained:

> First, recent work shows that those who are more prosocial and contribute more to groups are granted positions of status . . . in those groups. That higher status and leadership positions are also generally accompanied by larger material outcomes implies a negative relationship between selfishness and income. Similarly, many high paying jobs and occupations require the ability to empathize and work well with others. Given that such skills tend to be higher in those with prosocial emotions . . . we should expect prosocials to be better off economically.[33]

In other words, people want to work with those who are giving. Giving employees will invest more in mentoring and training and will contribute more overall, as they are generally happy to go above and beyond what is expected. It is no surprise that such employees are in high demand. And like all people and things in high demand, their economic value is high.

It is clear that *individual* extra milers are likely to do better economically than those who are not particularly giving. How about organizations that have a culture of giving? After September 11, the United States government tasked Richard Hackman of Harvard University with determining what makes its dozens of teams most effective. Professor Hackman and his colleagues interviewed hundreds of analysts across sixty-four different intelligence groups and went through a variety of factors that might account for effectiveness: resources, recognition, rewards, roles, responsibility, and team size.

The conclusion: None of those factors were determinative, or even close. The determinative factor was how giving the team members were. Professor Grant, in an analysis of Professor Hackman's study, wrote:

> In the highest performing teams, analysts invested extensive time and energy in coaching, teaching, and consulting with their

> colleagues. These contributions helped analysts question their own assumptions, fill gaps in their knowledge, gain access to novel perspectives, and recognize patterns in seemingly disconnected threads of information. In the lowest-rated units, analysts exchanged little help and struggled to make sense of tangled webs of data. Just knowing the amount of help-giving that occurred allowed the Harvard researchers to predict the effectiveness rank of nearly every unit accurately.

This finding has been shown across a variety of industries. The extent of a giving culture predicted success in pharmaceutical sales, bank profitability, retention in call centers, engineering creativity, productivity in paper mills, and customer satisfaction in restaurants.[34]

Giving Leads to Wealth #3: Financial Self-Confidence

Most people think that the question of whether one is wealthy can be easily answered by a calculation of financial assets. The twentieth-century essayist H. L. Mencken was not among them. He famously defined a wealthy man as one who earns at least $100 more a year than his wife's sister's husband.[35]

Was H. L. Mencken being clever and maybe cynical? Perhaps. But was he also correct? A 2005 study by Professor Ada Ferrer-i-Carbonell, now of the Barcelona School of Economics, found, "Individuals are happier the larger their income is in comparison with the income of the reference group." Indeed, studies from the United Kingdom and the United States show that the amount of money one has accounts for half of the information one processes to assess his wealth. The other half is how much he has by *comparison* with others in his reference group.[36]

The results are startling. A 2011 report from Boston College found only half of the members of a cohort with a minimum net worth is $25 million—and an average net worth is $78 million—considers themselves "financially secure."[37]

The lesson: One's perception of wealth is relative. How, then, can one *feel* wealthy? One possible answer is to move into a neighborhood where you are the wealthiest person. That would be a strange reason to make a life decision. Is there another way? A 2012 study by Professors Zoe Chance of

Yale, Michael Norton of Harvard, and Cassie Mogilner, then of Wharton, provides the answer.

They had one cohort of students do something prosocial—such as spend time on a Saturday morning writing notes to sick kids. They had a control cohort do something nonproductive (counting the "e"s in a Latin text), something entirely for themselves—or just allowed them to leave early.

The purpose was to determine how, if at all, these acts of giving changed the individual.

They found that students who performed prosocial acts were "less likely to view time as scarce and more likely to say they currently had some to spare." These students, they reported, felt "affluent" in the currency of time. This feeling of affluence had broad-based effects. Students who had given of their time were likely to report that their futures were "infinite."

With infinite futures and plenty of time to realize their potential, the students who gave had developed a particular attitude and worldview. Professors Chance, Norton, and Mogilner concluded that people who give "feel more capable, confident, and useful. They feel they've accomplished something and, therefore, that they can accomplish more in the future. And this self-efficacy makes them feel that time is more expansive."[38]

So, giving makes one feel more "capable, confident, useful" and "affluent." Why, in the context of accumulating objective wealth, does it matter whether someone *feels* like any of these things?

A 2017 article by Caroline Beaton in *New York* magazine reviewed recent studies in financial psychology. Ms. Beaton cites Professor Jiaying Zhao of the University of British Columbia, who points out that people with a scarcity mindset make shortsighted decisions. Professor Zhao's colleague Elizabeth Dunn points out that people who feel poor often make "brash" decisions and others that are "simply dumb"—like taking out a high-interest payday loan to pay for a car. As Ms. Beaton concludes, "If you feel like you have less, you may also feel like you have less to lose."[39]

Just as feeling poor induces wealth-destructive decisions, feeling wealthy appears essential for encouraging good financial decisions. A 2018 study by the Principal Financial Group and the behavioral psychologist Dan Goldstein found that each American makes an average of 35,000 decisions a day. However, 70 percent of Americans have not made a major financial decision in three years. Why do so many Americans, who have no problem making decisions about thousands of things, shy away from doing so when it comes to money?

Jerry Patterson, a senior executive at Principal, explained that the greatest determinant of whether one makes major financial decisions is unrelated to income or indebtedness. It is "really around whether they have confidence."[40]

Who is the most likely in a society to feel confident about their finances? Those who feel as if they are good builders of wealth. It is not possible to build wealth if one feels poor and makes bad financial decisions—as the *New York* article details. It is also not possible to build wealth by avoiding financial choices and depositing one's paycheck into a checking account. It is only possible to build wealth when one has the confidence to make investment and business decisions. The study by Professor Chance and her colleagues showed how that confidence can be cultivated: By giving, people develop the feelings of confidence, capability, self-efficacy, and affluence that are crucial for making good financial decisions.

Why might giving to charity be a confidence-building act? Perhaps the answer lies with Rabbi Abba bar Acha's analysis of the sin of the Golden Calf—when he distinguished between giving well and giving poorly. A donor who gives well will understand and appreciate the massive impacts of his charitable decisions. For instance, a donor could go to watsi.org, spend a few hundred dollars, and see how their gift has enabled a young mother to receive a Cesarean section and avoid death or debilitation and return as a healthy woman to her baby, husband, other children, and community. A donor could give to and volunteer at a soup kitchen and see how their generosity with time and money is able to bring sustenance to people who need it. A giver who appreciates how much impact he has by giving even a small amount of money will rightly conclude that he is good with money and develop the confidence necessary to make more of it.

Giving Leads to Wealth #4: "The Social Glue That Holds Business Relationships Together"

In 2007, Jennifer Openshaw published an analysis of what drives wealth—a subject that she had been studying and writing about for many years. She determined that the most likely determinant of whether one becomes a millionaire is "business contacts and relationships." She writes:

> The research found that millionaires actually do tap into their networks more effectively. This isn't about just going to some fancy club that costs $50,000 a year to hang-out with other ultra-rich people. No, the wealthy use the people, places, and resources around them.[41]

A person who would like to become a millionaire would logically ask two questions. First: What are the characteristics of these contacts and relationships that lead to wealth? Second: Where can I create these contacts and relationships?

The answer to the first question can be encapsulated in one word: trust. Francis Fukuyama wrote a book demonstrating that trust is the "social basis of prosperity," and Professors Jeanne Brett and Tyree Mitchell, respectively of Northwestern and Louisiana State University, write that trust is "the social glue that holds business relationships together." Trust is what allows people to do business together without the costly and cumbersome checking and contracting that is needed in its absence.[42]

Trust is created when people share a civic, humanitarian, existential, or public purpose that they sacrifice for and work toward together. And this is not all that is created by such a shared purpose. Mutual respect, affection, and a shared sense of belonging also develop. Probably *everyone* would rather do business with and increase the wealth of someone she respects, likes, trusts, and shares a purpose with than with someone who is just well-referred. The best place to build these kinds of relationships is through charitable and civic organizations—which bring people together around the shared values and common purpose that seed trusted relationships.

Giving Leads to Wealth (of a Different Kind) #5: What's Stronger Than Exercising Four Times a Week

We have seen that the Torah is right that acquiring wealth is one material blessing that will accrue to those who give enthusiastically. There is an even more fundamental material blessing: health. Does giving affect health?

In 2002, Professor Stephanie Brown of the University of Michigan found out. She published a study based upon longitudinal data from the

University of Michigan called the "Changing Lives of Older Couples Study," which began in 1987. At the beginning of the study, the researchers asked the participants questions to assess how active they were in providing and receiving help. Professor Brown found that those who provided no help to others were twice as likely to die in a five-year period as those who provided at least "some help." She concluded:

> If giving, rather than receiving, promotes longevity, then interventions that are designed to help people feel supported may need to be redesigned so the emphasis is on what people can do to help others . . . In other words, these findings suggest that it isn't what we get from relationships that makes contact with others so beneficial; it's what we give.[43]

These findings were validated by subsequent studies. Dr. Christine Carter of the University of California, Berkeley reports:

> People who volunteer tend to experience fewer aches and pains. Giving help to others protects overall health twice as much as aspirin protects against heart disease. People 55 and older who volunteer for two or more organizations have an impressive 44 percent lower likelihood of dying early—and that's after sifting out every other contributing factor, including physical health, exercise, gender, habits like smoking, marital status, and many more. This is a stronger effect than exercising four times a week or going to church.[44]

Who Gives

In Deuteronomy 15, Moses states that giving does not trade off but builds from one's brother to those in one's community to those he does not know. Was he right? It is obvious that married people, and particularly married people with children, usually have more claims on their time than do single people. One might think, therefore, that married people will be less engaged in volunteering or other civic activities than single people. Yet, data from the US Bureau of Labor Statistics shows that married people (especially those with children) both volunteer and vote at vastly higher rates than single adults.[45]

In 2016, the Pew Research Center released a study that reported that religious people are much more likely to volunteer their time and donate their money and goods than are secular people. Similarly, a study from the Lilly School of Philanthropy at Indiana University found that Americans with a religious affiliation give more than twice as much money to charity than do their secular counterparts—and that regular churchgoers give more than three times those who do not regularly attend religious services.[46]

To some extent, this data is not surprising. Religious people have communal institutions—houses of worship, among others—that require financial support. This is a classic manifestation of the notion of "brother" from Deuteronomy 15. Many are also drawn to support their co-religionists in need; this is the "poor one" in that biblical passage. Does it stop there? Karl Zinsmeister of *The Almanac of American Philanthropy* found that religious people give more frequently and in greater amounts to *secular* charities than do secular people. And Arthur Brooks of the American Enterprise Institute found that religious people are also much more likely to volunteer their time to secular causes than are secular people. The first dollar (or hour) that religious people give may be to their faith-based institution—but the practice of giving they develop there extends and manifests broadly.

"Help with Him" and Pathological Giving

As discussed, the Torah is clear that one's obligation to give only applies when the recipient engages *with* the giver. Why, according to science, is this the case? Giving, we see from the data, is the surest pathway to becoming happy, wealthy, and healthy. So who cares if the recipient does not reciprocate?

The hundreds of thousands of users of the collaboration software company Basecamp apparently do. All of them have access to the "snooze" feature that allows them to stop receiving messages from their colleagues that could be bids for assistance.

Why would Basecamp have this feature? The "extra miler" study cited earlier provides several reasons that might explain it.

The study analyzed three hundred organizations and found that "the distribution of collaborative work is often extremely lopsided." As discussed,

3 to 5 percent of employees account for up to 35 percent of collaborations. This *can* be good for the collaborative employees—who are more likely to get promoted and paid more than their less collaborative colleagues.

However, Professor Cross and his colleagues found that these collaborative employees are also likely to report less satisfaction and diminishing engagement—the consequences of stress and burnout. Consequently, an organization that does not simultaneously protect, acknowledge, and reward its collaborative employees risks losing them.[47]

This finding is amplified by a 2020 study on generosity conducted by Professor Kimmo Eriksson of Mälardalen University in Sweden and colleagues from around the world. They took data from the American General Social Survey and the European Social Survey that asked people to respond one way or the other to claims such as, "Personally assisting people in trouble is very important to me," "These days people need to look after themselves and not overly worry about others," and "In the past 12 months, how often did you get involved in work for voluntary or charitable organizations?"

They coded the responses as "prosocial" and "non-prosocial," and mapped them to the incomes of the respondents.

The American and European surveys revealed the same result. Those who are prosocial had significantly more income than those who were not. However, the story does not simply conclude with, "The more prosocial you are, the more money you will make."

Instead, the results showed that those who are "moderately prosocial" do even better financially than those who are completely prosocial.[48] This accords exactly with the Torah's notion of giving must not be conducted indiscriminately but "with" the recipients.

The challenge of indiscriminate giving extends well beyond the expensive problem of employee burnout. Indeed, the challenge is so widespread that it now has a name, "pathological altruism," which is the title of the 2012 collection of essays curated by a distinguished group of scholars from around the world and published by Oxford University Press.

The concept of pathological altruism is that giving, done indiscriminately, can backfire and *harm* the giver and the recipient. The legendary Harvard sociobiologist Edward O. Wilson called *Pathological Altruism* "one of the few books in evolutionary biology I've read in the past ten years that has taught me something completely new."[49] New—at least since Exodus 23:5, when God commands us to help someone whose donkey has fallen *with* him.

One of the major domains where this concept is operative is in foreign aid, which is a massive source of institutional giving. Foreign aid can have spectacular social, political, and humanitarian returns, as exemplified by the Marshall Plan and the President's Emergency Plan for AIDS Relief (PEPFAR).

However, the humanitarian and strategic success of the Marshall Plan and PEPFAR is not the norm. As William Easterly, the codirector of the NYU Development Research Institute, documented in *Foreign Policy*, foreign aid can significantly increase dependency, lead to lower growth in recipient countries, subsidize damaging policies, disincentivize needed reform, and cause resentment against the donor—while making it financially possible for countries to launch destructive military adventures.[50]

The dynamics of pathological giving extend well beyond national actors. Professor Shawn Burn of the California Polytechnic State University has studied the unintended consequences of giving. She writes:

> Our giving can compromise another's self-sufficiency and independence when they fail to develop normal age-appropriate competencies such as being financially responsible, taking care of their own basic needs for food and shelter, managing their emotions, dealing with life's bureaucracies, doing their share of the work, taking their share of responsibility, and cleaning up after themselves.[51]

Reflection

In 2023, David Wolpe concluded a long and remarkable career as a pulpit rabbi. He has counseled countless congregants through heartache, heartbreak, setbacks, and disappointments. At the end of his career, he reflected that the one thing no one ever said to him was, "Rabbi, I am experiencing financial problems because I have given too much to charity."

I have asked several friends in the clergy of other faiths if they ever had a congregant or parishioner say that they hit financial problems because they gave away too much. The reaction is always the same. The clergyperson thinks for a moment, and says, "Come to think of it, no one has ever come to me with anything like that." One Evangelical pastor did note, however, that he has met many people who regret *where* they gave. Rabbi Abba bar Acha would have understood.

These experiences from the clergy align with the claims of the Torah and the findings of social science. Giving is an enriching activity, in many ways. Just like other important and enriching activities—like parenting—it can be done better or worse.

The first question the giver of time and/or money needs to ask is: *Where should I allocate my gifts?* One answer to this question will be communal institutions, which include churches, synagogues, schools, and local sports leagues. These are vital for a vibrant and fulfilling life, and therefore command the contributions of each person who benefits from them. But they aren't really *tzedakah*, as much as they are dues. The evidence: Even the most generous donors generally contribute only to the institutions where they have a personal affiliation.

This issue surfaced in 2024, when the actress Alyssa Milano posted a GoFundMe for the benefit of her child's baseball team. She faced an abundance of criticism that she would not have faced if the fundraiser had been circulated only among fellow parents at the school, or if it were in support of the needy.[52]

As important as communal institutions and organizations are, contributions to them represent the *beginning* of the Torah's understanding of public-spirited engagement. *Tzedakah*, as discussed, is concerned with three things, each of which is fundamentally different from funding communal institutions: the creation of opportunity for the poor, the alleviation of suffering, and the saving of lives. Unfortunately, there are (and always will be) plenty of options that one can choose within each category. The option one chooses might come from personal experience, learning from a trusted friend, or from providential exposure. It might be the education of underprivileged children, emergency first response, food insecurity, the cure for a rare disease, diminishing the surgical deficit in Africa, or any number of countless others.

Any cause that *genuinely* creates opportunities for the poor, alleviates suffering, or saves lives is likely to be worthy of a giver's time and money. The next question the giver should ask is: *What organization—within the cause—is most worthy of my resources?*

This is virtually the same question that all investors and businesspeople ask. They both need to regularly decide where to put their time and money, and they make the decision with one overriding consideration. It is that of ROI—return on investment.

ROI asks the question: *How much can be generated with the dollars I commit?* As with financial investments, the potential and outcome of a social investment can be easily measured. The numerator is dollars in. The denominator is outcome units out. The outcome units may be children educated, lives saved, or surgeries performed. But it will always be something and will always be discernible. This ROI discipline is highly likely to lead someone to the right organization and avoid the pathological giving that, according to Rabbi Aba bar Acha, constituted the sin at the Golden Calf, and that William Easterly has determined constitutes much (but by no means all) of foreign aid.

The next question the giver needs to ask is*: What should I contribute?* In 2016, I was in Tanzania with two great Christian missionary doctors, Drs. Jon Fielder and Marc Jacobson. These men have devoted their entire adult lives, at enormous personal sacrifice, to bringing medical care to the poorest people in the world and to building institutions to ensure that more and better care will be continually available long into the future. We visited a nursing school that was affiliated with our hospital partner. I saw a bunch of high school lockers. I asked Dr. Jacobson what they were doing there. "That," he explained, "is what we call Junk for Jesus."

They explained that groups, thinking that they are doing good, sometimes send the random things that they no longer want. The missionary doctors accept the goods to sustain the relationship in the hope that the group will eventually send money—which can be used by the doctors on the ground to buy what they need most to serve their patients.

The same is the case with mission trips, which groups often want to take to do a week of service around our hospitals (or nearby churches and schools), often to clean or paint. These trips take a lot of resources from the local team to arrange and cost a lot of money for the participants to take. And they do not add much as there are plenty of local people who can paint and clean. The missionaries tolerate these trips—again, in the hope that the group will build or strengthen a relationship with the organization and provide meaningful support. It would be far better if these groups set aside the time they spend on these trips, and made as much money as they could at their jobs during that period—and donate it to the missionary hospitals, along with the money they spend on the trips.

I have seen a similar dynamic at United Hatzalah, Israel's corps of crowd-sourced volunteer first responders that I co-founded and Chair. After October 7, a lot of individuals and organizations reached out to us to contribute. Most offered money, and gave generously. But one Jewish group from a large investment bank told me that they wanted to do a communal volunteer activity in New York and Connecticut. They suggested packaging supplies for United Hatzalah. I told them that there were no issues packaging supplies, and that if there were it should be handled by high school students. As bankers—prosperous and wealthy people connected to others with money—their communal activity should be a fundraiser. This by no means suggests that the only way to fulfill one's biblical obligation for tzedakah is with financial support. Eli Beer, my co-founder and the leader of United Hatzalah, understands the importance of financial support as much as anyone. Yet, he often says that our most generous donors are the 7,000 volunteer medics—who leave their work, awake from their sleep, and rush from their Shabbat tables to help someone nearby who is having an emergency.

Erica and I say the same thing to potential donors about the Christian missionary doctors whose work we support in Africa. These missionary doctors give their lives—serving without much of what we Westerners would consider necessities—to answer the call of Jesus who, in the Book of Matthew, commanded his followers to serve "the least among us." The least we can do, from the comfort of our homes in these blessed United States, is to provide them with the financial resources they need to do their sacred work.

The opportunity to give from one's skills—as the medics in Israel and the doctors in Africa epitomize—is universal. In Exodus 4:17, God begins the freedom story of the Jewish people by telling Moses to take the "staff that is in your hand." God has put a staff in each our hands, to use for sacred purposes. For some people—like the aforementioned bankers—that staff is a checkbook. Similarly, one with expertise in drywall, electric, or plumbing can realize a remarkable return on their time by donating their services to build homes for the poor with Habitat for Humanity. A surgeon can, working with Samaritan's Purse for two weeks a year, perform life-changing operations on people in Africa who would otherwise suffer for a lifetime. A consultant, an attorney, or an accountant can donate her time to make an organization more efficient, effective, and transparent. A child with chess skills can alleviate the loneliness and exercise the brains of elderly people by going to elder care centers and playing with the residents. A software sales executive can work with a fundraising team to understand and implement donor acquisition and relationship strategies and structures—which are almost the same as those practiced by successful software companies with customers. The examples could keep coming, reflecting the Torah's teaching that everyone has something important and somewhere valuable to give.

The final question that everyone contemplating *tzedakah* will ask is: *How much should I contribute?* As ever, the Torah has the relevant guidance for us in Leviticus 22, when the instruction on giving is interjected between two sections on sacrifice.

In addition to the doctors in Africa and the medics in Israel, we were fortunate to see a sacrificial financial gift made. In 2019, when Erica spoke at the Tabernacle Church in Buffalo about African Mission Healthcare, the church did an offering for the benefit of AMH. A woman sitting a few pews back with clearly worn clothing put a $20 bill on the plate. At the end of the offering, one of the pastors told us about her. She was at a soup kitchen that morning when someone gave her $20. The woman, upon hearing from Erica about the Christian devotion of the missionary doctors, put the whole amount on the collection plate. We told our children that they had just met our most generous donor—as hers was a genuinely sacrificial gift.

That woman, whose name I wish I knew, has been a source of consistent inspiration. She helped us realize that we are not giving enough—whether time or money—unless we are sacrificing something we would otherwise enjoy. This something will be different for people of varying means. It might be having dinner out, a trip, a new car, a vacation home, flying business class or private, time spent at home or at an entertainment event, or something else one would otherwise enjoy.

As important and helpful (in knowing how much to give) the concept of sacrifice in *tzedakah* is, it comes with an irony—or at least a caveat. As God promises in Deuteronomy 15 and validated by contemporary social science, gifts of *tzedakah* are rewarded with blessings that we can take to the bank. Therefore, we can offer sacrificial gifts to *tzedakah* with the confidence that they will be followed by material blessings . . . meaning that they won't really be sacrifices at all. And that is perhaps the best deal of all time.

28

The Penultimate Curse of Deuteronomy and the Amygdala Hijack

The Torah and Science of Fear

The Most Common Instruction in the Bible

Everyone who has attended a Passover Seder is familiar with the ten plagues, which are the immediate prelude to the Jews being freed from Egyptian slavery. Given that the order or the sequence of things in the Torah is always important and instructive, a question emerges: Do the plagues ascend in severity?

Logic dictates that they do. God would not respond to the Pharaoh's refusal to free the Jews by *weakening* the plagues. Doing so would reward the Pharaoh's resistance, and convey that the pain is easing away in accordance with his recalcitrance. This logic is confirmed at least by the tenth plague: the slaying of the firstborn. There could be nothing more severe than that.

Accordingly, what is the *second* worst plague? The ninth plague is three days of darkness. This is, to be sure, unpleasant and undesirable, but is it worse than wild beasts running through the community (the fourth plague)? Or unrelenting pestilence (the fifth plague)? Or the destruction of the economy (the seventh plague)?

According to the Torah, it is. Darkness is the worst plague aside from the slaying of the firstborn. Why is darkness so bad?

Let's go to the text. The darkness, we learn in Exodus 10:22–23, was so "thick . . . [that] no man could see his brother nor could any rise from his place for a three-day period." This raises two questions that bring us to the most fundamental understanding of the plague.

First, if the plague were *only* of darkness, why didn't any Egyptian just light a candle? It wasn't a technical problem. Candles, according to the National Candle Association, were invented long before the Exodus, *in Egypt*. So, the Egyptians could have easily alleviated the second-worst plague Why didn't they?[1]

Second, if it were a plague *only* of darkness, why does the Torah say that no man could see his "brother" rather than "another"? If the problem were just darkness, it should not matter if the person each Egyptian could not see was his brother or anyone else. But the text specifies a very specific relationship. Why?

We can begin the investigation with the description of the plague. There were three days of "thick, tangible" darkness. Every child, and every parent, knows what that means. A universal characteristic of children is fear of the dark. And, as we will see, this fear is also common among adults.

Why is fear of the dark so persistent and pervasive? The primary sense that we use to escape danger is our sight. With our sight deactivated, something else takes the place of the reality we cannot see. This is our *imagination*, which creates, in the vacuum generated by our temporary blindness, an alternative reality. As an evolutionarily adaptive survival mechanism, our imagination is likely to generate potential threats, which result in fear that heightens awareness and compels action.[2]

The Egyptians, in a state of constant darkness during the ninth plague, could not light a candle because of the same reason that they could not recognize their "brothers." They were people in fear—disoriented, discombobulated, detached from reality, and consumed with concern about threats.

As people in fear, the Egyptians must have been so focused on imagined threats that they lost all of the qualities that are necessary to sustain any relationship, such as trust and affection. Hence, they could not even "see" their brothers. Bereft of relationships, no Egyptian was able to "rise from his place" (get out of bed) for the duration of the plague. They had fallen into what the author William Styron called "darkness visible," a deep and immobilizing depression.

The text thus teaches us the havoc fear can cause. The darkness unleashed the unrestrained imagination, which led to an immobilizing fear. Consumed by fear, the Egyptians were unable to even light a candle or "see" their brothers. The consequence was a depression that made them incapable of even arising. Who else cannot rise? A dead person.

No wonder that the biblical Author judged the plague of darkness/fear to be worse than every other one except for the slaying of the firstborn. What is so bad about fear? Why is fear so problematic?

The Sin of the Scouts: The Seven Lessons of Fear

Fast-forward to Numbers 13. God, whose spectacular actions through the Exodus freed the Jews after hundreds of years of slavery, presumably earned the trust of even the most devoted skeptics. It is now, God has made clear, time for the Jews to enter the Promised Land and to create, in the words of the Book of Exodus, "a kingdom of priests and a holy nation."

Moses, seemingly reluctantly, sends out scouts—leaders from each tribe—to venture into the land and return to report back on it. They return with a report that Moses does not expect: "The land through which we have passed, to scout it out, is a land that devours its inhabitants. All the people that we saw in it were huge! . . . We seemed like grasshoppers in our own eyes, and so we were in their eyes" (Numbers 13:32–33).

Why would the scouts compare themselves to grasshoppers specifically? Grasshoppers are not the smallest, weakest, or most defenseless creatures. But they jump high and far at the slightest provocation. The scouts, the leaders, felt like *grasshoppers*. And fear, as we saw with the ninth plague, is never contained or constrained.

With the leaders of every tribe having spoken, "the entire assembly raised up and issued its voice; the people wept that night." The "entire assembly"—*everyone*—spoke with a single voice and had one demand. "Let us return to Egypt" (Numbers 14:4).

God responds by forbidding the entire generation from going to the land, making an exception only for the two dissenting scouts, Joshua and Caleb. The people, acknowledging at this point that they had "sinned," tell Moses that they want to take the land after all. Moses tells them that God will not lift his edict. A people so susceptible to fear is ill-equipped to manifest the divine vision in the land. Some go anyway and get slaughtered. This short vignette teaches six lessons about fear.

- Fear is overwhelming. An unambiguous directive from God (in this case, to enter the land) seems like something every rational person should easily accept. But the scouts were afraid, and the fear proved more powerful than even God's unambiguous presence and guidance.
- Fear is indiscriminate. The scouts were the leaders of the tribes. They presumably had a clear understanding of the imperative to go to the Promised Land and of the significance of God's protection. But fear overcame them, depriving them of believing in what they must have told their followers many times before.
- Fear is contagious. When the fear was introduced to the public, it infected "everyone."
- Fear makes people stupid. The scouts did not acknowledge what they knew—that they were operating under the protection of God. Nor did they respond to their fear by requesting that Moses provide additional weaponry. Instead, they responded by yearning to go back to Egypt, where they had been brutally enslaved. These seasoned leaders, in fear, were willing to trade God's protection as a free people in their own land for slavery in Egypt.
- Fear has serious, tangible, and even irrevocable consequences. The Jews' fear results in God permanently denying them entrance into the land. This punishment makes them regret their actions, and they respond by saying that they now want to go and conquer the land—a desire that will remain unfulfilled.
- Fear can be conquered. Caleb and Joshua, who had the *same experience* as the other scouts, were not afraid. On the contrary, they said, "We can surely ascend the land!"

The Curse: "I Will Make Their Hearts Fearful."

In Leviticus 26:36, God communicates what Jewish thinkers have long called "The Admonishment." This is a list of curses that will befall those who defy the Torah. One of those curses will sound familiar to those who have pondered the sin of the scouts. But its language teaches us something new and crucial about fear:

> As for those of you who are left, I will make their hearts so fearful in the lands of their enemies that the sound of a windblown leaf will put them to flight. They will run as though fleeing from the sword, and they will fall, even though no one is pursuing them. So you will not be able to stand before your enemies.

As always, the meaning and practical guidance in this biblical passage is revealed in the nuance of its language. The curse is not "I will make them fear." It is "I will make their *hearts* fearful."

What is the difference? The curse of Leviticus is not fear per se. We are not cursed to fear charging lions or wild dogs. Such fears are proper responses to dangerous stimuli that go away as soon as the threat does. These legitimate fears are *short-term*.

The curse of Leviticus is that our *hearts* will be fearful—that we will be filled with and defined by an ever-present fear. The curse is that fear becomes a state of being, where we feel fear "even though no one is pursuing." These are *long-term* fears.

Deuteronomy is one big speech from Moses. Almost everything he says in Deuteronomy is an interpretation of something that happened in Exodus or Numbers. In Deuteronomy 28, Moses revisits the curses at the end of the Torah, as a reminder to the people of what to expect should they violate the word of God. The penultimate curse is, as it was with the plagues, fear.

Moses warns, "You will be frightened night and day, and you will not be sure of your purpose. In the morning you will say, 'Who can give back last night?!' And in the evening you will say, 'Who can give back this morning?,' for the fright of your heart that you will fear and the sight of your eyes you will never see."

Moses's substantive addition, born of years of reflection on fear, is deeply instructive. He says that fear will make otherwise centered people unsure of their very "purpose."

Accordingly, the most common instruction in the Torah—a guidebook devoted to helping us to live with purpose—is "Do not fear."[3]

The Science

Mr. Darwin Goes to the Zoo

Sometime in the nineteenth century, Charles Darwin went to the Reptile House at the London Zoological Gardens. He did not go to admire the animals. He was there on business. He wanted to study fear, with himself as the subject.

He approached the glass, where, on the other side, was the highly poisonous puff adder. With the glass separating him from the animal, Mr. Darwin, and presumably everyone else, realized that there were no grounds for fear. He approached the glass and jumped back "a yard or two." He continued the experiment, and had the same reaction from fear every time. He concluded, "My will and reason were powerless against the imagination of a danger which had never been experienced."[4]

Mr. Darwin's experiment was complete. The puff adder, he knew well, had no chance of striking him. It was, in Leviticus terms, a "windblown leaf." Yet, like the Egyptians of the ninth plague, he *imagined* that the puff adder should be feared. He recoiled every time, unable to convince himself to not fear the animal that was harmlessly on the other side of the glass. He presumably went to the zoo during the day, and therefore his experiment does not comment on when the imagination might be most active. For that, we have the Crown Plaza Hotel Group.

What Happens at 10:04 PM

In 2008, the Crown Plaza Hotel Group surveyed its guests. They did not seek to ascertain satisfaction with room cleanliness, the check-in process, or the quality of the breakfast. They surveyed the guests to ascertain when the guests considered themselves to be most creative. The answer: 10:04 PM.[5]

Nighttime creativity can be a blessing. Authors and artists whose creativity blossomed at night include Charles Dickens, Robert Frost, J. D. Salinger, Henri de Toulouse-Lautrec, William de Kooning, Pablo Picasso, and Pablo Neruda.[6]

As every parent knows, this is not the only kind of creativity that blossoms at night. We have all turned off the lights in our children's bedroom, leaving them peaceful and comfortable, only to come back to find that they have, essentially, conceived of a horror show in their cozy bed.

Fear of the dark is not like neophobia (fear of new food), which almost all children experience and outgrow. The science writer Cari Romm analyzed the literature concerning nyctophobia (fear of the night or dark) and concluded that fear of the dark is "shockingly common" among adults. A 2017 British poll revealed that *most* adults wake up twice a month feeling that something scary is in the room, and 20 percent check under their beds and close cupboards and drawers to protect against monsters before retiring. Given how frightening darkness can be to adults, we can see just how effective a fear-generating plague of three days of darkness must have been to the Egyptians in Exodus 10.[7]

What exactly are those who fear the dark afraid of? What did the Egyptians, pursuant to the ninth plague, fear? The text doesn't tell us for the simple reason that it could be anything, and therefore, it doesn't matter. The contemporary creative genre that is based on fear—horror movies—thrives on this dynamic. The horror film expert Josh Hrala says, "Good [horror movies] never directly show you the monster because your imagination makes something way scarier."[8]

The Physiology of Fear

Every decent child artist can draw a face in fear.

The eyes widen, with the outer corners slightly tilting downward. The pupils constrict, and the eyes quickly shift to the side, scanning for danger. The eyebrows knit together as the mouth opens wide.

These are reactions, the science writer Clara Moscowitz explains, of someone who is breathing in more air, seeking a wider view, and tracking targets more quickly.[9]

An analysis of fear by Professor Louise Delagran from the University of Minnesota describes the many physiological reactions that are manifest in the expression. Fear shuts down functions not immediately needed for survival (such as our digestive systems) and sharpens our functions needed to survive (such as eyesight). It increases our heart rate and blood flow to muscles so that we can run faster. The consequences can be cardiovascular damage, gastrointestinal problems such as irritable bowel syndrome and ulcers, decreased fertility, fatigue, accelerated aging, memory loss, and even brain damage.[10]

A 2017 analysis of fear by Professor Mary Moller of Pacific Lutheran University added to the litany of physical problems that stem from chronic fear. These include immune system dysfunction, endocrine system dysfunction, autonomic nervous system alterations, sleep/wake cycle disruption, and eating disorders. These pathologies progress rapidly, turning headaches into migraines, muscle aches into fibromyalgia (widespread muscle pain), body aches into chronic pain, and difficulty breathing into asthma.[11]

Chronic fear has equally serious implications for our mental health. Ms. Delagran writes, "Fear can interrupt processes in our brains that allow us to regulate emotions, read non-verbal cues and other information presented to us, reflect before acting, and act ethically. This impacts our thinking and decision-making in negative ways, leaving us susceptible to intense emotions and impulsive reactions. All of these effects can leave us unable to act appropriately."

And that's not all. Professor Moller found that fear can also lead to obsessive compulsiveness and the inability to have loving feelings.[12]

In other words, fear does just what the ninth plague says: It restricts our ability to recognize our "brother."

"You're Stupid"

In the Book of Numbers, we saw how fear influenced the thinking of the Jews in the desert. They return from their scouting mission afraid even as they know, with complete certainty, that God is on their side and wants them to conquer the land. They do not remind themselves of the divine support or even ask for another sign from God or additional weaponry from Moses. Instead, they demand to return to Egypt. How does this make sense?

Modern science has discovered two parts of the brain that exist in an inverse relationship. These are the amygdala (which processes certain emotions) and the prefrontal cortex (which enables rational thought). The amygdala is often called the "fear center," and the prefrontal cortex is often called "the thinking brain." When a person is emotionally charged, blood and oxygen will strongly activate the amygdala at the expense of the prefrontal cortex. The same exists in reverse.[13]

In 2008, Eric Hagerman explained in *WIRED* that fear causes "the amygdala, known as the fear center, one of the most primitive brain regions, [to] override the prefrontal cortex, which handles working memory and executive function."[14] This phenomenon is also known as the "amygdala hijack," as the amygdala, in response to fear, hijacks the brain and assumes complete control of it.

Professor Arash Javanbakht is a psychiatrist at Wayne State University who has reflected on how amygdala hijacking frequently affects people. He explains:

> Very often my patients with phobias start with: "I know it is stupid, but I am afraid of spiders." Or it may be dogs or cats, or something else. And I always reply: "It is not stupid, it is illogical." We humans have different functions in the brain, and fear often bypasses logic. There are several reasons. One is that logic is slow; fear is fast. In situations of danger, we ought to be fast: First run or kill, then think.[15]

The consequences are significant. Mr. Hagerman cites the psychiatrist Edward Hallowell who explained, "When those deep brain areas are active, they shanghai your cortical neurons. Your IQ plummets. Your creativity, your sense of humor, all of that disappears. You're stupid." The kind of stupidity that, perhaps, would lead a people protected by God en route to their Promised Land to yearn to return to slavery.[16]

The fear-induced mental contraction that presents as stupidity makes evolutionary sense. Psychologists, building on the early-twentieth-century work of the physiologist Walter Cannon, have determined that there are four reactions to fear: fawn, freeze, flight, or fight. When a real threat emerges, a person should not exercise analytical abilities, contemplate philosophical considerations, or weigh competing courses of action. He should use his brain power to immediately and effectively process the fear, and to respond with all possible resources to fawn, freeze, fight, or flee. We *want* the fear center to take over completely, and it does.[17]

Accordingly, it is not stupid to be afraid of something genuinely frightening. It is adaptive, and even smart. The problem is that the amygdala, when hijacking, is not responsive to whether one *should be* afraid in a given situation. It is only responsive to whether one afraid. The brain response does not calibrate differently if the fear is from a charging lion or the "wind-blown leaf" of Leviticus 26. The brain just registers fear and prepares us accordingly by shutting down rational thought.[18]

Clowns, Jaws, and the Color Purple

What might we fear? We can start with something that, according to a 2016 poll conducted by *Vox* and Morning Consult, is feared by 42 percent of Americans: clowns (coulrophobia). Americans are not content to deal with their coulrophobia as private citizens. Americans believe that state and local law enforcement should be "more" or "much more" active in anti-clown efforts, and more than a third believe that federal intervention is necessary.[19]

The executives at McDonald's are sensitive to this fear. A corporate spokesman announced in 2016, "McDonald's and franchisees in local markets are mindful of the current climate around clown sightings in communities. And as such are being thoughtful with respect to Ronald McDonald's participation in community events for the time being."[20]

It is unclear what specifically prompted this concern related to the friendliest clown imaginable. There is certainly no evidence of danger posed by Ronald McDonald or any of his counterparts. The clown scholar Ben Radford reported in late 2016 that clowns have not caused any serious harm.[21]

In 1974, the author Peter Benchley published the novel *Jaws*. A year later, the book became a movie made by a young director, Steven Spielberg. *Jaws* became a cinematic sensation within days of its release in the summer of 1975. Suddenly and persistently, sharks had been transformed in the public mind from a generally ignored fish to, in the words of *National Geographic*'s Stefan Lövgren, "stalking killing machines." This transformation was given a name by Professor Christopher Neff of the University of Sydney: The Jaws Effect.[22]

This effect has made millions of people afraid on the beach. Indeed, a 2015 Ipsos poll found that 51 percent of Americans are "absolutely terrified" of sharks, and that almost 40 percent are afraid to swim in the ocean because of them.[23]

The quick spark and rapid contagion of fear, warned about with the Sin of the Scouts, affected both people and, most profoundly, sharks. People have killed so many sharks since the movie that the population of large sharks along the Eastern Seaboard is half of what it was when *Jaws* was released. As of 2021, 77 percent of shark populations were threatened with extinction.

Meanwhile, the data on shark attacks, like all data from the past fifty years, has become more precise.

In 2020, there were ten unprovoked shark attacks *worldwide*, leading the shark researcher Cheryl McCarron to conclude, "You're more likely to be bitten by a New Yorker than to be bitten by a shark."[24]

The producers of *Jaws* have reflected on the consequences of the fear that they unintentionally generated. Steven Spielberg said, "I truly and to this day regret the decimation of the shark population because of the [*Jaws*] book and the film. I really, truly regret that." Peter Benchley became a shark activist. An unleashed fear, it turns out, is difficult to argue with or contain, and has real consequences.[25]

The fears of clowns and sharks have ample company. Fears prevalent enough to be discussed in psychological literature include anthrophobia (fear of flowers), barophobia (fear of gravity), batrachophobia (fear of amphibians), spargarophobia (fear of asparagus), chronomentrophobia (fear of clocks), triskaidekaphobia (fear of the number 13), octophobia (fear of the figure 8), porphyrophobia (fear of the color purple), selenophobia (fear of the moon), and phartophobia (fear of passing gas in a public place).[26]

Our "Age of Fear"

Though some of these fears may seem obscure, the category of fear is not. The psychologist Neha Shah wrote in 2021, "Research says that fear and anger are the most dominant emotions on the planet today." Or, as the title of a 2016 article in *Rolling Stone* proclaims, "We're Living in an Age of Fear."[27]

The fact that we are living in the age of fear is curious for a reason articulated by Lewis and Clark College president Barry Glassner. President Glassner is one of the nation's leading experts on the psychology and sociology of fear. He states, "Most Americans are living in the safest place at the safest time in human history."[28]

Indeed, much of what our grandparents feared the most—from polio outbreaks to state-sponsored persecution—are no longer of any personal concern for most readers of this book. And these fears have not been replaced by any genuinely equivalent dangers. Medical discoveries, advances in predictions, and safety innovations have made persistent dangers (from cancer to accidents to extreme weather) much less deadly.

Yet, for many people, it does not feel that way. Harvard professor Steven Pinker often points out the fact that the percentage of people who die as a result of violence is at an all-time low. Yet, he says, most people regard this fact as "somewhere between hallucinatory and obscene."[29]

Why do we live in an "age of fear" when its legitimate causes have declined? Moses gave us a potential answer in Deuteronomy. We could, he warned, *make* our hearts fearful even in the absence of legitimate fear.

Choosing Fearful Hearts

On March 4, 1933, President Franklin Roosevelt delivered his first inaugural address. It was in that speech when he delivered one of his most famous lines. He said, "There is nothing to fear but fear itself." These words would inspire a nation in the throes of the Great Depression and for generations to follow.[30]

Times have changed. At President Joseph Biden's inauguration on January 20, 2021, one of the speakers was a young poet named Amanda Gorman. Reflecting on her experience a year later in the *New York Times*, she revealed that she "almost declined" the invitation to read her poem at the inauguration. Why? She had been "terrified on a physical level." She explained:

> Covid was still raging, and my age group couldn't get vaccinated yet . . . I was going to become highly visible, which is a very dangerous thing to be in America, especially if you're Black and outspoken and have no Secret Service.
>
> It didn't help that I was getting DMs from friends telling me not so jokingly to buy a bulletproof vest. My mom had us crouch in our living room so that she could practice shielding my body from bullets. A loved one warned me to "be ready to die" if I went to the Capitol, telling me, "It's just not worth it." I had insomnia and nightmares, barely ate or drank for days . . .

It is understandable that the events of January 6 might have, *instinctively*, caused Ms. Gorman and her confidants some concern. However, Ms. Gorman and her confidants knew that she would be the most protected person in the most protected place in the world when she read from the inaugural stage. Moreover, it is unclear how Ms. Gorman's vaccination status was relevant to her reading a poem on the Capitol steps. Yet, there is a logic to her concerns. Fear, we learn in Leviticus, Numbers, and Deuteronomy, strikes indiscriminately, pervasively, and against rationality.

The question is how she would reflect on her fears well after the event had passed without any of her fears having been realized. Writing in the *New York Times* in early 2022, she said:

> The only thing we have to fear is *having no fear itself* [emphasis in original] . . . And yes, I still am terrified every day. Yet fear can be love trying its best in the dark. So do not fear your fear. Own it. Free it. This isn't a liberation that I or anyone can give you, it's a power you must look for, learn, love, lead and locate for yourself.[31]

Amanda Gorman glorified her fears—and did so by rebuking President Franklin Roosevelt's counsel to his country in his first inaugural address: "There is nothing to fear but fear itself." President Roosevelt's hope at his inauguration was specifically that Americans, then suffering through the Great Depression, would reject fear. The hope of the poet that President Biden chose for his inauguration is that Americans find their "power" to accept fear and liberate themselves to be "terrified every day."

Most people are not as articulate as Amanda Gorman and would not express a philosophy of fear as clearly and thoughtfully as she does. But it is clear that Ms. Gorman's embrace of Moses's curse—of a fearful heart—is not unique to her. It is a phenomenon in American cultural discourse of which Ms. Gorman is both a product and a spokesperson.

The Worst Mom in America

Who is America's "worst mom"? An internet search reveals the answer: Lenore Skenazy of New York City. Ms. Skenazy attained this appellation after writing an article in the *New York Sun* in 2008, "Why I Let My 9-Year-Old Ride the Subway Alone."[32]

So many readers were outraged that she let her son travel home from Bloomingdale's alone, after he expressed interest in doing so, that she earned the title of "America's worst mom."[33]

But Ms. Skenazy did not leave her child in Bloomingdale's out of laziness or carelessness. She wanted to opt out of what she identified as the "tsunami of fear" that was overwhelming parents and children, and for her son to develop independence in the only way possible: by doing independent things.

The controversy surrounding her decision to let her child go to a store and come home alone, inspired her to write a book, *Free-Range Kids: How Parents and Teachers Can Let Go and Let Grow*, and to start a movement by the same name. Just how countercultural is Ms. Skenazy that her ideas would form a named movement and earn her the appellation of "America's Worst Mom"?[34]

In 2013, a multi-year discussion on Quora began. It was, "What could you do as a child that you can't do now?" The list from the Missouri nurse Laura Wright includes: staying outdoors without a curfew on summer nights, camping, roaming in the woods, swimming in the lake, riding dirt bikes for miles and miles, boating, and hunting.

Other Quora posters offered: operating industrial equipment without much training, riding in the back of a pickup truck, climbing trees, using gymnastics equipment in gym class, riding while standing up in the back of a tractor, swinging across a creek on a rope to get to a tree branch, wandering through town, mowing grass for money with a power mower, and riding anywhere inside of a car (like I used to do, in the space under the back windshield of my father's 1979 Corvette).[35]

In the past nine years, there have been numerous contributions to the Quora post listing things people did in their childhood that would be unthinkable now. They come from men and women from cities, suburbs, and farms. The list only gets longer and is by no means exhaustive.

For instance, the list does not mention sleepovers, which were never contemplated in the context of fear during my childhood. In 2012, CNN and Parenting.com collaborated on "The New Playdate Parent Playbook." The questioner asked what to do if one's daughter is invited to sleep over at a friend's house, but the only parent home is the girl's divorced dad. The answer (called "Solution"): "Call and say, 'I'm sorry, and this is about me and not you, but I just don't feel comfortable with a man supervising an overnighter.'"[36]

What are the consequences of this "solution," which implies that a divorced father in the community should not be presumed to be a nice guy and a trustworthy care provider, but a potential pedophile? The children would be denied a sleepover. The child of divorce would see that respected adults in the community regard her father as a potential monster. And all children involved would be educated to fear unnecessarily. No wonder that we live in an "age of fear."

Numbers Speak: Are We Really More Afraid?

The Quora and CNN examples raise two questions. First, are parents now genuinely more restrictive than they were a generation ago? Second, do the fears of parents now at least roughly correspond with the associated risks?

In 2014, Jessica Grose and Hanna Rosin of *Slate* put these types of claims to an empirical test. They did a large survey to determine the ages at which people in different generations were able to do things unsupervised: walk one to five miles, go to a playground, stay home, use the stove or cook, and earn money. The data showed that parents today are significantly more protective and restrictive than were their parents.[37]

In 2010, NPR did a survey on what parents are most afraid of. The answer: stranger kidnapping.[38] An analysis in *Reason* showed that there are around sixty-five stranger kidnappings of children a year in the United States. Even this number may be overstated, as two-thirds of the stranger kidnappings occur in the residence of the child or the kidnapper. However the data is assessed, one is far more likely to choke to death, die in a motor vehicle accident, or be attacked by a dog than to have one's child kidnapped by a stranger. But stranger kidnapping remains the top parental fear, one around which they create and enforce rules.[39]

The night when stranger kidnapping is most feared is Halloween. In 2010, "parenting experts" on the *Today* show said that children should not trick-or-treat without parental supervision until they are thirteen years old.[40] This fear does not exist in a vacuum. The parental fear of Halloween is derived from a creative and ever-migrating array of fears, such as that the nice-seeming neighbor will load the candy with razor blades or lace it with rainbow fentanyl.[41]

What are these fears based on? Professor Elizabeth Letourneau of the Medical University of South Carolina investigated. She concluded, "There is zero evidence to support the idea that Halloween is a dangerous date for children . . . We almost called [our paper on the subject] 'Halloween: The Safest Day of the Year,' because it was just so incredibly rare to see anything happen on that day."[42]

Needless and baseless anxiety is not the only casualty of their modern-day fear of the windblown leaf. Attention to a false "danger" can mean inattention to *real* dangers. Bert Sperling, who analyzed Halloween safety data for the insurance company State Farm, said that parents should stop focusing on trick-or-treating and instead be sure that their children follow the usual rules governing pedestrian safety on streets full of cars.[43]

Of Library Stairs and Playground Swing Sets: Crime, Punishment, and Regulation

Individuals are free to develop a philosophy of fear, either intuitively or intentionally, and to act accordingly. However, a parent who effectively tells her child to fear the divorced dad of a friend, will invariably affect more than the child and her friends. We might be able to choose what fears we allow to enter our hearts, but we live in a broader society. And every society has laws that are, in part, based on consensus fears.

In December 2014, the Maryland couple Danielle and Alexander Meitiv allowed their six- and ten-year-old children to walk home from the local park in lovely Silver Spring without supervision. Who cares? The Montgomery County Child Protective Services did.

The Montgomery County authorities launched an investigation into the Meitivs on the grounds of "neglect." The Meitivs remained unafraid. The next year, they allowed their children to play at a park by themselves for two hours. In April 2015, the Meitivs were investigated again, and in this case, the children were held at Child Protective Services for five hours without being able to contact their parents.[44]

The ideology of fear that informed the actions of the Montgomery County Child Protective Services seems to be one thing that authorities in blue states and red states agree upon. Also in 2014, Debra Harrell, a single mother from South Carolina, was arrested and imprisoned for more than two weeks. Her alleged crime? Felony child neglect. The facts: While she worked her shift at McDonald's, she allowed her nine-year-old child to play without adult supervision in a nearby park that had a splash pad, a basketball court, a playground, and free food provided by volunteers.[45]

The experiences of Ms. Harrell and the Meitivs concerned the interpretation of criminal law. Is the culture of fear that they experienced representative of a larger trend in the legislative and executive processes? At least a partial answer was provided in 2014 when the *Spokesman-Review* (the newspaper of Spokane, Washington) reported, "Swing sets [are] becoming scarce on school playgrounds."[46]

Why? Steve Aagard, the spokesman for a nearby school district, explained, "It's just really a safety issue; swings have been determined to be the most unsafe of all the playground equipment on a playground."[47]

Mr. Aagard was not a freelancing paranoid, inflicting his ideology on an unwilling public. He was following what the *Argus Leader* of Sioux Falls called "a national trend" in phasing out or taking out swing sets. There hasn't been a newly discovered danger attributed to swing sets. In fact, they have gotten safer pursuant to voluntary compliance with the consumer safety standard ASTM F1148.[48]

Most people would likely say that a municipal library is a wholesome place for children to spend hours by themselves or with friends. But those people are at odds with policymakers in blue and red states including Oklahoma, New York, Florida, Wisconsin, Texas, Virginia, Minnesota, and Ohio. Numerous public libraries in those states and others have policies barring unsupervised children because children may "wander through the building and encounter hazards such as stairs, electrical equipment, doors, or furniture."[49]

How did such policies get to be so ubiquitous? It is not as if a disturbed librarian looked at a staircase and a desk, identified them as "hazards," and made a policy around it that somehow got copied around the country. It is not as if some evil bureaucrats in South Carolina had it out for Debra Harrell and invented a bizarre "crime" with which to charge her. It is not as if some anti-fun activists had a conference and decided to ban swing sets.

It is because of the widely adopted idea of safetyism, perhaps the most significant ever concession to fear in the heart.

Safetyism

Safetyism is a term coined by NYU professor Jonathan Haidt and Foundation for Individual Rights in Education President Greg Lukianoff in 2016. Safetyism, they wrote, is "a culture or belief system in which safety has become a sacred value, which means that people become unwilling to make trade-offs demanded by other practical and moral concerns. 'Safety' trumps everything else, no matter how unlikely or trivial the potential danger."[50]

The foundation of safetyism is, as they explain, the treatment of safety as a "sacred value." A sacred value is unyielding, absolute, and immune to competing claims.

An observant Jew, who views the Sabbath as sacred, would have no trouble turning down tickets to Game 7 of the NBA Finals if it falls on a Friday night, even if he's the biggest basketball fan in the world.

Sacred values are the exception to the usual rule that applies to ethics, which is, as articulated by Emory University professor Paul Wolpe, "a negotiation." It is literally childish to think that ethical decisions are between right and wrong. The genuine ethical challenges are between right and right and wrong and wrong. Sacred values, which are not open to negotiation, are above and outside ethical discussion and debate.[51]

Safety is, of course, a value that almost everyone holds dear. But does it have competition? Should it be open to negotiation? Those of us who let our children play by themselves on a playground, eat their Halloween candy, ride their bikes around town unsupervised, and take the subway around New York City certainly think so.

We acknowledge that our children, at least in the short term, would be safer if we ignored the statistics, indulged our fears, and based our parenting philosophy on the maximum elimination of risk. Yet, we also acknowledge that there are values that compete with safety. Those competing values include the cultivation of friendship, trust, independence, self-confidence, and problem-solving skills, as well as childhood fun.

The policy decisions that reflect the safetyist ideology, such as whether children should be able to spend an afternoon in the public library despite the risk that they will "encounter hazards such as stairs, electrical equipment, doors, or furniture," only occasionally made national news. And they did not cause an international reckoning concerning philosophies around fear and safetyism.

In an instant, that changed.

The Test: Covid-19 and Fear

Most people can remember where they were when they first grasped the seriousness of the Covid-19 pandemic. I was in the crowded parents' room of a scholastic chess tournament on March 8, 2020. I, along with presumably everyone in the room, was aware that a virus started in China and migrated to Italy and was probably coming to the United States. But it was abstract.

That's when I received an email from my friend Marty Makary, who is a surgeon at Johns Hopkins University and a careful, data-driven public health intellectual. He was planning a trip from Baltimore to New York, and we had plans for dinner on March 10. He told me that he was going to cancel.

"I'm very concerned about the pandemic and am planning to hunker down with a three-month food supply at home. Take care and be safe."

I read that email a few times to process it. Marty was "very concerned" and hunkering down with a season's worth of food about a virus that I considered only abstractly?

Within a few days, Covid had become the most important thing in the world, the subject around which most public and private discussions and actions revolved. The virus was new, contagious, and deadly. The early data on hospitalizations and death from Covid was instructive: The virus was especially dangerous for the elderly and the immunocompromised but was generally indistinguishable from influenza in the young, healthy, and middle-aged.

The contemplation of policy responses involved several considerations. Lockdowns and shutdowns would keep people apart to a significant extent, and slow, at least in the short term, the spread of this terrible virus. A safeytist approach, one that is governed by fear and treats safety as a sacred value to the exclusion of all other considerations, would argue for an indefinite lockdown.

But there were other considerations, which were widely known and undisputed going into Covid. The data from the New Orleans school closures from the 2005–6 school year (due to Hurricane Katrina) was clear: Students who missed a year of school suffered devastating and permanent learning loss.

There was also the guaranteed isolation. Loneliness had been declared an "epidemic" by the previous (and future) surgeon general, Vivek Murthy, in 2017. It was characterized by *Time* in 2018 as "a major threat to Americans' mental, physical and emotional well-being . . . [with] huge consequences for public health . . . ranging from substance abuse to heart disease."[52] And it was just as apparent that there would be enormous economic and health costs to shutting down businesses and limiting access to medical care.

It was clear from the beginning of Covid that its management would require a consideration of its dangers with that of the devastating consequences for education, mental health, physical health, and economics that a fear-driven reaction would guarantee. Some leaders acknowledged that their responsibility required just this consideration. In December 2020, Covid was raging in Rhode Island. The Democratic governor Gina Raimondo addressed her citizens. She acknowledged the fear. "I'm not going to sugarcoat this. Things are getting scary in Rhode Island."

Governor Raimondo continued. She discussed, in language the *New York Times* characterized as "harsh," the implications of "virtual learning." These included learning loss, increases in visits to pediatric emergency rooms, and suicidal ideation. She concluded, "Every day that a child is out of school is a problem for that child . . . To those of you who are throwing in the towel on our kids and going virtual, I think it's a shame. I really do. You're letting the children down, and I don't see any reason for it."[53]

Governor Raimondo's response was, as that *New York Times* analysis characterized it, "rare" among blue state political leaders. Many of these leaders were guided by the sentiment expressed by Professor Larisa DeSantis of Vanderbilt University in July of 2020. "If schools re-open in the fall, children will die, teachers will die, staff will die, and these deaths will have been preventable. This is hard to hear but it is true." There was no data to support this, but fear does not speak in the language of numbers.[54]

Starting in late 2020, a vaccine especially championed by blue-state officials began to be distributed. The vaccine was soon complemented by effective therapeutics that were made available for serious cases of Covid. This would have suggested a nationwide move to the philosophy and policies of Governor Raimondo. But the Torah's "fear in the heart" does not respond to logic. A *Vanity Fair* headline from March 2021 explained, "Biden's CDC Director: If You're Not Scared Shitless About COVID-19, You Should Be."[55]

The thinking driven by this fear persisted. In 2022, the US Supreme Court heard oral arguments for *National Federation of Independent Businesses v. United States Department of Labor* (a case about Covid). Justice

Sandra Sotomayor, a jurist who was confirmed by a bipartisan majority of the US Senate in part because of her reputation for being "thoroughly prepared," said in oral arguments, "We have over 100,000 children, which we've never had before, in serious condition and many on ventilators."[56]

If that were true, it would mean that more than 10 percent of hospital beds in the United States were being occupied by children in "serious condition" from Covid, with many being ventilated. Given that Covid patients on ventilators had a 50 percent chance of surviving their hospitalization, it would mean that huge numbers of children were dying of Covid in 2022. This was obviously not happening. Meanwhile, every review of the data confirmed what a *New York* magazine analysis concluded in mid-2021: "The kids were safe the whole time."[57]

The policies driven by fear persisted. By January 2022, Marty Makary had become one of the nation's leading authorities on Covid. He reviewed the policies of Georgetown, Amherst, Emerson, Princeton, and many other universities, which banned international travel, required twice-weekly testing, required double masking, severely limited leaving one's residence hall, and required even asymptomatic students who tested positive to be confined to a room in a special dorm for ten days. He concluded that these policies were "nonsensical, anti-scientific, and often downright cruel."[58]

Why would so many nice people want to implement policies that Dr. Makary, who had stocked up with three months of food in March of 2020, declared to be baseless and cruel? Dr. Lucy McBride is a Virginia-based physician who saw many patients during the Covid era. Writing in *The Atlantic* in August of 2021, she attributed these policies and pronouncements to people "marinating in fear" during the pandemic. Dr. McBride wrote:

> Being constantly wired [for fear] like this nevertheless carries a cost: Rational thought is hijacked. Our risk tolerance goes down. Our instinct to protect shifts into overdrive. We default to primitive thought patterns including black-and-white thinking . . . and catastrophizing.[59]

Shortly after Dr. McBride's warning, it became very clear that the fear-driven response to Covid was catastrophic. A variety of institutions issued reports on what the Brookings Institute called the "devastating impacts on learning" driven by the school closures, especially for those in poverty, those with disabilities, and those for whom English is a second language.[60] And the effects of the loss of connection are just as profound, with loneliness resulting in "social stuntedness" among the young to a variety of health effects in the elderly.[61]

In September 2023, Governor Gavin Newsom of California made an appearance on NBC's *Meet the Press*. He said of his Covid policies, "I think we would have done everything differently."[62]

This honest expression of regret is rare for a politician. But his sentiment is exactly that of the scouts in Numbers 14:39, when they feel "grief" after realizing what a bad political decision their fear had led them to.

The Contagion of Fear

In March 2020 when the pandemic was just starting, Professor Jacek Debiec of the University of Michigan knew what was coming. He wrote in *Fast Company*, "There's a pandemic of fear unfolding alongside the pandemic of the coronavirus."[63]

How was Professor Debiec, in the first week of the pandemic, able to diagnose this social phenomenon that would take two years to unfold? Because he understood the way that fear works in groups, just like the Author of the Torah who wrote about how ten of the scouts engendered fear in each other and soon the whole nation.

Professor Debiec, a neuroscientist, wrote that our brains are "hard-wired" to respond to threats in our environment. This is understandable. Fear is fundamental to threat detection and response, and one of its most important tools is sensitivity to the fear of others. If we notice that someone is afraid of a lion he thinks is around the corner, it makes evolutionary sense that he would immediately adopt that fear.

Professor Debiec explained the recently discovered brain science behind this phenomenon. It is all about contagion. He wrote:

> Experimental studies have identified a brain structure called the anterior cingulate cortex (ACC) as vital [to detect others' survival reactions]. It surrounds the bundle of fibers that connect the left and right hemispheres of the brain. When you watch another person express fear, your ACC lights up. Studies in animals confirmed that the message about another's fear travels from the ACC to the

> amygdala [the brain's "fear center"], where the defense responses are set off.[64]

In 2022, Professor Sarah Tashjian of the California Institute of Technology and a team of researchers published their research regarding the contagion of fear in an environment far more contained than that of the Covid pandemic. They had study participants enter a haunted house.

The team found that participants were, as measured by monitors on their waistbands, more afraid to the extent that they were with a larger group, and to the extent that the group contained friends. Professor Tashjian explained, "We interpreted this to reflect fear contagion, if your friends are around, your body picks up on their signals and has a higher level of arousal even in the absence of specific scares or startles."[65] This is precisely what happened with the scouts, whose fear immediately spread to "the entire congregation" in Numbers 14.

When Professor Debiec, based on his understanding of the science of fear and the unfolding dynamics of Covid, was able to predict that the virus was spawning a pandemic of fear, there was one thing he could not have known. Covid would not be the only thing to spark a pandemic of fear, with massive social and political ramifications, in 2020.

Fear of Police

On May 20, 2013, President Barack Obama delivered the commencement address at Morehouse College, one of the great historically black colleges and universities in the United States. It was, by any measure, a great speech.

President Obama neared the conclusion of his address by exhorting the audience to be "men who refuse to be afraid. Men who refuse to be afraid!"[66]

Eleven years later, President Biden delivered the commencement address at Morehouse. He took a very different approach to how the Morehouse men and their guests should think about fear. He said, "It's natural to wonder if democracy you hear about actually works for you. What is democracy if black men are being killed in the street?"[67]

Who is killing black men "in the street" to such an extent that the Morehouse men should question American democracy? President Biden did not specify or offer any data. But in 2014, the Amnesty International USA director Steven W. Hawkins issued a warning that might be what President

Biden was referencing: "The U.S. cannot continue to allow those obligated and duty-bound [the police] to protect, to become those who their [black] community fears most."[68]

Was Mr. Hawkins correct about the fear of the police within the black community? In 2019, the *Journal of Black Psychology* ran an article about how black youth regard the police. The headline: "That's My Number One Fear in Life. It's the Police." A 2019 survey by YouGov showed that 63 percent of black Americans answered yes to fearing that "you or someone in your family will be the victim of deadly force by a police officer."[69]

Two months after fear became the defining political emotion through Covid, the United States would confront another crisis. On May 25, 2020, several Minneapolis police officers arrested George Floyd for using a counterfeit bill. In the course of the arrest, Officer Derek Chauvin restrained Mr. Floyd by kneeling on his neck. Mr. Floyd pleaded for his life, saying, "I can't breathe." Onlookers pleaded with Chauvin to stop. Chauvin refused. Within ten minutes, George Floyd was dead.

There were protests in thousands of cities, characterized by the *Washington Post* on June 6, 2020 (when they were just getting started), as "the broadest in American history."[70] These occurred in every segment of America, from mostly white suburbs to largely black inner cities.

While most of these protests were peaceful, many were not. American cities from Minneapolis to New York, from Seattle to Philadelphia, from Portland to Oakland, saw protests turn to full-scale riots. Oscar Stewart, a thirty-year-old father of five, was burned to death when a pawnshop was set ablaze in Minneapolis. David Patrick Underwood, a Federal Protective Serviceman, was shot dead in Oakland. Barry Perkins was run over by a FedEx truck fleeing looters in St. Louis. Dozens of others were killed as well.

Insurance companies paid billions of dollars in claims to thousands of businesses that were damaged or destroyed, and that does not include the damage to the 40 percent of businesses that were uninsured and the many others that were underinsured. By early June of 2020, more than 200 American cities had imposed curfews, and more than 30 states had activated over 62,000 National Guard personnel.[71]

Why would one death, however tragic, lead to a summer of widespread violent riots? Shortly after Mr. Floyd's death, the media was full of politicians and commentators who said that the killing was not an isolated event.

It was an example of the "systemic racism" of which the police are a vanguard. For instance, Joe Biden, then the presumptive Democratic nominee for president, said on June 10, 2020, that there was "absolutely" systematic racism in law enforcement.[72]

If there is "systematic racism" with an armed police force as its vanguard, then there is ample reason for the extreme fear recorded in the aforementioned data from the *Journal of Black Psychology* and YouGov. As the psychologist Walter Cannon wrote a hundred years ago, a fight response—as witnessed on the streets of America in the summer of 2020—is one of the four responses to fear.

As we learn in the Torah, there is one question that must be asked about any fear. Is it fear of something genuine (a charging lion), or is it a "fear in the heart"? In the twenty-first century, we have data.

The Data

The canonical source of fatal police shootings is the *Washington Post*'s Police Shooting Database, which has rigorously cataloged and sorted every fatal police shooting in the United States since 2015. It offers a scientific way to assess whether the fear of the police resembles that of a charging lion or is (per Deuteronomy) "fear in the heart."

Given that George Floyd died in 2020, and the term "systemic racism" has become a common part of the lexicon, an analysis of the fear of police heading into the summer of 2020 can be conducted with regard to two datasets. First, the perception of how many unarmed black men were killed by the police in 2019, and second, the number that were *actually* killed by the police.

In early 2021, the Skeptic Research Center published the results of a survey of how Americans estimated the number of police killings of unarmed black men in 2019. They found that 16 percent of "very liberal" respondents believed that there were "about ten" such killings, while 54 percent believed that there were more than one thousand. The "very liberal" respondents also estimated that 60 percent of the people killed by the police were black. Meanwhile, 46 percent of the "conservative" respondents estimated "about ten," while 13 percent estimated more than one thousand. The "conservative" respondents estimated that 38 percent of those killed by the police were black.[73]

The *Washington Post* database has the facts. In 2019, there were 999 fatal police shootings—251 of those shot were black—12 of the 251 were unarmed. The *Washington Post* database also links to news articles about each killing. At least four of the twelve killings of unarmed black men in 2019 followed the deceased attacking the police officers. Several others faced extenuating circumstances. One case involved a suspect known to the police for previously shooting an officer, who then threatened to kill another officer. Thus, there were fewer than six cases of fatal police shootings of unarmed black citizens without extenuating violent circumstances in 2019—out of approximately 6.5 million contacts between the police and black citizens.[74]

Let's take those six deadly shootings. Each was a tragedy. But were they motivated by racism? There is nothing in the media stories, linked from the *Washington Post* site, to indicate that they were. Racism certainly may have been a factor in all, some, or none of them—just as extreme carelessness, uncontrolled fear, or pure sadism might have been significant or deciding factors.

And these possibilities are certainly worthy of consideration. For instance, in 2016, Arizona police officer Philip Brailsford arrested Daniel Leetin Shaver in a hotel for suspected possession of a gun. Officer Brailsford ordered Mr. Shaver to the ground, face down with empty hands spread wide in front of him. Mr. Shaver complied. Brailsford shot him dead anyway. It was, a video of the killing showed, the result of pure sadism. Both men were white.[75]

In 2023, Tyre Nichols was pulled over by police officers in Memphis. Mr. Nichols responded calmly and politely. The police officers beat and murdered him. Mr. Nichols and all of the police officers were black.

The statistics from the *Washington Post* database do not reveal the full extent of police shootings and violence. For instance, the database does not account for nonfatal shootings or deaths caused by something other than bullets. However, data from other studies is illustrative. Studies published between 2015 and 2021 from scholars at Georgia State, Harvard, and the University of Wyoming found that blacks are not more likely to be shot by the police than whites—with some finding that whites are more likely to be shot. A 2015 study by Harvard University economist Sendhil Mullainathan found that the race of police shooting victims corresponds with the race of arrestees in the area.[76]

Yet, the fear of police persists, with consequences that extend beyond the events of 2020.

The Consequences of Fear of Policing

The fear of police among black Americans has had at least five consequences.

Consequence #1: Mental Health

In September of 2020, Saleemah McNeil of the Oshun Family Center (a Pennsylvania organization devoted to helping the black community with life transitions) told ABC, "[Police killings] have affected people's everyday functioning. From people being hyper-vigilant when you're just going outside to the onset of having a panic attack when you're pulled over by the police, it has an effect."[77] This fear has a demonstrable effect on those it afflicts. According to the US Census Bureau, the rates of depression and anxiety (the usual accompaniments of fear) among black Americans increased by around 25 percent during the summer of 2020, meaning that around ten million black people were newly afflicted.[78]

Consequence #2: Less Engagement with Police

In 2016, Nikole Hannah-Jones became famous for creating the *New York Times* 1619 Project that was based on the premise that racism "is embedded in the DNA of this country."[79] In 2015, she wrote an article for ProPublica on the fear of the police among black Americans. She told of walking along the beach on July 4 with her family, another family, and a high school intern. Shots were fired on the beach. Ms. Jones saw her intern on the phone, and figured that she had called her mother. The intern corrected her; she was on the phone with the police. Ms. Jones wrote:

> My friends and I locked eyes in stunned silence. Between the four adults, we hold six degrees. Three of us are journalists. And not one of us had thought to call the police. We had not even considered it. We also are all Black. And without realizing it, in that moment, each of us had made a set of calculations, an instantaneous weighing of the pros and cons . . . Calling the police posed considerable risks.[80]

It is easy to imagine how reluctance and even refusal to call the police during a shooting could be very dangerous. It is also easy to understand why Ms. Jones did not want to call the police. The rational response to fear is to stay away from its source.

Consequence #3: Running from Danger

In 2015, the publication *In These Times* ran an interview with the University of Wisconsin sociologist Alice Goffman entitled "Why Black People Running from the Police Makes Perfect Sense." The presumption of the interview is that the police are a dangerous force to be feared. Thus, the rational response to a police encounter is to run from the danger. This, of course, poses *real* dangers to the person stopped. First, running might give rise to a police chase, which is always an unstable situation. Second, running from a a police officer trying to make a stop is a crime for which the person fleeing can expect to be arrested, convicted and punished. Consequently, one who exercises fear of the police by fleeing might get himself into serious trouble that he would otherwise have completely avoided.[81]

Consequence #4: Police Pull Back

In a healthy democracy like the United States, widespread fear of the police—whether warranted or not—will not remain silent or contained for long. It will trigger investigations of the police. In June 2020, Harvard Professor Roland Fryer and the data scientist Tanaya Devi reported their findings on what happens when police departments are investigated following a "viral event." A "viral event," in this context, is a deadly police action that becomes widely socialized. They determined that police officers, concerned that any interaction with a civilian could turn into a racially charged firestorm, just pull back, with devastating consequences.

Professor Fryer and Dr. Devi determined that investigations in five cities (Baltimore, MD; Chicago, IL; Cincinnati, OH; Riverside, CA; and Ferguson, MO) led to a decline of police–civilian interactions between 46 and almost 100 percent. They wrote in their paper that these investigations had led to 893 "excess homicides" (a measure of homicides during a particular period that exceed what would be expected based on historical data) and 34,000 excess non-homicidal felonies by the time of writing the paper.

In September 2020, Alec MacGillis published an analysis in *The Atlantic* of the phenomenon that Professor Fryer and Dr. Devi described. Writing about the police response to widespread accusations of police racism following the death of a black suspect (Freddie Gray) in Baltimore in 2015, Mr. MacGillis wrote:

> The protests flared into rioting and looting. Soon afterward, the city's chief prosecutor announced criminal charges against the officers involved in the arrest. The officers' colleagues responded by pulling back on the job, doing only the bare minimum in the following weeks. In the resulting void, crews seized new drug corners and settled old scores. Homicides surged to record levels and case-closure rates plunged. "The police stopped doing their jobs, and let people fuck up other people," Carl Stokes, a former Democratic city councilor in Baltimore, told me last year.[82]

This process takes a long time. Professor Fryer and Dr. Devi determined that it takes an average of 4.3 years following an investigation triggered by a viral event for police interactions to return to normal. Given that the clock was still running on several of the investigations at the time of their writing in 2020, Professor Fryer and Dr. Devi predicted that the investigations into police departments following the George Floyd killing would ultimately result in 1,244 excess homicides and tens of thousands of other felonies.[83]

Consequence #5: Focus

Fear demands one's focus and monopolizes one's attention. This makes evolutionary sense, as a hunter-gatherer threatened by a lion has the best chance to survive if he focuses on the lion.

When people focus their attention on the wrong issues, they often miss what's truly important. This principle can be observed in the widespread fear of police that emerged in the 2010s and continued into the 2020s. With the fear of being killed by a police officer dominating public discourse and policy considerations, a genuine problem with policing was effectively ignored.

Before the fateful night of May 25, 2020, Derek Chauvin had at least seventeen complaints filed against him. Chauvin's career "discipline" consisted of two reprimands, and yet, his terrible record did not preclude his serving as a police officer. Philip Brailsford was fired from the Mesa, Arizona, police department after he killed Mr. Shaver, but was subsequently reinstated so that he could apply for "medical disability" and receive a pension. Why did the Minneapolis police department persist in believing that Chauvin was a fit officer? Why did the Mesa police department reinstate Brailsford?[84]

A 2017 investigation by Reade Levinson of Reuters showed that police union contracts in forty-six of the eighty-two cities covered call for departments to erase disciplinary records—some after only six months. Fifteen unions did not need that in the contract, as the erasure was covered by state or local law. Police contracts in twenty cities allow officers accused of misconduct to forfeit sick leave or holiday and vacation time rather than serve suspensions, with this provision being state or local law in thirteen locales.[85]

Even with the unprecedented focus on policing since the murder of George Floyd, there has barely been a mention of Mr. Levinson's investigation—and few to the genuinely systemic problem he surfaced. Fear of police shootings, unsupported by the data, did what fear does—it dominated and distorted, with devastating consequences.

Climate Anxiety

Sometimes, fear arises in response to a specific circumstance, as with the scouts in Numbers, Covid, and George Floyd. But it is not the only way. Sometimes, as with the fear generated by the darkness in Exodus, it can emanate from anything and lead to pervasive and continuous dread.

Enter the Democrat House Whip Katherine Clark. In 2022, Congresswoman Clark told NBC about her experience as a mother: "I remember my middle child waking up with nightmares over concern around climate change."[86]

It is not only children who, afraid of climate change, come to their parents. In April 2021, the author Marta Zaraska wrote an article for *Discover* describing herself standing outside her daughter's room with her "heart pounding." She did not see a clown, was not imagining a monster, had not fled from an unwelcome animal, and had not heard a strange sound. She, like Congresswoman Clark's child, was thinking about the climate.

The title of Ms. Zaraska's article is "Chronic Fear of Environmental Doom: You're Not Alone," and that is certainly right. A feature on the environment in *Politico* in 2021 was titled "Get Scared." Lots of people are doing just that. A 2019 analysis in *Well and Good* states, "Climate anxiety is sweeping the planet."[87]

The data confirms this. A 2020 poll from the American Psychiatric Association showed that more than one-third of Americans are "extremely anxious" about the impact of climate change, and most of those state that their climate anxiety is "extremely" deleterious to their mental health. This fear is so pervasive that there is a large and growing profession of climate psychology, which itself is developing specialties, including "climate aware therapy" and "eco-anxious stories."[88]

An international team of researchers, in a paper published in *The Lancet* in late 2021 on "Climate Anxiety in Children," had similar findings. The researchers surveyed ten thousand people between the ages of sixteen and twenty-five in ten countries, and found that 75 percent said "the future is frightening [because of climate concerns]." Fifty-six percent believe that humanity "is doomed" because of climate change. And 45 percent said that their feelings about climate change negatively affect their "daily life and functioning." This is not surprising, at least to those familiar with the ninth plague, where fear made it impossible for people to "rise from their place."[89]

"Daily life and functioning" are not the only things being transformed by climate anxiety. It is the creation of life itself. In 2021, a Morgan Stanley analysis concluded, "The movement to not have children owing to fears over climate change is growing and impacting fertility rates quicker than any preceding trend in the field of fertility decline."[90]

Are these fears justified? For the purposes of considering fear, we can table the question as to whether extreme weather events are increasing, and if so, whether they are caused by human activity. Instead, we can turn to the one source of truth that should govern fears of climate events: the number of *fatalities* from climate-related events.

In 2011, Indur M. Goklany of the Reason Foundation published a study that looked at this question. He found that deaths from extreme weather, even without accounting for the 350 percent rise in global population from 1900 to 2010, declined by over 95 percent. These trends, according to a subsequent 2019 study from Giuseppe Formetta of the Fincons Group and Luc Feyen of the European Commission, have continued in the subsequent decade. The data would suggest that whatever the effect of human activity on the environment, there are fewer reasons to fear from the climate than ever before.[91]

Accordingly, some environmentalists, even those who believe that climate change is a significant concern, are counseling against "climate alarmism." Their concern is that fear is making it impossible to create the space for the dispassionate analysis and broad consensus that are necessary for effective and durable policies. But they have a very difficult opponent in fear that is overwhelming and contagious.[92]

Reflection

Rabbi Meir in the Talmud, speaking about the story of the scouts in the Torah, said, "No lie in which one does not speak at least some truth can be maintained."[93] In other words, every good lie is based on a little bit of truth. It is a truth that we all need fear to survive and thrive. The proper reaction to smelling fire in a home is to be afraid, and then to grab your loved ones and get out of there as soon as possible. More complex fears are also based on "at least some truth." Children do get kidnapped by strangers. Covid did kill a lot of people. And there are unjustifiable fatal police shootings.

It is equally true that some of the responses to our fears have been unambiguously positive. A combination of government regulation and social stigma has meant that we now wear helmets on bicycles and seat belts in cars, and have robust laws against drunk driving.[94]

How, then, do we distinguish between the legitimate and the illegitimate fears, both of which derive from "at least some truth"? What is the guiding principle, the line of distinction, that will allow us to permit our ten-year-old to walk home from school and to forbid him from riding in a car without a seat belt?

We can be guided by the early-twentieth-century Columbia University professor John Erskine, who proclaimed, "The moral obligation to be intelligent." We can counter the stupidity that fear induces with the basic intelligence that God has gifted us.[95]

How can we use our intelligence against fear? There are at least five ways.

1. Do Not Make Yourself Afraid

Rabbi Nachman of Breslov, the eighteenth-century Hasidic master, is revered by many Jews today. A teaching of his, now put to a popular song, is, "The whole world is a very narrow bridge, but the main thing is to not make yourself afraid."[96]

His instruction, which coheres with the biblical curse of fearing in the heart, is totally focused on the individual: Do not *make yourself* afraid. If one feels fear when a pit bull is charging, she is not making herself afraid. The pit bull is. However, if one prepares to read a poem in the most protected place in the world by telling themselves to be "prepared to die," she is making herself afraid. One must use their intellect to assess whether there is a threat stimulus right in front of them, or whether their thoughts are leading them astray.

How can we further use our intelligence to stop making ourselves afraid?

2. Distinguish Between Short and Long Fear

In his 2021 book, *The End of Trauma*, Columbia University professor George Bonanno wrote:

> Any emotion, fear included, is adaptive only insofar as it does its job quickly. When fear is prolonged, it becomes unmoored from its original purpose. It diffuses into a general sense of foreboding, an apprehension about what is yet to come. And eventually, if it persists long enough, it morphs into more dysfunctional states, such as anxiety or PTSD. When this happens, decision-making is seriously impaired, and it becomes increasingly difficult, if not impossible, to sort out when our actions are effective and when they are not.[97]

Professor Bonanno's insight: A legitimate fear "does its job quickly." This leads to a distinction that we can all make between short and long fear.

A short fear (e.g., that prompted by a charging lion) can be necessary and good. We can demote all other fears to *concerns*. When a potential bad outcome is a concern, we can pause and consider all the relevant facts, probabilities, and data. We can subject our concerns to dispassionate analysis and thoughtful and comprehensive consideration of the problem. This strategy would enable policymakers to focus on the real and important problems, with potential solutions including getting bad officers out of uniform, increasing safety for the poor, implementing broad-based environmental protections, and much more. It would allow a young adult consumed with climate fear to realize that historically, few people are suffering and dying from climate-related events, and the same systems and technologies that have accounted for this remarkable diminution continue to develop and protect us.

3. Strengthen Your Relationship with God

In Psalm 23, King David says, "Even though I walk through the valley of the shadow of death, I will fear no evil, for you are with me; your rod and your staff, they will comfort me."

The modern-day exemplar of this philosophy was Dr. Martin Luther King Jr. In what was his final speech, Dr. King said:

> Like anybody, I would like to live a long life. Longevity has its place. But I'm not concerned about that now. I just want to do God's will. And He's allowed me to go up to the mountain. And I've looked over. And I've seen the Promised Land. I may not get there with you. But I want you to know tonight that we, as a people, will get to the Promised Land! And so I'm happy tonight. I'm not worried about anything. I'm not fearing any man! Mine eyes have seen the glory of the coming of the Lord![98]

If one has full-time police protection, an ever-present doctor, and a food tester, one will fear less, as many of the avenues of danger are cut off. How much more so, like King David and Martin Luther King Jr., when one feels always accompanied by God. One who invites God on every journey would still fear an unaccompanied pit bull ten feet away. But he would not fear that speaking an unpopular truth will cost him status or money. He would not fear the reaction of what random people think of him as long as he is confident that God is proud.

4. Engage with the Sources of Fear

As discussed, the fear embedded in the ninth plague is associated with the result that "no man could recognize his brother." Fear, as is evident in the data of attitudes toward police among black Americans, fills a vacuum created by the absence of trust. In comes the story of Mike Collins and Michael Harris.

In August of 2016, Dallas police officer Mike Collins pulled over a black motorist, Michael Harris. Mr. Harris calmly told Officer Collins that he had a concealed carry permit and was carrying his weapon. Mr. Harris's seven-year-old daughter was in the car. She heard the conversation and became very afraid.

Officer Collins asked Mr. Harris and his daughter to come out of the car. He brought them to the police car. Officer Collins then gave the seven-year-old a sticker and let her activate the lights and sirens. Mr. Harris reported, "That made her feel a lot more comfortable with police officers."[99]

Also in 2016, a group of black children were playing basketball on a street in Gainesville, Florida, when the police were called for a noise complaint. Officer Bobby White—who is white—showed up. He approached the kids and asked for the ball and proceeded to play with them. They told him that they played there all the time. He told them to get ready, as he would be back another time, with police colleagues to join him.

The entire incident was captured on the camera on the dashboard of Officer White's police car. A colleague posted the video. By the next morning, it had been shared and viewed by three million people.

Officer White kept his word and returned with other officers. But he was not being fair. One of his teammates was a Florida reserve officer, Shaquille O'Neal. "Officer" O'Neal gave each of the kids $100 after each hit a free throw and, more importantly, a pep talk. This moment gave rise to the Basketball Cop Foundation, which enhances trust and diminishes fear between kids and officers through their shared love for the sport.[100]

The lessening of fear that Officers Collins, White, and O'Neal experienced is by no means unique to basketball. The International Association of Chiefs of Police counsels its members to "establish relationships with the community by fostering dialogue between law enforcement and residents. Successful strategies include convening monthly meetings with community members; increasing bicycle and foot patrols; and establishing programs that solicit involvement from residents, such as Coffee with a Cop, Neighborhood Watch, and National Night Out programs."[101]

5. Acquire for Yourself a Friend (Who Thinks Differently)

The Talmud, addressing another product of the imagination, specifies what one should do following a distressing dream: "One who sees a dream from which his soul is distraught, should go and have it interpreted before three [others]."[102]

A powerful way of dealing with negative products of the imagination, whether dreams or fear, is through the counsel of a trusted few. Indeed, the discipline of talking through one's fears with others is recommended by authorities ranging from Recovery Village in Colorado to the National Health Service in Great Britain.[103]

But the trusted few cannot be chosen casually or randomly. It has to be done in the spirit of Pirkei Avot, the ancient Jewish work of ethics. Pirkei Avot counsels, "*Acquire* for yourself a friend."[104] In other words, the selection of a friend must be pursued with the same rigor and thoughtfulness as any major acquisition. And given the pervasiveness and perniciousness of fear, one of the criteria for selecting a friend could be finding someone who is likely to challenge fears.

By acquiring a friend who thinks differently, one will curb fear's most potent property—its contagiousness. A reliable antidote is genuine diversity—bringing into one's circle of trust people who think differently, access different sources of information, and belong to distinct social groups. For instance, it is unlikely that Justice Sotomayor would have based her fear of Covid on a belief that more than 10 percent of US hospital beds are occupied by children sickened by the virus, if she were friends with the likes of Lucy McBride, Marty Makary, Gina Raimondo, or others who thought like them. The advice of a trusted friend, as counseled by Pirkei Avot, can go a long way to dispelling irrational fear and improving our assessments, even for the most intelligent, careful, and discerning amongst us.

29

Of the Enslaved Jews of the Exodus, Rejected Scientists, and Michael Jordan's Demolishment of the Washington Bullets

The Torah and Science of Antifragility

Jacob Progresses with a Limp

In Genesis 32, Jacob is in exile, fleeing from his brother Esau, who seeks to kill him for stealing their father's blessing.

Alone in a strange place, he engages in an all-night wrestling match with an unnamed man (whom the canonical commentators often designate as an angel). At dawn, Jacob is about to win the fight when his adversary takes a cheap shot, striking him in the hip socket and damaging the sciatic nerve. Injured but undeterred, Jacob holds on and continues to best his sparring partner who begs to be released. But Jacob has a condition before relenting: "I will not let you go until you bless me."

His adversary does not give him a traditional blessing. Instead, he tells Jacob, "Your name will no longer be Jacob, but Israel, because you have struggled with God and with man and have overcome."

We know this blessing is significant, if only because the Bible later refers to the Jews as "the Children of Israel." To be of the Children of Israel—to be a Jew—is to struggle and persevere.

What does victory after such a struggle look like? The text tells us. Jacob continues on his journey, with a limp. This limp would remain with him all his days, as would its lesson with us.

We are to struggle and overcome, but this does not mean that the struggle will become a distant memory. Like Jacob's limp, its scars may be with us for a long time. But the scars will not define us *negatively*. We will grow, persevere, and continue on our journeys with them—and, just maybe, *because* of them. Having established this principle, the Torah has prepared us for the foundational story of Exodus and all that follows.

More Affliction, More Growth?

In Exodus 1:8, a new Pharaoh—one who "did not know Joseph"—assumed power in Egypt. He decided that the Jews were becoming too powerful and might pose a threat to his regime. He responded by brutalizing, oppressing, and enslaving us.

We come to a very intriguing statement as the Torah proceeds to describe the dire state of the Jews in Egypt. In Exodus 1:12, the Torah says of the Jews, "The more they were afflicted, the more they multiplied and grew."

This is a seemingly illogical statement. The only reason to afflict someone is to weaken and diminish him. Even if an oppressor is incompetent, he should weaken the victim a little bit—and certainly not *strengthen* the people he afflicts. Yet, that is what the Torah says.

Was the narrator, in describing growth as connected to affliction, correct? We can turn to the censuses conducted in Numbers for some additional insight. One census was for the tribe of Levi and another was for the other eleven tribes. The Levites—the priest-teacher tribe—was not enslaved in Egypt according to the Midrash. This is inferred from the fact that Moses and Aaron—both Levites—traveled freely around Egypt while they negotiated with the Pharaoh. The census of the Levites counted every male older than one month. The general census for the other eleven tribes, all of which were enslaved, included only men twenty and older.

Among the eleven tribes, the smallest was Menasseh, with 32,200. The largest was Judah, with 74,500. The Levites numbered a mere 22,000. The one tribe who had not suffered Egyptian slavery was 70 percent smaller than the next smallest tribe.

True to Exodus 1:12, the enslaved tribes were the ones that "multiplied and grew." Hardship, it seems, can be beneficial to the one who encounters it.

Moses's Parting Speech

Moses does not mention these numbers in his farewell speech, which defines the book of Deuteronomy. Two seemingly incidental references, however, offer insight into the mindset he wishes us to adopt as we brace for the challenge of being a free people in our own land.

In Deuteronomy 4:20, Moses reminds us, "The Lord took you and brought you out of the iron crucible, out of Egypt, to be a people of His possession." Why would Moses specifically employ the metaphor of an "iron crucible"? Rashi explains that Moses wishes to compare the people to a precious metal, which enters the iron crucible as rough material, then gets burned and melted down before finally emerging purer and more valuable.[1]

Moses develops this theme in Deuteronomy 26. He recounts the Jewish experience through the lens of an imaginary farmer coming to offer his first fruits sometime in the future. The farmer declares that we "became there [Egypt] a great and mighty nation." This is an odd description considering we were an *enslaved* nation in Egypt. We coalesced as a people in Egypt, but surely we only became *great* in the desert (or even later upon entering the land!).

The thirteenth-century sage Nachmanides explained that the Torah is trying to teach us that we become great under pressure and amidst great challenges. Indeed, it was precisely because we were in this terrible situation in Egypt that we were able to identify, marshal, and understand the inner resources that we would need to become worthy of being God's emissary in the world. As Rav Joseph B. Soloveitchik wrote, "Had we not spent years in horror, we could not have become a great nation."[2]

Afflictions, Tests, and an Egg

The Jewish experience in the desert that characterizes much of Exodus and all of Leviticus and Numbers is marked by challenges and difficulties, some of which are self-inflicted, some of which are caused by enemies, and others that derive from desert conditions. In Deuteronomy, Moses sums them up in one sentence. He says, "And you shall remember the entire way in which the Lord, your God, led you these forty years in the desert, in order to afflict you in order to test you, to know what is in your heart" (Deuteronomy 8:2).

Moses's specific wording is, as ever, crucial and instructive. He tells us that an affliction will "test" us. And such a "test" will enable us to "know what is in your heart." Moses is essentially saying that the statement in Exodus that "the more we are afflicted, the more we will grow" is not unique to its context. It is a statement about people in all times and circumstances.

The notion that an affliction is a test that reveals who we really are has since become a staple of Jewish thought. The sixteenth-century sage Shlomo Ephraim ben Aaron Luntschitz (known as the Kli Yakar) notes that the word *l'nasotcha* (to test) derives from the word *ness* that means "banner." A banner is the flag we stand under, the symbol of who we truly are. So, too, the Kli Yakar said, is the notion of a test. Tests, struggles, and challenges all provide us with the opportunity to raise our banners and show who we really can be.[3]

In Proverbs 24:16, King Solomon wrote, "For though the righteous fall seven times, they rise again, but the wicked stumble when calamity strikes."

It is not a question whether someone will fall multiple times. It is a question of how he will react when he does. One can respond to a fall by playing the victim, wallowing in self-pity, blaming others, and growing bitter, resentful, and adversarial. Or one can respond to a fall by considering what one can learn and how one can grow and improve. This is the distinction, the proverb tells us, between wickedness and righteousness.[4]

The conviction that afflictions and falls provide the indispensable opportunity for growth became one of the most deeply held and important tenets of Jewish belief. The Talmud states, "No one can truly understand Torah unless he has stumbled in it." This applies to study, character, and action—because "Torah" encompasses all of them. A millennium and a half later, the eighteenth-century sage and founder of Hasidic Judaism, Israel ben Eliezer (known as the Baal Shem Tov), amplified this notion. He said that afflictions are necessary for us to become stronger and better.[5]

Every practicing Jew experiences and, indeed, eats this idea each year. The centerpiece of the Pesach table is the Seder plate. One of the items on every Seder plate is an egg. Why an egg? The nineteenth-century sage Moses Sofer (the Chatam Sofer) noted that most foods become softer to the extent that they are boiled. The egg, by contrast, becomes stronger. This, he said, describes the afflicted Jew. The more we are afflicted, the stronger we become.[6]

What to Do When Potentially Traumatized

One of the great questions of affliction is: How should we deal with it when the affliction is over? One answer—perhaps the intuitive one—is that we should try to blot it out of our minds and just move on. The Torah offers a very different solution.

In Numbers 21, the Canaanites attack the Jews and take captives. God enables us to win a military victory over them. The Jews respond by complaining about the food in the desert and demanding to return to Egypt. God's furious response is described in Numbers 21:6: "The Lord sent against the people the venomous snakes, and they bit the people, and many people of Israel died."

Many people died before the deadly snake attack ended with a prayer from Moses. God knows that this massive snake assault—likely witnessed by all of the people—could traumatize and thus weaken them. He has a solution. It is not to stop thinking about snakes. It is not to run from the word "snake" for fear that it will trigger the trauma of the attack. In Numbers 21:8, God instructs Moses, "Make a snake and put it up on a pole; anyone who is bitten can look at it and live." Moses does as instructed, specifically making a "copper snake."

Why does Moses make a *copper* snake? The answer is revealed in the Hebrew text. The word for "snake" is *nachash*, and the word for "copper" is *nechoshet*. The similarity is not coincidental. It is a way of shoving the snake in the people's face, creating what Rabbi David Kasher calls "a snakey snake." It is God's and Moses's way of telling the Jews to deal with their snake experience by looking at the source of their affliction directly—not as a painful memory but instead, as a symbol of overcoming adversity—*elevated* and placed up on a pole.[7]

Through the instruction of Numbers 21:8, God and Moses are teaching us about how to deal with trauma. We are not to run from it, but to face it and extract meaning from it. The result: "When anyone was bitten by a snake and looked at the bronze snake, they lived." A snake elevated on a pole remains the universally used medical symbol until this very day.[8]

How Abraham and Sarah Consider the Growing Independence of Their Child

Adults, who make their own decisions, will inevitably "fall seven times," as many choices prove to be wrong—even costly. One of the choices most adults face is how to approach King Solomon's proverb in relation to their children. Parents have always had to decide whether a child's growing independence, which invariably brings the risk of mistakes, should be cause for concern or something to nurture. The biblical Abraham had a clear point of view on this matter. Abraham and Sarah were the first in the Bible to experience a particularly heartbreaking affliction: the inability to conceive. In Genesis 18, their fortunes change. God tells Abraham he will have a son with Sarah. This is a spectacular revelation because Abraham is one hundred years old and Sarah is ninety. Their son, Isaac, has the responsibility of carrying the legacy of the Jewish people in a difficult and hostile world. If anything happened to Isaac—spiritually or physically—their legacy would end, as would God's project on earth. They had to protect and cultivate him, as much as any parent ever could. How would they do so?

In Genesis 21:8, we learn that Isaac had ceased breastfeeding. A child ceasing to breastfeed is not an interesting milestone we normally focus on. Why, then, would the Torah tell us about it? The answer starts with understanding what weaning really is: the *first* act of a child's independence. Abraham and Sarah's response to this event, then, demonstrates their attitude toward their child's increasing independence. In Genesis 21:8 we read: "Abraham made a great feast." A child's growing capacity for independence, according to Abraham, is to be celebrated.

Limits?

So, the Torah provides us with a robust understanding of human nature: humans grow under hardship, falling down and getting back up is a hallmark of righteousness, and independence—with all its unknown dangers—ought to be celebrated. But does the Torah recognize any limits? Is the Torah (and Jewish tradition) saying that more affliction and less protection from danger *always* leads to more growth?

One of the remarkable documents in twentieth-century Judaism is *Esh Kodesh.* This book, which means "Sacred Fire," is a memoir / Torah commentary from Rabbi Kalonymus Kalman Shapira. Rabbi Shapira was the Grand Rabbi of Piaseczno when the Nazis conquered Poland.

On September 25, 1939, Rabbi Shapira's only son, Elimelech Ben-Tzion, was sitting by a window when a shell fragment crashed through and seriously injured him. Rabbi Shapira and some others took the young man through the streets, which were being bombed, to bring him to a hospital. Rabbi Shapira, his daughter-in-law, and another relative spent the night at the entrance of the hospital. In the morning, Rabbi Shapira went to the home of a doctor to ask him to come to the hospital and treat his son. When Rabbi Shapira was gone, the entrance of the hospital was bombed. His daughter-in-law and the relative were killed and his son died shortly thereafter.

Rabbi Shapira did not say anything publicly for six weeks. On November 4, he gave a sermon. He began by quoting a Talmudic commentary from the eighteenth-century sage Menachem Mendel of Rimanov: "A covenant is made with salt, and a covenant is made with afflictions. Just as salt makes meat palatable, so too afflictions purify the individual of sin."

Rabbi Shapira explained, "Just as one cannot derive pleasure from meat that has been excessively salted . . . so too afflictions should be meted out only in such measure that they can be tolerated, and with an admixture of mercy."

Rabbi Shapira continued, citing Rashi on the death of Sarah in Genesis 23. Sarah, we can infer from the text, was a 127-year-old woman who died immediately upon hearing that her husband had taken their son to the mountain to be slaughtered. This affliction, Rabbi Shapira explained, was too much for Sarah to bear. The Torah, Rabbi Shapira said, "juxtaposed the death of Sarah to the binding of Yitzhak in order . . . to indicate what results from excessive afflictions, Heaven forbid, her soul burst forth."[9]

How much affliction is so much that it can no longer be a source of growth? Rabbi Shapira does not say. It is a question whose answer depends on the individual and the specific situation. But the centrality of the question itself speaks to the Torah philosophy: Affliction, even as severe as that described in Exodus 11, can and should be a source of growth and strength. But there are limits.

The Science

Nassim Nicholas Taleb's Best-Seller

In 2012, the mathematician and philosopher Nassim Nicholas Taleb published the book *Antifragile*, which became a critically acclaimed best-seller. He describes antifragility in the following manner:

> Some things benefit from shocks; they thrive and grow when exposed to volatility, randomness, disorder, and stressors and love adventure, risk, and uncertainty. Yet, in spite of the ubiquity of the phenomenon, there is no word for the exact opposite of fragile. Let us call it antifragile. Antifragility is beyond resilience or robustness. The resilient resists shocks and stays the same; the antifragile gets better.[10]

Some things are fragile. If we drop a piece of china on the floor, it will break. Other things are robust and resilient. If we drop a plastic bottle on the floor, it will neither diminish nor improve. Other things are antifragile. They improve when they are stressed or broken. If we tear our muscles through weightlifting, they will become stronger.

This dynamic leads to a great question. Are people psychologically fragile, resilient, or antifragile? The Torah is clear that people, psychologically, can be antifragile. Is this correct?

Why Darth Vader Couldn't Win and Michael Jordan Couldn't Lose

In 1977, George Lucas released *Star Wars Episode IV: A New Hope*. In the movie, Obi-Wan Kenobi is set to confront his younger and more powerful protégé (and now enemy), Darth Vader.

Darth says to his rival, "Your powers are weak, old man."

Obi-Wan has a ready response. "You can't win, Darth. If you strike me down, I shall become more powerful than you can possibly imagine."

In this scene, Obi-Wan Kenobi exhibits the logic of antifragility. One who accepts antifragility cannot lose. If Obi had won the fight, he would have been victorious. If he "lost" the fight, he would come back more powerful than Darth could possibly imagine.

A minute later, Darth Vader strikes Obi-Wan with his saber, but Obi-Wan vanishes before he can be killed, leaving behind only his cloak.

Obi-Wan will die, but he will not let Darth kill him. He is never seen again in the flesh, but he is able, from the beyond, to guide Luke Skywalker to an ultimate victory for the Jedi over Darth Vader. But the fictional Obi-Wan Kenobi is not the only one to have discovered the power of antifragility.

The potential and power of antifragility is so profound that the greatest athlete of all time went to a potentially unprecedented extreme to arouse it. On March 19, 1993, Michael Jordan was matched against LaBradford Smith of the Washington Bullets during a game in Chicago. Mr. Smith was a rookie who was averaging 8.5 points a game and Michael Jordan was . . . Michael Jordan. That night was special. Mr. Jordan scored 22 points, but Mr. Smith scored 37. On the way off the court, Mr. Smith supposedly said to Mr. Jordan, "Nice game, Michael."

The Bullets and the Bulls met again the next night, this time in Washington. Mr. Smith scored 15 points and had a rebound and no assists. Mr. Jordan scored 47 points, had 8 rebounds and 4 assists. And that was with Mr. Jordan sitting out the final twelve minutes, since the Bulls were up a safe twenty-two points after three quarters.

The interesting fact about that sequence was that Mr. Smith *did not say anything* to Mr. Jordan as he walked off the court on March 19. Mr. Jordan had, he later admitted, *imagined* the slight, in order to trigger the power of antifragility. This had become a standard technique for Michael Jordan.

If an opponent slighted Michael Jordan, the opponent had sentenced himself to basketball death—at least as the current or next game against the Bulls was concerned. If an opponent smartly kept quiet, he still risked becoming a victim of Michael Jordan's imagination. Mr. Jordan's biographer Mark Vancil explains, "These little slights were deep indignations to him. That's all he needs. That's like throwing meat to a tiger."[11]

Like so much of what Michael Jordan modeled, this would become standard practice for the best performers in basketball. Larry Bird felt disrespected and insulted when an opposing team assigned a white defender to guard him, and he would respond accordingly.[12] Kobe Bryant told the late-night TV host Jimmy Kimmel that not being drafted by the Los Angeles Clippers in 1996 "brought so much motivation."[13] Shaquille O'Neal readied himself to challenge the veteran star center David Robinson by inventing a story about Mr. Robinson refusing him an autograph when he was a boy.[14] A generation later, the Milwaukee Bucks star forward

Giannis Antetokounmpo admitted to *The Athletic* that he "killed . . . [and] dominated" an opponent by inventing a story of the other player having taunted him. In 2024, the University of Connecticut Coach Danny Hurley articulated his strategy for sustaining his string of NCAA championships. "I'm gonna mostly just either look for slights or create them that don't exist."[15]

In 2019, Tom Brady of the New England Patriots was the oldest quarterback ever to play in a Super Bowl. After he threw a touchdown, his teammate Julian Edelman came up to him on the bench and got in his face. "You're too fucking old!" Mr. Edelman yelled. The Patriots won the Super Bowl.[16]

It is a near surety that Bulls coach Phil Jackson did not tell Michael Jordan to invent slights and that Patriots coach Bill Belichick did not tell Julian Edelman to scream at Tom Brady. These star performers discovered it on their own or learned it from each other because of a psychological insight that guided them along their paths to greatness. Slights, insults, and rejections were not reasons to get discouraged. They were such powerful inducements to outstanding performance that they, in their absence, imagine them.

How does this strange tactic work?

Fragility and Growth

In the early 2000s, Stanford professor Carol Dweck conducted a series of studies with kindergarten and fifth-grade students. She and her colleagues gave the students an easy test, ensuring that they would score well. They curated the students from across the country to ensure they were capturing a culturally diverse cross section and controlling for any regional idiosyncrasies.

They then broke the students into two groups and a control. The psychologists praised one group for their intelligence, and praised another group for their effort. A third group (the control) was praised based on results and told, "Wow, that's a really good score," without reference to the students themselves. The students were then asked, "What do you want to work on now? I have some easier things here that you could work on, or I have some challenging problems. They're hard, and you'll make mistakes, but you'll learn some important things."[17]

The results were striking. The students who were praised for their intelligence opted for the easy problems, while the students who were praised for their effort opted for the more difficult ones.

Professor Dweck and her colleagues then gave the students in both groups a set of more difficult problems. Those who had been praised for their intelligence interpreted their struggle as a sign that they were stupid. Their self-esteem plummeted, and they reported not enjoying the work.

The students who had been praised for their effort concluded that the increased difficulty of the problem just called for more effort. Their motivation, and enjoyment of the work, continued until the end of the project, and they asked for more work that they could do at home.

At the conclusion of the experiment, Professor Dweck and her colleagues asked the students to report their scores. She found that 40 percent of those praised for their intelligence initially lied about their scores, always saying that they scored higher than they did.[18]

In 2017, Professor Dweck reflected on her research to a New York City parents group. She spoke of having visited many independent schools with "wonderful educators, wonderful programs, and many thriving students." But that is not where the story ended. She said:

> I have also seen many fragile and anxious students, students who are wounded by constructive feedback or who live in fear of not getting perfect grades and not getting into the "right" university. Even when they attend top universities, they don't always fare well. After a talk I gave at an independent school, a mother came up to me. She told me that her son had graduated from that high school the year before. He had been part of a group called the "geniuses." The geniuses had all gone to brand-name universities and almost all of them were on academic probation, that is, they were in danger of flunking out. They knew how to be geniuses but they didn't know how to confront challenges, to struggle, and to persevere when it mattered.[19]

When Papers Are Accepted and Rejected

In 2019, Professor Yang Wang of Northwestern University tested another group of learners. His subjects were not kindergarteners, but scientists. His paper "Early-Career Setback and Future Career Impact" investigated the lifetime accomplishments of scientists who had early successes and those who had early failures between 1990 and 2005. The study, correcting for people who had experienced early failures and had left the profession, measured the ten-year success of those who had "just made" the threshold to achieve NIH funding and those whose efforts were characterized as "near misses."

Professor Wang found that those who received the early grants received more funding than those who did not. This was not surprising, as they had a head start in receiving grants. Even still, those in the "near miss" group were more likely to publish "hit papers" (as defined by papers that were often cited) than those who achieved early success.

Professor Wang concluded, "Those who stick it out, on average, perform much better in the long term, suggesting that if it doesn't kill you, it really does make you stronger."[20]

The Pursuit of Happiness and the U-Shaped Curve

Professor Tal Ben-Shahar, who helped popularize the Positive Psychology course at Harvard, is one of the world's leading researchers in happiness studies. He has concluded that attempts to pursue happiness directly are bound to fail and may lead to depression. Does this mean that we should not seek happiness? No. In 2022, Professor Ben-Shahar discussed how happiness should be pursued. The title of his talk: "Don't Chase Happiness. Become Antifragile."[21]

Why might this be?

In 2011, Professor Mark Seery from the University at Buffalo conducted a study exploring how setbacks impact happiness. Professor Seery and his team tracked around 3,000 individuals over several years in the early 2000s to examine any connections between adversity and mental health or well-being.

The adversity experienced by study participants included divorce, death of a friend or parent, a serious illness, and being in a natural disaster. The measures of mental health and well-being included global distress, functional impairment, post-traumatic stress symptoms, and life satisfaction.[22]

Professor Seery discovered that the relationship between happiness and adversity is not linear, as in the less (or the more) adversity, the better mental health and well-being. It exists on a U-shaped curve. Those with the most robust mental health and well-being were those who had experienced a *moderate* amount of adversity. Those at the top ends of the U-shaped curve—those who had the most mental health challenges—were those who had experienced the least and the most adversity. A key to well-being, it seems, is to neither be protected from nor overwhelmed by adversity, but to experience a consistently moderate dose of it.[23]

Helicopter/Snowplow Parenting and the Cultivation of "Fragile Snowflakes"

If moderate challenge and adversity are beneficial for human flourishing, it stands to reason that humans should expose their children to it from an early age. In Genesis, Abraham and Sarah celebrated the first step in the independence of their son—his weaning—revealing to us their parenting philosophy regarding the burgeoning autonomy of their child. In 1969, the child psychologist and NYU professor Haim Ginott noticed a very different approach in American society. This is when he published the runaway best-seller *Between Parent and Child*, which made Dr. Ginott one of America's first popular child psychologists. In this book, Dr. Ginott identified an emerging phenomenon that has since entered the popular lexicon. Dr. Ginott quoted a teenager as saying, "Mother hovers over me like a helicopter, and I'm fed up with her noise and hot air. I'm entitled to sneeze without explanation."[24]

The phenomenon described became known as "helicopter parenting." Helicopter parents "hover" over their children, ready to swoop in and rescue their children from adversity. In 2019, the *New York Times* journalists Claire Cain Miller and Jason Bromwich identified a variant they called "snowplow parenting." Snowplow parents remove any challenges and obstacles from in front of their children. In 2022, Dr. Angela Mattke of the Mayo Clinic explained that helicopter and snowplow parents act from a simple conviction that the child "is too fragile to recover from failure."[25]

How prevalent is this philosophy of parenting? A 2007 study from the University of Texas determined that up to 60 percent of parents can be classified as helicopter parents. Other scholars put it at closer to 40 percent. Brown University professor Emily Oster, whose data-driven approach has made her one of America's most popular and influential experts on parenting, says future generations will regard helicopter parenting as the defining tactic of this generation of parents. Or, put slightly differently by Michael Shermer in a 2018 *Scientific American* analysis, "Kids Today Are Being Socialized to Think They're Fragile Snowflakes."[26]

Everyone acknowledges that parenting philosophies and practices have a significant effect on children. What are the effects of helicopter and snowplow parenting on American youth? In 2014, Professors Jill Bradley-Geist of the University of Colorado and Professor Julie Olson-Buchanan of California State University surveyed 482 college students to find out.

The students were asked to answer, on a scale of 1–5, questions that test for helicopter parenting, such as "My parents are too involved in my life." The researchers also gave the students hypothetical workplace challenges to see how they would respond to employer critiques and the like. The children of helicopter parents were less likely than the others to say that they would listen to the criticism and improve. They were more likely to say that they would quit the job, explain to the employer why the rating was unfair, or ask a parent to call the manager on their behalf. The results showed that the students with the *most* committed helicopter/snowplow parents believed in themselves the *least*.[27]

A variety of other studies have uncovered similar effects of helicopter and snowplow parenting.

A longitudinal study led by Harvard professor David Harrington in the 1980s showed that the toddlers whose parents gave them the most freedom exhibited more creativity, curiosity, initiative, confidence, and self-reliance five years later.[28]

A 2015 study by Professor Chris Segrin of the University of Arizona determined that children of helicopter parents are more likely to develop a sense of entitlement, less likely to believe that they can solve their problems, and less likely to be satisfied with their family's communication.[29]

A 2016 study led by Professor Kayla Reed of Florida State University determined that children of helicopter parents become less physically healthy adults because they never had to develop and maintain health habits themselves.[30]

A 2016 study led by Professor Ryan Hong of the National University of Singapore found that children of helicopter parents were afraid of making mistakes and became self-critical, anxious, and depressed when they inevitably did.[31]

A 2017 study led by Professor Julia Asbrand of the University of Freiburg found that children whose parents offer them help in a ten-minute puzzle exercise are more likely to develop social anxiety those who have to figure it out on their own.[32]

Other studies since 2011 have shown that children of helicopter parents are more likely to be anxious, take psychiatric medicine, and be unable to reliably regulate themselves emotionally. It is no wonder that the Author of the Torah had Abraham celebrate the independence of his beloved son Isaac with "a great feast."[33]

Helicopter Children in the Military

The children of helicopter parents, of course, often graduate from high school and leave home. How are institutions responding to these young people at this stage of their development, especially as they deal with the ramifications of helicopter parenting?

One institution faced with this question is the United States military. A pronouncement from the semi-official organization Marine Parents confronts a problem and delivers a sharp solution. "Simply put, helicopter parenting is no longer allowed. So mom and dad, no more hovering; take a step back. This is your time to learn how to let go a little bit more each day."[34]

In 2017, the *Military Review* (an official publication of the US Army) published an essay by the psychologist Major Lynn Marie Breckenridge on helicopter parenting. Major Breckenridge concluded that the Army is in danger of importing the culture of helicopter parenting and setting up a system designed to prevent failure at any cost. This, she writes, would be detrimental to the mission of the US Army. "By robbing children or subordinates of the opportunity to try new things and fail," she writes, "parents and commanders ruin the chance of developing a crucial psychological trait, self-efficacy."[35]

Major Breckenridge also notes that there is no evidence that this is a problem in the military yet. But it is such a problem outside of the military that the Army has an obligation to be sure that its systems are hardened against it. The essay was so well received that it won first place in the Army's Douglas MacArthur Leadership Writing Competition.

When Children of Snowplow and Helicopter Parents Enter College

Many young people enter the military after high school, but more go to college. College should be, for most students, the most carefree time of their lives. The primary tasks are intellectual exploration with scholars, teachers, and peers; rooting for sports teams populated by classmates; spending time with friends; attending parties; and participating in clubs and activities. The radical changes of puberty have settled. The challenges posed by physical breakdown, marital troubles, difficult children, aging parents, job insecurity, and financial pressures are generally far in the future. And all the activities of college are generally conducted with the blessings of youth, health, energy, idealism, and a long life of opportunity ahead.

But every experience is profoundly mediated by the attitude and worldview that one brings to it. How has this generation of college students who were raised by helicopter and snowplow parents adapted to the collegiate environment, where their parents can no longer shield them from every potential adversity? Boston College professor Peter Gray, the author of the canonical college textbook *Psychology*, has an instructive insight.

In 2015, Professor Gray told Jane Brody of the *New York Times* that his college counseling office saw a doubling of emergency calls in the previous five years. These calls, he said, were "mainly for problems kids used to solve on their own," like "being called a bad name by a roommate or finding a mouse in the room."[36]

Having had parents dissolve problems and smooth friction throughout their entire childhood, many of these students find themselves simply inexperienced at dealing with *any* adversity, and are thus incapable of doing so. Consequently, they reach out for help for everything that does not go as they had hoped.

The leaders of the military, noting the effects of helicopter and snowplow parenting, have reacted intentionally and sharply against it. These efforts have largely succeeded in turning young soldiers who might otherwise consider finding a mouse in their room to be a psychological emergency into courageous soldiers, sailors, and airmen. How have the adults in the academy—college administrators—responded?

Play-Doh, Coloring Books, and Puppy Videos

One of the things that happens to college students is that they meet classmates who disagree with them. In November 2014, Brown University hosted a debate between two well-known feminists, Wendy McElroy and Jessica Valenti, on the subject of rape on campus. Ms. Valenti has spoken out frequently about what she calls "rape culture," arguing that rape is the worst manifestation of a general misogyny in the culture. Wendy McElroy, the author of *The Big Lie of a "Rape Culture,"* argues that "rape culture" is an overbroad characterization that diminishes the accountability of rapists, creates undeserved mistrust between men and women, and directs resources away from genuine victims of sexual violence.[37]

This was an important debate to have for all of those who want to reduce sexual violence generally—and especially for college students. However, the Brown University Sexual Assault Task Force did not think so. They set up a "safe space" for the "students who may feel attacked by the viewpoints expressed at the forum." The safe space, intended for people who found comments "troubling," "triggering," and needed "a place to recuperate," was equipped with cookies, coloring books, bubbles, Play-Doh, calming music, pillows, blankets, a video of puppies, and trained professionals.[38]

How did the Brown University administration respond to the students' claim that they were too fragile to hear a contrary opinion and needed bubbles and blankets to help them through the talk? Brown University president Christina Paxson sent an email to all the students in advance of the event indicating her disagreement with Ms. McElroy and inviting them to another event on the same subject at the same time where the students could only hear one viewpoint.[39]

In September 2017, the conservative commentator Ben Shapiro was set to speak at the University of California at Berkeley. The university was ready. Executive Vice Chancellor and Provost Paul Alivisatos emailed the Berkeley community, "We are deeply concerned about the impact some speakers may have on individuals' sense of safety and belonging. No one should be made to feel threatened or harassed simply because of who they are or for what they believe. For that reason, the following support services are being offered and encouraged."[40]

Several months later, Mr. Shapiro was scheduled to speak at the University of Connecticut. In advance of Mr. Shapiro's appearance, Joelle Murchison (the Associate Vice President and Chief Diversity Officer of the University of Connecticut) emailed the student body, "We understand that even the thought of an individual coming to campus with the views that Mr. Shapiro expresses can be concerning and even hurtful." Ms. Murchison continued, emphasizing that there would be "many campus resources available to you should you want to talk through your feelings about this issue."[41]

Trigger Warnings

Associate Vice President Murchison's work to protect the University of Connecticut students from "hurtful" exposure to Ben Shapiro is part of a standard program that the university offers students. The University of Connecticut has an extensive program of "trigger" and "content" warnings. These warnings notify students that a video, a word, or picture that the student might find hurtful or harmful is coming. Following a trigger warning, students can leave the room, turn off the media, brace themselves for the harm, and/or schedule therapy sessions.

For instance, the University of Connecticut suggests that a professor issue a trigger warning before a student is assigned a reading about dozens of things—from the birth of a child to the death of an animal. The reason: Reading about these experiences is, according to the University of Connecticut Office of the Provost, "potentially distressing."[42]

In 2015, Jonathan Chait of *New York Magazine* wrote that trigger warnings were part of a growing movement on campus to "treat even faintly unpleasant ideas or behaviors as full-scale offenses." Indeed, an NPR survey from the same year found that 51 percent of college professors issue trigger warnings. This number is probably understated, given that the NPR survey did not include what it called "the elite private universities most often linked to the 'trigger warning' idea."[43]

One such elite university is Columbia University. In 2015, students from Columbia's Multicultural Advisory Board complained about the ancient Roman poet Ovid's *Metamorphosis*—the epic poem that influenced Dante, Chaucer, Shakespeare, and numerous Renaissance artists. These students said that this book "contains triggering and offensive material that marginalizes student identities in the classroom." The university did not require a trigger warning; it eliminated Ovid from the curriculum.[44]

Another such elite private university is Cornell. In 2023, the Cornell University Student Assembly voted *unanimously* to require "all instructors to provide content warnings on the syllabus for any traumatic content that may be discussed, including but not limited to, sexual assault, domestic violence, self-harm, suicide, child abuse, racial hate crimes, transphobic violence, homophobic harassment, xenophobia."[45]

Cornell president Martha Pollack determined that it would be impossible for professors to function if they were required to anticipate anything that might trigger a student, and overrode the resolution. She did not, however, prohibit Cornell professors from using trigger warnings if they chose, which they often do.

The prevalence of trigger warnings leads to a question: What is their effect? A 2018 study led by Professor Benjamin Ballet of Harvard and several colleagues demonstrated that trigger warnings actually *increase* anxiety by priming the brain to expect something negative.[46]

This was confirmed in a 2020 study by Professor Payton Jones of Harvard that found that trigger warnings increase the belief that trauma is an essential part of one's life story—which, according to the Association of Psychological Sciences, "research has shown is countertherapeutic." Trigger warnings, in other words, tell students to brace themselves even when they would not have been otherwise emotionally affected.[47]

The psychologist Todd Kashdan, who once supported trigger warnings, reviewed the data and changed his mind. Dr. Kashdan wrote, "Maybe it is not our youth that is fragile, but it is us, the parents, teachers, and adults enlisted with the hard task of guiding them to be stronger, flexible, and resilient to the trials and challenges that await them."[48]

The conclusions of Drs. Ballet, Jones, and Kashdan suggest something of a consensus around trigger warnings. In 2021, Professor Jeannie Suk Gersen of Harvard Law School did a comprehensive analysis of trigger warnings for the *New Yorker*. She wrote that psychological research "suggests that trigger warnings do not reduce negative reactions to disturbing material, and may increase them." Regardless, Professor Gersen reports that the use of trigger warnings is "steadily increasing."[49]

When Words Break

The fundamental idea behind trigger warnings is that words, even when removed from their context, have the power to harm and damage. This is a new phenomenon, coinciding with the rise of helicopter and snowplow parents in this century.

Harvard Law School professor Randall Kennedy is one of the nation's most well-respected scholars of race in America. He is also a devoted man of the left who in 2023 published an essay in the *New York Times* saying that opponents of affirmative action harbor "malign resentment at the sight of Black people getting ahead."[50]

In 2002, Professor Kennedy published a book, *N____: The Strange Case of a Troublesome Word*. Only: He used the full racial slur in the title, out of a conviction that "its actual meaning in any given instance always depends on surrounding circumstances." The book was very well received. There does not seem to have been any major criticism of his use of the N word in the title. Indeed, one liberal reviewer, Charles Taylor (writing in *Salon*), praised it, stating that efforts to erase usage of the N word in context is "stupidity masquerading as sensitivity."[51]

Words, as Professor Kennedy and Mr. Taylor insisted, must be understood in the context that they are used. Words by themselves, these men of the left insisted in the early 2000s, do not have the power to offend or break anyone.

Times have changed.

In December 2021, University of Illinois College of Law professor Jason Kilborn gave an examination related to employment discrimination. It included, as might be expected, two slurs. Both were redacted. They referenced a plaintiff being called "a 'n____' and 'b____' (profane expressions for African Americans and women)."

Professor Kilborn had used this example for the previous ten years, without issue. But in 2021, the student reaction was encapsulated by one young woman who said that she "had to seek counsel [sic] immediately after the exam to calm myself." Professor Kilborn was promptly investigated and suspended. His reinstatement depended on his attending long diversity training seminars whose materials, ironically, contained the same redacted slur as that which caused him to be suspended.[52]

In 2020, Professor Greg Patton of the University of Southern California was teaching a class on filler words in various languages. English filler words include "err," "um," and "like." During his lecture, Patton explained that in Mandarin Chinese, a common filler phrase is "*neige*" (那个), which translates to "that" and is often repeated in conversation. This word sounds phonetically similar to a racial slur in English.

There was an immediate uproar from many of the students. An unnamed group of students sent a letter of complaint titled "A Callous, Reckless Illustration in Management Communication" to the office of Dean Geoffrey Garrett. The letter said that the incident violated "their sense of peace and mental well-being."[53]

Dean Garrett was ready with a response. "It is simply unacceptable for faculty to use words in class that can marginalize, hurt, and harm the psychological safety of our students. [Professor Patton] repeated several times a Chinese word that sounds very similar to a vile racial slur in English. Understandably, this caused great pain and upset among students, and for that I am deeply sorry."[54]

Ninety-four alumni, many of whom are Chinese people living in China, wrote a letter to Dean Garrett. "We unanimously recognize Professor Patton's use of '*na ge*' as an accurate rendition of common Chinese use, and an entirely appropriate and quite effective illustration of the use of pauses."[55]

Professor Patton responded by apologizing several times for "the discomfort and pain I have caused members of our Community." His apologies did him no good. The university suspended him. Still, it remained unclear whether the students who the administration sympathetically said might be "marginalized, hurt and harmed" by hearing the Chinese filler word wanted the school to stop teaching Chinese, or China to change its language.

How to Get a Diversity Consultant Fired

Michael McElroy is an African American actor, professor, and diversity consultant. In 2020, he was hired by the Juilliard School, the renowned New York City–based performing arts university, to teach within their EDIB (Equity, Diversity, Inclusivity, and Belonging) program. In September 2020, Mr. McElroy led a three-day virtual "Roots to Rep" workshop to explore how "the Negro spiritual . . . is the foundation of so many musical genres today."

Mr. McElroy began the workshop by issuing a "trigger warning" of offensive words in the sessions to come, as the slave masters being portrayed would use racial slurs. Mr. McElroy's trigger warning was followed by a reminder of the "law of two feet," granting permission to any students who chose to leave the online sessions.

Mr. McElroy began the instruction by playing an audio of a slave auction, taken from *Roots*, the acclaimed and award-winning 1977 miniseries that was, in full or part, watched by 85 percent of American households. It was celebrated by Maya Angelou in the *New York Times*, and seemingly every other critic.[56]

It was rebroadcast by the Black Entertainment Network in 2013, in honor of Black History Month, where it was seen by another eleven million households. Its broadcast and rebroadcasts generated only praise, no controversy.

But times have changed since 2013. The students did not avail themselves of the chance to leave after the trigger warning. When the audio from *Roots* was played, the Juilliard students texted each other in the language of fragility, saying, for instance, that they were "utterly broken." They FaceTimed each other after the exercise, and were so overwhelmed with tears that they could not speak. They protested to the administration, and Mr. McElroy was immediately fired.[57]

The head of the Drama Division, Evan Yionoulis, addressed the matter in an email to the Juilliard community on April 23, more than six months after the workshop. She did not make the point that Juilliard students presumably heard rap songs that used the N word without being traumatized. She did not make the point that it is educationally and morally compelling to teach the history of slavery and racism, and that using the language of slave masters is essential for doing so accurately. She certainly did not take this as a teaching moment to instruct students in the benefits of antifragility.

Instead, she said that she was "deeply sorry for the trauma it caused," and recounted the remedial efforts. "We took steps immediately following the exercise to support our community and facilitate healing, including canceling the remainder of the workshop, holding community meetings, facilitating discussions, and providing counseling resources."

The president of Juilliard, Damian Woetzel, agreed. As President Woetzel put it, Mr. McElroy's subjecting the students to the reenactment of slavery was "extremely distressing and problematic." He reiterated the school's commitment to provide guidance and support to those who listened to the audio from *Roots*.[58]

Rob Weinert-Kendt, the editor in chief of *American Theater*, also agreed. In an analysis of the situation he published in April 2021, he called Mr. McElroy's presentation "pointlessly traumatic."[59]

The Wages of Fragility

So: college students, shielded by their helicopter parents from conflict and adversity, enter an environment where their fragility is validated, indulged, and amplified. The psychologist Satya Doyle Byock described the consequences in her 2022 book, *Quarterlife: The Search for Self in Early Adulthood*. She writes, "Crippling anxiety, depression, anguish, and disorientation are effectively the norm."[60]

The data underlying the concerns of Professor Gray and Dr. Byock are stark. A report from the American College Health Association in 2019 found that (at some point in the previous year) 87 percent of college students felt "overwhelmed by all they do"; 66 percent felt overwhelming anxiety; 65 percent felt very lonely; 56 percent felt that things were hopeless; 45 percent felt so depressed that "it is hard to function"; 13 percent considered suicide (with 2 percent actually attempting it); and 9 percent intentionally bruised, cut, burned, or otherwise injured themselves.[61]

A study from Professor Sarah Lipson of the Boston University School of Public Health, based on a massive dataset collected from 2013 to 2021, shows that the rate of mental illness at universities has steadily and significantly increased during that period. Even by 2017, a report in STAT News concluded that colleges "can't meet the soaring needs for mental healthcare."[62]

The Response

How are university administrators responding to the mental health crisis on campus? There are three primary responses.

Response One: "Just Hire More Therapists"

According to a 2022 analysis in *Inside Higher Ed*, the "mainstream thinking" about the mental health crisis on campus is to just hire more therapists. There is a problem with this. Michael Gerard Mason, an associate dean at the University of Virginia and an experienced counselor, said in 2022, "[At UVA], our counseling staff has almost tripled in size, but even if we continue hiring, I don't think we could ever staff our way out of this challenge."[63]

The math suggests that Dr. Mason is right. There are approximately twenty million college students in the United States. The aforementioned data from the American College Health Association makes it clear that at least half of college students need therapy.

If the students who need therapy received it once a week, there would be a demand for ten million therapy sessions every week. Assuming that each therapist can see thirty patients a week, there is a demand for approximately 350,000 therapists to serve college students. This means that 2 percent of the American workforce is needed to provide mental healthcare to college students, who constitute less than 5 percent of the population.[64]

This dynamic has expanded beyond the campus and into general society. In 2022, the *Washington Post* published the results of an inquiry into "why it's so hard to find mental health counseling right now." The report showed how would-be patients (including those willing to pay cash) in places as diverse as Oklahoma, Los Angeles, Boston, and Ohio have to join nearly year-long wait lists to receive therapy.[65]

Response Two: "Depressed? Get Out!"

A second response is suggested by a 2006 *Washington Post* article on mental health on campus pursuant to a policy at George Washington University, "Depressed? Get Out!" The article describes the case of Jordan Nott, who in 2004 sought treatment for suicidal ideation. Within days, the university charged him with "endangering behavior," with his suicidal ideation being the behavior that "endangered" his classmates. The university suspended him and threatened to have him arrested for trespassing if he set foot on campus.[66]

Was this an aberrant policy or one that was quickly adjusted when the *Washington Post* covered it?

In 2015, Luchang Wang was a Yale student. She became seriously depressed. She was given an involuntary leave from the university, and told that she would need to reapply if she wanted to return. She bought a one-way ticket to San Francisco, and wrote a note:

> "Dear Yale, I loved being here. I only wish I could've had some time. I needed time to work things out and to wait for new medication to kick in, but I couldn't do it in school, and I couldn't bear the thought of having to leave for a full year, or of leaving and never being readmitted. Love, Luchang."

She then jumped to her death from the Golden Gate Bridge.[67]

In 2021, Dartmouth freshman Elizabeth Reimer was hospitalized pursuant to a mental health diagnosis. Shortly after being discharged, the college placed her on involuntary medical leave. She was not permitted back into her dorm room and was excluded from campus. Ms. Reimer attempted to resist her exclusion. She posted on a Dartmouth forum about the mental health authorities: "I told them numerous times that being sent home would be the worst thing for my mental health."[68]

The administration either did not agree or care, and maintained the order of exclusion. Elizabeth Reimer committed suicide.

In late 2022, the *Washington Post* ran a long feature on how Yale University still handled students with suicidal ideation. The title of the article is taken from the first words spoken by a Yale student upon waking up in the hospital after having swallowed twenty pills in an attempt to kill herself: "What If Yale Finds Out?"[69]

Her concern was justified. Several months before, Yale freshman Rachael Shaw-Rosenbaum killed herself after contemplating that her suicidal ideation was going to result in a forced withdrawal from the university.

This was not a unique case. The *Washington Post* chronicled dozens of Yale students who, when their struggles with suicidal ideation became known, were forced to withdraw without any support, guarantee, or even expectation of readmission. These occurred in the years following the death of Luchang Wang.[70]

What is the logic behind this policy? There are at least two reasons. The first was articulated by a Dartmouth dean: "Students who are on medical leave do not live on campus because it is in their best interest to put their studies on hold and focus on their recovery."[71]

It is hard to imagine that this policy could have been designed by any knowledgeable person who cares about students with mental health challenges. Psychologists widely agree that individuals with mental health challenges have the best chance of recovery within a trusted, supportive community, while isolation from community can significantly worsen their outcomes.[72]

Moreover, college administrators presumably want students who are suffering from mental health problems to seek treatment. The threat of being removed from the community, having one's education suspended and social network destroyed, is quite an incentive to suffer in silence and not seek treatment.

The second reason has nothing to do with the students who need help. It concerns their classmates.

In 2015, a student at Northern Michigan University, Katerina Klawes, visited the campus counseling center for treatment after a sexual assault. Following an initial counseling session, she received an email from Mary Brundage, Associate Dean of Students with "Conduct Policy Reminder" in the subject line. The note read:

> I received a report that others are worried about your well-being . . . Engaging in any discussion of suicidal or self-destructive thoughts or actions with other students interferes with, or can hinder, their pursuit of education and community. It is important that you refrain from discussing these issues with other students . . . If you involve other students in suicidal or self-destructive thoughts or actions, you will face disciplinary action.

Why would sexual assault victims face disciplinary action for discussing the assault with peers? Dean Brundage explained to a newspaper reporter, "Relying on your friends can be very disruptive to them."[73]

In other words, students are so fragile that engaging with their friends who have suffered can break them.

Response Three: Have the Suicide Hotline on Speed Dial

The Graduate Outcomes Survey is conducted by the Social Research Centre in Australia to assess the experience of graduate students. The project, funded by the Australian government, asks benign questions such as "What aspects of your course were most in need of improvement?" and "Overall, how well did your course prepare you for your job?"[74]

At the end of the survey, graduates are given the following message: "Thank you again for your time completing the Graduate Outcomes

Survey. Everyone's experiences are different, if the questions in this survey have raised anything that you would like support for, you could contact: Beyondblue on 1300 22 46 36/ • Lifeline on 13 11 14."[75]

Beyondblue and Lifeline are suicide hotlines. The professionals at the Social Research Centre apparently believe that just thinking about one's graduate school experience may lead survey respondents to contemplate suicide.

This is surely not an Australian phenomenon. Indeed, it is more likely to be an Australian adaptation of an American phenomenon.

One of the leading American authorities on mental health and youth is Professor Eugene Beresin of Harvard Medical School. In addition to being a professor at Harvard Medical School, Dr. Beresin directs a center at Massachusetts General Hospital focused on cultivating young and healthy minds. His influence is both popular and professional, as he has consulted for *ER* and *Law & Order* and edits *Academic Psychiatry* and the *Journal of Graduate Medical Education.*

In 2021, Professor Beresin released a video on conversation starters that parents should use with their children in college. The conversation starters did not regard what classes were engaging, which professors were inspiring, which speakers were interesting, or what postgraduate opportunities seem compelling. Instead, Dr. Beresin introduced the video on conversation starters by saying, "Today we have a major crisis in college mental health with increases in depression, anxiety, stress, loneliness, and suicide." He followed by saying, "It's a tough thing," and then suggested the conversation starters.

"How's college going? Do you think that your academics are going okay? Are you stressed out by other aspects of your life? How is your social life? Your relationships? Do you feel like you are getting adequate support in college? Have you felt so bad that you've thought about taking your own life? Have you turned to substances like alcohol or drugs just to chill out? What supports your well-being? Is there someone you'd like to talk with about mental health?"[76]

America's Favorite Diagnosis

Why would a well-regarded authority like Dr. Beresin advise parents to *expect* their children in college to be suffering severe mental distress? Why are so many professors getting suspended and fired for saying things that were uncontroversial ten years ago? Why would Rob Weinert-Kendt, an impartial observer and leader of one of the leading publications in theater, call a presentation based on *Roots* "pointlessly traumatic"?

Enter Professor Nick Haslam, perhaps the world's leading authority on psychiatric classification. Professor Haslam studied the classification of six psychological terms from the mid-twentieth century to the present. They are: abuse, bullying, mental disorder, addiction, prejudice, and trauma. He observed that each of these concepts has steadily expanded both horizontally and vertically. Horizontal expansion occurs when concepts are expanded to include new things. For instance, bullying has expanded from verbal and physical assaults to including social exclusion.

Vertical expansion occurs when terms are recharacterized to include milder versions of the same thing. For instance, "prejudice" once referred to direct dislike or discrimination against certain kinds of people. It now includes microaggressions, implicit bias, institutional bias, and subtle stereotyping—none of which even necessitate the awareness of the person supposedly harboring the prejudice.[77]

The expansion of the definition of "trauma"—culminating in Juilliard's designation of *Roots* as traumatizing—can be easily traced through the bible of modern psychology: the *Diagnostic and Statistical Manual of Mental Disorders* (DSM). This manual, which is updated every ten to fifteen years to reflect the changing perspectives of the psychological profession, provides guidelines for clinicians to diagnose and treat mental disorders.

Trauma was acknowledged in the first edition of the DSM in 1953. The original DSM spoke of trauma as generated by gross force, electricity, infection, poison, or congenital factors.

In 1980, the DSM-III expanded the scope of trauma, but still required that the stressor be something that "would evoke significant symptoms of distress in most people." The criteria further clarified that the stressor "is generally outside the range of such common experiences as simple bereavement, chronic illness, business losses, or marital conflict."[78]

By 1994, however, the DSM-IV had expanded the definition to include purely psychological events. A stressor for trauma could be "witnessing an event that involves death, injury, or a threat to the physical integrity of another person; or learning about the unexpected or violent death, serious harm, or threat of death or injury experienced by a family member or other close associate."

This final clause provides a basis for the "Depressed? Get Out!" policies. If, per the DSM-IV, one could be traumatized by "learning about" a "serious harm" like the sexual assault of a classmate, then it makes sense to shield these students from trauma by forbidding sexual assault victims from talking to their classmates about their trauma.[79]

By the twenty-first century, the psychological diagnosis of trauma has been expanded to include incidents that one would rightly assume fall well within what the DSM previously called the "usual human experience." The psychological and popular literature on trauma includes the death of a terminally ill elderly relative, daily misogyny (like catcalling), learning about other people's trauma, and a child being refused puberty blockers.[80]

The idea that one can be easily traumatized, which would have been nonsensical to the psychologists who wrote the original DSM, is now fully assimilated into popular understanding. The book *The Body Keeps the Score: Brain, Mind, and Body in the Healing of Trauma* has been a best-seller for years, with more than three million copies sold. It has, a 2023 magazine cover declares, "made trauma America's favorite diagnosis." There are more than 5,550 podcasts devoted specifically to the theme of trauma.[81]

In 2006, the satirical publication *The Onion* ran an article about people suffering from "*pre-traumatic* stress syndrome." A decade later, it was no joke. In 2015 and 2016, *US News, Health* and *Psychology Today* each published articles about the concerns aroused by "pre-traumatic stress syndrome." In the years that followed, *Vice*, the *British Medical Journal*, and Johns Hopkins's Project Muse published analyses of "climate-related pre-traumatic stress syndrome," which is the trauma caused by contemplating the potential effects of climate change.[82]

No wonder that *Vox* was able to publish a feature in 2022 entitled "How Trauma Became the Word of the Decade."[83]

Professor Bonnano's Response: Antifragility and Potentially Traumatic Events

What are the implications of the belief that people are easily traumatized? A massive study done in 2016 authored by thirty-two researchers from around the world concluded that more than 70 percent of people have witnessed a traumatic event. And their definition of trauma is, by contemporary standards, restrictive—it does not include things like learning about other people's trauma.[84]

According to the logic of the DSM-IV, which has been essentially adopted and amplified by the academy, all of these people are traumatized. Is this even possible? Given that we live in the most peaceful time known to mankind, the implication is that almost everyone went through life in a state of trauma for almost all of human history. If almost everyone is traumatized, then how is trauma distinctive or meaningful?

Enter Professor George Bonanno of Teachers College at Columbia University, who has spent the past twenty-five years researching trauma. His research goes right to the heart of the question of whether people are fundamentally fragile, resilient, or antifragile.

In 2020, Professor Bonanno published the results of a study that he and his colleagues conducted using rats. They took a population of fifty-eight rats and subjected them to a shock while they listened to a tone. The purpose was to learn how the rats would respond to the tone when they were not being exposed to electric shock.

The study found that 57 percent of the rats stopped reacting to the tone after a few trials, 32 percent stopped after some more trials, and 10 percent maintained their fear after two hundred trials. Rats, in other words, experienced trauma after the visceral shock, but most shed the effects of the trauma naturally.[85]

What does this have to do with humans? It turns out: Everything. Professor Bonanno conducted and reviewed numerous studies of responses to events including the 9/11 attacks, injury, natural disaster, and combat. He found that humans, in response to these intense events, are more resilient than were the rats who were shocked. In other words, the normal human response to a terrible event is *not* being traumatized. He writes:

> PTSD is what happens when traumatic stress doesn't go away, when it festers and expands and eventually stabilizes into a more enduring state of distress. But this outcome is not nearly as common as we might think. Research over the past several decades has shown incontrovertibly that most people exposed to violent or life-threatening events do not develop long-term PTSD. And

> that can only mean that the events themselves are not inherently traumatic. In fact, no event, not even a violent or life-threatening event, is inherently traumatic. Such events are only "potentially traumatic." A good part of the rest of it is up to us.[86]

The precision in Professor Bonanno's language is important. Terrible events, he says, are not traumatic, but "potentially traumatic." He does not say that the existence of trauma is *entirely* up to the individual. He claims only that "a good part" of it is.[87]

Resilience is not the only alternative to trauma. As Nassim Nicholas Taleb has shown, there is antifragility. Antifragility is sometimes categorized in the psychological literature as "post-traumatic growth" (PTG). PTG occurs when one responds to what Professor Bonnano identifies as a *potentially* traumatic event (PTE) by becoming stronger. Those with PTG experience the same PTE, but use it to be like Jacob in Genesis 32, who always bore the mark of his struggle as he progressed—stronger—to his ultimate goal.

Scott Barry Kaufman, writing in *Scientific American*, explains the many opportunities of PTG, including a greater appreciation of life, strengthening of close relationships, increased compassion and altruism, the identification of new possibilities or purpose in life, greater awareness and utilization of personal strengths, enhanced spiritual development, and creative growth.[88]

And these opportunities are widely available. A 2018 study led by Professor Xiaoli Wu of the Xiangya School of Public Health at Central South University in China suggests that half of the people respond to potentially traumatic events with post-traumatic growth.[89]

A classic description of post-traumatic growth comes from Rabbi Harold Kushner. In 1977, Rabbi Kushner's fourteen-year-old son, Aaron, died after a lifelong struggle with progeria, or "rapid aging." Five years later, Rabbi Kushner chronicled his experience in his book *Why Bad Things Happen to Good People*. He wrote, "I am a more sensitive person, a more effective pastor, a more sympathetic counselor because of Aaron's life and death than I would ever have been without it."

This does not mean that Rabbi Kushner believed that the experience of losing his son to a terrible disease was positive. The logic of PTG would never suggest such a thing. Instead, it is embodied in an explanation he provided: "I would give up all of those gains in a second if I could have my son back. If I could choose, I would forgo all of the spiritual growth and depth which has come my way because of our experiences . . . But I cannot choose."[90]

He could, however, choose whether to respond with fragility or antifragility, and he chose the latter. In doing so, Rabbi Kushner chose to accept the blessing that the angel gave to Jacob/Israel in Genesis 32, when our patriarch emerged from a struggle with a limp, continuing with renewed strength on his journey that ultimately led the Jewish people to the Promised Land.

Why the Concept of Potentially Traumatic Events Matters

Why does it matter whether Professor Bonanno (or anyone else) thinks in terms of trauma or potential trauma? There are at least four reasons.

The first derives from what the twentieth-century sociologist Robert Merton called a "self-fulfilling prophecy," which he defined as "a belief or expectation, correct or incorrect, [that] could bring about a desired or expected outcome."[91] If the sufferer expects trauma to follow a potentially traumatic event, his chances of being traumatized increase. If the sufferer knows that resilience and antifragility are much more likely, he will position himself to avoid the devastating effects of lasting trauma, and be more open to post-traumatic growth.

The second reason why the definition of trauma matters is offered in Deuteronomy 4:2, where Moses says, "Do not add to what I command you and do not subtract from it, but keep the commands of the Lord your God that I give you." The logic of addition, Moses teaches, necessitates subtraction. When we add to something, we generally diminish its essence. Sometimes that's fine, as when we put a serving of salt on food, diminishing its essence and making it taste better.

But often, as Moses knew, it is not fine. There is a lot of genuine trauma in the world. Many people suffer from and need treatment for PTSD—caused by sexual abuse, war, and other events that are outside the norm of human experience. There is nothing new about this; this terrible condition has nothing to do with the contemporary culture of fragility. The ancient Greek historians Herodotus and Plutarch each identified cases of severe

PTSD, as did the early twentieth-century psychologists who diagnosed "shell shock" in World War I veterans.[92]

A good society would work to help those who genuinely suffer from PTSD. The resources for these services are, like those for all valuable things, limited. If a university has to devote mental health resources to help students who are "traumatized" by seeing a mouse, it will not have the sufficient resources to help students who are severely depressed or have been raped.

The third reason why it matters how we relate to the concept of trauma relates to Professor Bonanno's point regarding human responses. Whether one responds to a PTE with resilience, trauma, or PTG, is rarely automatic or predetermined. Surely, those who are resilient or antifragile share a quality, a mentality, a discipline—*something*—that accounts for their response, and that can be taught and learned. What is it?

Dr. Melissa Thomas of Yale New Haven Hospital, who has studied three decades of mental and physical health data of her fellow veterans, explains: "A lot of research on stress and trauma focused on negative outcomes. But by focusing on successful resilience we can learn a lot about how to build prevention strategies." The presumption of fragility and its manifestations has led researchers away from asking what innate characteristics predict resilience and antifragility, and toward discovering how we can inculcate these qualities.[93]

The fourth reason why our attitude toward trauma matters derives from a truism stated by Professor Jeffrey Kahn of the University of Minnesota: "Public Health and Politics Don't Mix."[94] An expanded definition of trauma, accompanied by special concern to all those who are "traumatized," creates a "Trauma Olympics," just like the "Oppression Olympics" discussed in the chapter on diversity.

In January 2020, *The Advocate* (a publication serving the gay community) ran an article, "In Gay We Trust: How Do We Tackle PTSD in the LGBTQ+ Community?" The article reported, "Eighty-six percent of LGBTQ+ youth said that recent politics have negatively impacted their well-being." The photograph accompanying the article was of a combat soldier.[95]

The data is not sourced, and it is hard to ascertain what these pervasively traumatic "recent politics" could have been in January 2020. All of the major candidates for president in 2020 proudly proclaimed their commitment to a pro-gay philosophy and politics. When the (gay) diplomat Richard Grenell tweeted in August 2020 that Donald Trump was the "most pro-gay President in American history," President Trump immediately responded, "My great honor!"[96]

This line of thinking was reflective of the general politics of the United States at the end of the first quarter of the century. As the renowned historian of gay America James Kirchick wrote in 2022, "In our increasingly polarized society, one of the few issues about which there appears to be any consensus is equality for gay people."[97]

Still, *The Advocate* claims that being gay in twenty-first-century America is a traumatic experience, akin to being in a combat zone.

Exposure Therapy

There are two very general responses to potentially traumatic events (however one defines them). One is to do as Moses modeled in Numbers after the snake attack in the desert—elevate the source of the trauma and seek meaning from it. The other is that of trigger warnings—which encourages avoidance of anything that could be conceivably considered traumatic. The avoidance technique is, according to the American Psychological Association, the one that people will "tend to."[98] Is this the right response? The psychologist Eric Patterson does not think so. He writes that avoidant behaviors can lead sufferers to "faulty thoughts," which include leading them to amplify dangers and imagine the "worst case scenario."[99]

What is the alternative? One is exposure therapy, defined by Drs. Johanna Kaplan and David Tobin, writing in *Psychiatric Times*, as "any treatment that encourages the systematic confrontation of feared stimuli, which can be external (e.g., feared objects, activities, situations) or internal (e.g., feared thoughts, physical sensations)."[100]

According to the Cleveland Clinic, there are several ways to conduct exposure therapy. These include imaginal therapy (imagining the event happening again), VR therapy (experiencing the event through a virtual reality headset), and in vivo therapy (doing the act that one fears).[101]

For instance, the Fear of Flying program conducted by the Anxiety and Phobia Treatment Center at White Plains (NY) Hospital has sufferers share their concerns, walk through simulated security, experience flying through VR, and then fly from New York to Boston. The program has a 90 percent success rate, which is the rate that the Cleveland Clinic says can be expected through exposure therapy generally.[102]

Moses, it turns out, knew what he was doing when he had the Jews respond to the snake attack by putting a snake on a pole so that the afflicted could stare their trauma in the eye.

Reflection

One question that nearly every couple must consider is how they plan to raise their children. It may be in premarital counseling with a clergyman, it may be before or after the engagement, it may be with the first pregnancy. It may be an ongoing conversation.

The couple might consider how they can make their children happy, secure, successful, generous, socially conscious, and devoted to the faith of the family. They should add, however, a commitment to antifragility.

The couple will need to contemplate what this means. It means that they will let their children walk home from the park alone, ride their bikes through town or the subway through the city, and negotiate problems with peers and teachers with only light guidance from adults. It means that they will teach their children that words must be considered in context and can never break anyone, that potentially traumatic events usually do not result in trauma. It means that they will teach that self-assured young men and women can withstand and indeed grow from more than they probably know.

This commitment to antifragility, particularly as it is so countercultural, will invariably inform the way that parents think, act, and speak. In May 2024, the concept of antifragility came up in the Torah class that I teach for primarily Evangelical Christians every Tuesday through Eagles Wings. The host, Pastor Doug Reed of the Tabernacle Church in Buffalo, said that he and his wife had recently changed the way they speak to their children. They no longer tell their children before an exercise of independence, "Be careful." Instead, they say, "Be brave."

Pastor Reed acknowledged that this is not easy, adding that he and his wife "sometimes hold our breath" when they tell their children to be brave. But they concluded that *encouraging* their children to exercise independence by telling them to "be brave" and do the activity is what they should do as parents. The biblical Abraham would have agreed.

As Doug and Samantha Reed acknowledge, this commitment to antifragility means that the parents will sometimes worry about what is happening to their children when they exercise independence. But there is, as the college mental health data demonstrates, a far greater risk to helicopter or snowplow parenting. A parent who decides to use the wonderful Christian expression "Let go and let God" can take comfort in what they are preparing their children to do and who they are enabling them to become. A parent who cultivates and encourages antifragility in her children is giving them the best chance to become confident, self-assured people who can comfortably manage the inevitable setbacks, disappointments, offenses, and afflictions that they will experience.

The embrace of antifragility can and should continue into young adulthood. A young adult, whether or not he has been raised by a helicopter/snowplow parent, has a choice. He can, as in the aforementioned example from Juilliard, declare himself to be "broken" after seeing a film clip. Or he can follow the logic of President Obama, who said in his 2013 commencement address at Morehouse College:

> Nobody cares how tough your upbringing was. Nobody cares if you suffered some discrimination. And moreover, you have to remember that whatever you've gone through, it pales in comparison to the hardships previous generations endured, and they overcame them. And if they overcame them, you can overcome them, too . . . You now hail from a lineage and legacy of immeasurably strong men.[103]

President Obama's words were greeted with rousing applause. If the biblical Jacob heard those words, he would have applauded as well.

30

Moses's Nickname and the Creation of *Star Wars*

The Torah and Science of Education

The Insight of Hoover and Boon

What are Jews best known for? One answer comes from the classic 1978 movie *Animal House*:

> **Hoover:** "We're in trouble. I just checked with the guys at the Jewish house and they said that every one of our answers on the psych test was wrong."
>
> **Boon:** "Every one? [looks at Bluto and D-Day] Those assholes must have stolen the wrong fucking exam!"

Why did Hoover check with the "guys at the Jewish house"? Because the notion that Jews are good at education is embedded in our cultural understanding and is borne out by data. Jews are the most highly educated of the world's religious groups and are significantly more educated than the local population in every country where there are Jews. Jews compose 0.2 percent of the world's population and have won 22 percent of Nobel Prizes. Jews are even more likely to win the Turing Award, the primary prize in computer science. And Jews are overrepresented by 700 to 1,000 percent in fields that require significant education, such as medicine and engineering.[1]

The only slightly contrary response that Boon could have given to Hoover was that he should consult the women in the Jewish house as well. Jewish women are better educated than Jewish men.[2]

Moses Rabbenu

How did the Jews become so famously good at education? There is one simple answer: The Torah commands education.

In Exodus 10, Egypt has just been devastated by seven plagues. Following this, the Egyptian people pressure Pharaoh to release the Jews. The Pharaoh, seemingly ready to acquiesce in part, asks Moses, "Who will be going?"

Moses proceeds to make perhaps the most revolutionary and consequential statement uttered in the Bible: "We will leave with our young and with our old."

The *young* would come first.

The idea that the young would come first—that children would be the primary focus of a society—was a new and radical idea that Moses introduced into the world. Like all major principles, it led to the question of how it would be implemented.

Moses had just the answer. In Exodus 12, God kills the firstborn in every Egyptian household. The Pharaoh subsequently decides to let the Jews leave Egypt. This sounds good, but the Pharaoh has relented before, only to change his mind and keep the Jews enslaved. The Jewish People must escape quickly, before the Pharaoh invariably reconsiders his decision.

Yet, with no time to waste, Moses stops to give a speech about how the people should educate future generations: "You shall tell your son on that day, saying, 'It is because of this that Hashem acted on my behalf when I left Egypt . . . And it shall be when your son will ask you at some future time, 'What is this?' you shall say to him, 'By strength of hand the Lord brought us out of Egypt, from the house of bondage'" (Exodus 13:8–14) Moses had delayed the Exodus to give a speech about the importance of education. It was as if he was saying: "There's no purpose in leaving unless we get this right and clear." And by saying, "*When* your son will ask you"—rather than "*If* your son will ask you"—he is telling the people that a child's natural curiosity will provide the pathway for adults to fulfill their duty to educate.

This commitment to education is furthered in Deuteronomy 6:7–9, where Moses commands the people regarding the transmission of Torah: "You shall teach them diligently to your children, and you shall talk of them when you sit in your house, and when you walk by the way; when you lie down, and when you rise . . . You shall write them on the doorposts of your house and on your gates."

The Jewish people, he said, would be sustained by making education an always and forever endeavor. Whether we are rising or retiring, whether we are sitting or walking, we should always be educating.

But the last part of this commandment, which Jews honor through affixing a mezuzah on our doorposts to this day, is simply astonishing. It presumes that everyone would be able to read the writing on the doorposts. But when Moses decreed it, writing was still in its infancy and reserved for only the elite in most cultures. Indeed, literacy was so marginal that there is no report of any of the major biblical figures in the Torah prior to him—even Joseph, an administrative genius—reading or writing *anything*.

Moses decided to bet the survival and vitality of the Jewish people on a commitment to something that was entirely new. His strategy of perpetuation, therefore, had no basis to work from, no ingrained support, no history of success, and was seemingly impossible to accomplish. But Moses was not deterred.

It is no surprise how Moses would become known in the Jewish tradition. He is not called Moses our Leader, Moses our Founder, or Moses our Prophet. He is known as *Moshe Rabbenu*—Moses our teacher.

"A Jew, However Poor . . ."

This commitment to education would continue throughout all of Tanakh—the five books of the Torah and the subsequent prophetic and historical writings. The Book of Chronicles refers to "anointed ones," but does not specify who they are. The rabbis in the Talmud, however, all agree that the Chronicler (King David) must have been referring to schoolchildren. How did they know this? They explained that the world "only exists because of the breath of schoolchildren." Therefore, they are "anointed," chosen as it were, to sustain the world. The Talmud also specifies that children could not be interrupted from their studies even to build the Holy Temple.[3]

By at least the first century AD, and possibly long before, formal education was compulsory for Jewish children by the age of six. A town without children in school was to be excommunicated from the Jewish community. This rule coheres with the Talmudic characterization of children as "builders" and of teachers as "protectors." A town devoid of builders and protectors would be unwelcome in any community.[4]

Josephus, the first-century Jewish historian, wrote, "Should anyone of our nation be asked about our laws, he will repeat them as readily as his own name. The result of our thorough education in our laws from the very dawn of intelligence is that they are, as it were, engraved on our souls."[5]

This commitment and discipline continued, undiluted, after Jews were scattered through the world in the mid-second century. In the early twelfth century, an Egyptian Jewish woman about to die wrote a letter to her sister:

> My greatest wish is that you should take care of my little daughter and make an effort for her to study. Indeed I know that I am imposing a heavy burden on you. We do not have the means for her upkeep, let alone the cost of tuition. But we have an example from her mother and teacher, a servant of God.[6]

Gentile observers throughout the world observed this curious Jewish dedication to education. A Christian monk in France wrote, "A Jew, however poor, if he had ten sons, would put them all to letters, not for gain, as the Christians do, but for the understanding of God's law; and not only his sons but his daughters too." Histories of eastern European Jewish life are full of stories recounting how Jewish parents would sacrifice everything, even food, to provide schooling for their children.[7]

Moshe Rabbenu, the Radical

Moses's commitment to children and education, which has been sustained by his people forever, was not just novel. It was radical. When Moses decreed that the youth would come first and that Jewish society would be constructed around the education of children, few other societies valued either. Gautama (later known as Buddha) sought enlightenment by *leaving* his son, Rahula. Moses's contemporaries in China worshipped their ancestors. Filicide—the sacrificial killing of children—was prevalent in Greek and

Roman mythology, which characterized the world around Moses (which is why the Torah issues so many prohibitions against it). This continued longer after in societies from Africa to India to South America—until the practice was stopped, often by Christian missionaries.[8]

Moses's revolution was not only in prioritizing children philosophically, but also in educating them practically through mass literacy. Mass literacy empowers people to access and develop new ideas, fostering the ability to doubt dubious philosophies and challenge corrupt systems. Consequently, elites in many societies sought to maintain widespread illiteracy by discouraging and criminalizing efforts to educate citizens in reading and writing.

Socrates was executed in 399 BCE for "corrupting the youth"—a euphemism for his educational practices. These actions were similar to those mandated by Moses. In 1391, King Richard II and the British Parliament enacted a law stating, "No serf or villein [peasant farmer] . . . should put his children to school." Seventeen years later, the British clergy enacted the Constitutions of Oxford, which deemed translating the Bible into English an act of heresy.

The great master of the English language, William Shakespeare, lived two hundred years later. His daughters were illiterate. This was not due to Shakespeare being sexist, a negligent father, a bad teacher, or financially unable to provide education for his children. The creator of Portia, Beatrice, Lady Macbeth, and Viola valued strong women and had ample resources. He was just a man of his time. A generation after Shakespeare's death, a survey of the English diocese of Norwich showed that no women were literate.[9]

Meanwhile, the Jews—from Moses on, without interruption—regarded education with utmost seriousness, as though preparing for the dialogue between Boon and Hoover in *Animal House*.[10]

How to Educate

By itself, the Torah's commitment to education could not explain the *Animal House* dialogue and the Nobel and Pew numbers. Like everything else, the effectiveness of even the best idea (which universal education is) depends entirely on its execution. This fact is especially salient with education, given that there are many different educational theories and practices that, like any set of tactics, cannot all be equal to one another.

Thus, the Jewish theory and practice of *how* to educate is as important as the Jewish commitment to educate. What, then, is the Jewish philosophy about how to educate?

Moses elucidates in Exodus 12:26–27 when he tells the people, "And when your children ask you, 'What does this service mean to you?' then tell them, 'It is the Pesach festival for you.'"

This verse is the biblical basis for one of our most important holiday practices—the recitation of the Exodus story on the festival of Pesach (or Passover). Pesach, known as the "Festival of Freedom," is the authentic Jewish New Year—the most important night of the Jewish year, and our annual spring festival. And the focal point of the holiday, also ordained in Exodus 12, is the Pesach Seder.

The Seder is the most widely observed Jewish holiday practice and its central purpose, first stated in Exodus 12 and 13, is very clear: to educate our children. Jews are guided through the Seder by a small book, the Haggadah ("The Telling"). This extraordinary book provides, among other things, a master class in *how* to educate.

Consequently, a list of ten Torah-based educational principles follows. Many of them are exemplified in the Haggadah and lived at the Seder.

Principle 1: Order and Structure

The first principle of Jewish education is embedded in the name of the evening, Seder, which means "order." And the fundamental text of the Seder night is the Haggadah, which means "telling." The Haggadah, like most books, has a table of contents. The table of contents in most books is either ignored or consulted briefly for referential purpose. This is not so with the Haggadah. We begin the Seder evening by *singing* the table of contents.

Jews don't do this with any other book. Consequently, this practice is so strange that we must inquire: Why are we singing the table of contents? The answer becomes apparent when one considers the name of the ceremony itself. We call our central event on the Festival of Freedom "order," and we sing the table of contents to remind ourselves and to teach our children to rejoice in the fact that education must be conducted in a structure. And this structure must be known and articulated at the beginning of the educational process.

Following the singing of the table of contents, the main activities of the evening commence. The wine is poured and drunk, the matzah is broken and served, and the children are encouraged, and even required, to ask questions. This is not *seder*; there is nothing orderly about (inevitably) spilled wine, crumbling matzah, and open questioning! It is pure freedom.

Freedom and its ally, creativity, we learn, are not the opposite of order. Order is what makes freedom possible and creativity flourish. For instance, Billy Joel and I each have the "freedom" to play the piano right now, but only one of us has the freedom to do so meaningfully.

The order and structure of ancient Jewish education is reflected in the many rules governing it. How large should class sizes be? The answer from the Talmud: no more than twenty-five.[11]

Principle 2: Education Begins at Home

The second principle of education derives from where the Seder is held and who leads it. We celebrate most of our major holidays—Rosh Hashanah, Yom Kippur, even Purim—in the synagogue, under the guidance of rabbis. It is possible, and probably more efficient, to host a Seder in a synagogue, as a rabbi could lead a Seder for many congregants. But that is not where or how we usually conduct it. We do it in the home, where the leaders are likely to be the parents. Why do we do this? The Bible is clear about who the primary teachers of a child are. As Moses instructs in Deuteronomy 6, "And *you* shall teach them diligently to your children."

The responsibility of the parent to educate coheres precisely with the Jewish conception of where children learn most. The Talmudic sage Abaye said, "Yes, as people say, the speech of a child in the marketplace is learned either from that of his father or from that of his mother."[12] "As the people say" is an illustrative introduction, as it indicates that what follows is conventional wisdom.

The Torah tradition inculcates the belief that the education in the home occurs comprehensively and pervasively, when parents are directly teaching and when they are not. In Proverbs 1:8, King Solomon declared, "Hear, my son, the instruction of thy father and forsake not the teaching of thy mother."

In a 1977 eulogy for the mother of his eldest son-in-law, the twentieth-century sage Rav Joseph B. Soloveitchik discussed what this proverb meant for him. His father instructed him in the Torah text. As for the "teaching" of his mother:

> I used to have long conversations with my mother. In fact, it was a monologue rather than a dialogue. She talked and I "happened" to overhear. What did she talk about? I must use a halakhic term in order to answer this question: she talked about *inyanei de-yoma* (the issues of the day). I used to watch her arranging the house in honor of a holiday. I used to see her recite prayers; I used to watch her recite the sidra every Friday night and I still remember the nostalgic tune. I learned from her very much. Most of all I learned that Judaism expresses itself not only in formal compliance with the law but also in a living experience. She taught me that there is a flavor, a scent and warmth to *mitzvot*. I learned from her the most important thing in life, to feel the presence of the Almighty and the gentle pressure of His hand resting upon my frail shoulders. Without her teachings, which quite often were transmitted to me in silence, I would have grown up a soulless being, dry and insensitive.[13]

Principle 3: The Teacher Must Be a Textperson

The kind of teaching that Rav Soloveitchik received from his mother is deeply rooted in the Torah tradition. Indeed, it derives directly from Exodus.

Later, in Exodus 25:11, God commands the Jewish people, regarding the building of the holy ark, "From within and from without you shall cover it." Why does God command a *double* coating of the ark? One cannot see the internal coating!

The fourth-century sage Rava explained that the instruction is about Torah observance more broadly since the ark was the home of the tablets that Moshe wrote. He explains that the double coating teaches us that "any Torah scholar whose inside is not like his outside (i.e., whose outward expression of righteousness is insincere), is not to be considered a Torah scholar."[14] In other words, one must *live* that which he teaches.

The idea that education is a function of instruction *and* modeling was developed 1,600 years later, by the twentieth-century Rabbi Abraham Joshua Heschel. Rabbi Heschel explained:

> To guide a pupil into the promised land, [the teacher] must have been there himself. When asking himself: Do I stand for what I

> teach? Do I believe what I say? He must be able to answer in the affirmative. What we need more than anything else is not textbooks but text-people. It is the personality of the teacher which is the text that the pupils read; the text that they will never forget.[15]

It is in this vein that Rabbi YY Jacobson said that of the thousands of classes a teacher may give, he really has "only one" and it is "the way he lives."[16]

The twentieth-century American sage Rabbi Yaakov Kamenetsky was once asked how he taught his children to be stringent about saying *brachot* (blessings) on food. The great scholar did not cite any biblical verses, quote any ancient sages, speak about the importance of gratitude, or even reference God. He said, "I made brachot, my wife made brachot, the kids always saw us making brachot. It's no surprise they also make brachot!"[17]

The teaching that one imparts through "the way he lives" is by no means limited to ritual practices. Rabbi Moshe Scheiner of the Palm Beach Synagogue tells the story of a colleague, Rabbi Moshe Bryski, who was on a trip with a bunch of students. An adult in the room dropped a dollar. One of the young men picked it up and pocketed it. The student standing next to him took a dollar out of his pocket, dropped it on the floor, and tapped the man and said, "Sir, I think you dropped this," and gave it to him.

Rabbi Bryski asked the second student why he did that. The student said that he spent his childhood with his grandfather at his store. The student said that he once saw a customer drop a dollar on the floor. The student, like his classmate, picked it up and put it in his pocket. His grandfather, without saying anything, dropped a dollar on the floor, tapped the customer on the shoulder, and said, "You just dropped this."[18]

Principle 4: Knowledge Is Crucial, and It Begets Knowledge

In Pirkei Avot, it is taught that "one who learns as a child is compared to what? To ink written on new parchment. And one who learns as an elder is compared to what? To ink written on muddled parchment."[19]

Children, in other words, are born knowing nothing. Teachers are obliged to fill students with knowledge, just as a writer must fill parchment with ink. The early acquisition of knowledge prepares the learner to benefit from future knowledge, and one should never think that a student will simply discover knowledge or skills on their own. Moses emphasizes this idea in Deuteronomy 11:13 when he says, "If you have *heard*, you will *hear* my mitzvot [commands]."[20]

The switch in tenses (the past tense of *heard* to the future tense of *hear*) is instructive. We will hear (or learn) to the extent that we have heard (or learned). Our rate of learning, the Torah is telling us, is dynamic and compounding. The more we know about a subject, the easier it is to learn more.

This insight is reflected in the Talmudic dictum "One cannot compare one who learns something for the 101st time to someone who learned it for the 100th time."[21] Why does the Talmud use 101 and 100 rather than, say, 2 and 3? Because most people recognize that we gain lots of knowledge in the early stages of learning, but ignore the value in constant repetition past the point of knowledge acquisition. The Talmud is teaching us that when a learner has accumulated *a lot* of knowledge, she is primed for creative breakthroughs. We *cannot even compare* the level of knowledge between the 100th and 101st review.

This conviction is effectively pronounced at each Seder. The Haggadah has us read, "And even were we all wise, intelligent, aged, and knowledgeable in the Torah, still the command would be upon us to tell of the Exodus from Egypt. The more one tells of the Exodus from Egypt, the more praiseworthy is he."

There is, the Haggadah is reminding us, always more to learn. And those with the most knowledge about a subject are best equipped to learn new ideas, process new information, and arrive at new insights. Hence, they are the most praiseworthy.

Principle 5: The Importance of Questions

The tone for the Seder is set by one of the most beloved parts of the Haggadah, when the youngest child asks the Four Questions. It might seem counterintuitive that an evening devoted to the transmission of a religious faith should emphasize questions. Questions might be seen as a liability for a religious system, especially on the night whose purpose is transmission of our heritage to the next generation. Questions invite doubt and often lead to criticism and challenge.

By welcoming questions, the Seder leader is telling his children that he respects their inquiries and welcomes their challenges. And he is showing them that he is so confident in the Jewish tradition that he believes its transmission will be *strengthened* through the challenges their questions will inevitably bring.

The section on the Four Questions concludes with a fascinating subtlety. There is no section entitled "The answer." More, the questions do not receive a direct answer! Instead, the response is a long and intertwined recitation of thought-provoking Talmudic anecdotes. Why would the authors of the Haggadah have a section called the "Four Questions" with no direct answers? To teach us that the emphasis in education should be on questions, not answers, and that questions invariably lead to more questions and greater interest.

The importance of questions is further highlighted in the Jewish experience following the Exodus. To sustain the people in the desert, God sends food from heaven known simply as *man*, or in English, manna. According to the twelfth-century sage Samuel ben Meir (known as Rashbam), the manna that fell from heaven was so named because the Egyptian word *man* means "what." The people saw this strange food, asked "What is this?" and named it accordingly.[22]

The nineteenth-century sage Yehudah Aryeh Leib Alter (known as the Sfat Emet) explains that the experience of ingesting "what food" was a way for God to prepare the Children of Israel to be a free people in the Promised Land. This explains why the Talmud states that "the Torah was only given to the generation who ate the manna." The Torah, in other words, belongs to those who live off questions.[23]

This insistence on questioning in the Jewish tradition was manifested in the teachings of a well-known first-century rabbi, Jesus of Nazareth. In his magnificently titled book *Jesus Is the Question*, Martin Copenhaver of the Andover Newton Theological School points out that Jesus asks questions forty times as often as he answers them directly, and offers indirect answers twenty times as often as he does direct answers.[24]

The success that rabbi Jesus enjoyed with questioning would continue forever and is reflected in the data on Jewish Nobel Prize winners. Isidor Isaac Rabi was born in Poland in 1898. He won the Nobel Prize for Physics in 1944 for his discovery of nuclear magnetic resonance. This enabled magnetic resonance imaging (MRI), which allow doctors to examine our organs, tissues, and skeletal systems.

An interviewer asked Dr. Rabi for the secret to his success. He said that when his classmates in grade school came home from school, their parents would ask, "What did you learn today?" That was not, he said, the question his mother asked. He recalled: "'Izzy,' my mother would say, 'did you ask a good question today?' That . . . made me become a scientist."[25]

Principle 6: Know Thy Student

In Genesis 25, Rebecca gives birth to twins, Esau and Jacob. We know immediately how different they are. Esau emerges "red, like a hairy mantle." Jacob emerges without any such description, just grasping the heel of his older twin. Sure enough, we later learn that they are very different. Esau becomes a "master hunter" and Jacob "dwells in tents."

The Torah then tells us that "the boys grew up," which sounds innocuous enough, but not to the nineteenth-century sage Rabbi Samson Raphael Hirsch. He said that it indicates that the boys grew up totally together and were educated in the same way by their parents who paid no regard to their distinctiveness. Rabbi Hirsch suggests that this failure of parenting leads to the problems that soon develop within the family—culminating in an attempt by one brother to murder the other.[26]

Jewish education incorporates the lessons that we can learn from the mistake of Isaac and Rebecca. In Proverbs 22:6, King Solomon says, "Educate a child according to his way, and when he is old he will not depart from it." King Solomon could have said, "Educate a child according to *the* way," but he doesn't. King Solomon says *his* way, emphasizing the singularity of the student. Different people learn in different ways, and the job of the educator is to teach accordingly.

This idea is also expressed in the Passover Seder. One of the opening sections of the Haggadah is that of the four sons—the wise son, the wicked son, the simple son, and the son who does not know how to ask a question. These sons ask very different questions, and are given distinct and responsive answers.

This teaching has been taken up by the Israel Defense Forces. The motto of the IDF Education Corps is: 100 percent content to 100 percent of the students. Corporal David Wolfowicz, a former commander in the IDF Education Corps, explains its meaning. The role of the teacher in Jewish philosophy is to bring all of the material to the student, which necessarily means presenting the content with sensitivity and responsiveness to the unique capabilities, challenges, proclivities, and interests of each student. Some students learn better visually, some textually, some through discussion, some through videos, some while exercising, and some while sitting. The teacher must identify how the student learns best and teach the material accordingly. But the students never get left behind with a "lesser version" of the content.[27]

Rav Joseph B. Soloveitchik lived this principle in his family. He was, as discussed in the chapter of this book on future orientation, determined to fulfill his Jewish responsibilities as a grandfather to teach his grandchildren Torah. He also knew that his grandsons were Boston Red Sox fans. Rav Soloveitchik had no interest in sports but got tutored about baseball and the Red Sox before he saw his grandchildren so that he would be able to teach them "according to their way."[28]

Principle 7: Cultivate Enthusiasm

The seventh lesson of education is reflected in the activities of the Seder—a night of serious learning that is full of games, songs, performances, challenges, and culinary delights.

In the Talmud, Rabbi Yehuda HaNasi is quoted as saying, "A person can learn Torah only from a place that his heart desires, as it is stated: But his delight is in the Torah of the Lord" (Psalm 1:2, authored by King David)."[29]

The Torah provides a litmus test for success in teaching with passion. Deuteronomy 11:19 commands us to "teach them [words of Torah] to your children, to speak of them." Since teaching and speaking words of Torah are seemingly synonymous, the command must be referring to cause and effect. We must, the Torah guides us, teach our children so that they are excited to speak and share them.

In many communities, this practice begins with a ritual. A child starts learning by licking a chart of Hebrew letters covered in honey and receives honey cake for good performance. Consequently, the Yiddish word for honey cake (*lekach*) likely derives from the German word *lecken* (meaning "lick").[30] At the Seder, parents are similarly advised to give their children nuts and other treats that can keep them awake and engaged with the learning experience. Learning should, in the first instance, be associated with sweetness and enjoyment.[31]

Principle 8: Learn by Teaching

In Exodus 10:2, God instructs, "And that you may tell in the ears of your son, and of your son's son, what things I have wrought in Egypt, and my signs which I have done among them; that you may know that I am the Lord."

The twenty-first-century Israeli Rabbi Yisrael Meir Druck noted something strange about this verse. One would expect it to read, "Tell it in the ears of your son . . . so *he* will know that I am the Lord." Instead, it says, "Tell it in the ears of your son . . . so that *you* may know that I am the Lord."[32] The Torah is telling us that we learn by teaching.

In the same breath, God teaches us how this process works. We are not to lecture our children but to "tell in the ears of your son." The teaching process is best conducted as a personal and intimate conversation with the child, with the material being distilled so that the individual child can understand, appreciate, and rejoice in it. When we engage in this personalized type of learning, we ourselves are forced to understand the material from new and unique perspectives, thus providing the parent or teacher with constant opportunities to learn.

Principle 9: Learning Is Multifaceted

In Genesis 25:27, we learn about the education of Jacob. This son of Isaac and Rebecca, the text tells us, "dwells in tents." What did he do in the tents? The majority of classical and modern commentators understand this to refer to study.

Interestingly, the word "tents" is plural, indicating that Jacob sought multiple viewpoints and learned multiple subjects. His study of multiple subjects served him well. In Genesis 30, he is able to achieve great wealth through a highly sophisticated use of selective breeding, which would be officially "discovered" by Gregor Mendel in the nineteenth century.[33]

The understanding that Jacob studied multiple subjects coheres with what we later learn about God. In Exodus 33, Moses asks God to reveal himself. God answers, "I will cause my goodness to pass in front of you." Maimonides learned from this verse that "the knowledge of the works of God is the knowledge of His attributes, by which He can be known."

Many of those attributes are to be found in science, which seeks to explain how things work in God's physical world. Rabbi Israel Drazin, summarizing Maimonides's view, writes, "The true worship of God requires Jews to study the sciences."[34]

This accords with the criteria that Maimonides lists for serving on a Jewish court. He said that only "wise and understanding men" could sit on the court. In order to possess the wisdom and understanding necessary to interpret Jewish law, Maimonides said, "They must be experts in Torah law, with a wide breadth of knowledge. They must also know secular subjects like medicine, mathematics, astrology, and astronomy."[35]

The requirement that Jewish judges be knowledgeable in multiple academic disciplines is not just theoretical. All of the rabbis of the Talmud and the Middle Ages had professions and trades. Rabbi Akiva was a shepherd; Rabbi Joshua was a blacksmith; Hillel the Elder was a woodcutter; Rabbi Judah HaNasi was a property owner; Don Isaac Abarbanel was a statesman; Rashi was in the wine business; and Maimonides, Nachmanides, and Judah Halevi were physicians. In the early modern period, Rabbi Elijah Ben Solomon Zalman, known as the Vilna Gaon, wrote a mathematics textbook.

These greatest of rabbis did not work in their profession for purely economic reasons. They did so for religious reasons. Rabbi Akiva's knowledge of how sheep act informed his theory of Jewish leadership. Rabbi Judah HaNasi's knowledge of landholding enabled him to understand and teach the Torah's laws regarding leaving the land fallow every seven years. Rashi's knowledge from the wine business enabled him to explain the requirements for wine libations in Leviticus and Numbers. Maimonides's knowledge of weather forecasting enabled him to develop a theory of prophecy. Nachmanides's knowledge of medicine enabled him to create leniencies within Jewish law for pregnant women on fast days.[36]

The lives of our greatest rabbis illustrate why Jacob "dwells in *tents*." These rabbis were each able to develop breakthroughs in Torah understanding and teaching because they had immense knowledge of the Torah *and* of other disciplines. As a result of their multifaceted mastery, they were able to make unique associations that resulted in creative breakthroughs.

Principle 10: Revere Teachers

The ancient Jewish regard for teachers is evident in how, in Jewish tradition, teachers are likened to parents.

We are, pursuant to the Fifth Commandment, required to honor our parents. The Talmud interprets this commandment so strictly that one is commanded to pass up the opportunity to make a fortune if doing so would require disturbing a parent from a nap.[37]

And teachers, as the co-educators (with parents) of children, are accorded the same respect, if not more. Maimonides writes, "Just as a person is commanded to honor and revere his father, so he is under an obligation to honor and revere his teacher, even to a greater extent than his father, for his father gave him life in this world, while his teacher who instructs him in wisdom secures for him life in the world to come."[38]

There is nothing abstract or theoretical about this reverence. Students, Maimonides writes (drawing from ancient sources), must not recline in the presence of their teachers, but "should sit before him as one would sit before a king." Students, Maimonides continues, should greet the teacher by bowing and saying, "with awe and reverence, 'Peace be upon you, my master.'" The teacher can waive these (and many other) signs of respect, but the student must continue to demonstrate reverence in all of their interactions.[39]

The Science

Moses's idea to prioritize and educate all children in a culture of universal literacy might be the most radical idea a leader ever proposed. It might also be the most successful.

It took several thousand years, but the world is now with him. Massachusetts became the first US state to require universal education in 1852 and Mississippi became the last state in 1918. France required universal schooling in 1959, as did England in 1996. In 2017, a United Nations report castigated member states for failing to meet literacy targets, emphasizing that achieving progress would require "drastic measures." The global literacy rate that prompted the UN concern was 86 percent, with 91 percent among youth.[40]

Cultures that do not support universal education for children, such as the Taliban, are widely considered to be primitive, oppressive, or downright evil.

Many of the specific and once radical educational concepts in the Torah are now widely accepted. Several are discussed below, followed by a consideration of one Torah-based idea on education that remains highly contested—with very significant implications.

Class Size

As noted, the Talmud requires that class size be limited to twenty-five pupils. In 2022, the education blog *Chalkbeat* reports, "There's little debate among teachers that class size matters."

Why would this be?

In 1985, a research team from Tennessee began the "Lasting Benefits Study." More than 11,000 students were randomly assigned to smaller or larger classes from kindergarten to third grade. The researchers determined that the students in smaller classes performed better in the first year, with benefits that kept growing in subsequent years. While all kinds of students showed the benefits of being in smaller classes, those from underprivileged backgrounds experienced the most profound benefits. Studies in other states from all over the country have shown similar results. The benefits include higher test scores, higher attendance, more engagement, and a greater likelihood to attend college. Class size is so important that it is mandated in the Florida Constitution, with the maximum number for high school students being the Talmud's number: twenty-five.[41]

Respect for Teachers

Democrats disagreed with much of what President Ronald Reagan said and did, but there was no disagreement when he chose a teacher as the civilian to accompany the professional astronauts on the space shuttle.

Republicans disagreed with a lot of what President Barack Obama said and did, but no one disagreed when he said at the 2013 White House Teacher of the Year event: "I cannot think of something more important than reaching that child who maybe came in uninspired, and suddenly, you've inspired them."[42]

There is plenty of debate about how society should express its respect for teachers, but not about whether teachers do sacred work. And the United States is not even the leading country, with nations including China,

Indonesia, Russia, Singapore, Turkey, and Korea ranking ahead of the United States in respect accorded to teachers.[43]

Enthusiasm

As noted, Jewish tradition is not only concerned with the technical aspects of education, but with the heart and soul of learning as well. Why would Moses, King David, and the rabbis of the Talmud have insisted so adamantly that students be taught enthusiastically? In 1993, Professor Elaine Hatfield of the University of Hawaii identified the phenomenon of "emotional contagion," which she defined as "the tendency to automatically mimic and synchronize expressions, vocalizations, postures, and movements with those of another person and, consequently, to converge emotionally." Intangibles, like emotions and attitudes, travel from person to person with a fluency that is worthy of the term "contagion."[44]

In 2011, the psychologist Dr. David Hamilton wrote about how this works. He wrote that emotional contagion operates through the mirror neuron system (MNS) in the brain, which both records the emotions of others and mirrors them in the observer.[45]

In 2014, Professor Qin Zhang of Fairfield University showed how this discovery is relevant in the context of education when she published the results of her study on the effects of teacher enthusiasm on communications students. The emotional contagion generated by an enthusiastic teacher has educational consequences far beyond how the students regard the material. Professor Zhang concluded, "Results indicate that teacher enthusiasm is an effective predictor of student behavioral, cognitive, and emotional engagement, intrinsic goal orientation, and academic self-efficacy."[46]

The benefits of enthusiastic teaching expand further than most people would even consider. For instance, a 2015 study from Hungary shows that students cheat less in a class led by an enthusiastic teacher.[47]

Learning by Teaching

As discussed, God commands in Exodus 10:2 to "tell it in the ears of your son . . . so that *you* may know that I am the Lord." We learn best, the Torah asserts, by teaching.

In the 1980s, the French scholar of teaching Jean-Pol Martin pioneered the technique of "Learning by Teaching" (LdL). Professor Martin developed this method for teaching foreign language lessons in Germany. It has since enjoyed wide applications and is the idea powering group presentations, peer teaching, and service learning.[48]

The Torah posits that the teacher learns through the process of distilling the subject for the uninitiated to understand it. Cornell professor Richard Feynman, who was one of the great physicists of the twentieth century, would have agreed. He won the Nobel Prize in 1965 for his discoveries in quantum electrodynamics. His approach to learning the most complex subjects has now been named the Feynman technique. The Feynman technique has the learner study a subject until they can explain it to a child, often by using simple analogies to make it understandable.

The Feynman technique has been expanded even further. A companion method is the plastic platypus technique, where the learner teaches the subject to an inanimate object. This technique has been widely adapted by software engineers who solve problems by explaining the issues to a rubber duck (or teddy bear). This is so popular that, in 2018, the engineering education site Stack Exchange introduced its avatar: a plastic duck.[49]

Knowledge Begets Knowledge

There is, however, one main area of disagreement regarding the Torah's philosophy of education. The Torah emphasizes that the fundamental purpose of education is the acquisition of knowledge. When one knows a lot about a subject, his rate of learning about the subject increases. Especially if he knows a lot about multiple subjects—if he is a proverbial Jacob "dwelling in *tents*"—he will be positioned for creative breakthroughs, as he will be able to associate knowledge from multiple domains to generate a discovery.

This idea has been under assault since 1763, when Jean-Jacques Rousseau wrote *Emile, or On Education*. The enduring significance of *Emile*, which Mr. Rousseau called his "best and most important book," is remarkable. The renowned nineteenth-century British educator R. H. Quick called *Emile* "perhaps the most influential book ever written on the subject of education." More recent assessments have agreed, with some educational theorists saying that it is one of the three books that compose the canon on education (the other two are Plato's *Republic* and John Dewey's *Democracy and Education*).[50]

Mr. Rousseau imagined a child named Emile and envisioned an ideal education for each stage of his life. This ideal education would consist of minimal instruction. The child should be encouraged to learn through amusement, experiences, and exploration and not with requirements, demands, or a notion of scholarship. Creativity, in this view, is constrained or destroyed by formal education and traditional learning, and by any requirement or expectation that the student master an enormous body of knowledge. Mr. Rousseau did not agree with the Talmud that studying the same material for the 101st time is incomparable with studying it for the 100th time. He wrote:

> The only habit the child should be allowed to acquire is to contract none . . . Prepare in good time from the reign of freedom and the exercise of his powers, by allowing his body its natural habitats and accustoming him always to be his own master and follow the dictates of his will as soon as he has a will of his own.[51]

If a child should "always be his own master and follow the dictates of his will as soon as he has a will of his own," what is the significance of the teacher? Or of a body of knowledge that the child is expected to master? Suffice it to say that Mr. Rousseau's answers to these questions are entirely different from those of the Torah.

"What School Could Be"

We see Mr. Rousseau's influence on education almost everywhere, including the girls' soccer field. In October 2021, I and other parents of eight-year-old girls received an email from the West Side Soccer League, before the third game of the season.

"Get ready," the email instructed, for "SILENT SOCCER this weekend!" I played youth soccer in the 1980s and was entirely unfamiliar with this term. The email explained, "Silent soccer is the cornerstone of a child-centered soccer philosophy. We let the kids play, show off what they have learned so far this season, and take leadership and responsibility for playing as a team. Coaches do not coach, but referees do ref."

I looked it up, and silent soccer is supported by the American Youth Soccer Organization, which sponsors our daughter's West Side Soccer

League. Silent soccer is played throughout the country—although not the world, as Brazilian friends were stunned by it.

Like all thoughtfully conceived policies, silent soccer has a philosophy behind it. It comes right from *Emile*. It is a manifestation of what is alternatively called minimally guided education, discovery-based education, or child-centered learning. The fact that it has gone by multiple names is, as we'll see, instructive.

Perhaps the two most important contemporary theorists of minimally guided education are Ted Dintersmith and the late Ken Robinson, who was knighted by the United Kingdom in 2003 for his contributions to education. Sir Ken Robinson's TED Talk, "Do Schools Kill Creativity?," is the most popular TED Talk of all time. Why would schools kill creativity? The answer is encapsulated in a pronouncement from Mr. Robinson: "Creativity is as important as literacy, and we should treat it with the same status."[52]

Schools naturally teach literacy as a foundation for learning. However, Mr. Robinson argued that creativity is distinguished from and often competes with literacy, suggesting that educators need to choose one or the other.

This philosophy derives from Emile and is precisely the opposite of the Torah's philosophy of, "If you have *heard*, you will *hear* my mitzvot [teachings]," which holds that creativity is not opposed to literacy (or knowledge) but derives from it.

Ted Dintersmith spent the 2015–2016 school year visiting two hundred schools in all fifty states. He concluded, "[Students] don't need to be taught. Given the right challenges and devices, they'll learn. These budding competencies can become decisive life advantages, equipping graduates to capitalize on machine intelligence."[53]

This is a concise and articulate presentation of Mr. Rousseau's philosophy of education. It is also a direct repudiation of the Torah's philosophy of education, which holds that children do not learn by themselves, but through an ordered system oriented around teachers systematically conveying abundant knowledge.

One of the most influential schools of thought within discovery-based education is the Reggio Emilia approach, which focuses on very young children, infants, toddlers, and preschoolers. There are more than a hundred centers in the United States devoted to it and thousands of educators around the world who practice the approach—from Thailand to Italy. It is based on the premise that even very young children are "competent and capable of constructing their own learning."[54]

Consequently, in the words of an Atlanta-based Reggio Emilia preschool director quoted in the *New York Times*, an educator should acknowledge that children are "not empty vessels who need to be filled." Adults should not, accordingly, regard the imparting of knowledge as a top priority. They should instead, according to a Reggio Emilia school publication that articulates its approach, "consider themselves collaborators and facilitators [who should] . . . observe, document, and engage in dialogue with the children to better understand and support their learning."[55]

When a child graduates from a Reggio Emilia institution, parents may consider enrolling them in one of the many discovery-based learning schools that extend through high school. A prominent example of such an institution is Acton Academy, based in Texas with campuses worldwide. Acton Academy replaces traditional teachers with "guides" and refers to its learners not as students but as "heroes" or "geniuses." These heroes and geniuses don't require teachers, only guides to help navigate the knowledge they will acquire independently.[56]

The debate between the Torah and Mr. Rousseau is set. Now the question is: Who, given the benefit of modern social science, is right?

The Zombie of Education

In 2015 (and again in 2017), the National Assessment of Educational Progress, which is conducted by the United States Department of Education, reported that one-third of American fourth graders cannot read at a basic level and that fewer than 40 percent are proficient in reading.[57]

Why is this? One theory is that poor reading derives from poverty. But the poverty rate of American children is nowhere near 40 percent. In 2015, Jack Silva, the Chief Academic Officer of Bethlehem, Pennsylvania, noticed that his students were performing in line with these terrible national numbers. He set out to investigate. He found significant deficiencies in reading from students in the wealthier areas as well. He dispatched a new director of literacy, Kim Harper, to find out why. Ms. Harper visited one of the lowest performing schools in the district and observed how reading was being taught. An NPR report details what she observed.

> The teachers were talking about how students should attack words in a story. When a child came to a word she didn't know, the teacher would tell her to look at the picture and guess. The most important thing was for the child to understand the meaning of the story, not the exact words on the page. So, if a kid came to the word "horse" and said "house," the teacher would say, that's wrong. But, Harper recalls, "if the kid said 'pony,' it'd be right because pony and horse mean the same thing."
>
> Harper was shocked. First of all, pony and horse don't mean the same thing. And what does a kid do when there aren't any pictures?[58]

The method of instruction that Kim Harper observed is known as the "three-cueing" system, which is based on the premise that students should learn to read by making what an analysis in *Education Week* calls "strategic guesses."[59] The three-cueing technique (sometimes called "balanced literacy") is the favored reading instruction approach within discovery-based learning—as it encourages young readers to use a variety of techniques to figure out a word with minimal guidance. It is distinct from, and often contrasted with, phonics. The phonics approach, often referred to as the "science of reading," focuses on students sounding out words with explicit instruction from teachers.

Why did the Bethlehem teachers decide to use the triple cue method? They were just teaching in accordance with the prevailing philosophy of their profession; *Education Week* found that more than 70 percent of K–2 teachers teach reading using the "balanced literacy" approach. One curriculum devoted to balanced literacy, Lucy Calkins's "Units of Study," is used in around 25 percent of American elementary schools—earning her what one teacher described as "rock star" status among teachers.[60]

This classic application of the consequences of discovery-based learning for reading did not receive much attention in 2017. That changed five years later, when the education journalist Emily Hanford released a podcast series, *Sold a Story.* Ms. Hanford's series developed based on a Covid phenomenon: Everyone was at home, and parents got to observe firsthand how their children were being taught to read.

One of those parents was Corine Adams, a Rhode Island mother of a kindergartener. As Ms. Hanford reported, "In kindergarten and again in first grade, her son and his classmates were taught that when they came to a word they didn't know, they should look at the first letter, look at the picture in the book, and think of a word that would make sense. They weren't told to sound out the word."

The prevalence of "balanced literacy" is belied by the fact that it has been, as Ms. Hanford explained in a *New York Times* essay, "contradicted by decades of scientific research"—which she links to.[61] The decades of scientific research that confirmed the superiority of phonics was not just buried in scientific journals. In 2013, Mississippi overhauled its reading instruction to require phonics. The result was that Mississippi jumped from forty-ninth to twenty-ninth in fourth-grade reading results in six years.[62]

Ms. Hanford's reporting, backed by parents who discovered their children's reading deficiencies during Covid, is leading to a widespread rethinking of the balanced literacy approach in blue and red states alike. In 2023, the New York City Commissioner of Education David Banks said that the city's previous approach was "fundamentally flawed," and that there would be a "massive turnaround" to phonics.[63] In the same year, the Tennessee governor, Bill Lee, advanced a bill that would require that young schoolchildren "be taught phonics as the primary form of reading instruction."[64]

Even Lucy Calkins is conducting what the *New York Times* called a "major retreat." She said, "All of us are imperfect. The last two or three years, what I've learned from the science of reading work has been transformational."[65]

The prevalence of balanced literacy, despite the evidence against it, aligns with the principles of the discovery-based learning, of which it is an important part. In 2004, Professor Richard Mayer of the University of California at Santa Barbara published his review of several decades of studies on variations of discovery learning. He titled his review "Should There Be a Three-Strikes Rule Against Pure Discovery Learning?"

Professor Mayer addressed one of the core claims of the Rousseauian school of thought: that students develop the most and in the best possible way when they are given the license to discover, with minimal guidance, what they want to learn. He concluded:

> When students have too much freedom, they may fail to come into contact with the to-be-learned material. There is nothing

> magical to ensure that simply working on a problem or simply discussing a problem will lead to discovering its solution. If the learner fails to come into contact with the to-be-learned material, no amount of activity or discussion will be able to help the learner make sense of it.

Still, he said, "Like some zombie that keeps returning from its grave, pure discovery continues to have its advocates. However, anyone who takes an evidence-based approach to educational practice must ask the same question: Where is the evidence that it works?"[66]

Six year later, Professor Paul Kirschner of the Open University of the Netherlands and his colleagues published a long analysis of the research on what they called "Constructivist, Discovery, Problem-Based, Experiential, and Inquiry-Based Teaching." They reviewed hundreds of studies regarding discovery-based education in fields ranging from law to medicine to neuroscience. They found that discovery-based learning leads to students feeling lost, frustrated, and suffering from unmanageable "cognitive loads," which result when students approach new material without a sufficient basis to process it. Moreover, discovery-based learning is "inefficient," as students experience "false starts" and pursue tangential topics they came across without having first grasped the core concept. These students also have trouble retaining knowledge, as there are no mechanisms to reinforce foundational ideas. They concluded:

> After a half-century of advocacy associated with instruction using minimal guidance, it appears that there is no body of research supporting the technique. In so far as there is any evidence from controlled studies, it almost uniformly supports direct, strong instructional guidance rather than constructivist-based minimal guidance during the instruction of novice to intermediate learners.[67]

Still, as they acknowledged, discovery-based education remains popular and pervasive, even outside of the schools that are expressly devoted to it.

The question of whether education should be knowledge based has surprisingly widespread implications, extending beyond teaching methods whose importance became evident in 2020 when parents realized that their children were struggling to read. In the 2021–2022 school year, 41 percent of New York City students were chronically absent. This had a predictable impact on their learning. In 2022, the New York comptroller's office studied the reading, writing, and mathematics test scores of high school *graduates* and determined that only 57 percent of them were "college ready."[68]

Yet, the public high school graduation rate in New York City has steadily increased every year from 2011 to 2022 (when 84 percent of students graduated). At the same time the graduation rate increased, the rate of test exemptions escalated, to 70 percent, in 2021.[69]

How could the New York City Board of Education deem so many students who did not attend class regularly *or* pass examinations deserving of a diploma?

The stated philosophy of the New York City Department of Education provides the answer: "Culturally responsive-sustaining education (CR-SE)." This, in addition to discovery-based learning, is another alternative to the Torah's philosophy of knowledge-based cumulative learning. According to the NYC DOE:

> The DOE uses an educational strategy that embraces students' identities. We call it "culturally responsive-sustaining education (CR-SE)." It is a way of seeing diversity as a source of knowledge. With CR-SE, students use their own identity to get education. They learn using aspects of their race, social class, gender, language, sexual orientation, nationality, religion, or ability. Studies show that students learning with CR-SE are more active in class. They graduate more often.[70]

As we will see in the chapter on diversity, the Torah has a very rich and highly developed of diversity. But diversity is different from knowledge. In the New York schools context, knowledge would come from academic subjects that educate the student, provide a foundation to engage the world, and prepare him for a lifetime of continual learning.

The Secret of the Great Achievers

In 2022, the Stanford University Encyclopedia identified the twentieth-century German sociologist Max Weber as one of the three "principal architects of modern social science."[71]

In 1918, Professor Weber rose to a lectern at Munich University. His lecture, "Science as a Vocation," addressed the ways that new ideas, or what we could call creativity, are generated. He said:

> Ideas occur to us when they please, not when it pleases us. The best ideas do indeed occur to one's mind in the way that Ihering describes it: when smoking a cigar on the sofa . . . [or] when taking a walk on a slowly ascending street; or in a similar way. In any case, ideas come when we do not expect them, and not when we are brooding and searching at our desks. Yet ideas would certainly not come to mind had we not brooded at our desks and searched for answers with passionate devotion.[72]

Creativity, Weber said, comes in sometimes unexpected and extraordinary bursts, but these are *only possible* after an enormous amount of scientific work, exactly as Moses suggested in Deuteronomy when he said, "If you heard, you will hear."

Shortly after Professor Weber's lecture, a team of Soviet psychologists did a study on memory. They presented chess masters and intelligent non-masters with a chess board that was arranged based on an actual game. They shortly thereafter asked both groups to reconstruct the board. The chess masters could do so easily, while the non-masters could not.

Did this mean that chess masters achieved their status because of their remarkable memories? The researchers tested that hypothesis and found that the chess masters were no better than the non-masters at general memory activities. This study has been replicated many times over the intervening decades, always with the same results.[73]

Professor Paul Kirschner and his colleagues, in the aforementioned study, discovered why chess masters *seem* to have great memories. They identified two components to memory: working memory and long-term memory.

Working memory is not "memory" in the conventional sense. It is more like immediately accessible knowledge, such as what guitarists rely on when they start to play or cashiers use when they count bills. The working memory, which is what we use to process information in real time, is very limited. Some researchers attribute its limit to the "magical number seven," with seven being the maximum number of items that we can carry in our brains at one time.[74]

Long-term memory, by contrast, can hold vast amounts of information. When we learn, we deposit the knowledge in the long-term memory, which is available for withdrawal. A cashier, for instance, will use his working memory to count bills and his long-term memory to use the point of sale system, the procedures for handling cash, and the prices of items.

This, Professor Kirschner explains, shows how chess masters can easily reconstruct the placement of pieces while those with equivalent memories but no chess knowledge could not. "These [chess] results suggest that expert problem solvers derive their skill by drawing on the extensive experience stored in their long-term memory and then quickly select and apply the best procedures for solving problems."[75]

When a chess master looks at a board, his long-term memory is flooded with patterns from previous games, making it easier to understand the current position and remember where the pieces are. This extensive long-term memory is what makes the chess master proficient. It allows him to recall which moves have succeeded or failed in the past, enabling him to apply those lessons in the present game and thus leverage the value of experience. With a long-term memory rich in chess knowledge, a master can come up with moves that might elude a less-experienced player.

Professors Kirschner, Clark, and Sweller explained that this finding is not specific to chess but reflects a contemporary understanding of how the mind works and how insights are created. The chess experiments may have been among the first, and perhaps the most frequently repeated, demonstrations of how performance improves as more knowledge is stored in long-term memory. However, the purest demonstration might not be an experiment at all but rather the career of hockey player Wayne Gretzky, known as "The Great One."

Wayne Gretzky won eight consecutive MVP Awards, set and broke his own records for goals and assists through the 1980s, and still holds (by far) the record for most career goals and assists. He is universally recognized as the best hockey player of all time, worthy of his nickname. Yet, as a profile by Ben McGrath in the *New Yorker* in 2018 contended, Mr. Gretzky was "never particularly strong or fast."[76]

So, how did Wayne Gretzky become The Great One? Mr. McGrath provided one answer: He "skated to where the puck was going." Another answer was provided by the company MasterClass. MasterClass could have selected anyone from any field to give its class on creativity. The company executives chose Wayne Gretzky. It was a good choice as he regularly did things like flip a puck over the net, against the back of the goalkeeper's neck, and into the net.[77]

How did Mr. Gretzky know where the puck was going? How did he become so creative? There is one answer to both questions.

When Wayne Gretzky was three years old, his father, Walter Gretzky, began systematically coaching him. By age four, Wayne was already charting the movements of the puck during games he watched. This disciplined study continued, and over time, Wayne, much like the aforementioned chess masters, developed a long-term memory filled with hockey plays that his working memory could instantly access during a game. The more he studied—using his own games as a significant part of his education—the more knowledge he accumulated and internalized.

Wayne Gretzky entered the National Hockey League (NHL) in 1979 at eighteen years old. He was named the MVP in his rookie season with the Edmonton Oilers, an award he would go on to win for the next seven consecutive seasons. In his classic book on the 1980–1981 Edmonton Oilers, Peter Gzowski explains that Mr. Gretzky was able to "summon up from his bank account of knowledge the fact that in a particular situation, someone is likely to be in a particular spot, and if he is not there now he will be presently."[78]

Mr. Gretzky's creativity was not distinguished from or contrary to his knowledge. His creativity derived from his knowledge, which came from the systematic study of his craft. As Moses might have said, Wayne Gretzky heard—and thus could hear.

Everything Is a Remix

The equivalent of the MVP in the sciences is the Nobel Prize. Each winner of a scientific Nobel Prize has made a major discovery and has had extensive and formal training in his or her discipline. But that is also true of scientists who did not receive their field's highest honor.

What, then, accounts for the special excellence of Nobel Prize winners? In 2022, Professors Robert and Michele Root-Bernstein of Michigan State studied 773 Nobel Prize winners in a variety of disciplines from 1901 to 2008 to find out. They emerged with an important discovery.

They found that Nobel Prize winners in the sciences are nine times more likely than other scientists to be *trained* in seemingly unrelated crafts such as woodworking and metalworking. They wrote, "The vast majority of laureates have or had formal . . . education in more than one discipline, developed intensive and extensive hobbies, and changed fields. Most importantly, we found, they have intentionally sought out useful connections among their diverse activities as a formal strategy for stimulating creativity."[79] With enormous amounts of systematically acquired knowledge across multiple disciplines, these scientists associate concepts from one field with those from another and emerge with creative breakthroughs. This data would have made a lot of sense to Kirby Ferguson, a Canadian filmmaker who has written, spoken, and produced films on the creative process. In 2015, he released a documentary whose title reveals his key finding: *Everything Is a Remix.* Mr. Ferguson said of creativity, "[It] isn't magic. It happens by applying ordinary tools of thought to existing material."[80]

Mr. Ferguson shows how the logic of remixing applies to all kinds of innovation. For instance, *Star Wars,* which is one of the most enduring and creative works of cinematic arts. Mr. Ferguson shows how *Star Wars* is a remix of themes, techniques, and even scenes from other films, including Joseph Campbell on myth; the films of Flash Gordon and Akira Kurosawa; *The Searchers*; *The Good, the Bad and the Ugly*; *633 Squadron*; *Metropolis*; *The 7th Voyage of Sinbad*; *Forbidden Planet*; *2001: A Space Odyssey*; *Silent Running*; *Triumph of the Will*; and *The Bridges at Toko-Ri.*

This is not to take anything away from George Lucas. Quite the contrary! As a creative genius, he should be expected to have learned, combined, and integrated knowledge derived from mastering a huge number of movies from a variety of genres. And school, contrary to Ken Robinson, did not kill Mr. Lucas's creativity; he is a proud graduate of the University of Southern California School of Cinematic Arts.

The remix theory accounts for most, if not nearly all, innovations. Throughout history, the most creative individuals did not stumble upon discoveries through exploration and experimentation; instead, they achieved them due to their vast knowledge bases.

Johannes Gutenberg was a professional goldsmith who lived in the winemaking region of France in the fifteenth century. He associated his knowledge of metal with his knowledge of wine pressing, and invented the printing press. Thomas Edison did not invent the light bulb. His patent was on "Improvement in Electric Lamps." James Watt's invention of the separate condenser steam engine was a modification of Thomas Newcomen's steam engine, which was based on Thomas Savery's invention of a steam pump to extract water from mines. Gunpei Yokoi combined technology from calculators with that of credit cards, and the result was Nintendo. Alexis Carrel's knowledge of embroidery enabled him to develop vascular surgical techniques that won him the 1912 Nobel Prize in Medicine.[81]

All of these inventions came as the result of the *learned* innovator seeing one thing, associating it with something else he systematically mastered, and realizing that the combination of the two would produce something new and special.

Why Die Progress Units Are Compressing

We see that creative breakthroughs are the result of innovators having an enormous amount of systematically acquired knowledge, often garnered from mastering a variety of disciplines. This validation of Moses's claim in Deuteronomy that we will learn in accordance with what we know has enormous implications for society.

Enter the futurist Tim Urban, and his concept of the "die progress unit" (DPU). A DPU is the amount of years a time traveler would have to go ahead to be so shocked that he would just keel over and die.

Mr. Urban explains, "Imagine that you got in a time machine back to 1750, grabbed someone alive then, and then brought them back to the present to show him around. Everything we take for granted, cars, tall buildings, iPhones, live sports broadcasts, recorded music, Google Maps, would blow his mind in such a major way that he wouldn't just be shocked, he might actually die."[82]

The amount of time it takes to constitute a die process unit has been radically shortening.

Mr. Urban writes that a time traveler from 100,000 BCE could survive for 85,000 years before accumulating enough DPUs to metaphorically die from shock upon encountering fire and language. Similarly, a visitor from 12,000 BCE, prior to the First Agricultural Revolution, would not reach a fatal DPU threshold until arriving somewhere between AD 1500 and 1750—and seeing things like the printing press, the Scientific Revolution, and globalization. However, a visitor from 1750 would accumulate enough DPUs to "die" of shock just 250 years later (and possibly fewer).

Mr. Urban's theory is, appropriately, a creative adaptation from the work of others, including the twentieth-century architect R. Buckminster Fuller and the twenty-first-century inventor Ray Kurzweil. In 1981, Buckminster Fuller estimated that human knowledge doubled from the year 1 to 1500, doubled again between 1500 and 1750, and again between 1750 and 1900. In 2001, Dr. Kurzweil identified "the Law of Accelerating Returns," which holds that "we won't experience 100 years of progress in the twenty-first century, it will be more like 20,000 years of progress (at today's rate)."[83]

Estimates now have knowledge doubling at every twelve to thirteen months, and accelerating so quickly that knowledge will eventually double every twelve hours. The implications for almost every field are profound. According to a 2011 report from Dr. Peter Densen of the University of Iowa, medical knowledge is doubling every seventy-three *days*. These estimates were conceived before the mass adoption of artificial intelligence, which will accelerate the rate of learning faster and further than even Tim Urban could have imagined when he originated the concept of the DPU.[84]

Why does the Law of Accelerating Returns exist? It's for the same reason Tim Urban's time traveler would experience shock much sooner than in the past. We have accumulated more knowledge, expanding our collective long-term memory. The more information stored in our long-term memory, the more we can draw upon to facilitate creative breakthroughs and significant discoveries. As the Talmud teaches, the 101st learning of something is incomparable to the 100th.

Reflection

There are a few certainties in American politics that hold true across any era. One of these is that every candidate, whether running for town council or the presidency, will express his commitment to education. This declaration is typically followed by an explanation of why his education policies are superior. Moses would be delighted to see that his once-radical vision of the importance of education has become deeply ingrained in American culture, expectations, and aspirations. It's also beneficial when education policies are clearly articulated and debated, as they can be the deciding factor between successful and unsuccessful educational experiences for many students.

While education policies are crucial, education *principles*—which can inform a wide range of policies—are also deeply consequential. These principles shape teaching in all settings, whether at home by parents or in schools by teachers. The correct principles are found in the Torah and validated by contemporary social science. True to the nature of the Torah, our ultimate guide, these principles are simple to understand and implement.

A teacher should be excited by his subject and convey his enthusiasm to his student, especially when the student asks a good question. Our family does this at our Passover Seder, when we ask the guests to celebrate a child who asks a good question by throwing a marshmallow across the room at him!

A teacher should recognize the sacred uniqueness of each student and tailor his instruction to match those interests. For example, if a student is a baseball enthusiast, the teacher might teach statistics using batting averages and ERAs, and suggest the student read and write a report on *Moneyball*.

A teacher should realize that his most important lesson will be instructed through how he lives his life. A teacher may do a lot of things right—he may convey abundant material to the student in just the way the student learns best, he may teach with infectious enthusiasm, he may inspire probing questions. But if one of those questions is, "Why does our teacher behave that way?"—if the teacher is not a text-*person*, he will inevitably fail.

A teacher should use these principles to actualize an additional principle: that knowledge begets knowledge. The teacher can, by enthusiastically teaching with regard to the sacred uniqueness of each student, enable the student to learn *a lot* of facts. When a student knows a lot about a particular subject, it is easier for him to learn more about that subject. When a student knows a lot about *multiple* subjects, he will be primed for being able to realize that A (a fact about one subject) combined with B (a fact about another subject) yields C (a creative breakthrough).

The teacher will likely have to reject a lot of bad educational ideas to fulfill the promise of the Torah and social science. The legacy of Mr. Rousseau's *Emile* may take the name of minimally guided education, child-centric learning, or discovery-based education—all of which may sound appealing and attractive. Whatever it is called, this method accounts for—among many other things—the horror experienced by many during Covid when they discovered how poorly their young children read. One who is devoted to systematic learning will fulfill the promise of "If you have heard, you will hear," and position himself to be the Wayne Gretzky of his chosen profession.

31

When God Weeps and College Students Learn Nothing

The Torah and Science of Education's Limits

The Torah, through Moses, invented the idea of mass education and universal literacy. Our great guidebook continually emphasized its existential importance by embedding it deeply in Jewish thought and practice. The rabbis, acting accordingly, constructed a Jewish life centered around education.

But that does not tell the full story of the Torah and education. As if channeling its teaching on marriage, where God creates Eve for Adam as a "help against him," the Torah creates a companion for education. It can be called the Limits of Education. The Torah's description and development of this idea can be categorized in three ways.

Limits of Education I: Why God Saves Only Rabbi Elazar

The Talmud articulates the Limits of Education with stark clarity: "One who concerns himself solely with [study of] Torah is as one who has no God."[1]

Another section of the Talmud shows just how deeply inculcated this notion was among our ancient sages. Around 135 CE, rabbis Hanina and Elazar were arrested by the Roman authorities for crimes related to their teaching of Torah. Rabbi Elazar was arrested, the Talmud tells us, "on five charges," while Rabbi Hanina was arrested on one.

Yet, Rabbi Hanina told his colleague that he (Rabbi Elazar) was more likely to receive divine intervention and be saved. Rabbi Hanina explained,

"You concerned yourself with both Torah and *gmilut hasadim* (acts of kindness) whereas I concerned myself solely with Torah." Rabbi Hanina's premonition proved true. The Romans killed him, but spared Rabbi Elazar.[2]

Rabbi Hanina knew that he had lived suboptimally not only because of his Torah study, but also in comparison to the life choices of other great sages. As discussed in the previous chapter, our ancient sages—and their successors in rabbinic leadership—had secular occupations. These occupations deepened their Torah understanding just as their Torah understanding informed their work. Their engagement in the everyday activities of society gave them opportunities for frequent acts of kindness and allowed them to live a full Jewish life, neither of which a life of full-time study would allow.

This ancient teaching would become manifest in a classic Jewish (true) story. Rabbi Schneur Zalman of Liadi (known as the Ba'al Ha-Tanya), who founded the Chabad movement in Judaism, was studying Torah in the end room of his railroad flat in the early 1800s. His son (Dovber Schneuri, the Mittler Rebbe) was studying in the next room, and his infant grandson (Menachem Mendel, who became the Tzemach Tzedek) was sleeping in the other room. The Ba'al Ha-Tanya heard the baby cry and went to tend to the child. On his way back, he stopped by the room of his son. His son stated that he, immersed in his studying, had not heard the baby crying.

It was then the Ba'al Ha-Tanya gave his son advice that would resonate through the generations. He said, "If someone is studying Torah and fails to hear a baby's cry, there is something very wrong with his learning."

This spirit would inspire a sage in the next century, who led a very different kind of Orthodox Judaism. In 1968, Rav Yehuda Amital founded the Gush Yeshiva in Israel. He saw that the original plans for the Beit Midrash (study hall) in the Yeshiva did not have windows. The architects had apparently believed that windows would be a distraction for the students immersed in learning. Rav Amital ordered the installation of large windows, explaining that a Beit Midrash must always enable the students to hear the cries from outside.[3]

Limits of Education II: When God Cries

The Talmud specifies that there are "three types of people for whom the Holy One, Blessed be He, cries every day."[4]

One of these is "a leader who lords over the community." It is easy to understand why God would mourn when one of his children abuses his power over others.

Another is "one who is able to engage in Torah study and does not engage in it." It is similarly easy to understand—consistent with the Torah's emphasis on education—why God would mourn the loss of potential when a promising student does not engage in Torah learning.

The third reason why God cries every day is for "one who is *unable* to engage in Torah study and nevertheless endeavors and engages in it." Given that the earliest Jewish educational systems required universal education for children as young as six or seven, this must apply to those doing what we would call higher education.

The third source of God's tears accords with King Solomon's instruction that education should be designed with regard to the sacred individuality of each student. God loves and commands Torah study and acknowledges that there are many people who are not constituted to pursue it full time. God has given these people other talents and gifts, which they should develop and deploy to contribute to society.

Limits of Education III: An Elixir of Life . . . or a Deadly Poison

In Genesis 4, we are introduced to Lamech, a fifth-generation descendant of Adam and Eve. Lamech has quite a family. One of his grandchildren invented "stringed instruments and pipes"—in other words, culture. Another of his grandchildren invented "tools out of bronze and iron"—a reference to technology. How does Lamech, the progenitor of these great leaps in culture and technology, respond? Lamech, we learn in Genesis 4:23, speaks to his wives:

> Adah and Zilhah, listen to me;
> wives of Lamech, hear my words.
> I have killed a man for wounding me
> a young man for injuring me

The Author of the Torah thus introduces us to one of the crucial lessons of education: One can create an environment of extraordinary cultural and technological advancement and take pride not in its development—but in murdering people.

This characteristic, we learn in Numbers 22, is not unique to Lamech. Balaam, a gentile sorcerer, is dispatched by King Balak to destroy the Jews and is intent on fulfilling his mission. The ancient commentary, the *Sifrei*, says that Balaam was a prophet as talented as Moses. Moreover, Balaam fully understood the sovereignty and power of God. Yet, he uses his knowledge and intelligence to devise new ways to destroy the Jews. He would have succeeded if it were not for the heroism of Pinchas (as discussed in the chapter of this book on bystanding).[5]

The problem of Lamech and Balaam seems to be on Moses's mind during his parting speech. In Deuteronomy 4:39, Moses instructs the people of Israel regarding the Torah's dictates to "know and return it to your heart." This passage is so important that it is recited by observant Jews thrice daily as part of the *alenu* prayer. Why is it so important to both know *and* "return it to your heart"? What does Moses even mean by it?

In a 1971 sermon, the twentieth-century sage Rabbi Norman Lamm explained, "In Hebrew, *daat* [knowledge] means more than just intellectual cognition. 'Knowledge' in the Biblical scheme means total knowledge, which includes the physical, spiritual, the material, the psychological, and the intellectual. It is a quality of the heart that necessarily leads one to act righteously."[6]

The Jewish tradition makes very clear just how distinct and unrelated learning and righteous behavior are. In the Talmud, Rabbi Benah, drawing from two verses in Proverbs, says that Torah learning can either be "an elixir of life" or "a deadly poison." The Talmud also refers to people whose substantial learning is not reflected in their character as "book carrying donkeys."[7]

The eighteenth-century sage Elijah ben Solomon Zalman, known as the Vilna Gaon, noted that the Torah is so often compared to water. He explained that water makes anything grow, from the most fruitful trees to poisonous plants.[8]

The idea that Torah knowledge can be a "deadly poison" refers to a case where one's knowledge covers for the deficiencies of his heart. But this is not the only limit of education suggested by the Jewish tradition. Our ancient sages were also concerned with other abuses of Torah knowledge. In the ancient work Pirkei Avot (Ethics of our Fathers), we read: "Rabbi Zadok said, 'Do not make them [words of Torah] a crown for self-exaltation, nor a spade with which to dig.' So too Hillel used to say, 'And he that puts the crown to his own use shall perish.'"[9]

In other words, one can learn immense amounts of Torah, and use that learning to show off, justify one's previous conclusions, or advance one's self-interest.

Reflection

Until very recently, the assumption that attending a four-year college is right for almost all Americans went unquestioned, unchallenged, and even unconsidered. This assumption was eloquently articulated by university officials, supported by politicians, and funded by parents, philanthropists, taxpayers, and the students themselves. Meanwhile, the voice of the Torah—the book that invented the idea of universal education and continually emphasized its importance—was sounding two warnings. First: It matters *what* students are learning, both academically and morally. Second: A baseline of education is for everyone, but full-time "higher" learning is not.

As of this writing in 2024, the Torah's philosophy is having a moment against the "higher education for all" view of Presidents Obama and Biden. Is this because students and parents have determined, perhaps from persistent debt, that college is a terrible financial investment for many people? Is it because they have realized how little so many students learn in college? Is it because they acknowledge how college students spend their time, and have concluded that the lack of studying (and abundance of partying) suggests that there are better uses for this crucial time in a person's life? Is it because they realized that there are now many ways to learn skills, and that a college education is often an inefficient way to do so? Is it because they have concluded that some subjects are not worthy of studying—such as "Bodies, Gender, Sexualities: Critical Perspectives" (Amherst), "Black Life. Trans Life." (Northwestern), "The Gendered Workplace" (Cornell), and "Spectacular Sex" (Williams)?

Surely, some parents and students have answered yes to each question. Whatever the answer in each case, one thing is clear from Mr. Tough's data: Americans, like the Author of the Torah, value education, and are coming to appreciate its limits.

This appreciation both begins a discussion and complicates a decision. In the era when the American expectation was that every young person should graduate from high school and go straight to college, the only questions that families faced was what college the student should attend and how they should finance it.

Now, the decision of what a young person should do after graduating high school is far more nuanced. Consistent with King Solomon's advice, "Educate a child according to *his* way," there are no rules or formulas that can be easily applied to help make that decision. But there are some questions that every family can ask that can guide them toward an answer.

These include:

- Is the student sufficiently inspired by academics and self-motivated to study, that he is likely to become deeply engaged in the intellectual pursuits that should be at the center of university life?
- Does the student envision a career where higher education is a genuine necessity (such as being a litigator, a physician, or a physicist)? Or does he envision a career where a higher education is not necessary (such as with most roles in the trades and even in business)?
- Am I, as a parent, teaching my child to respect people based on their character and contributions rather than their academic pedigree? There is *no reason* why professors should be respected more than plumbers. But in a culture that places no limits on the value of education, they invariably are, as parents in such a society would generally be much prouder to say "My daughter is a professor" than "My daughter is a plumber." Young people, in consultation with older people who love and guide them, will be better off if their decision is not distorted by an indefensible sense as to how they will earn the respect and admiration of those they care about.
- The perversities (drinking, partying, sexual abuse) that characterize much of American college life are not prevalent in Israel. This is likely because Israelis enter college after two or three years of military service. Might the student be better off doing something meaningful and nonacademic (from military service to construction work) in the years immediately following high school? If a student and his family decide to send him to college, what should he

study there? A parent should not feel satisfied or proud because his child is "going to Harvard." A student interested in the Humanities who goes to Harvard and studies Queer Theory will get one kind of education. The same student who goes to Harvard and studies Shakespeare will get an entirely different kind of education. How will the college culture, peer groups, and choice of academic concentration influence a student's character development? One student can attend an "elite" college and emerge with a victim mentality, convinced that the world is divided into oppressors and oppressed, and that, as a member of an "oppressed group," the world owes him. His roommate can attend the same college and emerge with an understanding of complexity, a sense of gratitude, a feeling of obligation, and a determination to develop real skills that he can deploy in service of the less fortunate. A student's experience in college will be mediated by his attitude and influenced by his choice of friends—both of which should be of great interest to anyone who wants their child to have a valuable experience.

The more that these types of questions are asked, the better chance God will not have to weep for a student who is engaged in full-time learning who should not be.

32

Why God Hates the Tower of Babel and HBCUs Produce So Many STEM Graduates

The Torah and Science of Diversity

Babbling in Unison: The Destructive Power of Uniformity

By Genesis 10, the world had just been repopulated in the generations following the great flood that destroyed all people except for Noah and his family. What became of the post-flood people?

In Genesis 11:1, we learn, "The whole earth was of one language and of a common set of words." This seems amazing! Seemingly perfect unity achieved, and the Torah has barely begun.

There is something in the text of the verse that foreshadows God's displeasure with the situation. Why would Genesis 11:1 say that everyone spoke the same language *and* used the same "set of words"? There must be a difference between the two, and it must be of sufficient importance to warrant inclusion at the start of this very short and important story.

We do not have to wait long to find out. In Genesis 11:3, the Torah says, "The people said to each other, 'Let us brick bricks.'" This is odd for two reasons.

First, all of the people are saying the same thing to each other. This is not how conversations work. In a conversation, one person says something and the other person responds by saying something different. Why would these people be saying the same thing to each other? The text has already told us. They used one "set of words." A supposed dialogue that uses just "one set of words" is not a dialogue at all. It is an exercise in voicing an approved idea, with no entrance point for another "set of words" that would convey different ideas or perspectives.[1]

Second, "Let us brick bricks" is even stranger in Hebrew than it is in English. It is a tongue twister. Why, in the context of people who speak with a common "set of words," would the Author of the Torah speak with tongue twisters? To teach us the irony of linguistic and ideological uniformity. When people speak with a common "set of words," they may seem unified, but are just mimicking and repeating each other without thinking. They sacrifice the opportunity of conversation, which is an exchange of ideas that leads to growth and progress. And the result of speaking "the same set of words" is as ridiculous, and confusing, as a tongue twister.

Words, even confusing and ridiculous ones, create reality. The Torah tells us what happened when people spoke with a "common set of words." The people decide to build a tower "with its top in the heavens" and a desire to "make a name for ourselves, lest we be dispersed across the whole earth" This is a direct repudiation of God's instruction—first to Adam and then to Noah—to "fill the earth" (Genesis 1:28; 9:1; 11:4).

What was the point of building a tower that would reach the heavens? Rashi suggests that it was to reach God—an endeavor that should have seemed ridiculous and problematic to anyone giving it a moment's thought. Did anyone in Genesis 11 suggest that God is everywhere, not just "in the heavens"? Did anyone point out the ridiculousness of working to build a tower where they would be able to knock on God's door and say hello? Did anyone object and say that they should build a name for God, and not for themselves? Did anyone question the wisdom of a building project designed to prevent being "dispersed across the whole earth" when God had specifically commanded—twice—that people fill it? There is no indication anyone raised any of these obvious questions, teaching us that uniformity of language leads to uniformity of thought and not to unity.

Accordingly, the people begin building the structure, which becomes known as the Tower of Babel. Beyond the desire to reach the heavens, the builders of the tower, we are told, wanted to make for themselves *a* name. Yet, the previous chapter of Genesis (Genesis 10) is one long list of names, most of whom have no role in the Torah other than being named. That chapter is so monotonous that many readers just skip over it. Indeed, the fact that one guy is named Togarmah and another Sabetka seems to be inconsequential. But the fact that each individual has a name—the quintessential signifier of specialness and uniqueness—is itself part of the message. The people traded names for "*a* name," indicating that they opted to jettison their individuality in favor of a group identity. It is what Rav Joseph Soloveitchik identified as "uniformity," which he sharply distinguished from "unity."[2]

This, as Rav Soloveitchik wrote, is deeply consequential. A society that values uniformity is one that "does not believe that each individual has his own approach to life and his own unique talents." And a society that denies individuality and discourages variety will, as rabbis Shlomo Riskin and Michael Hattin independently identify, become totalitarian.[3] It does not seem to have occurred to anyone, in all the commentary on Babel over thousands of years, that the builders shared ideas because they were all men of the same ethnicity. Their uniform thought is a construct of their own making.

God's response is telling. He does not knock down the tower, indicating that the structure is not God's main concern. He does not, as he often does, criticize the people for sinning—as if there is another point he wants to emphasize. Instead, he confuses their language and disperses them throughout the world. This change in language and location will inevitably lead to significant differences in perceptions, experiences, culture, perspective, and much else. These differences constitute, in modern parlance, *diversity*. Diversity, we learn, is God's chosen alternative to the kind of uniformity he hates.

Still, one question remains: Why doesn't God knock down the tower? Perhaps God is being careful not to center the tower in the narrative. The people, having decided to make "a name for themselves" using "a common set of words," could have easily done something other than make a tower. Whatever it was would have been just as stupid and wrong. Intellectual uniformity, God is saying, is the root of all kinds of bad things. The cure is not knocking down a tower, but instituting diversity.

The distinction between unity and uniformity that the Torah introduces in Genesis is amplified in Exodus. In Exodus 19:6, God gives us our ultimate mission: to become "a kingdom of priests and a holy nation." The fact that it says *a* holy nation, signifying oneness, is crucial. Our goal is unity, not uniformity, and, as God makes clear in Genesis 11, it can be achieved through diversity.

This concept—that unity requires diversity—seems counterintuitive and even paradoxical or contradictory. But this is the Torah, where there is always logic. So, how might we achieve unity *through* diversity? Again, the Torah, our great guidebook, answers very clearly.

The Tabernacle and the Camp of Israel: Unity-Oriented Diversity

The most important place for the Jews in the desert was the Tabernacle. Constructed by the people in Exodus, it is the central place in the Torah of covenantal rites, worship, sacrifice, and revelation for all Jews. It was the place where God wanted to "dwell within [our] midst." It is the quintessentially unifying structure.

In Numbers 1, the Tabernacle is fully operational. God orders a census of the Jewish nation. A census, which attributes one number to the entire nation, is also an expression of unity. One would expect a census count to be straightforward, with the administrative authority just counting heads. But this is not what God instructs. Instead, he tells Moses to have everyone counted "by the number of names, every male by their polls." And the precise term for "count" is also instructive. It is to "raise up by the heads." The nation, God insists, must consist of *individuals*, with each person's individuality being emphasized as part of the collective.

How, practically speaking, can unity be created from individuality? We do not have to wait long to learn.

In Numbers 2:2, God instructs Moses and Aaron to be sure that the Children of Israel encamp around the Tabernacle, "each man by his banner according to the insignia of their father's household." God then tells Moses and Aaron where he wants each tribe to be seated around the Tabernacle. There were assigned seats, and the assignments were determined by tribe.[4]

Thus, we learn *how* unity can be achieved through diversity. The Tabernacle of the Testimony is situated in the center of the camp. *After* people have a unifying force in the center of the camp, they are counted individually and the banners signifying their group identities are raised. God, it is clear, wants us to achieve unity through diversity by orienting our differences around a shared ideal and toward a unifying aspiration.

Given how complicated people are and given how many kinds of differences we have, this raises some questions. What types of difference (or diversity) lead toward divine unity? How can we direct our differences toward the common goal, and achieve unity through diversity?

The Torah offers very clear and instructive guidance.

Arguing with God: Diversity of Viewpoint

The first type of diversity was revealed at the Tower of Babel. God changes the language and location of the people at Babel after witnessing that their togetherness produced one mindset. The opposite of one mindset at Babel is many mindsets. This is known, in modern parlance, as viewpoint diversity.

The essence of viewpoint diversity is disagreement. How does God, who desires unity, regard disagreement—a core component of strife, discord, and division? God answers with an example, provided just seven chapters after Babel.

In Genesis 18, God decides to destroy the cities of Sodom and Gomorrah, whose sins are "very grievous." Abraham approaches God and says, "Far be it from You to do such a thing, to bring death upon the innocent as well as the guilty, so that innocent and guilty fare alike. Far be it from You! Shall not the Judge of all the earth deal justly?"

"Far be it from You to do such a thing"! How does God respond to the audacity of Abraham that seems to amount to insubordination? He engages in a negotiation with Abraham, and ultimately agrees to save the city if there are just ten righteous people there. God, we see, welcomes disagreement.

In Genesis 25, we are introduced to Jacob and Esau, the twin sons of Isaac and Rebecca. Jacob, we learn, "dwells in tents." As noted in the chapter on education, the use of the plural "tents," instead of "tent," is instructive. Rashi says that the plural of "tents" indicates that Jacob learned from multiple teachers, presumably with a range of viewpoints.[5]

In Exodus 32, Moses ascends Mount Sinai to receive the Ten Commandments. The people respond to Moses's absence by constructing a Golden Calf and having an orgy on their idol. God says that he wants to destroy the people and start over with Moses. Moses responds in an even more audacious manner than Abraham. He tells God to forgive the people—and, if God refuses, to "blot me out of your Torah!" God responds by acquiescing to Moses's demand and forgiving the people.

One might say that God accepts vigorous disagreement from Abraham and Moses because they are his closest and most-beloved partners. How about ordinary people?

In Numbers 9, a group of nameless men have an issue. They are aggrieved that they cannot celebrate the Pesach holiday due to being in a state of ritual impurity. These ordinary men take their complaint directly to Moses. They say, "Why should we be diminished by not offering Hashem's offering in the appointed time among the children of Israel?" (Numbers 9:7).

Moses, apparently thinking this question is too important and too difficult to answer himself, takes it to God. God tells Moses that the men are right. He decrees a backup holiday, Pesach Sheni (the second Pesach), which can be celebrated by people who could not celebrate the first one. But that's not all. In granting the request of these ordinary men, God essentially says: "You don't know how right you are!" In articulating the laws of the new festival, God includes other potential celebrants—not just those who are contaminated by a corpse, but also those who are on a "distant road."

Who are those on a "distant road"? In the traditional cantillation, there is an accent over the phrase "distant road," indicating that the beneficiaries of this holiday are not only those who are physically distant. It includes those who are at the threshold of the celebration and, for whatever reason, cannot bring themselves to join.[6]

In these stories from Genesis, Exodus, and Numbers, God not only shows how he welcomes disagreement and cultivates viewpoint diversity. He also shows its purpose. If God embodies truth, and viewpoint diversity can lead even God to change his mind, then viewpoint diversity must be the way for us to search for and arrive at truth.

The imperative of viewpoint diversity continues to animate Torah-based teaching long after Deuteronomy concludes. The two most important academies in the Talmud are Beit Hillel and Beit Shammai. They disagreed on almost everything. The Talmud states that Beit Hillel and Beit Shammai once disagreed for three years over an issue of Jewish law. The specific issue is lost to history, but the ruling is not.

A Divine Voice emerged. It proclaimed, "Both these and those are the words of the living God. However, the *halacha* [law] is in accordance with the opinion of Beit Hillel." There is a right and a wrong when it comes to application of the law—but even the view that is not accepted legally contains insights and truths that can enlighten and improve the world.[7]

The indispensability of disagreement, the core of viewpoint diversity, became a key component of Jewish moral and social thought. Rabbi Nachman of Breslov, the eighteenth-century Ukrainian sage, proclaimed, "A disagreement is a kind of creation of the world." And there was nothing theoretical about this. The ancient Jewish court, the Sanhedrin, had at least twenty-three judges for capital cases. If *all* of the judges voted to convict, the defendant was acquitted. Why? Because, the ancient sages concluded, unanimity is so abnormal that it could only be the result of judicial collusion or error.[8]

One of the great works of Jewish law is the *Arukh HaShulchan*, authored by the nineteenth-century sage Yechiel Michel Epstein. In the introduction to his work, Rav Epstein explores the Jewish value of disagreement:

> And all the disputes of the Tannaic, Amoraic, Gaonic and later sages are, in truth, to the one who understands the matter correctly—the words of the living God. And they all have a place in Halacha. The exact opposite [of what you may think regarding disputes] is true: This is the glory of our holy and pure Torah. And the entire Torah is called a song [in Deuteronomy 31], and the glory of a song is when the voices are different from each other (harmony), and this is the essence of the pleasantness. And whoever wanders in the sea of the Talmud—will see all types of pleasures in all the different voices from each other.[9]

It is this sentiment that inspired the twentieth-century sage Abraham Isaac Kook, the religious leader of early modern Zionism. Rav Kook thought a lot about the messianic era and considered the formation of a modern state of Israel to be a major part of its unfolding. Many of Rav Kook's contemporaries disagreed. They saw no way to accommodate the opinions and approaches of the secular Zionists, with whom they disagreed completely on basically all religious matters (broadly defined). Rav Kook had a response: "It is precisely the multiplicity of opinions which derive from variegated souls and backgrounds which enriches wisdom and brings about its enlargement. In the end all matters will be properly understood and it will be recognized that it was impossible for the structure of peace to be built without those trends which appeared to be in conflict."[10]

The coming of the Messiah, the ultimate manifestation of unity, is only possible through a diversity of viewpoint so vigorous that it will *appear* as conflict.

Diversity of Skillset

In Genesis 6, God decides to destroy the world with a flood. He decides to save Noah and his family—commanding his designated survivor to build an enormous ark that will accommodate the family and a huge number of animals for the duration of the flood. Generations of biblical commentators have sought to determine why God selects Noah—centering around the question: Was Noah objectively righteous, or was he just righteous in comparison to everyone else? Rabbi David Wolpe suggests that God chose Noah for something other than his righteousness altogether. God selects Noah, at least in part, because he is good at building things. An equally righteous person who was not capable of building the ark could not have been God's partner here. The fact that this explanation might not be not readily apparent educates the reader about something he lacks—an appreciation for a skillset that he, and others around him, might lack.[11]

An appreciation of different skillsets, however, is not something that God lacks. In Genesis 33, the Torah tells us about the monumental reunion between Jacob and Esau after years of separation. Jacob, the intellectual who "dwells in tents," had been forced to flee the murderous wrath of his twin brother Esau, described as a "master hunter" and "man of the field." As they brace for the long-awaited encounter, Jacob, we learn, "raised his eyes" and saw his brother. Four verses later, we learn Esau's reaction. Esau "raised his eyes."

Why do both brothers raise their eyes? It cannot be a physical description. Either one is shorter than the other and must raise his eyes, or they are the same height and neither would need to raise his eyes. What is certain is that each would not need to raise his eyes to see the other.

The Torah must therefore be referring to a philosophical raising of the eyes and teaching us how people should relate to each other. Jacob and Esau each looked up to each other as greater in some way. Each saw the other as having a quality or skill that he, himself, lacked. Jacob likely came to appreciate Esau's skills as a hunter, and Esau came to appreciate Jacob's skills as an intellectual. Their appreciation of each other's skills, and of the concept of skillset diversity, enabled the reconciliation of the most fraught relationship.

In Exodus 31, God directly addresses skillset diversity. It is here that God provides Moses with a list of professions to include in the building of the Tabernacle. They include weavers, perfumers, artists, metal workers, carvers, and engravers. Why would God list so many professions individually, when he could have trusted Moses and his team to figure out who was needed to perform the task?

God explains, "I have granted skills to all who are skillful." Everyone who is skillful at *anything* has a gift from God.

And each person's gift comes with *responsibility*. The twentieth-century sage Rebbe Menachem Mendel Schneerson noted the Talmudic teaching that "all Israel are guarantors for one another."[12] Often, this phrase is understood to mean that each Jew is responsible for the well-being of others in the community. While that is true, the Rebbe noted that the specific language here warrants additional explanation.

What, the Rebbe asked, qualifies one to guarantee another? Anyone who has guaranteed the rent on a child's apartment knows: The guarantor must be wealthier than the person whose obligation he is guaranteeing. The Rebbe said, "If the Talmud says that *all* Jews serve as guarantors to each other [sic], this means that in every Jew, there is a quality in which he or she is superior to all others." It is incumbent upon every Jew to identify what he is the best at, cultivate that skill, and use it in service of something greater than himself. Similarly, it is incumbent upon every Jew to accord others who develop and contribute their skills the appropriate respect.[13]

It is from the Torah's teaching on diversity of skillset that we can understand its doctrine of respect. Respect is not accorded vertically by profession. It is allocated horizontally by qualities that can be realized in any profession—such as humility, honesty, industriousness, and productivity. Divine unity can be achieved when each person hones his unique skills and makes contributions based on them within a society that appreciates and values each skill.

We see this notion at work in Numbers 4:49, where God tells Moses to count the Levites who work as priest-teachers in the Temple. The Torah uses very specific language to describe the count. "He [Moses] counted them at the word of God, through Moses, each and every man over his work and over his burden; and his count [was] as God had commanded Moses."

The multiple references to God in this one verse teach us that this particular way of counting is important to God. What could be so important to God? The answer is provided in the other intriguing part of this verse. The text is explicit that God wants Moses to count the Levite workers by acknowledging "each and every man."

The thirteenth-century sage Moses ben Nachman (known as Nachmanides) wrote that the emphasis on the singularity of each individual worker indicates how God regards each contribution. Each individual, Nachmanides reasoned, has a distinct and divinely provided skill that he should appreciate, cultivate, and contribute. The singers should be singers, the clothiers should be clothiers, and the doormen should be doormen—with everyone comfortable and confident in his role and secure that his contributions are integral for the functioning of the sacred Tabernacle.[14]

It is also instructive that the Torah emphasizes this kind of counting must be done for the Levites. The Levites were the spiritual leaders and the moral examples for the nation. They were, in Rabbi Abraham Joshua Heschel's term, the original *textpeople*: those who have to teach by the example they set. If the Levites were to count workers in the Tabernacle by emphasizing the distinct contributions of each person, then the rest of the Jewish nation, then and now, should do the same.

Moses learned this lesson well. In Deuteronomy 33, he delivers his final blessings to each of the tribes. He gives every tribe a singular blessing, except for the two tribes blessed in 33:18–19. Moses says, "Rejoice, O Zebulun, in your excursions, and Issachar in your tents."

Zebulun, we learn, is a tribe of international businessmen—while Issachar is a tribe of scholars. Moses stipulated that these two tribes, which have very different skills and missions, should be blessed together.

Diversity of Approach

In Exodus 3, God gives Moses his most important assignment. Moses is to be God's partner in liberating the Jews from slavery in Egypt. The first thing that God must do is help Moses articulate the message to the enslaved Jews. God instructs, "Say to the Israelites, 'The God of your fathers, the God of Abraham, the God of Isaac and the God of Jacob, has sent me to you.'"

One of the principles of Jewish biblical understanding is that every word in the Torah is meaningful. Why, then, would God speak of "the God *of* Abraham, the God *of* Isaac and the God *of* Jacob" rather than the "God of Abraham, Isaac, and Jacob?" Indeed, why does God need to list them at all? Surely the people know who their forefathers are!

The same question is raised twelve chapters later.

In Exodus 15:2, the Exodus has succeeded. The Jews, who had just crossed the Red Sea, are a unified nation, and express their solidarity and their gratitude in song. They sing, "This is my God and I will glorify him."

Why—particularly while singing at this moment of unity—do the Jews refer to the Lord as "*my* God" and not "*our* God"? For the same reason that the Lord is referred to as the God *of* Abraham, the God *of* Isaac, and the God *of* Jacob. There is one God, with whom everyone has a unique, distinct, and sacred relationship.

This notion of diversity of approach is so important that God emphasizes it just five verses later. In Exodus 20:15, God gives the Torah to the Jews. It is a moment so spectacular that "all of the people saw the sounds." The awesomeness of the occasion discombobulated our senses to the extent that we could actually *see* sounds.

The ancient commentary known as the Targum Yonatan reflects on the fact that "sounds" is in the plural. The Targum Yonatan writes that when God gave the Torah, everyone heard his or her own sound. God gave us one Torah, and everyone a customized portal of entry.[15]

In Numbers 27:16, Moses calls upon God to choose the leader by saying, "Let the Lord, the God of the spirits of all flesh, set a man over the congregation." This is the first time he calls upon God in his capacity as "the God of the spirits of all flesh." What could be meant by this original and strange locution?

Rashi explains that Moses was asking God to use his unique knowledge of every human personality to choose the right leader for the Jews. The leader, Moses was instructing us, is tasked with appreciating and harnessing the diversity amongst his followers for the benefit of the whole.

The same celebration of the diversity of approach is evident in Judaism's most important post-biblical book, the Haggadah. The Haggadah, which guides us through the Passover Seder, is a Greatest Hits of Jewish Thought, curated to enable us to live happier, more fulfilling and meaningful lives. One of the most famous parts of the Haggadah is the section concerning the four sons, which serve as archetypes for different modes of questioning. If the night were longer, the Haggadah could have listed four thousand sons. What is important is that there are multiple sons.

These sons have very different questions, reflecting their diversity of attitudes, styles, and approaches. By including multiple sons, the Haggadah teaches us every year anew that there is no one way to seek God. There are people who are more musical and more mystical, more intellectual and more prayerful, more creative and more mechanical. These types, and infinitely more, all constitute the diversity of approaches to God that he expects and desires.

The Torah's respect for diversity of approach also informs the Jewish relationship to other religions. We do not seek to convert anyone to Judaism because we believe that God regards other faiths as legitimate access points to him. God does not want everyone to be Jewish. He wants everyone to be righteous and to connect with him through different channels. It is a staple of Jewish theology that the righteous of all the nations have a "share in the world to come." The Jewish messianic vision is expressed by the prophet Isaiah, who said:

> And foreigners who bind themselves to the Lord, to minister to him, to love the name of the Lord, and to be his servants, all who keep the Sabbath without desecrating it and who hold fast to my covenant, these I will bring to my holy mountain and give them joy in my house of prayer. Their burnt offerings and sacrifices will be accepted on my altar; for my house will be called a house of prayer for all nations. (Isaiah 56:6–7)

The Jewish messianic vision, therefore, is one where "all the nations" come together, with all of their differences and disagreements, around their shared source of allegiance to the one true God.

The Absent Diversity

The twenty-first-century sage Rabbi Jonathan Sacks noted that the Torah speaks as much in its absences as it does in its content. "Recall," Rabbi Sacks wrote, "the famous remark of Sherlock Holmes."

> "I draw your attention," he said to Dr Watson, "to the curious incident of the dog at night." "But the dog did nothing at night," said Watson. "That," said Holmes, "is the curious incident."[16]

Torah understanding, per Rabbi Sacks, often requires an attention to what the sacred text does *not* say. As it pertains to diversity, there is an enormous, and enormously significant, omission.

In Numbers 11, freed from Egyptian slavery, we complain about the miraculous food provided by God and express a longing to return to our former slave masters. In an effort to manage the people and prevent a further descent into rebellion, God commands Moses to "assemble for Me seventy men of the elders of Israel, whom you know to be the people's elders and officers, and you shall take them to the Tent of Meeting, and they shall stand there with you."

This command is intriguing. The biblical Israelites were organized according to tribal membership. Tribal affiliation accounted for how we camped in the desert, inherited land, brought sacrifices, and would eventually settle in the land of Israel. There were thirteen tribes as Joseph was subdivided into Ephraim and Manasseh. The math is telling. Seventy (the number of elders whom Moses said would govern) is not divisible by thirteen. This means that there could not be equal tribal representation among the elders. There is not even a mention of this being an issue. All we have is a number that precludes anyone even trying for equality of representation.

The successor body to the seventy elders was the Sanhedrin, which governed the post-biblical Jewish nation. This body had educational, political, and judiciary powers. It was the Congress, the Supreme Court, the electoral college, and more, all in one. It had seventy-one members—again, a number that is not divisible by thirteen.

As with great political bodies everywhere, there were many requirements for serving on the Sanhedrin. A member had to have children in his care—either biological offspring or students. A member had to be able to argue both sides of a matter. A member had to be a Torah scholar with significant knowledge of math and science. A member was required to be faithful, incorruptible, wise, humble, and well-respected. A member had to understand sorcery, to refute quackery. A member had to be physically imposing. And he had to speak multiple languages so that he could hear testimony from witnesses directly.[17]

There is a dog that does not bark amidst all of these requirements. Despite the importance of the tribal system in ancient Jewish life, there is no requirement that any (let alone all) tribes have representation on the Sanhedrin. This is striking. One might think that at least the Levites, designated in the Torah as the priest-teachers, would be guaranteed a spot on the Sanhedrin. Maimonides, in his Laws of the Sanhedrin, said, "It is a [special] mitzvah to have priests and Levites included in the Great Sanhedrin" but was explicit that it was not required to have any for the court to be valid.[18]

There was no discussion, let alone requirement, regarding representation from any of the other tribes either. Consequently, the Sanhedrin could have consisted of all Simeonites or no Simeonites, all Levites or no Levites. Even though the society of ancient Israel was tribally based, tribal identity was completely irrelevant when it came to membership on the Sanhedrin. All that mattered was whether an individual was wise, incorruptible, multilingual, knowledgeable about Torah and secular subjects, projected authority, and personally invested in the next generation.[19]

The rabbis in the Talmudic era vigorously debated seemingly everything, from whether one could urinate in public to what constituted a permitted textile. Consequently, one might think that the rabbis might have debated whether the Sanhedrin should embody tribal diversity. A rabbi could have said that it was important that each tribe be proportionally represented so that the young people would have role models to whom they could relate.

Yet no one seems to have even *suggested* any notion of tribal diversity with regard to service in the national body.

Given the Torah's emphasis on the value of diversity since the Tower of Babel, why would it not include any provision for tribal diversity on the Sanhedrin? It seems to have never come up, so we cannot know for sure.

Perhaps the answer is revealed, however, through the story of Korach's Rebellion. Korach, we learn in Numbers 16, is a Levite who instigated and led the most serious rebellion against Moses in the Bible. Even though Korach forms his following with a significant group of Levites and the neighboring Reubenites, there are plenty of people from those tribes—including his own sons—who opted out. Given that Korach's Rebellion shows that there can be diversity *within* a group, it would make no sense to require each group's members to be represented in the nation's main political body. A man could not be expected to rule, or even think, a certain way just because he was from a particular tribe.

Whatever the reason, the exquisitely detailed, thoughtfully conceived, and plentiful requirements for membership on the Sanhedrin do not include tribal membership. Tribal affiliation was simply irrelevant when it came to selecting who would govern and judge the people. We thus have the Torah's template for diversity: God conspicuously omits tribal diversity and seeks diversity of viewpoint, skillset, and approach—all in service of unity and as a bulwark against uniformity.

The Science

The concept of diversity is as important in contemporary American life as it was in ancient Jewish society. Political leaders from Nancy Pelosi to Chris Christie and institutions from the United States Army to the United Nations, from Harvard Medical School to the Sacramento Kings, have reiterated an expression that is familiar to practically every student, soldier, company employee, and even sports fan: "Diversity is our strength."[20]

According to leading institutions across various fields, diversity makes companies prosperous, soldiers lethal, citizens healthy, students thrive, employees creative, and everyone smile more.[21] Few things have ever been so emphasized as the cause of all that is good and the bulwark against all that is bad.

Accordingly, most significant institutions in the United States have oriented themselves around the cultivation and promotion of diversity. Diversity is now a major determinant of who gets admitted to universities, who gets hired at companies, who receives government contracts, and who qualifies for a variety of other perks, rewards, and privileges in society.

In 2023, the *Yale Daily News* reported that increasing diversity was President Peter Salovey's "top priority." And he allocated funding commensurate with this conviction; between 2019 and 2023, Yale committed more than $125 million to Diversity, Equity, and Inclusion (DEI) programs and personnel.[22]

Yale is hardly alone in its commitment and willingness to staff and fund accordingly. In 2021, dozens of universities from red and blue states (including Stanford, Ohio State, Indiana, Duke, and Virginia Tech) had more than fifty full-time DEI personnel. And the profession was growing. The University of Michigan, which had 163 full-time DEI personnel in 2021, tripled its DEI staff over the next three years. The Michigan DEI leader, Dr. Robert Sellers, made more than $400k in 2002. Two of his counterparts at the University of Virginia were paid more than $500k in 2003.[23]

Universities have been joined by corporations in this funded commitment to diversity. In January 2022, LinkedIn reported that the fastest growing job title on its site was "Vaccine Specialist." Number two: "Diversity and Inclusion Manager." And those are just full-time jobs. Clutch, an online marketplace devoted to identification of business services companies, lists over one thousand "top" diversity consulting firms.[24]

Diversity has become both a civic religion, in that everyone is expected to swear allegiance to it, as well as a magic wand, in that it supposedly makes everything better. As we saw in the Torah discussion, diversity is indeed a powerful and important concept, but it is one that does not define itself. The Torah puts forth several distinct notions of diversity. Accordingly, the first question about diversity today is: What is it? When leaders intone, "Diversity is our strength," what are they talking about?

What Is Diversity?

If one does an image search for diversity or looks at a section on diversity in a corporate or university publication, what should one expect to find? It will not be a photo of several people engaged in a discussion, demonstrating viewpoint diversity. It will not be of people from different professions—one in a doctor's coat, a soldier's uniform, a clergyman's garb, a lifeguard's bathing suit, and a worker's hard hat, demonstrating skillset diversity. It will not be of one person praying, one person studying, one person taking a long walk, and another person doing an act of service, demonstrating diversity of approach. It will be of people of different genders, races, and sexual orientations doing anything—or nothing.

This is reflected in a 2021 survey conducted by the software company Ongig on the "diversity goals" in corporate America. The companies in the survey included Netflix, Microsoft, Hilton, McDonald's, the NBA, Target, Amazon, and others.

All of the diversity initiatives analyzed and discussed in the Ongig survey were focused *solely* on hiring and spending more with members of certain races, ethnicities, genders, or sexual orientations. *None* of these diversity programs mention viewpoint diversity, skillset diversity, or diversity of approach. In other words, the *only* kind of diversity manifest in these programs is the *one* kind of diversity absent from the Bible—that of immutable characteristics.[25]

The findings of this survey were confirmed by another survey from 2021, done by the employment company Indeed. Indeed listed the "Seven Types of Diversity in the Workplace." These are race, gender, religion, sexual orientation, age, disability, and culture.[26]

The sole emphasis on what we might term "identity diversity" in corporate America is shared by other institutions. In 2016, the United States Department of Education published a report on "Advancing Diversity and Inclusion in Higher Education." It pertains *entirely* to immutable characteristics—race, gender, sexuality, and ethnicity.[27]

Who Qualifies?

The first question to ask about "diversity" as understood today is: Who qualifies? The answer seems simple: those of a preferred race, gender, sexual orientation, or whatever other characteristic. But the reality is much more complicated.

In 2012, Harvard Law School professor Elizabeth Warren ran for the United States Senate. The *Boston Herald* reported that Senator Warren, who certainly seems "white," had identified as a Native American when she began her career in legal education.

She explained that there was "family lore" of a Cherokee past. Cherokee chief Bill John Baker, himself 1/32 Cherokee, welcomed Professor Warren's affiliation, stating that he wished that more people "had a kinship or felt a kinship" with the Cherokee Nation.[28]

Eight years later, the issue resurfaced when then senator Warren ran for president. She took a DNA test, administered by the Stanford University geneticist Carlos Bustamante. Professor Bustamante attested that Senator Warren had a Native American ancestor between six and ten generations ago. Senator Warren said that this proved she was correct all along.[29]

However, there was an immediate firestorm, including among the Cherokee Nation, of which Bill John Baker was no longer chief. A spokesperson for the Cherokee Nation told the *New York Times*, "Using a DNA test to lay claim to any connection to the Cherokee Nation or any tribal nation, even vaguely, is inappropriate and wrong." Senator Warren apologized "for the harm I have caused."[30]

This was not the first time a question of racial category was raised. In 1956, the Conference of Negro-African Writers and Artists was held in Paris. The head of the American delegation was John Preston Davis. The French chairperson pointed out that Mr. Davis looked white. The great novelist James Baldwin explained, "He is a Negro, of course, from the remarkable legal point of view which obtains in the United States."[31]

This "remarkable legal point of view" is the "one drop rule," which holds that an individual with *any* ancestor of a race or ethnicity is considered to be in that group. This "remarkable" assertion has a long history. Starting with Maryland in 1664, every southern colony (and later, state) passed a law prohibiting interracial marriage. A problem, though, is that race can be amorphous. Could someone who was, say, 1/8 or 1/16 black marry a white person? In 1883, Alabama passed a law ordering "imprisonment or hard labor" for two to seven years for a "white person and a negro" who married, and defined a "negro" as one who has a great-grandparent who was black.

By the 1920s, many intellectuals and legislators thought that Alabama's race categorization was insufficient. Perhaps the most influential of those was Madison Grant, whose 1916 *The Passing of the Great Race* was considered by Adolph Hitler to be his "bible" and became the first foreign book published by the Nazis when they came to power. In the book, Grant said that "the mixture of two races . . . gives us a race reverting to the . . . lower type." He believed that descendants of interracial couples should forever be considered of the "lower type."[32]

This view became codified in the Racial Integrity Act (passed in Virginia in 1924). It is defined as white anyone "who has no trace whatsoever of any blood other than Caucasian." Another Virginia law, passed in 1928, codified what had become known as the "one drop rule." It stated that the term "colored" would apply to anyone with "any ascertainable degree of negro blood, or who is descended on the part of the father or mother from negro ancestors, without reference to or limit of time or number of generations removed."[33]

Thankfully—blessedly—times have changed. Among many other things, the Supreme Court ruled in 1967 that laws prohibiting interracial marriages are unconstitutional. There has been a spectacular rise in the number of interracial couples since then, with 19 percent of marriages in 2019 being interracial. As we'll see, Hispanics are marrying non-Hispanics at even greater rates. This means that the question of who qualifies as a member of a group that benefits from diversity is rising in importance as well, as there will be more and more Americans who come from parents of different races and ethnicities.[34]

However, there is one thing about race in America that has not changed since the Virginia race laws of the 1920s: how race is determined. The diversity programs at American institutions use the US census definition of race. The 2020 census classified as black "a person having origins in any of the Black racial groups of Africa." And it defines as Hispanic/Latino "a person of Cuban, Mexican, Puerto Rican, South or Central American, or other Spanish culture or origin regardless of race."

All it takes to qualify for a contemporary diversity benefit, in the contemporary official understanding, is "one drop" of racial/ethnic blood, just as Madison Grant and his legislative followers prescribed. And neither proof nor standards are required; the census is clear that one can "self-identify" with any category, and that "respondent self-identification should be facilitated to the greatest extent possible." The criteria are even more broad for American Indians and Native Alaskans, where "community attachment" is sufficient.[35]

So, Elizabeth Warren, in declaring herself to be a Native American when she applied to teach at Harvard Law School, was justified by both official criteria. She satisfied the "one drop rule," *and* she felt a "community attachment." As a senator, she has been a devoted supporter of diversity policies, in accordance with the official definition. It is unclear, therefore, why she apologized for accepting a benefit that she was unquestionably qualified for.

There must be a significant benefit that is worth the cost of this illogic. What could it be?

A Stronger New York City

The most significant part of any government budget can be encapsulated in one word: purchasing. Governments have to buy all kinds of things, from payroll services to concrete barriers to paper clips. Government purchasing is usually done by contracting with private sector companies.

By 2020, New York City had a well-established program to provide preferences in government contracting to vendors who are female, black, Asian, Hispanic, or Native American. Although this program offered diversity benefits to a significant *majority* of the population, the New York City authorities decided in 2021 that it was insufficient. They expanded the program to include "LGBTQ+" people.[36]

Why would New York City decide to give preferences in government contracts to LGBTQ+ individuals and their businesses? Seemingly every survey of the most LGBTQ+-friendly cities in the world lists New York City in the top ten. Moreover, gay men are far better educated than straight men, and employed gay men (the subset of gays who can compete for city contracts) are much wealthier than employed straight men. And lesbians enjoy a 9 percent "wage premium" over their straight counterparts.[37]

Jonnel Doris, the commissioner of the NYC Department of Small Business Services, had an explanation. He said, "A diverse vendor pool makes a stronger New York City."[38]

Such a claim leads to a few questions. How is New York made "stronger" by awarding paving contracts to men who are attracted to men and women over men who are attracted only to women? How is a company whose majority shareholder has transitioned from male to female likely to install parking meters better than someone who is fine with his birth gender?

Of course, these questions are not limited to preferences based on sexuality and gender. Should a Jew whose grandparents escaped the Holocaust through Mexico en route to New York receive preferential treatment over a Jew whose grandparents escaped the Holocaust through Canada? Is New York made "stronger" by providing a preference to a vendor who has a Chinese or Argentinian grandparent over a competitor whose grandparents all came from Italy?

Jonnel Doris did not offer any data, or reasoned argument, to answer (or even address) any of these questions. Instead, he just said, "A diverse vendor pool makes a stronger New York City," as if it is an obvious fact that every decent citizen should easily understand and appreciate.

This kind of "diversity" program is by no means limited to New York, or even to like-minded jurisdictions. The federal Small Business Development Program, which governs the awarding of tens of billions of dollars a year in federal contracts and has thrived under Republican and Democrat administrations, administers the 8(a) program. This program promotes the development and growth of small businesses that are majority owned by the "socially and economically disadvantaged" by giving them preference in the federal government contracting program. These benefits include limiting competition, making awards irrevocable, and allowing for higher pricing.

There are dozens of groups who qualify as "socially and economically disadvantaged." They include black, Hispanic, Pacific Islander, Asian, and Native American. And that is not all. A potential contractor who is not a member of the group can submit a narrative backed by an "adequate" and "reasonably" compelling story of how he or she has suffered from "prejudice, bias, or discriminatory practices."

A Hasidic Jew applied under such an exception, but was rejected. The SBA explained, "The bias they suffered in the marketplace as a result of that cultural distinctiveness stems from adherence to religious doctrine."[39]

Many LGBTQ+ business owners have been more fortunate, with the SBA judging a self-reported experience with homophobia to be sufficient to win special treatment in the awarding of federal contracts. Indeed, the SBA encourages LGBTQ+ business owners to seek counseling from the SBA about how to craft narratives to win 8(a) set-asides.[40]

There is one categorical winner of the diversity game hosted by the SBA. The winner is not black or Hispanic Americans, women or homosexuals. It is . . . Alaska Natives. Alaska Natives, who compose 18 percent of the state, alone can win direct awards *without* competition, and have no enforceable caps on contract size. This has minted fortunes. For instance, the Arctic Slope Regional Corporation earned \$3.7 billion in revenue from federal contracts in 2020.

Why would Alaska Natives, who few people ever think about, receive such privilege in the awarding of federal contracts? In 2009 and 2010,

Senator Claire McCaskill (a Democrat from Missouri) wondered that. She sought to limit eligibility to companies with revenues of under $3.5 million.

Senator Mark Begich of Alaska angrily accused his colleague of "targeting" the Alaskan "way of life" and of "simply refusing to try and understand the history and culture of a great state like Alaska." His spirited support was joined by Alaskan representatives of both parties. Senator McCaskill lost, and these policies favoring Alaska Natives persist.[41]

Major allocations of capital, concerning far smaller sums than those in government contracts, are generally justified with abundant data that is subject to rigorous analysis. Yet, Jonell Doris did not offer any data to demonstrate why bisexuals should get preferences when applying for New York City contracts. And Senator Begich did not offer any data to show how asking Alaskan Natives to compete equally for federal contracts reflects a misunderstanding of "a great state like Alaska."

They did not have to, as the diversity policies they embodied are not subject to the usual tests of logic, data, and evidence. They are claims of faith. This faith, summarily rejected by the Torah in the lack of tribal representation on the Sanhedrin, has significant and wide-ranging ramifications beyond the allocation of public resources.

The Ramifications of Modern Diversity: Present Discrimination

There are always a limited number of university slots, government contracts, and corporate jobs. Therefore, if one person gets an advantage because of his race, gender, or ethnicity, another will receive a disadvantage because of his.

Most proponents of diversity (as it is commonly understood today) theoretically oppose discrimination. Therefore, they generally do not acknowledge the fact that the programs they support or demand require discrimination against people based on their race, ethnicity, and sexuality. Ibram X. Kendi is not one of those people. Professor Kendi, the founding leader of the Boston University Center for Anti-Racist Research, is the author of the enormously influential best-seller *How to Be an Antiracist* and his companion children's book, *Antiracist Baby*. He fully acknowledges the logic of the diversity policies he supports, stating, "The only remedy to past discrimination is present discrimination."[42]

How extensive and effective is this discrimination? An inquiry can start with a group that was, in the twentieth century, the subject of systematic and widespread discrimination but is never a beneficiary of diversity policies: the Jews.

Between 1900 and 1922, the percentage of the Harvard student body that was Jewish increased from 7 to 27.5 percent. The presence of so many Jews, according to Harvard president A. Lawrence Lowell, risked "ruin[ing] the college." He asked the Committee on Admissions to raise the admissions standards for members of the "Hebrew Race."[43]

The Committee chose a more subtle approach. They realized that Jews were not evenly distributed throughout the country, and that Harvard could achieve its goal by diminishing objective criteria (standardized tests) and optimizing for geographic diversity. Consequently, the percentage of Jews at Harvard declined precipitously and stayed at around 15 percent for the next thirty years.[44]

By the 1990s, Harvard and comparable colleges were back up to being around 25 percent Jewish. Then came the "diversity" push. Unlike in the 1920s, no one (including the Jews) was *specifically* discriminated against.

In 2021, Princeton Dean of Admission Karen Richardson proudly announced that 68 percent of its incoming freshmen were "people of color," 52 percent were women, and 14 percent were international.[45] As Jews are now considered "white," that does not leave many spots for Jewish men. By discriminating in favor of so many others, the enrollment of Jews at Princeton and Harvard is down by almost 50 percent since 1980, and is significantly lower than President Lowell ever dreamed of when he instituted his "geographic diversity" discrimination against Jews.[46]

And Jews are far from the only group that is disadvantaged by what Professor Kendi calls "present discrimination." There are Asians, which is simply a weird category. Asia is a massive continent that contains countries as different as Korea, Japan, China, India, Indonesia, Thailand, and Singapore. These countries have often warred against each other, with lingering animosity between their citizens. Perhaps the only thing that "Asians" have in common is that they are all considered the same in American diversity calculations. This confusion might explain a strange fact about this category: Asians are often favored in government diversity programs and disfavored in university diversity programs.[47]

Still, there is no doubt that they were discriminated against in university diversity programs. A 2009 review of SAT data by Princeton sociologists

Thomas Espenshade and Alexandria Walton Radford showed that Asians need SAT scores 140 points higher than whites, 270 points higher than Hispanics, and 450 points higher than blacks to be considered equally for college admissions.[48]

One might respond to Professor Kendi's call for "present discrimination" by telling the disadvantaged groups to just deal with it, and to do what Jews did when discriminated against in the twentieth century (which was to create businesses, firms, and other alternate institutions). But it is not so simple, for several reasons.

First, there can be downstream effects of discrimination. It may have limited impact if a heterosexual Jewish candidate for a teaching position in Dance is at a significant disadvantage to a peer in a preferred group. But data from the Association of Medical Colleges shows that admission to medical schools is governed by the same kind of diversity criteria as are colleges. The results can be seen in the acceptance rate of applicants to American medical schools with average GPAs and MCAT scores between 2013 and 2016: 20.6 percent of Asian students, 29 percent of white students, 59.5 percent of Hispanic students, and 81.2 percent of black students were accepted.[49]

The consequences are stark. Dr. Jennifer Lucero is the vice chair for Justice, Equity, Diversity, and Inclusion (JEDI) for the Department of Anesthesiology and Perioperative Medicine at the David Geffen UCLA School of Medicine. In 2020, she became the dean of admissions. She made diversity a top priority for admissions. Among other things, she responded to the rejection of a Native American student by requiring the admissions committee to sit through a two-hour lecture on Native American history (delivered by her sister). She called out those who challenged the candidacy of certain "minority" candidates by accusing them of acting from privilege and requiring them to receive diversity training. The result of her work: far fewer Asian students and a massive increase in the failure rate of UCLA medical students on the standardized "shelf" exams, which measure medical knowledge, application of basic science, clinical reasoning, and problem-solving skills at the end of a rotation.[50]

Second, "present discrimination" can degrade the confidence of the "beneficiaries" of diversity programs. In 2014, Professors Lisa Leslie of NYU, David Mayer of the University of Michigan, and David Kravitz of

George Mason University published a meta-analysis of several dozen studies of the effects of affirmative action programs on those impacted. They found that "the possibility that members of the groups the AAP [affirmative action program] targets were hired or promoted due to their demographics, not their qualifications" is likely to lead to feelings of self-doubt and incompetence on the part of the supposed beneficiary. They found that this lack of self-confidence may inhibit job performance. This self-doubt often presents as impostor syndrome, the phenomenon where people deem themselves unworthy of their positions of achievement. The wide-ranging impacts of impostor syndrome are explored in a separate dedicated chapter of this book.

But impostor syndrome, as serious as it is, is not the only discovery that this team found in their meta-analysis. They also found that recipients of diversity benefits are likely to be viewed by others in the organization as lacking competence and warmth.[51]

This is nonintuitive. It is predictable that one who receives a benefit based on irrelevant criteria he did not earn (like skin color or gender) would suffer from impostor syndrome. But why would others view such a person as lacking competence and warmth? A 2016 study by Professors Tessa Dover, Brenda Major, and Cheryl Kaiser (of Portland State University, UCSB, and the University of Washington, respectively) yields a potential explanation. They had a group of white students apply to a hypothetical company with a stated diversity commitment and to another hypothetical company without one.

They found that "participants applying to the pro-diversity company exhibited greater cardiovascular threat, expressed more concerns about being discriminated against, and made a poorer impression during the interview relative to white men applying to a neutral company."[52]

This was the case regardless of the political views of the participants. It turns out that most people, even if they say they favor diversity, are at least uncomfortable with a system that awards advantages due to immutable criteria that are irrelevant to the tasks at hand. Thus, it is not surprising that their discomfort may translate into muted ill will toward those who might have received their position as a result of "present discrimination."

So, having discovered the depth and extent of discontent with preferences, Professor Mayer came up with a solution. It was not to follow the

Torah's guidance, by omitting preferences based on tribal membership from its rich notion of diversity. Instead, he argues that organizations with diversity programs should just deny that anyone received any diversity benefit. The organization managers should say that the diversity programs are "an outreach effort to cast a wider net in the community and find qualified job applicants from every walk of life."[53]

Most untruths are hard to sustain, and this one is especially so. For example, 71 percent of black students at Harvard come from families who are considered "wealthy"—i.e., in the top 20 percent of income. This is no outlier. In 2023, David Leonhardt of the *New York Times* reported that fewer than 15 percent of the student bodies at "elite" universities, including UVA, Brown, Oberlin, and Wake Forest, qualify for Pell Grants (the largest federal aid program). The fact that the students at the "elite" universities come from the same kinds of privileged backgrounds, regardless of their racial identities, is apparent to everyone on campus. No one will be fooled that diversity is about "casting a wider net."[54]

The obfuscation of diversity programs that manifests in the recommendation that they be recast as an "outreach effort" extends beyond universities. IBM, like most corporations of its size, has a large and public commitment to diversity, with a sizable staff to implement it. Its materials do not speak of discriminating against anyone. In fact, a 2020 diversity report from IBM proudly features a 1951 letter from the company founder (Tom Watson) committing the company to hiring talent "regardless of race, color or creed."[55]

The reality is quite different. In 2023, a video of a Zoom session between IBM chairman and CEO Arvind Krishna, IBM subsidiary Red Hat chairman Paul Cormier, and communications executive Allison Showalter was leaked. Mr. Krishna said, "I'm not trying to finesse this." He stated that managers who hire more black, Hispanic, and female candidates will get a bigger bonus and those who do not will "lose" part of their bonus, and that Asian candidates should not be included in diversity goals. Mr. Cormier responds by boasting that he has fired "multiple leaders" for "not living up to the DEI standards that we set up in this space. This conversation takes place every single day. And a lot of it is behind the scenes."[56]

Neither Mr. Krishna nor Mr. Cormier specified why IBM executes its diversity policies "behind the scenes." But it is clear that IBM's diversity policies are all about identity characteristics, leaving no room for diversity of opinion about "DEI standards," and have nothing to do with casting a wider net.

The Creation of the Oppression Olympics

In the 2010 United States census, 53 percent of people of "Hispanic origin" identified as "only white." In the 2020 census, just 20 percent of people of "Hispanic origin" identified as "only white." It is interesting that Hispanic identification has increased at the same time as the Hispanic community has become more ethnically diverse. According to the National Research Center on Hispanic Children and Families, 27 percent of Hispanics in 2019 were married to people of another ethnic background. Most of those people, of course, got married long before 2019. The rate of Hispanics marrying non-Hispanics has risen dramatically in recent years. Forty-two percent of Hispanics who wed in 2015 married a non-Hispanic person, and that number is even higher among those who were born in the United States.[57]

Why, then, did so many more *begin* identifying themselves as Hispanic in this ten-year span? It is simple. If society awards benefits, admissions slots, jobs, and contracts (among other things) on the basis of immutable characteristics that serve as a proxy for grievances, then its members will emphasize those characteristics in their self-definition. This might seem harmless, but it leads to what is widely identified as "the Oppression Olympics." This is, according to Tashi Copeland of the Central Indiana Community Foundation, "the idea that marginalization is a competition of determining the relative weight of overall oppression of individuals or groups, based on identity. Simply put, it's comparing who has it worse."[58]

The person who can demonstrate, on the basis of an immutable characteristic, that he "has it worse" wins diversity points that can get him a desired slot, a job, a contract, or (in some circles) respect. Consequently, the diversity agenda has incentivized and conditioned those who seek societal benefits to identify with a status that will help in the Oppression Olympics.

And it's working. In polls taken in 2014 and 2024, the Pew Research Center found that large numbers of people in a wide variety of groups—blacks, whites, women, men, Jews, Hispanics, gays, Evangelicals, and Catholics—believe that they are victims of discrimination. As a *Washington Post* analysis of this data concluded, "The Most Discriminated Against People in America? It's People Like You, Of Course."[59]

The consequences of having this victim mindset are discussed in an earlier chapter of this book.[60]

Lessons from STEM

According to a 2021 study by Bankrate, the top twenty-five college degrees by pay and demand are *all* in STEM (science, technology, engineering, and math). This should be good news for black and Hispanic students. According to the University of San Diego law professor Gail Heriot, "Study after study has found . . . that African-American and Hispanic students are slightly more interested in pursuing science and engineering degrees than white students are."[61]

Yet, numerous reports have pointed out that minority students are underrepresented in STEM. Indeed, black college graduates aged thirty-five or younger are 36 percent as likely as their white peers to hold a STEM degree, and 15 percent as likely to have a PhD in STEM. Hispanic graduates are 41 percent as likely to have graduated with a STEM degree, and 26 percent less likely to have a PhD in STEM.

What accounts for the incoming interest in STEM and yet the lack of degrees? In a word: attrition. Professor Heriot's explains:

> While African Americans and Hispanics have higher rates of initial interest than whites, they are less likely to follow through with that interest. Somewhere in college, the intention to graduate with a degree in science or engineering withers and dies. In one study of elite colleges and universities, for example, 70 percent of Asians persisted in their ambition, while 61 percent of whites, 55 percent of Hispanics, and 34 percent of blacks did.[62]

What accounts for the non-persistence of STEM interest among black and Hispanic students as they progress through college? A clue exists in the data regarding where black students stay with their STEM commitments: historically black colleges and universities (HBCUs). These universities enroll 10 percent of black college students, graduate 20 percent of black college students, and produce almost 30 percent of all black STEM grads. The United Negro College Fund reports that 46 percent of black women who received STEM degrees between 1995 and 2004 graduated from HCBUs.

And many of these STEM graduates continue in their fields, earning PhDs in STEM from a broad array of universities.[63]

So, why would black students persist in STEM in HBCUs to a much greater extent than in non-HBCUs? A variety of studies have demonstrated that a student with STEM interest is likely to persist in pursuit of a STEM degree to the extent that his *incoming* STEM credentials (for instance, math SAT score) are the same as or better than that of his peers.[64] A student who enters a university with interest in STEM, but finds that she is less prepared than her classmates, is unlikely to persist. This is often due to the fact that STEM knowledge is cumulative, meaning that one who starts behind will likely fall further behind as their more knowledgeable peers increase in knowledge faster. The student who started behind, therefore, will quite understandably become discouraged and switch to a different major.

The STEM attrition problem, therefore, is inevitable in institutions that admit students on the basis of criteria unrelated to STEM knowledge. The result: University "diversity" policies effectively steer students away from STEM disciplines and toward majors that are less cumulative, more subjective, and lead to less remunerative careers. These issues do not exist at HBCUs, which admit students on the basis of academic merit, have high rates of STEM persistence and achievement, and have graduated some of America's most distinguished physicians and scientists.

Can Identity-Based Diversity Work?: Professor Allport's Tabernacle

Can diversity policies based on immutable characteristics have *any* positive and even unifying consequences? The answer is clearly: Yes. The story of this "yes" begins with one man, Gordon Allport, who taught at Dartmouth and Harvard for over forty years until his death in 1967. He is the pioneer of contact theory, which posits that diverse people(s) will feel substantially better about each other when they are brought together.

His investigation of this theory began in 1946, with a study of white Merchant Marines who served in World War II. He found that two-thirds of white sailors who had never served with black sailors harbored racist prejudices. This was a terrible number, but it was not fixed. This percentage decreased to 54 percent for those white sailors who shipped out once with black comrades, 38 percent for those who shipped out twice, and 18 percent for those who shipped out five or more times. The racism of the white Merchant Marines diminished to the extent that they spent more time with their fellow black sailors.

Was this an anomaly? A 1949 study of the US Army by Professor Allport tested this finding with data relating to another question for white soldiers: Did they support the integration of the United States military? Professor Allport found that 62 percent of white soldiers who had no contact with black soldiers in World War II opposed integrating their platoons. That number plummeted to 7 percent when the question was given to white soldiers who had already served with black soldiers.[65]

Does this mean that prejudice can be relieved by simply bringing people from a discriminating group in contact with others? Professor Allport's research led him to a definitive answer: No. In fact, his research led him to conclude that, often, "The more contact, the more trouble."[66] How, then, can more contact lead to *less* trouble, and even affection? He explained:

> Only the type of contact that leads people *to do* [emphasis in original] things together is likely to result in changed attitudes . . . The principle is clearly illustrated in the multi-ethnic athletic team. Here the goal is all-important, the ethnic composition of the team is irrelevant. It is the cooperative striving for the goal that engenders solidarity. So too, in factories, neighborhoods, housing units, schools, common participation and common interests are more effective than the bare fact of equal-status contact.[67]

There have been hundreds of studies exploring Professor Allport's theory. In the mid- to late twentieth century, Professor Allport's protégé Thomas Pettigrew became a dominant figure in the world of contact theory. Professor Pettigrew was attracted to this field by his hatred of racial prejudice, which was triggered by a seminal moment in his youth. His black caretaker, Mildred Adams, took him to a movie in Virginia. They were turned away because the theater barred blacks from entry.[68]

Professors Gordon Hodson and Miles Hewstone of Brock College and Oxford University discussed the life work of Professor Pettigrew in their book, *Advances in Intergroup Contact*. They wrote, "Specifically, he [Professor Pettigrew] argued that initial contact is optimized when group representatives interact as individuals (through *de-categorization*, de-emphasizing group relations)." [Italics in original.][69]

Prejudice is reduced, in other words, to the extent that people identify with each other as individuals working together to achieve a goal or solve a problem. Diversity, these hundreds of studies showed, can be our strength, so long as—as the Torah showed in Numbers—there is a Tabernacle in the middle.

I have seen this firsthand over the past fifteen years, with the Israeli-Palestinian conflict. There have been countless initiatives to bring Jews and Arabs together to discuss their differences and/or similarities. There is no evidence that any such initiative has had any positive impact. But there is something that worked.

I am the cofounder and chairman of United Hatzalah of Israel, the country's crowd-sourced volunteer first-response force that ensures that everyone in the country will be treated within the three minutes separating life from death, following a trauma like a heart attack, stroke, choking incident, or car accident. The volunteers, who all undergo the same rigorous training before being given their equipment, come from all sectors of Israel's diverse society, including secular and observant Jews, Arab Muslims, Christians, and Druze. Volunteers are homemakers, rabbis, imams, business executives, college students, medical translators, real estate developers, police officers—everyone.

The volunteers are united by a commitment to save lives, ameliorate pain, and otherwise aid their fellow citizens who are in any kind of distress. With the volunteers developing respect and admiration for each other on the basis of working together in service of their shared commitment, the relationships follow. Invitations to each other's weddings, Seders, Iftar celebrations, and Shabbat dinners are offered and accepted.

Discussions of group identity and the attendant politics often follow—and always in the context of genuine curiosity, great respect, and sometimes good humor. I have never seen or heard of anyone being offended or otherwise put off during such a conversation. Indeed, the opposite is true, and predictable, in line with the discovery of Professor Allport.

In Professor Allport's work, the Tabernacle was the United States Army and the great nation it protects. The Tabernacle is, in the work of United

Hatzalah, the commitment to saving lives and ameliorating pain. And such Tabernacles abound.

The Tabernacle of Public Safety: Police in Chicago and Miami

Everyone should agree that society has an obligation to protect its citizens from the ravages of crime, while maximizing goodwill between police officers and citizens. A key question is: How to do so?

In 2020, a team of social scientists from the University of Pennsylvania studied police interactions in Chicago. They worked with a large dataset, consisting of 1.6 million enforcement actions by 7,000 officers from 2012 to 2015. They found that black officers made 20 to 30 percent fewer arrests than did their white colleagues, and the differences were largest in majority-black neighborhoods.[70]

This is not necessarily good, as it could suggest that black officers tolerate more criminal activity without consequence than their white colleagues. But that does not appear to be the case, as there was no variation in arrests between white and black officers concerning violent criminals. It is likely that black officers are better able to understand conflicts that arise in black communities, and diffuse or correctly interpret situations that would otherwise end in arrest.

Does that mean that police departments that serve black communities should prefer black people when selecting officers? Yes, so long as the black candidates have the background that yields the kind of deep cultural knowledge that is reflected in the Chicago data.

This hypothesis is strengthened by an insight from Major Albert Guerra of the Miami Police Department. In 2018, he said, "In Miami, we have a large Latin population. Latin people sometimes speak to each other in close proximity that would make someone of a different culture uncomfortable."[71]

A 2017 study published in the *Journal of Cross-Cultural Psychology* about personal spaces granted around the world confirms that there are significant variations in the distances that people in different cultures grant each other when conversing, especially among strangers. In the dozens of countries surveyed, the two cultures where strangers converse most closely together are Peru and Argentina. Mayor Guerra was exactly right.[72]

Does this suggest that a police department with jurisdiction over a large number of Hispanic residents should take affirmative action to hire more Hispanic officers? Probably. But nuances matter and details are determinative.

For instance, a young person with a Mexican grandfather who grew up in Short Hills, New Jersey, would qualify as Hispanic by the standards of the US census. But he would likely not have the cultural knowledge that Major Guerra is looking for. Similarly, a white or black person who grew up in Miami's Little Havana would likely have that cultural sensitivity. But most of the people who can distinguish between a harmlessly animated conversation and a dangerously escalating situation in a Latin neighborhood will be Hispanic, and police departments should recruit accordingly. As everyone is invested in safer neighborhoods and better policing, such an identity diversity policy is unifying.

The Tabernacle in Business: Women in Venture Capital

In recent years, august business organizations have declared, "The Business Case for Diversity Is Now Overwhelming" (World Economic Forum) and "Diversity Wins" (McKinsey reports published in 2015, 2018, 2020, and 2023). Can a business, therefore, perform better by hiring more women, blacks, Hispanics, or homosexuals?[73]

Professors Jeremiah Green of Texas A&M and John R. M. Hand of the University of North Carolina conducted a rigorous analysis of the McKinsey studies, which have been very influential. They emerged with questions about the McKinsey methodologies. For instance, McKinsey measured financial performance at the beginning of a period and diversity at the end. This approach likely indicated that profitable companies had resources to invest in diversity programs, rather than diversity programs driving profitability.

When Professors Green and Hand replicated the McKinsey study, they found "no statistically significant difference between the likelihood of financial outperformance" that accrues to the companies McKinsey judges as diverse. This conclusion applied to all of the major metrics that account for company performance: industry-adjusted profit margins, industry-adjusted sales growth, gross margin, return on assets, return on equity, and total shareholder returns.[74]

Who is right? A research team led by Professor Greg Filbeck of Penn State looked at the ultimate source of truth for financial performance: long-term stock prices. Professor Filbeck and his colleagues, in a 2017 analysis published in *Advances in Accounting*, examined the stock performances of the Diversity 50. These are the top fifty companies in diversity, as determined by DiversityInc.

They found that inclusion in the DiversityInc 50 produces an "announcement effect" that results in an immediate stock price bump. This reflects the popularity that accrues to being recognized as a diverse employer. However, the research team found (as did Professors Green and Hand) that diversity efforts were not reflected in improved financial accounting results. They also found that, after the "announcement effect" had waned, the "diverse" companies did not outperform a matched sample. They concluded, "Diversity for diversity's sake may not be a wise investment."[75]

Does this mean that a business should never pursue identity-based diversity? No. The results of a 2018 study of gender and venture capital by Harvard Business School professor Paul Gompers are illustrative. Professor Gompers concluded, "Academic research shows that VC firms with 10% more female investing partner hires make more successful investments at the portfolio company level; have 1.5% higher fund returns; and see 9.7% more profitable exits."[76]

Why would this be? An insight from Michael Silverstein and Kate Sayre of the Boston Consulting Group offers a possible explanation: "Knowing whom you're targeting and what she looks for in the marketplace can be a tremendous source of advantage."[77]

Who knows what consumers "look for in the marketplace"? The data is clear: women. According to data from Chain Store Age and the OECD, women make 85 percent of household purchase decisions, and even more in home furnishings, vacations, and home purchases.[78]

So, a woman is likely to have better insights than a man into whether customers buy this product at the price point and in the places that the entrepreneurs claim. However, a woman would have no better insights than a man into, say, whether a hardware manufacturer is likely to adopt a new kind of semiconductor being developed by an entrepreneur. Thus, an investor considering allocating to a venture capital firm that focuses on the consumer should pay attention to the gender of the partners, while an investor in a firm that focuses on industrial hardware should not.

Identity diversity *can* work, so long as it is calibrated, nuanced, and targeted toward a Tabernacle in the middle (like, in the business case, making money).

Viewpoint Diversity

In December of 2014, Professors Cass Sunstein and Reid Hastie of the University of Chicago published an essay in the *Harvard Business Review* called "Making Dumb Groups Smarter." It is a classic study of decision-making in groups that do not have viewpoint diversity. This was exemplified at the Tower of Babel, where the participants used a "common set of words" to say the same thing to each other ("let us brick bricks") until they found themselves doing something that any observer would have identified as futile and stupid (building a tower to reach God).

The essay begins by stating that human beings everywhere and throughout all time have made decisions in groups. These groups are diverse and include church groups, political parties, juries, regulatory agencies, faculties, internet discussion groups, and talk radio communities.

How do these groups, which are composed of individuals coming together to make a decision, perform? Often very badly. Professors Sunstein and Hastie write, "Companies bet on products that are doomed to fail, miss out on spectacular opportunities, pursue unsuccessful competitive strategies. In governments, policy judgments misfire, hurting thousands or even millions of people in the process."[79]

How do groups so often fail, with often spectacular consequences? They often fall into what Professor Sunstein called elsewhere "the law of group polarization."[80] This is the phenomenon that occurs when "members of a deliberating group predictably move toward a more extreme point in the direction." Groups move to the extreme when their participants enter the discussion with the same "pre-deliberation tendencies," i.e., without viewpoint diversity.

The dynamic by which participation in a homogenous group pulls its participants to the extreme has been demonstrated in areas as diverse as opposition to a war, concern about global warming, identification of racism, and even among federal judges, who are more likely to rule pursuant to an "ideological voting pattern" when sitting with judges from the same party.[81]

This finding, of course, prompts the question: Why do groups, in the absence of viewpoint diversity, become more entrenched and extreme? Professor Sunstein posits two explanations, both of which could be operative in a given scenario.

One is social comparison. This occurs when members of a homogenous group want to be perceived by others and by themselves as convicted believers and bold advocates who are passionate and courageous, rather than nuanced challengers.[82]

The other explanation is persuasive arguments. An individual in a group without viewpoint diversity will be exposed to "a disproportionate number of arguments supporting that same direction." Without anyone advocating a contrary position, the contrary position is vulnerable to either being ignored or caricatured. The uninterrupted cascade of arguments in favor of the dominant position will draw advocates further to the extreme.[83]

Fortunately, there is an alternative. It is what God established at Babel, when he reacted to everyone speaking the same way by changing their languages and dispersing them across the world to have different experiences and create different cultures.

Viewpoint Diversity Works (but Does Not Feel Good)

In 2008, Professors Kathryn Williams Phillips, Katie Liljenquist, and Margaret Neale of Northwestern University placed three members of the same fraternity or sorority in a room and gave them twenty minutes to solve a murder mystery. After five minutes, a fourth person came into the room. Half the time, it was a fellow member of the fraternity or sorority. Half the time, it was a newcomer. The consequence: Half of the groups were diverse and half were homogeneous.[84]

At the conclusion of the project, the students reported two things. First, the more diverse groups reported being *less* comfortable. They judged their interactions to be less effective than did the groups that had all members of the same society. Moreover, the diverse groups were less confident in their answers than were the nondiverse groups.

But the story takes an interesting turn. The diverse groups performed *much better*. In fact, they were more than twice as likely to come to the right answer as were the homogenous groups.

Why? A *Harvard Business Review* analysis led by the neuroscientist David Rock suggests an interesting possibility. Dr. Rock and his colleagues concluded that participants in a homogenous group experience what they call "the fluency heuristic."

The "fluency heuristic" manifests when we gravitate to stories, songs, food, and other things that have become easy and comfortable. It also applies to people and ideas. The fluency heuristic leads people to gravitate to individuals, groups, and ideas that are easy and comfortable. The problem is that there is no positive correlation between what is comfortable and what is right. And there just might be a negative correlation.

Dr. Rock and his colleagues write, "In fact, working on diverse teams produces better outcomes precisely *because* it's harder . . . confronting opinions you disagree with might not seem like the quickest path to getting things done, but working in groups can be like studying (or exercising): no pain, no gain."[85]

Why might viewpoint diversity have worked so well for the Northwestern students? First, the Northwestern students in the diverse group wanted to arrive at the truth; they wanted to solve the murder mystery. They probably did not become emotionally invested in their hypotheses or fear social sanction from challenging another participant. In other words, the disagreements that they likely had in their quest were what the Talmud called "arguments for the sake of heaven," those not designed to prevail or embarrass but to arrive at the truth.

Second, the Northwestern students in diverse groups were not comfortable with each other. Therefore, they likely had to reason carefully, articulate clearly, and listen closely in order for their ideas to be understood and acted upon.

Viewpoint Diversity in the Age of Identity Diversity

The evidence and the reasons for it are in: Viewpoint diversity enables more refined thinking and better decision-making, whereas its absence, for reasons that Professor Sunstein identified, leads to suboptimal and sometimes even downright stupid conclusions. What has society done in response to these twenty-first-century social scientific confirmations of biblical claims?

A useful place to begin the investigation is with universities, where ideas are conceived, developed, and taught to young people.

According to data from the Carnegie Commission and UCLA, college professors were between 50 and 100 percent more likely to identify as liberal than conservative from the 1970s to the 1990s. The diversity push, which purportedly included viewpoint diversity, started in earnest in the 2000s. Indeed, by 2016, the numbers had changed. College professors were then around 600 percent more likely to be liberal than conservative.[86]

In 2017, a team of researchers led by Professor Mitchell Langbert of Brooklyn College analyzed the voter registration data of professors at fifty-one of the leading liberal arts colleges as determined by *U.S. News & World Report*. They found that Democrats outnumbered Republicans by 10.4 to 1, and that includes the service academies and outright conservative institutions such as Thomas Aquinas College. The data also showed significant variation between disciplines. Democrats outnumbered Republicans by 1.6 to 1 in engineering departments, where political and social ideas should be irrelevant. However, Democrats outnumbered Republicans by 8 to 1 in politics, 17 to 1 in psychology, 48 to 1 in English, and 70 to 1 in religion. There were no Republicans in anthropology and communications.[87]

There was also some variation among colleges. Williams College, which has around one full-time diversity employee per hundred students including a "dialogue facilitator," has a faculty Democrat–Republican ratio of 132 to 1. Other institutions with a similar commitment to "diversity" include Swarthmore (120 to 1), Barnard (98 to 1), and Amherst (34 to 1).[88]

This study included only liberal arts colleges, but the numbers seem to be the same at universities. A 2015 analysis of political giving conducted by the *Harvard Crimson* showed that 96 percent of donations from professors in the Harvard undergraduate faculty went to Democratic candidates, as did 98 percent of donations from Harvard Law professors. Michael Smith, the Dean of the Harvard Faculty of Arts and Sciences, said that he was "amazed" by the statistics.

It is unclear why a dean at Harvard, who presumably has attended dozens of workshops and discussions on diversity, would be amazed with a statistic demonstrating the lack of viewpoint diversity at his school. Does his amazement derive from him having thought that the faculty was full of Republicans, or that he had not thought of viewpoint diversity? The analysis does not specify.[89]

The executives at the leading admissions advisory company Ivy Coach do not seem to have been "amazed" at the lack of viewpoint diversity on campus. In 2017, they wrote that "highly selective colleges, and especially their admissions offices, seek to enroll a diverse and talented group of students each year. Diversity of opinion is part of this diversity these colleges seek."

Consequently, Ivy Coach concluded, "We anticipate that our nation's most highly selective colleges will make even greater efforts to appeal to conservative applicants and their families this admissions cycle, and in the cycles to come."[90]

Their prediction was wrong. Precinct data for the top twenty universities in the United States puts President Biden's share of the 2020 presidential vote at 88 percent. Yet, that understates the extent of the support for left-of-center candidates among students at elite universities. For instance, President Biden received only 87 percent of support from Harvard freshmen because Howie Hawkins, the Green Party candidate, received 6.7 percent of the vote.[91]

Data like this does not seem to concern college administrators. There are *countless* diversity initiatives and programs. As of this writing (in late 2023), there does not seem to be *any* program or initiative geared toward attracting more students or faculty whose views could align it with the diversity in American society.

It would not be hard to do. There are significantly more National Merit Scholars at the University of Alabama in Tuscaloosa and the University of Florida than there are at Yale, Harvard, and Princeton. Many of the students at the University of Alabama and the University of Florida are conservative. An Ivy League administration interested in viewpoint diversity could presumably recruit some of the conservative National Merit Scholars who are headed to Alabama or Florida. However, no such effort seems to have been considered.[92]

This phenomenon is not limited to the academy. NPR is as committed to "diversity" as any university. In 2021, its CEO (John Lansing) said that "diversity" is its "North Star" that "filters through everything that we do with all our work."[93]

It was around that time when Uri Berliner, an award-winning journalist who had been at NPR for more than twenty years, surveyed the voter registration of the employees at their headquarters. There were eighty-seven Democrats and zero Republicans. He presented his findings at an all-hands meeting, suggesting that this was a diversity problem. His colleagues sent him messages of what he called "oh wow, that's weird" variety, but no one considered it a problem. One colleague emailed to tell him that she had raised the issue of the lack of "diversity of thought" at NPR, and got "skewered." She told him that they should "be careful about how we discuss this publicly."[94]

Uri Berliner did not take that advice. In 2024, he published an essay in the *Free Press* about his experience and its implications for NPR. The new CEO, Katherine Maher, promptly suspended him. Mr. Berliner subsequently resigned, stating that he could not work in an environment where he was publicly disparaged by the CEO.

"It's Not Our Job to Make Sure That All Viewpoints Flourish"

So, the evidence is clear that the same institutions that push so insistently for the one kind of diversity shunned in the Torah effectively reject the fundamental kind that is celebrated by it. This leaves a question: Is identity diversity absent in the Torah because it conflicts with viewpoint diversity? Conversely, can viewpoint diversity coexist with modern notions of identity diversity?

One place to begin the investigation may be diversity statements, which are required of professors applying for jobs at almost half of the large universities in the United States.[95] These statements make it very clear how the university administrators conceive of diversity, what answers they expect, and how important they are for one's candidacy.

As of 2024, Columbia University requires "diversity statements" from faculty candidates and publishes a "Sample Candidate Evaluation Tool for Faculty Searches" to guide the relevant committees in their assessments.[96] There are four categories in which candidates are to be assessed: research, teaching, service, and diversity. Within the diversity category, each candidate should be judged by "knowledge of, experience with, and interest in dimensions of diversity that result from different identities, such as ethnic, socioeconomic, racial, gender, sexual orientation, disability, and cultural differences." There is no mention of viewpoint diversity.

The University of California at Berkeley also requires diversity statements. Its Office of Faculty Equity and Welfare, on its website, tells its applicants what kinds of statements will earn which kinds of scores.

The Office explains that a general statement such as, "Diversity is important for science," will earn the lowest score. An average score will incorporate support for diversity initiatives along with plans for "outreach" with "expected outcomes." A high score will include a description of "multiple activities in depth, with detailed information about both their role in the activities and the outcomes."[97] The University of California at Berkeley, in Tower of Babel terms, supplies the "common set of words" that applicants must use to describe their beliefs about diversity.

How important is a candidate's willingness to use "a common set of words"? A 2023 *New York Times* analysis cited research that showed that 75 percent of applicants in life sciences and environmental sciences and management policy at the University of California at Berkeley were rejected solely because of their diversity statements.[98]

As suggested in the Babel story, an enforced way of speaking becomes a required way of thinking. The *Times* told the story of Professor Yoel Inbar of the University of Toronto. In 2023, he was expected to receive a position at Berkeley due to his widely respected scholarship and pursuant to the "partner hire" policy (as his life partner had just received a professorship there). However, students surfaced a podcast where he questioned the intellectual validity of diversity statements, and another statement where he said that professional societies should not reject people based on their views on abortion. The students signed a letter stating that "his hiring would threaten ongoing efforts to protect and uplift individuals of marginalized backgrounds," and demonstrated that he was not committed to a "safe, welcoming and inclusive environment."

How did the University of California administrators respond to this rejection of the principle of viewpoint diversity? Professor Brian Soucek led the University of California system-wide Committee on Academic Freedom in the early 2020s, and won the Chancellor Achievement Award for Diversity and Community in 2023. Professor Soucek told the *New York*

Times "It's our job to make sure people of all identities flourish here. It's not our job to make sure that all viewpoints flourish."[99]

James Damore's A-

Professor Soucek's philosophy of diversity is not unique to the academy. In August of 2017, the Google software engineer James Damore attended a corporate diversity program that solicited feedback in accordance with Google's longtime stated commitment to tolerance and openness. Mr. Damore provided feedback through a memo he wrote on a flight to China. He stated that Google executives attribute the gender gap in technology jobs entirely to bias. Mr. Damore wrote that biases are *part* of the answer, but that there are more general differences between men and women that could explain some of these discrepancies as well.

Many of the differences that he stated, including that women are more empathic, people oriented, cooperative, and less driven by status, are those invoked to argue for more women on corporate boards and executive roles. All of his claims were supported with citations from mainstream social science literature. Professor Geoffrey Miller of the University of New Mexico, who later reviewed the memo, concluded, "Graded fairly, his memo would get at least an A- in any masters' level psychology course. It is consistent with the scientific state of the art on sex differences."[100]

Still, the memo created an immediate controversy. The Google message board rang with posts like, "I intend to silence these views. They are violently offensive." Google's VP of Diversity, Danielle Brown, responded, "Part of building an open, inclusive environment means fostering a culture in which those with alternative views, including different political views, feel safe sharing their opinions. But that discourse needs to work alongside the principles of equal employment found in our Code of Conduct, policies and anti-discrimination laws."

So, viewpoint diversity is *encouraged* . . . so long as it does not lead to the questioning of any of the assumptions of immutable diversity. What happens, practically, when the exercise of viewpoint diversity leads to challenging immutable diversity? The CEO of Google, Sundar Pichai, cut short his vacation to deal with the fallout, which included firing Mr. Damore.[101]

Why might, per Professor Soucek and the executives at Google, a commitment to identity diversity be at odds with a commitment to viewpoint diversity?

Denise Young Smith, once the VP of Diversity and Inclusion at Apple, found out.

The Tower of Babel Comes to Cupertino

In May 2017, Apple demonstrated its commitment to diversity by creating a VP-level position for Diversity and Inclusion. The position reported directly to the CEO, Tim Cook.

Five months later, the newly installed VP for Diversity and Inclusion, Denise Young Smith, went to Bogota, Colombia, to speak at the One Young World Summit. On a panel about fighting racial injustice, she said, "Diversity is the human experience. I get a little bit frustrated when diversity or the term 'diversity' is tagged to the people of color, or the women, or the LGBT."

She was greeted with applause.

She elaborated, "I've often told people a story, there can be twelve white, blue-eyed, blonde men in a room and they're going to be diverse too because they're going to bring a different life experience and life perspective to the conversation."[102]

Ms. Young Smith's remarks in Bogota quickly got to Apple headquarters in California. A firestorm of opposition immediately developed. She issued an apology for her "poor choice of words," even though she had prefaced her remarks by saying that she had "often" made the point. Her apology did not do her much good. Her twenty-year career at Apple was over by the end of the year.

Denise Young Smith's statement was obviously offensive to those who advocate diversity, so much so that it got her effectively fired. But was she right? To evaluate Ms. Young Smith's statement, let's imagine that the following people were in the same room at the same time: Justin Bieber, Ron DeSantis, Volodymyr Zelensky, Bernie Sanders, Tucker Carlson, Tim Cook, Bill Maher, Anthony Fauci, David Wolpe, Luka Dončić, Stephen King, and Hunter Biden. All of these people are, by the categorization of contemporary diversity, white males. Yet would it be a diverse room?

Abortion is a subject that many consider "the quintessential women's issue."[103] But what do women really think about it? In 2019, *Vox* conducted a survey and an analysis on gender and abortion views. The headline of the article: "Men and Women Have Similar Views on Abortion." This is true globally, as people in different countries have very different views on abortion, but men and women in each country have substantially the same views.[104]

Another significant political issue is the death penalty. Governor Gavin Newsom of California says that the death penalty is "infected with racism." Yet, half of black Americans support it.[105]

The same pattern can be seen with voter ID laws. The (black) Democrat Stacey Abrams considers voter ID laws to be racist—a view that the (black) former Ohio Secretary of State Ken Blackwell considers "ridiculous." Black Americans are split on voter ID laws, with approximately two-thirds of blacks supporting them.[106]

But what do those committed to DEI say? Professor Erec Smith of York College has an insight, derived from his time leading DEI at a liberal arts college. He explains, "I was talking to the president of the university at the time, and it came up in conversation that . . . black people aren't a monolith. We have different lifestyles, different religious affiliations, all kinds of different things. And he looked at me like I had four heads, like I said the craziest thing ever."[107]

Why do DEI devotees, from Erec Smith's college president to Denise Young Smith's bosses, resist the truth that there is diversity within groups? Perhaps the answer is that the claim that diversity exists within groups subverts the very logic of immutable identity diversity. If individual blacks, gays, women, Hispanics, Jews, or whomever think differently, have different experiences, and even respond to the same stimuli differently, one cannot claim that a group will be made "stronger" (or anything at all) on the basis of the race, gender, ethnicity, or sexuality of a new member.

Skillset Diversity

In December 2007, Mike Mason concluded a twenty-two-year career at the FBI. His final job was as executive assistant director. This meant that half of the FBI's operational resources were under his command, including 6,500 workers in Washington and employees at over one hundred field offices in the United States. Upon retirement, he became an executive at Verizon where he worked for thirteen years.

Upon the completion of a very successful career in the public and private sectors, Mr. Mason was ready for a third career. He became a bus driver for autistic children with the Chesterfield Public Schools in Northern Virginia. When people wondered why such a storied law enforcement officer and successful corporate executive would become a bus driver, Mr. Mason had an answer: "I think in our society we need to get used to the idea that there are no unimportant jobs."[108] And his important job was giving special needs children a loving start to a school day.

Mr. Mason's appreciation of skillset diversity is precisely aligned with that of the Torah, where all kinds of jobs—from weaving to leading—are specifically distinguished by God. But if Mr. Mason had said, instead, "Diversity is our strength," and joined in a chorus to demand that some institution increase its numbers of this or that group, no one would have noticed. Yet, his lived articulation of skillset diversity made national news. Why?

An investigation can begin with a 2021 YouGov survey of what people from different countries want in the careers of their children. The survey found that approximately three times as many Americans would "be happy" if their child became an architect, musician, teacher, or lawyer than a truck driver or a police officer.[109]

This cannot be because the professions of policing and truck driving are unimportant. Almost everything that we consume depends on truck drivers, and the functioning of society depends on police officers. And it cannot be financial. Truck drivers get paid more than teachers and most musicians. Could it be lifestyle, in that parents do not want their children to have to spend time on the road and away from their families? This answer is also unsatisfactory. Parents are generally happy when their children become consultants, lawyers, and bankers—all professions that involve a lot of time away from home. It must be that Americans simply value some professions more than others.

The lack of appreciation for skillset diversity is not an American phenomenon. Respondents everywhere want their children to be doctors, scientists, and corporate executives. How about social media influencers? Urban Indians are very encouraging, Americans are skeptical and Spaniards are highly discouraging. Nurses? Americans are very proud, whereas Poles are not. Miners? Yes in Australia, no in Italy. Builders? Yes in the UK, no in Spain.

The striking commonality across nations is that people everywhere value some professions much more than others. There is no country where all professions are even close to being regarded equally. No country, when it comes to skillset diversity, approaches the vision of the Torah and the lived conviction of Mike Mason.

In 2020, we discovered a profound irony in the lack of appreciation for skillset diversity. In the early days of Covid, the Brookings Institute scholars Hannah Van Drie and Richard Reeves noted that the term "essential worker" had entered the popular lexicon to describe those upon whose presence in the workplace society depended. They noticed that there is no correlation between the occupations deemed "essential" and those receiving much and little prestige. Numerous jobs were simultaneously considered essential and unworthy of respect—such as bus station custodians and grocery store clerks.[110]

There is at least one example of how an organization can respect and seek skillset diversity, and benefit everyone in the process. Israel is like other countries, where citizens value some professions significantly over others. Not surprisingly, the Jewish state has one of the highest ratios of doctors to citizens. What is interesting and distinctive, however, is the approach that the Israeli military, perhaps unique among militaries, has taken regarding skillset diversity.[111]

The American, British, Australian, and Canadian militaries all have diversity initiatives that are similar to those in their corporations and universities, with the same proclamations ("Diversity is our strength") and focus around race, gender, ethnicity, and sexual preferences.[112]

New recruits in the Israeli Defense Forces are often asked a simple question: What is the purpose of the IDF? Many give answers such as, "to defend the Jewish state" or "to fulfill my legal obligation." But those are not correct. The right answer is simple: "to win wars."[113]

Accordingly, the IDF has an initiative called *Ro'im Rachok* (Hebrew for "seeing into the distance"). It is focused on recruiting autistic young men and women. Some of these recruits are routed to Unit 9900, an elite intelligence unit that has a special purpose for individuals with autism. Why would the IDF specifically recruit autistic young men and women?

Autistic people, in the words of Duke professor Geraldine Dawson, "may compensate for lagging social development by developing stronger than average perceptual skills, excelling in visually and systematically oriented activities like puzzles and drawings." This, the IDF determined, is ideal for excelling in "the highly specialized task of aerial analysis."[114]

For instance, Air Force intelligence might produce photographs of the same ground day after day. A neurotypical soldier might not notice anything different. But a soldier on the autism spectrum could detect tiny changes that indicate that the enemy is moving somewhere and planning something.

The IDF, attuned to how everyone has a different skill to offer in the work of winning wars, also has a "Special in Uniform" program. This initiative includes soldiers with Down syndrome and other such conditions. How could these soldiers help Israel win wars?

An IDF commander explained that there are soldiers, probably eighteen-year-old recruits, who always want to go home or are perpetually tardy. The commander matches that soldier with a Special in Uniform soldier. "Now that soldier has a responsibility to someone who has a disability and feels ashamed to run home when these guys are trying so hard." The result: "an incredible increase in morale."[115]

Despite the United States military's pronouncement that "diversity is our strength," backed by numerous diversity initiatives, there is no such program that utilizes the unique strengths of autistic soldiers. And people with Down syndrome are ineligible for service in the United States military.[116]

Reflection

It surely will not be long before the next public figure declares, "Diversity is our strength." The answer from the Torah and social science is clear: "It can be."

The Torah, validated by social science, offers us guidance as to how we can unleash the awesome power of diversity.

First, members of a community (or a society or nation) should decide on a meaningful task it wants to accomplish. The task (or goal) could be anything that every member of the community believes is important. In the Torah, it was the building of the Tabernacle and the conduct of the activities within it. In the United States that Gordon Allport wrote about, it was the defense of the free world against the Axis powers. At United Hatzalah of Israel, it is the saving of lives and amelioration of pain that all of our volunteers—Jewish, Christian, Muslim, and Druze—believe is sacred.

While the stakes do not need to be existential, they need to be deeply important to everyone involved. It could be the creation of a company, the growth of a charity, or an addition to a church. The Torah's formula for diversity applies to all shared tasks and goals that are purposeful to those involved.

With the unifying purpose—the Tabernacle in the center of the camp—set, each member of the group should identify the distinct contribution that he can best and perhaps uniquely bring to the task. Let's imagine a young pastor or rabbi who wants to build a church or synagogue to serve a community in a large American city. The building of the institution requires architecture, painting, legal services, plumbing, carpentry, electrical work, money, and lots of other things.

The role of the leader is to identify the diverse talents and capabilities within his community and to cultivate them. This will entail the leader showing each person how important their contribution to the shared task would be. This is not hard to do; I don't think anyone would want to join a church or synagogue that does not have functional plumbing, lights, seats, and lots of other things. The leader will know that he is doing *his* task well when he has created a culture of members who greatly respect each other's differences—when the carpenter, the lawyer, the electrician, and the main funder realize that the shared task can be best and perhaps *only* accomplished because of the unique contribution of each member.

The pastor or rabbi will also, of course, pay attention to the activities that he dreams will happen in the institution. He should acknowledge that his intended parishioners will connect with God, and with each other, in diverse ways. Some will experience God primarily through prayer, some through service, some through study, some through fellowship, some through music. An inclusive community, which is best poised for fidelity and growth in its mission, will recognize this truth institutionally. That will mean having a diverse array of programming, supported by lay leaders (perhaps serving on the institution's board) who primarily connect with God in each of the different ways, to ensure that the church or synagogue is serving all members of the community well.

It is inevitable that the community, particularly if it grows, will become a venue for theological and political disputes. The leader may have a strongly held conviction on one of these disputes. The leader, even if so inclined, will not succeed or even be taken seriously, if he pretends that such disagreements do not exist. He therefore has a choice. He can simply rule on an issue, sending a clear message to those who do not agree that they do not belong. Or he can establish a culture of viewpoint diversity, and make it clear that a multitude of views (even, or perhaps especially, those he disagrees with) will be welcome.

He might find that merely "welcoming" multiple views is not enough. Especially in this era when viewpoint diversity is countercultural, he might need to educate his congregants in its virtues. He might also have to educate his members about *how* to approach viewpoint diversity. He could start with a 2017 *New York Times* column by Bret Stephens, which explored the idea of "disagreeing well." Mr. Stephens writes:

> To disagree well you must first *understand* well. You have to read deeply, listen carefully, watch closely. You need to grant your adversary moral respect; give him the intellectual benefit of doubt; have sympathy for his motives and participate empathically with his line of reasoning. And you need to allow for the possibility that you might yet be persuaded of what he has to say.[117]

A pastor (or rabbi) may find his congregation roiled by a political issue that won't, despite his wishes and efforts, stop at the institution's front door. He could educate his congregants that the Bible does not provide answers to contemporary political questions. Instead, the Bible provides guidance for how to think about them, which can result in open-minded believers of goodwill coming to different conclusions.

For instance: immigration. A member who advocates a welcoming immigration policy might cite the abundant teachings from the Torah and the New Testament that beckon us to be compassionate, hospitable, and loving to the stranger. The pastor or rabbi could emphasize that these teachings are core to the faith and incumbent upon all believers to incorporate into their lives. He could continue, educating his followers that these teachings are not all the Torah tradition says about immigration. In Deuteronomy 32–33, Moses makes it clear that there should be national boundaries whose "locks" should be made of "iron and brass." The authoritative sixteenth-century Shulchan Aruch (Code of Jewish Law) accordingly ruled that a Jew is commanded to violate even the Sabbath in order to fortify a border against a potential adversary. And Jewish law is also very clear that only immigrants who keep the seven Noahide commandments—the foundational principles of every good society, incumbent on Jews and gentiles—should be welcome.[118]

Every believer, the pastor or rabbi could emphasize, should consider all teachings, as well as the contemporary economic analysis—in formulating an opinion on immigration policy. It's quite possible that such a conversation will not result in anyone's mind being changed. But it is highly probable that it will result in each person appreciating the complexity of the issue, understanding the costs and benefits of each side, respecting the other position and those who hold it—enriching his position with insights from the other side and being drawn closer to the institution that encouraged viewpoint diversity.

The skin color, gender, sexuality, and national origin of any of the members are not included in this parable for one simple reason. Just as the Torah teaches us by having no reference to tribal membership on the Sanhedrin, these characteristics are not components of meaningful diversity. How should we reflect, as of this writing in 2024, about "diversity" as is commonly understood in American language and culture?

"Diversity" is a dynamic concept. Just as no economic forecaster in 2000 would have predicted that the second fastest growing profession two decades later would be Diversity and Inclusion Manager, predictions and projections about the future of diversity need to be made with appropriate humility.

But there are a few certainties. In 2023, the diversity policies governing admissions at universities received a shock. Nine years before, Students for Fair Admissions (SFAA) sued Harvard University, claiming that its admissions policies illegally discriminated against Asian American students. In 2022, the United States Supreme Court heard the case and decided in favor of SFAA the following year. Chief Justice John Roberts wrote, "Harvard's and UNC's admissions programs cannot be reconciled with the guarantees of the Equal Protection Clause. Both programs lack sufficiently focused and measurable objectives warranting the use of race, unavoidably employ race in a negative manner, involve racial stereotyping, and lack meaningful end points."[119]

The ruling, which was opposed by the leaders of most elite colleges, applies just to college admissions. It does not affect diversity policies in the hiring of professors, government contracting, or anything in business. Still, the ruling has required colleges to make changes in their admissions policies. It remains to be seen how substantive and lasting these changes will be. In 1996, the citizens of California voted in Proposition 209, which made illegal any consideration of race, sex, color, ethnicity, or national origin in public education, contracting, and employment. Yet, the aforementioned UCLA David Geffen Medical School admissions policies that gave such significant preferences to members of select groups were instituted in the 2020s.

Already in 2024, we have at least a provisional glimpse into how universities are responding to SFAA. Some, such as the University of North Carolina and the University of Florida, have either significantly downsized or completely eliminated their DEI apparatus. The Harvard leaders, while saying that they will "certainly comply" with the Court's decision, also stipulated they remained "steadfast" in their commitment to the "diversity" conception and goals they previously had. That being said, the Harvard admissions application for the Class of 2029 asks students to write about a time they "strongly disagreed" with someone else—and to explain how they engaged with the disputant, and what they learned from the experience.[120]

Still, the "elite" colleges and universities have not scaled back, let alone eliminated, the DEI staff that have grown massively in the second and third decades of this century. Many have diminished quantitative criteria and emphasized essays that describe the "holistic" student. For instance, the Mayo Clinic Alix School of Medicine requires applicants to answer, "Tell us how your diversity is reflected not only in your personal and professional activities, but also in your relationship with others, particularly in diverse learning environments." Many other medical schools, from Pittsburgh to Miami, require answers to similar questions.[121]

It is unlikely that "Diversity and Inclusion Manager" will be the #2 fastest growing profession in companies again. Many companies have filled DEI departments, others are letting them shrink alongside other departments in response to economic pressures, and a few have eliminated them.

The policies of governments will derive from the convictions of the elected leaders at any given point—with some (like Florida) taking broad steps to eliminating DEI and others (like New York) taking equally broad steps to expanding it.[122]

There is at least one thing we know for sure, as it is posited in the Torah and confirmed in social science: Diversity, properly defined, can be our strength.

33

Why Yisrael Salanter Jumped Out a Window and Venezuela Failed

The Torah and Science of Corruption

One of the most well-known statements in political thought is from the nineteenth-century historian and politician Lord Acton: "Power corrupts, and absolute power corrupts absolutely." There is nothing cynical about this quotation. It is an accurate description of the political world, with ancient provenance.

The political advisor Kautilya was, in the words of Nilay Singh of the University of Allahabad, "the brains behind the establishment of the [pan-Indian] Mauryan Empire." In the third-century BCE work *Arthashastra*, Kautilya recognized the problem of corruption but treated it as a necessary evil: "Just as it is impossible not to taste the honey or the poison that finds itself at the tip of the tongue, so it is impossible for a government servant not to eat up at least a bit of the king's revenue."[1]

Corruption was also rampant in ancient Egypt, China, Rome, and Greece. In ancient Greece and China, even the gods were corruptible—and people bribed them for everything from gaining favor to winning wars. Corruption was so prevalent in the ancient Olympics that athletes, their trainers, and fathers had to pledge not to "sin against the games." Many did anyway, through bribery and doping. When they were caught, they were fined, but their victories were not rescinded.[2]

It was into this world that another ancient people, the Jews, entered. And we do not have to get very far in the Torah to understand its philosophy of corruption. In Genesis 14, we learn of a regional war of four kingdoms against five. There is no good side in this conflict. However, Abraham's nephew Lot had been living in Sodom and had been captured by the four kingdoms. Abraham, who had just 318 men, conducts a daring nighttime raid, defeats the four kings, and rescues his nephew.

The king of Sodom comes to greet Abraham and offers him what are presumably the spoils of war. Abraham responds:

> With raised hand I have sworn an oath to the Lord, God Most High, Creator of heaven and earth, that I will accept nothing belonging to you, not even a thread or the strap of a sandal, so that you will never be able to say, "I made Abram rich." I will accept nothing but what my men have eaten and the share that belongs to the men who went with me, to Aner, Eshkol and Mamre. Let them have their share.

Abraham, as a servant of God, wants to make it very clear that his actions in the war are motivated solely by a desire to rescue his nephew. He wants the world to know that he hates corruption so much that he will not even—after victory in a war—accept a "thread." His men would take their "share"—their legitimate army wages—but no more.

What did the king of Sodom think of this act of anti-corruption, which would have been as foreign to him as it was to every other ruler in the ancient world? The reader is left to wonder. But Abraham's act of anti-corruption would be one that would animate the rest of the Torah.

Why a Great Rabbi Jumped Out the Window

In Exodus, God establishes the example set by Abraham as a fundamental Jewish law. In Exodus 23:8, God instructs, "You shall not take a bribe, for a bribe blinds the clear-sighted and subverts the cause of the just." Moses believes that this statement is so important for the people as they prepare to enter the land, that he emphasizes it in Deuteronomy 16:19, reiterating that "bribery blinds the eyes of the wise."

The prohibition on taking bribes is simple enough. But the clause that follows in both Exodus and Deuteronomy is deeply instructive. God and Moses are expressly not speaking about people who are confused or wicked. They direct the prohibition to those who are clear-sighted and just—precisely the kinds of people we would presume to not be susceptible to bribes.

The belief behind this clause is clear: *Everyone*, the Torah contends—even the clear-sighted, just, and wise—is susceptible to bribery. This conviction will animate numerous stories of the Torah and much of the Jewish teaching that is based on it.

In Exodus 38:21, Moses orders that the counting of the monies in the Tabernacle be done by *Levites* (plural). Not even he (the political leader) nor the high priest (the religious leader) is allowed to do so by himself.

The ancient Mishnah teaches that this kind of practice became standard among priests in the Temple. Priests could not enter the Holy Temple wearing "a bordered cloak or shoes or tefillin or an amulet." They could only wear clothing where there was no place to hide any valuables. Similarly, the Mishnah states that the priests charged with counting money in the Temple would only do so in groups of three.[3]

In Numbers 32:22, Moses is negotiating with the tribes of Reuben and Gad, who have asked to settle on the east side of the Jordan. Moses insists that these tribes must publicly demonstrate their willingness to fight for all of Israel. In so doing, they will establish themselves as being "clean before the Lord and before Israel."

Why not just clean before God? God, after all, knows everything. One who is clean before God *is* clean regardless of what others think. But apparently Moses did not think that was enough. In stating the importance of being clean "before Israel," Moses emphasizes that the nation cannot tolerate even the appearance or the possibility of corruption.

Moses's statement that we must be "clean before the Lord and before Israel" became the biblical basis for the ancient Jewish concept of *marit ayin*, "appearance to the eye." According to this principle, we should act in a way where no one could plausibly say that we are doing something corrupt. An individual should be so embarrassed by the prospect of being considered *potentially* corrupt that he would not do anything to arouse the suggestion.

This discipline was exemplified by the nineteenth-century sage Rabbi Yisrael Salanter. He paid a visit to a former student, by then a banker, who was not expecting him. The student, surprised to see his great teacher, rushed out of the room to get properly dressed. Rabbi Salanter saw an open money box in the room vacated by the banker and jumped out of a window.[4]

Moses's prohibition on the priests of the Tabernacle counting money alone and Rabbi Yisrael Salanter jumping out of the window show how our best leaders live and, through their example, teach the conviction that corruption can "blind the clear-sighted." But "blinding the clear-sighted" is not all that Exodus 38:21 teaches regarding the dangers of bribery. It also "subverts the cause of the just," making good governance impossible. In Numbers 16, Moses shows just how deeply he understood and incorporated this teaching.

"Not a Single Donkey"

In Numbers 16, Moses faces Korach's Rebellion, which threatens to depose him. The stakes could not be higher. If the revolution succeeded, the Jewish people would have traded our master leader, teacher, and prophet for a demagogue—ensuring the destruction of God's project on earth before we got out of the desert.

The rebellion is easy to refute intellectually. The rebels have no positive agenda. They propose no new policies or political structure. They do not even have a specific complaint against Moses. Their only complaint was that there is *a* leader, which violated their populist notion that "all the people are holy." Any one of these points would have been grounds for an effective response from Moses. Yet he makes none of them. Instead, he says, "I have not taken a single donkey of theirs."

Moses had his supporters and detractors, but no one had ever questioned his integrity. Indeed, the Torah had already characterized him as "the humblest man ever to live" (Numbers 12:3) and would soon identify him as the greatest prophet ever to live (Deuteronomy 34:10). These are not descriptions of someone who thinks that he deserves more than he has, let alone one who is willing to use his public position for private gain.

So, why would Moses base the continuation of his rule (and the future of the Jewish people) on rebutting an accusation that no one has made? There are several possibilities, all of which can be true. He might have believed that ancient peoples would assume that leaders are corrupt. He might have believed that people, even if they think they have to tolerate it, hate corruption. He might have believed that *any* corruption (even taking a single donkey) is destructive for a society. And he might have believed that citizens have a right, and even the obligation, to depose any leader who is at all corrupt. He probably considered all of those reasons and resolved to publicly anchor his leadership in the image of incorruptibility.

The final biblical word on corruption belongs to King Solomon. He said in Proverbs 29:4, "By justice a king brings stability to a land, but a man who demands 'contributions' demolishes it."

Can corruption—"contributions"—really *demolish* a society?

The Science

Venezuela

In 1950, Venezuela had a per capita GDP of $7,424. That made it the fourth richest country in the world, right behind the United States, Switzerland, and New Zealand. In the 1950s, the Standard Oil Company made a promotional film encouraging investment in Venezuela, stating that "Venezuela does have something the rest of the free world needs . . . some of the world's most precious resources, oil, iron ore, and other minerals." In short, Venezuela had everything going for it—it was resource rich, growth oriented, internationally celebrated, and had a basis to continue to grow from strength to strength.[5]

No one in the 1950s would have predicted what the University of Pennsylvania professor William Burke-White would say of Venezuela in 2016: "The experience of the everyday citizen in Venezuela on the ground today is one of hunger and starvation."[6]

By 2020, it was the poorest country in the Americas, with 96 percent of its population living in poverty and 70 percent in extreme poverty. Its poverty is in spite of its oil wealth, even with oil being more than twice as valuable in 2020 as it was in 1950 on an inflation-adjusted basis.[7]

When Venezuela was thriving in 1950, Taiwan and South Korea were among the poorest nations in the world, with a GDP per capita of $922 and $876 respectively. West Germany and Japan were still in ruins after being destroyed by the Allies in World War II, and East Germany even more so by the Soviets in the generation that followed. Yet Taiwan, South Korea, Germany, and Japan are now among the richest countries.[8]

What can explain these startling changes? Professor Richard Florida of the University of Toronto answers in two digits. Professor Florida has determined that there is a .81 correlation between a nation's Gross Domestic

Product and its Corruption Perception Index rating (which is determined by Transparency International).

Indeed, Venezuela is ranked by Transparency International at 177 (out of 180) in terms of corruption. As the US Department of Justice puts it, Venezuela is "plagued by corruption." South Korea, Taiwan, Germany, and Japan all rate as fundamentally non-corrupt.[9]

The Implications of .81

The very high correlation of .81 between wealth and corruption that Professor Florida posits is manifested in seemingly every measure of the wealth and poverty of nations. A country with significant access to the sea has important economic advantages, one of the most significant of which is that it makes global trade easier and cheaper. However, wealthy countries such as Austria, Luxembourg, Lichtenstein, and Switzerland are landlocked. Somalia, one of the world's poorest countries, has a large and glorious coastline—perfectly constituted for international trade and beachfront tourism. The difference: Somalia is, according to Transparency International, one of the three most corrupt countries in the world. Austria, Luxembourg, Lichtenstein, and Switzerland are non-corrupt.

Another massive economic advantage in the cultivation of wealth is natural resources. A country with abundant natural resources has wealth right in its ground. Yet, countries such as Israel, Switzerland, Taiwan, Japan, and Singapore that have very few natural resources have vibrant economies, with high GDP per capita as a result. Other countries such as Russia, Iraq, Democratic Republic of the Congo, and Sierra Leone are blessed with abundant resources, but have weak economies with low GDP per capita. The difference? The former are fundamentally non-corrupt and the latter are fundamentally corrupt.

In 2023, the economist Bjorn Lomborg published a book called *Best Things First*, which described the results of a study he conducted of leading economists to determine the twelve most efficient ways to deploy money to improve the world. These high-returning investments included spending in maternal/child health, agricultural R&D, tuberculosis, chronic diseases, and childhood immunization. These all qualified for the top twelve, but none were at the top of the list. Number one—the *best* investment in improving the world—was "E-procurement systems."

Dr. Lomborg explains, "While it's impossible to establish precisely, corruption has an estimated global cost of $1 trillion annually." He cites the World Bank's 2020 Enterprise Survey that showed that, across countries, 23.7 percent of companies said that they are expected to "give gifts" to secure government contracts, with significant variation between countries. Dr. Lomborg and his colleagues found that instituting "an online e-procurement system makes it much more difficult for private entities to garner special treatment." This is due to the digital fingerprint that reveals how the procurement decision was made, features in these systems that can surface red flags for corruption, the transparency these systems provide for outside monitors to detect corruption, and the way that they expand government contracting to vastly more parties.[10]

The analysis of Dr. Lomborg coheres with the observation of Farah Stockman, a *New York Times* journalist who reported extensively from Afghanistan. In September 2023, Ms. Stockman wrote that political leaders often divide nations into autocracies and democracies. However, she writes, there is a "more important division." It is between countries where corruption is tolerated and countries where "corruption is the exception rather than the rule."[11]

And the ways that corruption can, per King Solomon, "demolish" a society are seemingly endless.

Health

In the early 2010s, the UK physician Dr. David Berger volunteered at a small hospital in North India. In 2014, he wrote of his experience in the *British Medical Journal*. He ordered an electrocardiogram for a patient, following which a young doctor demanded to sign the script. Dr. Berger soon learned the reason for the doctor's urgency: The clinic that administers the electrocardiogram pays a kickback to the doctor who ordered it, with an envelope of cash.

There was nothing unique about this experience. Dr. Berger noticed that young people were admitted to medical school as a result of making huge donations, causing decades of indebtedness. Doctors ordered "totally unnecessary" tests, from which they received kickbacks, a great expense to "desperately poor people." And pharmaceutical companies provided doctors with cash, goods, and sometimes prostitutes. Consequently, the healthcare system he observed lost the trust of citizens, while driving its costs up and its legitimacy down. When he discussed the situation with others at the hospital, he would be met by "apologetic shrugs and half smiles," with explanations like, "The corruption strangles everything, Sir. It's like a cancer."[12]

There is nothing unique to India about Dr. Berger's experience. A 2018 report from the European Proceedings concluded that "Russia is one of the most corrupt nations in the world. It ranks only after African and Asian countries. The scale of Russian corruption is enormous. It can equal the amount of the federal budget . . . The corruption exists at all levels of the healthcare system, from nurses to high-level officials of the Ministry of Healthcare."[13]

The consequences? A 2018 analysis by Oliver Bullough in *Al Jazeera* found that the Russian rate of HIV prevalence and growth is "unprecedented for a European country." Mr. Bullough writes, "It is spread by drug use, prostitution, and a poor healthcare system, all of which are a result of the country's rampant corruption." The same analysis shows that corruption is at the root of outbreaks of ebola in Sierra Leone and Liberia, multidrug resistant tuberculosis in Central Asia, and polio in Ukraine.[14]

This tragic data keeps coming. A 2022 report from Dr. Emily Glynn of the University of Washington shows that corrupt countries have higher infant and child mortality rates, lower life expectancy, lower immunization rates, higher rates of antibiotic resistance, worse mental health, and a lower perception of their actual health.[15]

Education

The same countries that suffer from corruption in the healthcare sector also see it in the classroom. In 2013, the World Bank published a report entitled "The Hidden Cost of Corruption: Teacher Absenteeism and Loss in Schools." Countries including Kenya, India, Uganda, and Senegal have teacher absenteeism rates that approach 30 percent. The cost of absenteeism can be 25 percent of a school system's budget, and pervasive absenteeism makes it very difficult for the students who regularly show up to school to receive an education when there is no one there to teach them.

The reasons for this absenteeism can be teachers missing class to "moonlight," and being called by politicians to perform "electioneering." The costs of "absenteeism" or "ghost teachers" to the taxpayer are quantifiable. The costs to the students, in terms of a diminished education, are not—but they are surely greater.[16]

This phenomenon of "ghost teachers" is just one example of education corruption. Reports from the Christian Michelsen Institute in Norway and UNESCO show how corruption permeates education finance (leakage of funds), construction (inflation of costs and selection of inferior vendors), graduation (diploma mills, examination fraud), information systems (manipulating data), nepotism (unqualified teachers), and sexual harassment (two-thirds of girls in Botswana in 2001 reported being sexually harassed by teachers). The extent of this corruption is remarkable. One anti-cheating campaign waged by the Romanian government led to a 50 percent reduction in the pass rate.[17]

Corruption in education does what corruption always does. It raises costs, reduces quality, and calls into question the legitimacy of the thing it infects. A uniquely pernicious effect of corruption in education is articulated in a United Nations report. Students in a corrupt system will question why they should apply any effort, given that the system does not reward academic performance or hard work, but bribes. In addition, students learn the most important lessons, as they always do, by observing what the adults in their environment do. The UN report says, "Moreover, students develop the understanding that the system works in corrupt ways and that bribes are necessary to get things done—a modus operandi which students later transfer to their professional and daily activities." Hence, it makes sense that this UN analysis of "corruption in education" was issued by a *seemingly* unrelated entity: the United Nations Office on Drugs and Crime.[18]

Criminality

In 2019, Interpol (the global policing organization) published a study on corruption and organized crime in East Africa. Interpol concluded that corruption "facilitates a wide array of illicit activities notably drug trafficking, trafficking in human beings and people smuggling, wildlife crimes, the trade of stolen motor vehicles and small arms and light weapons." And there is nothing unique to East Africa about this dynamic, as the report also concludes, "It is highly likely that corruption acts in the Eastern African region are similar in almost all criminal markets."[19]

How does corruption facilitate such broad and deep lawbreaking? A country can have laws against drug trafficking, human trafficking, and arms sales, but they are meaningless if criminals can buy off the authorities.

The crime bred by corruption leads people to seek order at all costs. Consequently, another Interpol analysis concluded that corruption provides a "fertile ground for terrorism." Indeed, the Carnegie Endowment reports that Afghan elders who aligned with the terrorist Taliban government did so more because of governmental corruption than because of religious commitment. Other organizations that have developed and thrived because of the corruption of the centralized authorities include Boko Haram, ISIS, Hezbollah, and Hamas, whose "success," the attorney Magd Lh wrote in 2021, "[is] because the majority of Palestinians were disgusted with the blatant corruption of the Palestinian Authority (PA) under the Fatah party."[20]

Moses's Single Donkey, in Modern Times

When people think of corruption, the power to confiscate an enormous amount often comes to mind. There is the Palestinian leader Yasser Arafat who died a billionaire; the Nigerian leader Sani Abacha, who concluded his five-year reign with at least $1.5 billion; the Tunisian president Zine El Abidine Ben Ali who, during his twenty-four-year reign, stole $11 to 17 billion; and Vladimir Putin, who might be the world's richest man despite never having worked in the private sector. Government leaders are not the only parties to big corruption. The European conglomerate Siemens, investigators in 2006 concluded, gained its global market share by paying $1.4 billion in bribes.[21]

Every country that ranks high on the Transparency International Corruption Index has had spectacular acts of what is known as "grand corruption." But this is not the only kind of corruption that exists in society. Moses does not remind the people at Korach's Rebellion that he did not take all of the gold out of the Tabernacle. He tells them that he did not take "a single donkey."

This kind of transparency stands to refute another kind of corruption, which may be characterized as "petty corruption." The term "petty corruption" reflects the belief that there must be a kind of corruption that can be overlooked. Is there a corruption equivalent of petty cash? Or, per the Torah, does the tolerance of any level of corruption become so pervasively corrosive that it ultimately defines the character of the society and the behavior of its members?

In 2019, Professor Dan Ariely of Duke and Ximena Garcia-Rada of Texas A&M conducted a study where students entered a game of dice for the chance to win money. Some students were offered the chance to "illegally" bribe the researchers to potentially earn more money than if they did not pay the bribe. They also allowed students to cheat within the game. They found that the mere exposure to the possibility of a bribe led students to cheat. They concluded that "corruption is contagious."[22]

It stands to reason that corruption should be contagious. Corruption is, at its core, the arrogation of public resources for private purposes. Most people value their private interests (in which they have an entire stake) over the public good (in which they have a very small stake). If people see that society tolerates taking public goods to advance private interests, individuals will easily convince themselves that it is okay to do so themselves.

In a state system, this inevitable contagion can become organized and systemic. The former US Department of Justice attorney Jacob Steiner explains, "The low-level official demanding a bribe at the point of service might be required to give a cut of the bribes (or salary) to the next person up the chain, who might be required to do the same, and so forth." Mr. Steiner concludes, "Corruption at any level legitimizes and normalizes wrongful behavior, threatening the rule of law and making anti-corruption efforts all the more difficult."[23]

Seemingly every analysis on the subject comes to the same conclusion about one of its effects: Corruption exacts disproportionate suffering on a society's poor. A country in which it is commonplace for a police officer to take a bribe instead of writing a ticket will generally not have an income-based pricing schedule. Consequently, poor people in corrupt countries will spend a significant percentage of their low income on paying bribes.

A 2012 report from Transparency International revealed that the average Kenyan paid 23 euro per bribe and the average Mexican paid 9.7 euro per bribe. This accumulation of bribes cost the average Mexican household 14 percent of its income, with poorer families paying 33 percent of their income. The regressive tax that corruption imposes on the poor exists throughout the world.[24]

Moses's Single Donkey Comes to New York

The problem of corruption in Kenya and Mexico is unlikely to be ameliorated by new laws. Both countries have laws and enforcement mechanisms to prevent and combat corruption. This is common. In 2003, the United Nations adopted a Convention Against Corruption. Signatory nations committed to a robust system of anti-corruption, including the enactment of laws, rigorous internal enforcement mechanisms, and international cooperation. Kenya and Mexico adopted it immediately.

Over the next twenty years, the convention was adopted by Afghanistan, Bangladesh, the Democratic Republic of the Congo, Haiti, Russia, South Sudan, Turkmenistan, Venezuela, Yemen, and other countries still considered "Highly Corrupt" by Transparency International. Many of these countries have gone even further than required by the convention, and have adopted anti-corruption provisions into their national constitutions.

Sometimes, such a commitment, expressed in law, is worse than meaningless. These are the instances where anti-corruption laws can become a weapon for corrupt officials to use against their political opponents. Vladimir Putin, for instance, has long imprisoned political opponents for being "corrupt."[25]

The persistence of corruption in a society that formally condemns it would not have surprised the Author of the Torah, who decreed that an anti-corrupt legal system must be accompanied by a *cultural* intolerance for corruption. It is easy to see if a society has a law against corruption and formal enforcement mechanisms. It is harder to know whether, and how deeply, a society has a culture of anti-corruption. The ideal test of the culture would be whether public officials would act corruptly in the absence of any legal sanction, whether, in order words, corruption would embarrass them and their colleagues.

Fortunately, twenty-first-century social science has produced exactly that test. In 2006, Professors Raymond Fisman of Boston University and Edward Miguel of the University of California at Berkeley took to an obscure dataset on behalf of the National Center for Economic Research: the parking violations incurred by diplomats in New York City between 1997 and 2002. This dataset is instructive because diplomats during that period enjoyed immunity from any fines or other penalties. They could violate New York parking laws with no legal consequence.

In their paper, "Cultures of Corruption: Evidence from Diplomatic Parking Tickets," Mr. Fisman and Mr. Miguel found that diplomats from some countries (including Sweden, Norway, Denmark, Canada, Israel, Australia, Switzerland, the Netherlands, and New Zealand) had 0.1 or fewer unpaid tickets per diplomat. By contrast, diplomats from other countries (including Egypt, Chad, Sudan, Mozambique, Pakistan, and Senegal) had dozens and in some cases hundreds of unpaid tickets per diplomat. They concluded:

> We find that this measure is strongly correlated with existing measures of home country corruption. This finding suggests that cultural or social norms related to corruption are quite persistent: even when stationed thousands of miles away, diplomats behave in a manner highly reminiscent of officials in the home country. Norms related to corruption are apparently deeply ingrained, and factors other than legal enforcement are important determinants of corruption behavior.[26]

Reflection

One of the most powerful politicians in New York in the late nineteenth and early twentieth centuries was George Washington Plunkitt. In 1905, State Senator Plunkitt gave a now famous address near the New York County Courthouse. It is entitled "Honest Graft." He said:

> Everybody is talkin' these days about Tammany men growin' rich on graft, but nobody thinks of drawin' the distinction between honest graft and dishonest graft. There's all the difference in the world between the two. Yes, many of our men have grown rich in politics. I have myself. I've made a big fortune out of the game, and I'm gettin' richer every day, but I've not gone in for dishonest graft, blackmailin' gamblers, saloonkeepers, disorderly people, etc., and neither has any of the men who have made big fortunes in politics. There's an honest graft, and I'm an example of how it works. I

> might sum up the whole thing by sayin', "I seen my opportunities and I took 'em." Just let me explain by examples. My party's in power in the city, and it's goin' to undertake a lot of public improvements. Well, I'm tipped off, say, that they're going to lay out a new park at a certain place. I see my opportunity and I take it. I go to that place and I buy up all the land I can in the neighborhood. Then the board of this or that makes its plan public, and there is a rush to get my land, which nobody cared particularly for before. Ain't it perfectly honest to charge a good price and make a profit on my investment and foresight? Of course, it is. Well, that's honest graft.[27]

Times have changed. In 2016, Rachel Freier became the first Hasidic Jewish woman to hold public office in the United States when she became a civil court judge in George Washington Plunkitt's state. In the ten years before becoming a judge, she had founded three charitable organizations. One serves poor Jewish families, one serves at-risk youth, and one is an all-female ambulance service. Yet, she had to stop raising money for all of them because judges in New York are prohibited from raising money, even for a charity.[28]

This sensitivity to corruption is not a New York phenomenon. If an American wants to wish his postman a happy birthday, he has to do so in accordance with The Code of Federal Regulations Standards of Ethical Conduct for Employees of the Executive Branch, Part 2635, Subpart B. "The appreciative homeowner cannot give cash or cash equivalent, but can give a donut, cookie or a fruit platter . . . so long as the platter is intended to be shared with other postal workers and is valued at less than $20."[29]

The concern solved by the rules governing judges raising money for charity and gifts given to postal workers is likely not one of substance. Could a judge theoretically raise money for a charity without having her rulings compromised? Sure. Would a postman be corrupted by accepting a $50 gift card from a customer who appreciated how he delivered the mail in the sleet, snow, and heat? It is unlikely. But the American devotion to anti-corruption (akin to the concept of *marit ayin*) is so deep that the regulation is uncontroversial.

This is not to say that the United States has solved the corruption problem. There are still United States officials and their family members of both parties who use their public office for private gain, and even do so in brazen ways (hidden gold bars, kickbacks to school principals, cash stashed in freezers and jacket pockets, no-show jobs, shell companies, etc.). The persistence of these acts does not mean that nothing has changed. The response to them demonstrates that *everything* has changed.

First, the conception of what is corrupt and how it should be punished is now wider than ever. In 2007, New Orleans councilman Oliver Thomas was sentenced to thirty-seven months in prison for taking a $15K bribe; in 2014, the Illinois state representative Derrick Smith spent five months in prison for receiving $7K for writing a letter in support of a vendor; in 2019, the Chicago alderman William Cochran went to prison for a year for expropriating $14K from a charity; in 2019, numerous parents went to prison for paying thinly veiled bribes to get their children into college.

Many of these men offered defenses, but none said any variant of "everyone does it" or "it's not that big a deal." They knew that any such excuse or other justification would be unconvincing and even offensive in our culture, which has incorporated the belief that even expropriating a contemporary equivalent of "a single donkey" is completely unacceptable.

Second, there is just one expected and customary response to corruption, including when conducted by one's political ally. This is swift condemnation, followed by a vigorous prosecution and a significant penalty. The intolerability of any corruption is one of the few things that Democrats and Republicans, from all wings of both parties, agree on completely.

Many countries are with the United States in their culturally ingrained rejection of corruption. Others are not. But just as New York City could not be farther away from when "honest graft" was celebrated, there is hope for other countries who are presently rife with corruption. The analysis of Rwanda by Michael Rubin of the American Enterprise Institute is instructive.

Rwanda was once one of the most corrupt countries in the world—on par with Russia and worse than Yemen, Libya, and Iran. It is now on par with the Czech Republic, and less corrupt than Italy and Greece. What happened?

Dr. Rubin explains that, in 1997, Rwanda established a National Tender Board and they led the Rwanda Public Procurement Authority to establish honesty and decentralization in government transactions. The Rwanda Revenue Authority reformed tax collection and ended privileges that the elites enjoyed. The Bureau of the Auditor General was established and rid the government of thousands of public "employees" who were not doing anything. Other committees and boards were established to monitor the wealth of government officials, promote meritocracy, and monitor public perception of corruption.[30]

The success of Rwanda is largely due to the leadership of President Paul Kagame. However, relying on a singular leader, who serves for decades, is not a dependable or replicable formula for anti-corruption. In 2007, the Sudanese-British entrepreneur Mo Ibrahim created the Ibrahim Prize—a $5 million award given to an African leader who is democratically elected, serves out his term and then leaves and is devoted to anti-corruption. Winners have included former leaders of Niger, Liberia, Cabo Verde, Namibia, Botswana, and Mozambique.

There is not one formula for fighting corruption. The corruption temptation and problem can be presumed to exist everywhere—from New Jersey to Rwanda. In all places and times, anti-corruption must start with leaders echoing Moses, who said, "I have not taken a single donkey"—and for a culture to be established accordingly.

ACKNOWLEDGMENTS

My gratitude for this book will begin with Eagles' Wings, the Evangelical parachurch ministry devoted to Christian Zionism and philo-Semitism. Eagles' Wings, which has a network of 10,000+ (and fast growing) churches, has been one of the best friends and partners the Jewish people have *ever* had.

And it has been one of the best friends and partners this Jewish person has ever had! Each week, Eagles' Wings hosts Torah Tuesday (at 12 PM EST), where I teach Torah to primarily Evangelical pastors and parishioners from around the world. We go through each line in the Torah, extracting the practical lessons and real-world guidance that it offers us. In the course of preparing for and teaching these sessions, I was struck by how much of the guidance offered in each Torah verse has been addressed by the social science that has captured the public imagination throughout this century.

This was far from the only gift that Torah Tuesdays has granted me. Each Torah Tuesday session has an Evangelical pastor affiliated with Eagles' Wings as its host. The real-time questions, challenges, and insights from these Christian clergymen has consistently enriched my Torah understanding and its application to the decisions and dynamics that shape our day-to-day lives. The wisdom and insights I gleaned from these pastors was so consistently incisive and interesting that I took to opening a second screen because I knew a host would say something I would want to note for this book.

I would like to thank the Torah Tuesday pastors, many of whom have become—as with other Evangelical leaders I have met through Eagles'

Wings—dear friends. These pastors include Samuel Bentley, Cameron Brice, Luke Cobrae, Juan Diaz, Malik Edwards, Joe Green, Josh Hamlin, Justin Hamilton, Ken Hansen, Bryce Harper, Rusty Nelson, Juan Rivera, Doug Reed, Micah Wood, Kaylen Xiong, and a crowd favorite despite the fact that he makes everyone turn on their cameras, Marcus McFolling. My friendships with these Christian leaders has enriched my life, deepened my Torah understanding, and made me a better Jew.

I am also grateful to my Jewish friends—from whom I have learned much Torah, in person and through their teachings over many years. These include Rabbis Shmuley Boteach, Kenneth Brander, Matt Gewirtz, Efrem Goldberg, Shmully Hecht, Moshe Scheiner, Meir Soloveitchek, Mark Wildes, Ambassador Michael Oren, Cantor Howard Stahl, Doron Spielman, Jeff Ballabon, and Mitch Horowitz.

In addition to teaching Torah Tuesdays, I lead a Torah study every Saturday morning (to primarily Jews). I am grateful to all of those who have studied with us over the past ten years, for the biblical insights I have gained from the preparation and the teaching—and for enabling our children to grow up in Torah.

There is Aviva (now nine), who went from excitedly recounting her first escalator ride without someone carrying her (at Barnes and Noble on 83rd Street) to offering her perspectives on Pinchas driving a spear through Zimri and Cozbi as they were having sex on the Tabernacle steps in Numbers 25.

There is Talia (now twelve), reminding me that I said, "This is one of the most important lines in the Torah" dozens of times—and me trying to explain that it very well might be right with each of them. And there is Elijah (now fourteen), who I will always remember as the six-year-old boy climbing onto my chair to pound me until I gave him Torah questions (he got a dollar a question answered correctly).

There is Joshua (now sixteen), who a couple of years ago told me before Torah study that he did not want to come. This was familiar, but he came as he always does. During that Torah study, I saw him taking abundant notes. I wondered what was going on. When it concluded, he showed me what he was doing. He had diagrammed my teaching, having recorded 29 points in 58 minutes. He categorized them into ones that he "predicted" and "knew" (based on previous years teachings), one that was "dumb," one that "made absolutely no sense," and three that were "new." He calculated that teaching him the new points would have taken just six minutes.

I had his sheet framed—as its presentation is a masterpiece in design thinking and early teenage Torah understanding. Maybe one point was "dumb" and one "made absolutely no sense"—but I think that an annual reconsideration of two dozen good Torah points and learning three new ones is worth a fourteen year old's 58 minutes! Anyway, I put Joshua's page on godwasright.com for anyone to consider.

My last book, *The Telling: How Judaism's Essential Book Reveals the Meaning of Life*, was published in the spring of 2021. When the book tour was completed, I had the general idea for this book. I asked Rabbi Benji Levy in Jerusalem if he knew anyone who could work with me on research for this book.

He said that he had the perfect person, and introduced me to David Wolfowicz. Wow, was Benji right! David, who served as a commander in the IDF Education Corps, is extraordinarily learned in all things Jewish—and has put his encyclopedic knowledge in a framework that is at once exceptionally structured, rigorous, creative, and accessible (he has seemingly perfect recall). David has, remarkably and fortuitously, the same knowledge base, and accompanying talents, in social science. We have done Zoom sessions six days a week for three years (usually with me in New York and he in Jerusalem), with follow-up on email throughout each day. He has the knowledge, wisdom, range, and insights that would be staggering in a generational talent twice his age, and I am deeply fortunate to be able to work with him now.

I would also like to thank my agent, Urbahn of Javelin, and the terrific team that he has assembled. I am especially grateful for their landing this work with BenBella Books. BenBella's founder/CEO Glenn Yeffeth has built a remarkable company, with systems, processes, discipline, and amazing professionals in every department. They are great at *everything*, from production to design to strategy. BenBella—which, I can say as a businessman myself, has commercial lessons to teach probably every company—does all of that while maintaining a deep respect for the book, and the creative process that an author needs to produce the best one he can. I am fortunate to have Glenn and his colleagues not just as my publisher and friends, but as my partners.

In addition to Glenn, I'm delighted to extend my gratitude to the outstanding BenBella team of Madeline Griggg, Susan Welte, Alicia Kania, Lindsay Marshall, Monica Lowry, Rick Chillot, and Leah Wilson. And I am especially thankful for Joe Rhatigan, who edited this book for BenBella. Joe's careful eye, trenchant insights, incisive questions, fresh perspective, and disciplined editorial methodology has made this a much better book.

I am also grateful to people I don't know and probably never will, but who made it possible to write this book. There are so many people I could thank here, so I'll have to settle with a too-short list. I start each day by studying Torah on the treadmill for an hour (six miles now; I get a little slower every year). I am grateful for the manufacturers of all of the treadmills I have used around the world in the three years it took to write this book. I am grateful to whomever invented double-speed on audio and video files.

I am also grateful to all of those who made the internet so amazing—those at Google who made searching so easy and good, those at Google Docs who enabled me to write regardless of where I was and easily return to earlier versions, those at Amazon Kindle who made every book a click away, those at Zoom who enabled me to meet with David six days a week, those at ChatGPT, which came on strong in the past six months, and those who uploaded every social science study and other document that I used.

I would also like to thank those who enabled me to find my writing groove. These include those at Zyn (and its many excellent competitors) and Spotify—the latter by making Elvis, Sinatra, the Statler Brothers, Emmy Lou Harris, The Cathedrals, and others in primarily upbeat country and gospel music always available.

I am also deeply indebted to my parents, Susan and Michael Gerson. In the course of giving me really the perfect upbringing, they instilled in me a love of our Jewish heritage, of learning, and of the search for truth. I have quoted their wisdom directly in this book, and its ever presence was with me throughout its writing. Their guidance, in what they taught me through their words and their actions, has always been invaluable and deeply appreciated—and it has been *especially* helpful here, given my mother's profession as a writing instructor and my father's profession as a psychologist and their eagerness to critically read every draft I shared.

And then there is my wife, Rabbi Erica Gerson. She has taught me, and all who know her, the essential virtues of our Jewish faith through her example. Her devotion to truth and commitment to speaking and spreading it, her mindful and successful creation of a magnificent Jewish home, her living and modeling the Torah teachings and principles on spousehood and parenthood, her kindness, compassion, rationality, competence and generosity, her reverence for the old and embrace of the new, her learning and her leadership—she *is* the biblical "Woman of Valor." As our eighteenth anniversary approaches, I realize that my goal in life is to make her proud. I hope that this book, which is dedicated to her, has done that.

All of the author's proceeds from this book will go to African Mission Healthcare, which I co-founded in 2010 with Dr. Jon Fielder. We co-founded AMH after Jon had been a missionary doctor in Kenya and Malawi for almost a decade, and saw that very few people in Africa have access to decent healthcare. He also identified a solution. There are Christian missionary physicians at Christian hospitals throughout Africa who, inspired by their faith, devote their entire lives to provide care to those who Jesus called in the Book of Matthew, "the least among us." These doctors have, for a variety of reasons that could be the subject of another book, been effectively abandoned in the field.

We created African Mission Healthcare to partner with these holy men and women to provide clinical care, enable training, build infrastructure, and do administration at Christian hospitals throughout east and central Africa. After years of working with African Mission Healthcare and its doctors every day, Erica and I know that the highest return on investment in the world (measured by output/dollars invested)—in business, investing, or philanthropy—is through support of these missionary doctors through AMH.

Consequently, we are delighted to commit all of the proceeds of this book to the AMH SAFE (Surgical Access for Everyone) program. Every purchase of this book, therefore, will help a mother in need of a Caesarian section or birth injury repair, a girl who fell and broke her leg, a boy who got burned in a (common) kitchen fire and whose fingers are fused together, a child with cleft palate or bow legs, a laborer who developed a hernia and suffers immobilizing pain—and many other such patients.

Without the support of AHM, in partnership with Christian missionary physicians, these surgeries simply would not happen. For an average cost of $319, a donor can enable one of these surgeries—and save a life, ameliorate great pain, enable a mother to return healthy to her children, a child to get back to school, and a man to return to work so he can support his family.

If there is one biblical verse that is incumbent upon all faithful Jews and Christians, it is Deuteronomy 10: "You shall love the stranger." If there is one principle incumbent upon devotees of social science and other rationalists, it is the maximization of Return on Investment (ROI). This is the measure of how much can be accomplished per unit of resource expended—be it time, money or something else.

If anyone wants to learn more about African Mission Healthcare, please email amh@godwasright.com, and we'll look forward to a discussion.

NOTES

Introduction

1. Debbie Maimon, "Rescued Sifrei Torah Carry Secrets of Jewish Eternity," *Yated Ne'eman*, February 8, 2023.
2. From discussions with Imam Mohammed Jebara.
3. John Adams, "Letter to Benjamin Rush," National Archives, February 2, 1807, https://founders.archives.gov/documents/Adams/99-02-02-5166.

Chapter 1

1. See Rashi, Genesis 9:23.
2. J. B. Soloveitchik, in H. Schachter, *Nefesh Harav* (Reishis Yerushalayim, 1993), 272–273.
3. Mishna, Avot 5:3.
4. Maimonides, Commentary to Avot 5:3.
5. Sfat Emet, Lech Lecha 2.
6. Ramban, Exodus 20:12; Abraham bar Hiyya, *Higayon Hanefesh Haatzuva* (The Logic of the Melancholy Soul), 36; Rashi, Song of Songs 4:5.
7. Rabbenu Bechaye, Exodus 20:14.
8. See Rashi, Exodus 32:6.
9. S. Held, "Parashat Ki Tissa: The Importance of Character," *Hadar*, 2014, https://www.hadar.org/torah-resource/importance-character.
10. Babylonian Talmud, Nazir 23a.
11. Babylonian Talmud, Kiddushin 31a; Y. Hutner, *Pachad Yitzchak*, Rosh Hashanah 74.
12. J. B. Soloveichik, *Kol Dodi Dofek: Listen-my Beloved Knocks*, trans. D. Z. Gordon and J. R. Woolf (Ktav Publishing, 2006), 113–114.

13. Tanchuma, Parshas Ki Teitzei 9; Sefer HaMaamarim 5679, 294.
14. Maimonides, Mishneh Torah, Laws of Substitutions 4:13.
15. Orchot Tzaddikim, Introduction, 19.
16. Vilna Gaon, Even Shleimah 2.
17. Sforno, Deuteronomy 10:17, Exodus 34:6; Nachmanides, Deuteronomy 23:19.
18. Bereshit Rabbah 87:7.
19. Shaarei Teshuvah 3:70.
20. A. Ghoniem and W. Hofmann, "Yielding to Temptation: How and Why Some People Are Better at Controlling Themselves," *The Inquisitive Mind* 27, (2015), https://www.in-mind.org/article/yielding-to-temptation-how-and-why-some-people-are-better-at-controlling-themselves.
21. A. H. Mokdad, J. S. Marks, D. F. Stroup, and J. L. Gerberding, "Actual Causes of Death in the United States, 2000," *JAMA* 291, no. 10 (2004): 1238; R. L. Keeney, "Personal Decisions Are the Leading Cause of Death," *Operations Research* 56, no. 6, (2008): 1335–1347.
22. H. J. Parry and H. M. Crossley, "Validity of Responses to Survey Questions," *Public Opinion Quarterly* 14, no. 1 (1950): 61–80.
23. Seth Stephens-Davidowitz, "Everybody Lies: How Google Search Reveals Our Darkest Secrets," *The Guardian*, July 9, 2017, https://www.theguardian.com/technology/2017/jul/09/everybody-lies-how-google-reveals-darkest-secrets-seth-stephens-davidowitz; B. Carlson, "Everybody Lies: Pollster Edition—A Wealth of Common Sense," *A Wealth of Common Sense*, November 5, 2020, https://awealthofcommonsense.com/2020/11/everybody-lies-pollster-edition/.
24. M. Kataria, "Men Slower Than They Think," University of Gothenburg, June 8, 2017, https://www.gu.se/en/news/men-slower-than-they-think, https://www.sciencedirect.com/science/article/abs/pii/0001691881900056?via%3Dihub.

    C. Halton, "Self-Enhancement: Meaning, Examples, Disadvantages," Investopedia, September 29, 2022, https://www.investopedia.com/terms/s/selfenhancement.asp; R. Reid, "Are You Above Average? The Lake Wobegon Effect," University of Dayton, June 13, 2022, https://udayton.edu/blogs/erma/2022/06/lakewobegon.php.

    R. W. Robins and D. L. Paulhus, "The Character of Self-Enhancers: Implications for Organizations," in *Personality Psychology in the Workplace* (American Psychological Association, 2001), 193–219, https://priceonomics.com/why-do-we-all-think-were-above-average/.
25. C. May, "Most People Consider Themselves to Be Morally Superior," *Scientific American*, February 2, 2017, https://www.scientificamerican.com/article/most-people-consider-themselves-to-be-morally-superior/; J. D. Brown, *The Self* (McGraw-Hill, 1998), 62.
26. W. Hofmann and R. R. Fisher, "How Guilt and Pride Shape Subsequent Self-Control," *Social Psychological and Personality Science* 3, no. 6 (2012): 682–690.

27. S. Shalvi, F. Gino, R. Barkan, and S. Ayal, "Self-Serving Justifications," *Current Directions in Psychological Science* 24, no. 2 (2015): 125–130.
28. C. May, January 31, 2017, *op. cit.*
29. T. Bianchi, "Most Popular Websites Worldwide as of November 2022, by Total Visits," Statista, August 29, 2023, https://www.statista.com/statistics/1201880/most-visited-websites-worldwide/.
30. I. Hogben, "I Had a Helicopter Mom. I Found Pornhub Anyway," *Free Press*, August 29, 2023, https://www.thefp.com/p/why-are-our-fourth-graders-on-pornhub.
31. B. Resnick, "The Myth of Self-Control," *Vox*, November 24, 2016, https://www.vox.com/science-and-health/2016/11/3/13486940/self-control-psychology-myth.
32. R. F. Baumeister et. al., "Ego Depletion: Is the Active Self a Limited Resource?" *Journal of Personality and Social Psychology* 74, no. 5 (1998): 1252–1265.
33. H. Ledford, "How Thinking Hard Makes the Brain Tired," *The Economist*, August 11, 2022, https://tinyurl.com/35ppb7db.
34. K. McGonigal, *The Willpower Instinct* (Penguin Publishing Group, 2013), 56.
35. M. Inzlicht and M. Friese, "Willpower Is Overrated," *The Behavioral and Brain Sciences* 44, p. e42 (2021). Emphasis added.
36. V. M. Patrick and H. Hagtvedt, "'I Don't' Versus 'I Can't': When Empowered Refusal Motivates Goal-Directed Behavior," *Journal of Consumer Research* 39, no. 2 (2012): 371–381.
37. A. Gersh, "Guard Yourselves Very Well," *My Jewish Learning*, https://www.myjewishlearning.com/article/guard-yourselves-very-well/.
38. See S. Yanklowitz, "An Obesity Problem in the Orthodox Community?" Jewish Telegraphic Agency, April 25, 2012, https://www.jta.org/2012/04/25/ny/an-obesity-problem-in-the-orthodox-community; Y. Arbel, C. Fialkoff, and A. Kerner, "Are Ultra-Orthodox Jews Healthier Than Secular Jews? Gender Differences, Cohort Effect, Lifestyle and Obesity," *Contemporary Jewry* 42, no. 1 (2022): 113–137.
39. P. K. Newby, K. L. Tucker, and A. Wolk, "Risk of Overweight and Obesity Among Semivegetarian, Lactovegetarian, and Vegan Women," *American Journal of Clinical Nutrition* 81, no. 6 (2005): 1267–1274; E. Becker, S. Kozmér, M. B. Aulbach, and N. S. Lawrence, "The Relationship Between Meat Disgust and Meat Avoidance—A Chicken-and-Egg Problem," *Frontiers in Nutrition* 9, (2022): 958248.
40. G. De Clercq, "French 'Backpack Hero' Says His Faith Gave Him Strength to Fight Knifeman," Reuters, June 9, 2023, https://www.reuters.com/world/europe/france-hails-backpack-hero-who-fought-annecy-knife-attacker-2023-06-09.
41. A. P. J. Smyth, K. M. Werner, M. Milyavskaya, A. Holding, and R. Koestner, "Do Mindful People Set Better Goals? Investigating the Relation Between Trait

Mindfulness, Self-Concordance, and Goal Progress," *Journal of Research in Personality* 88 (2020): 104015.

42. Z. Rom and Z. Rom, "The Psychology of Setting Motivating and Satisfying Goals," *Trail Runner Magazine*, January 2, 2024, https://www.trailrunnermag.com/training/mental-training-training/the-psychology-of-setting-motivating-and-satisfying-goals/; R. Koestner, N. Lekes, T. A. Powers, and E. Chicoine, "Attaining Personal Goals: Self-Concordance plus Implementation Intentions Equals Success," *Journal of Personality and Social Psychology* 97, no. 5 (2008): 1105–1116. doi: 10.1037/0022-3514.97.5.1105.
43. Associated Press, "Former UCLA Bruins Coach John Wooden Named Sports' Greatest Coach by Sporting News," ESPN, July 29, 2009, https://www.espn.com/mens-college-basketball/news/story?id=4365068; C. Impelman, "Why Enthusiasm Is a Powerful Tool for Success," *SUCCESS*, April 19, 2017, https://www.success.com/why-enthusiasm-is-a-powerful-tool-for-success/.
44. D. Sirota, L. A. Mischkind, and M. I. Meltzer, "Nothing Beats an Enthusiastic Employee," *Globe and Mail*, July 29, 2005, https://www.theglobeandmail.com/report-on-business/nothing-beats-an-enthusiastic-employee/article984108/.

Chapter 2

1. Sifrei, Deuteronomy 357.
2. Babylonian Talmud, Yoma 52b.
3. Sholom Dovber Schneersohn, *Overcoming Folly*, chapter one.
4. Plato, Timaeaus 30a.
5. S. Cave, "On the Dark History of Intelligence as Domination," *Aeon*, February 21, 2017, https://aeon.co/essays/on-the-dark-history-of-intelligence-as-domination.
6. Plato, *Phaedrus*, 246a-b.
7. D. Ebrey and R. Kraut, *The Cambridge Companion to Plato* (Cambridge University Press, 2022), 32.
8. John Milton, *Areopagitica* (1644).
9. J. Smith, "Freedom of Expression and the Marketplace of Ideas Concept from Milton to Jefferson," *Journal of Communication Inquiry* 7, no. 1 (1981): 47–63.
10. M. Cannon, "Accidental Scientific Discoveries and Breakthroughs," *InterFocus*, December 14, 2015, https://www.mynewlab.com/blog/accidental-scientific-discoveries-and-breakthroughs/.
11. Francis Bacon, *Novum Organon XLVI* (1620).
12. James Madison, "Federalist 49," *The Federalist Papers*, February 5, 1788.
13. David Hume, *A Treatise of Human Nature*, 3.3.3 (1739).

14. C. Mooney, "The Science of Why We Don't Believe Science," *Mother Jones*, March 2011, https://www.motherjones.com/politics/2011/04/denial-science-chris-mooney/.
15. K. Komarnitsky, "Cognitive Dissonance and the Resurrection of Jesus," Westar Institute, 2014, https://www.westarinstitute.org/editorials/cognitive-dissonance-resurrection-jesus; S. Perry, "When Facts Fail: UFO Cults, 'Birthers' and Cognitive Dissonance," *MinnPost*, April 28, 2011, https://www.minnpost.com/second-opinion/2011/04/when-facts-fail-ufo-cults-birthers-and-cognitive-dissonance/.
16. Field Guide: brief bio of Edgar Whisenant, *Field Guide to World Religions*, http://www.isitso.org/guide/whise.html.
17. Field Guide.
18. C. G. Lord, L. Ross, and M. R. Lepper, "Biased Assimilation and Attitude Polarization: The Effects of Prior Theories on Subsequently Considered Evidence," *Journal of Personality and Social Psychology* 37, no. 11 (1979): 2098–2109.
19. Lord, Ross, and Lepper, "Biased Assimilation and Attitude Polarization."
20. L. Festinger, H. W. Riecken, and S. Schachter, *When Prophecy Fails* (University of Minnesota Press, 1956).
21. J. Haidt, *The Righteous Mind* (Random House, 2012), 39.
22. Haidt, *The Righteous Mind*, 45.
23. The On Being Project, "Jonathan Haidt—The Psychology of Self-Righteousness," The On Being Project, 2020, https://onbeing.org/programs/jonathan-haidt-the-psychology-of-self-righteousness-oct2017/.
24. W. E. Buffett, "Letter to the Shareholders of Berkshire Hathaway Inc.," Berkshire Hathaway Inc., February 28, 1989, https://www.berkshirehathaway.com/letters/1988.html; T. Gillies, "Warren Buffett: Buy, Hold and Don't Watch Too Closely," CNBC, December 4, 2018, https://www.cnbc.com/2016/03/04/warren-buffett-buy-hold-and-dont-watch-too-closely.html.
25. M. Darbyshire, "Emotions Cost Investors Dear, Research Finds," *Financial Times*, October 23, 2020, https://www.ft.com/content/ad548fde-7ee2-42e4-89d7-97cbef068c56; J. Meyers, "New Report Finds Almost 80% of Active Fund Managers Are Falling Behind the Major Indexes," CNBC, March 27, 2022, https://www.cnbc.com/2022/03/27/new-report-finds-almost-80percent-of-active-fund-managers-are-falling-behind.html.
26. "Don't Fall in Love with Your Business," American Express Business Trends and Insights, January 2, 2012.
27. R. Colom, S. Karama, R. E. Jung, and R. J. Haier, "Human Intelligence and Brain Networks," *Dialogues in Clinical Neuroscience* 12, no. 4 (2010): 489–501.
28. B. Hansen, *The Truth About Us: The Very Good News About How Very Bad We Are* (Baker Books, 2020), 58.

29. M. Shermer, "Smart People Believe Weird Things," *Scientific American*, September 1, 2002, https://www.scientificamerican.com/article/smart-people-believe-weir/.
30. G. Morse, "Decisions and Desire," *Harvard Business Review*, January 2006, https://hbr.org/2006/01/decisions-and-desire.
31. D. Baer, "How Only Being Able to Use Logic to Make Decisions Destroyed a Man's Life," *The Cut*, June 14, 2016, https://www.thecut.com/2016/06/how-only-using-logic-destroyed-a-man.html.
32. M. Lenzen, "Feeling Our Emotions," *Scientific American Mind* 16, no. 1 (April 1, 2005): 14–15.
33. D. Westen et. al., "Neural Bases of Motivated Reasoning: An fMRI Study of Emotional Constraints on Partisan Political Judgment in the 2004 U.S. Presidential Election," *Journal of Cognitive Neuroscience* 18, no. 11 (2006): 1947–1958; S. M. Hermer, "The Political Brain," *Scientific American*, July 1, 2006, https://www.scientificamerican.com/article/the-political-brain/.
34. N. Tec, "It Was My Duty," *Under the Gables*, October 3, 2021, https://underthegables.blogspot.com/2021/10/it-was-my-duty.html.
35. N. Tec, "Righteous Gentiles," *YIVO*, https://yivoencyclopedia.org/article.aspx/Righteous_Gentiles.
36. M. Mietkiewicz, "The Righteous Among the Nations: Why Did They Do It?" *Canadian Jewish News*, April 12, 2018, https://thecjn.ca/perspectives/the-righteous-among-the-nations-why-did-they-do-it/.
37. S. P. Oliner and P. M. Oliner, *The Altruistic Personality: Rescuers of Jews in Nazi Europe* (Free Press, 1988), 172.
38. S. P. Oliner, "Ordinary Heroes," *YES!*, November 6, 2001, https://www.yesmagazine.org/issue/love-save-world/opinion/2001/11/06/ordinary-heroes. See also S. P. Oliner and P. M. Oliner, *The Altruistic Personality: Rescuers of Jews in Nazi Europe* (Free Press, 1988).
39. C. Fiennes, "Presenting Assessments of a Charity's Performance Doesn't Necessarily Increase Donations," Third Sector, September 17, 2014, https://www.thirdsector.co.uk/caroline-fiennes-presenting-assessments-charitys-performance-doesnt-necessarily-increase-donations/fundraising/article/1329772.

Chapter 3

1. Sha'ar Bat Rabim, Deuteronomy 28:2.
2. Rabbenu Nissim, Derashot HaRan 3.
3. The people might have counted the day of Moses's departure as his first day—meaning that, in their counting, he was not back when he said that he would be; S. C. Kesselman, "What Was the Golden Calf?" Chabad.org, March 9, 2017,

https://www.chabad.org/library/article_cdo/aid/3613047/jewish/What-Was-the-Golden-Calf.htm.

4. J. Sacks, "Shemini: When Weakness Becomes Strength," *Covenant and Conversation*, The Rabbi Sacks Legacy Trust, 2018, https://www.rabbisacks.org/covenant-conversation/shemini/when-weakness-becomes-strength/.
5. Rashi, Leviticus 9:7.
6. J. Sacks (2018), *op. cit.*
7. Quoted in Y. Smith, "Parashat Ki Tisa 5782: The Inherent Value of the Individual," *Pardes from Jerusalem*, February 13, 2022, https://elmad.pardes.org/2022/02/parashat-ki-tisa-5782-the-inherent-value-of-the-individual/.
8. Babylonian Talmud, Berachot 5b.
9. P. R. Clance and S. A. Imes, "The Imposter Phenomenon in High Achieving Women: Dynamics and Therapeutic Intervention," *Psychotherapy* 15, no. 3 (1978): 241–247, https://www.hrmagazine.co.uk/content/news/two-thirds-of-women-experience-imposter-syndrome/; https://march8.com/articles/78-of-business-leaders-experience-imposter-syndrome.
10. Clance and Imes, "The Imposter Phenomenon in High Schieving Women."
11. J. Ma, "25 Famous Women on Impostor Syndrome and Self-Doubt," *The Cut*, January 12, 2017, https://www.thecut.com/2017/01/25-famous-women-on-impostor-syndrome-and-self-doubt.html; A. Pervez et. al., "An Empirical Investigation of Mental Illness, Impostor Syndrome, and Social Support in Management Doctoral Programs," *Journal of Management Education* 45, no. 1 (2021): 126–158, https://leaders.com/articles/personal-growth/imposter-syndrome/.
12. J. Leonard, "How to Handle Impostor Syndrome," *Medical News Today*, September 30, 2020, https://www.medicalnewstoday.com/articles/321730.
13. R. Gardner and J. Bednar, "4 Ways to Combat Imposter Syndrome on Your Team," *Harvard Business Review*, October 18, 2022, https://hbr.org/2022/10/4-ways-to-combat-imposter-syndrome-on-your-team.
14. W. B. Johnson and D. G. Smith, "Mentoring Someone with Imposter Syndrome," *Harvard Business Review*, February 22, 2019, https://hbr.org/2019/02/mentoring-someone-with-imposter-syndrome; "Ditching Imposter Syndrome, 'Want to Become a Certified Imposter Syndrome Master Coach?'" *Ditching Imposter Syndrome*, https://ditchingimpostersyndrome.com/imposter-syndrome-mentor-training/.
15. D. Wolpe, "The Great Book of Grievance," *Mosaic Magazine*, May 25, 2017, https://mosaicmagazine.com/observation/religion-holidays/2017/05/the-great-book-of-grievance/.

Chapter 4

1. A. Smith, *The Theory of Moral Sentiments* 3.1.46 (1759).

2. "Satire of the Trades," in A. Erman, *The Literature of the Ancient Egyptians: Poems, Narratives, and Manuals of Instruction, From the Third and Second Millennia B.C.* (Methuen and Co., 1927), 67.
3. V. E Frankl, *Man's Search for Meaning* (Washington Square Press, 1946), 86.
4. *Ibid.*, 178–79.
5. R. Phillips, "Viktor Frankl on Reframing Suffering," Robin Mark Phillips, November 24, 2015, https://robinmarkphillips.com/viktor-frankl-reframing-suffering/; S. Robatmili, F. Sohrabi, et al., "The Effect of Group Logotherapy on Meaning in Life and Depression Levels of Iranian Students," *International Journal for the Advancement of Counseling* 37, no. 1 (2015): 54–62; H., Delavari, M. Nasirian, and K. Baezegar Bafrooei, "Logotherapy Effect on Anxiety and Depression in Mothers of Children with Cancer," *Iranian Journal of Pediatric Hematology and Oncology* 4, no. 2 (2014): 42–48; T. E. Zuehlke and J. T. Watkins, "Psychotherapy with Terminally Ill Patients," *Psychotherapy: Theory, Research and Practice* 14, no. 4 (1977): 403–410; Pavel G. Somov, "Meaning of Life Group: Group Application of Logotherapy for Substance Use Treatment," *The Journal for Specialists in Group Work* 32, no. 4 (2007): 316–345; S. M. Southwick, et. al. "Logotherapy as an Adjunctive Treatment for Chronic Combat-Related PTSD: A Meaning-Based Intervention," *American Journal of Psychotherapy* 60, no. 2 (2006): 161–174.
6. Beck Institute for Cognitive Behavior Therapy, *Cognitive Restructuring in CBT*, YouTube, April 30, 2014, https://www.youtube.com/watch?v=_dAPW9j3UW4.
7. D. David, I. A. Cristea, and S. G. Hofmann, "Why Cognitive Behavioral Therapy Is the Current Gold Standard of Psychotherapy," *Frontiers in Psychiatry* 9 (2018): 4.
8. J. Lemoncelli, "Australian Olympian Fixed Kayak with a Condom, Threw Up and Won Gold," *New York Post*, July 30, 2021, https://nypost.com/2021/07/29/olympics-2020-jess-fox-won-kayak-gold-thanks-to-condom-fix/.
9. K. Brander, "When the Lubavitcher Rebbe Met Rep. Shirley Chisholm (Parshat Re'eh)," *The Blogs: Times of Israel*, August 12, 2020, https://blogs.timesofisrael.com/when-the-lubavitcher-rebbe-met-rep-shirley-chisholm-parshat-reeh/.
10. L. E. McCutcheon, "A New Test of Misconceptions about Psychology," *Psychological Reports* 68, no. 2 (1991): 647–653.
11. M. Johnson, "The Idea That Opposites Attract Is BS," *VICE*, February 21, 2018, https://www.vice.com/en/article/j5bv5y/the-idea-that-opposites-attract-is-bs.
12. J. R. Jones, B. W. Pelham, M. Carvallo, and M. C. Mirenberg, "How Do I Love Thee? Let Me Count the Js: Implicit Egotism and Interpersonal Attraction," *Journal of Personality and Social Psychology* 87, no. 5 (2004): 665–683.
13. B. W. Pelham, M. C. Mirenberg, and J. T. Jones, "Why Susie Sells Seashells by the Seashore: Implicit Egotism and Major Life Decisions," *Journal of Personality and Social Psychology* 82, no. 4 (2002): 469–487.

14. B. Laeng, O. Vermeer, and U. Sulutvedt, "Is Beauty in the Face of the Beholder?," *PLoS ONE* 8, no. 7 (2013).
15. Bureau of Labor Statistics, "Volunteering in the United States—2015," U.S Department of Labor, February 25, 2016, https://www.bls.gov/news.release/pdf/volun.pdf.
16. D. Mesch, "Do Women Give More? Findings from Three Unique Data Sets on Charitable Giving," The Indiana University Lilly Family School of Philanthropy, 2015, https://scholarworks.iupui.edu/server/api/core/bitstreams/bf45c65c-41e5-46e7-9d46-da8490942907/content.
17. Philanthropy Roundtable, *Who Gives Most to Charity?*, https://www.philanthropyroundtable.org/almanac/who-gives-most-to-charity/.
18. Pew Research Center, "How Religious Is Your State?" Pew Research Center, February 29, 2016, https://www.pewresearch.org/short-reads/2016/02/29/how-religious-is-your-state/?state=alabama.
19. K. Zinsmeister, "Less God, Less Giving?" *Philanthropy Roundtable*, 2019, https://www.philanthropyroundtable.org/magazine/less-god-less-giving/; M. Lipka and B. Wormald, "How Religious Is Your State?" Pew Research Center, February 29, 2016, https://www.pewresearch.org/short-reads/2016/02/29/how-religious-is-your-state/?state=alabama, https://www.hoover.org/research/religious-faith-and-charitable-giving.
20. *Ibid.*
21. N. Kristof, "Evangelicals Without Blowhards," *New York Times*, July 30, 2011, https://www.nytimes.com/2011/07/31/opinion/sunday/kristof-evangelicals-without-blowhards.html.
22. An excellent analysis is, characteristically, offered by Rabbi Jonathan Sacks. J. Sacks, "Vayigash: Reframing," *Covenant and Conversation*, The Rabbi Sacks Legacy Fund, 2022, https://rabbisacks.org/reframing-vayigash-5776/.

Chapter 5

1. Institute for Statistics of the United Nations Educational, Scientific and Cultural Organization, *The 2009 UNESCO Framework for Cultural Statistics (FCS)* (United Nations, 2010), 9, https://unstats.un.org/unsd/statcom/doc10/Bg-FCS-e.pdf.
2. Babylonian Talmud, Nedarim 3a; See also D. Fohrman, "Origins of the Firstborn Nation," *Aleph Beta*, 2018, https://www.alephbeta.org/playlist/origins-of-the-firstborn-nation.
3. Maimonides, Mishneh Torah, *Human Dispositions* 5:11.
4. B. Campbell and J. Manning, "Microaggression and Changing Moral Cultures," *The Chronicle of Higher Education* 61, no. 41 (2015): A25.
5. Babylonian Talmud, Gittin 36b.

6. E. Goldberg, "Vayeitzei: When He Feels Far Away, He Is Closer Than Ever," *Parsha Perspectives*, (November 9, 2021), https://www.listennotes.com/podcasts/parsha-perspectives/vayeitzei-when-he-feels-far-soU7WQ01fvj/.
7. E. Goldberg, "Va'eira: Knowing in the Heart," *Parsha Perspectives*, January 12, 2021, https://www.listennotes.com/podcasts/parsha-perspectives/vaeira-knowing-in-the-heart-gFwIPBkq7NR/.
8. W. Goldstein, "Pinchas: Where Does Leadership Begin?," *The Language of Tomorrow*, July 9, 2020, https://www.listennotes.com/podcasts/chief-rabbi-warren/pinchas-where-does-2SyI5ojWtbU/.
9. Y. Smith, "Parashat Ki Tisa 5782: The Inherent Value of the Individual," *Pardes from Jerusalem*, February 13, 2022, https://elmad.pardes.org/2022/02/parashat-ki-tisa-5782-the-inherent-value-of-the-individual/.
10. A. Gordimer, "Post-Pittsburgh: Capital Punishment, and Jews with Guns," *Israel National News*, November 2, 2018, https://www.israelnationalnews.com/news/351531.
11. M. Begin, "Menachem Begin on the Lessons of the Holocaust," *Aish*, 1981, https://aish.com/menachem-begin-on-the-lessons-of-the-holocaust/.
12. B. Leff, "Is the Torah Anti-Semitic?," *Aish*, https://aish.com/is-the-torah-anti-semitic/.
13. A. Males, "Rabbi's Diary: Chocolate and Eagles and Lions, Oh My!," *Jewish Action*, 2015, https://jewishaction.com/religion/jewish-law/chocolate-and-eagles-and-lions-oh-my/.
14. D. Peel, "Lion Anatomy—The Eye," *Safari Guide Online*, October 3, 2011, https://danielpeel.wordpress.com/2011/10/03/lion-anatomy-the-eye/.
15. Mishna, Avot 5:20.
16. Syed, "Where Do Lions Sleep?," *Animals Truth*, August 13, 2022, https://animalstruth.com/where-do-lions-sleep/.
17. Bali Safari, "How Lions Hunt Their Prey," *Bali Safari Marine Park*, August 30, 2019, https://www.balisafarimarinepark.com/how-lions-hunt-their-prey/.
18. A. T. Hardy, *China Versus the US: Who Will Prevail?* (World Scientific Publishing Company, 2020), 135.
19. A. Saxenian, "Silicon Valley Versus Route 128," *Inc.*, February 1, 1994, https://www.inc.com/magazine/19940201/2758.html.
20. P. Ujvári, *Magyar Zsidó Lexikon (Hungarian Jewish Lexicon)*, trans. A. Manchin and R. Pastor, (1929), 562; M. M. Kovács, *Liberal Professions and Illiberal Politics: Hungary from the Habsburgs to the Holocaust* (Woodrow Wilson Center Press, 1994).
21. C. Hirschman, "Demographic Trends in Peninsular Malaysia, 1947–75," *Population and Development Review* 6, no. 1 (1980): 103–125.
22. T. Sowell, "Race, Culture, and Equality," *Hoover Institution*, July 17, 1998, https://www.hoover.org/research/race-culture-and-equality.

23. American Community Survey, "2021: ACS 1-Year Estimates Selected Population Profiles," *United States Census Bureau*, 2021, https://www.census.gov/programs-surveys/acs/technical-documentation/table-and-geography-changes/2021/1-year.html.
24. A. Hsin and Y. Xie, "Explaining Asian Americans' Academic Advantage Over Whites," *Proceedings of the National Academy of Sciences* 111, no. 23 (2014): 8416–8421.
25. *The Nigerian Diaspora in the United States*, Migration Policy Institute, 2015, migrationpolicy.org/sites/default/files/publications/RAD-Nigeria.pdf., https://www.chron.com/news/article/Data-show-Nigerians-the-most-educated-in-the-U-S-1600808.php; I. Jackson-Obot, "What Makes Nigerians in Diaspora So Successful?," *Financial Times*, October 29, 2020, https://www.ft.com/content/ca39b445-442a-4845-a07c-0f5dae5f3460., https://imdiversity.com/diversity-news/the-most-successful-ethnic-group-in-the-u-s-may-surprise-you/.
26. A. Brune, "Why Nigerian-Americans Strive So Hard at School," *Ozy*, June 13, 2018, http://adrianbrune.com/ozycom.
27. S. Kramer, "U.S. Has World's Highest Rate of Children Living in Single-Parent Household," *Pew Research Center*, December 12, 2019, https://www.pewresearch.org/fact-tank/2019/12/12/u-s-children-more-likely-than-children-in-other-countries-to-live-with-just-one-parent/; S. Sun, "National Snapshot: Poverty Among Women and Families," National Women's Law Centre, February 16, 2023, https://nwlc.org/resource/national-snapshot-poverty-among-women-families/#; "Poverty Rate of Married-Couple Families in the United States Who Live below the Poverty Line from 1990 to 2022," Statista, 2023, https://www.statista.com/statistics/204962/percentage-of-poor-married-couple-families-in-the-us/.
28. R. Haskins, "Three Simple Rules Poor Teens Should Follow to Join the Middle Class," Brookings, March 13, 2013, https://www.brookings.edu/opinions/three-simple-rules-poor-teens-should-follow-to-join-the-middle-class/., https://sutherlandinstitute.org/what-you-need-to-know-about-the-success-sequence/.
29. B. Goesling, H. Inanc, and A. Rachidi, "Success Sequence: A Synthesis of the Literature," *OPRE Report 2020–41*, 2020, https://www.acf.hhs.gov/sites/default/files/documents/opre/Success_sequence_review_2020_508_0.pdf.
30. B. Caplan, "What Does the Success Sequence Mean?," *Econlib*, February 22, 2021, https://www.econlib.org/the-meaning-of-the-success-sequence/.
31. M. Dirda, "Tocqueville's 'Democracy in America,' Read Anew in 2020, Feels Prophetic—and in Some Ways, Hopeful," *Washington Post*, October 14, 2020, https://www.washingtonpost.com/entertainment/books/tocquevilles-democracy-in-america-read-anew-in-2020-feels-prophetic—and-in-some-ways-hopeful/2020/10/14/a104c752-0d73-11eb-8074-0e943a91bf08_story.html.

32. J. Asher, B. Horwitz, and T. Monkovic, "Why Does Louisiana Consistently Lead the Nation in Murders?," *New York Times*, February 15, 2021, https://www.nytimes.com/2021/02/15/upshot/why-does-louisiana-consistently-lead-the-nation-in-murders.html.
33. F. Butterfield, "Ideas & Trends: Southern Curse; Why America's Murder Rate Is So High," *New York Times*, July 26, 1998, https://www.nytimes.com/1998/07/26/weekinreview/ideas-trends-southern-curse-why-america-s-murder-rate-is-so-high.html.
34. G. G. Johnson, *Ante-Bellum North Carolina: A Social History* (University of North Carolina Press, 1937), 45.
35. D. B. Smith, "Celebrate President's Day with a History Lesson: What Is the Story behind Dueling in America?," Grateful American Foundation, 1937, https://gratefulamericanfoundation.org/11483/.
36. B. Franklin, "From Benjamin Franklin to Thomas Percival, 17 July 1784," National Archives, July 17, 1784, https://founders.archives.gov/documents/Franklin/01-42-02-0265#BNFN-01-42-02-0265-fn-0002.
37. B. McKay and K. McKay, "Manly Honor Part IV—The Gentlemen and the Roughs: The Collision of Two Honor Codes in the American North," The Art of Manliness, November 12, 2021, https://www.artofmanliness.com/character/behavior/manly-honor-part-iv-the-gentlemen-and-the-roughs-the-stoic-christian-code-of-honor-in-the-american-north/.
38. H. Carter, *Southern Legacy* (Louisiana State University Press, 1950), 48–59.
39. M. E. L. Renwick, J. A. Stanley, J. Forrest, and L. Glass, "Boomer Peak or Gen X Cliff? From SVS to LBMS in Georgia English," *Language Variation and Change* 35, no. 2 (2023): 175–197.
40. D. Cohen, R. E. Nisbett, B. F. Bowdle, and N. Schwarz, "Insult, Aggression, and the Southern Culture of Honor: An 'Experimental Ethnography,'" *Journal of Personality and Social Psychology* 70, no. 5 (1996): 945–960.
41. O. Patterson, "The Real Problem with America's Inner Cities," *New York Times*, May 9, 2015, https://www.nytimes.com/2015/05/10/opinion/sunday/the-real-problem-with-americas-inner-cities.html.
42. R. Manguel, personal communication, 2022; L. L. Finley, *Encyclopedia of School Crime and Violence: Volume 1* (ABC-CLIO, 2011), 462.
43. D. Shor (@davidshor), Twitter (now X), March 29, 2022, https://twitter.com/davidshor/status/1508774997246058502.
44. Y. Lin, N. Caluori, E. B. Öztürk, and M. J. Gelfand, "From Virility to Virtue: The Psychology of Apology in Honor Cultures," *Proceedings of the National Academy of Sciences* 119, no. 41 (2022): 1-e2210324119.
45. D. Strong, "7 Ways Anger Is Ruining Your Health," *Everyday Health*, May 29, 2015, https://www.everydayhealth.com/news/ways-anger-ruining-your-health/.
46. C. Morton, "The 10 Friendliest Cities in the U.S: 2023 Readers' Choice Awards,"

Condé Nast Traveler, November 21, 2023, https://www.cntraveler.com/gallery/2015-08-11the-2015-friendliest-and-unfriendliest-cities-in-the-us.; "States with 'Cultures of Honor,'" ABC News, August 15, 2011, https://abcnews.go.com/Health/states-considered-honor-cultures/story?id=14302664.

47. R. Brown, *Honor Bound: How a Cultural Ideal Has Shaped the American Psyche* (Oxford University Press, 2016), 33–34; See also D. Cohen, J. Vandello, S. Puente, and A. Rantilla, "'When You Call Me That, Smile!' How Norms for Politeness, Interaction Styles, and Aggression Work Together in Southern Culture," *Social Psychology Quarterly* 62, no. 3 (1999): 257–275.
48. Fields Center Fellows, Carl A. Fields Center for Equality + Cultural Understanding—Princeton University, http://fieldscenter.princeton.edu/center-fellows.
49. Poster at Fields Center, photographed by my wife at Princeton (where she was for our son's chess tournament) in November of 2022.
50. "How to Stop Ruminating Thoughts," Medical News Today (November 8, 2019), https://www.medicalnewstoday.com/articles/326944; "Rumination: A Cycle of Negative Thinking," APA Blogs, American Psychiatric Association, March 5, 2020, https://www.psychiatry.org/news-room/apa-blogs/rumination-a-cycle-of-negative-thinking; T. Ehring, "Thinking Too Much: Rumination and Psychopathology," *World Psychiatry* 20, no. 3 (2021): 441–442.
51. S. Pagones, "Threat Specialist Known as the 'Grim Reaper' Explains How Authorities Can Stop Mass Shootings," *New York Post*, July 7, 2023, https://nypost.com/2023/07/07/threat-specialist-patrick-prince-explains-how-to-stop-mass-shootings/.
52. E. M. Zitek, A. H., Jordan, B. Monin, and F. R. Leach, "Victim Entitlement to Behave Selfishly," *Journal of Personality and Social Psychology* 98, no. 2 (2010): 245–255.
53. B. Warmke, "The Psychology of Moral Grandstanding," *Big Think*, May 22, 2019, https://www.youtube.com/watch?v=pNQqst5o3X4&ab_channel=BigThink; B. Warmke and J. Tosi, "Moral Grandstanding and Virtue Signaling: The Same Thing?," *Psychology Today*, August 11, 2020, https://www.psychologytoday.com/us/blog/moral-talk/202008/moral-grandstanding-and-virtue-signaling-the-same-thing.
54. F. Manjoo and D. Arthur, "Opinion: We All Live in 'South Park' Now," *New York Times*, June 26, 2023, https://www.nytimes.com/2023/06/26/opinion/we-all-live-in-south-park-now.html.
55. "The World Wide Privacy Tour," *South Park* Season 26, Episode 2, February 15, 2023.
56. E. Megginson, "When I Applied to College, I Didn't Want to 'Sell My Pain,'" *New York Times*, May 9, 2021, https://www.nytimes.com/2021/05/09/opinion/college-admissions-essays-trauma.html.

57. E. Benedek, "White People Are Going to Colonize Mars, and Other Fears from Today's Campuses," *Tablet Magazine*, January 3, 2024, https://www.tabletmag.com/sections/news/articles/antisemitism-dei-cuny-hillel.
58. E. Gorelick and W. Porayouw, "Salovey Names DEI, Health and Fundraising Top Priorities for 2023," *Yale Daily News*, January 26, 2023, https://yaledailynews.com/blog/2023/01/26/salovey-names-dei-health-and-fundraising-top-priorities-for-2023/; J. S. Rosenberg, "The Art of the Dean," *Harvard Magazine*, October 28, 2021, https://www.harvardmagazine.com/2021/08/jhj-art-of-the-dean.
59. B. Mason, "Making People Aware of their Implicit Biases Doesn't Usually Change Minds. But Here's What Does Work," *PBS News Hour*, June 10, 2020, https://www.pbs.org/newshour/nation/making-people-aware-of-their-implicit-biases-doesnt-usually-change-minds-but-heres-what-does-work, https://www.washington.edu/news/1998/09/29/roots-of-unconscious-prejudice-affect-90-to-95-percent-of-people-psychologists-demonstrate-at-press-conference/.
60. M. Fitzgerald, "Implicit Bias—How We Hold Women Back," TEDx Talks, March 1, 2018, https://www.youtube.com/watch?v=YM1MBSczyzI.
61. B. Mason, "Curbing Implicit Bias: What Works and What Doesn't," *Knowable Magazine*, June 4, 2020, https://knowablemagazine.org/content/article/mind/2020/how-to-curb-implicit-bias.
62. B. Mason, "Making People Aware of Their Implicit Biases Doesn't Usually Change Minds. But Here's What Does Work," *PBS News Hour*, June 10, 2020, https://www.pbs.org/newshour/nation/making-people-aware-of-their-implicit-biases-doesnt-usually-change-minds-but-heres-what-does-work; C. L. Eisgruber, "Letter from President Eisgruber on the University's Efforts to Combat Systemic Racism," Princeton University, September 6, 2020, https://www.princeton.edu/news/2020/09/02/letter-president-eisgruber-universitys-efforts-combat-systemic-racism.
63. "Bias Education and Response," American University, https://www.american.edu/ocl/bias-education.cfm; "Bias Incident Policy," Wheaton College, https://www.wheaton.edu/life-at-wheaton/kingdom-diversity/bias-incident-policy/; "Annual Report on Diversity," Office of Equity and Inclusion Reports, University of Rochester, 2018, https://www.rochester.edu/diversity/reports/annual-report-on-diversity-2018/.
64. "Bias Response and Referral Network," Frequently Asked Questions, University of Minnesota, https://bias-response.umn.edu/frequently-asked-questions; "Frequently Asked Questions," Office of Institutional Equity and Diversity, Brown University, https://www.brown.edu/about/administration/institutional-diversity/incident-reporting/bias-incidents/frequently-asked-questions.
65. FAQs on Discrimination and/or Harassment, Inclusive Princeton, https://inclusive.princeton.edu/addressing-concerns/faqs.

66. N. Confessore, "The DEI Reckoning," *New York Times*, October 16, 2024, https://www.nytimes.com/2024/10/16/magazine/dei-university-michigan.html.
67. S. Yenor, "At Texas A&M, a Different Kind of 'Climate Change,'" The James G. Martin Center for Academic Renewal, February 22, 2023, https://www.jamesgmartin.center/2023/02/at-texas-am-a-different-kind-of-climate-change/.
68. Campus Demands "The Demands," National Demands, 2016, https://web.archive.org/web/20201231162844/https://www.thedemands.org/; G. Orfield, "What Are Students Demanding?," *Higher Education Today*, January 13, 2016, https://www.higheredtoday.org/2016/01/13/what-are-students-demanding/.
69. I. Stanley-Becker, "Yale's President Responds to Protesters' Demands, Announces New Initiatives to Ease Racial Tension," *Washington Post*, November 18, 2015, https://www.washingtonpost.com/news/grade-point/wp/2015/11/18/yales-president-responds-to-protesters-demands-announces-new-initiatives-to-ease-racial-tension/.
70. C. Dunson, "Abolish Yale," *Yale Daily News*, December 10, 2021, https://yaledailynews.com/blog/2021/12/10/abolish-yale/.
71. J. M. Keynes, *The General Theory of Employment, Interest and Money* (Macmillan, 1936), 383.
72. "Born This Way? The Rise of LGBT as a Social and Political Identity," CSPI Report no. 6, CSPI Center, May 30, 2022, https://cspicenter.org/reports/born-this-way-the-rise-of-lgbt-as-a-social-and-political-identity/#.
73. CSPI Report no. 6, *op. Cit.*, https://bi.org/en/articles/study-finds-bi-women-are-the-most-likely-to-be-liberal-but-why1561060510.
74. C. Skelding, "New-Age Cuomo Daughter Has Booming Online Spirituality Biz," *New York Post*, February 19, 2022, https://nypost.com/2022/02/19/new-age-cuomo-daughter-has-booming-online-spirituality-biz/.
75. A. Mahdawi, "What Does The Dawn of Demisexuals Tell Us? How Sex-Drenched Society Has Become," *Guardian*, September 8, 2021, https://www.theguardian.com/society/commentisfree/2021/jul/13/what-does-the-dawn-of-demisexuals-tell-us-how-sex-drenched-society-has-become.
76. M. Cuomo, Instagram, June 4, 2021, http://tinyurl.com/4zuy5ts2.
77. M. Smith, "The 10 Fastest-Growing Jobs in the United States—Some Pay Over $100,000 a year," CNBC, January 19, 2022, https://www.cnbc.com/2022/01/19/the-10-fastest-growing-jobs-in-the-united-states-and-how-much-they-pay.html.
78. M. Mallick, "How to Support Your Jewish Colleagues Right Now," *Harvard Business Review*, December 15, 2022, https://hbr.org/2022/12/how-to-support-your-jewish-colleagues-right-now.
79. N. Bell, "Trump's Victim Mentality Strikes a Chord with Some," *The Interpreter*, October 24, 2016, https://www.lowyinstitute.org/the-interpreter/trump-s-victim-mentality-strikes-chord-some.

80. H. R. Clinton, *What Happened* (Simon & Schuster, 2017), 15, 114.
81. E. Dovere, "Hillary Clinton Says She Warned You About Trump," *The Atlantic*, October 9, 2020, https://www.theatlantic.com/politics/archive/2020/10/hillary-clinton-doing-now-2020/616668/; B. Haring, "Hillary Clinton Claims 'Funny Things' That Happened to Her During the 2016 Election 'Will Not Happen Again,'" Deadline, September 27, 2019, https://deadline.com/2019/09/hillary-clinton-cbs-morning-news-interview-jane-pauley-1202746179/.
82. D. J. Trump, "President Trump: 'We're all victims,'" *The Hill*, December 5, 2020, https://www.youtube.com/watch?v=raymu9S5qEg&ab_channel=TheHill.
83. H. Allen, "Former President Trump Announces 2024 Presidential Bid: Transcript," *Rev*, November 16, 2022, https://www.rev.com/blog/transcripts/former-president-trump-announces-2024-presidential-bid-transcript.
84. J. Singal, "Have Microaggression Complaints Really Launched a Whole New Sort of 'Victimhood Culture'?" *The Cut*, September 14, 2015, https://www.thecut.com/2015/09/microaggression-complaints-and-victimhood.html.
85. T. E. Hill, "Kantian Perspectives on the Rational Basis of Human Dignity" in *The Cambridge Handbook of Human Dignity: Interdisciplinary Perspectives*, ed. M. Duwell, et al. (Cambridge University Press, (2014), 215–221.
86. J. A. Ruddiman, "'A Mere Youth:' James Monroe's Revolutionary War," *Journal of the American Revolution*, August 12, 2021, https://allthingsliberty.com/2021/08/a-mere-youth-james-monroes-revolutionary-war/.
87. D. L. Dreisbach, "The 'Vine and Fig Tree' in George Washington's Letters: Reflections on a Biblical Motif in the Literature of the American Founding Era," *Anglican and Episcopal History* 76, no. 3 (2007): 299–326.
88. G. Washington, "From George Washington to the Hebrew Congregation in Newport, Rhode Island, 18 August 1790," National Archives, August 18, 1790, https://founders.archives.gov/documents/Washington/05-06-02-0135.
89. D. Shultziner and G. E. Carmi, "Human Dignity in National Constitutions: Functions, Promises and Dangers," *The American Journal of Comparative Law* 62, no. 2 (2014): 461–490.
90. M. L. King Jr., *I've Been to the Mountaintop*, April 3, 1968, https://www.americanrhetoric.com/speeches/mlkivebeentothemountaintop.htm.
91. W. Echikson, "Preserving Jewish Identity in Christian Docieties," *Christian Science Monitor*, October 16, 1984, https://www.csmonitor.com/1984/1016/101618.html.
92. S. Clemence, "Is There Racism in the Deed to Your Home?," *New York Times*, August 17, 2021, https://www.nytimes.com/2021/08/17/realestate/racism-home-deeds.html.
93. U. Heilman, "Miami Beach Loves the Jews, but It Wasn't Always This Way," Jewish Telegraphic Agency, February 3, 2014, https://www.jta.org/2013/10/23/lifestyle/miami-beach-loves-the-jews-but-it-wasnt-always-this-way.

Chapter 6

1. Bereshit Rabbah 80:11.
2. Most translations insist that the verb *ta'arotz* is a version of "fear" or "terror." This is possible, but given that Deuteronomy 1:29 uses this verb *in addition* to the traditional word for "fear," *yir'ah*, an alternative translation of "admire" is warranted.
3. Babylonian Talmud, Berachot 5b.
4. T. Gross, "Whose Side Was She On? 'American Heiress' Revisits Patty Hearst's Kidnapping," NPR, August 3, 2016, https://www.npr.org/2016/08/03/488373982/whose-side-was-she-on-american-heiress-revisits-patty-hearst-s-kidnapping.
5. C. Klein, "Stockholm Syndrome: The True Story of Hostages Loyal to Their Captor," History, August 23, 2013, https://www.history.com/news/stockholm-syndrome; L. Martin, "'Clark' Shows What We've Been Getting Wrong About Stockholm Syndrome," *Esquire*, May 5, 2022, https://www.esquire.com/uk/culture/a39915265/netflix-clark-true-story-stockholm-syndrome/; D. Beaulieu, "The Bizarre, Six-Day Bank Heist That Spawned 'Stockholm Syndrome,'" *Washington Post*, August 23, 2023, https://www.washingtonpost.com/history/2023/08/23/stockholm-syndrome-bank-robbery-jan-erik-olsson/.
6. J. Frankel, "Exploring Ferenczi's Concept of Identification with the Aggressor: Its Role in Trauma, Everyday Life, and the Therapeutic Relationship," *Psychoanalytic Dialogues* 12, no. 1, (2008): 101–139.
7. "Can DV Survivors Adopt Stockholm Syndrome?," Domestic Shelters, May 9, 2016, https://www.domesticshelters.org/articles/identifying-abuse/can-dv-survivors-have-stockholm-syndrome.
8. "Top 25 Movies About Stockholm Syndrome," IMDb, 2022), https://www.imdb.com/list/ls094936772/.
9. "Why Do I Love My Abuser?," National Domestic Violence Hotline, https://www.thehotline.org/resources/why-do-i-love-my-abuser/; "Stockholm Syndrome," Cleveland Clinic, https://my.clevelandclinic.org/health/diseases/22387-stockholm-syndrome.
10. Domestic Shelters, *op. cit.*
11. S. Hargreaves, P. A. Bath, S. Duffin, and J. Ellis, "Sharing and Empathy in Digital Spaces: Qualitative Study of Online Health Forums for Breast Cancer and Motor Neuron Disease (Amyotrophic Lateral Sclerosis)," *Journal of Medical Internet Research* 20, no. 6 (2018): e222.
12. *Ibid.*
13. "Borrowing Experience," The John Maxwell Company, October 6, 2011, https://www.johnmaxwell.com/blog/borrowing-experience/.

Chapter 7

1. Y. Wolbe, "Parsha: Noach—The Flood and the Fish," *Rabbi Yaakov Wolbe Podcast Collection*, October 27, 2022, https://www.listennotes.com/podcasts/rabbi-yaakov-wolbe/parsha-noach-the-flood-and-wOgQATEY_L0/.
2. Rashi, Numbers 3:29; 16:1.
3. Psalms 60:9; 1 Chronicles 12:32; Judges 5:14.
4. Mishna, Pirkei Avot 1:7.
5. Mishna, Pirkei Avot 2:9.
6. Maimonides, Mishneh Torah, *Laws of Human Dispositions* 6:1.
7. See chapter 22.
8. Babylonian Talmud, Shevuot 39a; A. Weiss, "Why Are We Called Yehudim?," *Torah Library of Yeshivat Chovevei Torah*, May 25, 2016, https://library.yctorah.org/2016/05/why-are-we-called-yehudim/.
9. Babylonian Talmud, Keritot 6b.
10. S. E. Crispe, "Finding Ourselves Through Others: The Meaning of Community," *The Jewish Woman,* May 25, 2016, https://www.chabad.org/theJewishWoman/article_cdo/aid/978160/jewish/Finding-Ourselves-Through-Others.htm.
11. S. Riskin, "Torah Portion: Hukat," *Southern New England Jewish Ledger*, June 29, 2011, http://www.jewishledger.com/2011/06/torah-portion-hukat/.
12. Babylonian Talmud, Sanhedrin 71a; Maimonides, Mishneh Torah, *Foreign Worship and Customs of the Nations* 4:6.
13. S. Rubin, "Jewish Opposition to the Ancient Gladiatorial Games," *Hakira* 26 (2019): 287–300.
14. Cited in J. Shwartz, "Points to Ponder—Shelach 5778," *YU Torah*, June 6, 2018, https://www.yutorah.org/sidebar/lecture.cfm/902045/rabbi-dr-jonathan-schwartz/points-to-ponder-shelach-5778/.
15. L. R. Kass, "A Woman for All Seasons," *Commentary*, 1991, https://www.commentary.org/articles/leon-kass/a-woman-for-all-seasons/.
16. J. Dean, "Solomon Asch Conformity Experiment Shows Effect of Social Pressure," *PsyBlog*, March 7, 2023, https://www.spring.org.uk/2021/06/asch-conformity-experiment.php.
17. G. S. Berns, J. Chappelow, C. F. Zink, G. Pagnoni, M. E. Martin-Skurski, and J. Richards, "Neurobiological Correlates of Social Conformity and Independence During Mental Rotation," *Biological Psychiatry* 58, no. 3 (2005), 245–25.
18. S. S. Wang, "Peer Pressure for Teens Paves the Path to Adulthood," *Wall Street Journal*, June 17, 2013, https://www.wsj.com/articles/SB10001424127887324520904578551462766909232.
19. D. Albert, J. Chein, and L. Steinberg, "The Teenage Brain: Peer Influences on Adolescent Decision Making," *Current Directions in Psychological Science* 22, no. 2 (2013): 114–120.

20. B. Peçi, "Peer Influence and Adolescent Sexual Behavior Trajectories: Links to Sexual Initiation," *European Journal of Multidisciplinary Studies* 2, no. 3 (2017): 96–105; C. T. Leshargie et. al. "The Impact of Peer Pressure on Cigarette Smoking Among High School and University Students in Ethiopia: A Systemic Review and Meta-Analysis," *PloS One* 14, no. 10 (2019): e0222572; A. J. Rose, R. A. Schwartz-Mette, G. C. Glick, R. L. Smith, and A. M. Luebbe, "An observational study of co-rumination in adolescent friendships," *Developmental Psychology* 50, no. 9 (2014): 2199–2209; S. Abrutyn, A. S. Mueller, and M. Osborne, "Rekeying Cultural Scripts for Youth Suicide: How Social Networks Facilitate Suicide Diffusion and Suicide Clusters Following Exposure to Suicide," *Society and Mental Health* 10, no. 2 (2020): 112–135; L. Steinberg and K. C. Monahan, "Age Differences in Resistance to Peer Influence," *Developmental Psychology* 43, no. 6 (2007): 1531–1543; D. C. Geary, "Understanding the Rise of Transgender Odentities," *Quillette*, February 10, 2023, https://quillette.com/2023/02/10/social-contagion-and-transgender-identities/; L. Littman, "Rapid-Onset Gender Dysphoria in Adolescents and Young Adults: A Study of Parental Reports," *PloS One* 13, no. 8 (2018): e0202330.
21. N. J. Goldstein, R. B. Cialdini, and V. Griskevicius, "A Room with a Viewpoint: Using Social Norms to Motivate Environmental Conservation in Hotels," *Journal of Consumer Research* 35, no. 3 (2008): 472–482.
22. R. McDermott, J. H. Fowler, and N. A. Christakis, "Breaking Up Is Hard to Do, Unless Everyone Else Is Doing It Too: Social Network Effects on Divorce in a Longitudinal Sample," *Social Forces* 92, no. 2 (2013): 491–519.
23. N. A. Christakis and J. H. Fowler, "The Collective Dynamics of Smoking in a Large Social Network," *New England Journal of Medicine* 358, no. 21 (2008): 2249–2258; R. McDermott, et al., "Breaking Up Is Hard to Do," *op. cit.*
24. J. T. Cacioppo, J. H. Fowler, and N. A. Christakis, "Alone in the Crowd: The Structure and Spread of Loneliness in a Large Social Network," *Journal of Personality and Social Psychology* 97, no. 6 (2009): 977–991; N. R. Smith, P. N. Zivich, and L. Frerichs, "Social Influences on Obesity: Current Knowledge, Emerging Methods, and Directions for Future Research and Practice," *Current Nutrition Reports* 9, no. 1 (2020): 31–41.
25. Pew Research Center, "Marriage, Families and Children among U.S. Jews," Pew Research Center's Religion and Public Life Project, May 11, 2021, https://www.pewresearch.org/religion/2021/05/11/marriage-families-and-children/.

Chapter 8

1. Maharal, Tiferet Yisrael 3:4.
2. D. Baron, "The Meaning of 'Adam': Insights into the Hebrew Language," *Aish*, May 11, 2021, https://aish.com/48956911/#.

3. D. Wolpe, "Parashat Vayetzeh: Transformation," *Jerusalem Post*, November 30, 2020, https://www.jpost.com/judaism/torah-portion/parashat-vayetzeh-transformation-650352.
4. Maimonides, Mishneh Torah, *Laws of Repentance* 5:2.
5. J. Sacks, "A Stiff-Necked People," *Covenant & Conversation,* The Rabbi Sacks Legacy Trust, 2008, https://rabbisacks.org/covenant-conversation/ki-tissa/a-stiff-necked-people/.
6. Babylonian Talmud, Shabbat 156a.
7. Jerusalem Talmud, Terumot 8:10.
8. *Tanchuma Metzora.*
9. Babylonian Talmud, Shabbat 88a.
10. Ha'Emek Davar, Numbers 25:12.
11. Sefer Hachinuch, 16:2.
12. M. Luzzatto, *Mesilat Yesharim* 7:14.
13. Maimonides, Commentary on Mishnah, Pirkei Avot 3:15.
14. M. Ben-Avie, Y. Ives, and K. Loewenthal, *Applied Jewish Values in Social Science and Psychology* (Springer International, 2015), 135.
15. Jerusalem Talmud, Taanit 1:11.
16. J. Quoidbach, D. T. Gilbert, and T. D. Wilson, "The End of History Illusion," *Science* 339, no. 6115 (2013): 96–98.
17. B. W. Roberts and D. Mroczek, "Personality Trait Change in Adulthood," *Current Directions in Psychological Science* 17, no. 1 (2008): 31–35.
18. *Ibid.*
19. "One in Three People Born Stubborn (and If You Don't Agree, Tough)," *Scotsman*, January 2, 2008, https://www.scotsman.com/news/one-in-three-people-born-stubborn-and-if-you-dont-agree-tough-2471007.
20. "Turning Stubbornness into a Positive Personality Trait," BetterHelp, November 9, 2022, https://www.betterhelp.com/advice/general/turning-bad-mad-and-stubborn-into-positive-personality-traits/.
21. C. Pulver, "Episode 447," *Hoop Heads Podcast*, March 21, 2021, https://hoopheadspod.com/clint-pulver-author-of-i-love-it-here-how-coaches-can-create-a-program-that-players-never-want-to-leave-episode-447/.
22. A. Lansley, "Response to NHS Future Forum's Second Report," Department of Health, January 10, 2012, 5.
23. B. Gardner, P. Lally, and J. Wardle, "Making Health Habitual: The Psychology of 'Habit-Formation' and General Practice," *British Journal of General Practice: The Journal of the Royal College of General Practitioners* 62, no. 605 (2012): 664–666.
24. *Ibid.*
25. J. Gaeng, "The Largest Animal Brain on the Planet," AZ Animals, June 8, 2022, https://a-z-animals.com/blog/the-largest-animal-brain-on-the-planet/.

26. I. Asimov, "In the Game of Energy and Thermodynamics You Can't Even Break Even," *Smithsonian Institute Journal*, 1970, 10.
27. "MIT Researcher Sheds Light on Why Habits Are Hard to Make And Break," MIT News, October 20, 1999, https://news.mit.edu/1999/habits.
28. N. Mathers, "Compassion and the Science of Kindness: Harvard Davis Lecture 2015," *British Journal of General Practice: The Journal of the Royal College of General Practitioners* 66, no. 648 (2016): e525–e527.
29. S. Watson, "Dopamine: The Pathway to Pleasure," Harvard Health, July 20, 2021, https://www.health.harvard.edu/mind-and-mood/dopamine-the-pathway-to-pleasure?utm_content=buffer992e3&utm_medium=social&utm_source=linkedin&utm_campaign=buffer.
30. S. Parker, "The Science of Habits," *Knowable Magazine*, July 15, 2021, https://knowablemagazine.org/article/mind/2021/the-science-habits.
31. P. Lally, et. al., "How Are Habits Formed: Modelling Habit Formation in the Real World," *European Journal of Social Psychology* 40, no. 6 (2010): 998–1009.

Chapter 9

1. *Daat Zekenim*, Genesis 27:15.
2. Likkutei Sichos, Vol. II, 411–413.
3. Babylonian Talmud, Berakhot 19b.
4. Babylonian Talmud, Menahot 43b.
5. M. Soloveitchik, "Fringes and Flags," *Bible365*, 2022, https://bible365podcast.com/bible-365/fringes-and-flags/.
6. "Penguins Logo History," Hockey Central, http://www.hockeycentral.co.uk/penguins/history/Pit-Uni-History.php.
7. M. G. Frank and T. Gilovich, "The Dark Side of Self- and Social Perception: Black Uniforms and Aggression in Professional Sports," *Journal of Personality and Social Psychology* 54, no. 1 (1988): 74–85.
8. S. Boxer, "DARK FORCES," *Sports Illustrated Vault*, April 17, 1989, https://vault.si.com/vault/1989/04/17/dark-forces-are-teams-that-are-dressed-in-black-really-meaner-and-tougher-than-their-more-cheerfully-clad-brethren-a-scientific-study-comes-up-with-some-somber-findings.
9. H. Adam and A. D. Galinsky, "Enclothed Cognition," *Journal of Experimental Social Psychology* 48, no. 4, (2012): 918–925, cited in https://www.nytimes.com/2012/04/03/science/clothes-and-self-perception.html.
10. L. Clydesdale, "How Feeling Insecure in a Swimsuit Can Hurt Your Capability," Laura Clydesdale, February 5, 2017, https://www.lauraclydesdale.com/blog-native/body-image-feeling-insecure-social-comparisons-can-hurt-math-scores-capability-swimsuit-study; B. L. Fredrickson et. al., "That Swimsuit Becomes You: Sex Differences in Self-Objectification, Restrained Eating, and Math

Performance," *Journal of Personality and Social Psychology* 75, no. 1 (1998): 269–284.

11. R. A. Smith, "Why Dressing for Success Leads to Success," *Wall Street Journal*, February 21, 2016, https://www.wsj.com/articles/why-dressing-for-success-leads-to-success-1456110340.
12. M. L. Slepian et. al. "The Cognitive Consequences of Formal Clothing," *Social Psychological and Personality Science* 6, no. 6 (2015): 661–668.
13. B. Hannover and U. Kühnen, "'The Clothing Makes the Self' Via Knowledge Activation," *Journal of Applied Social Psychology* 32 (2006): 2513–2525.
14. K. Pine, *Mind What You Wear* (Amazon Singles, 2014), 23.
15. M. Sebra, "Your Morning Shot: Deion Sanders," *GQ*, August 14, 2013, https://www.gq.com/story/your-morning-shot-deion-sanders.
16. C. Callahan, "How to Dress While Working from Home, According to the Experts," NBC10 Philadelphia, March 24, 2020, https://www.nbcphiladelphia.com/news/coronavirus/how-to-dress-while-working-from-home-according-to-the-ex.xperts/2338451/.
17. J. L. Ferguson, "How Clothing Choices Affect and Reflect Your Self-Image," *HuffPost*, February 5, 2016, https://www.huffpost.com/entry/how-clothing-choices-affect-and-reflect-your-self-image_b_9163992.
18. Pine, *Mind What You Wear*, 32–39.
19. "Why You Should be Dressing for Success," The University of Texas at Austin September 8, 2022, https://sites.utexas.edu/discovery/2022/09/08/why-you-should-be-dressing-for-success/.
20. K. Aniket and D. Roshan, "Cosplay Costumes Market Size, Share—Industry Report by 2030," Allied Market Research, 2021, https://www.alliedmarketresearch.com/cosplay-costumes-market-A13135.
21. R. T. Muller, "Becoming Another Person Through Cosplay," *Psychology Today*, December 7, 2021, https://www.psychologytoday.com/us/blog/talking-about-trauma/202112/becoming-another-person-through-cosplay.
22. A. Mertes, "History of Sports Merchandise," Quality Logo Products, July 23, 2020, https://www.qualitylogoproducts.com/promo-university/history-of-sports-merchandise.htm.
23. "$39.8 Billion Worldwide Licensed Sports Merchandise Industry to 2027—Featuring Columbia Sportswear, Fanatics, Hanesbrands and Nike Among Others," Business Wire, October 5, 2022, https://tinyurl.com/254pdaz6.
24. T. Layden, "We Are What We Wear: How Sports Jerseys Became Ubiquitous in the U.S.," *Sports Illustrated*, February 1, 2016, https://www.si.com/nfl/2016/02/01/mlb-nba-nhl-sports-jersys-rise-popularity.
25. P. Chris, *From Makeup to Breakup: My Life in and out of Kiss* (Simon and Schuster, 2012), 74.

26. A. Roberts, "Why Does Tiger Woods Always Wear Red on Sundays on the PGA Tour?," *Golf Magic*, January 18, 2022, https://www.golfmagic.com/pga-tour/why-does-tiger-woods-always-wear-red-sundays-pga-tour.
27. M. Jordan, "NBA 2K14 Michael Jordan Uncensored Part II Admires Hakeem Olajuwon," *HipHopGamer*, YouTube, November 14, 2013, https://www.youtube.com/watch?v=Beq7jjtrsV0&ab_channel=HipHopGamer.
28. G. Hughes, "Look: Jordan Wore His UNC Practice Shorts in Every NBA Game," 247 Sports, September 23, 2020, https://247sports.com/college/north-carolina/Article/Michael-Jordan-Wore-UNC-Practice-Shorts-Under-Jersey-During-Every-NBA-Game-Chicago-Bulls-151830390/.
29. Personal correspondence with Alexandra Wolfe Schiff.

Chapter 10

1. Babylonian Talmud, Menachot 44a.
2. Ibn Ezra, Deuteronomy 5:18.
3. "Why Do Some Ideas Prompt Other Ideas Later on Without Our Conscious Awareness?" The Decision Lab, https://thedecisionlab.com/biases/priming; J. A. Bargh and P. Pietromonaco, "Automatic Information Processing and Social Perception: The Influence of Trait Information Presented Outside of Conscious Awareness on Impression Formation," *Journal of Personality and Social Psychology* 43, no. 3 (1982): 437–449.
4. J. A. Bargh, M. Chen, and L. Burrows, "Automaticity of Social Behavior: Direct Effects of Trait Construct and Stereotype Activation on Action," *Journal of Personality and Social Psychology* 71 (1996), 230–244.
5. D. Ariely, G. Loewenstein, and D. Prelec, "Arbitrarily Coherent Preferences" in *The Psychology of Economic Decisions, Volume 2: Reasons and Choices* (CEPR Press, 2004), 131–161.
6. S. W. S. Lee and N. Schwarz, "Dirty Hands and Dirty Mouths: Embodiment of the Moral-Purity Metaphor Is Specific to the Motor Modality Involved in Moral Transgression," *Psychological Science* 21, no. 10 (2010): 1423–1425.
7. D. Kahneman, *Thinking Fast and Slow* (Farrar, Straus & Giroux, 2011): 53.
8. P. Chatterjee and R. L. Rose, "Do Payment Mechanisms Change the Way Consumers Perceive Products?," *Journal of Consumer Research* 38, no. 6 (2012): 1129–1139.
9. D. Malhotra, "(When) Are Religious People Nicer? Religious Salience and the 'Sunday Effect' on Pro-Social Behavior," *Judgment and Decision Making* 5 (2010): 138–143.
10. E. P. Duhaime, "Is the Call to Prayer a Call to Cooperate? A Field Experiment on the Impact of Religious Salience on Prosocial Behavior, *Judgment and Decision Making* 10, no. 6 (2015): 593–596.

11. T. Bianchi, "Most Popular Websites Worldwide as of November 2022, by Total Visits," Statista, August 29, 2023, https://www.statista.com/statistics/1201880/most-visited-websites-worldwide/.
12. P. O'Rourke, "74 Percent of Pornhub's Canadian Traffic Came from Mobile Devices in 2017," MobileSyrup, January 9, 2018, https://mobilesyrup.com/2018/01/09/pornhub-canada-2017-mobile-stats/; "Top 100: The Most Visited Websites in the US [2023 Top Websites Edition]," *Semrush Blog*, https://www.semrush.com/blog/most-visited-websites/.
13. K. Sollee, "Most Porn Is Bought on This Day of the Week (Hint: It's Not Sunday)," *Bustle*, August 25, 2015, https://www.bustle.com/articles/106180-most-porn-is-bought-on-this-day-of-the-week-hint-its-not-sunday.
14. B. Edelman, "Markets: Red Light States: Who Buys Online Adult Entertainment?," *Journal of Economic Perspectives* 23, no. 1 (2009): 209–220; "The 2019 Year in Review," Pornhub Insights December 11, 2019, https://www.pornhub.com/insights/2019-year-in-review.
15. Confraternity of Our Lady of Fatima, Pilgrimage, https://www.livefatima.io/pilgrimage/.
16. Dashboard Jesus, Archie McPhee, https://mcphee.com/products/dashboard-jesus.

Chapter 11

1. L. Kass, *The Beginning of Wisdom: Reading Genesis* (Free Press, 2003), 545.
2. Rashi, Genesis 40:23.
3. For an excellent discussion of responsibility in this context see M. Feuer, "5780—Miketz: Righteous are the foundation of the world," *Pardes from Jerusalem*, December 22, 2019, https://www.listennotes.com/podcasts/pardes-from/5780-miketz-righteous-are—2hinSwN5xp/.
4. Y. Gefen, "Judah—Taking Responsibility," *Aish*, 2019, https://www.aish.com/tp/i/gl/Judah-Taking-Responsibility.html.
5. Mizrachi, Exodus 6:9.
6. E. Goldberg, "Korach: Don't Be on the Take, Be on the Give," *Parsha Perspectives*, June 23, 2022, https://www.listennotes.com/podcasts/parsha-perspectives/korach-dont-be-on-the-take-xyvUHg4mzN5/.
7. See Abarbanel, Leviticus 4:22.
8. Ba'al Haturim, Leviticus 4:12.
9. E. Goldberg, "Naso: Wisdom from the South," *Parsha Perspectives*, June 2, 2020, https://www.listennotes.com/podcasts/parsha-perspectives/naso-wisdom-from-the-south-lQLZ5VRNXbm/.
10. Maimonides, Mishneh Torah, *Laws of Repentance* 2:3.

11. M. Comer, "Confession and Venting as a Leader," The Hayes Group International, 2017, https://www.thehayesgroupintl.com/2017/01/12/confession-venting-leadership/#content_jump.
12. Maimonides, Mishneh Torah, *Laws of Repentance* 2:10.
13. Maimonides, Mishneh Torah, *Laws of Repentance* 7:8.
14. S. Rosenblatt, "Yom Kippur: A Day of Reconciliation," *Aish*, https://aish.com/48970706/#.
15. I. Kershner, "19 Yemeni Jews Arrive in Israel, Ending Secret Rescue Operation," *New York Times*, March 21, 2016, https://www.nytimes.com/2016/03/22/world/middleeast/yemen-jews-israel.html; Ma'ot Chittin—"Wheat Money," Passover 2023 (Pesach), https://www.chabad.org/holidays/passover/pesach_cdo/aid/1170218/jewish/Maot-Chitim-Wheat-Money.htm.
16. J. Sacks, "Lech Lecha: The Heroism of Ordinary Life," *Covenant and Conversation*, The Rabbi Sacks Legacy Trust, 2008, https://www.rabbisacks.org/covenant-conversation/lech-lecha/the-heroism-of-ordinary-life/.
17. Associated Press, "Baldwin: 'Someone Is Responsible' for Shooting, but 'Not Me,'" ABC4, December 4, 2021, https://www.abc4.com/news/entertainment-news/baldwin-someone-is-responsible-for-shooting-but-not-me/.
18. M. Memmott, "It's True: 'Mistakes Were Made' Is the King of Non-Apologies," NPR, May 14, 2013, https://www.npr.org/sections/thetwo-way/2013/05/14/183924858/its-true-mistakes-were-made-is-the-king-of-non-apologies.
19. D. Wolpe, "Terumah: Why Do We Need a Tabernacle?," Sinai Temple, February 1, 2014, https://www.sinaitemple.org/worship/sermons/terumah-need-tabernacle/; S. Nenkov, "Short-Term Thinking Is a Long-Term Problem," World Quant, February 6, 2019, https://www.worldquant.com/ideas/short-term-thinking-is-a-long-term-problem/.
20. T. G. Okimoto, M. Wenzel, and K. Hedrick, "Refusing to Apologize Can Have Psychological Benefits (and We Issue No Mea Culpa for This Research Finding)," *European Journal of Social Psychology* 43, no. 1 (2013): 22–31.
21. K. Wong, "Why It's So Hard to Admit You're Wrong," *New York Times*, May 22, 2017, https://www.nytimes.com/2017/05/22/smarter-living/why-its-so-hard-to-admit-youre-wrong.html.
22. N. J. Fast and L. Z. Tiedens, "Blame Contagion: The Automatic Transmission of Self-Serving Attributions," *Journal of Experimental Social Psychology* 46, no. 1 (2010): 97–106.
23. Conversation with Congressman Gonzalez.
24. D. Wuerffel (@DannyWuerffel), Twitter (now X), October 13, 2015, https://twitter.com/DannyWuerffel/status/653754325911633921.
25. D. Murphy, "Question on Gomes Sparks Calhoun's Tirade," Daily Orange, January 17, 2004, https://dailyorange.com/2004/01/question-on-gomes-sparks-calhoun-s-tirade/.

26. K. Schumann and C. S. Dweck, "Who Accepts Responsibility for Their Transgressions?," *Personality and Social Psychology Bulletin* 40, no. 12 (2014): 1598–1610.
27. E. Bruenig (@ebruenig), Twitter (now X), March 16, 2021, https://archive.md/tXbu4#selection-3007.0-3014.0.
28. A. Romano, "Is There Room for Forgiveness in Today's 'Cancel Culture' Era?," *Vox*, March 22, 2022, https://www.vox.com/22969804/forgiveness-gibson-logan-paul-jk-rowling.
29. J. Canfield, "Taking 100% Responsibility for Your Life," Jack Canfield, March 22, 2022, https://jackcanfield.com/blog/taking-100-responsibility-for-your-life/.
30. G. Aimard, *The Freebooters: A Story of the Texan War* (Ward and Locke, 1861), 57.
31. M. B. Crawford, "The Case for Working with Your Hands," *New York Times*, May 23, 2009, https://www.nytimes.com/2009/05/24/magazine/24labor-t.html.
32. M. B. Crawford, *Shop Class as Soulcraft: An Inquiry Into the Value of Work* (Penguin, 2009), 8.
33. M. B. Crawford, "Shop Class as Soulcraft," C-SPAN, March 19, 2010, https://www.c-span.org/video/?292685-11/shop-class-soulcraft.
34. Y. Y. Jacobson, "How to Forgive," *YEHUDI*, YouTube, October 21, 2016, https://www.youtube.com/watch?v=tlCL_R2V7Y4.

Chapter 12

1. Ibn Habib, *Introduction to Ein Yaakov.*
2. D. Perez, "The Most Important Passuk in the Torah," Mizrachi World Movement, October 21, 2016, https://mizrachi.org/festivals/the-most-important-passuk-in-the-torah/.
3. Gates of Ethics, *Ethical Wills of the Sages of Israel*, Vol. 1, 105.
4. Babylonian Talmud, Brachot 26b.
5. E. Goldberg, "Vayeitzei: How Far Apart Are the Real You and the Best Version of You?," *Parsha Perspectives*, December 3, 2019, https://www.listennotes.com/podcasts/parsha-perspectives/vayeitzei-how-far-apart-are-R_0qolxX-KZ/.
6. M. Scheiner, "Foundations of Judaism," Palm Beach Synagogue, YouTube, May 2, 2023, https://www.youtube.com/watch?v=2FxR9gl7FOs&ab_channel=PalmBeachSynagogue.
7. A. Kovac, "A Year Without Hanukkah? It's a Mathematical Certainty in the Year 3031," *Forward*, December 21, 2022, https://forward.com/fast-forward/529156/a-year-without-hanukkah-its-a-mathematical-certainty-in-the-year-3031/.
8. Babylonian Talmud, Kiddushin 40b; See also Babylonian Talmud, Shabbat 31a.
9. Mishna, Zevachim 10:1.

10. E. Goldberg, "Ki Savo: A World of Gratitude," *Parsha Perspectives*, August 24, 2021, https://www.listennotes.com/podcasts/parsha-perspectives/ki-savo-a-world-of-gratitude-z9t8D0e5E-A/.
11. Babylonian Talmud, Yoma 12b.
12. N. Lamm, "Aharei Mot: Something Different for a Change," Jewish Center, 1973, https://archives.yu.edu/gsdl/collect/lammserm/index/assoc/HASH8eb6.dir/doc.pdf.
13. N. Lamm, "Aharei Mot."
14. Babylonian Talmud, Niddah 31b.
15. Ezekiel 46:9.
16. W. Goldstein, "Va'etchanan: What Is a Mezuzah?," *Language of Tomorrow*, August 14, 2019, https://www.listennotes.com/podcasts/the-language-of/vaetchanan-what-is-a-mezuzah-kHqMjceif8G/.
17. Babylonian Talmud, Brachot 26a; 29b.
18. Babylonian Talmud, Brachot 29b.
19. D. E. Mercer and G. E. Woody *Therapy Manuals for Drug Addiction Series Individual Drug Counseling*, University of Pennsylvania and Veterans Affairs Medical Center, U.S. Department of Health and Human Services, 1999.
20. E. Frank, J. M. Gonzalez, and A. Fagiolini, "The Importance of Routine for Preventing Recurrence in Bipolar Disorder," *American Journal of Psychiatry* 163, no. 6 (2006): 981–985.
21. H. I. Lanza, and D. Drabick, "Family Routine Moderates the Relation Between Child Impulsivity and Oppositional Defiant Disorder Symptoms," *Journal of Abnormal Child Psychology* 39, no. 1 (2011): 83–94.
22. Hao, "Kobe Bryant: Daily Routine," Balance the Grind, April 27, 2021, https://www.balancethegrind.com.au/daily-routines/kobe-bryant-daily-routine/.
23. M. Oshin, "The Daily Routine of 20 Famous Writers (and How You Can Use Them to Succeed)," Medium, November 2, 2020, https://medium.com/the-mission/the-daily-routine-of-20-famous-writers-and-how-you-can-use-them-to-succeed-1603f52fbb77; https://www.newyorker.com/magazine/1996/03/25/the-third-man-4.
24. G. Sulli, M. T. Y. Lam, and S. Panda, "Interplay Between Circadian Clock and Cancer: New Frontiers for Cancer Treatment," *Trends in Cancer 5*, no. 8 (2019): 475–494.
25. B. Haas, A. G. Doumouras, D. Gomez, C. de Mestral, D. M. Boyes, L. Morrison, and A. B. Nathens, "Close to Home: An Analysis of the Relationship Between Location of Residence and Location of Injury," *Journal of Trauma and Acute Care Surgery* 78, no. 4 (2015),: 860–865; "Survey Finds Vehicle Crashes Most Likely to Occur Close to Home," Autoweek, May 8, 2002, https://www.autoweek.com/news/a2108966/survey-finds-vehicle-crashes-most-likely-occur-close-home/; Dolphin Technologies, "Study by Dolphin Technologies Reveals

a Quarter of All Car Accidents Happen in the First Three Minutes of Driving," PR Newswire, September 17, 2020, https://www.prnewswire.com/news-releases/study-by-dolphin-technologies-reveals-a-quarter-of-all-car-accidents-happen-in-the-first-three-minutes-of-driving-301132286.html; Office of Energy Efficiency and Renewable Energy "FOTW #1042, August 13, 2018: In 2017 Nearly 60% of All Vehicle Trips Were Less than Six Miles," Energy.gov, August 13, 2018, https://www.energy.gov/eere/vehicles/articles/fotw-1042-august-13-2018-2017-nearly-60-all-vehicle-trips-were-less-six. The DMV reference to "quite hard" is no longer online as of the final edit of this book.

26. S. G. Charlton and N. J. Starkey, "Driving on Familiar Roads: Automaticity and Inattention Blindness," *Transportation Research Part F: Traffic Psychology and Behaviour* 19 (2013): 121–133, https://www.psychologicalscience.org/news/motr/navigating-familiar-roads-may-lead-to-driving-on-autopilot.html.
27. Rovshan, "Topic 43: Unsafe Acts/Conditions During Routine Tasks in Platforms/Offshore and How to Avoid Them," iMechanica, 2012, https://imechanica.org/node/13705.
28. Rovshan, "Topic 43."
29. B. E. Ruark, "The Risk of Routine," *Training Magazine*, February 17, 2021, https://trainingmag.com/the-risk-of-routine/.
30. Ruark, "The Risk of Routine."
31. S. L. Koen and J. Wiltfong, "Safety Leadership: The Risks with Routine," *Safety+Health*, November 25, 2017, https://www.safetyandhealthmagazine.com/articles/16381-safety-leadership-the-risks-with-routine.
32. M. Allen and O. Pierce, "Medical Errors Are No. 3 Cause of U.S Deaths, Researchers Say," NPR, May 3, 2016, https://www.npr.org/sections/health-shots/2016/05/03/476636183/death-certificates-undercount-toll-of-medical-errors.
33. A. Gawande, *The Checklist Manifesto: How to Get Things Right* (Metropolitan Books, 2009): 37–38.
34. B. C. Fletcher and K. Pine, *Flex: Do Something Different* (University of Hertfordshire Press, 2012), 105.

Chapter 13

1. L. S. Zierler, "Yitro: A Considered Climb," *Jewish Standard*, February 10, 2012, https://jewishstandard.timesofisrael.com/yitro-a-considered-climb/.
2. Babylonian Talmud, Sanhedrin 21b.
3. Sifrei Bamidbar 89.
4. Babylonian Talmud, Bava Metzia 38a; Mishna, Pirkei Avot 5:23.
5. E. Dessler, *Strive for Truth*, trans. A. Carmell (Feldheim Publishers), 127.
6. Babylonian Talmud, Kiddushin 41a.

7. M. I. Norton, D. Mochon, and D. Ariely, "The IKEA Effect: When Labor Leads to Love," *Journal of Consumer Psychology* 22, no. 3 (2012): 453–460.
8. D. Ariely, "What Makes Us Feel Good About Our Work?," TED-Ed, YouTube, December 6, 2013, https://www.youtube.com/watch?v=c8iswsLT3Jc.
9. L. T. Hamilton, "More Is More or More Is Less? Parental Financial Investments During College," *American Sociological Review* 78, no. 1 (2013): 70–95.
10. J. M. Jennings, "What IKEA, Subway, and Build-A-Bear Can Teach Us About Ourselves," John M. Jennings, January 18, 2021, https://johnmjennings.com/what-ikea-subway-and-build-a-bear-can-teach-us-about-ourselves/.
11. J. Caporal, "Kevin O'Leary Is Concerned about Leaving Too Large an Inheritance—So Are Two-Thirds of High-Net-Worth Individuals," Motley Fool, October 12, 2021, https://www.fool.com/research/high-net-worth-inheritance/.
12. A. Cooper, *The Howard Stern Show*, March 31, 2014, https://tinyurl.com/nhh4yf82.
13. J. L. Zagorsky, "Do People Save or Spend Their Inheritances? Understanding What Happens to Inherited Wealth," *Journal of Family and Economic Issues* 34 (2013): 64–76.
14. Focus for Health Foundation, "The Lottery: The Poor Are Playing, and the Wealthy are Winning," Focus for Health, 2013, https://www.focusforhealth.org/the-lottery-the-poor-are-playing-and-the-wealthy-are-winning/.
15. M. Weber, "Science as a Vocation," *Wissenschaft als Beruf from Gesammlte Aufsaetze zur Wissenschaftslehre*, Tubingen, 1922, 524–555.

Chapter 14

1. Sforno, Exodus 12:2.
2. Mishna, Rosh Hashana 2:7.
3. C. Boeckmann, "Why the Week Has Seven Days," Almanac, November 12, 2021, https://www.almanac.com/content/why-week-has-seven-days; S. Courtois, N. Werth, et. al., *The Black Book of Communism: Crimes, Terror, Repression* (Harvard University Press, 1999), 172.
4. D. Nosowitz, "Why Can't We Get Rid of the 7-Day Week?," Atlas Obscura, September 17, 2015, https://www.atlasobscura.com/articles/why-cant-we-get-rid-of-the-7day-week.
5. Babylonian Talmud, Nedarim 49b
6. Keter Shem Tov, Appendix 169; J. Sacks, "The Deep Power of Joy," *Covenant and Conversation*, The Rabbi Sacks Legacy Trust, 2016, https://www.rabbisacks.org/covenant-conversation/reeh/deep-power-of-joy/.
7. Maimonides, *Shemoneh Perakim*, Chapter 5; B. Gesundheit, "Maimonides' Appreciation for Medicine," *Rambam Maimonides Medical Journal* 2, no. 1

(2011), e0018. See also the scholar Mitchell First's analysis of Rashi's profession and commentary: https://jewishlink.news/rashi-insights-into-his-life-and-works/.

8. Rabbi Moshe Scheiner provides a characteristically outstanding analysis here. M. Scheiner, "Foundations of Judaism—December 13, 2022," Palm Beach Synagogue, YouTube, December 14, 2022, https://www.youtube.com/watch?v=14vJPtbd-PY.
9. Babylonian Talmud, Yoma 22a.
10. Babylonian Talmud, Berachot 57b.
11. Rashi, Genesis 37:11.
12. P. Peli, *On Repentance: The Thought and Oral Discourses of Rabbi Joseph Dov Soloveitchik* (Rowman and Littlefield Publishers, 1984), 88.
13. E. Goldberg, "Vayakhel/Pekudei: Subjective Shabbos," *Parsha Perspectives*, March 15, 2023, https://www.listennotes.com/podcasts/parsha-perspectives/vayakhelpekudei-subjective-s1YKe-4IjdA/.
14. D. Fohrman, "Shabbat: Why Do We Rest?," *Aleph Beta*, 2013, https://www.alephbeta.org/playlist/shabbat-why-do-we-rest.
15. Y. Goldstein, "Shabbos-Intimacy on Friday Night," *Kedushas Habayis*, December 9, 2020, https://shulchanaruchharav.com/halacha/shabbos-intimacy-on-friday-night/#_ftn1.
16. Juvenal, *The Satires XIV.*
17. A. Kalmanofsky, "Ki Tissa—Kept By Shabbat," Torah Commentary, March 2, 2018, https://www.jtsa.edu/torah/kept-by-shabbat/.
18. Personal correspondence.
19. L. Neary, "A Cup of Ambition and Endurance: '9 to 5' Unites Workers Across Decades," NPR, July 11, 2019, https://www.npr.org/2019/07/11/738587297/a-cup-of-ambition-and-endurance-9-to-5-unites-workers-across-decades.
20. J. Kirkland, "Elizabeth Warren Used Dolly Parton's '9 to 5' Without Her Permission," *Esquire*, March 12, 2019, https://www.esquire.com/entertainment/music/a26795885/dolly-parton-elizabeth-warren-9-to-5/.
21. S. Crabtree, "Worldwide, 13% of Employees Are Engaged at Work," Gallup, October 8, 2013, https://news.gallup.com/poll/165269/worldwide-employees-engaged-work.aspx.
22. T. W. Smith, "Job Satisfaction in the United States," NORC/University of Chicago, 2007, 1.
23. "Start Smiling: It Pays to Be Happy at Work," *Forbes*, August 14, 2010, https://www.forbes.com/2010/08/13/happiest-occupations-workplace-productivity-how-to-get-a-promotion-morale-forbes-woman-careers-happiness.html?sh=22f95fb9efb4.

24. T. Amabile and S. Kramer, "Do Happier People Work Harder?," *New York Times*, September 2, 2011, https://www.nytimes.com/2011/09/04/opinion/sunday/do-happier-people-work-harder.html.
25. "Start Smiling."
26. J. Austen, *Mansfield Park*, Classics in Literature (The Electric Book Co, 1998), 243.
27. M. A. Killingsworth, D. Kahneman, and B. Mellers, "Income and Emotional Well-Being: A Conflict Resolved," *Proceedings of the National Academy of Science—PNAS*, 120, no. 10 (2023): e2208661120–e2208661120; J. Robison, "Happiness Is Love—and $75,000," Gallup, November 17, 2011, https://news.gallup.com/businessjournal/150671/happiness-is-love-and-75k.aspx.
28. T. W. Smith, "Job Satisfaction in the United States," NORC/University of Chicago, 2007, 5.
29. Amabile and Kramer, "Do Happier People Work Harder?"; S. Achor, A. Reece, G. Rosen Kellerman, and A. Robichaux, "9 Out of 10 People Are Willing to Earn Less Money to Do More-Meaningful Work," *Harvard Business Review*, November 6, 2018, https://hbr.org/2018/11/9-out-of-10-people-are-willing-to-earn-less-money-to-do-more-meaningful-work.
30. M. Nikolova and F. Cnossen, "What Makes a Job Meaningful?," Brookings, April 8, 2020, https://www.brookings.edu/blog/up-front/2020/04/08/what-makes-a-job-meaningful/; T. Bromley, T. Lauricella, and B. Schaninger, "Making Work Meaningful from the C-Suite to the Frontline," McKinsey and Company, June 28, 2021, https://www.mckinsey.com/capabilities/people-and-organizational-performance/our-insights/the-organization-blog/making-work-meaningful-from-the-c-suite-to-the-frontline.
31. S. Achor et. al., "9 Out of 10 People."
32. A. Wrzesniewski, "Job Crafting—Amy Wrzesniewski on Creating Meaning in Your Own Work," *re:Work*, YouTube, November 10, 2014, https://www.youtube.com/watch?v=C_igfnctYjA.
33. B. Schwartz, *Why We Work* (TED Books, 2015), 14.
34. J. E. Dutton and A. Wrzesniewski, "What Job Crafting Looks Like," *Harvard Business Review*, March 12, 2020, https://hbr.org/2020/03/what-job-crafting-looks-like.
35. J. Byerly, "The Janitor Who Helped Put a Man on the Moon," From the Green Notebook, November 4, 2017, https://fromthegreennotebook.com/2017/11/04/the-janitor-who-help-put-a-man-on-the-moon/.
36. C. Moore, "What Is Job Crafting? (Incl. 5 Examples and Exercises)," *Positive Psychology*, May 17, 2019, https://positivepsychology.com/job-crafting/.
37. N. J. Fryer, *Correlates and Outcomes of Task Crafting: Linking Task Crafting to Promotion* (University of Leeds, 2019), iii.

38. T. Veblen, *The Theory of the Leisure Class: An Economic Study of Institutions (*Mentor Books, 1953), 42–43.
39. J. M. Keynes, "Economic Possibilities for Our Grandchildren" in *Essays in Persuasion* (Harcourt Brace, 1930), 358–373.
40. B. Lord, "Innovation Used to Benefit Workers. Can It Again?," Inequality.org, December 26, 2018, https://inequality.org/great-divide/can-innovation-benefit-workers/.
41. "The Only Way to Travel Is Cadillac Style," Cadillac, YouTube, 1989, https://www.youtube.com/watch?v=W7XEg0kqmCM&ab_channel=ewjxn; A. Luft, "Ad Break: 1988 Cadillac Style Commercial Is . . . Stylish," GM Authority, October 9, 2012, https://gmauthority.com/blog/2012/10/ad-break-1988-cadillac-style-commercial-is-stylish/.
42. W. Powers, *Hamlet's BlackBerry: Building a Good Life in the Digital Age* (Harper Perennial, 2011), 213.
43. T. Kreider, "The 'Busy' Trap," *New York Times*, June 30, 2012, https://archive.nytimes.com/opinionator.blogs.nytimes.com/2012/06/30/the-busy-trap/.
44. S. Bellezza, N. Paharia, and A. Keinan, "Research: Why Americans Are So Impressed by Busyness," *Harvard Business Review*, December 15, 2016, https://hbr.org/2016/12/research-why-americans-are-so-impressed-by-busyness.
45. Thecoreclub.com, zerobondny.com Aman New York Policies, https://www.aman.com/sites/default/files/2022-04/Aman-New-York-Policies.pdf.
46. M. Kivimäki et. al, "Long Working Hours, Socioeconomic Status, and the Risk of Incident Type 2 Diabetes: A Meta-Analysis of Published and Unpublished Data from 222 120 Individuals," *Lancet: Diabetes and Endocrinology* 3, no. 1 (2015): 27–34.
47. F. Pega, et. al., "Global, Regional, and National Burdens of Ischemic Heart Disease and Stroke Attributable to Exposure to Long Working Hours for 194 Countries, 2000–2016: A Systematic Analysis from the WHO/ILO Joint Estimates of the Work-related Burden of Disease and Injury," *Environment International* 154 (2021): 106595.
48. M. Virtanen, et. al., "Long Working Hours and Cognitive Function: The Whitehall II Study," *American Journal of Epidemiology* 169, no. 5 (2009): 596–605.
49. J. Pencavel, "The Productivity of Working Hours," IZA Discussion Paper No. 8129, 2014.
50. C. W., "Proof that You Should Get a Life," *Economist*, December 9, 2014, https://www.economist.com/free-exchange/2014/12/09/proof-that-you-should-get-a-life.
51. B. Daisley, "Hacks for Bringing Joy to Your Job," *Great Leadership With Jacob Morgan*, 2020, https://www.listennotes.com/podcasts/great-leadership/hacks-for-bringing-joy-to-Q4tbaGAk-lJ/.

52. R. Sharp, "Long Working Hours Crush Creativity," *HR Magazine*, March 22, 2018, https://www.hrmagazine.co.uk/content/news/long-working-hours-crush-creativity; Pencavel, "The Productivity of Working Hours"; T. Garrity, "Does Ditching Your Phone for Three Days Actually Rewire Your Brain?," InsideHook, December 20, 2023, https://www.insidehook.com/wellness/detox-your-phone.
53. Babylonian Talmud, Bava Metzia 83b.
54. D. Hampton, "The Science Behind Why You Should Switch Off Your Thinking Brain to Spark Creativity and Smart Decisions," The Best Brain Possible, April 29, 2018, https://thebestbrainpossible.com/brain-creativity-decisions-default-mode-network-aha/; A. Hurt, "What Is the Default Mode Network?," *Discover Magazine*, March 3, 2023, https://www.discovermagazine.com/mind/what-is-the-default-mode-network.
55. M. Frenzel, "Rest Is Productive—Better Humans," Medium, May 27, 2020, https://betterhumans.pub/rest-is-productive-1348b2b7eeb0.
56. "Dopamine," Cleveland Clinic, https://my.clevelandclinic.org/health/articles/22581-dopamine.
57. S. Weinschenk, "Shopping, Dopamine, and Anticipation," *Psychology Today*, October 22, 2015, https://www.psychologytoday.com/ca/blog/brain-wise/201510/shopping-dopamine-and-anticipation; "What Is Dopamine and How Does It Keep Me Using?," The Coleman Institute, January 14, 2022, https://thecolemaninstitute.com/tci-blog/72-dopamine-the-anticipation-molecule/.
58. F. T. Moura, "Dopamine: More Than Pleasure, the Secret Is the Anticipation of a Reward," Live Innovation, April 2, 2020, https://liveinnovation.org/dopamine-more-than-pleasure-the-secret-is-the-anticipation-of-a-reward/; "Global Digital Marketing Report," Razorfish, 2015, 27; P. Jedras, A. Jones, and M. Field, "The Role of Anticipation in Drug Addiction and Reward," *Neuroscience and Neuroeconomics* 3 (2014): 1.

Chapter 15

1. Babylonian Talmud, Chullin 91a.
2. M. M. Schneerson, *Likkutei Sichot*, vol. 13, 108.
3. J. B. Soloveitchik, "A Tribute to the Rebbetzin of Talne," *Tradition* 17, no. 2 (1978): 73–82.
4. Y. M. Druck, *Eish Tamid*, Leviticus 1:1.
5. M. Gellman, "What Are You Looking For?," *First Things*, 1997, https://www.firstthings.com/article/1997/03/002-what-are-you-looking-for.
6. Mishnah, Avot 4:2.
7. Babylonian Talmud, Kiddushin 40b.
8. Maimonides, Mishneh Torah, *Laws of Repentance* 3:4.

9. B. Miller, "Masterpiece Cakeshop Owner Says He's Lost 40% of Business, Welcomes SCOTUS Hearing," ABC Denver 7 Colorado News, June 26, 2017, https://www.denver7.com/news/politics/masterpiece-cakeshop-owner-says-hes-lost-40-of-business-welcomes-scotus-hearing.
10. B. Foldy, "How an Ordinary Guy Took a $3,000 Case to the Supreme Court," *Wall Street Journal*, May 2, 2024, https://www.wsj.com/us-news/small-claims-case-goes-to-supreme-court-b24ac380.
11. E. N. Lorenz, "Deterministic Nonperiodic Flow," *Journal of the Atmospheric Sciences* 20, no. 2 (1963): 130–141.
12. G. Herman, *Chaos Theory, Edward Lorenz, and Deterministic Nonperiodic Flow* (2015), http://schumacher.atmos.colostate.edu/gherman/ATS780FA2015_Lorenz_V2.pdf.
13. E. N. Lorenz, "Predictability: Does the Flap of a Butterfly's Wings in Brazil Set off a Tornado in Texas," American Association for the Advancement of Science, 1972, http://gymportalen.dk/sites/lru.dk/files/lru/132_kap6_lorenz_artikel_the_butterfly_effect.pdf.
14. *Ibid.*
15. J. L. Vernon, "Understanding the Butterfly Effect," *American Scientist*, 2017, https://www.americanscientist.org/article/understanding-the-butterfly-effect.
16. C. Sparks, "Introducing: The Small Things Often Podcast," The Gottman Institute, February 14, 2020, https://www.gottman.com/blog/introducing-the-small-things-often-podcast/.
17. R. D. Goodwin et. al., "Trends in U.S. Depression Prevalence from 2015 to 2020: The Widening Treatment Gap," *American Journal of Preventive Medicine* 63, no. 5 (2022): 726–733.
18. D. J. Brody, L. A. Pratt, and J. P. Hughes, "Prevalence of Depression Among Adults Aged 20 and Over: United States, 2013–2016,"*NCHS Data Brief No. 303*, 2018, https://www.cdc.gov/nchs/products/databriefs/db303.htm; G. N., Bratman, et. al., "Nature Experience Reduces Rumination and Subgenual Prefrontal Cortex Activation," *Proceedings of the National Academy of Sciences of the United States of America* 112, no. 28 (2015): 8567–8572.
19. R. Malka, "When Rebbitzen Jungreis Came to Town," Rivka Malka Coaching, 2015, https://rivkamalka.com/when-rebbitzen-jungreis-came-to-town/.
20. N. Spector, "Smiling Can Trick Your Brain into Happiness—and Boost Your Health," NBC News, November 28, 2017, https://www.nbcnews.com/better/health/smiling-can-trick-your-brain-happiness-boost-your-health-ncna822591.
21. G. L. Kelling and J. Q. Wilson, "Broken Windows," *The Atlantic*, March 1982, https://www.theatlantic.com/magazine/archive/1982/03/broken-windows/304465/; C. Ruhl, "Broken Windows Theory of Criminology," *Simply Psychology*, August 1, 2023, https://www.simplypsychology.org/broken-windows-theory.html.

22. Post Editorial Board, "Restore 'Broken Windows' Policing to Close the Window on Crime," *New York Post*, July 26, 2023, https://nypost.com/2023/07/26/restore-broken-windows-policing-to-close-the-window-on-crime/; A. Maas, "Fix Broken Windows, Both the Concept and on the Subway," *Police1*, January 5, 2021, https://www.police1.com/patrol-issues/articles/fix-broken-windows-both-the-concept-and-on-the-subway-bXGpKM7En7KpSHwH/.
23. N. S. Riley, "It's Time for a 'Broken Windows' Policy for Schools," *New York Post*, December 16, 2023, https://nypost.com/2023/12/16/opinion/its-time-for-a-broken-windows-policy-for-schools/.
24. D. N. Bass, "Rates of Crime and Violence Spike 24% in NC Public High Schools," *Carolina Journal*, March 3, 2023, https://www.carolinajournal.com/crime-and-violence-spike-24-in-nc-public-high-schools/.
25. J. Seaman and E. Hernandez, "Rising Violence Makes Denver Schools Reconsider Campus Police," *Governing*, June 13, 2023, https://www.governing.com/community/rising-violence-makes-denver-schools-reconsider-campus-police.
26. B. Jones, "'It Can't Just Be Violent Game of Whack-A-Mole': Akron Teachers Raise Concerns over Violence in Schools," ABC News 5 Cleveland, December 8, 2022, https://www.news5cleveland.com/news/local-news/it-cant-just-be-violent-game-of-whack-a-mole-akron-teachers-raise-concerns-over-violence-in-schools.
27. Riley, "It's Time for a 'Broken Windows.'"
28. M. Puma, "Bear Bryant 'Simply the Best There Ever Was,'" ESPN Classic, 2022, https://www.espn.com/classic/biography/s/Bryant_Bear.html; P. Williams, *The Pursuit* (Regal, 2008), 140.
29. A. Tallent, "25 Greatest Head Coaches in NFL History," *Athlon Sports*, March 1, 2021, https://athlonsports.com/nfl/25-greatest-head-coaches-nfl-history.
30. Williams, *The Pursuit*, 140.
31. D. Flemming, "From the Archives: The Building of Bill Belichick," ESPN, October 4, 2016, https://www.espn.com/espn/feature/story/_/id/17703210/new-england-patriots-coach-bill-belichick-greatest-enigma-sports.
32. J. Kerr, *Legacy: What the All Blacks Can Teach Us About the Business of Life* (Constable, 2013), 18.
33. M. Slater, "Marginal Gains Underpin GB Cycling Dominance," BBC Sport, August 8, 2012, https://www.bbc.com/sport/olympics/19174302.
34. M. Imai, *Kaizen: The Key to Japanese Competitive Success* (Random House, 1986), https://www.techtarget.com/searcherp/definition/kaizen-or-continuous-improvement.
35. D. Do, "What Is Continuous Improvement (Kaizen)?," *The Lean Way*, August 5, 2017, https://theleanway.net/what-is-continuous-improvement; "What Companies Use Kaizen?," Creative Safety Supply, https://www.creativesafetysupply.com/qa/kaizen/what-companies-use-kaizen.

Chapter 16

1. E. Goldberg, "Shemos: Connecting the Dots," *Parsha Perspectives*, January 10, 2023, https://www.listennotes.com/podcasts/parsha-perspectives/shemos-connecting-the-dots-dOU_8-AvFu6/.
2. This insight is from David Wolfowicz from his conversations with Rabbi Noah Kunin.
3. D. Simons, "Selective Attention Test," Daniel Simons, YouTube, March 10, 2010, https://www.youtube.com/watch?v=vJG698U2Mvo&list=PLB228A1652CD49370&ab_channel=DanielSimons.
4. D. Simons, "The 'Door' Study," Daniel Simons, YouTube, March 14, 2010, https://www.youtube.com/watch?v=FWSxSQsspiQ.
5. Z. Stambor, "Right before Our Eyes," *Monitor on Psychology* 37, no. 9 (2006): 30.
6. B. C. Hamilton, L. S. Arnold, and B. C. Tefft, "Distracted Driving and Perceptions of Hands-Free Technologies: Findings from the 2013 Traffic Safety Culture Index," AAA Foundation for Traffic Safety, 2013; "Distracted Driving—Injury Facts," Injury Facts, National Safety Council, May 4, 2023, https://injuryfacts.nsc.org/motor-vehicle/motor-vehicle-safety-issues/distracted-driving/.
7. J. K. Caird, S. M. Simmons, K. Wiley, K. A. Johnston, and W. J. Horrey, "Does Talking on a Cell Phone, with a Passenger, or Dialing Affect Driving Performance? An Updated Systematic Review and Meta-Analysis of Experimental Studies," *Human Factors* 60, no. 1 (2018),: 101–133; Y. Ishigami and R. M. Klein, "Is a Hands-Free Phone Safer than a Handheld Phone?," *Journal of Safety Research* 40, no. 2 (2009): 157–164.
8. B. Charny, "Cell Phones May Cause 'Tunnel Vision,'" ZDNET, July 25, 2007, https://www.zdnet.com/article/cell-phones-may-cause-tunnel-vision/; FiveThirtyEight, "Driving? Your Phone Is a Distraction Even If You Aren't Looking at It," Association for Psychological Science, June 25, 2018, https://www.psychologicalscience.org/news/driving-your-phone-is-a-distraction-even-if-you-arent-looking-at-it.html.
9. "Facts + Statistics: Motorcycle Crashes," Insurance Information Institute, https://tinyurl.com/y3pr8p6u.
10. "3 Reasons Motorcycle Accidents Are More Dangerous Than Car Accidents," Rossman Law Group, https://rossmanlaw.com/3-reasons-motorcycle-accidents-are-more-dangerous-than-car-accidents/.
11. K. Pammer, S. Sabadas, and S. Lentern, "Allocating Attention to Detect Motorcycles: The Role of Inattentional Blindness," *Human Factors* 60, no. 1 (2018): 5–19; Human Factors and Ergonomics Society, "Why Drivers May Fail to See Motorcycles in Plain Sight," *ScienceDaily*, January 5, 2018, www.sciencedaily.com/releases/2018/01/180105082243.htm.

12. D. Simons and C. F. Chabris, "Gorillas in Our Midst: Sustained Inattentional Blindness for Dynamic Events," *Perception* 28, no. 9 (1999): 1059–1074; D. Simons and D. T. Levin, "Failure to Detect Changes to People During Real-World Interaction," *Psychonomic Bulletin and Review* 5 (1998): 644–649.
13. N. Briscoe, "Why Bikers Make Better Car Drivers Than the Rest of Us," *Irish Times*, May 4, 2016, https://www.irishtimes.com/life-and-style/motors/why-bikers-make-better-car-drivers-than-the-rest-of-us-1.2633465.
14. M. Ocrant, "Madoff Tops Charts; Skeptics Ask How," *MARHedge*, 2001, https://nakedshorts.typepad.com/files/madoff.pdf; E. E. Arvedlund, "Don't Ask, Don't Tell: Bernie Madoff Attracts Skeptics in 2001," *Barron's*, May 7, 2001, https://www.barrons.com/articles/SB989019667829349012.
15. H. Markopolos, "The World's Largest Hedge Fund Is a Fraud," Submission to the SCC, November 7, 2005, https://math.nyu.edu/~avellane/madoffmarkopoulos.pdf.
16. J. Gottman and J. Schwartz Gottman, "Here's the No. 1 Phrase Used in Successful Relationships, Say Psychologists Who Studied 40,000 Couples," CNBC, January 20, 2023, https://www.cnbc.com/2023/01/20/the-no-1-phrase-that-makes-relationships-successful-according-to-psychologists-who-studied-40000-couples.html.
17. S. Possing, "13 Ways to Be Observant," wikiHow, September 11, 2021, https://www.wikihow.com/Be-Observant.

Chapter 17

1. D. Fohrman 'The Meaning of You Shall Not Boil a Kid In Its Mother's Milk: Understanding Basar B'chalav," *AlephBeta*, https://members.alephbeta.org/playlist/basar-bchalav.; Sefer HaChinuch, *Mitzvah 313*.
2. Babylonian Talmud, Niddah 51b.
3. Y. Y. Jacobson, "Fins and Scales," Chabad.org, https://www.chabad.org/library/article_cdo/aid/137607/jewish/Fins-and-Scales.htm; E. Goldberg, "Re'eh: A Jew Need Fins and Scales," *Parsha Perspectives*, August 3, 2021, https://www.listennotes.com/podcasts/parsha-perspectives/reeh-a-jew-need-fins-and-OPQf32RLiB_/.
4. J. Sacks, "The Power of a Curse: Behar," *Covenant and Conversation*, The Rabbi Sacks Legacy Fund, 2020, https://rabbisacks.org/covenant-conversation/behar/the-power-of-a-curse/.
5. H. Wouk, *The Will to Love On: This Is Our Heritage* (HarperCollins, 2000), 13.
6. B. McNeil, S. Pauker, H. Sox, Jr., and A. Tversky, "On the Elicitation of Preferences for Alternative Therapies," *New England Journal of Medicine* 306 (1982): 1259–1262.

7. A. Ledgerwood, "Getting Stuck in the Negatives (and How to Get Unstuck)," TEDxUCDavis, TEDx Talks, June 22, 2013, https://www.youtube.com/watch?v=7XFLTDQ4JMk&ab_channel=TEDxTalks.
8. M. Shermer, "Negativity Bias," *Edge*, 2017, https://www.edge.org/response-detail/27025.
9. T. A. Ito, J. T. Larsen, N. K. Smith, and J. T. Cacioppo, "Negative Information Weighs More Heavily on the Brain: The Negativity Bias in Evaluative Categorization," *Journal of Personality and Social Psychology* 75, no. 4 (1998): 887–900; D. Binder, "Counting Thoughts, Part I," Exploring the Problem, January 1, 2017, https://www.exploringtheproblemspace.com/new-blog/2017/1/1/counting-thoughts-part-i.
10. "Negativity Bias—The Decision Lab," The Decision Lab, https://thedecisionlab.com/biases/negativity-bias.
11. A. Levitt, "Hate Vegetables? Blame Your Parents," *The Takeout*, November 15, 2019, https://thetakeout.com/vegetable-taste-genetics-american-heart-association-1839892751; A. W. Logue, I. Ophir, K. E. Strauss, "The Acquisition of Taste Aversions in Humans," *Behaviour Research and Therapy* 19, no. 4 (1981): 319–333; A. Fleming, "Food Aversions: Why They Occur and How You Can Tackle Them," *Guardian*, August 2, 2018, https://www.theguardian.com/lifeandstyle/wordofmouth/2013/jun/18/food-aversions-why-occur-how-tackle; M. S. Haley, S. Bruno, A. Fontanini, and A. Maffei, "LTD at Amygdalocortical Synapses as a Novel Mechanism For Hedonic Learning," *eLife*, 2020, 9.
12. A. Thomas, "The Secret Ratio That Proves Why Customer Reviews Are So Important," *Inc.*, February 26, 2018, https://www.inc.com/andrew-thomas/the-hidden-ratio-that-could-make-or-break-your-company.html; N. Patel, "Your Business Needs More Negative Reviews. Here's Why," Neil Patel, 2018, https://neilpatel.com/blog/your-business-needs-negative-reviews/.
13. A. Horne, "Gottman's 'Art and Science of Love,'" *Positive Psychology News*, November 3, 2009, https://positivepsychologynews.com/news/amanda-horne/200911034418.
14. A. F. Shariff and M. Rhemtulla, "Divergent Effects of Beliefs in Heaven and Hell on National Crime Rates," *PloS One* 7, no. 6 (2012): e39048.
15. Cited in M. Shermer, *Conspiracy: Why the Rational Believe the Irrational* (Johns Hopkins University Press, 2022), 90–91.
16. J. Mandelaro, "When Campaign Ads Go Low, It Often Works," University of Rochester News Center, November 3, 2016, https://www.rochester.edu/newscenter/when-campaign-ads-go-low-it-often-works/.
17. R. Schelenz, "Why Negative Campaigning Works—and How to Fight It," University of California, September 12, 2019, https://www.universityofcalifornia.edu/news/why-negative-campaigning-works-and-how-fight-it; Business Communication Practices, 216.

18. R. Kwok, "How Much Do Campaign Ads Matter?," *Kellogg Insight*, November 1, 2021, https://insight.kellogg.northwestern.edu/article/how-much-do-campaign-ads-matter.
19. D. Rozado, R. Hughes, and J. Halberstadt, "Longitudinal Analysis of Sentiment and Emotion in News Media Headlines Using Automated Labelling with Transformer Language Models," *PLoS ONE* 17, no. 10 (2022): e0276367.
20. J. B. Merrill and W. Oremus, "Five Points for Anger, One for a 'Like': How Facebook's Formula Fostered Rage and Misinformation," *Washington Post*, October 26, 2021, https://www.washingtonpost.com/technology/2021/10/26/facebook-angry-emoji-algorithm/; R. Pomeroy, "Negative, Emotionally Manipulative News Headlines Have Skyrocketed Since 2000," *Big Think*, October 21, 2022, https://bigthink.com/the-present/negative-media-headlines-skyrocketed/.
21. M. Trussler and S. Soroka, "Consumer Demand for Cynical and Negative News Frames," *International Journal of Press/Politics* 19, no. 3, (2014): 360–379.
22. S. Soroka, P. Fournier, and L. Nir, "Cross-National Evidence of a Negativity Bias in Psychophysiological Reactions to News," *Proceedings of the National Academy of Sciences of the United States of America* 116, no. 38 (2019): 18888–18892.
23. P. Srivastava, G. P. Currie, and J. Britton, "Smoking Cessation," *British Medical Journal* 332, no. 7553 (2006): 1324–1326.
24. K. Rubel, "Read the Surgeon General's 1964 Report on Smoking and Health," *PBS News Hour*, January 12, 2014, https://www.pbs.org/newshour/health/first-surgeon-general-report-on-smokings-health-effects-marks-50-year-anniversary; https://www.govinfo.gov/features/anniversary-report-smoking-health.
25. M. C. Jensen, "Tobacco: A Potent Lobby," *New York Times*, February 19, 1978, https://www.nytimes.com/1978/02/19/archives/tobacco-a-potent-lobby-lobby.html.
26. A. O. Sulzberger, "Smoking Warnings Called Ineffective," *New York Times*, May 22, 1981, https://www.nytimes.com/1981/05/22/us/smoking-warnings-called-ineffective.html.
27. L. T. Kozlowski, "Origins in the USA in the 1980s of the Warning That Smokeless Tobacco Is Not a Safe Alternative to Cigarettes: A Historical, Documents-Based Assessment with Implications for Comparative Warnings on Less Harmful Tobacco/Nicotine Products," *Harm Reduction Journal* 15, no. 1 (2018): 21.
28. J. F. Thrasher, A. Osman, and D. Anshari, "Images in Cigarette Warning Labels: How Should They Warn?," *Virtual Mentor* 15, no. 8 (2013), 704–712.
29. "Tobacco Warning Labels Around the World," CNN Health, CNN, August 15, 2019, https://edition.cnn.com/2012/08/16/business/gallery/tobacco-warning-labels/index.html.
30. M. E. Cornelius, C. G. Loretan, A. Jamal, et al., "Tobacco Product Use Among Adults—United States, 2021," *CDC Morbidity and Mortality Weekly Report* 72

(2023): 475–483, https://www.cdc.gov/mmwr/volumes/72/wr/mm7218a1.htm; G. Bentley, "Youth Smoking Nears Zero," *Reason*, November 2, 2023, https://reason.com/2023/11/02/youth-smoking-nears-zero/; American Lung Association, *Tobacco Trends Brief*, https://www.lung.org/research/trends-in-lung-disease/tobacco-trends-brief/overall-tobacco-trends.

31. Z. Sheikh, "13 Best Quit-Smoking Tips Ever," WebMD, October 11, 2013, https://www.webmd.com/smoking-cessation/ss/slideshow-13-best-quit-smoking-tips-ever.
32. https://www.cdc.gov/healthyweight/effects/index.html.
33. A. Van Dam, "Why Are Americans Getting Shorter?," *Washington Post*, December 15, 2023, https://www.washingtonpost.com/business/2023/12/15/why-are-americans-getting-shorter/; https://www.wionews.com/science/research-shows-nearly-half-of-all-cancer-cases-are-linked-to-obesity-720324.
34. D. Glickman and D. Mozaffarian, "Our Food Is Killing Too Many of Us," *New York Times*, September 11, 2019, https://www.nytimes.com/2019/08/26/opinion/food-nutrition-health-care.html. CSPI, "Why Good Nutrition Is Important," Center for Science in the Public Interest, https://www.cspinet.org/eating-healthy/why-good-nutrition-important.
35. "Adult Obesity," Harvard University School of Public Health, https://www.hsph.harvard.edu/obesity-prevention-source/obesity-trends-original/obesity-rates-worldwide/; "Childhood Obesity Facts," Centers for Disease Control and Prevention, May 17, 2022, https://www.cdc.gov/obesity/data/childhood.html.
36. E. Barclay, J. Belluz, and J. Zarracina, "It's Easy to Become Obese in America. These 7 Charts Explain Why," *Vox*, August 9, 2018, https://www.vox.com/2016/8/31/12368246/obesity-america-2018-charts.
37. D. Blumenthal and S. Seervai, "Rising Obesity in the United States Is a Public Health Crisis," Commonwealth Fund, April 24, 2018, https://www.commonwealthfund.org/blog/2018/rising-obesity-united-states-public-health-crisis; D. Desilver, "How America's Diet Has Changed over Time," Pew Research Center, December 13, 2016. B. Lin, J. Guthrie, and T. Smith, "Dietary Quality by Food Source and Demographics in the United States, 1977–2018," Economic Research Service, Department of Agriculture, March 2023.
38. P. Attia, "How to Live Longer and Healthier with Dr. Peter Attia," *Honestly with Bari Weiss*, June 1, 2023, https://www.listennotes.com/podcasts/honestly-with-bari/how-to-live-longer-and-QK7hGxEwSsH/; L. R. Goldberg and T. J. Gould, "Genetic Influences Impacting Nicotine Use and Abuse During Adolescence: Insights from Human and Rodent Studies," *Brain Research Bulletin* 187 (2022): 24–38; L. Stahl, "Recognizing and Treating Obesity as a Disease," *60 Minutes*, CBS News, January 1, 2023, https://www.cbsnews.com/news/weight-loss-obesity-drug-2023-01-01/.

39. G. Kolata, "Food Deserts and Obesity Role Challenged," *New York Times*, April 12, 2012, https://www.nytimes.com/2012/04/18/health/research/pairing-of-food-deserts-and-obesity-challenged-in-studies.html.
40. A. E. Carroll, "The Failure of Calorie Counts on Menus," *New York Times*, November 30, 2015, https://www.nytimes.com/2015/12/01/upshot/more-menus-have-calorie-labeling-but-obesity-rate-remains-high.html; L. J. Harnack et al., "Effects of Calorie Labeling and Value Size Pricing on Fast Food Meal Choices: Results from an Experimental Trial," *International Journal of Behavioral Nutrition and Physical Activity* 5, no. 1 (2008): 63; C. Berry et. al. "Understanding the Calorie Labeling Paradox in Chain Restaurants: Why Menu Calorie Labeling Alone May Not Affect Average Calories Ordered," *Journal of Public Policy and Marketing* 38, no. 2 (2019): 192–213; A. Hartocollis, "Calorie Postings Don't Change Habits, Study Finds," *New York Times*, October 6, 2009, https://www.nytimes.com/2009/10/06/nyregion/06calories.html.
41. T. Tompson et. al., "Obesity in the United States: Public Perceptions," Associated Press-NORC Center for Public Affairs Research 2013; Duke University Medical Center, "Fewer Americans Think Smoking a Pack a Day Poses a Great Health Risk: Risk Perception Dropped from 2006 to 2015, Declining More Quickly in Women," *ScienceDaily*, February 27, 2018, www.sciencedaily.com/releases/2018/02/180227125719.htm; M. Gannon, "What, Me Fat? Most Americans Don't Think They're Overweight, Poll Finds," *Live Science*, June 11, 2014, https://www.livescience.com/46246-most-americans-dont-think-theyre-overweight.html; L. Saad, "A Half-Century of Polling on Tobacco: Most Don't Like Smoking but Tolerate It," in *The Public Perspective* 9 (1998): 1–4.
42. D. A. McIntyre, "This Is America's Most-Loved TV Personality," 247 Wallst, April 16, 2021, https://247wallst.com/media/2021/04/16/oprah-winfrey-is-americas-most-loved-tv-personality/; K. Salari, "The Dawning Era of Personalized Medicine Exposes a Gap in Medical Education," *PLoS Medicine* 6, no. 8 (2009): e1000138.
43. M. McKinnon, "Weight Watchers Becomes WW: Wellness That Works," *Simple Nourished Living*, September 25, 2018, https://simple-nourished-living.com/weight-watchers-becomes-ww-wellness-that-works/.
44. C. Wischhover, "Weight Watchers Changes Its Name to WW as 'Dieting' Becomes More Taboo," *Vox*, September 24, 2018, https://www.vox.com/the-goods/2018/9/24/17897114/weight-watchers-ww-wellness-rebranding.
45. E. Adams, *Healthy at Last: A Plant-Based Approach to Preventing and Reversing Diabetes and Other Chronic Illnesses* (Hay House, 2021), 4.
46. *Ibid.*, 10.
47. E. G. Fitzsimmons, "Weight Discrimination Is Banned by New York City," *New York Times*, May 26, 2023, https://www.nytimes.com/2023/05/26/nyregion/weight-discrimination-law-nyc.html.

48. "Mayor Adams Signs Legislation to Prohibit Height or Weight Discrimination in Employment, Housing," Press Office, The Official Website of the City of New York, https://www.nyc.gov/office-of-the-mayor/news/364-23/mayor-adams-signs-legislation-prohibit-height-weight-discrimination-employment-housing-#/0.
49. K. Cherry, "What Is Body Positivity?" Verywell Mind, 2023, https://www.verywellmind.com/what-is-body-positivity-4773402.
50. "Fatphobia," Boston Medical Center, n.d., https://www.bmc.org/glossary-culture-transformation/fatphobia; J. Gassam Asare, "The Unplug Collective Explores How Diet Culture Is Rooted in Anti-Blackness," *Forbes*, 2020, https://www.forbes.com/sites/janicegassam/2020/09/13/the-unplug-collective-explores-how-diet-culture-is-rooted-in-anti-blackness; "How Racism Shapes Our Perceptions of Healthy Food," Science Friday, 2023, https://www.sciencefriday.com/articles/racism-healthy-food/; "Racism Needs to Be Part of the Conversation About Dismantling Diet Culture," *Shape*, 2021, https://www.shape.com/lifestyle/mind-and-body/racism-diet-culture.
51. H. Carlan, "'Fearing the Black Body: The Racial Origins of Fat Phobia,' by Sabrina Strings, Review," UCLA Center for the Study of Women, November 23, 2020, https://csw.ucla.edu/2020/11/23/fearing-the-black-body-the-racial-origins-of-fat-phobia-by-sabrina-strings-nyu-press-2019/.
52. T. Gross, "Diet Culture Can Hurt Kids. This Author Advises Parents to Reclaim the Word 'Fat,'" NPR, April 25, 2023, https://www.npr.org/transcripts/1171112216; L. Miller, "Let Them Eat . . . Everything," *New York Times*, April 24, 2024, https://www.nytimes.com/2024/04/21/well/eat/fat-activist-virginia-sole-smith.html.
53. L. Lumsden and A. Lee, "11 Women Who Prove Wellness Isn't 'One Size Fits All,'" *Cosmopolitan*, January 1, 2021, https://www.cosmopolitan.com/uk/body/a34915032/women-bodies-wellness-healthy-different-shape-size/.
54. J. Ducharme, "No One Knows How to Talk About Weight Loss Anymore," *TIME*, May 8, 2024, https://time.com/6973988/how-to-talk-about-weight-loss-ozempic/.
55. G. Boucher, "Bill Maher Weighs in on U.S. Obesity: Fat Shaming 'Needs to Make a Comeback,'" *Deadline*, September 6, 2019, https://deadline.com/2019/09/bill-maher-weighs-in-on-u-s-obesity-fat-shaming-needs-to-make-a-comeback-1202728488/.
56. S. Chavkin, C. Gilbert, A. Tsui, and A. O'Connor, "As Obesity Rises, Big Food and Dietitians Push 'Anti-Diet' Advice," *Washington Post*, April 3, 2024, https://www.washingtonpost.com/wellness/2024/04/03/diet-culture-nutrition-influencers-general-mills-processed-food/.
57. V. H. Smith, "The US Spends $4 Billion a Year Subsidizing 'Stalinist-Style' Domestic Sugar Production," American Enterprise Institute, June 25, 2018,

https://www.aei.org/articles/the-u-s-spends-4-billion-a-year-subsidizing-stalinist-style-domestic-sugar-production/.

58. C. Means (@calleymeans), Twitter (now X), December 30, 2022, https://twitter.com/calleymeans/status/1608618928561074177?lang=en, https://www.cato.org/briefing-paper/snap-high-costs-low-nutrition, https://www.npr.org/sections/thesalt/2018/10/29/659634119/food-stamps-for-soda-time-to-end-billion-dollar-subsidy-for-sugary-drinks.
59. I. Goyanes, "Coca-Cola to Face Criticism for Food Stamp Lobbying," *Miami New Times*, April 24, 2013, https://www.miaminewtimes.com/restaurants/coca-cola-to-face-criticism-for-food-stamp-lobbying-6583712.
60. "What Is Theory of Change?" Theory of Change, n.d., https://www.theoryofchange.org/what-is-theory-of-change/.

Chapter 18

1. E. Goldberg, "Shoftim: Put It Down and Let It Go," *Parsha Perspectives*, August 18, 2020, https://www.listennotes.com/podcasts/parsha-perspectives/shoftim-put-it-down-and-let-FIyEqwN9dPc/.
2. Babylonian Talmud, Shabbat 31a.
3. Toldot Yaakov Yosef, *Parashat Shoftim.*
4. Maimonides, Sefer HaMitzvot, *Positive Command* 177.
5. Babylonian Talmud, Sotah 35a.
6. S. R. Hirsch, *Numbers 16:12.*
7. J. Kulp, *Mishnah Yomit*, 2013, https://www.sefaria.org/English_Explanation_of_Pirkei_Avot.1.6.2?lang=bi.
8. Babylonian Talmud, Ta'anit 24a; Kli Yakar, Genesis 24:14.
9. Mishan, Pirkei Avot 2:9.
10. Maimonides, *The Guide for the Perplexed* 3:14.
11. M. Scheiner, "The Man Who Told His Wife 'Drop Dead,'" Palm Beach Synagogue, YouTube, April 28, 2023, https://www.youtube.com/watch?v=_QGFHhSNbC8.
12. I. Shatz, "The Principle of Charity: Assume the Best Interpretation of People's Arguments," *Effectivology*, 2023, https://effectiviology.com/principle-of-charity/; N. L. Wilson, "Substances without Substrata," *The Review of Metaphysics* 12, no. 4 (1959): 521–539.
13. A. Bloch, *Murphy's Law, Book Two: More Reasons Why Things Go Wrong* (Price/Stern/Sloan Publishers, 1980), 52.
14. I. Shatz, *op. cit.*
15. D. W. Sue, et. al., "Racial Microaggressions in Everyday Life: Implications for Clinical Practice," *American Psychologist* 62, no. 4 (2007): 271–286.
16. *Ibid.*

17. T. DeAngelis, "Unmasking 'Racial Micro Aggressions,'" *American Psychological Association* 40, no. 2 (2009): 42, https://www.apa.org/monitor/2009/02/microaggression.html.
18. L. Z. Schlosser, "Microaggressions in Everyday Life: The American Jewish Experience," Seton Hall University, 2008, https://www.bjpa.org/content/upload/bjpa/micr/microaggressions.pdf.
19. S. O'Neal, *Graham Bensinger*, YouTube, November 20, 2015, https://www.youtube.com/watch?v=KobLv1BL5JI&ab_channel=GrahamBensinger.
20. G. Bensinger, "Jtube: Shaquille O'Neal's Jewish Financial Advisor," *Aish*, 2015, https://aish.com/jtube-shaquille-oneals-jewish-financial-advisor/.
21. "Understanding Racial Microaggression and Its Effect on Mental Health," Pfizer, https://www.pfizer.com/news/articles/understanding_racial_microaggression_and_its_effect_on_mental_health; "What Are Microaggressions?," Health Essentials, Cleveland Clinic, February 2, 2022, https://health.clevelandclinic.org/what-are-microaggressions-and-examples/; A. Limong, "Microaggressions Are a Big Deal: How to Talk Them Out and When to Walk Away," NPR, June 9, 2020, https://www.npr.org/2020/06/08/872371063/microaggressions-are-a-big-deal-how-to-talk-them-out-and-when-to-walk-away; B. Lord and F. Baker, "From Microaggressions to Triggers," National Cancer Institute, February 28, 2023, https://dceg.cancer.gov/about/diversity-inclusion/inclusivity-minute/2023/microaggression-triggers.
22. L. Rice, "For the Sake of Argument," Harvard Law School, July 23, 2020, https://hls.harvard.edu/today/for-the-sake-of-argument/.
23. L. Wolfe, "Don't Use the Term 'Trap House' in Your Party Invite at Yale Law School," *Reason.com*, October 13, 2021, https://reason.com/2021/10/13/dont-use-the-term-trap-house-in-your-party-invite-at-yale-law-school/.
24. C. Carberg, "Crack Cocaine Statistics—Facts on Crack Abuse by Demographics," Addiction Help, January 13, 2023, https://www.addictionhelp.com/crack/statistics/.
25. D. Lat, "The Latest (Ridiculous) Controversy at Yale Law School," *Original Jurisdiction*, October 14, 2021, https://davidlat.substack.com/p/the-latest-ridiculous-controversy.
26. A. Sibarium, "Convulsions at Yale Law School: Administrators Do Damage Control as Faculty Members Slam School's Dishonesty," *Washington Free Beacon*, October 18, 2021, https://freebeacon.com/campus/convulsions-at-yale-law-school-administrators-do-damage-control-as-faculty-members-slam-schools-dishonesty/.
27. L. Espinosa, "Who Is the Happiest at the 'Happiest College in America'?," *The Student Life*, 2019, https://tsl.news/opinions5116/.

28. E. Shire, "P.C. Police Tearing Apart California's Claremont McKenna College," *Daily Beast*, April 13, 2017, https://www.thedailybeast.com/pc-police-tearing-apart-californias-claremont-mckenna-college.
29. J. Haidt and G. Lukianoff, 2019, *op. cit.*, 55.
30. Master Etymology, *Etymology Geek*, https://etymologeek.com/eng/master.
31. History, University of Oxford, https://www.ox.ac.uk/about/organisation/history.
32. J. Fraser, "Gov. Hochul Announces More CNY Teachers to Join the Master Teacher Program," Local SYR, February 4, 2022, https://www.localsyr.com/news/local-news/gov-hochul-announces-more-cny-teachers-to-join-the-master-teacher-program/.
33. S. Cannon, "Pharrell Is Teaching a New Class on Racism, Social Justice," *New York Post*, November 12, 2020, https://nypost.com/2020/11/12/pharrell-launching-new-masterclass-on-racism-social-justice/.
34. P. Salovey, "Decisions on Residential College Names and 'Master' Title," Yale University: Office of the President, April 27, 2016, https://president.yale.edu/president/statements/decisions-residential-college-names-and-master-title; "News' View: Drop the Title 'Master,'" *Yale Daily News*, September 2, 2015, https://yaledailynews.com/blog/2015/09/02/news-view-drop-the-title-master/.
35. S. Franklin, "The Biggest Bedroom Is No Longer a 'Master,'" *New York Times*, August 5, 2020, https://www.nytimes.com/2020/08/05/realestate/master-bedroom-change.html.
36. C. Olson, "Is the Term 'Master Bedroom' Problematic?," *House Beautiful*, July 17, 2021, https://www.housebeautiful.com/lifestyle/fun-at-home/a1087/master-bedroom-politically-incorrect/.
37. J. Passy, "Real-Estate Reckoning on 'Master Bedrooms' as a Racist Term Took Place After Years of Discussion—Yet Many Home Builders Dropped the Term Years Ago," *Market Watch*, August 8, 2020, https://www.marketwatch.com/story/the-real-estate-industry-may-finally-be-abandoning-master-bedrooms-after-years-of-discussion-2020-08-05.
38. J. Levine, "JPMorgan Chase's Woke DEI Style Guide Nixes Terms Like 'Manpower,' 'Blacklist,'" *New York Post*, April 27, 2024, https://nypost.com/2024/04/27/us-news/jpmorgan-chase-dei-style-guide-nixes-terms-like-manpower-and-blacklist/.
39. L. Gandhi, "The Extraordinary Story of Why a 'Cakewalk' Wasn't Always Easy," NPR, December 23, 2013, https://www.npr.org/sections/codeswitch/2013/12/23/256566647/the-extraordinary-story-of-why-a-cakewalk-wasnt-always-easy.
40. B. N. Singh "Increased Heart Rate as a Risk Factor for Cardiovascular Disease," *European Heart Journal Supplements* 5, (2003): 3–9.

41. F. Barbash, "The War on 'Microaggressions:' Has It Created a 'Victimhood Culture' on Campuses?," *Washington Post*, October 28, 2015, https://www.washingtonpost.com/news/morning-mix/wp/2015/10/28/the-war-over-words-literally-on-some-american-campuses-where-asking-where-are-you-from-is-a-microaggression/.
42. D. Jasielska, R. Rogoza, M. B. Russa, J. Park, and A. Zajenkowska, "Happiness and Hostile Attributions in a Cross-Cultural Context: The Importance of Interdependence," *Journal of Happiness Studies: An Interdisciplinary Forum on Subjective Well-Being* 22, no. 1 (2021): 163–179.
43. D. Jasielska, R. Rogoza, M. B. Russa, et al., "Happiness and Hostile Attributions in a Cross-Cultural Context: The Importance of Interdependence," *Journal of Happiness Studies* 22 (2021): 163–179.
44. J. Klemz, "How Dr. Gottman Can Predict Divorce (with 94% Accuracy)," *Real Life Counseling*, 2018, https://reallifecounseling.us/blog/predict-divorce-gottman.
45. E. E. Smith, "The Secret to Love Is Just Kindness," *The Atlantic*, June 12, 2014, https://www.theatlantic.com/health/archive/2014/06/happily-ever-after/372573/.
46. I. Shatz, *op. cit.*
47. D. Wolpe, *Making Loss Matter: Creating Meaning in Difficult Times* (Penguin, 2000), 92.

Chapter 19

1. Babylonian Talmud, Yoma 23a.
2. *Orchot Tzaddikim*, *Gate of Cruelty*, 8:4.
3. E. Goldberg, "Vayeira: The License to Protest and Object to Hashem," *Parsha Perspectives*, October 30, 2018, https://www.listennotes.com/podcasts/parsha-perspectives/vayeira-the-license-to-UHrkTxDLunG/.
4. Chizkuni, Leviticus 19:18.
5. D. Fohrman, "How Can I Achieve True Love?," *Aleph Beta*, 2017, https://www.alephbeta.org/playlist/love-your-neighbor-meaning.
6. J. Sacks, "Vayigash: The Birth of Forgiveness," Covenant and Conversation, The Rabbi Sacks Legacy Trust, 2012, https://www.rabbisacks.org/covenant-conversation/vayigash/the-birth-of-forgiveness/; Maimonides, Mishneh Torah, *Laws of Repentance* 2:2.
7. Maimonides, Mishneh Torah, *Laws of Repentance* 2:9.
8. Maimonides, Mishneh Torah, *Laws of Repentance* 2:4; S. Himeles, "It Takes Two to Do Teshuvah," *Unpacked*, December 22, 2021, https://jewishunpacked.com/it-takes-two-to-do-teshuvah/.
9. Mishnah, *Bava Metzia* 4:10.

10. K. B. Stratton, "Narrating Violence, Narrating Self: Exodus and Collective Identity in Early Rabbinic Literature," *History of Religions* 57, no. 1 (2017): 68–92.
11. Quoted in B. Lester, "The Gift of Forgetting—D'var Torah for Shabbat Shuvah (Ha'azinu)," *Bet Am Shalom*, White Plains, NY, September 25, 2020; M. Drelich, "The Gift of Forgetting: How and When. Haazinu/Shabbat Shuva 5784—Rabbi Dr. D.," YouTube, September 20, 2023, https://www.youtube.com/watch?v=aWelCQLlSRA&ab_channel=MosheDrelich.
12. D. Wolpe, "Ha'azinu—Learning to Forget," Sinai Temple, September 30, 2006, https://www.sinaitemple.org/worship/sermons/haazinu-learning-forget/.
13. S. Vanbuskirk, "The Mental Health Effects of Holding a Grudge," *Verywell Mind*, August 19, 2021, https://www.verywellmind.com/the-mental-health-effects-of-holding-a-grudge-5176186.
14. G. Dvorsky, "Why Your Brain Can't Let Go of a Grudge," Gizmodo, August 30, 2018, https://gizmodo.com/why-your-brain-cant-let-go-of-a-grudge-1828421174.
15. "What Does Holding a Grudge Do to Your Health?" Piedmont, https://www.piedmont.org/living-real-change/what-does-holding-a-grudge-do-to-your-health.
16. "Forgiveness: Your Health Depends on It," Johns Hopkins Medicine, Johns Hopkins University, https://www.hopkinsmedicine.org/health/wellness-and-prevention/forgiveness-your-health-depends-on-it.
17. C. vanOyen Witvliet, T. E. Ludwig, and K. L. V. Laan, "Granting Forgiveness or Harboring Grudges: Implications for Emotion, Physiology, and Health," *Psychological Science*12, no. 2 (2001): 117–123.
18. "Forgiveness: Your Health Depends on It," Johns Hopkins Medicine, Johns Hopkins University, https://www.hopkinsmedicine.org/health/wellness-and-prevention/forgiveness-your-health-depends-on-it; E. Messias et. al., "Bearing Grudges and Physical Health: Relationship to Smoking, Cardiovascular Health and Ulcers," *Social Psychiatry and Psychiatric Epidemiology* 45 (2010): 183–187.
19. G. Dvorsky, "Why Your Brain Can't Let Go of a Grudge," Gizmodo, August 30, 2018, https://gizmodo.com/why-your-brain-cant-let-go-of-a-grudge-1828421174; E. Messias, et. al., "Bearing Grudges and Physical Health: Relationship to Smoking, Cardiovascular Health and Ulcers," *Social Psychiatry and Psychiatric Epidemiology* 45 (2010): 183–187, https://www.everydayhealth.com/emotional-health/big-ways-forgiveness-is-good-for-your-health/.
20. X. Zheng, et. al., "The Unburdening Effects of Forgiveness: Effects on Slant Perception and Jumping Height," *Social Psychological and Personality Science* 6, no. 4 (2015): 431–438.
21. A. Cabotaje, "Is Holding a Grudge Bad for Your Health?," Right as Rain by UW Medicine, August 1, 2019, https://rightasrain.uwmedicine.org/mind/well-being/holding-a-grudge.

22. B. M. Law, "Probing the Depression-Rumination Cycle: Why Chewing on Problems Just Makes Them Harder to Swallow," *American Psychological Association*, 36, no. 10 (2005): 38; R. A. Sansone and L. A. Sansone, "Rumination: Relationships with Physical Health," *Innovations in Clinical Neuroscience* 9, no. 2 (2012): 29–34; B. L. Alderman et. al., "Rumination in Major Depressive Disorder Is Associated with Impaired Neural Activation During Conflict Monitoring," *Frontiers in Human Neuroscience*, no. 9 (2015): 269.
23. B. J. Bushman, et. al., "Chewing on It Can Chew You Up: Effects of Rumination on Triggered Displaced Aggression," *Journal of Personality and Social Psychology* 88, no. 6 (2005): 969–983; M. E. McCullough, P. Orsulak, A. Brandon, and L. Akers, "Rumination, Fear, and Cortisol: An In Vivo Study of Interpersonal Transgressions," *Health Psychology* 26, no. 1 (2007): 126–132.
24. D. E. Forster, et al., "Experimental Evidence That Apologies Promote Forgiveness by Communicating Relationship Value," *Scientific Reports* 11, no. 1 (2021): 13107–13107.
25. https://www.ncbi.nlm.nih.gov/pmc/articles/PMC10120569/; "Forgiveness: Your Health Depends on It," Johns Hopkins Medicine, https://www.hopkinsmedicine.org/health/wellness-and-prevention/forgiveness-your-health-depends-on-it.
26. P. Streep, "When You Should and Should Not Forgive," *Psychology Today*, October 6, 2014, https://www.psychologytoday.com/us/blog/tech-support/201410/when-you-should-and-shoul.
27. L. B. Luchies, et al., "People Feel Worse About Their Forgiveness When Mismatches Between Forgiveness and Amends Create Adaptation Risks," *Journal of Social and Personal Relationships* 36, no. 2 (2017): 681–705; P. Streep, "When You Should and Should Not Forgive," *Psychology Today*, October 6, 2014, https://www.psychologytoday.com/us/blog/tech-support/201410/when-you-should-and-should-not-forgive.
28. R. De Vogli, T. Chandola, and M. G. Marmot, "Negative Aspects of Close Relationships and Heart Disease," *Archives of Internal Medicine* 167, no. 18 (2007): 1951–1957; L. Barhum, "Serious Ways Toxic Relationships Can Do Damage to Your Body," *Health Digest*, January 27, 2023, https://www.healthdigest.com/292616/serious-ways-toxic-relationships-can-do-damage-to-your-body/; S. Novak, "Do Relationships Affect Our Physical Health?," *Discover Magazine*, May 24, 2023, https://www.discovermagazine.com/mind/do-relationships-affect-our-physical-health; C. Jarrett, "Red Flags: Is There Any Science to Spotting a Toxic Relationship?," *BBC Science Focus Magazine*, November 8, 2022, https://www.sciencefocus.com/news/red-flags-is-there-any-science-to-spotting-a-toxic-relationship; E. Scott, "What to Know If You're Concerned About a Toxic Relationship," *Verywell Mind*, November 3, 2023, https://www.verywellmind.com/toxic-relationships-4174665.

29. C. Jarrett, "Red Flags: Is There Any Science to Spotting a Toxic Relationship?," *BBC Science Focus Magazine*, November 8, 2022, https://www.sciencefocus.com/news/red-flags-is-there-any-science-to-spotting-a-toxic-relationship; E. Scott, "What to Know If You're Concerned About a Toxic Relationship," *Verywell Mind*, November 3, 2023, https://www.verywellmind.com/toxic-relationships-4174665.
30. Canadian Institute for Advanced Research, "Forgetting Can Make You Smarter," ScienceDaily, June 21, 2017, www.sciencedaily.com/releases/2017/06/170621132910.htm.
31. T. Siegfried, "Why Forgetting May Make Your Mind More Efficient," *Knowable Magazine*, January 14, 2019, https://knowablemagazine.org/content/article/mind/2019/why-we-forget.
32. B. A. Richards and P. W. Frankland, "The Persistence and Transience of Memory," *Neuron* 94, no. 6, (2017): 1071–1084.
33. Canadian Institute for Advanced Research, "Forgetting Can Make You Smarter," ScienceDaily, June 21, 2017, www.sciencedaily.com/releases/2017/06/170621132910.htm, https://time.com/6171190/new-science-of-forgetting/.
34. A. L. Le Cunff, "Memory Bias: How Selective Recall Can Impact Your Memories," Ness Labs, 2020, https://nesslabs.com/memory-bias.
35. T. Siegfried, "Why Do We Forget Things? It May Make the Mind More Efficient," *Discover Magazine*, February 18, 2019, https://www.discovermagazine.com/mind/why-do-we-forget-things-it-may-make-the-mind-more-efficient.

Chapter 20

1. S. Held, "Daring to Dream with God," *Forward*, September 22, 2010, https://forward.com/opinion/131500/daring-to-dream-with-god/.
2. S. Held, "Can We Be Grateful and Disappointed at the Same Time?," *Hadar*, https://www.hadar.org/torah-resource/can-we-be-grateful-and-disappointed-same-time.
3. Cited in E. Goldberg, "Vayeitzei: Carving a Unique Relationship With Hashem," *Parsha Perspectives*, November 23, 2020, https://www.listennotes.com/podcasts/parsha-perspectives/vayeitzei-carving-a-unique-YSq1OrosJ04/.
4. Exodus Rabbah 9:10.
5. Cited in A. Morinis, "Path of the Soul #3: Gratitude," *Aish*, https://aish.com/48906987/.
6. Hai Gaon, *Sheiltot, Vayishlach 26*.
7. https://www.chabad.org/library/article_cdo/aid/1211258/jewish/Perpetual-Joy.htm.
8. A. Steinsaltz, *Talks on the Parsha*, (Koren, 2015), 74.

9. M. Posner, "Shimon Peres, 93, Proclaimed Centrality of Judaism to Israel and the Jewish People," Chabad.org, September 28, 2016, https://www.chabad.org/news/article_cdo/aid/3448647/jewish/Shimon-Peres-93-Proclaimed-Centrality-of-Judaism-to-Israel-and-the-Jewish-People.htm; D. Wolpe, "Rabbi Wolpe: Shimon Peres Left a Legacy of Innovation and Openness," *TIME*, September 28, 2016, https://time.com/4512054/shimon-peres-legacy-rabbi-david-wolpe/.
10. Mishna, Avot 4:1; B. Sofer, "The Human Spirit: A Roll This Side of Heaven," *Jerusalem Post*, December 24, 2010, https://www.jpost.com/opinion/columnists/the-human-spirit-a-roll-this-side-of-heaven.
11. D. Fohrman, "What Does Dayenu Mean?: Dayenu in the Pesach Haggadah," *Aleph Beta*, 2010, https://www.alephbeta.org/playlist/meaning-of-dayeinu-song-lyrics.
12. J. Sacks, "Tzav: Giving Thanks," *Covenant and Conversation*, The Rabbi Sacks Legacy Trust, 2018, https://www.rabbisacks.org/covenant-conversation/tzav/giving-thanks/.
13. M. Seligman, *Authentic Happiness: Using the New Positive Psychology to Realize Your Potential for Lasting Fulfillment* (Free Press, 2002), 46; E. Weil, "Happiness Inc.," *New York Times*, April 22, 2013, https://www.nytimes.com/2013/04/21/fashion/happiness-inc.html.
14. E. Batista, "Sonja Lyubomirsky and the How of Happiness," *Social Media Today*, February 9, 2009, https://www.socialmediatoday.com/content/sonja-lyubomirsky-and-how-happiness.
15. P. Gene, "Benefits of Gratitude: 31 Powerful Reasons to be More Grateful," *Happier Human*, March 17, 2023, https://www.happierhuman.com/benefits-of-gratitude/.
16. R. A. Emmons and M. E. McCullough, "Counting Blessings Versus Burdens: An Experimental Investigation of Gratitude and Subjective Well-Being in Daily Life," *Journal of Personality and Social Psychology* 84, no. 2 (2003): 377–389; L. H. Chen and C. H. Wu, "Gratitude Enhances Change in Athletes' Self-Esteem: The Moderating Role of Trust in Coach," *Journal of Applied Sport Psychology* 26, no. 3 (2014): 349–362; B. L. Fredrickson, M. M. Tugade, C. E. Waugh, and G. R. Larkin, "What Good Are Positive Emotions in Crisis? A Prospective Study of Resilience and Emotions Following the Terrorist Attacks on the United States on September 11th, 2001," *Journal of Personality and Social Psychology* 84, no. 2 (2003): 365–376; T. B. Kashdan and W. E. Breen, "Materialism and Diminished Well-Being: Experiential Avoidance as a Mediating Mechanism," *Journal of Social and Clinical Psychology* 26, no. 5 (2007): 521–539; J. T. Wilson, "Brightening the Mind: The Impact of Practicing Gratitude on Focus and Resilience in Learning," *Journal of Scholarship of Teaching and Learning* 16, no. 4 (2016): 1–13.
17. E. Brown, "How Can I Increase My Serotonin Levels Quickly?," *Verywell Health*, December 1, 2023, https://www.verywellhealth.com/how-to-increase-serotonin

-food-pills-natural-tips-5209264; A. Korb, *The Upward Spiral* (New Harbinger Publications, 2015), 154–55; S. Watson, "Dopamine: The Pathway to Pleasure," *Harvard Health*, April 18, 2024, https://www.health.harvard.edu/mind-and-mood/dopamine-the-pathway-to-pleasure.

18. Z. Brittle, "G Is for Gratitude," The Gottman Institute, March 31, 2014, https://www.gottman.com/blog/g-is-for-gratitude/.
19. D. DeSteno, *Emotional Success: The Power of Gratitude, Compassion and Pride* (Mariner Books, 2018).
20. C. M. Karns, W. Moore, and U. Mayr, "The Cultivation of Pure Altruism via Gratitude: A Functional MRI Study of Change with Gratitude Practice," *Frontiers in Human Neuroscience* 11 (2017).
21. S. Samuel, "Gratitude Can Make Your Brain More Charitable, Generous, and Altruistic," *Vox*, November 24, 2020, https://www.vox.com/future-perfect/2019/11/27/20983850/gratitude-altruism-charity-generosity-neuroscience.
22. T. Andrews, "Which Language Is Richest in Words?," *Interpreters and Translators Inc.*, May 1, 2023, https://ititranslates.com/blog/which-language-is-richest-in-words/.
23. John Templeton Foundation, "The Science of Gratitude," Greater Good Science Center, University of California, Berkeley, (2012, https://greatergood.berkeley.edu/images/uploads/JTF_GRATITUDE_REPORTpub.doc.
24. A. Lincoln, "Proclamation 97—Appointing a Day of National Humiliation, Fasting, and Prayer," The American Presidency Project, March 30, 1863, https://www.presidency.ucsb.edu/documents/proclamation-97-appointing-day-national-humiliation-fasting-and-prayer.
25. K. Kettenring, "The Serious Pursuit of Happiness," *Commune with God*, May 2, 2017, https://communewithgod.org/blog/the-serious-pursuit-of-happiness/.
26. E. H. Zeigler, "Hit Songs Offer Window into Society's Psyche," University of Kentucky College of Arts and Sciences, March 22, 2011, https://psychology.as.uky.edu/hit-songs-offer-window-societys-psyche-0.
27. C. N. DeWall, R. S. Pond, Jr., W. K. Campbell, and J. M. Twenge, "Tuning In to Psychological Change: Linguistic Markers of Psychological Traits and Emotions over Time in Popular U.S. Song Lyrics," *Psychology of Aesthetics, Creativity, and the Arts* 5, no. 3 (2011): 200–207, https://journals.sagepub.com/doi/10.1177/0022022112455100.
28. https://n-continuum.blogspot.com/2009/03/take-narcissistic-personality-inventory.html.
29. J. M. Twenge and J. D. Foster, "Birth Cohort Increases in Narcissistic Personality Traits Among American College Students, 1982–2009," *Social Psychological and Personality Science* 1, no. 1 (2010): 99–106.
30. K. Child, March 15, 2022, *op. cit.*

31. Z. Carter, "Is Social Media Turning Everyone into a Narcissist?," *RELEVANT*, March 29, 2023, https://relevantmagazine.com/life5/are-you-accidentally-a-narcissist-on-social-media/.
32. S. Meslow, "Taking a Stand Against Frank Sinatra's 'My Way,'" *GQ*, August 13, 2016, https://www.gq.com/story/my-way-is-the-worst.
33. W. Friedwald, "Sinatra v. My Way," *Wall Street Journal*, June 2, 2009, https://www.wsj.com/articles/SB124389543795174079.
34. S. Hurd, "6 Signs You May Have a Victim Mentality (Without Even Realizing It)," *Learning Mind*, May 19, 2017, https://www.learning-mind.com/victim-mentality-signs/.
35. Fields Center Fellows, Carl A. Fields Center for Equality + Cultural Understanding—Princeton University, http://fieldscenter.princeton.edu/center-fellows.
36. Poster at Fields Center, photographed by my wife at Princeton (where she was for our son's chess tournament) in November of 2022.
37. B. M. Brenan, "Record-Low 38% Extremely Proud to Be American," Gallup, June 29, 2022, https://news.gallup.com/poll/394202/record-low-extremely-proud-american.aspx.
38. "Happiness Among Americans Dips to Five-Decade Low," University of Chicago News, June 16, 2020, https://news.uchicago.edu/story/happiness-among-americans-dips-five-decade-low; T. B. Edsall, "Conservatives Are Happier Than Liberals. Discuss," *New York Times*, October 20, 2021, https://www.nytimes.com/2021/10/20/opinion/conservatives-liberals-happiness.html.
39. K. M. Newman, "World Happiness Report Finds That People Are Feeling Worse," *Greater Good*, March 20, 2019, https://greatergood.berkeley.edu/article/item/world_happiness_report_finds_that_people_are_feeling_worse.
40. C. Ingram, "New Data Shows Americans More Miserable Than We've Been in Half a Century," *The Why Axis*, January 28, 2022, https://thewhyaxis.substack.com/p/new-data-shows-americans-more-miserable.
41. World Happiness Report 2019, https://s3.amazonaws.com/happiness-report/2019/WHR19.pdf.
42. O. Winfrey, "Oprah's Gratitude Journal—Oprah on Gratitude," October 25, 2012, https://www.oprah.com/spirit/oprahs-gratitude-journal-oprah-on-gratitude.

Chapter 21

1. E. Goldberg, "Vayeira: The License to Protest and Object to Hashem," *Parsha Perspectives*, October 30, 2018, https://www.listennotes.com/podcasts/parsha-perspectives/vayeira-the-license-to-UHrkTxDLunG/.
2. Epicurus, *Letter to Menoeceus*; Mishnah, Sanhedrin 10:1.

3. L. Palatnik, "Blessing the Children," *Aish.com*, https://aish.com/shabbat-blessing-the-children/.
4. See Bereshit Rabbah 68–74, which constantly refers to Israel as "Saba." The Kabbalah emphasizes the point by using Yisrael Saba as the name of the wisdom we can access.
5. Babylonian Talmud, Kiddushin 30a.
6. J. Sacks, "Covenant and Conversation: The Blessings of Grandchildren," *OU Torah*, December 18, 2010, https://outorah.org/p/915/.
7. https://www.youtube.com/watch?v=9dMILHy7x0Q&ab_channel=TheRabbiSacksLegacy.
8. Or HaChaim, Deuteronomy 26:1; Midrash Lekach Tov, Deuteronomy 27:2.
9. M. Kaiserman, "From Strength to Strength: A Shabbat Message from Rabbi Mark Kaiserman," 6 Points Sci-Tech Academy, August 3, 2019, https://6pointsscitech.org/2019/08/03/from-strength-to-strength-a-shabbat-message-from-rabbi-mark-kaiserman/.
10. J. Sacks, "Future Tense: How The Jews Invented Hope," The Rabbi Sacks Legacy Trust, April 1, 2008, https://www.rabbisacks.org/archive/future-tense-how-the-jews-invented-hope/.
11. See Samson Raphael Hirsch's commentary, Deuteronomy 32:7.
12. M. Tartakovsky, "Why Ruminating Is Unhealthy and How to Stop," Psych Central, 2018, https://www.psychiatry.org/news-room/apa-blogs/rumination-a-cycle-of-negative-thinking.
13. A. E. Joubert, et. al., "Understanding the Experience of Rumination and Worry: A Descriptive Qualitative Survey Study," *British Journal of Clinical Psychology* 61, no. 4 (2022): 929–946; APA Blogs "Rumination: A Cycle of Negative Thinking," American Psychiatric Association, March 5, 2020, https://www.psychiatry.org/news-room/apa-blogs/rumination-a-cycle-of-negative-thinking.
14. S. Coelho, "Can't Help Thinking About the Past? 3 Tips to Stop Ruminating," PsychCentral, February 7, 2022, https://psychcentral.com/blog/how-to-stop-ruminating-on-the-past; T. Ehring, "Thinking Too Much: Rumination and Psychopathology," *World Psychiatry* 20, no. 3 (2021): 441–442; T. Christiansen, "Rumination," The Recovery Village, July 12, 2023, https://www.therecoveryvillage.com/mental-health/rumination/.
15. "Ervin McKinness, Aspiring Rapper, Tweets 'YOLO' About Driving Drunk and Dies Minutes Later," *HuffPost*, September 13, 2012, https://www.huffpost.com/entry/ervin-mckinness-driving-drunk-tweet-yolo-dies-car-crash-dui_n_1880348.
16. Š. Lyócsa, E. Baumöhl, and T. Výrost, "YOLO Trading: Riding with the Herd during the GameStop Episode," *Finance Research Letters* 46 (2022): 102359.
17. A. E. Navidad, "Stanford Marshmallow Test Experiment," *Simply Psychology*, 2023, https://www.simplypsychology.org/marshmallow-test.html.

18. S. R. Johnson, R. W. Blum, and T. L. Cheng, "Future Orientation: A Construct with Implications for Adolescent Health and Wellbeing," *International Journal of Adolescent Medicine and Health* 26, no. 4 (2014): 459–468.
19. R. Servidio, C. Scaffidi Abbate, A. Costabile, and S. Boca, "Future Orientation and Symptoms of Anxiety and Depression in Italian University Students during the COVID-19 Pandemic: The Role of Resilience and the Perceived Threat of COVID-19," *Healthcare* 10, no. 6 (2022): 974. See also J. K. Hirsch, P. R. Duberstein, K. R. Conner, M. J. Heisel, A. M. Beckman, N. Franus, and Y. Conwell, "Future Orientation and Suicide Ideation and Attempts in Depressed Adults Ages 50 and Over," *American Journal of Geriatric Psychiatry: Official Journal of the American Association for Geriatric Psychiatry* 14, no. 9 (2006): 752–757; E. C. Chang, O. D. Chang, T. Martos, and V. Sallay, "Future Orientation and Suicide Risk in Hungarian College Students: Burdensomeness and Belongingness as Mediators," *Death Studies* 4, (2017): 284–290; N. M. Petry, W. K. Bickel, and M. A. Arnett, "Shortened Time Horizons and Insensitivity to Future Consequences in Heroin Addicts," *Addiction* 93, no. 5 (1998): 729–38; E. Hejazi, A. H. Moghadam, Z. Naghsh, and R. A. Tarkhan, "The Future Orientation of Iranian Adolescents Girl Students and Their Academic Achievement," *Procedia—Social and Behavioral Sciences* 15 (2011): 2441–2444; L. Zheng, S. Lippke, Y. Chen, D. Li, and Y. Gan, "Future Orientation Buffers Depression in Daily and Specific Stress," *PsyCh Journal* 8, no. 3 (2019): 342–352.
20. E. Kapogli and J. Quoidbach, "Stranger or a Clone? Future Self-Connectedness Depends on Who You Ask, When You Ask, and What Dimension You Focus On," *Current Opinion in Psychology* 43 (2022): 266–270.
21. "Dopamine," Cleveland Clinic, https://my.clevelandclinic.org/health/articles/22581-dopamine.
22. S. Weinschenk, "Shopping, Dopamine, and Anticipation," *Psychology Today*, October 22, 2015, https://www.psychologytoday.com/ca/blog/brain-wise/201510/shopping-dopamine-and-anticipation.
23. "What Is Dopamine and How Does It Keep Me Using?," The Coleman Institute, January 14, 2022, https://thecolemaninstitute.com/tci-blog/72-dopamine-the-anticipation-molecule/.
24. F. T. Moura, "Dopamine: More Than Pleasure, The Secret Is the Anticipation of a Reward," *Live Innovation*, April 2, 2020, https://liveinnovation.org/dopamine-more-than-pleasure-the-secret-is-the-anticipation-of-a-reward/.
25. "Global Digital Marketing Report," *Razorfish*, 2015, 27.
26. P. Monaghan and E. R. Ivimey-Cook, "No Time to Die: Evolution of a Post-Reproductive Life Stage," *Journal of Zoology* 321 (2023): 1–21.
27. J. Compton and R. A. Pollak, "Family Proximity, Childcare, and Women's Labor Force Attachment," *Journal of Urban Economics* 79 (2014): 72–90.

28. M. Á. T. Marcos, "Grandmothers and the Gender Gap in the Mexican Labor Market," *Journal of Development Economics* 162 (2023): 10301; "The Age of the Grandparent Has Arrived," *Economist*, January 12, 2023, https://www.economist.com/international/2023/01/12/the-age-of-the-grandparent-has-arrived.
29. Pastor Chanda, "Beware of Cynicism in Old Age," *Zambia Daily Mail*, April 29, 2017, http://www.daily-mail.co.zm/beware-of-cynicism-in-old-age/.
30. S. Hilbrand, D. A. Coall, D. Gerstorf, and R. Hertwig, "Caregiving Within and Beyond the Family Is Associated with Lower Mortality for the Caregiver: A Prospective Study," *Evolution and Human Behavior* 38, no. 3 (2017): 397–403; L. Esposito, "The Health Benefits of Having (and Being) Grandparents," *US News & World Report*, September 13, 2017, https://health.usnews.com/wellness/articles/2017-09-13/the-health-benefits-of-having-and-being-grandparents.
31. M. Lewis and R. Correa, "SMART LIVING: National Grandparents' Day—Grandma and Grandpa Matter," 90 WAFB, September 9, 2022, https://www.wafb.com/2022/09/09/smart-living-national-grandparents-day-grandma-grandpa-matter/.
32. T. Li and P. Siu, "Relationship with Grandparents and Young Adults' Attitudes About Aging and Future-Oriented Tendencies," *Innovation in Aging* 4 (2020): 883.
33. See, for instance, J. B. Yorgason, L. Padilla-Walker, and J. Jackson, "Nonresidential Grandparents' Emotional and Financial Involvement in Relation to Early Adolescent Grandchild Outcomes," *Journal of Research on Adolescence* 21 (2011): 552–558; S. M. Moorman and J. E. Stokes, "Solidarity in the Grandparent-Adult Grandchild Relationship and Trajectories of Depressive Symptoms," *The Gerontologist* 56, no. 3 (2016): 408–420; A. Lall, "Children Who Grow Up with Their Grandparents Are Happier and More Secure," *Woman's World*, March 3, 2019, https://www.womansworld.com/posts/family/grandparent-grandchild-relationship-benefits-169833.

Chapter 22

1. R. I. Rothstein, "The Power of Jewish Blessings," *My Jewish Learning*, 2019, https://www.myjewishlearning.com/article/blessings-a-conduit-of-infinite-potential/.
2. S. Chong, "Making Room for the Bible's Maternal Images of God," *Think Christian*, May 9, 2017, https://thinkchristian.net/making-room-for-the-bibles-maternal-images-of-god.
3. Babylonian Talmud, Shabbat 88a-88b.
4. J. Sacks "Spirituality: An Introduction," *Covenant and Conversation*, The Rabbi Sacks Legacy Trust, 2022, https://www.rabbisacks.org/covenant-conversation/spirituality-an-introduction/.

5. Sifrei, Bamidbar 89.
6. Sifrei Devarim 301; Passover Haggadah.
7. Psalm 91:15.
8. M. Gerson, *The Telling: How Judaism's Essential Book Reveals the Meaning of Life* (St. Martin's Press, (2021), 66.
9. Jeremiah 31:3.
10. T. Ruggiero, "Whitehead's Observations on Religion," PhilosophicalSociety .com, January 27, 2002, https://philosophicalsociety.com/Archives/Whitehead's %20Observations%20On%20Religion.htm.
11. Babylonian Talmud, Ta'anit 7a.
12. *Ibid.*
13. Babylonian, Brachot 21b.
14. E. Goldberg, "Acharei Mos/Kedoshim: Also Being Sensitive to Hashem," *Parsha Perspectives*, July 26, 2022, https://rabbiefremgoldberg.org/acharei-mos -kedoshim-also-being-sensitive-to-hashem.
15. Babylonian Talmud, Yevamot 63a.
16. "Nisan 9," *Aish.com*, 2023, https://aish.com/nisan-9/.
17. Babylonian Talmud, Kiddushin 29b.
18. Babylonian Talmud, Yevamot 63a.
19. "The True Story of Wilson the Volleyball," Wilson Sporting Goods, September 13, 2022, https://www.wilson.com/en-us/blog/volleyball/behind-scenes /true-story-wilson-volleyball; A. Martinez, "Volleyball from 'Cast Away' Sells for Over $300,000 at Auction," NPR, November 11, 2021, https://www.npr.org /2021/11/11/1054615049/volleyball-from-cast-away-sells-for-over-300-000-at -auction.
20. S. Gannett, "The Case for Sleeping with Stuffed Animals as an Adult," Wirecutter, *New York Times*, February 6, 2024, https://www.nytimes.com/wirecutter /blog/adults-who-sleep-with-stuffed-animals/; D. Linton, "'I Love Him So Much I Could Cry': Adults Who Have Cuddly Toys," *Guardian*, November 19, 2022, https://www.theguardian.com/lifeandstyle/2022/nov/19/adults-who-have -cuddly-toys-comfort-objects.
21. M. Kim, "Boredom's Link to Mental Illnesses, Brain Injuries and Dysfunctional Behaviors," *Washington Post*, July 17, 2021, https://www.washingtonpost.com /health/boredom-mental-health-disconnected/2021/07/16/c367cd30-9d6a-11eb -9d05-ae06f4529ece_story.html.
22. S. F. Lee, et. al. "The Association Between Loneliness and Depressive Symptoms Among Adults Aged 50 Years and Older: A 12-Year Population-Based Cohort Study," *Lancet Psychiatry* 8, no. 1 (2021): 48–57.
23. N. K. Valtorta, M. Kanaan, S. Gilbody, S. Ronzi, and B. Hanratty, "Loneliness and Social Isolation as Risk Factors for Coronary Heart Disease and Stroke:

Systematic Review and Meta-analysis of Longitudinal Observational Studies," *Heart* 102, no. 13 (2016): 1009–1016.

24. https://www.cigna.com/static/www-cigna-com/docs/health-care-providers/resources/loneliness-index-provider-flyer.pdf, The Cigna Group Newsroom, "Loneliness in America," The Cigna Group, https://newsroom.thecignagroup.com/loneliness-in-america; F. U. Jung and C. Luck-Sikorski "Overweight and Lonely? A Representative Study on Loneliness in Obese People and Its Determinants," *Obesity Facts* 12, no. 4 (2019): 440–447.
25. M. Makary, "Covid Prescription: Get the Vaccine, Wait a Month, Return to Normal," *Wall Street Journal*, March 10, 2021, https://www.wsj.com/articles/covid-prescription-get-the-vaccine-wait-a-month-return-to-normal-11615401516; A. Gawande, "Praise for 'Together'" in V. H. Murthy, *Together: The Healing Power of Human Connection in a Sometimes Lonely World* (Harper Wave, 2020).
26. V. Murthy, "Work and the Loneliness Epidemic," *Harvard Business Review*, September 26, 2017, https://hbr.org/2017/09/work-and-the-loneliness-epidemic.
27. J. A. Lam, et. al., "Neurobiology of Loneliness: A Systematic Review," *Neuropsychopharmacology* 46, no. 11 (2021): 1873–1887; D. G. Smith, "How Loneliness Affects the Brain," *New York Times*, May 9, 2024, https://www.nytimes.com/2024/05/09/well/mind/loneliness-brain-dementia-isolation.html.
28. L. Mineo, "Over Nearly 80 Years, Harvard Study Has Been Showing How to Live a Healthy and Happy Life," *Harvard Gazette*, April 11, 2017, https://news.harvard.edu/gazette/story/2017/04/over-nearly-80-years-harvard-study-has-been-showing-how-to-live-a-healthy-and-happy-life/; R. Waldinger, "What Makes a Good Life? Lessons from the Longest Study on Happiness," TED, YouTube, January 25, 2016, https://www.youtube.com/watch?v=8KkKuTCFvzI.
29. G. E. Vaillant, *Triumphs of Experience: The Men of the Harvard Grant Study* (Harvard University Press, 2012), 41.
30. W. Wang, "The Share of Never-Married Americans Has Reached a New High," *Institute for Family Studies*, September 9, 2020, https://tinyurl.com/mr2bc73j; A. DeBarros, "A Visual Breakdown of America's Stagnating Number of Births," *Wall Street Journal*, June 1, 2023, https://www.wsj.com/articles/a-visual-breakdown-of-americas-stagnating-number-of-births-9a2e6e2d.
31. "More Than Half of Americans Say Marriage Is Important but Not Essential to Leading a Fulfilling Life," Pew Research Center, 2020, https://www.pewresearch.org/short-reads/2020/02/14/more-than-half-of-americans-say-marriage-is-important-but-not-essential-to-leading-a-fulfilling-life/.
32. B. L. Cohen, *The Nuclear Option* (Plenum Press, 1990), 120; M. Gallagher, "Why Marriage Is Good for You," *City Journal*, 2000, https://www.city-journal.org/article/why-marriage-is-good-for-you; H. Marano, "Debunking the Marriage Myth: It Works for Women, Too," *New York Times*, August 4, 1998, https://

www.nytimes.com/1998/08/04/science/debunking-the-marriage-myth-it-works-for-women-too.html

33. R. Shmerling, "The Health Advantages of Marriage," *Harvard Health*, November 30, 2016, https://www.health.harvard.edu/blog/the-health-advantages-of-marriage-2016113010667.
34. S. Peltzman, "The Socio Political Demography of Happiness," *George J. Stigler Center for the Study of the Economy & the State Working Paper No. 331*, 2023, 21, https://www.chicagobooth.edu/review/marriage-may-be-key-happiness; O. Khazan, "Why Married People Are Happier," *The Atlantic*, August 31, 2023, https://www.theatlantic.com/ideas/archive/2023/08/does-marriage-make-you-happier/675145/.
35. O. Khazan, "Why Married People Are Happier," *The Atlantic*, August 31, 2023, https://www.theatlantic.com/ideas/archive/2023/08/does-marriage-make-you-happier/675145/.
36. M. Gallagher, 2000, *op. cit.*; J. E. Uecker, "Marriage and Mental Health Among Young Adults," *Journal of Health and Social Behavior* 53, no. 1 (2012): 67–83.
37. Post Staff Report, "The Top 10 Greatest NYC Sitcoms Ever," *New York Post*, June 9, 2014, https://nypost.com/2014/06/07/the-top-10-greatest-nyc-sitcoms-ever/.
38. "The Engagement," *Seinfeld*, Season 7, Episode 1, 1995, https://www.seinfeldscripts.com/TheEngagement.html.
39. M. Salam, "Seinfeld' Ended 25 Years Ago: Its View of Adulthood Endures," *New York Times*, May 12, 2023, https://www.nytimes.com/2023/05/12/arts/television/seinfeld-finale-anniversary.html.
40. E. St. James, "How *Friends* Ruined TV comedy," *Vox*, September 19, 2019, https://www.vox.com/2014/9/29/6857745/friends-ruined-tv-25th-anniversary.
41. D. L. Hammond, "11 Reasons Why You Need to Be More Independent," *LifeHack*, November 27, 2013, https://www.lifehack.org/articles/productivity/11-reasons-why-you-need-more-independent.html; S. Weiss, "7 Signs You Don't Want a Life Partner, and Why That's OK," *Bustle*, December 12, 2017, https://www.bustle.com/p/7-signs-you-dont-want-a-life-partner-why-thats-ok-7427779.
42. D. A. Cox, "The State of American Friendship: Change, Challenges, and Loss," *The Survey Center on American Life*, June 8, 2021, https://www.americansurveycenter.org/research/the-state-of-american-friendship-change-challenges-and-loss/; K. Gray, "America's 'Friendship Recession' Is Weakening Civic Life," *The Survey Center on American Life*, 2023, https://www.americansurveycenter.org/newsletter/americas-friendship-recession-is-weakening-civic-life/.
43. K. Gray, "America's 'Friendship Recession' Is Weakening Civic Life," *The Survey Center on American Life*, 2023, https://www.americansurveycenter.org/newsletter/americas-friendship-recession-is-weakening-civic-life/.
44. Netherlands Organization for Scientific Research, "Half of Your Friends Lost

in Seven Years Social Network Study Finds," *ScienceDaily*, May 27, 2009, www.sciencedaily.com/releases/2009/05/090527111907.htm.

45. S. Degges-White, "Not All Friendships Last Forever," *Psychology Today*, June 29, 2017, https://www.psychologytoday.com/us/blog/lifetime-connections/201706/not-all-friendships-last-forever; D. French, "Being There," *New York Times*, September 24, 2023, https://www.nytimes.com/2023/09/24/opinion/friendship-loneliness.html; Z. Gervis, "Why the Average American Hasn't Made a New Friend in 5 Years," *New York Post*, May 10, 2019.
46. R. Bell, "What Is a Self-Marriage Ceremony and Should You Have One?," *Brides*, October 25, 2021, https://www.brides.com/story/sologamy-why-women-are-marrying-themselves; D. Braff, "I, Take Me, to Love Forever: Some Women Are Marrying Themselves, Complete with White Dresses, Cakes, and Lavish Parties," *Insider*, March 12, 2022, https://www.insider.com/women-marrying-themselves-sologamy-pandemic-self-love-covid-2022-3; P. Garcia, "Why Women Are Choosing to Marry Themselves," *Vogue*, October 6, 2017, https://www.vogue.com/article/women-marrying-themselves-sologamy; F. Karimi, "These Women Wanted a Symbolic Expression of Self-Love. So They Married Themselves," CNN, May 31, 2023, https://edition.cnn.com/2023/05/28/us/sologamy-self-marriage-women-cec/index.html.
47. A. C. Moors, A. N. Gesselman, and J. R. Garcia, "Desire, Familiarity, and Engagement in Polyamory: Results from a National Sample of Single Adults in the United States," *Frontiers in Psychology* 12 (2021).
48. D. Bergner, "A 20-Person Polycule on Boundaries, Relationships and Intimacy," *New York Times*, April 15, 2024, https://www.nytimes.com/interactive/2024/04/15/magazine/polycule-polyamory-boston.html; J. Angelini, "Everything You've Ever Wondered About Polycules In Polyamory, Explained," *Women's Health*, April 9, 2024, https://www.womenshealthmag.com/relationships/a60410228/what-is-a-polycule/.
49. H. Tsukayama, "Your Facebook Friends Have More Friends Than You," *Washington Post*, February 3, 2012, https://www.washingtonpost.com/business/technology/your-facebook-friends-have-more-friends-than-you/2012/02/03/gIQAuNUlmQ_story.html.
50. Office of Governor Gavin Newsom, "First Partner Jennifer Seibel Newsom," California Governor, https://www.gov.ca.gov/about-firstpartner/#:~:text=Jennifer%20Siebel%20Newsom%20is%20the,advocate%2C%20and%20mother%20of%20four.
51. *Modern Family*, Season 4, Episode 13.
52. K. Markowicz, "Our Falling Birth and Marriage Rates Reflect the Lie That Only Singles Have Fun," *New York Post*, December 2, 2022, https://nypost.com/2022/12/01/our-falling-birth-and-marriage-rates-reflect-the-lie-that-only-singles-have-fun/.

Chapter 23

1. Babylonian Talmud, Sanhedrin 109b.
2. E. Dessler, *Strive for Truth: Volume 1*, trans. A. Carmell (Felheim, 1978), 127–131.
3. D. Wolpe, "We Are Defining Love the Wrong Way," *Time*, February 16, 2016, https://time.com/4225777/meaning-of-love/; D. Wolpe, "Love as Sacrifice," *New York Jewish Week*, November 13, 2012, https://blogs.timesofisrael.com/love-as-sacrifice/.
4. J. Levine, "'Creepy' Joe Biden Offers Unsolicited Dating Advice to Young Girl in Awkward Photo Op," *New York Post*, October 15, 2022, https://nypost.com/2022/10/15/joe-biden-tells-young-girl-no-serious-guys-until-youre-30/.
5. U.S. Census Bureau, "Percent Married Among 18-to 34-Year-Olds: 1978 and 2018," Census.gov, 2018. Retrieved from https://www.census.gov/library/visualizations/2018/comm/percent-married.html.
6. S. S. J. Lee, "Does More Dating Lead to a Happier Marriage?," Penn State University, October 10, 2016, https://sites.psu.edu/siowfa16/2016/10/10/does-more-dating-lead-to-a-happier-marriage/; J. Mackey, "What Is the Average Length of an Engagement?," *Brides*, May 8, 2023, https://www.brides.com/story/how-long-should-you-be-engaged-before-marriage.
7. D. Smith-Garcia, "What to Expect from the Egg Freezing Process," *Healthline*, August 17, 2022, https://www.healthline.com/health/egg-freezing-process#timeline.
8. B. Stanek, "How Male Fertility Changes with Age," *Forbes Health*, August 9, 2023, https://www.forbes.com/health/mens-health/male-fertility-by-age/.
9. Rutgers University, "Older Fathers Put Health of Partners, Unborn Children at Risk: Men Who Delay Fatherhood Should Consult Their Doctor and Consider Banking Sperm Before Age 35," *Science Daily*, May 13, 2019, www.sciencedaily.com/releases/2019/05/190513081409.htm.
10. E. Jong, *Fear of Flying* (Holt, Rinehart and Winston, 1972), 10.
11. J. Naftulin, "Young People Are Having Less Casual Sex and Spending More Time Scrolling on Social Media," *Insider*, March 26, 2021, https://www.insider.com/teens-less-casual-sex-generation-parents-did-2021-3; K. Julian, "Young People Are Having Less Sex," *The Atlantic*, 2018, https://www.theatlantic.com/magazine/archive/2018/12/the-sex-recession/573949/; N. Yau, "Married People Have More Sex," *Flowing Data*, 2017, https://flowingdata.com/2017/07/03/married-people-sex/.
12. R. Black, "One in Three Guys Prefers Video Games to Sex: Study," *New York Daily News*, April 3, 2009, https://www.nydailynews.com/life-style/health/guys-prefers-video-games-sex-study-article-1.359202; S. J. South and L. Lei, "Why Are Fewer Young Adults Having Casual Sex?," *Socius* 7 (2021).
13. D. Cox, "How Prevalent Is Pornography?," Institute for Family Studies, May

3, 2022, https://ifstudies.org/blog/how-prevalent-is-pornography; M. Castleman, "How Much Time Does the World Spend Watching Porn?," *Psychology Today*, October 31, 2020, https://www.psychologytoday.com/us/blog/all-about-sex/202010/how-much-time-does-the-world-spend-watching-porn; M. Klein, "Less Curious, and Less Interested in Courting," *Psychology Today*, August 2, 2022, https://www.psychologytoday.com/us/blog/sexual-intelligence/202208/why-todays-teens-are-having-so-much-less-sex.

14. R. Weiss, "Porn-Induced Erectile Dysfunction," *Psychology Today*, April 12, 2021, https://www.psychologytoday.com/us/blog/love-and-sex-in-the-digital-age/202104/porn-induced-erectile-dysfunction; B. Levine, "Does Using Porn Lead To Erectile Dysfunction?," EverydayHealth.com, January 16, 2024, https://www.everydayhealth.com/erectile-dysfunction/pornography-habit-is-linked-to-erectile-dysfunction-research-suggests.
15. R. Black, "One in Three Guys Prefers Video Games to Sex: Study," *New York Daily News*, April 3, 2009, https://www.nydailynews.com/life-style/health/guys-prefers-video-games-sex-study-article-1.359202.
16. Zava, "One Night Only," *ZAVA UK*, https://www.zavamed.com/uk/one-night-only.html.
17. D. Rickman, "Erica Jong on Feminism, Sex Addiction and Why There Is No Such Thing as a Zipless F**k," *HuffPost UK*, January 6, 2012, https://www.huffingtonpost.co.uk/2011/11/07/erica-jong-no-such-thing-as-zipless-fuck_n_1079222.html.
18. "Sexual Offense Prevention Policy (SOPP) & Title IX," Antioch College, https://antiochcollege.edu/campus-life/sexual-offense-prevention-policy-title-ix/.
19. D. R. King, "Is It Date Rape," SNL Transcripts Tonight, October 8, 2018, https://snltranscripts.jt.org/93/93bdaterape.phtml.
20. S. F. Colb, "Withdrawing Consent During Intercourse: California's Highest Court Clarifies the Definition of Rape," *FindLaw*, January 15, 2003, https://supreme.findlaw.com/legal-commentary/withdrawing-consent-during-intercourse.html.
21. F. J. Fleming (@IMAO), Twitter (now X), September 29, 2014, https://twitter.com/IMAO_/status/516669307254996993.
22. From conversations with Dr. Peresky; R. Tracinski, "California's Neo-Victorian Feminism," *Federalist*, October 3, 2014, https://thefederalist.com/2014/10/03/californias-neo-victorian-feminism/; N. Anderson and S. Clement, "College Sexual Assault: 1 in 5 College Women Say They Were Violated," *Washington Post*, June 12, 2015, https://www.washingtonpost.com/sf/local/2015/06/12/1-in-5-women-say-they-were-violated/.
23. M. Koss and A. Rutherford, "What Surveys Dating Back Decades Reveal About Date Rape," *The Atlantic*, September 26, 2018, https://www.theatlantic.com/ideas/archive/2018/09/what-surveys-dating-back-decades-reveal-about-date-rape/571330/; V. I. Rickert and C. M. Wiemann, "Date Rape Among Adolescents

and Young Adults," *Journal of Pediatric and Adolescent Gynecology* 11, no. 4 (1998): 167–175; E. Gerstmann, "The Stat That 1 in 5 College Women Are Sexually Assaulted Doesn't Mean What You Think It Means," *Forbes*, January 27, 2019, https://www.forbes.com/sites/evangerstmann/2019/01/27/the-stat-that-1-in-5-college-women-are-sexually-assaulted-doesnt-mean-what-you-think-it-means/?sh=27ab2e232217.

24. K. Weir, "The Pain of Social Rejection—As Far as the Brain Is Concerned, a Broken Heart May Not Be So Different from a Broken Arm," *American Psychological Association* 43, no. 4 (2012): 50.
25. C. Pearson, "How Online Dating Apps Can Lead to Burnout," *New York Times*, August 31, 2022, https://www.nytimes.com/2022/08/31/well/mind/burnout-online-dating-apps.html.
26. E. Kross, M. G. Berman, W. Mischel, E. E. Smith, and T. D. Wager, "Social Rejection Shares Somatosensory Representations with Physical Pain," *Proceedings of the National Academy of Sciences—PNAS*108, no. 15 (2011): 6270–6275.
27. S. Marie, "Should You Ever Give an Ultimatum In a Relationship?," Psych Central, March 30, 2022, https://psychcentral.com/blog/should-you-ever-give-an-ultimatum-in-a-relationship#definition.
28. N. Shakhnazarova, "Olympian Lolo Jones on Why She's Decided to Start IVF: 'I'm Running Out of Time,'" *Page Six*, August 4, 2022, https://pagesix.com/2022/08/04/olympian-lolo-jones-explains-why-shes-decided-to-start-ivf/.
29. T. E. DiDonato, "Are Couples That Live Together Before Marriage More Likely to Divorce?," *Psychology Today*, January 27, 2021, https://www.psychologytoday.com/us/blog/meet-catch-and-keep/202101/are-couples-that-live-together-before-marriage-more-likely-to; "A Decade of Change in Shares of Single, Cohabiting, and Married Individuals, 2012–2022," (no date), https://www.bgsu.edu/ncfmr/resources/data/family-profiles/julian-decade-change-shares-single-cohabiting-married-2012-2022-fp-23-07.html; T. Mitchell and T. Mitchell, "1. The Landscape of Marriage and Cohabitation in the U.S.," Pew Research Center, 2024, https://www.pewresearch.org/social-trends/2019/11/06/the-landscape-of-marriage-and-cohabitation-in-the-u-s/; A. Kuperberg, "Premarital Cohabitation and Direct Marriage in the United States: 1956–2015," *Marriage & Family Review* 55 no. 5 (2019): 447–475.
30. C. A. Agbro, "Celebs Who Have Said They'll Never Get Married," Buzzfeed, 2024, https://www.buzzfeed.com/chantelleadanna/celebs-who-said-theyll-never-get-married; B. Wilcox, "The Awfulness of Elite Hypocrisy on Marriage," *The Atlantic*, February 13, 2024, https://www.theatlantic.com/ideas/archive/2024/02/elitism-marriage-rates-hypocrisy/677401/.
31. T. Mitchell and T. Mitchell, "Marriage and Cohabitation in the U.S.," Pew Research Center, 2024, https://www.pewresearch.org/social-trends/2019/11/06/marriage-and-cohabitation-in-the-u-s/.

32. T. Mitchell and T. Mitchell, "4. How Married and Cohabiting Adults See Their Relationships," Pew Research Center, 2024, https://www.pewresearch.org/social-trends/2019/11/06/how-married-and-cohabiting-adults-see-their-relationships.
33. W. D. Manning, "Cohabitation and Child Wellbeing," *Future Child*, 25 no. 2 (Fall 2015): 51–66; R. V. Reeves and E. Krause, "Cohabiting Parents Differ from Married Ones in Three Big Ways," Brookings, April 5, 2017, https://www.brookings.edu/research/cohabiting-parents-differ-from-married-ones-in-three-big-ways/; J. Anderson, "The Impact of Family Structure on the Health of Children: Effects of Divorce," *Linacre Q.* 81 no. 4 (November 2014): 378–87; S. McLanahan, I. Garfinkel, and R. Mincy, "Marriage and Child Wellbeing Revisited: Introducing the Issue (Princeton University, 2015), https://futureofchildren.princeton.edu/sites/g/files/toruqf2411/files/media/marriage_and_child_wellbeing_revisited_25_2_full_journal.pdf; W. B. Wilcox, "Suffer the Little Children: Cohabitation and the Abuse of America's Children," The Public Discourse, 2024, https://www.thepublicdiscourse.com/2011/04/3181/.
34. Research Releases, "Majority of Americans Now Believe in Cohabitation," Barna Group, June 24, 2016, C. N. Nugent and J. Daugherty, "A Demographic, Attitudinal, and Behavioral Profile of Cohabiting Adults in the United States, 2011–2015," Centers for Disease Control and Prevention, May 31, 2018, https://www.cdc.gov/nchs/data/nhsr/nhsr111.pdf.
35. S. M. Stanley, G. K. Rhoades, P. R. Amato, H. J. Markman, and C. A. Johnson, "The Timing of Cohabitation and Engagement: Impact on First and Second Marriages," *Journal of Marriage and Family* 72, no. 4 (August 1, 2010): 906–918.
36. M. J. Rosenfeld and K. Roesler, "Premarital Cohabitation and Marital Dissolution: A Reply to Manning, Smock, and Kuperberg," *Journal of Marriage and Family* 83, no. 1 (2021): 268–279; Stanley, Rhoades, Amato, Markman, and Johnson, "The Timing of Cohabitation and Engagement."
37. M. Jay, "The Downside of Cohabiting Before Marriage," *New York Times*, April 14, 2012, https://www.nytimes.com/2012/04/15/opinion/sunday/the-downside-of-cohabiting-before-marriage.html.
38. B. Luscombe, "The Divorce Rate Is Dropping. That May Not Actually Be Good News," *Time*, November 26, 2018, https://time.com/5434949/divorce-rate-children-marriage-benefits/; C. Bieber, "Revealing Divorce Statistics in 2024," *Forbes Advisor*, January 8, 2024, https://www.forbes.com/advisor/legal/divorce/divorce-statistics/.
39. B. Hollar, "Regular Church Attenders Marry More and Divorce Less Than Their Less Devout Peers," Institute for Family Studies, March 4, 2020, https://ifstudies.org/blog/regular-church-attenders-marry-more-and-divorce-less-than-their-less-devout-peers.
40. P. Paul, "Why Divorce? Just Stay Separated," *New York Times*, July 30, 2010, https://www.nytimes.com/2010/08/01/fashion/01Undivorced.html.

41. R. Taibbi, "Why Separations Usually Lead to Divorce," *Psychology Today*, August 8, 2020, https://www.psychologytoday.com/us/blog/fixing-families/202008/why-separations-usually-lead-divorce.
42. E. Barker, "The Science of 'Happily Ever After': 3 Things That Keep Love Alive," *Barking Up the Wrong Tree*, 2015, https://bakadesuyo.com/2014/04/happily-ever-after/.
43. IDFA, "Why People Divorce and What Are the Reasons for Divorce?," Institute for Divorce Financial Analysts, https://institutedfa.com/Leading-Causes-Divorce.
44. M. Zheng, J. K. Marsh, J. V. Nickerson, and S. Kleinberg, "How Causal Information Affects Decisions," *Cognitive Research: Principles and Implications* 5, no. 1 (2020): 6.
45. "Information Overload, Why It Matters and How to Combat It," The Interaction Design Foundation, https://www.interaction-design.org/literature/article/information-overload-why-it-matters-and-how-to-combat-it.
46. "Why Arranged Marriages Are Considered Better Than Love Marriages in Indian Society," *Times of India*, March 17, 2021, https://timesofindia.indiatimes.com/life-style/relationships/love-sex/why-arranged-marriages-are-considered-better-than-love-marriages-in-indian-society/articleshow/81549410.cms.
47. A. Zuckerman, "56 Marriage Statistics: 2020/2021 Global Data, Analysis & Trends," *CompareCamp*, May 31, 2020, https://comparecamp.com/marriage-statistics/.
48. Ians, "Indians Swear by Arranged Marriages," *India Today*, March 4, 2013, https://www.indiatoday.in/lifestyle/relationship/story/indians-swear-by-arranged-marriages-155274-2013-03-03.
49. "Why Arranged Marriages Are Considered Better Than Love Marriages in Indian Society."
50. D. Page, "Struggling to Find Marriage Material? Here's What to Look For," NBC News, June 30, 2017, https://www.nbcnews.com/better/pop-culture/why-you-should-treat-marriage-more-business-ncna778551; https://www.sciencedirect.com/science/article/abs/pii/S0190740920321496.
51. L. R. Emery, "What Modern Arranged Marriages Really Look Like," *Brides*, September 27, 2022, https://www.brides.com/story/modern-arranged-marriages.
52. H. Benson and S. McKay, "Does Religion Help Couples Stay Together?," The Marriage Foundation, 2016, https://marriagefoundation.org.uk/wp-content/uploads/2016/11/MF-paper-Religion-and-stability-final.pdf; R. Vink, "Muslim Women Have Winning Recipe for Relationship Success," Marriage Foundation, November 19, 2016, https://marriagefoundation.org.uk/muslim-women-have-winning-recipe-for-relationship-success/.
53. R. Epstein, "Fall in Love and Stay That Way," *Scientific American*, January 1, 2010, https://www.scientificamerican.com/article/how-science-can-help-love/.

Chapter 24

1. J. Sacks "Va'Etchanan: A Tiny, Treasured People," *Covenant and Conversation*, The Rabbi Sacks Legacy Trust, 2012, https://rabbisacks.org/covenant-conversation/vaetchanan/a-tiny-treasured-people/.
2. A. Klein, "Parashat Behar-Behukotai," *Lectures on the Torah Reading by the faculty of Bar-Ilan University*, 1998, https://www2.biu.ac.il/JH/Parasha/eng/bahar/kle.html.
3. M. Ringelmann, "Recherches sur les moteurs animés: Travail de l'homme [Research on animate sources of power: The work of man]," *Annales de l'Institut National Agronomique*, 2nd series 12 (1913): 1–40.
4. T. Van Schneider, "The Psychological Theory That Explains Why You're Better Off Working Solo," *Quartz*, November 30, 2016, https://qz.com/848267/the-ringelmann-effect-productivity-increases-when-youre-working-solo-rather-than-on-a-team.
5. M. De Rond, "Why Less Is More in Teams," *Harvard Business Review*, August 6, 2012, https://hbr.org/2012/08/why-less-is-more-in-teams.
6. Knowledge at Wharton, "Research Roundup: Team Performance, Demystifying Market Composition and the Reality vs. Hype of Sponsored Search," Knowledge at Wharton, University of Pennsylvania, January 18, 2012, https://knowledge.wharton.upenn.edu/article/research-roundup-team-performance-demystifying-market-composition-and-the-reality-vs-hype-of-sponsored-search/.
7. Ibid.
8. N. Penn, "An Oral History of the 2004 'Dream' Team," *GQ*, July 27, 2012, https://www.gq.com/story/2004-olympic-basketball-dream-team; "'What Did We Just Watch?'—The Bronze That Broke USA Basketball," ESPN.com, August 30, 2019, https://www.espn.com/nba/story/_/id/27462338/what-did-just-watch-bronze-broke-usa-basketball.
9. Roster Continuity, Basketball-Reference.com, https://www.basketball-reference.com/friv/continuity.html.
10. *Ibid.*
11. Z. Lowe, "NBA Windows: The Rockets' Missing Third Superstar and the NBA's Continuity Problem," *Grantland*, September 30, 2014, https://grantland.com/the-triangle/nba-windows-houston-rockets-james-harden-dwight-howard/.
12. B. Holmes, "Kobe Bryant of Los Angeles Lakers Envious of Continuity of San Antonio Spurs," ESPN, November 14, 2014, https://www.espn.com/los-angeles/nba/story/_/id/11875566/kobe-bryant-los-angeles-lakers-envious-continuity-san-antonio-spurs.
13. S. Smith (@scottsbucs), Twitter (now X), January 14, 2021, https://twitter.com/scottsbucs/status/1349802141209264129.

14. C. H. Heller, "Weakness into Strength: Overcoming Strategic Deficits in the 1948 Israeli War for Independence," *The Strategy Bridge*, September 24, 2018, https://thestrategybridge.org/the-bridge/2018/9/24/weakness-into-strength-overcoming-strategic-deficits-in-the-1948-israeli-war-for-independence.
15. "Why the Arabs Were Defeated," *Al Jazeera*, July 13, 2009, https://www.aljazeera.com/news/2009/7/13/why-the-arabs-were-defeated.

Chapter 25

1. M. Leiber, *The Torah Treasury* (Artscroll Mesorah Publishers, 2002), 433.
2. E. Goldberg, "Mattos/Masei: Kashering Ourselves," *Parsha Perspectives*, July 26, 2022, https://www.listennotes.com/podcasts/parsha-perspectives/mattosmasei-kashering-Rw_JHmcBhrs/.
3. Rashi, Numbers 30:2.
4. Babylonian Talmud, Pesachim 3a.
5. M. Kalmenson, "The Rebbe's Unusual Word Choice—Chapter 10 of Positivity Bias," Chabad.org, 2022, https://www.chabad.org/therebbe/article_cdo/aid/4405210/jewish/Chapter-10-The-Rebbes-Unusual-Word-Choice.htm.
6. Babylonian Talmud, Arakhin 15b.
7. E. Goldberg, "Tazria/Metzora: Are Girls Twice as Good as Boys?," *Parsha Perspectives*, April 12, 2018, https://www.listennotes.com/podcasts/parsha-perspectives/tazriametzora-are-girls-bWAgHmZP3Nh/.
8. Mishna, *Nagaim*, 12:5; M. Scheiner, "Three Strikes and You're Out," Palm Beach Synagogue, YouTube, April 20, 2023, https://www.youtube.com/watch?v=2potRoJrH-A.; Mishna, Negaim 12:5; Sifra, Metzorah 5:10.
9. G. Dennis, "Jewish Curses," *My Jewish Learning*, June 14, 2017, https://www.myjewishlearning.com/article/jewish-curses/.
10. S. Brombacher, "A Pillow Full of Feathers," Chabad.org, 2017, https://www.chabad.org/library/article_cdo/aid/812861/jewish/A-Pillow-Full-of-Feathers.htm.
11. Rashi's, Proverbs 27:14.
12. Maimonides, Mishneh Torah, *Laws of Human Dispositions*, 7:4.
13. Or Ha-Chaim, Leviticus 19:16; see also *Chafetz Chaim 10:1.*
14. *Chafetz Chaim 1:10:2.*
15. Shemirat HaLashon, Book I, *The Gate of Remembering 11:8.*
16. A. Newberg and M. R. Waldman, *Words Can Change Your Brain* (Penguin Publishing Group, 2012), 3.
17. "Emotional and Health Benefits of Saying I Love You," *HiRoad*, February 10, 2022, https://www.hiroad.com/blog/living-mindfully/health-benefits-of-saying-I-love-you.; D. A. Tod, R. Thatcher, M. McGuigan, and J. Thatcher, "Effects of Instructional and Motivational Self-Talk on the Vertical Jump," *Journal of Strength and Conditioning Research* 23, no. 1 (2009): 196–202.

18. A. Newberg and M. R. Waldman, 2012, *op. cit.*, 35.
19. S. Gottfried, "The Science Behind Why People Gossip—and When It Can Be a Good Thing," *Time*, September 25, 2019, https://time.com/5680457/why-do-people-gossip/.
20. "Can You Kiss and Hug Your Way to Better Health?," Penn Medicine, January 8, 2018, https://www.pennmedicine.org/updates/blogs/health-and-wellness/2018/february/affection.
21. N. Brondino, L. Fusar-Poli, and P. Politi, "Something to Talk About: Gossip Increases Oxytocin Levels in a Near Real-Life Situation," *Psychoneuroendocrinology* 77 (2017): 218–224.
22. R. I. M. Dunbar, "Gossip in Evolutionary Perspective," *Review of General Psychology* 8, no. 2 (2004): 100–110.
23. J. Schafer, "Why People Like to Gossip," *Psychology Today*, June 24, 2021, https://www.psychologytoday.com/us/blog/let-their-words-do-the-talking/202106/why-people-gossip.
24. S. Farley, "Is Gossip Power? The Inverse Relationships Between Gossip, Power, and Likability," *European Journal of Social Psychology* 41 (2011): 574–579.
25. E. Martinescu, O. Janssen, and B. A. Nijstad, "Self-Evaluative and Other-Directed Emotional and Behavioral Responses to Gossip About the Self," *Frontiers in Psychology* 9 (2019): 1–16.
26. *Ibid.*
27. M. L. Fisher, "The Influence of Female Attractiveness on Competitor Derogation," *Journal of Evolutionary Psychology* 7 (2009): 141–155.
28. S. Melwani, *A little Bird Told Me So . . . : The Emotional, Attributional, Relational and Team-Level Outcomes of Engaging in Gossip* (ProQuest Dissertations Publishing, 2012).
29. K. Georganta, E. Panagopoulou, and A. Montgomery, "Talking Behind Their Backs: Negative Gossip and Burnout in Hospitals," *Burnout Research* 1, no. 2 (2014): 1–6.

Chapter 26

1. E. Goldberg, "Pinchas: Battling the Yetzer Every Morning and Every Evening," *Parsha Perspectives*, July 7, 2020, https://www.listennotes.com/podcasts/parsha-perspectives/pinchas-battling-the-yetzer-QskU2rTZ3VA/.
2. Babylonian Talmud, Yoma 9b.
3. Babylonian Talmud, Gittin 56a.
4. E. Goldberg, "Ki Seitzei: Staying Within Our Moral Boundaries, "*Parsha Perspectives,* August 25, 2020, https://www.listennotes.com/podcasts/parsha-perspectives/ki-seitzei-staying-within-zFRDGXbNV0x/.
5. E. Goldberg, "Eikev: Wearing Your Heart On Your Sleeve," *Parsha Perspectives*,

April 11, 2018, https://www.listennotes.com/podcasts/parsha-perspectives/eikev-wearing-your-heart-on-FWJr5CxVcGd/.

6. T. Potier, "Holocaust Remembrance: What the Holocaust Means to Me," 349th Air Mobility Wing, April 15, 2009, https://www.349amw.afrc.af.mil/News/Article-Display/Article/185511/holocaust-remembrance-what-the-holocaust-means-to-me.
7. "New Surveillance Video Released of Teens Watching and Laughing as a Man Drowns," ABC News, YouTube, July 22, 2017, https://www.youtube.com/watch?v=hx8n95R0EiQ.
8. B. M. Tarm, "Facebook Live Attack Stirs Questions About Witnessing Crimes Online," *Chicago Tribune*, March 23, 2017, https://www.chicagotribune.com/news/breaking/ct-facebook-live-attack-stirs-questions-about-witnessing-crimes-online-20170323-story.html.
9. W. Mansell, "7 Charged in Stabbing Death of 16-Year-Old Broadcast on Snapchat as Dozens Watched," ABC News, September 28, 2019, https://abcnews.go.com/US/killed-snapchat-teens-charged-gang-assault-connection-stabbing/story?id=65923337.
10. T. Kingkade, "Why Would Anyone Film a Rape and Not Try to Stop It," *HuffPost*, April 24, 2016, https://www.huffpost.com/entry/why-film-a-rape_n_5717b957e4b0c9244a7a8e07; L. You, and Y. Lee, "The Bystander Effect in Cyberbullying on Social Network Sites: Anonymity, Group Size, and Intervention Intentions," *Telematics and Informatics* 45 (2019): 101284.
11. T. Dixon, "Key Studies: Darley and Latane—Bystanderism (1968)," *IB Psychology*, October 5, 2016, https://www.themantic-education.com/ibpsych/2016/10/05/key-studies-darley-and-latane-bystanderism-1968/.
12. G. Barron and E. Yechiam, "Private E-Mail Requests and the Diffusion of Responsibility," *Computers in Human Behavior* 18, no. 5 (2002): 507–520.
13. D. A. Prentice and D. T. Miller, "Pluralistic Ignorance and Alcohol Use on Campus: Some Consequences of Misperceiving the Social Norm," *Journal of Personality and Social Psychology* 64, no. 2 (1993): 243–256.
14. J. Grass and R. Trust, "From Bystanding to Standing Up," *Wharton Magazine*, February 6, 2014, https://magazine.wharton.upenn.edu/digital/from-bystanding-to-standing-up/.
15. J. Harris, "The Heroics of Lenny Skutnik," *The Southern Voice*, April 13, 2021, https://thesouthernvoice.com/the-heroics-of-lenny-skutnik/.
16. J. Fifield, "Why It's Hard to Punish 'Bad Samaritans,'" *Stateline*, September 19, 2017, https://stateline.org/2017/09/19/why-its-hard-to-punish-bad-samaritans/.
17. *Ibid.*
18. C. Angyal and M. Hui, "Sexual Misconduct: The New Rules," *Princeton Alumni Weekly*, September 16, 2015, 2015https://paw.princeton.edu/article/sexual-misconduct-new-rules-0.

Chapter 27

1. "Charity," *Oxford Advanced American Dictionary*, https://www.oxfordlearnersdictionaries.com/definition/american_english/charity.
2. Babylonian Talmud, Sukkah 49b.
3. B. Blech, "Judgment Day on Wall Street," *Aish*, October 6, 2022, https://aish.com/48951701/.
4. Babylonian Talmud, Ta'anit 9a.
5. Maimonides, Mishneh Torah, *Gifts to the Poor* 10:2.
6. M. M. Schneerson, *Sichas Purim 5747*, 1987.
7. Babylonian Talmud, Bava Batra 9b, Riva, Genesis 26:12.
8. L. Cox, "God's Palindrome," Kathy Harris Books, April 21, 2013, https://kathyharrisbooks.com/gods-palindrome/.
9. Babylonian Talmud, Brachot 63a.
10. D. Greenberg, "The Man Who Changed His Life after Reading His Obituary," Chabad.Org, 2005, https://www.chabad.org/library/article_cdo/aid/271383/jewish/The-Man-who-Changed-his-Life.htm.
11. M. Scheiner, "You're not complete without . . . ," Palm Beach Synagogue, YouTube, March 13, 2020, https://www.youtube.com/watch?v=ARyGhyvboGg.
12. Y. T. Weil, *Marbeh L'Saper*, Commentary to Passover Haggadah.
13. Conversation with Rabbi David Wolpe.
14. E. Jungreis, "When Rebbitzen Jungreis Came to Town," *Rivka Malka*, 1974, https://rivkamalka.com/when-rebbitzen-jungreis-came-to-town/.
15. Shulchan Arukh, *Yoreh De'ah 249:1.*
16. Sifra, *Emor 13:11.*
17. Babylonian Talmud, Bava Metzia 32a.
18. Jerusalem Talmud, Shekalim 1:1.
19. T. Wu, and B. Kayser, "High Altitude Adaptation in Tibetans," *High Altitude Medicine and Biology* 7, no. 3 (2006): 193–208.
20. A. Krebs and R. M. Thomas, "Notes on People; Some Disunity Along the United Way," *New York Times*, September 19, 1981, https://www.nytimes.com/1981/09/19/nyregion/notes-on-people-some-disunity-along-the-united-way.html.
21. "Charitable Giving Statistics," National Philanthropic Trust, July 8, 2022, https://www.nptrust.org/philanthropic-resources/charitable-giving-statistics/; J. M. Jones, "Percentage of Americans Donating to Charity at New Low," Gallup, May 14, 2020, https://news.gallup.com/poll/310880/percentage-americans-donating-charity-new-low.aspx.
22. M. Halpert, "Nearly Half of Americans Now Describe Their Financial Situation as Bad, Poll Finds," *Forbes*, October 12, 2022, https://www.forbes.com/sites/madelinehalpert/2022/10/12/nearly-half-of-americans-now-describe-their-financial-situation-as-bad-poll-finds/?sh=7fb66d0c8721; E. Rosenbaum, "Millions

of Americans Are Only $400 Away from Financial Hardship. Here's Why," CNBC, May 23, 2019, https://www.cnbc.com/2019/05/23/millions-of-americans-are-only-400-away-from-financial-hardship.html.

23. E. Norris, "Top 10 Most Common Financial Mistakes," *Investopedia*, June 14, 2022, https://www.investopedia.com/personal-finance/most-common-financial-mistakes/.
24. E. Kirkham, "23 Reasons Why You Will Always Be Poor," *Inquirer*, June 24, 2015, https://www.inquirer.com/philly/business/personal_finance/23_Reasons_Why_You_Will_Always_Be_Poor.html.
25. https://www.doughroller.net/personal-finance/dr-100-100-ways-improve-finances-10-minutes/.
26. "Volunteerism and Charitable Giving in 2009—Executive Summary," Fidelity Charitable Gift Fund 2009, https://faunalytics.org/wp-content/uploads/2015/05/Volunteerism-Charitable-Giving-2009-Executive-Summary.pdf; "Giving Makes You Rich," *Entrepreneur*, October 17, 2007, https://www.entrepreneur.com/business-news/giving-makes-you-rich/185662.
27. J. Moll et. al., "Human Fronto-Mesolimbic Networks Guide Decisions About Charitable Donation," *Proceedings of the National Academy of Sciences of the United States of America* 103, no. 42 (2006): 15623–15628.
28. Health Essentials "Why Giving Is Good for Your Health," Cleveland Clinic, January 5, 2023, https://health.clevelandclinic.org/why-giving-is-good-for-your-health/; A. Chatterjee, "Orgasm for Dummies: Neuroscience Explains Why Sex Feels Good," *Salon*, November 9, 2013, https://www.salon.com/2013/11/09/orgasm_for_dummies_neuroscience_explains_why_sex_feels_good/; P. A. Smeets et. al., "Effect of Satiety on Brain Activation During Chocolate Tasting in Men and Women," *American Journal of Clinical Nutrition* 83, no. 6 (2006): 1297–1305.
29. D. Moynihan, "Virtue Rewarded: Helping Others at Work Makes People Happier," University of Wisconsin-Madison, July 29, 2013, https://news.wisc.edu/virtue-rewarded-helping-others-at-work-makes-people-happier/.
30. P. B. Lester, "Top Performers Have a Superpower: Happiness," *MIT Sloan Management Review*, February 16, 2022, https://sloanreview.mit.edu/article/top-performers-have-a-superpower-happiness/?utm_source=release&utm_medium=pr&utm_campaign=lest0222.
31. N. Li, H. H. Zhao, S. L. Walter, X. A. Zhang, and J. Yu, "Achieving More with Less: Extra Milers' Behavioral Influences in Teams," *Journal of Applied Psychology* 100, no. 4 (2015): 1025–1039.
32. R. Cross, R. Rebele, and A. Grant, "Collaborative Overload," *Harvard Business Review*, 2016, https://hbr.org/2016/01/collaborative-overload.
33. K. Eriksson, I. Vartanova, P. Strimling, and B. Simpson, "Generosity Pays:

Selfish People Have Fewer Children and Earn Less Money," *Journal of Personality and Social Psychology* 118, no. 3 (2020): 532–544.

34. A. Grant, "Givers Take All: The Hidden Dimension of Corporate Culture," *McKinsey Quarterly*, 2013, 1–13.
35. M. Shermer, "(Can't Get No) Satisfaction," *Scientific American*, March 1, 2007, https://www.scientificamerican.com/article/cant-get-no-satisfaction/#.
36. A. Gasiorowska, "The Relationship Between Objective and Subjective Wealth Is Moderated by Financial Control and Mediated by Money Anxiety," *Journal of Economic Psychology* 43 (2014): 64–74.
37. G. Wood, "Secret Fears of the Super-Rich," *The Atlantic*, April 2011, https://www.theatlantic.com/magazine/archive/2011/04/secret-fears-of-the-super-rich/308419/; S. Agarwal, et. al., "Peers' Income and Financial Distress: Evidence from Lottery Winners and Neighboring Bankruptcies," *Review of Financial Studies* 33, no. 1 (2020): 433–472.
38. C. Mogilner, "You'll Feel Less Rushed If You Give Time Away," *Harvard Business Review*, 2012, https://hbr.org/2012/09/youll-feel-less-rushed-if-you-give-time-away.
39. C. Beaton, "Why You Feel Richer or Poorer Than You Really Are," *The Cut*, August 3, 2017, https://www.thecut.com/article/why-you-feel-richer-or-poorer-than-you-really-are.html.
40. A. Coombes, "3 Simple Strategies to Contributing the Maximum to Your 401(K) Each Year," *USA Today*, December 26, 2018, https://www.usatoday.com/story/money/personalfinance/retirement/2018/12/26/maximum-401-k-contributions-3-strategies-save-most/2361406002/.
41. J. Openshaw, "Power of Networking: How the Rich Do It," LinkedIn, September 28, 2015, https://www.linkedin.com/pulse/power-networking-its-key-next-job-success-jennifer-openshaw/.
42. J. M. Brett and T. Mitchell, "Research: How to Build Trust with Business Partners from Other Cultures," *Harvard Business Review*, January 31, 2020, https://hbr.org/2020/01/research-how-to-build-trust-with-business-partners-from-other-cultures.
43. Eureka Alert, "People Who Give, Live Longer: U-M Study Shows," *EurekAlert!*, November 12, 2002, https://www.eurekalert.org/news-releases/887795.
44. C. Carter, "What We Get When We Give," *Greater Good Magazine*, February 18, 2010, https://greatergood.berkeley.edu/article/item/what_we_get_when_we_give.
45. "Volunteering in the United States—2015," U.S. Bureau of Labor Statistics, February 25, 2016, https://www.bls.gov/news.release/volun.nr0.htm.
46. M. Lipka, "How Highly Religious Americans' Lives Are Different from Others," *Pew Research Center*, April 14, 2024, https://www.pewresearch.org/short-reads/2016/04/12/how-highly-religious-americans-lives-are-different-from-others/;

"Less God, Less Giving?," Philanthropy Roundtable, 2024, https://www.philanthropyroundtable.org/magazine/less-god-less-giving/.

47. R. Cross, R. Rebele, and A. Grant, 2016, *op. cit.*
48. See tables 1 and 2 in K. Eriksson, I. Vartanova, Strimling, and B. Simpson, "Generosity Pays: Selfish People Have Fewer Children and Earn Less Money," *Journal of Personality and Social Psychology* 118, no. 3 (2020): 532–544.
49. Approbation to B. Oakley, A. Knafo, G. Madhavan, and D. S. Wilson, eds., *Pathological Altruism* (Oxford University Press, 2012).
50. W. Easterly, "Think Again: Debt Relief," *Foreign Policy*, November 16, 2009, https://foreignpolicy.com/2009/11/16/think-again-debt-relief/.
51. S. M. Burn, *Unhealthy Helping: A Psychological Guide to Overcoming Codependence, Enabling, and Other Dysfunctional Giving* (CreateSpace Independent Publishing Platform, 2016), 48.
52. M. A. Melendez, "Alyssa Milano Responds to Backlash over Son's GoFundMe Campaign, Slams Troll for Commenting," CBS8, February 2, 2024, https://www.cbs8.com/article/entertainment/entertainment-tonight/alyssa-milano-responds-to-backlash-over-sons-gofundme-campaign-slams-troll-for-commenting.

Chapter 28

1. "History," National Candle Association, July 23, 2020, https://candles.org/history/.
2. J. A. Krisch, "How Monsters Under the Bed Became a Universal Childhood Fear," *Fatherly*, December 28, 2022, https://www.fatherly.com/health/monsters-under-the-bed-childhood-fears.
3. D. Greenberg, "Do Not Fear," Chabad.org, https://www.chabad.org/multimedia/video_cdo/aid/1916012/jewish/Do-NotFear.htm.
4. J. Bourke, "Fear: A Cultural History," *The Age*, May 7, 2005, https://www.theage.com.au/entertainment/books/fear-a-cultural-history-20050507-ge040y.html.
5. M. Moore, "Brainwave Most Likely to Strike at 10.04pm," *Telegraph*, October 20, 2008, https://www.telegraph.co.uk/news/newstopics/howaboutthat/3228009/Brainwave-most-likely-to-strike-at-10.04pm.html.
6. M. Shoard, "Writing at Night," *Guardian*, August 21, 2019, https://www.theguardian.com/books/booksblog/2010/dec/21/writing-at-night.
7. "A Surprising Number of Adults Are Still Scared of the Dark," *Mirror*, November 14, 2017, https://www.mirror.co.uk/news/weird-news/surprising-number-adults-still-scared-11520336; C. Romm, "Why Some People Never Grow Out of a Fear of the Dark," *The Cut*, October 26, 2016, https://www.thecut.com/2016/10/why-are-people-afraid-of-the-dark.html.

8. J. Hrarla, “There’s an Evolutionary Reason Why We’re Afraid of the Dark,” *Science Alert*, February 15, 2016, https://www.sciencealert.com/here-s-the-evolutionary-reason-why-we-re-afraid-of-the-dark.
9. C. Moskowitz, “The Face of Fear Explained,” *Live Science*, June 15, 2008, https://www.livescience.com/2608-face-fear-explained.html.
10. L. Delegran, “Impact of Fear and Anxiety,” University of Minnesota, https://www.takingcharge.csh.umn.edu/impact-fear-and-anxiety.
11. J. Rosenberg, “The Effects of Chronic Fear on a Person’s Health,” *AJMC*, December 19, 2020, https://www.ajmc.com/view/the-effects-of-chronic-fear-on-a-persons-health.
12. *Ibid.*
13. A. Cuncic, “Amygdala Hijack and the Fight or Flight Response,” *Verywell Mind*, June 22, 2021, https://www.verywellmind.com/what-happens-during-an-amygdala-hijack-4165944.
14. E. Hagerman, “Don’t Panic—It Makes You Stupid,” *WIRED*, April 21, 2008, https://www.wired.com/2008/04/gs-08dontpanic/.
15. A. Javanbakht, “The Politics of Fear: How It Manipulates Us to Tribalism,” *The Conversation*, January 11, 2019, https://theconversation.com/the-politics-of-fear-how-it-manipulates-us-to-tribalism-113815.
16. E. Hagerman, “Don’t Panic—It Makes You Stupid,” *WIRED*, April 21, 2008, https://www.wired.com/2008/04/gs-08dontpanic/.
17. C. Malchiodi, “Understanding Fight, Flight, Freeze, and the Feign Response,” *Psychology Today*, June 13, 2021, https://www.psychologytoday.com/us/blog/arts-and-health/202106/understanding-fight-flight-freeze-and-the-feign-response.
18. A. Rowden, “What to Know About Amygdala Hijack,” *Medical News Today*, April 19, 2021, https://www.medicalnewstoday.com/articles/amygdala-hijack#summary.
19. Z. Crockett, “Americans Are More Afraid of Clowns Than Climate Change, Terrrorism, and . . . Death,” *Vox*, October 21, 2016, https://www.vox.com/2016/10/21/13321536/clown-scare-sightings-2016.
20. M. Hyde, “Ronald McDonald’s Not Lovin’ the Creepy Clown Craze,” *Guardian*, October 13, 2016, https://www.theguardian.com/lifeandstyle/lostinshowbiz/2016/oct/13/ronald-mcdonald-not-lovin-creepy-clown-craze.
21. C. H. Russo, “Minnesota Police Chief Has a Stern Message for Creepy Clowns,” *HuffPost*, October 7, 2016, https://www.huffpost.com/entry/minnesota-clown-sighting-police_n_57f6ea85e4b068ecb5dd71b1.
22. C. Neff “The *Jaws* Effect: How Movie Narratives Are Used to Influence Policy Responses to Shark Bites in Western Australia,” *Australian Journal of Political Science* 50, no. 1 (2015): 114–127; S. Lovgren, “Jaws at 30: Film Stoked Fear,

Study of Great White Sharks," *National Geographic News*, June 15, 2005, http://news.nationalgeographic.com/news/2005/06/0615_050615_jawssharks.html.

23. Ipsos Public Affairs, "Sharks: Half (51%) of Americans Are Absolutely Terrified of Them and Many (38%) Scared to Swim in the Ocean Because of Them . . . ," *Ipsos*, July 7, 2015, https://www.ipsos.com/en-us/sharks-half-51-americans-are-absolutely-terrified-them-and-many-38-scared-swim-ocean-because-them.
24. M. Salazar, "If You Think Sharks Are Scary, Blame Hollywood, New Study Suggests," *Mongabay Environmental News*, February 3, 2023, https://news.mongabay.com/2021/09/if-you-think-sharks-are-scary-blame-hollywood-new-study-suggests/.
25. Harriet, "Oceanic Shark and Ray Populations Decline by 71%. Let's Dive In!," *Shark Guardian*, February 4, 2021, https://www.sharkguardian.org/post/oceanic-shark-and-ray-populations-decline-by-71-let-s-dive-in; M. Papenfuss, "Steven Spielberg 'Truly Regrets' Decimation of Shark Population After 'Jaws,'" *HuffPost*, December 18, 2022, https://www.huffpost.com/entry/steven-spieberg-shark-decimation-jaws-regrets_n_639fce3ee4b0e2fa1a45ff11.
26. L. Fritscher, "Prevalence of Phobias in the United States," *Verywell Mind*, March 9, 2020, https://www.verywellmind.com/prevalence-of-phobias-in-the-united-states-2671912.
27. N. Strauss, "Why We're Living in the Age of Fear," *Rolling Stone*, October 6, 2016, https://www.rollingstone.com/politics/politics-features/why-were-living-in-the-age-of-fear-190818/.
28. *Ibid.*
29. B. Stetka, "Steven Pinker: This Is History's Most Peaceful Time—New Study, 'Not So Fast,'" *Scientific American*, November 9, 2017, https://www.scientificamerican.com/article/steven-pinker-this-is-historys-most-peaceful-time-new-study-not-so-fast/.
30. Franklin Roosevelt, *Inaugural Address*, March 4, 1933.
31. A. Gorman, "Why I Almost Didn't Read My Poem at the Inauguration," *New York Times*, January 20, 2022, https://www.nytimes.com/2022/01/20/opinion/amanda-gorman-poem-inauguration.html.
32. L. Skenazy, "Why I Let My 9-Year-Old Ride the Subway Alone," *New York Sun*, April 1, 2008, https://www.nysun.com/article/opinion-why-i-let-my-9-year-old-ride-subway-alone.
33. https://archive.nytimes.com/well.blogs.nytimes.com/2015/01/19/advice-from-americas-worst-mom/.
34. N. Power and R. Noone, "Just Let Your Child Run Wild," *Daily Telegraph*, May 4, 2012, https://www.dailytelegraph.com.au/free-range-parenting-advocate-lenore-skenazy-says-fear-is-crippling-parents-and-depriving-children-of-fun/news-story/4e1b74d7b4cce786e2bce2bfdcb4ec97.

35. "What Could You Do as a Child That You Can't Do Now?," *Quora*, https://www.quora.com/What-could-you-do-as-a-child-that-you-cant-do-now.
36. D. Skolnik, "The New Playdate Playbook," CNN, January 27, 2012, https://www.cnn.com/2012/01/27/living/new-playdate-playbook-p.
37. J. Grose and H. Rosen, "Don't Go There, Don't Do That: Kids Today Have a Lot Less Freedom Than Their Parents Did," *Slate Magazine*, August 6, 2014, http://www.slate.com/articles/life/family/2014/08/slate_childhood_survey_results_kids_today_have_a_lot_less_freedom_than_their.2.html.
38. M. Voss, "5 Worries Parents Should Drop, and 5 They Shouldn't," NPR, August 30, 2010, https://www.npr.org/sections/health-shots/2010/08/30/129531631/5-worries-parents-should-drop-and-5-they-should?sc=fb&cc=fp/.
39. E. N. Brown, "Enough Stranger Danger! Children Rarely Abducted by Those They Don't Know," *Reason*, March 31, 2017, https://reason.com/2017/03/31/kidnapping-stats/.
40. E. Anderssen, "When Should Kids Trick-or-Treat on Their Own?," *Globe and Mail*, October 20, 2011, https://www.theglobeandmail.com/life/parenting/when-should-kids-trick-or-treat-on-their-own/article558263/.
41. G. Heyward, "Unfounded Fears About Rainbow Fentanyl Become the Latest Halloween Boogeyman," NPR, October 31, 2022, https://www.npr.org/2022/10/31/1132737831/rainbow-fentanyl-halloween-candy/.
42. L. Skenazy, "Online Only: The Scariest Thing about Halloween," *Daily Messenger*, October 24, 2010, https://www.mpnnow.com/story/opinion/2010/10/24/online-only-scariest-thing-about/45010916007/.
43. K. Painter, "'The Real Danger on Halloween': Kids Hit by Cars," *USA Today*, October 28, 2012, https://www.usatoday.com/story/news/nation/2012/10/28/halloween-kids-pedestrian-deaths/1652807/.
44. D. St. George, "'Free Range' Parents Cleared in Second Neglect Case After Kids Walked Alone," *Washington Post*, June 22, 2015, https://www.washingtonpost.com/local/education/free-range-parents-cleared-in-second-neglect-case-after-children-walked-alone/2015/06/22/82283c24-188c-11e5-bd7f-4611a60dd8e5_story.html.
45. "S.C. Mom's Arrest over Daughter Alone in Park Sparks Debate," CBS News, July 28, 2014, https://www.cbsnews.com/news/south-carolina-moms-arrest-over-daughter-alone-in-park-sparks-debate/.
46. J. Lawrence-Turner, "Swing Sets Becoming Scarce on School Playgrounds," *Spokesman Review*, October 8, 2014, https://www.spokesman.com/stories/2014/oct/08/spokane-school-district-removing-swings-from/.
47. A. Homer, "Washington Town Bans Swings from School Playgrounds," *The Inquisitr*, October 3, 2014, https://www.inquisitr.com/1517164/washington-town-bans-swings-from-school-playgrounds/.

48. J. Sneve, "Swings Staying Put in Sioux Falls Playgrounds, Despite National Trends," *Argus Leader*, February 26, 2020, https://www.argusleader.com/story/news/2020/02/25/swings-staying-put-sioux-falls-playgrounds-despite-national-trends/4867195002/.
49. City of Denison, "Unattended Children Policy," Denison, Texas: Library, 2022, https://www.cityofdenison.com/library/page/unattended-children-policy.
50. J. Haidt and G. Lukianoff, *The Coddling of the American Mind* (Penguin Books, 2019), 29.
51. W. C. Wallach, "Making Decisions When Values Conflict or Are Prioritized Differently, with Paul Root Wolpe," Carnegie Council for Ethics in International Affairs, May 10, 2022, https://www.listennotes.com/podcasts/carnegie-council/making-decisions-when-values-nfi0xp374YA/.
52. J. Ducharme, "Young Americans Are the Loneliest, According to a New Study," *Time*, May 1, 2018, https://time.com/5261181/young-americans-are-lonely/.
53. S. Dominus, "Rhode Island Kept Its Schools Open. This Is What Happened," *New York Times*, February 10, 2021, https://www.nytimes.com/2021/02/10/magazine/school-reopenings-rhode-island.html.
54. L. R. G. DeSantis, "How Many Children and Teachers Are We Willing to Sacrifice to Open Schools Again?," *The Tennessean*, July 15, 2020, https://www.tennessean.com/story/opinion/2020/07/15/reopening-schools-williamson-county-middle-tennessee-coronavirus/5437767002/.
55. B. Levin, "Biden's CDC Director: If You're Not Scared Shitless About COVID-19, You Should Be," *Vanity Fair*, March 29, 2021, https://www.vanityfair.com/news/2021/03/rochelle-walensky-covid-19-warning.
56. J. Ludden and L. Weeks, "Sotomayor, 'Always Looking Over My Shoulder,'" NPR, May 26, 2009, https://www.npr.org/2009/05/26/104538436/sotomayor-always-looking-over-my-shoulder; G. Kessler, "Sotomayor's False Claim That 'Over 100,000' Children Are in 'Serious Condition' with Covid," *Washington Post*, January 10, 2022, https://www.washingtonpost.com/politics/2022/01/08/sotomayors-false-claim-that-over-100000-children-are-serious-condition-with-covid/.
57. F. Michas, "Number of All Hospital Beds in the U.S. from 1975 to 2020", Statista, March 20, 2023, https://www.statista.com/statistics/185860/number-of-all-hospital-beds-in-the-us/; S. Thompson, "We're Tired of Watching People Die: The 6 Stages of Critical COVID-19 Care," *Nebraska Medicine Omaha*, January 26, 2022, https://www.nebraskamed.com/COVID/were-tired-of-watching-people-die-the-6-stages-of-critical-covid-19-care; https://nymag.com/intelligencer/2021/07/the-kids-were-safe-from-covid-the-whole-time.html.
58. M. Makary, "Universities' Covid Policies Defy Science and Reason," *Common Sense with Bari Weis*, January 4, 2022.
59. L. McBride, "When COVID-19 Puts Kids at Risk, Parents May Overreact," *The*

Atlantic, August 13, 2021, https://www.theatlantic.com/ideas/archive/2021/08/children-delta-covid-19-risk-adults-overreact/619728/.

60. M. Kuhfeld, J. Soland, K. Lewis, and E. Morton, "The Pandemic Has Had Devastating Impacts on Learning. What Will It Take to Help Students Catch Up?," *Brookings*, March 3, 2022, https://www.brookings.edu/articles/the-pandemic-has-had-devastating-impacts-on-learning-what-will-it-take-to-help-students-catch-up/.
61. C. Skopeliti, "'Socially Stunted': How Covid Pandemic Aggravated Young People's Loneliness," *Guardian*, June 19, 2023, https://www.theguardian.com/society/2023/jun/19/socially-stunted-how-covid-pandemic-aggravated-young-peoples-loneliness; J. Barshay, "The Science of Catching Students Up After COVID Learning Loss," *The 74*, October 14, 2021, https://www.the74million.org/article/students-covid-learning-loss-science-catching-up/; Office for Civil Rights, "Education in a Pandemic: The Disparate Impacts of COVID-19 on America's Students," United States Department of Education, 2021, https://www2.ed.gov/about/offices/list/ocr/docs/20210608-impacts-of-covid19.pdf; A. Stuart, et. al., "Loneliness in Older People and COVID-19: Applying the Social Identity Approach to Digital Intervention Design," *Computers in Human Behavior Reports* 6 (2022): 100179.
62. C. Cadelago, "'We Would've Done Everything Differently': Newsom Reflects on Covid Approach," *Politico*, September 10, 2023, https://www.politico.com/news/2023/09/10/newsom-covid-california-00114888.
63. J. Debiec, "Evolution Explains Why We're Falling Victim to Fear Contagion as COVID-19 Spreads," *Fast Company*, March 16, 2020, https://www.fastcompany.com/90477966/evolution-explains-why-were-falling-victim-to-fear-contagion-as-covid-19-spreads.
64. *Ibid.*
65. A. Ionescu, "Fear Is a Contagious Emotion That Is Amplified in a Group," *Earth.com*, February 2, 2022, https://www.earth.com/news/fear-is-a-contagious-emotion-that-is-amplified-in-a-group/#google_vignette; S. M. Tashjian, V. Fedrigo, T. Molapour, D. Mobbs, and C. F. Camerer, "Physiological Responses to a Haunted-House Threat Experience: Distinct Tonic and Phasic Effects," *Psychological Science* 33, no. 2 (2022): 236–248.
66. B. Obama, "Remarks by the President at Morehouse College Commencement Ceremony," The White House: Office of the Press Secretary, May 19, 2013, https://obamawhitehouse.archives.gov/the-press-office/2013/05/19/remarks-president-morehouse-college-commencement-ceremony.
67. J. Biden, "Remarks by President Biden at the Morehouse College Class of 2024 Commencement Address," The White House: Office of the Press Secretary, May 19, 2024, https://www.whitehouse.gov/briefing-room/speeches-remarks/2024/05/19/remarks-by-president-biden-at-the-morehouse-college-class-of-2024-commencement-address-atlanta-ga/.

68. "Amnesty International Joins Moment of Silence for Victims of Police Brutality," Amnesty International USA, August 14, 2014, https://www.amnestyusa.org/press-releases/amnesty-international-joins-moment-of-silence-for-victims-of-police-brutality/.
69. J. R. Smith Lee and M. A. Robinson, "'That's My Number One Fear in Life. It's the Police': Examining Young Black Men's Exposures to Trauma and Loss Resulting from Police Violence and Police Killings," *Journal of Black Psychology* 45, no. 3 (2019): 143–184; K. Frankovic, "More African-Americans Fear Victimization by Police Than Fear Violent Crime," *YouGov*, 2019, https://today.yougov.com/topics/politics/articles-reports/2019/03/15/black-americans-police.
70. L. Putnam and E. Chenoweth, "The Floyd Protests Are the Broadest in U.S. History, and Are Spreading to White, Small-Town America," *Washington Post*, June 6, 2020, https://www.washingtonpost.com/politics/2020/06/06/floyd-protests-are-broadest-us-history-are-spreading-white-small-town-america/.
71. L. Beckett, "At Least 25 Americans Were Killed During Protests and Political Unrest in 2020," *Guardian*, October 31, 2020, https://www.theguardian.com/world/2020/oct/31/americans-killed-protests-political-unrest-acled; J. A. Kingson, "Exclusive: $1 Billion-Plus Riot Damage Is Most Expensive in Insurance History, *Axios*, September 16, 2020, https://www.axios.com/2020/09/16/riots-cost-property-damage; B. Polumbo, "George Floyd Riots Caused Record-Setting $2 Billion in Damage, New Report Says. Here's Why the True Cost Is Even Higher," *Foundation for Economic Education*, September 16, 2020, https://fee.org/articles/george-floyd-riots-caused-record-setting-2-billion-in-damage-new-report-says-here-s-why-the-true-cost-is-even-higher/.
72. K. Watson, "Biden Says There's 'Absolutely' Systemic Racism in Law Enforcement and Beyond," CBS News, June 10, 2020, https://www.cbsnews.com/news/joe-biden-systemic-racism-exists-law-enforcement/.
73. K. McCaffree and A. Saide, "How Informed Are Americans About Race and Policing?," *Skeptic Research Center*, CUPES007, 2021.
74. E. Harrell and E. Davis, "Contacts Between Police and the Public, 2018, Statistical Tables," U.S. Department of Justice, Bureau of Justice Statistics, 2023.
75. "Video Shows Officer Shoot Unarmed Man [Video]," CNN, December 11, 2017, https://edition.cnn.com/videos/us/2017/12/10/daniel-shaver-philip-brailsford-shooting-bodycam-video-sandoval-pkg-newday-new.cnn; M. O'Connor, "Mesa Cop Calls People 'Idiots' for Bringing Up Shaver Shooting on Facebook," *Phoenix New Times*, October 17, 2019, https://www.phoenixnewtimes.com/news/daniel-shaver-mesa-brailsford-shot-dead-police-facebook-flanigan-11374239.
76. R. VerBruggen, "Fatal Police Shootings and Race: A Review of the Evidence and Suggestions for Future Research," *Manhattan Institute*, 2022; S. Mullainathan, "Police Killings of Blacks: Here Is What the Data Say," *New York Times*, October

16, 2015, https://www.nytimes.com/2015/10/18/upshot/police-killings-of-blacks-what-the-data-says.html.

77. R. Shepard, "Black American Anxiety at All-Time High, Experts Say," ABC News, September 5, 2020, https://abcnews.go.com/US/black-american-anxiety-time-high-experts/story?id=72651176.
78. A. Fowers and W. Wan, "Depression and Anxiety Spiked Among Black Americans After George Floyd's Death," *Washington Post*, June 12, 2020, https://www.washingtonpost.com/health/2020/06/12/mental-health-george-floyd-census/.
79. D. Douglas, "The Atlantic Interview: Nikole Hannah-Jones," *The Atlantic*, December 14, 2017, https://www.theatlantic.com/education/archive/2017/12/progressives-are-undermining-public-schools/548084/.
80. N. Hannah-Jones, "Yes, Black America Fears the Police. Here's Why," ProPublica, March 2015, https://www.propublica.org/article/yes-black-america-fears-the-police-heres-why.
81. N. Viswanathan, "Why Black People Running from the Police Makes Perfect Sense," In These Times, April 28, 2015, https://inthesetimes.com/article/why-black-people-running-from-the-police-makes-perfect-sense.
82. A. MacGillis, "How to Stop a Police Pullback," *The Atlantic*, September 3, 2020, https://www.theatlantic.com/ideas/archive/2020/09/how-stop-police-pullback/615730/.
83. R. G. Fryer and T. Devi, "Policing the Police: The Impact of 'Pattern-or-Practice' Investigations on Crime," *NBER Working Paper Series*, 2020. Some have attributed the increase in murder rate to Covid policies. The excess killings, however, did not start until after the death of George Floyd—and are not present in any other country. See P. Moskos, "The Murder Spike of 2020: When Police Pull Back," *Wall Street Journal*, July 23, 2021, https://www.wsj.com/articles/the-murder-spike-of-2020-when-police-pull-back-11626969547.
84. R. R. Ortega, "Man Says Derek Chauvin Pointed Gun at Him as a Teenager," *Daily Mail Online*, June 1, 2020, https://www.dailymail.co.uk/news/article-8377407/Minneapolis-man-says-Derek-Chauvin-pointed-gun-teen-Nerf-dart-shot-car-window.html; T. Law, "49 Years After the Kent State Shootings, New Photos Are Revealed," *Time*, May 5, 2019, https://time.com/5583301/kent-state-photos/.
85. "Bill of Rights in Action," Constitutional Rights Foundation, https://www.crf-usa.org/bill-of-rights-in-action/bria-9-3-and-4-a-let-us-reason-together-lyndon-johnson-master-legislator.html/; R. Levinson, "Special Report: Police Union Contracts Offer Shield of Protection," Reuters, January 13, 2017, https://www.reuters.com/investigates/special-report/usa-police-unions/.
86. J. Chasmar, "Incoming Democrat Whip Katherine Clark Recalls Child 'Waking Up with Nightmares' Over Climate Change," *New York Post*, December 7, 2022,

https://www.politico.com/news/2021/08/09/climate-change-scientists-report-disastrous-502799, https://nypost.com/2022/12/06/katherine-clark-recalls-child-waking-up-with-nightmares-over-climate-change/.

87. M. Zaraska, "Chronic Fear Of Environmental Doom? You're Not Alone," *Discover Magazine*, April 10, 2021, https://www.discovermagazine.com/mind/chronic-fear-of-environmental-doom-youre-not-alone.
88. J. Reinl, "One in Four Americans Skipping Children and Other Life Plans Over Fears of Climate Change: Study," *Daily Mail Online*, January 11, 2023, https://www.dailymail.co.uk/news/article-11623605/One-four-Americans-skipping-children-life-plans-fears-climate-change-study.html; APA Public Opinion Poll, Annual Meeting 2020, American Psychiatric Association, https://www.psychiatry.org/newsroom/apa-public-opinion-poll-2020; S. Osaka, "Should You Not Have Kids Because of Climate Change? It's Complicated," *Washington Post*, December 2, 2022, https://www.washingtonpost.com/climate-environment/2022/12/02/climate-kids/.
89. C. Hickman, et. al., "Climate Anxiety in Children and Young People and Their Beliefs About Government Responses to Climate Change: A Global Survey," *Lancet: Planetary Health* 5, no. 12 (2021): 863–873.
90. S. Osaka, "Should You Not Have Kids Because of Climate Change? It's Complicated," *Washington Post*, December 2, 2022, https://www.washingtonpost.com/climate-environment/2022/12/02/climate-kids/.
91. M. Goklany, "Wealth and Safety: The Amazing Decline in Deaths from Extreme Weather in an Era of Global Warming: 1900–2010," *Reason*, Policy Study 393, 2011, https://pubmed.ncbi.nlm.nih.gov/31417231/; G. Formetta and L. Feyen, "Empirical Evidence of Declining Global Vulnerability to Climate-Related Hazards," *Global Environmental Change—Human and Policy Dimensions* 57 (2019): 101920.
92. J. Jowit, "Don't Exaggerate Climate Dangers, Scientists Warn," *Guardian*, March 18, 2007, https://www.theguardian.com/environment/2007/mar/18/theobserver.climatechange.
93. Babylonian Talmud, Sotah 35a.
94. T. Goldman, "Women's Soccer Stars Concerned About Trauma from Repetitive Head Impact," NPR, September 5, 2019, https://www.npr.org/2019/09/05/757935739/womens-soccer-stars-concerned-about-trauma-from-repetitive-head-impact#:~:text=Still%2C%202017%20research%20by%20the,That%27s%20where%20Dr; "Comparing Head Impacts in Youth Tackle and Flag Football," CDC Injury Center, https://www.cdc.gov/traumaticbraininjury/pubs/youth_football_head_impacts.html.
95. J. Neusner, "'The Glory of God Is Intelligence': A Theology of Torah Learning in Judaism," in *The Glory of God Is Intelligence: Four Lectures on the Role of Intellect*

in Judaism (Brigham Young University, 1978), 1–12; J. Erskine, *The Moral Obligation to Be Intelligent and Other Essays* (Duffield and Company, 1915).

96. Rebbe Nachman of Breslov, *Likkutei Maharan*, Part II, 48:2.
97. G. Bonanno, *The End of Trauma: How the New Science of Resilience Is Changing How We Think About PTSD* (Basic Books, 2021), 191.
98. M. L. King, Jr., "I've Been to the Mountaintop," Address Delivered at Bishop Charles Mason Temple, in *A Call to Conscience: The Landmark Speeches of Dr. Martin Luther King Jr.*, ed. K. Shepard, and C. Carson (Grand Central Publishing, 2001).
99. C. Thorbecke, "Officer Calms Girl Who Is Afraid of Police During Traffic Stop," ABC News, August 26, 2016, https://abcnews.go.com/Lifestyle/officer-calms-girl-afraid-police-traffic-stop/story?id=41667522.
100. Basketball Cop Foundation, "Our Story," *Basketball Cop*, January 15, 2016, https://basketballcop.net/; F. Karimi, "Shaq, Florida Officer Surprise Kids with a Basketball Game," CNN, January 24, 2016, https://www.cnn.com/2016/01/24/us/florida-shaq-police-officers-game/index.html.
101. International Association of Chiefs of Police, "Steps to Building Trust," IACP, August 15, 2018, https://www.theiacp.org/resources/steps-to-building-trust.
102. Babylonian Talmud, Berakhot 55b.
103. R. Deveny, "How to Help a Friend with Phobias," The Recovery Village Drug and Alcohol Rehab, May 26, 2022, https://www.therecoveryvillage.com/mental-health/phobias/related/how-to-help-a-friend-with-phobias/; NHS Inform, "10 Ways to Fight Your Fears," National Health Service, January 4, 2023, https://www.nhsinform.scot/healthy-living/mental-wellbeing/fears-and-phobias/ten-ways-to-fight-your-fears.
104. Mishna, Pirkei Avot 1:7.

Chapter 29

1. Rashi, Deuteronomy 4:20.
2. E. Goldberg, "Ki Savo: Count Your Blessings," *Parsha Perspectives*, August 29, 2023, https://www.listennotes.com/podcasts/parsha-perspectives/ki-savo-count-your-blessings-bGXCLl2Edh4/.
3. Kli Yakar, Deuteronomy 8:2.
4. Malbim, Proverbs 24:16.
5. Babylonian Talmud, Gittin 43a; E. Goldberg, "Vayeira (Slonimer): Mesirus Nefesh vs. Mesirus Ha'Guf," *Parasha Perspectives*, October 30, 2018, https://www.listennotes.com/podcasts/parsha-perspectives/vayeira-slonimer-mesirus-bJI61TaRoN5/.
6. I. Klein, "The Laws of Passover," Jewish Theological Seminary, February 11, 2013, https://www.jtsa.edu/torah/the-laws-of-passover/.

7. D. Kasher, "Snakes on a Plain—Parshat Chukat," *ParshaNut*, July 14, 2016, https://parshanut.com/post/147400228141/snakes-on-a-plain-parshat-chukat.
8. S. Sweeny Silver, "The Biblical Caduceus, Symbol of Medicine," *Early Church History*, https://earlychurchhistory.org/medicine/the-biblical-caduceus-symbol-of-medicine/.
9. H. Abramason, *Torah from the Years of Wrath 1939–43: The Historical Context of the Aish Kodesh* (Sam Sapozhnik Publishers, 2017), 80.
10. N. N. Taleb, *Antifragile: Things That Gain from Disorder* (Random House Publishing, 2012), 3.
11. J. Zillgitt, "'The Last Dance': Why Michael Jordan Invented Slights for Motivation," *USA Today*, May 11, 2020, https://www.usatoday.com/story/sports/nba/2020/05/10/the-last-dance-why-michael-jordan-invented-slights-for-motivation/3103843001/.
12. H. Volarevic, "'Who's Guarding Me?'—When Larry Bird Got Insulted Because a 'White Boy' Guarded Him," *Basketball Network*, October 26, 2022, https://www.basketballnetwork.net/old-school/when-larry-bird-got-insulted-because-a-white-boy-guarded-him.
13. K. Bryant, "Kobe Bryant Up Close Interview with Jimmy Kimmel [FULL INTERVIEW]," *All Honesty*, August 26, 2013, https://www.youtube.com/watch?v=ORhcTM80e0A.
14. D. Kulkarni, "Shaquille O'Neal on David Robinson, 'He Is My Favorite Player Ever. I Loved Him So Much I Had to Make Up a Fake Story to Play Against Him,'" *Fadeaway World*, February 15, 2022, https://fadeawayworld.net/nba-media/shaquille-oneal-on-david-robinson-he-is-my-favorite-player-ever-i-loved-him-so-much-i-had-to-make-up-a-fake-story-to-play-against-him.
15. A. Zagoria, "Dan Hurley Will Continue to 'Look for Slights, or Create Them' as UConn Bids for a Three-Peat," Nj.com, July 6, 2024, https://www.nj.com/sports/2024/07/dan-hurley-will-continue-to-look-for-slights-or-create-them-as-uconn-bids-for-a-three-peat.html.
16. NFL Films (@NFLFilms), Twitter (now X), January 24, 2019, https://twitter.com/NFLFilms/status/1088198508811829249.
17. C. VanDeVelde, "Carol Dweck: Praising Intelligence: Costs to Children's Self-Esteem and Motivation," Stanford University Bing Nursery School, November 1, 2007, https://bingschool.stanford.edu/news/carol-dweck-praising-intelligence-costs-childrens-self-esteem-and-motivation.
18. *Ibid.*
19. C. Dweck, "Growth Mindset and the Future of Our Children," Parents League of New York, September 26, 2017, https://www.parentsleague.org/blog/growth-mindset-and-future-our-children.
20. K. Stoner, "Science Proves That What Doesn't Kill You Makes You Stronger," *Northwestern*, October 1, 2019, https://tinyurl.com/2vcebfvf

21. T. Ben-Sahar, "Don't Chase Happiness. Become Antifragile," *Big Think*, YouTube, January 26, 2022, https://www.youtube.com/watch?v=e-or_D-qNqM&ab_channel=BigThink.
22. M. D. Seery, E. A. Holman, and R. Cohen Silver, "Whatever Does Not Kill Us: Cumulative Lifetime Adversity, Vulnerability, and Resilience," *Journal of Personality and Social Psychology* 99, no. 6 (2010): 1025–1041; B. Carey, "Mind: Past Adversity May Aid Emotional Recovery," *New York Times*, February 4, 2013, https://www.nytimes.com/2011/01/04/health/04mind.html.
23. University at Buffalo, "Study Confirms: Whatever Doesn't Kill Us Can Make Us Stronger," *ScienceDaily*, October 15, 2010, www.sciencedaily.com/releases/2010/10/101015125645.htm.
24. H. G. Ginott, *Between Parent and Child: New Solutions to Old Problems* (Macmillan, 1965), 18; A. Ang, "Helicopter Parenting 2.0: Hovering Around, Yet Letting the Kids Take Some Risks," Nanyang Business School, May 30, 2022, https://www.ntu.edu.sg/business/news-events/news/story-detail/helicopter-parenting-2.0-hovering-around-yet-letting-the-kids-take-some-risks.
25. A. Mattke, "Stepping Back from Helicopter Parenting," Mayo Clinic, February 24, 2022, https://mcpress.mayoclinic.org/parenting/stepping-back-from-helicopter-parenting/.
26. M. Shermer, "Kids Today Are Being Socialized to Think They're Fragile Snowflakes," *Scientific American*, December 1, 2018, https://www.scientificamerican.com/article/kids-today-are-being-socialized-to-think-theyre-fragile-snowflakes/; S. Schwartz, "Helicopter Parenting: From Good Intentions to Poor Outcomes," The Gottman Institute, August 15, 2018, https://www.gottman.com/blog/helicopter-parenting-good-intentions-poor-outcomes/; E. Oster, "Bad Moms with Emily Oster," *Honestly with Bari Weiss*, January 25, 2023 https://www.listennotes.com/podcasts/honestly-with-bari/bad-moms-with-emily-oster-7xMBWGCAthr/.
27. J. Bradley-Geist and J. Olson-Buchanan, "Helicopter Parents: An Examination of the Correlates of Over-Parenting of College Students," *Education & Training* 56, no. 4 (2014): 314–328; P. Gray, "Helicopter Parenting & College Students' Increased Neediness," *Psychology Today*, June 14, 2019, https://www.psychologytoday.com/us/blog/freedom-learn/201510/helicopter-parenting-college-students-increased-neediness.
28. D. M. Harrington, J. H. Block, and J. Block, "Testing Aspects of Carl Rogers's Theory of Creative Environments: Child-Rearing Antecedents of Creative Potential in Young Adolescents," *Journal of Personality and Social Psychology* 52 (1987): 851–856.
29. C. Segrin, "Parents: Don't Hover, Let Your College Student Be Free," *University of Arizona News*, August 26, 2015, https://news.arizona.edu/blog/parents-dont-hover-let-your-college-student-be-free.

30. K. Reed, et al., "Helicopter Parenting and Emerging Adult Self-Efficacy: Implications for Mental and Physical Health," *Journal of Child and Family Studies* 25 (2016): 3136–3149.
31. A. Packham, "Intrusive Parents Make Kids More Anxious, Study Suggests," *HuffPost UK*, July 4, 2016, https://www.huffingtonpost.co.uk/entry/helicopter-parents-make-children-anxious_uk_577a3961e4b0f7b5579582ce.
32. J. Asbrand, J. Hudson, and J. Schmitz, "Maternal Parenting and Child Behaviour: An Observational Study of Childhood Social Anxiety Disorder," *Cognitive Therapy and Research* 41 (2017): 562–575.
33. Terri LeMoyne and Tom Buchanan, "Does 'Hovering' Matter? Helicopter Parenting and Its Effect on Well-being," *Sociological Spectrum* 31, no. 4 (2011): 399–418; A. M. Luebbe, K. J. Mancini, E. J. Kiel, B. R. Spangler, J. L. Semlak, and L. M. Fussner, "Dimensionality of Helicopter Parenting and Relations to Emotional, Decision-Making, and Academic Functioning in Emerging Adults," *Assessment* 25, no. 7 (2018): 841–857; J. E. Barker, A. D. Semenov, L. Michaelson, L. S. Provan, H. R. Snyder, and Y. Munakata, "Less-Structured Time in Children's Daily Lives Predicts Self-Directed Executive Functioning," *Frontiers in Psychology* 5 (2014): 593.
34. J. W. Kohler, "Helicopter Parenting," *Marine Parents*, https://rp.marineparents.com/bootcamp/helicopter.asp.
35. L. M. Breckenridge, "Curbing the 'Helicopter Commander': Overcoming Risk Aversion and Fostering Disciplined Initiative in the U.S. Army," *Army University Press*, 2017, https://www.armyupress.army.mil/Journals/Military-Review/English-Edition-Archives/July-August-2017/Breckenridge-Curbing-the-Helicopter-Commander/.
36. J. E. Brody, "Parenting Advice from 'America's Worst Mom,'" *New York Times*, January 19, 2016, https://archive.nytimes.com/well.blogs.nytimes.com/2015/01/19/advice-from-americas-worst-mom/.
37. W. McElroy, "The Big Lie of a 'Rape Culture,'" The Future of Freedom Foundation, April 7, 2014, https://www.fff.org/explore-freedom/article/the-big-lie-of-a-rape-culture/.
38. J. Valenti, "Why We Need to Keep Talking About 'Rape Culture,'" *Washington Post*, March 28, 2014, https://www.washingtonpost.com/opinions/why-we-need-to-keep-talking-about-rape-culture/2014/03/28/58acfec4-b5bf-11e3-8cb6-284052554d74_story.html; J. Saffron, "An Intellectual Cocoon," *National Review*, November 20, 2014, https://www.nationalreview.com/phi-beta-cons/intellectual-cocoon-jesse-saffron/; J. Shulevitz, "Opinion: In College and Hiding from Scary Ideas," *New York Times*, March 21, 2015, https://www.nytimes.com/2015/03/22/opinion/sunday/judith-shulevitz-hiding-from-scary-ideas.html.
39. Email from President Christina Paxson to the Brown Community, November 14,

2014, https://www.thefire.org/research-learn/email-president-christina-paxson-brown-community.

40. "Ben Shapiro Visit: Safe Navigation, Other Logistics and Resources," *Berkeley News*, October 30, 2018, https://news.berkeley.edu/campus-update-on-ben-shapiro-event/.
41. C. Powell, "UConn's PC Hysteria Invites a Nervous Breakdown," *The Day Newspaper*, January 27, 2018, https://www.theday.com/columnists/20180127/uconns-pc-hysteria-invites-a-nervous-breakdown/.
42. Office of the Provost, "Trigger and Content Warning Guidance," University of Connecticut, 2022, https://provost.uconn.edu/trigger-warning/.
43. J. Chait, "Not a Very P.C. Thing to Say," *Intelligencer*, January 27, 2015, https://nymag.com/intelligencer/2015/01/not-a-very-pc-thing-to-say.html; A. Kamenetz, "Half of Professors in NPR Ed Survey Have Used 'Trigger Warnings,'" NPR, September 7, 2016, https://www.npr.org/sections/ed/2016/09/07/492979242/half-of-professors-in-npr-ed-survey-have-used-trigger-warnings.
44. M. Moynihan, "Western Lit, Shot to Death by 'Trigger Warnings,'" *Politico*, July 18, 2015, https://www.politico.eu/article/western-lit-shot-to-death-by-trigger-warnings/; M. E. Miller, "Columbia Students Claim Greek Mythology Needs a Trigger Warning," *Washington Post*, May 14, 2015, https://www.washingtonpost.com/news/morning-mix/wp/2015/05/14/columbia-students-claim-greek-mythology-needs-a-trigger-warning/.
45. Student Assembly, "Resolution 31: Mandating Content Warnings for 2 Traumatic Content in the Classroom," Cornell University, March 23, 2023, https://assembly.cornell.edu/sites/default/files/resolution_31_-_content_warnings.pdf.
46. B. W. Bellet, P. J. Jones, and R. J. McNally, "Trigger Warning: Empirical Evidence Ahead," *Journal of Behavior Therapy and Experimental Psychiatry* 61 (2018): 134–141.
47. "The Following News Release Contains Potentially Disturbing Content: Trigger Warnings Fail to Help and May Even Harm," Association for Psychological Science, June 9, 2020, https://www.psychologicalscience.org/news/releases/trigger-warnings-fail-to-help.html.
48. T. B. Kashdan, "How Science Changed My View on Trigger Warnings," *Psychology Today*, October 5, 2021, https://www.psychologytoday.com/us/blog/curious/202110/how-science-changed-my-view-trigger-warnings.
49. J. S. Gersen, "What if Trigger Warnings Don't Work?," *New Yorker*, September 28, 2021, https://www.newyorker.com/news/our-columnists/what-if-trigger-warnings-dont-work.
50. R. Kennedy, "The History Behind Debates Around Affirmative Action," *New York Times*, June 7, 2023, https://www.nytimes.com/2023/06/07/opinion/resistance-black-advancement-affirmative-action.html.

51. C. Taylor, "The N Word," *Salon*, January 22, 2002, https://www.salon.com/2002/01/22/kennedy_22/; G. Early, "The Way Out of Here," *New York Times*, March 3, 2002, https://www.nytimes.com/2002/03/03/books/the-way-out-of-here.html.
52. FIRE, "LAWSUIT: Professor Suspended for Redacted Slurs in Law School Exam Sues University of Illinois Chicago," The Foundation for Individual Rights and Expression, January 27, 2022, https://www.thefire.org/news/lawsuit-professor-suspended-redacted-slurs-law-school-exam-sues-university-illinois-chicago; J. Stossel, "Speech Is Not Violence," *Reason*, July 21, 2021, https://reason.com/2021/07/21/speech-is-not-violence/.
53. J. McGahan, "How a Mild-Mannered USC Professor Accidentally Ignited Academia's Latest Culture War," *Los Angeles Magazine*, October 21, 2020, https://www.lamag.com/citythinkblog/usc-professor-slur/.
54. C. Friedersdorf, "The Fight Against Words That Sound Like, but Are Not, Slurs," *The Atlantic*, September 21, 2020, https://www.theatlantic.com/ideas/archive/2020/09/fight-against-words-sound-like-are-not-slurs/616404/.
55. The letter transliterated the phrase differently than did Professor Garrett. See C. Flaherty, "Professor Suspended for Saying Chinese Word That Sounds Like an English Slur," *Inside Higher Ed*, September 7, 2020, https://www.insidehighered.com/news/2020/09/08/professor-suspended-saying-chinese-word-sounds-english-slur.
56. M. Angelou, "Haley Shows Us the Truth of Our Conjoined Histories," *New York Times*, January 23, 1977, https://timesmachine.nytimes.com/timesmachine/1977/01/23/issue.html.
57. C. Eberhart, "Julliard School Forced Students to Take Part in 'Slavery Saturday' Workshop," *Daily Mail*, May 27, 2021, https://www.dailymail.co.uk/news/article-9626169/Julliard-School-forced-students-Slavery-Saturday-workshop.html.
58. D. Woetzel, "A Message from President Woetzel," Juilliard, April 23, 2021, https://www.juilliard.edu/news/149411/message-president-woetzel.
59. R. Weinert-Kendt, "A Teaching Moment for Juilliard," *American Theatre*, April 30, 2021, https://www.americantheatre.org/2021/04/30/a-teaching-moment-for-juilliard/.
60. D. Blum, "How to Navigate a 'Quarterlife' Crisis," *New York Times*, August 15, 2022, https://www.nytimes.com/2022/07/29/well/family/quarter-life-crisis.html.
61. "National College Health Assessment II: Reference Group Executive Summary," American College Health Association, 2022, https://www.acha.org/documents/ncha/NCHA-II_SPRING_2019_US_REFERENCE_GROUP_EXECUTIVE_SUMMARY.pdf.
62. M. Thielking, "A Dangerous Wait: Colleges Can't Meet Soaring Student Needs for Mental Health Care," *STAT*, December 7, 2017, https://www.statnews.com/2017/02/06/mental-health-college-students/.

63. Z. Abrams, "Student Mental Health Is in Crisis. Campuses Are Rethinking Their Approach," *Monitor on Psychology* 53, no. 7 (2022): 60, https://www.apa.org/monitor/2022/10/mental-health-campus-care.
64. Good Therapy Editor Team, "Is There a Shortage of Mental Health Professionals in America?," *Good Therapy*, March 26, 2020, https://www.goodtherapy.org/for-professionals/personal-development/become-a-therapist/is-there-shortage-of-mental-health-professionals-in-america.
65. L. Bernstein, "This Is Why It's So Hard to Find Mental Health Counseling Right Now," *Washington Post*, March 6, 2022, https://www.washingtonpost.com/health/2022/03/06/therapist-covid-burnout/.
66. "Depressed? Get Out!," *Washington Post*, March 13, 2006, https://www.washingtonpost.com/archive/opinions/2006/03/13/depressed-get-out/9338d3fa-4ceb-4e8d-baf9-47c82c3a3860.
67. A. Giambrone, "When Mentally Ill Students Feel Alone," *The Atlantic*, March 2, 2015, https://www.theatlantic.com/education/archive/2015/03/when-mentally-ill-students-feel-alone/386504/.
68. E. P. Janowski, "Sent Away," *Chronicle of Higher Education*, June 27, 2022, https://www.chronicle.com/article/sent-away#:~:text=Dartmouth%20officials%20sent%20Elizabeth%20Reimer,mental%20health%2C%E2%80%9D%20she%20wrote.
69. W. Wan, "What If Yale Finds Out?," *Washington Post*, November 11, 2022, https://www.washingtonpost.com/dc-md-va/2022/11/11/yale-suicides-mental-health-withdrawals/.
70. *Ibid.*
71. E. P. Jankowski, June 27, 2022, *op. cit*,
72. S. Gilbert, "The Importance of Community and Mental Health," *NAMI: National Alliance on Mental Illness*, November 18, 2019, https://www.nami.org/Blogs/NAMI-Blog/November-2019/The-Importance-of-Community-and-Mental-Health.
73. J. Haidt and G. Lukianoff, 2019, *op. cit.*, 196.
74. G. Challice, "Graduate Outcomes Survey," *QILT*, 2022, https://www.qilt.edu.au/surveys/graduate-outcomes-survey-(gos), 63.
75. D. Wolfowicz, personal communication, May 8, 2023.
76. G. Beresin, "Your College Student—Conversation Starters," *MGH Clay Center*, YouTube, December 20, 2021, https://www.youtube.com/watch?v=4WtMiobqMr0.
77. T. B. Edsall, "The Happiness Gap Between Left and Right Isn't Closing," *New York Times*, May 8, 2024, https://www.nytimes.com/2024/05/08/opinion/conservatives-liberals-depression-anxiety.html; M. Cikara, "Concept Expansion as a Source of Empowerment," *Psychological Inquiry* 27, no. 1 (2016): 29–33.
78. American Psychiatric Association, *Diagnostic and Statistical Manual of Mental Disorders*, 3rd ed. (1980).

79. American Psychiatric Association, *Diagnostic and Statistical Manual of Mental Disorders*, 4th ed. (1994).
80. A. Ghorayshi, "Doctors Debate Whether Trans Teens Need Therapy Before Hormones," *New York Times*, January 13, 2022, https://www.nytimes.com/2022/01/13/health/transgender-teens-hormones.html; A. Reuben, "'Secondary Trauma': When PTSD is Contagious," *The Atlantic*, December 14, 2015, https://www.theatlantic.com/health/archive/2015/12/ptsd-secondary-trauma/420282/.
81. L. Pandell, "How Trauma Became the Word of the Decade, and the Covid-19 Pandemic," *Vox*, January 25, 2022, https://www.vox.com/the-highlight/22876522/trauma-covid-word-origin-mental-health; D. Carr, "Tell Me Why It Hurts," *New York Magazine*, July 31, 2023, https://nymag.com/intelligencer/article/trauma-bessel-van-der-kolk-the-body-keeps-the-score-profile.html.
82. "Report: More U.S. Soldiers Suffering from Pre-Traumatic Stress Disorder," The Onion, 2023, https://theonion.com/report-more-u-s-soldiers-suffering-from-pre-traumatic-1819568807/; E. A. Kaplan, "Is Climate-Related Pre-Traumatic Stress Syndrome a Real Condition?," *American Imago* 77, no. 1 (2020): 81–104; J. E. Lipton, "Pre-Traumatic Stress Disorder," *Psychology Today*, June 20, 2016, https://www.psychologytoday.com/us/blog/peace-and-war/201606/pre-traumatic-stress-disorder; "Our Children Face 'Pretraumatic Stress' from Worries About Climate Change," *The BMJ Opinion*, November 19, 2020, https://blogs.bmj.com/bmj/2020/11/19/our-children-face-pretraumatic-stress-from-worries-about-climate-change/#content; D. Oberhaus, "Climate Change Is Giving Us 'Pre-Traumatic Stress,'" *Vice*, February 4, 2017, https://www.vice.com/en/article/vvzzam/climate-change-is-giving-us-pre-traumatic-stress.
83. L. Pandell, January 25, 2022, *op. cit.*
84. C., Benjet, et. al., "The Epidemiology of Traumatic Event Exposure Worldwide: Results from the World Mental Health Survey Consortium," *Psychological Medicine* 46, no. 2 (2016): 327–343.
85. K. Armstrong, "Remarkable Resiliency: George Bonanno on PTSD, Grief, and Depression," *Association for Psychological Science*, January 29, 2020, https://www.psychologicalscience.org/observer/bonanno.
86. G. A. Bonanno, *The End of Trauma: How the New Science of Resilience Is Changing How We Think About PTSD* (Basic Books, 2021), 14.
87. G. A.Bonanno, 2021, *op. cit.*
88. S. B. Kaufman, "Post-Traumatic Growth: Finding Meaning and Creativity in Adversity," *Scientific American*, April 20, 2020, https://blogs.scientificamerican.com/beautiful-minds/post-traumatic-growth-finding-meaning-and-creativity-in-adversity/.
89. X. Wu, A. C. Kaminga, W. Dai, J. Deng, Z. Wang, X. Pan, and A. Liu, "The Prevalence of Moderate-to-High Posttraumatic Growth: A Systematic Review and Meta-Analysis," *Journal of Affective Disorders* 243 (2019): 408–415.

90. H. S. Kushner, *When Bad Things Happen to Good People* (Schocken Books, 1981), 133–134.
91. "Self-fulfilling Prophecies | World Problems & Global Issues," *The Encyclopedia of World Problems*, http://encyclopedia.uia.org/en/problem/140824.
92. W. Shipp, "How Did Ancient Warriors Deal with Post Traumatic Stress Disorder?," *Australian Army Research Centre*, February 12, 2019, https://researchcentre.army.gov.au/library/land-power-forum/how-did-ancient-warriors-deal-post-traumatic-stress-disorder.
93. "What West Point Graduates Can Teach Us About Stress and Resilience," Yale School of Medicine, January 2, 2022, https://medicine.yale.edu/news-article/what-west-point-graduates-can-teach-us-about-stress-and-resilience/.
94. J. P. Kahn, "Why Public Health and Politics Don't Mix," *American Journal of Bioethics* 7, no. 11 (2007): 3–4.
95. R. Jackson, "In Gay We Trust: How Do We Tackle PTSD in the LGBTQ+ Community?," *Advocate*, September 1, 2020, https://www.advocate.com/commentary/2020/9/01/gay-we-trust-how-do-we-tackle-ptsd-lgbtq-community.
96. S. Sonoma, "Trump Bafflingly Says It's 'Great Honor' to Be "Most Pro-Gay President in America,'" *Them*, August 20, 2020, https://www.them.us/story/log-cabin-republicans-trump-tweet.
97. J. Kirchick, "The First Amendment Created Gay America," May 31, 2022, https://www.thefp.com/. https://www.thefp.com/p/the-first-amendment-created-gay-america.
98. "What is Exposure Therapy?," American Psychological Association, 2017, https://www.apa.org/ptsd-guideline/patients-and-families/exposure-therapy.pdf.
99. E. Patterson, "Exposure Therapy: How It Works and What to Expect," *Choosing Therapy*, August 10, 2023, https://www.choosingtherapy.com/exposure-therapy/.
100. J. S. Kaplan and D. F. Tolin, "Exposure Therapy for Anxiety Disorders," *Psychiatric Times* 28, no. 9, September 6, 2011, https://www.psychiatrictimes.com/view/exposure-therapy-anxiety-disorders.
101. Cleveland Clinic, "Exposure Therapy," https://my.clevelandclinic.org/health/treatments/25067-exposure-therapy.
102. T. Murphy, "For Fear of Flying, Therapy Takes to the Skies," *New York Times*, July 24, 2007, https://www.nytimes.com/2007/07/24/health/psychology/24fear.html.
103. B. Obama, May 19, 2013, *op. cit.*

Chapter 30

1. A. Aziz, "Why Are There So Many Jewish Nobel Winners?," *Jewish Chronicle*, December 8, 2022, https://www.thejc.com/lets-talk/why-are-there-so-many-jewish-nobel-winners-ctycke48.

2. "Jewish Educational Attainment Around the World," Pew Research Center's Religion & Public Life Project, December 13, 2016, https://www.pewresearch.org/religion/2016/12/13/jewish-educational-attainment/.
3. Babylonian Talmud, Shabbat 119b.
4. Babylonian Talmud, Bava Batra 21a; Maimonides, Mishneh Torah, *Laws of Talmud Torah 2:1*; Babylonian Talmud, Brachot 64a.
5. T. M. Jonquière, *Prayer in Josephus* (Brill, 2007), 104.
6. T. Freeman, "Eight Great Things About Jewish Mothers. Really," Chabad.org, 2007, https://www.chabad.org/library/article_cdo/aid/3976582/jewish/Eight-Great-Things-About-Jewish-Mothers-Really.htm.
7. B. Smalley, *The Study of the Bible in the Middle Ages* (University of Notre Dame Press, 1964), 78; J. Neusner, *Understanding Jewish Theology: Classical Issues and Modern Perspectives* (Global Publications, 2001), 57; M. Zborowski and E. Herzog, *Life Is with People: The Culture of the Shtetl* (Schocken, 1988), 294.
8. K. Romey, "Exclusive: Ancient Mass Child Sacrifice May Be World's Largest," *National Geographic*, April 26, 2018, https://www.nationalgeographic.com/news/2018/04/mass-child-human-animal-sacrifice-peru-chimu-science/.
9. M. Roser and E. Ortiz-Ospina, "Literacy," *Our World in Data*, September 20, 2018, https://ourworldindata.org/literacy.
10. For Jews and education generally (including the discussion of Shakespeare), see "The Craziest Dream Comes True: How We Live in Moses's World." M. Gerson, *The Telling: How Judaism's Essential Book Reveals the Meaning of Life* (St. Martin's Press, 2021), 25–35.
11. Babylonian Talmud, Bava Batra 21a; J. Sacks, "Parshat Matot: Judaism Believes That Children Are the Future," *Algemeiner*, July 29, 2019, https://www.algemeiner.com/2019/07/29/parshat-matot-judaism-believes-that-children-are-the-future/; A. Pařík, "Jewish Education," Jewish Museum in Prague, December 3, 2006, https://www.jewishmuseum.cz/en/program-and-education/exhibits/archive-exhibits/328/.
12. Babylonian Talmud, Sukkah 56b.
13. E. Krakowski, "On Mothers," *Jewish Action*, 2018, https://jewishaction.com/family/relationships/on-mothers/.
14. Babylonian Talmud, Yoma 72b.
15. A. J. Heschel, *I Asked for Wonder: A Spiritual Anthology* (Crossroad, 1983), 62.
16. Y. Y. Jacobson, "How Do We Inspire Our Children? Parsha Va'eschanan," Rabbi Y. Y. Jacobson, YouTube, https://www.youtube.com/watch?v=UU8YEGiqDKc.
17. D. Kaplan, "Parshat Vayeira: Abraham's Hospitality—Rabbi David Kaplan," *Hidabroot—Torah & Judaism*, June 23, 2016, https://www.youtube.com/watch?v=akBGmxb3UT8.
18. M. Scheiner, "The F of Father's Day," Palm Beach Synagogue, YouTube, June 16, 2024, https://www.youtube.com/watch?v=_c_WlXUqYL4&t=220s.

19. Mishna, Avot 4:20.
20. Standard translations render the verse: "and it will be, if you *surely* hear my commands." My translation, based on Rashi's commentary, reflects the literal meaning of the Hebrew text which employs a double usage of the verb "to hear."
21. Babylonian Talmud, Chigaga 9b.
22. Rashbam, Exodus 16:15.
23. Sefat Emet, Beshalach 31.
24. P. Wehner, "Why Jesus Never Stopped Asking Questions," *New York Times*, December 23, 2021, https://www.nytimes.com/2021/12/23/opinion/christmas-jesus-questions.html.
25. D. Sheff, "Izzy, Did You Ask a Good Question Today?," *New York Times*, January 19, 1988, https://www.nytimes.com/1988/01/19/opinion/l-izzy-did-you-ask-a-good-question-today-712388.html.
26. Rabbi Samson Raphael Hirsch, Genesis 25:27.
27. From discussions with Corporal David Wolfowicz, a former commander in the IDF's Education Corps.
28. E. Goldberg, "Vayechi: Finding Closure," *Parsha Perspectives*, December 29, 2020, https://www.listennotes.com/podcasts/parsha-perspectives/vayechi-finding-closure-d1QB3MRfVrt/.
29. Babylonian Talmud, Avoda Zarah 19a.
30. L. Gottlieb, "The History of Honey Cake," *My Jewish Learning*, 2021, https://www.myjewishlearning.com/the-nosher/the-history-of-honey-cake.
31. Maimonides, Mishneh Torah, *Laws of Leavened and Unleavened Bread*, 7:3.
32. E. Goldberg, "Emor: Inspire Yourself to Inspire Others and Inspire Others to Inspire Yourself," *Parsha Perspectives*, April 27, 2021, https://www.listennotes.com/podcasts/parsha-perspectives/emor-inspire-yourself-to-l6vUBEG7p1J/.
33. Rashi, Genesis 25:27; J. D. Pearson, "A Mendelian Interpretation of Jacob's Sheep," *Science & Christian Belief* 13, no. 1 (2001): 51–58.
34. I. Drazin, "Maimonides View on the Proper Way to Worship God," *Dr Israel Drazin*, January 20, 2022, https://booksnthoughts.com/maimonides-view-on-the-proper-way-to-worship-god/.
35. Maimonides, Mishneh Torah, *The Sanhedrin and the Penalties within Their Jurisdiction*, 2:1.
36. D. Schwartz, "Jewish Traditions and Practices in the Medieval World," in M. Heiduk, K. Herbers, and H. Lehner, eds., *Prognostication in the Medieval World: A Handbook* (De Gruyter, 2021), 686–688.
37. Babylonian Talmud, Kiddushin 31a.
38. R. J. Sacks, "Pinchas: On Parents and Teachers," *Covenant and Conversation*, The Rabbi Sacks Legacy Trust, 2007, https://www.rabbisacks.org/covenant-conversation/pinchas/on-parents-and-teachers/.
39. Maimonides, Mishneh Torah, *Laws of Torah Study*, 5:6.

40. UNESCO, "Literacy Rates Continue to Rise from One Generation to the Next," UNESCO Institute for Statistics, 2017, https://uis.unesco.org/sites/default/files/documents/fs45-literacy-rates-continue-rise-generation-to-next-en-2017_0.pdf.
41. S. Konstantopoulos and V. Chung, "What Are the Long-Term Effects of Small Classes on the Achievement Gap? Evidence from the Lasting Benefits Study," *American Journal of Education* 116, no. 1 (2009): 125–154; M. Barnum, "Does Class Size Really Matter?," *Chalkbeat*, June 10, 2022, https://www.chalkbeat.org/2022/6/10/23162544/class-size-research; Florida Department of Education, "Class Size," fldoe.org, https://www.fldoe.org/finance/budget/class-size/.
42. M. Slack, "President Obama Honors the 2013 National Teacher of the Year," The White House: President Barak Obama, April 23, 2013, https://obamawhitehouse.archives.gov/blog/2013/04/23/president-obama-honors-2013-national-teacher-year.
43. V. Strauss, "Where in the World Are Teachers Most Respected? Not in the U.S., a New Survey Shows," *Washington Post*, November 15, 2018, https://www.washingtonpost.com/education/2018/11/15/where-world-are-teachers-most-respected-not-us-new-survey-shows/.
44. E. Hatfield, J. T. Cacioppo, and R. L. Rapson, "Emotional Contagion," *Current Directions in Psychological Science* 2, no. 3 (1993): 96–100.
45. D. R. Hamilton, "Emotional Contagion: Are Your Feelings 'Infecting' Others?," *HuffPost*, July 19, 2011, https://www.huffpost.com/entry/emotional-contagion_b_863197.
46. Q. Zhang, "Assessing the Effects of Instructor Enthusiasm on Classroom Engagement, Learning Goal Orientation, and Academic Self-Efficacy," *Communication Teacher* 28, no. 1 (2014): 44–56.
47. G. Orosz, et. al., "Teacher Enthusiasm: A Potential Cure of Academic Cheating," *Frontiers in Psychology* 6 (2014): 318–318.
48. J. G. Hood, "Service-Learning in Dental Education: Meeting Needs and Challenges," *Journal of Dental Education* 73, no. 4 (2009): 454–463; S. Aslan, "Is Learning by Teaching Effective in Gaining 21st Century Skills? The Views of Pre-Service Science Teachers," *Educational Sciences: Theory & Practice* 15, no. 6 (2015): 1441–1457.
49. "Stack Exchange Has Been Taken over by a Rubber Duck!," Stack Exchange, 2018, https://meta.stackexchange.com/questions/308564/stack-exchange-has-been-taken-over-by-a-rubber-duck/308578#308578.
50. J. J. Rousseau, *The Confessions*, J. M. Cohen, trans. (Penguin, 1953), 529–30; C. Hendrick, "Ten Books Every Teacher Should Read," *Guardian*, August 15, 2017, https://www.theguardian.com/teacher-network/2017/aug/15/ten-books-every-teacher-should-read.
51. Rousseau, *Émile*, Book I.

52. K. Robinson, "Do Schools Kill Creativity?," James Clear (Originally delivered at TED2016), 2016, https://jamesclear.com/great-speeches/do-schools-kill-creativity-by-ken-robinson.
53. T. Dintersmith, *What School Could Be* (Princeton University Press, 2018), 23; K. Robinson, "Creativity Is as Important as Literacy," *Learning by Design*, 2018, https://pubs.royle.com/publication/?i=675590&article_id=3778465&view=articleBrowser.
54. "Exploring the Reggio Emilia Approach to Early Childhood Education," Explorers Early Learning, April 28, 2023, https://eel.com.au/family/blog/exploring-the-reggio-emilia-approach-to-early-childhood-education/.
55. North American Reggio Emilia Alliance, https://www.reggioalliance.org/; "Everything There Is to Know About the Reggio Emilia Approach to Learning," Little Sunshine's Playhouse and Preschool: A Reggio Emilia School, March 14, 2024, https://littlesunshine.com/everything-there-is-to-know-about-the-reggio-emilia-approach-to-learning/; K. Hobson, "What Are Reggio Emilia Schools?," *New York Times*, April 19, 2020, https://www.nytimes.com/2020/04/19/parenting/reggio-emilia-preschool.html.
56. K. Moody, "Top 10 Reasons Why Every Young Hero Needs to Be in a Learner-Driven Environment: Reason 1," Acton Academy Palm Harbor, May 10, 2022, https://www.actonacademyph.com/blog/top-10-reasons-why-every-young-hero-needs-to-be-in-a-learner-driven-environment.
57. NAEP Reading: National Achievement-Level Results, n.d., https://www.nationsreportcard.gov/reading_2017/nation/achievement/?grade=4.
58. E. Hanford, "Why Millions of Kids Can't Read and What Better Teaching Can Do About It," NPR, January 2, 2019, https://www.npr.org/2019/01/02/677722959/why-millions-of-kids-cant-read-and-what-better-teaching-can-do-about-it.
59. S. Schwartz, "Is This the Dnd of 'Three Cueing?," *Education Week*, April 2, 2024, https://www.edweek.org/teaching-learning/is-this-the-end-of-three-cueing/2020/12.
60. H. Kurtz, et al., "Early Reading Instruction Results of a National Survey of K-2 and Elementary Special Education Teachers and Postsecondary Instructors," *Education Week*, 2020, https://epe.brightspotcdn.com/1b/80/706eba6246599174b0199ac1f3b5/ed-week-reading-instruction-survey-report-final-1.24.20.pdf; K. Hurley, "The Decadeslong Travesty That Made Millions of Americans Mistrust Their Kids' Schools," *Slate Magazine*, October 15, 2023, https://slate.com/human-interest/2023/10/reading-phonics-literacy-calkins-curriculum-public-school.html; L. Robinson, "Episode 4: The Superstar," *Sold a Story*, November 3, 2022, https://www.listennotes.com/podcasts/sold-a-story/4-the-superstar-l4Jab6ePA57/.

61. E. Hanford, "School Is for Learning to Read," *New York Times*, September 1, 2022, https://www.nytimes.com/2022/09/01/opinion/us-school-reading.html.
62. "Kids' Reading Scores Have Soared in Mississippi 'Miracle,'" *PBS Newshour*, 2023, https://www.pbs.org/newshour/education/kids-reading-scores-have-soared-in-mississippi-miracle.
63. T. Closson, "New York Is Forcing Schools to Change How They Teach Children to Read," *New York Times*, May 23, 2023, https://www.nytimes.com/2023/05/09/nyregion/reading-nyc-schools.html.
64. D. Waters, "Politics of Phonics: How a Skill Becomes a Law," The Institute for Public Reporting: Memphis, May 10, 2021, https://www.psrmemphis.org/politics-of-phonics-how-a-skill-becomes-a-law/.
65. D. Goldstein, "In the Fight Over How to Teach Reading, This Guru Makes a Major Retreat," *New York Times*, May 22, 2022, https://www.nytimes.com/2022/05/22/us/reading-teaching-curriculum-phonics.html.
66. R. E. Mayer, "Should There Be a Three-Strikes Rule Against Pure Discovery Learning?: The Case for Guided Methods of Instruction," *The American Psychologist* 59, no. 1 (2004): 14–19.
67. P. A. Kirschner, J. Sweller, and R. E. Clark, "Why Minimal Guidance During Instruction Does Not Work: An Analysis of the Failure of Constructivist, Discovery, Problem-Based, Experiential, and Inquiry-Based Teaching," *Educational Psychologist* 41, no. 2 (2006): 75–86.
68. A. Zimmerman, "41% of NYC Students Were Chronically Absent Last School Year," *Chalkbeat*, September 16, 2022, https://www.chalkbeat.org/newyork/2022/9/16/23357144/chronic-absenteeism-pandemic-nyc-school/; C. Bamberger, "Many NYC Public School Grads Aren't Ready for College, State Audit Finds," *New York Post*, October 4, 2022, https://nypost.com/2022/10/04/many-nyc-public-school-grads-arent-ready-for-college-comptroller/.
69. A. Zimmerman, "NYC's 2022 Graduation Rate Rises as State Officials Relax Graduation Requirements," *Chalkbeat*, February 3, 2023, https://www.chalkbeat.org/newyork/2023/2/2/23583538/nyc-2022-school-graduation-rate-regents-exam-requirement/; C. Bamberger, "NY High School Graduation Rates May Have Been 'Inflated' During COVID Pandemic: Report," *New York Post*, August 8, 2022, https://nypost.com/2022/08/08/ny-high-school-graduation-rates-may-have-been-inflated-during-covid-pandemic/.
70. "Culturally Responsive-Sustaining Education," NYC Public Schools, https://www.schools.nyc.gov/about-us/vision-and-mission/culturally-responsive-sustaining-education.
71. S. H. Kim, "Max Weber," in E. N. Zalta and U. Nodelman, eds., *The Stanford Encyclopedia of Philosophy* (2022), https://plato.stanford.edu/archives/win2022/entries/weber/.

72. M. Webber, *Science as a Vocation: The Vocation Lectures*, trans. R. Livingstone (Hackett Publishing Company, 2004), 9.
73. W. D. Wall, "Memory and Chess," Bill Wall, http://billwall.phpwebhosting.com/articles/memory_and_chess.htm.
74. G. A. Miller, "The Magical Number Seven, Plus or Minus Two: Some Limits on Our Capacity for Processing Information," *Psychological Review* 63 (1956): 81–97.
75. P. A. Kirschner, J. Sweller, and R. E. Clark, "Why Minimal Guidance During Instruction Does Not Work: An Analysis of the Failure of Constructivist, Discovery, Problem-Based, Experiential, and Inquiry-Based Teaching," *Educational Psychologist* 41, no. 2 (2006): 75–86.
76. B. McGrath, "Wayne Gretzky and the Mysteries of Athletic Greatness," *New Yorker*, November 14, 2018, https://www.newyorker.com/sports/sporting-scene/wayne-gretzky-and-the-mysteries-of-athletic-greatness.
77. "Gretsky's Goals," *Orlando Sentinel*, March 6, 1994, https://www.orlandosentinel.com/1994/03/06/gretzkys-goal/.
78. M. Gladwell, "The Physical Genius," *New Yorker*, July 25, 1999, https://www.newyorker.com/magazine/1999/08/02/the-physical-genius; J. Gatehouse, "Wayne Gretzky on the Love of His Life," *Maclean's*, October 6, 2016, https://macleans.ca/sports/wayne-gretzky-on-the-love-of-his-life/.
79. M. Root-Bernstein and R. Root-Bernstein, "Nobel Prizes Most Often Go to Researchers Who Defy Specialization—Winners Are Creative Thinkers Who Synthesize Innovations from Varied Fields and Even Hobbies," The Conversation, October 3, 2022, https://theconversation.com/nobel-prizes-most-often-go-to-researchers-who-defy-specialization-winners-are-creative-thinkers-who-synthesize-innovations-from-varied-fields-and-even-hobbies-186193.
80. K. Ferguson, "Embrace the Remix," TED Talks, 2012, https://www.ted.com/talks/kirby_ferguson_embrace_the_remix?language=en.
81. S. Johnson, *Where Good Ideas Come From: The Natural History of Innovation* (Riverhead Books, 2010), 151–153; M. Alt, "How Gunpei Yokoi Reinvented Nintendo," *Vice*, November 12, 2020, https://www.vice.com/en/article/pkdbx7/how-gunpei-yokoi-reinvented-nintendo; L. Tomasovic, "Beyond the Renaissance: Nobel Laureates and their Creative Pursuits," *Biomedical Odyssey: Life at the Johns Hopkins School of Medicine*, January 10, 2024, https://biomedicalodyssey.blogs.hopkinsmedicine.org/2024/01/beyond-the-renaissance-nobel-laureates-and-their-creative-pursuits/.
82. P. McCormick, "Compounding Crazy," *Not Boring*, August 2, 2021, https://www.notboring.co/p/compounding-crazy.
83. R. Kurzweil, "The Law of Accelerating Returns," *Kurzweil*, March 7, 2001, https://www.kurzweilai.net/the-law-of-accelerating-returns.

84. D. R. Schilling, "Knowledge Doubling Every 12 Months, Soon to be Every 12 Hours," *Industry Tap*, 2017, https://www.industrytap.com/knowledge-doubling-every-12-months-soon-to-be-every-12-hours/3950; P. Densen "Challenges and Opportunities Facing Medical Education," *Transactions of the American Clinical and Climatological Association* 122 (2011): 48–58; J. Y. Yang, "Most of What You Learned in Medical School Is Wrong. And That's OK," *KevinMD*, September 10, 2019, https://www.kevinmd.com/2019/09/most-of-what-you-learned-in-medical-school-is-wrong-and-thats-ok.html.

Chapter 31

1. Babylonian Talmud, Avodah Zara 17b.
2. Babylonian Talmud, Avodah Zara 17b.
3. Y. S. Freedman, "Stories Rav Amital Told," *Yeshivat Har Etzion*, 2010, http://www.haretzion.org/45-torah/harav-yehuda-amital-ztl-life-and-work/114-hesped-yonatan-freedman.
4. Babylonian Talmud, Chagigah 5b.
5. Sifrei Deuteronomy 357:40.
6. N. Lamm, "How to Read the Torah," *YU Torah*, October 15, 1971, https://www.yutorah.org/lectures/lecture.cfm/982413/rabbi-norman-lamm/how-to-read-the-torah/.
7. Babylonian Talmud, Avodah Zarah 5b.
8. Babylonian Talmud, Taanit 7; Even Sheleima 1:11.
9. Mishna, Pirkei Avot 4:5.

Chapter 32

1. Netziv, *Ha'emek Davar*, Genesis 11:1;3.
2. J. D. Soloveitchik, *Abraham's Journey*, ed. D. Shatz, J. B. Wolowelsky, and R. Zeigler, eds., (Ktav, 2008), 37.
3. A. J. Gerber, "The Kosher Bookworm the Tower of Babel and Its Totalitarianism Tradition," *The Jewish Star*, October 18, 2012, https://www.thejewishstar.com/stories/The-Kosher-BookwormThe-Tower-of-Babel-and-its-Totalitarianism-Tradition,3619; M. Hattin, "Noach: The Tower of Bavel," *Torat Har Etzion VBM*, September 21, 2014, https://etzion.org.il/en.
4. "The Encampment of the Tribes of Israel," *Bible History*, https://bible-history.com/old-testament/encampment-of-israel.
5. Rashi, Genesis 25:27.
6. M. Gerson, *The Telling: How Judaism's Essential Book Reveals the Meaning of Life* (St. Martin's Press, 2021), 294.
7. Babylonian Talmud, Eruvin 13b.

8. Rabbi Nachman of Breslov, *Likkutei Moharan 64:4*. See Maharitz Chajes' commentary to Babylonian Talmud, Sanhedrin 17a.
9. *Arukh HaShulchan, Introduction to Choshen Mishpat.*
10. Text Study, "These and Those Are the Words of the Living God," Central Synagogue, https://www.centralsynagogue.org/assets/downloads/Enduring_Disagreements_Discussion_1_Text_Study.pdf.
11. https://www.listennotes.com/podcasts/off-the-pulpit/noach-noah-and-the-tower-a-MhPdeV8Ks4C/.
12. Babylonian Talmud, Sanhedrin 27b.
13. Y. Tauber, "Nitzavim: Summary and Commentary," Chabad.org, https://w2.chabad.org/media/pdf/56/kZJi561539.pdf.
14. Nachmanides, Numbers 4:49.
15. Aruch HaShulchan, *Choshen Mishpat: Introduction*; Jonathan Targum, *Exodus 20:15.*
16. R. J. Sacks, "Nitzanim: Defeating Death," *Covenant and Conversation*, The Rabbi Sacks Legacy Trust, 2014, https://www.rabbisacks.org/covenant-conversation/nitzavim/defeating-death/.
17. Babylonian Talmud, Sanhedrin 17a.
18. Maimonides, Mishneh Torah, *The Sanhedrin and the Penalties within Their Jurisdiction*, 2:2.
19. Maimonides, Mishneh Torah, *The Sanhedrin and the Penalties within Their Jurisdiction*, 2:1–7.
20. M. Falcone, "The Winter of Chris Christie's Discontent," ABC News, January 21, 2014, https://abcnews.go.com/blogs/politics/2014/01/the-winter-of-chris-christies-discontent-the-not; UN News "Diversity, a 'Source of Strength,' UN Chief Tells Security Council," United Nations, October 15, 2021, https://news.un.org/en/story/2021/10/1102842; A. Aguilastratt, "Diversity Is Our Army's Strength," *Army University Press*, 2022, https://www.armyupress.army.mil/Journals/NCO-Journal/Archives/2020/October/Diversity-is-Our-Armys-Strength/.
21. V. Singh, A. Atrey, and S. Hegde, "Do Individuals Smile More in Diverse Social Company?: Studying Smiles and Diversity Via Social Media Photos," *MM '17: Proceedings of the 25th ACM International Conference on Multimedia* (2017): 1818–1827; J. Garamone, "Diversity, Equity, Inclusion Are Necessities in U.S. Military," U.S. Department of Defense, February 9, 2022, https://www.defense.gov/News/News-Stories/Article/Article/2929658/diversity-equity-inclusion-are-necessities-in-us-military/; S. S. Levine and D. Stark, "Diversity Makes You Brighter," *New York Times*, December 9, 2015, https://www.nytimes.com/2015/12/09/opinion/diversity-makes-you-brighter.html; D. Rock, "Why Diverse Teams Are Smarter," *Harvard Business Review*, November 4, 2016, https://hbr.org/2016/11/why-diverse-teams-are-smarter.

22. "With $85 Million, Yale Intensifies Commitment to a Premier, Diverse Faculty," *Yale News* December 10, 2019, https://news.yale.edu/2019/12/10/85-million-yale-intensifies-commitment-premier-diverse-faculty.
23. J. Greene and J. Paul, "Diversity University: DEI Bloat in the Academy," The Heritage Foundation, July 27, 2021, https://www.heritage.org/education/report/diversity-university-dei-bloat-the-academy; H. Raleigh, "DEI-Obsessed Universities Overprice Degrees and Under-Deliver on Them," *The Federalist*, March 12, 2024, https://thefederalist.com/2024/03/12/dei-obsessed-universities-overprice-degrees-and-under-deliver-on-them/.

    The Heritage Data only covers the universities with easily accessible data on the staff, which explains why it mostly covers public universities. It does not cover any of the Ivy League universities, or many other "elite" schools, many of which are the most committed to DEI.
24. LinkedIn News, "LinkedIn Jobs on the Rise 2022: The 25 U.S. Roles That Are Growing in Demand," LinkedIn, January 18, 2022, https://www.linkedin.com/pulse/linkedin-jobs-rise-2022-25-us-roles-growing-demand-linkedin-news/?trackingId=5M2WH4CgErXx9T%2F6rqczmg%3D%3D; Business and Management Consulting, Top Diversity Consulting Firms—July 2024 Reviews, *Clutch*, https://clutch.co/consulting/diversity-inclusion.
25. H. Barbour, "25 Examples of Awesome Diversity Goals," *Ongig Blog*, April 18, 2023, https://blog.ongig.com/diversity-and-inclusion/diversity-goals/.
26. Indeed Editorial Team, "7 Types of Diversity in the Workplace," *Indeed Career Guide*, April 21, 2023, https://www.indeed.com/career-advice/career-development/types-of-diversity-in-workplace.
27. Office of the Under Secretary, "Advancing Diversity and Inclusion in Higher Education: Key Data Highlights Focusing on Race and Ethnicity and Promising Practices," Office of Planning, Evaluation and Policy Development Office of the Under Secretary U.S. Department of Education.
28. A. Blake, "Why the Cherokee Nation's Rebuke of Elizabeth Warren Matters," *Washington Post*, October 16, 2018, https://www.washingtonpost.com/politics/2018/10/16/why-cherokee-nations-rebuke-elizabeth-warren-matters/.
29. M. L. Kelly, "Warren Releases DNA Results, Challenges Trump over Native American Ancestry," NPR, October 15, 2018, https://www.npr.org/transcripts/657468655.
30. T. Kaplan, "Elizabeth Warren Apologizes at Native American Forum: 'I Have Listened and I Have Learned,'" *New York Times*, August 19, 2019, https://www.nytimes.com/2019/08/19/us/politics/elizabeth-warren-native-american.html.
31. A. Harris, "Louisiana Court Sees No Shades of Gray in Woman's Request," *Washington Post*, May 21, 1983, https://www.washingtonpost.com/archive

/politics/1983/05/21/louisiana-court-sees-no-shades-of-gray-in-womans-request/ddb0f1df-ba5d-4141-9aa0-6347e60ce52d/; F. J. Davis, *Who Is Black? One Nation's Definition* (Pennsylvania State University Press, 1991), 13–16.

32. M. Grant, *The Passing of the Great Race or The Racial Basis of European History* (Charles Scribner's Sons, 1923), 18; Stefan Kühl, *Nazi Connection: Eugenics, American Racism, and German National Socialism* (Oxford University Press, 1994).
33. Brendan Wolfe, "Racial Integrity Laws (1924–1930)" in *Encyclopedia Virginia*, 2020, https://encyclopediavirginia.org/entries/racial-integrity-laws-1924-1930.
34. K. Parker and A. Barroso, "How Kamala Harris Reflects America's Changing Demographics," Pew Research Center, February 25, 2021, https://www.pewresearch.org/short-reads/2021/02/25/in-vice-president-kamala-harris-we-can-see-how-america-has-changed/.
35. R. L. Revesz, *Federal Register* 88, no. 18 (2023); United States Census Bureau, "About the Topic of Race," United States Census Bureau, 2022, https://www.census.gov/topics/population/race/about.html.
36. M. Lavietes, "New York City Opens Billions in Contracts to LGBT+ Business, U.S," Reuters, January 20, 2021, https://www.reuters.com/article/us-lgbt-business-new-york/new-york-city-opens-billions-in-contracts-to-lgbt-business-idUSKBN29P2MW.
37. D. Paquette, "The Surprising Reason Why Lesbians Get Paid More Than Straight Women," *Washington Post*, February 25, 2016, https://www.washingtonpost.com/news/wonk/wp/2016/02/25/the-surprising-reason-why-lesbians-get-paid-more-than-straight-women/; F. Olito, "The 10 Best Cities for Same-Sex Couples in the US," *Insider*, June 4, 2020, https://www.insider.com/best-cities-for-same-sex-couples-2020-6#san-diego-california-tied-with-albuquerque-for-seventh-place-8.
38. J. Kaplan, "New York Just Became the Biggest City to Make LGBT-Owned Businesses Eligible for Billions in Government Contracts for Minority Entrepreneurs," *Business Insider*, January 19, 2021, https://www.businessinsider.com/new-york-biggest-city-recognize-lgbt-owned-businesses-minority-contracts-2021-1.
39. B. Gallob, "Jewish Organizations Challenge SBA Decision to Bar Aid to Hasidic Businessmen's Group," *JTA Daily News Bulletin*, February 18, 1981, https://www.jta.org/archive/jewish-organizations-challenge-sba-decision-to-bar-aid-to-hasidic-businessmens-grou.
40. U.S. Small Business Administration, *LGBTQ-Owned Businesses*, https://www.sba.gov/business-guide/grow-your-business/lgbtq-owned-businesses.
41. B. Everett, "Begich: McCaskill Doesn't Get It," *Politico*, July 2, 2014, https://www.politico.com/story/2014/07/mark-begich-claire-mccaskill-alaska-108537.

42. I. X. Kendi, "Ibram X. Kendi Defines What It Means to Be an Antiracist," *Penguin Extracts*, June 8, 2020, https://www.penguin.co.uk/articles/2020/06/ibram-x-kendi-definition-of-antiracist.
43. I. Shapira, "Before Asian Americans Sued Harvard, the School Once Tried Restricting the Number of Jews," *Washington Post*, October 28, 2021, https://www.washingtonpost.com/news/retropolis/wp/2018/09/14/before-asian-americans-sued-harvard-the-school-tried-restricting-the-number-of-jews/.
44. P. Jacobs, "Harvard Is Being Accused of Treating Asians the Same Way It Used to Treat Jews," *Business Insider*, December 4, 2014, https://www.businessinsider.com/the-ivy-leagues-history-of-discriminating-against-jews-2014-12.
45. Office of Communications, "In an Extraordinary Year, Princeton Offers Admission to 1,498 Students for the Class of 2025," Princeton University, April 6, 2021, https://www.princeton.edu/news/2021/04/06/extraordinary-year-princeton-offers-admission-1498-students-class-2025.
46. A. Hendershott, "Are the Doors to Elite Universities Still Open to Jewish Students?," *Minding the Campus*, June 22, 2019, https://www.mindingthecampus.org/2019/06/22/are-the-doors-to-elite-universities-still-open-to-jewish-students/.
47. B. Stoke, "Hostile Neighbors: China vs. Japan," Pew Research Center, September 13, 2016, https://www.pewresearch.org/global/2016/09/13/hostile-neighbors-china-vs-japan/.
48. D. Saffran, "Fewer Asians Need Apply: How the Ivy League Discriminates Against Top-Achieving Students," *City Journal*, 2016, https://www.city-journal.org/article/fewer-asians-need-apply.
49. M. J. Perry, "New Chart Illustrates Graphically the Racial Preferences for Blacks, Hispanics Being Admitted to US Medical Schools," The American Enterprise Institute, June 25, 2017, https://www.aei.org/carpe-diem/new-chart-illustrates-graphically-racial-preferences-for-blacks-and-hispanics-being-admitted-to-us-medical-schools/.
50. A. Sibarium, "'A Failed Medical School': How Racial Preferences, Supposedly Outlawed in California, Have Persisted at UCLA," *Washington Free Beacon*, May 23, 2024, https://freebeacon.com/campus/a-failed-medical-school-how-racial-preferences-supposedly-outlawed-in-california-have-persisted-at-ucla/.
51. L. M. Leslie, D. M. Mayer, and D. A. Kravitz, "The Stigma of Affirmative Action: A Stereotyping-Based Theory and Meta-Analytic Test of the Consequences for Performance," *Academy of Management Journal* 57, no. 4 (2014): 964–989.
52. T. L. Dover, B. Major, and C. R. Kaiser, "Members of High-Status Groups Are Threatened by Pro-Diversity Organizational Messages," *Journal of Experimental Social Psychology* 62 (2016): 58–67.

53. B. Leonard, "Affirmative Action Policies Can Perpetuate Stigmas," *SHRM*, August 25, 2014, https://www.shrm.org/topics-tools/news/inclusion-diversity/affirmative-action-policies-can-perpetuate-stigmas.
54. D. Leonhardt, "Social Class Is Not About Only Race," *New York Times*, July 5, 2023, https://www.nytimes.com/2023/07/05/briefing/affirmative-action.html.
55. *IBM 2020 Diversity & Inclusion Report*, IBM, 2020, https://www.ibm.com/impact/be-equal/pdf/IBM_Diversity_Inclusion_Report_2020.pdf.
56. J. O'Keefe (@JamesOKeefeIII), Twitter (now X), December 12, 2023, https://twitter.com/JamesOKeefeIII/status/1734374423124176944?s=20.
57. G. Livingston and A. Brown, "Intermarriage in the U.S. 50 Years After *Loving v. Virginia*," Pew Research Center, May 18, 2017, https://www.pewresearch.org/social-trends/2017/05/18/intermarriage-in-the-u-s-50-years-after-loving-v-virginia/; D. Ordway, "Intermarriage and U.S. Hispanics: New Research," *The Journalist's Resource*, August 3, 2017, https://journalistsresource.org/politics-and-government/interracial-intermarriage-hispanic-population-research/.
58. T. Copeland, "Oppression Olympics: The Game That Needs to End," Central Indiana Community Foundation, August 2, 2021, https://www.cicf.org/2021/08/02/oppression-olympics-the-game-that-needs-to-end/.
59. A. Blake, "The Most Discriminated-Against People in America? It's People Like You, Of Course," *Washington Post*, September 22, 2014, https://www.washingtonpost.com/news/the-fix/wp/2014/09/22/the-most-discriminated-against-people-in-america-its-people-like-you-of-course/; P. Bump, "White Republicans Think Whites, Blacks and Hispanics Face About the Same Amount of Discrimination," *Washington Post*, April 15, 2019, https://www.washingtonpost.com/politics/2019/04/15/white-republicans-think-whites-blacks-hispanics-face-about-same-amount-discrimination/; R. Nadeem and R. Nadeem, "1. Views on Discrimination in Our Society," Pew Research Center, 2024, https://www.pewresearch.org/2024/04/02/views-on-discrimination-in-our-society/.
60. T. Copeland, "Oppression Olympics: The Game That Needs to End," Central Indiana Community Foundation, August 2, 2021, https://www.cicf.org/2021/08/02/oppression-olympics-the-game-that-needs-to-end/.
61. J. Ostrowski, "The Most Valuable College Majors in 2021, Ranked," *Bankrate*, October 4, 2021, https://www.bankrate.com/loans/student-loans/most-valuable-college-majors/?utm_source=Twitter&utm_medium=organic_socia; G. Heriot, "A 'Dubious Expediency': How Race-Preferential Admissions Policies on Campus Hurt Minority Students," The Heritage Foundation, August 31, 2015, https://www.heritage.org/civil-rights/report/dubious-expediency-how-race-preferential-admissions-policies-campus-hurt.
62. *Ibid.*

63. D. K. Hawkins, "Impact of HBCUs on Diversity in STEM," US Black Engineer Information Technology, May 19, 2022, https://www.blackengineer.com/article/impact-of-hbcus-on-diversity-in-stem/; TECH-Levers, "HBCUs Produce the Most Black Alums Who Receive Doctorates in Science and Engineering," HBCU TECH-Levers, June 19, 2013, https://hbcu-levers.blogspot.com/; "The Impact of HBCUs on Diversity in STEM Fields, UNCF, 2024, https://uncf.org/the-latest/the-impact-of-hbcus-on-diversity-in-stem-fields#.
64. J. Radunzel, K. Mattern, P. Westrick, "The Role of Academic Preparation and Interest on STEM Success," *Act Research Series* 8 (2016): 1–56; C. W. Kohler, "Persistence in STEM Majors: Investigating Whether and When High-Performing Students Leave STEM during Undergraduate Studies," *Journal of Research in STEM Education* 3, no. 1 (2017): 17–33.
65. G. W. Allport, *The Nature of Prejudice* (Addison-Wesley Publishing Company, 1954), 276.
66. Allport, *The Nature of Prejudice.*
67. Allport, *The Nature of Prejudice.*
68. E. Lake, "Thomas F. Pettigrew: Faculty Profile," *The Harvard Crimson*, April 9, 1964, https://www.thecrimson.com/article/1964/4/9/thomas-f-pettigrew-pa-little-over/.
69. G. Hodson and M. Hewstone, eds., *Advances in Intergroup Contact* (Psychology Press, 2013), 7. Italics in original.
70. N. Yancey-Bragg and G. Hauck, "Police Don't All Act 'The Same Way': White Officers Use Force More Often, Chicago Police Study Finds," *USA Today,* February 11, 2021, https://www.usatoday.com/story/news/nation/2021/02/11/chicago-police-study-white-cops-more-likely-arrest-use-force/4439259001/.
71. B. Flavin, "Police Officers Explain Why Diversity in Law Enforcement Matters," Rasmussen University, December 10, 2018, https://www.rasmussen.edu/degrees/justice-studies/blog/diversity-in-law-enforcement/.
72. A. Sorokowska et. al., "Preferred Interpersonal Distances: A Global Comparison," *Journal of Cross-Cultural Psychology* 48, no. 4 (2018): 577–592.
73. "Diversity Wins: How Inclusion Matters," McKinsey & Company, 2020, https://www.mckinsey.com/featured-insights/diversity-and-inclusion/diversity-wins-how-inclusion-matters; V. Eswaran, "The Business Case for Diversity in the Workplace Is Now Overwhelming," World Economic Forum, 2019, https://www.weforum.org/agenda/2019/04/business-case-for-diversity-in-the-workplace/.
74. J. Green and J. R. M. Hand, "Diversity Matters/Delivers/Wins Revisited in S&P 500® Firms," *SSRN*, 2021, 4, https://econjwatch.org/File+download/1296/GreenHandMar2024.pdf?mimetype=pdf.

75. G. Filbeck, B. Foster, D. Preece, and X. Zhao, "Does Diversity Improve Profits and Shareholder Returns? Evidence from Top Rated Companies for Diversity by DiversityInc," *Advances in Accounting* 37 (2018): 94–102.
76. P. Gompers and S. Kovvali, "The Other Diversity Dividend," *Harvard Business Review*, July 2018, https://hbr.org/2018/07/the-other-diversity-dividend.
77. M. J. Silverstein and K. Sayre, "The Female Economy," *Harvard Business Review*, September 2009, https://hbr.org/2009/09/the-female-economy.
78. D. Berthiaume, "Study: Women Influence 85% of All Purchases," *Chain Store Age*, June 18, 2014, https://chainstoreage.com/news/study-women-influence-85-all-purchases; OECD Data, "Household Spending," *OECD*, 2022, https://data.oecd.org/hha/household-spending.htm.
79. C. R. Sunstein, "Making Dumb Groups Smarter," *Harvard Business Review*, December 2014, https://hbr.org/2014/12/making-dumb-groups-smarter.
80. C. R. Sunstein, "The Law of Group Polarization," *Journal of Political Philosophy* 10, no. 2 (2002): 175–195.
81. *Ibid.*
82. Lyn M. Van Swol, "Extreme Members and Group Polarization," *Social Influence* 4, no. 3 (2009): 185–199.
83. C. R. Sunstein, "Deliberative Trouble? Why Groups Go to Extremes," *Yale Law Journal* 110, no. 1 (2000): 71–119.
84. K. Phillips, K. Liljenquist, and M. Neale, "Is the Pain Worth the Gain? The Advantages and Liabilities of Agreeing with Socially Distinct Newcomers," *Personality & Social Psychology Bulletin* 35 (2009): 336–350.
85. D. Rock, H. Grant, and J. Gray, "Diverse Teams Feel Less Comfortable, and That's Why They Perform Better," *Harvard Business Review*, September 22, 2016, https://hbr.org/2016/09/diverse-teams-feel-less-comfortable-and-thats-why-they-perform-better.
86. P. W. Magness and D. Waugh, "The Hyperpoliticization of Higher Ed: Trends in Faculty Political Ideology, 1969–Present," *The Independent Review* 27, no. 3 (2022): 359–369.
87. M. Langbert, "Homogenous: The Political Affiliations of Elite Liberal Arts College Faculty," National Association of Scholars, 2018, https://www.nas.org/academic-questions/31/2/homogenous_the_political_affiliations_of_elite_liberal_arts_college_faculty.
88. *Ibid.*
89. K. M. Aspelund, M. P. Bernhard, D. Freed, I. M. Kahloon, and A. H. Patel, "Harvard Faculty Donate to Democrats by Wide Margin," *Harvard Crimson*, May 1, 2015, https://www.thecrimson.com/article/2015/5/1/faculty-political-contributions-data-analysis/.

90. "Conservatism in Ivy League College Admissions," *Ivy Coach*, November 10, 2017, https://www.ivycoach.com/the-ivy-coach-blog/college-admissions/conservatism-ivy-league-college-admissions/.
91. M. Yglesias, "Education Polarization Is Only Growing—and It's Making Everyone Mad All the Time," *Slow Boring*, September 27, 2021, https://www.slowboring.com/p/education-polarization.
92. The University of Alabama Student Life, *Niche*, https://www.niche.com/colleges/the-university-of-alabama/students/; *2018–2019 Annual Report*, National Merit Scholarship Corporation, October 31, 2019, https://web.archive.org/web/20210805191249/https://www.nationalmerit.org/s/1758/images/gid2/editor_documents/annual_report.pdf?gid=2&pgid=61&sessionid=c211e88d-8f77-40dc-8cea-f6e3d3c2f118&cc=1.
93. T. Falk, "CEO John Lansing Discusses NPR's Diversity Efforts, Budget Deficit and Growing Podcast Competition," *Current*, February 4, 2021, https://current.org/2021/02/ceo-john-lansing-discusses-nprs-diversity-efforts-budget-deficit-and-growing-podcast-competition/.
94. U. Berliner, "NPR Editor Uri Berliner: Here's How We Lost America's Trust," *The Free Press*, April 9, 2024, https://www.thefp.com/p/npr-editor-how-npr-lost-americas-trust.
95. R. Quinn, "MIT Stops Asking Faculty Applicants for Diversity Statements," Inside Higher Ed, 2024, https://www.insidehighered.com/news/quick-takes/2024/05/08/mit-stops-asking-faculty-applicants-diversity-statements.
96. Equal Opportunity and Affirmative Action, "Assessing Candidate Contributions to Diversity, Equity, & Inclusion (DEI)," Columbia University, https://eoaa.columbia.edu/sites/default/files/content/docs/Assessing_Candidate_DEI_Contributions.pdf; Equal Opportunity and Affirmative Action, "Sample Candidate Evaluation Tool for Faculty Searches," Columbia University, https://eoaa.columbia.edu/sites/default/files/content/docs/Sample_Candidate_Evaluation_Tool_for_Faculty_Searches.pdf?utm_source=substack&utm_medium=email.
97. UC Berkeley, "Rubric for Assessing Candidate Contributions to Diversity, Equity, Inclusion, and Belonging," Berkeley Office for Faculty Equity and Welfare, https://ofew.berkeley.edu/recruitment/contributions-diversity/rubric-assessing-candidate-contributions-diversity-equity.
98. M. Powell, "D.E.I. Statements Spark Debate at UCalifornia and Other Universities," *New York Times*, September 8, 2023, https://www.nytimes.com/2023/09/08/us/ucla-dei-statement.html.
99. *Ibid*.
100. P. Lewis, "'I See Things Differently': James Damore on His Autism and the Google Memo," *The Guardian*, December 17, 2017, https://www.theguardian.com/technology/2017/nov/16/james-damore-google-memo-interview-autism-regrets;

"The Google Memo: Four Scientists Respond," *Quillette*, August 7, 2017, https://quillette.com/2017/08/07/google-memo-four-scientists-respond/.

101. S. Emerson and L. Matsakis, "Google on Anti-Diversity Manifesto: Employees Must 'Feel Safe Sharing Their Opinions,'" *Vice*, August 6, 2017, https://www.vice.com/en/article/vbv54d/google-on-anti-diversity-manifesto-employees-must-feel-safe-sharing-their-opinions.
102. A. Mohdin, "Apple's First Ever VP of Diversity and Inclusion Says She Focuses on Everyone, Not Just Minorities," *Quartz*, October 9, 2017, https://qz.com/1097425/apples-first-ever-vp-of-diversity-and-inclusion-says-she-focuses-on-everyone-not-just-minorities.
103. A. A. Matthews, R. J. Kreitzer, and E. U. Schilling, "Gender Polarization Fuels Abortion Policymaking in the States," University of Minnesota, October 13, 2020, https://genderpolicyreport.umn.edu/gender-polarization-fuels-abortion-policymaking-in-the-states/.
104. M. Yglesias, "Abortion Gender Gap: Men and Women Have Similar Views," *Vox*, May 20, 2019, https://www.vox.com/2019/5/20/18629644/abortion-gender-gap-public-opinion.
105. A. Beam, "California Governor: Death Penalty 'Infected by Racism,'" Associated Press, October 27, 2020, https://apnews.com/article/california-discrimination-race-and-ethnicity-racial-injustice-gavin-newsom-a7d0ac3aef1e3f689a2c6ebb6bf41975; "Most Americans Favor the Death Penalty Despite Concerns About Its Administration," Pew Research Center, July 14, 2021, https://www.pewresearch.org/politics/2021/06/02/most-americans-favor-the-death-penalty-despite-concerns-about-its-administration/.
106. K. Blackwell, "Claiming State Voting Reforms Are Racist Is Ridiculous. I Should Know," *USA Today,* April 8, 2021, https://www.usatoday.com/story/opinion/voices/2021/04/08/voter-id-laws-and-racism-democrats-just-muddling-debate-column/7113493002/.
107. G. Loury, "A Peek Behind the DEI Curtain," Glenn Loury, Substack, November 28, 2023, https://glennloury.substack.com/p/a-peek-behind-the-dei-curtain.
108. S. Hartman, "'There Are No Unimportant Jobs': This Retired FBI Boss Became a School Bus Driver Amid Shortage," CBS News, October 15, 2021, https://www.cbsnews.com/news/steve-hartman-on-the-road-mike-mason-fbi-school-bus-driver/.
109. M. Smith and J. Ballard, "Scientists and Doctors Are the Most Respected Professions Worldwide," YouGov, February 8, 2021, https://today.yougov.com/topics/economy/articles-reports/2021/02/08/international-profession-perception-poll-data.
110. H. Van Drie and R. V. Reeves, "Many Essential Workers Are in 'Low-Prestige' Jobs. Time to Change Our Attitudes, and Policies?," Brookings Institute, May

28, 2020, https://www.brookings.edu/articles/many-essential-workers-are-in-low-prestige-jobs-time-to-change-our-attitudes-and-policies/.

111. T. Velmer, "Doctor Remains Most Prestigious Profession," *Ynetnews*, March 27, 2012, https://www.ynetnews.com/articles/1,7340,L-4202913,00.html.
112. See, for instance, Ministry of Defence (@defencehq), Twitter (now X), June 24, 2016, https://twitter.com/defencehq/status/746327245422198784; General / Général Wayne Eyre Twitter (now X), February 11, 2021, https://twitter.com/CDS_Canada_CEMD/status/1359743611349438464; J. Garamone, "Diversity, Equity, Inclusion Are Necessities in U.S. Military," U.S. Department of Defense, February 9, 2022, https://www.defense.gov/News/News-Stories/Article/Article/2929658/diversity-equity-inclusion-are-necessities-in-us-military/.
113. As relayed to me by David Wolfowicz, a former commander in the IDF Education Corps.
114. S. Rubin, "The Israeli Army Unit That Recruits Teens with Autism," *The Atlantic*, January 6, 2016, https://www.theatlantic.com/health/archive/2016/01/israeli-army-autism/422850/.
115. "Unit 9900, Autistic Teens Join the Israeli Army," *Hadassah, the Women's Zionist Org of America*, October 22, 2018, https://my.hadassah.org/news-stories/unit-9900-autistic-teens-join-israeli-army.html.
116. 3rd Infantry Division Public Affairs, "Diversity Is Our Strength: African American History Month," US Army, February 11, 2021, https://www.army.mil/article/243203/diversity_is_our_strength_african_american_history_month.
117. B. Stephens, "The Dying Art of Disagreement," *New York Times*, September 26, 2017, https://www.nytimes.com/2017/09/24/opinion/dying-art-of-disagreement.html.
118. Shulchan Aruch, *Orach Chaim*, 329:6.
119. Supreme Court of the United States, *Students for Fair Admissions Inc. v. President and Fellows of Harvard College*, Certiorari to the United States Court of Appeals for the First Circuit, 4o, 2022, https://www.supremecourt.gov/opinions/22pdf/20-1199_hgdj.pdf.
120. William, "Supreme Court Decision," Harvard Admissions Lawsuit, June 29, 2023, https://www.harvard.edu/admissionscase/2023/06/29/supreme-court-decision/; C. Gay, "President-Elect Claudine Gay Message to the Community," Harvard University, June 29, 2023, https://www.youtube.com/watch?v=AoGjh3tbPm4; A. Sabes, "Harvard to Ask Undergraduate Applicants About Time 'They Strongly Disagreed With Someone,'" *Campus Reform*, August 8, 2024, https://www.campusreform.org/article/harvard-ask-undergraduate-applicants-time-they-strongly-disagreed-someone/26079 .
121. J. Greene and J. Paul, July 27, 2021, *op. cit.*; "University of Pittsburgh School

of Medicine Secondary Questions," Prospective Doctor, 2023, https://www.prospectivedoctor.com/university-of-pittsburgh-school-of-medicine-secondary/; Shemmassian Academic Consulting, *Minnesota*, 2023, https://www.shemmassianconsulting.com/blog/medical-school-secondary-essay-prompts; A. A. Smith, "CSU Panel Recommends Eliminating the Use of SAT and ACT Exams for Admission," *EdSource*, January 27, 2022, https://edsource.org/2022/csu-panel-recommends-eliminating-the-use-of-sat-and-act-exams-for-admission/66651.

122. J. Diaz, "Florida Gov. Ron DeSantis Signs a Bill Banning DEI Initiatives in Public Colleges," NPR, May 15, 2023, https://www.npr.org/2023/05/15/1176210007/florida-ron-desantis-dei-ban-diversity; New York State Senate, *NY State Senate Bill 2023-S108A*, https://www.nysenate.gov/legislation/bills/2023/S108/amendment/A.

Chapter 33

1. N. Singh, "Kautilya's Relevance in the 21st Century," *International Journal of Creative Research Thoughts* 6, no. 1 (2018): 1275–1277; B. Venkatappiah, "Misuse of Office," in D. L. Stills, ed., *International Encyclopedia of the Social Sciences*, vol. II (Macmillan Company and the Free Press), 272.
2. A. K. Biswas and C. Tortajada, "From Our Ancestors to Modern Leaders, All Do It: The Story of Corruption," The Conversation, September 7, 2018, https://theconversation.com/from-our-ancestors-to-modern-leaders-all-do-it-the-story-of-corruption-102164.
3. Mishnah, *Shekalim 3:2.*
4. E. Goldberg, "Tzav (Purim): Hashem from Beginning to End," *Parsha Perspectives*, March 15, 2022, https://www.listennotes.com/podcasts/parsha-perspectives/tzav-purim-hashem-from-NHlBRWu2b7X/.
5. Periscope Film, *Journey to Venezuela: 1950s Standard Oil Co. Travelogue Film Caracas 94224*, YouTube, https://www.youtube.com/watch?v=Fb7mYfHqRpI.
6. Knowledge at Wharton Staff, "How Venezuela Fell Apart," *Knowledge at Wharton*, University of Pennsylvania, July 12, 2016, https://knowledge.wharton.upenn.edu/article/how-venezuela-fell-apart/.
7. G. Gorder, "What Are the Most Corrupt Countries in Latin America?," *InSight Crime*, February 11, 2022, https://insightcrime.org/news/what-are-the-most-corrupt-countries-in-latin-america/.
8. L. Venture, "The World's Richest and Poorest Countries 2023," *Global Finance Magazine*, May 2, 2023, https://www.gfmag.com/global-data/economic-data/worlds-richest-and-poorest-countries.

9. Office of Public Affairs, "Nicolás Maduro Moros and 14 Current and Former Venezuelan Officials," Department of Justice, March 27, 2020, https://www.justice.gov/opa/pr/nicol-s-maduro-moros-and-14-current-and-former-venezuelan-officials-charged-narco-terrorism; Transparency International, *Corruption Perceptions Index*, 2022, https://www.transparency.org/en/cpi/2022.
10. B. Lomborg, *Best Things First: The 12 Most Efficient Solutions for the World's Poorest and Our Global SDG Promises* (Copenhagen Consensus Center, 2023), 145–157.
11. F. Stockman, "Corruption Is an Existential Threat to Ukraine, and Ukrainians Know It," *New York Times*, September 10, 2023, https://www.nytimes.com/2023/09/10/opinion/ukraine-war-corruption.html.
12. D. Berger, "Corruption Ruins The Doctor-Patient Relationship in India," *BMJ* 348 (2014): g3169.
13. A. Archipova, "Corruption in Healthcare System of Russia: Challenges and Effects," in I. B. Ardashkin, B. Vladimir Iosifovich, and N. V. Martyushev, eds., *Research Paradigms Transformation in Social Sciences* 50, European Proceedings of Social and Behavioural Sciences (2018): 50–56.
14. O. Bullough, "Four Reasons Why Corruption Matters," *Al Jazeera*, January 9, 2018, https://www.aljazeera.com/opinions/2018/1/9/four-reasons-why-corruption-matters.
15. E. H. Glynn, "Corruption in the Health Sector: A Problem in Need of a Systems-Thinking Approach," *Frontiers in Public Health* 10 (2022): 910073–910073.
16. H. A. Patrinos, "The Hidden Cost of Corruption: Teacher Absenteeism and Loss in Schools," *World Bank Blogs*, October 1, 2013, https://blogs.worldbank.org/education/hidden-cost-corruption-teacher-absenteeism-and-loss-schools.
17. M. Kirya, "Education Sector Corruption: How to Assess It and Ways to Address It," *Chr. Michelsen Institute*, April 28, 2019, https://www.u4.no/publications/education-sector-corruption-how-to-assess-it-and-ways-to-address-it.pdf; Etico, "Mapping of Risks: Platform on Ethics and Corruption in Education," UNESCO, https://etico.iiep.unesco.org/en/mapping-risks.
18. UNODC, "Anti-Corruption Module 9 Key Issues: Costs of Corruption in Education," United Nations Office on Drugs and Crime, https://www.unodc.org/e4j/en/anti-corruption/module-9/key-issues/costs-of-corruption-in-education.html.
19. INTERPOL, "Corruption as a Facilitator for Organized Crime in the Eastern African Region," *enact* October 15, 2019, https://tinyurl.com/2p8nvp6v.
20. M. Lh, "A Closer Look at Corruption, Hamas, and Violence in the Gaza Strip," *GAB: The Global Anticorruption Blog*, June 28, 2021, https://globalanticorruptionblog.com/2021/06/28/a-closer-look-at-corruption-hamas-and-violence-in-the-gaza-strip/.

21. B. Venard, "Lessons from the Massive Siemens Corruption Scandal One Decade Later," *The Conversation*, December 13, 2018, https://theconversation.com/lessons-from-the-massive-siemens-corruption-scandal-one-decade-later-108694.
22. D. Ariely and X. Garcia-Rada, "Corruption Is Contagious," *Scientific American*, September 1, 2019, https://www.scientificamerican.com/article/corruption-is-contagious/.
23. J. Steiner, "'Petty' Corruption Isn't Petty," *GAB: The Global Anticorruption Blog*, December 29, 2017, https://globalanticorruptionblog.com/2017/12/29/petty-corruption-isnt-petty/.
24. Transparency International, "Poor Families Hit Hardest by Bribery, Even in Rich Countries, Finds New TI Poll," Transparency.org, December 5, 2007, https://www.transparency.org/en/press/20071205-poor-families-hit-hardest-by-bribery-even-in-rich-countries-finds.
25. M. Popova, "Putin-Style 'Rule of Law' & the Prospects for Change," *Daedalus* 146, no. 2 (2017): 64–75.
26. R. Fisman and E. Miguel, "Cultures of Corruption: Evidence from Diplomatic Parking Tickets," *Institute of Public Affairs* 58, no. 3 (2006): 42.
27. G. W. Plunkitt, "Honest Graft," *Lapham's Quarterly*, 1905, https://www.laphamsquarterly.org/city/honest-graft.
28. R. Freier, "The Hasidic Superwoman of Night Court—Judge Ruchie Freier," *Living Lechaim*, YouTube, July 17, 2022, https://www.youtube.com/watch?v=38ufpik7hx8.
29. T. Murse, "How to Pick the Right Gift for Your Mail Carrier," *ThoughtCo*, October 3, 2022, https://www.thoughtco.com/the-right-gift-for-the-mailman-3321106.
30. M. Rubin, "Rwanda Should Be the Model to Defeat Corruption," American Enterprise Institute, April 13, 2021, https://www.aei.org/op-eds/rwanda-should-be-the-model-to-defeat-corruption/.

ABOUT THE AUTHOR

Mark Gerson, a New York–based entrepreneur and philanthropist, is the cofounder of Gerson Lehrman Group, 31 Members, United Hatzalah of Israel, and African Mission Healthcare—where he and his wife, Rabbi Erica Gerson, made the largest gift ever to Christian medical missionaries. A graduate of Williams College and Yale Law School, Mark is the author of the national bestseller *The Telling: How Judaism's Essential Book Reveals the Meaning of Life*. His articles and essays have been published in *The New Republic*, USA Today, Commentary, Fox News, *The Wall Street Journal* and Christian Broadcast Network. Mark lives in New York City with his wife and their four children.